**2025–2026**

# Private Pilot
# TEST PREP

## Pass your test the first time

AVIATION SUPPLIES & ACADEMICS, INC.
NEWCASTLE, WASHINGTON

*Private Pilot Test Prep*
2025–2026 Edition

Aviation Supplies & Academics, Inc.
7005 132nd Place SE
Newcastle, Washington 98059
asa@asa2fly.com | 425.235.1500 | asa2fly.com

Visit **asa2fly.com/TPP** for additional information and resources related to this book.

Sample Federal Aviation Administration (FAA) questions herein contain information as of: September 2024. Stay informed of changes since the book was printed: **asa2fly.com/testupdate**

None of the material in this publication supersedes any documents, procedures or regulations issued by the Federal Aviation Administration.

Aviation Supplies & Academics, Inc. (ASA), assumes no responsibility for any errors or omissions. Neither is any liability assumed for damages resulting from the use of the information contained herein.

Cover photo: Naris Vachiranantavat/Shutterstock.com

**ASA-TP-P-25**
ISBN   978-1-64425-434-9

Additional format available:
eBook PDF ISBN   978-1-64425-435-6

Printed in the United States of America

2025    2024              5   4   3   2   1

## About the Contributor

**Jackie Spanitz**
General Manager
Aviation Supplies & Academics, Inc.

As ASA General Manager, Jackie Spanitz oversees maintenance and development of the books and pilot supplies in the ASA product line. Ms. Spanitz has worked with airman training and testing for more than 30 years, including participation in the Airman Certification Standards (ACS) committees. Jackie holds a Bachelor of Science in Aviation Technology from Western Michigan University, a Master of Science from Embry-Riddle Aeronautical University, and Instructor and Commercial Pilot certificates. She is the technical editor for ASA's Test Prep and FAR/AIM series.

**Aviation Supplies & Academics, Inc. (ASA)** is an industry leader in the development and sale of aviation supplies and publications for pilots, flight instructors, aviation mechanics, aircraft dispatchers, air traffic controllers, and drone operators. ASA has provided trusted training materials to millions of aviators resulting in successful airman certification for over 80 years. Visit **asa2fly.com** to learn more.

Stay informed with ASA online resources.

| Website | Updates | Blog | Author Talks |
|---|---|---|---|
|  |  |  |  |
| asa2fly.com | asa2fly.com/testupdate | learntoflyblog.com | asapresents.net |

**Follow, like, share.**

instagram.com/asa2fly
facebook.com/asa2fly
youtube.com/asa2fly
linkedin.com/company/asa2fly

# Contents

## Cross References

## FAA Figures

Airman Knowledge Testing Supplement for Sport
Pilot, Recreational Pilot, Remote Pilot, and Private
Pilot (FAA-CT-8080-2H)

# Updates and Practice Tests

## Free Test Updates for the One-Year Life Cycle of Test Prep Books

The FAA modifies tests as needed throughout the year. ASA keeps abreast of changes to the tests and posts free Test Updates on the ASA website. Before taking your test, be certain you have the most current information by visiting the ASA Test Updates webpage: **asa2fly.com/testupdate**. Additionally, sign up for free email notifications, which are sent when new Test Updates are available.

## We Invite Your Feedback

After you take your FAA exam, let us know how you did. Were you prepared? Did ASA's products meet your needs and exceed your expectations? We want to continue to improve these products to ensure applicants are prepared and become safe aviators. Send your feedback to: **cfi@asa2fly.com**.

# Introduction

Welcome to the Aviation Supplies & Academics, Inc., (ASA) Test Prep Series. This series has been helping pilots prepare for the FAA Knowledge Tests for more than 60 years with great success. We are confident that with proper use of this book you will score very well on your Private, Sport, or Recreational Pilot certificate test.

Begin your studies with a classroom or home-study ground school course, which will involve reading a comprehensive textbook. Visit the Reader Resources for this Test Prep (**asa2fly.com/TPP**) and become familiar with the FAA guidance materials available for this certification exam. Then use this Test Prep to prepare for your exam: read the question, select your choice for the correct answer, and then read the explanation. Use the references that conclude each explanation to identify additional resources for further study of a subject. Upon completion of your studies, take practice tests at **prepware.com** (see inside the front cover for your activation code).

The questions in this book have been arranged into chapters based on subject matter to promote better understanding, aid recall, and provide a more efficient study guide. Place emphasis on questions most likely to be included in your test (identified by the aircraft category above each question). For example, a pilot preparing for the Private Airplane test would focus on the questions marked "ALL" and "AIR," and a pilot preparing for the Private Helicopter test would focus on the questions marked "ALL" and "RTC." See the Description of the Tests section for more on planning your studies.

Prior to taking an FAA Airman Knowledge Test, all applicants must establish an FAA Tracking Number (FTN) by creating a profile in the Integrated Airman Certification and Rating Application (IACRA) system at **iacra.faa.gov**. Then visit **faa.psiexams.com** to register for your exam and take FAA-created practice tests to become familiar with the computer testing platform.

It is important to answer every question assigned on your FAA Knowledge Test. If in their ongoing review, the FAA decides a question has no correct answer, is no longer applicable, or is otherwise defective, your answer will be marked correct no matter which one you chose. However, you will not be given the automatic credit if you have not marked an answer. Unlike some other exams you may have taken, there is no penalty for guessing in this instance.

The FAA exams are "closed tests" which means the exact database of questions is not available to the public. The question and answer choices in this book are based on our extensive history and experience with the FAA testing and airman certification process. You might see similarly worded questions on your official FAA exam, or answer stems might be rearranged from the order you see in this book. Therefore, be sure to fully understand the intent of each question and corresponding answer while studying, rather than memorizing the letter associated with the correct response. You may be asked a question that has unfamiliar wording; studying and understanding the information in this book and the associated references will give you the tools to answer question variations with confidence.

If your study leads you to question an answer choice, we recommend you seek the assistance of a local instructor. We welcome your questions, recommendations, and concerns—send them to:

**Aviation Supplies & Academics, Inc.**
7005 132nd Place SE
Newcastle, WA 98059-3153
Phone: 425.235.1500
Email: cfi@asa2fly.com
Website: asa2fly.com

The FAA appreciates testing experience feedback. You can contact them at:

**Federal Aviation Administration**
Training & Certification Group,
Testing Standards Section
PO Box 25082
Oklahoma City, OK 73125
Email: TestingStandardsComments@faa.gov

# Description of the Tests

The FAA Knowledge Exam is an objective, multiple choice test. Each question can be answered by one of the three choices. Each test question is independent of the others—a correct response to one question does not depend on the correct response to another. You must score at least 70 percent to pass the test.

As stated in 14 CFR §61.63, an applicant does not need to take an additional knowledge test if they already hold an airplane, rotorcraft, powered-lift, weight-shift control aircraft, powered parachute, or airship rating at that pilot certificate level. For example, an applicant transitioning from gliders to airplanes will need to take the test. An applicant transitioning from weight-shift or powered parachute to airplane will need to take the test. But an applicant transitioning from airplanes to gliders, from airplanes to helicopters, or from airplanes to weight-shift or powered parachute, will *not* be required to take the test.

The table below lists the number of questions and allotted time for each test. Each question in this book is preceded by a category. Use these categories to study the content that may appear on your test. For example, if you are seeking a Private Pilot—Airplane Certificate, study questions marked ALL and AIR; if you are seeking a Recreational Pilot—Helicopter Certificate, study questions marked ALL, RTC, and REC. The content of questions marked ALL could appear on *any* Private Pilot Certificate exam.

| Test Code | Test Name | Test Prep Study | Number of Questions | Min. Age | Allotted Time (hrs) |
|---|---|---|---|---|---|
| RPA | Recreational Pilot—Airplane | ALL, AIR, REC | 50 | 15 | 2.0 |
| RPH | Recreational Pilot—Helicopter | ALL, RTC, REC | 50 | 15 | 2.0 |
| RPG | Recreational Pilot—Gyroplane | ALL, RTC, REC | 50 | 15 | 2.0 |
| PAR | Private Pilot—Airplane | ALL, AIR | 60 | 15 | 2.0 |
| PRH | Private Pilot—Helicopter | ALL, RTC | 60 | 15 | 2.5 |
| PRG | Private Pilot—Gyroplane | ALL, RTC | 60 | 15 | 2.5 |
| PGL | Private Pilot—Glider | ALL, GLI | 60 | 14 | 2.5 |
| PBH | Private Pilot—Balloon–Hot Air | ALL, LTA | 60 | 14 | 2.5 |
| PBG | Private Pilot—Balloon–Gas | ALL, LTA | 60 | 14 | 2.5 |
| PLA | Private Pilot—Airship | ALL, LTA | 60 | 15 | 2.5 |
| PPP | Private Pilot Powered Parachute | ALL, PPC | 60 | 15 | 2.5 |
| PWS | Private Pilot Weight-Shift Control | ALL, WSC | 60 | 15 | 2.5 |
| PAT | Private Pilot Airplane/ Recreational Pilot—Transition | ALL, AIR | 30 | 15 | 1.5 |
| PGT | Private Pilot Gyroplane/ Recreational Pilot—Transition | ALL, RTC | 30 | 15 | 1.5 |
| PHT | Private Pilot Helicopter/ Recreational Pilot—Transition | ALL, RTC | 30 | 15 | 1.5 |
| PCP | Private Pilot Airplane Canadian Conversion* | ALL, AIR | 40 | 16 | 2.0 |
| PCH | Private Pilot Helicopter Canadian Conversion* | ALL, RTC | 40 | 16 | 2.0 |
| PEP | Private Pilot Airplane EU Part–FCL Conversion* | ALL, AIR | 40 | 16 | 2.0 |

| SPA | Sport Pilot Airplane | SPO, LSA | 40 | 15 | 2.0 |
|-----|---------------------|----------|----|----|----|
| SPB | Sport Pilot Lighter-Than-Air (Balloon) | SPO, LSL | 40 | 15 | 2.0 |
| SPI | Sport Pilot Glider | SPO, LSG | 40 | 15 | 2.0 |
| SPL | Sport Pilot Lighter-Than-Air (Airship) | SPO, LSL | 40 | 15 | 2.0 |
| SPP | Sport Pilot Powered Parachute | SPO, LSP | 40 | 15 | 2.0 |
| SPW | Sport Pilot Weight-Shift Control | SPO, LSW | 40 | 15 | 2.0 |
| SPY | Sport Pilot Gyroplane | SPO, LSR | 40 | 15 | 2.0 |

* This test focuses on U.S. regulations, airspace, ATC services and practices, communications, and emergency procedures.

# Knowledge Test Registration

The FAA testing provider authorizes hundreds of test center locations that offer a full range of airman knowledge tests. For information on authorized testing centers and to register for the knowledge test, visit **faa.psiexams.com**.

When you contact a knowledge testing center, be prepared to select a test date and make payment. You may register for test(s) several weeks in advance online or by phone, and you may cancel in accordance with the testing center's cancellation policy.

Regardless of your registration method, you will need an FAA Tracking Number (FTN) prior to registering for the FAA Airman Knowledge Test. This FTN will follow you throughout your aviation career. You will obtain your FTN as part of the test registration process, by creating a profile in the Integrated Airman Certificate and Rating Application (IACRA) system at **iacra.faa.gov/IACRA**. This FTN will be printed on your Airman Knowledge Test Report (AKTR).

The test registration process includes collection of this information: name, FTN, physical address, date of birth, email address, photo identification, phone number, test authorization (credentials of the individual such as an instructor endorsement), and previous number of test attempts.

Step 1: Create a profile using the IACRA system and login to obtain your FTN.
Step 2: Register for your knowledge test with PSI by phone or online.

For more information, contact:
**PSI Services LLC**
844-704-1487 or examschedule@psionline.com
faa.psiexams.com

# Knowledge Test Eligibility

When you take your FAA Knowledge Test you will be required to show proper identification that includes your photograph, signature, and home address, as well one of the following:

- A certificate of graduation from a pilot training course conducted by an FAA-approved pilot school, or a statement of accomplishment from the school certifying the satisfactory completion of the ground-school portion of such a course.

- A written statement from an FAA-certified ground or flight instructor, certifying that you have satisfactorily completed the required ground instruction. (See the examples below.)

- Logbook entries by an FAA-certified ground or flight instructor, certifying satisfactory completion of the required ground instruction.

- A certificate of graduation or statement of accomplishment from a ground school course conducted by an agency such as a high school, college, adult education program, the Civil Air Patrol, or a Reserve Officers' Training Corp (ROTC) Flight Training Program.

- A certificate of graduation from a home-study course developed by the aeronautical enterprise providing the study material.

Complete two Prepware practice tests with scores of 80% or higher to get your knowledge test endorsement for any pilot rating directly from ASA. Visit **asa2fly.com/prepware** or **prepware.com** for more details.

If you are taking the test again, you must present the unsatisfactory AKTR (if failed) or register after 30 days (if seeking a higher passing score). See Retesting Procedures for more details.

If a flight or ground instructor is providing your endorsement, they may adapt one of the following statements:

### Private or Recreational Endorsement

I certify that *(First name, MI, Last name)* _____ has received the required training in accordance with (Private 14 CFR §61.105 *or* Recreational §61.97). I have determined he/she is prepared for the *(Test name; e.g., Private Pilot – Airplane)* _____ _____ knowledge test.

Signed _____ Date _____

CFI Number _____ Expires _____

### Sport Endorsement

I certify that *(First name, MI, Last name)* _____ has received the required aeronautical knowledge training of §61.309. I have determined he/she is prepared for the Sport Pilot *(category)* _____ knowledge test.

Signed _____ Date _____

CFI Number _____ Expires _____

## Acceptable Materials

The applicant may use test aids and materials within the guidelines listed below during the test, if actual test questions or answers are not revealed.

| Acceptable Materials | Unacceptable Materials | Notes |
|---|---|---|
| Supplement book provided by proctor. | Written materials that are hand-written, printed, or electronic. | Testing centers may provide calculators and/or deny the use of personal calculators. |
| All models of aviation-oriented calculators or small electronic calculators that perform only arithmetic functions. | Electronic calculators incorporating permanent or continuous type memory circuits without erasure capability. | Test proctor may prohibit the use of your calculator if he or she is unable to determine the calculator's erasure capability. |
| Calculators with simple programmable memories, which allow addition to, subtraction from, or retrieval of one number from the memory; or simple functions, such as square root and percentages. | Magnetic cards, magnetic tapes, modules, computer chips, or any other device upon which pre-written programs or information related to the test can be stored and retrieved. | Printouts of data must be surrendered at the completion of the test if the calculator incorporates this design feature. |
| Scales, straight-edges, protractors, plotters, navigation computers, blank log sheets, holding pattern entry aids, and electronic or mechanical calculators that are directly related to the test. | Dictionaries. | Before, and upon completion of the test, while in the presence of the test proctor, actuate the ON/OFF switch or RESET button, and perform any other function that ensures erasure of any data stored in memory circuits. |
| Manufacturer's permanently inscribed instructions on the front and back of such aids, such as formulas, conversions, regulations, signals, weather data, holding pattern diagrams, frequencies, weight and balance formulas, and ATC procedures. | Any booklet or manual containing instructions related to use of test aids. | Test proctor makes the final determination regarding aids, reference materials, and test materials. |

## Testing Procedures for Applicants Requesting Special Accommodations

If you are an applicant with a learning or reading disability, you may request approval from the local FAA office to take an airman knowledge test, using the special accommodations procedures outlined in the most current version of FAA Order 8080.6 Conduct of Airman Knowledge Tests.

Prior to approval of any option, the FAA Aviation Safety Inspector must advise you of the regulatory certification requirement of being able to read, write, speak, and understand the English language.

## Test Reports

Your test will be graded immediately upon completion and your score will display on the computer screen. You will receive your Airman Knowledge Test Report (AKTR), which will state your score. See sample AKTR on the next page.

Visit **faa.psiexams.com** to request a duplicate or replacement AKTR due to loss or destruction.

Airman Knowledge Test Reports are valid for 24 calendar months. If the AKTR expires before completion of the practical test, you must retake the knowledge test.

Your AKTR lists the ACS code (if an ACS is available for the certificate and rating specific to the test) or Learning Statement Code (LSC) (if a Practical Test Standard is in effect for the certificate and rating specific to the test) for questions answered incorrectly. The total number of ASCs/LSCs shown on the AKTR is not necessarily an indication of the total number of questions answered incorrectly. Study these knowledge areas to improve your understanding of the subject matter. See Cross-Reference B in the back of this book for a listing of ASCs and LSCs and their associated questions.

Your instructor is required to provide instruction on each of the knowledge areas listed on your AKTR and to complete an endorsement of this instruction. You must present this to the examiner prior to taking the practical test. During the oral portion of the practical test, the examiner is required to evaluate the noted areas of deficiency.

## Retesting Procedures

Applicants retesting *after failure* are required to submit the applicable AKTR indicating failure, along with an endorsement (on the test report) from an authorized instructor, who gave the applicant the additional training, certifying the applicant is competent to pass the test. The original failed AKTR and retest endorsement presented as authorization shall be retained by the proctor and attached to the applicable sign-in/out log. The latest test taken will reflect the official score.

Applicants retesting *in an attempt to achieve a higher passing score* may retake the same test for a better grade after 30 days. The latest test taken will reflect the official score. Applicants are required to submit the original applicable AKTR indicating previous passing score to the testing center prior to testing. Testing center personnel must collect and destroy this report prior to issuing the new test report.

## Cheating or Other Unauthorized Conduct

Computer testing centers must follow strict security procedures to avoid test compromise. These procedures are established by the FAA and are covered in FAA Order 8080.6 Conduct of Airman Knowledge Tests. The FAA has directed testing centers to terminate a test at any time a test proctor suspects a cheating incident has occurred. An FAA investigation will then be conducted. If the investigation determines that cheating or unauthorized conduct has occurred, then any airman certificate or rating that you hold may be revoked, and you will be prohibited for one year from applying for or taking any test for a certificate or rating under 14 CFR Part 61.

## U.S. DEPARTMENT OF TRANSPORTATION
### Federal Aviation Administration
### Airman Knowledge Test Report

**NAME:** TAYLOR SMITH

**FAA TRACKING NUMBER (FTN):** C1234567     **EXAM ID:** 98765432109876543

**EXAM:** Private Pilot – Airplane (PAR)

**EXAM DATE:** 09/15/2024     **EXAM SITE:** ABC12345

**SCORE:** 88%     **GRADE:** Pass     **TAKE:** 1

The Airman Certification Standards (ACS) codes listed below represent incorrectly answered questions. These ACS codes and their associated Areas of Operation/Tasks/Elements may be found in the appropriate ACS document at http://www.faa.gov/training_testing/testing/acs.

A single code may represent more than one incorrect response.

PA.I.C.K3a    PA.I.C.K3k    PA.I.F.K1    PA.III.A.K1    PA.III.A.K8    PA.VI.A.K2    PA.VI.A.K5c

**EXPIRATION DATE:** 09/30/2026

# DO NOT LOSE THIS REPORT

----

AUTHORIZED INSTRUCTOR'S STATEMENT: (if applicable)

On _____ (date) I gave the above named applicant _____ hours of additional instruction, covering each subject area shown to be deficient, and consider the applicant competent to pass the knowledge test.

Name _____

Cert. No. _____ *(print clearly)*

Type of instructor certificate _____

Signature _____

**FRAUDULENT ALTERATION OF THIS FORM BY ANY PERSON IS A BASIS FOR SUSPENSION OR REVOCATION OF ANY CERTIFICATES OR RATINGS HELD BY THAT PERSON.**
**ISSUED BY: PSI Services LLC**
**FEDERAL AVIATION ADMINISTRATION**

**THIS INFORMATION IS PROTECTED BY THE PRIVACY ACT. FOR OFFICIAL USE ONLY.**

Sample Airman Knowledge Test Report

# Test-Taking Tips

Prior to launching the actual test, the test proctor's testing software will provide you with an opportunity to practice navigating through the test. This practice (or tutorial) session may include a "sample" question(s). These sample questions have no relation to the content of the test, but are meant to familiarize you with the look and feel of the system screens, including selecting an answer, marking a question for later review, time remaining for the test, and other features of the testing software.

Follow these time-proven tips, which will help you develop a skillful, smooth approach to test-taking:

- Visit **faa.psiexams.com** to take a small sample test to become familiar with the latest PSI exam interface you will see on your actual FAA knowledge test.

- Be careful to fully understand the intent of each question and corresponding answer while studying, rather than memorizing the A, B, C answer choice—answer stems may appear in a different order than you studied and have some wording differences.

- Remember to bring a sign-off from an instructor, photo I.D., the testing fee, calculator, flight computer (ASA's E6-B or CX-3 Flight Computer), plotter, magnifying glass, and a sharp pointer, such as a safety pin.

- Your first action when you sit down should be to write any formulas and information you can remember from your study on the scratch paper they will provide. Remember, some of the formulas may be on your E6-B.

- Read each question carefully before looking at the possible answers. You should clearly understand the problem before attempting to solve it.

- After formulating an answer, determine which answer choice corresponds the closest with your answer. The answer chosen should completely resolve the problem.

- From the answer choices given, it may appear that there is more than one possible answer. However, there is only one answer that is correct and complete. The other answers are either incomplete, erroneous, or represent popular misconceptions.

- Answer each question in accordance with the latest regulations and guidance publications.

- If a certain question is difficult for you, tag it for review and proceed to the other questions. After you answer the less difficult questions, return to those which you tagged and answer them. Be sure to untag these questions once you have answered them. The review marking procedure will be explained to you prior to starting the test. Although the computer should alert you to unanswered questions, make sure every question has an answer recorded. This will allow you to use the available time to your maximum advantage.

- Perform each math calculation twice to confirm your answer. If adding or subtracting a column of numbers, reverse your direction the second time to reduce the possibility of error.

- When solving a calculation problem, select the answer nearest to your solution.

- Remember that information is provided in the Legends and Figures contained within the Airman Knowledge Testing Supplement (FAA-CT-8080 document) you'll be using during the test.

- Remember to answer every question, even the ones with no completely correct answer, to ensure the FAA gives you credit for a bad question.

- Take your time and be thorough but relaxed. Take a minute off every half-hour or so to relax your brain and body. Stay hydrated.

- Your test will be graded immediately upon completion.

# Pilot Certificate Eligibility Requirements

If you are pursuing a **Student Pilot Certificate**, you should review §61.83 "Applicability and Eligibility Requirements: General," for additional detailed information pertaining to eligibility.

If you are pursuing a **Sport Pilot Certificate**, you should review Part 61 Subpart J for eligibility and operating limitation information.

If you are pursuing a **Recreational Pilot Certificate**, you should review §61.96 "Applicability and Eligibility Requirements: General," for additional detailed information pertaining to eligibility.

If you are pursuing a **Private Pilot Certificate**, you should review §61.103 "Applicability and Eligibility Requirements: General," for additional detailed information pertaining to eligibility.

If you are pursuing a **Recreational Pilot** or **Private Pilot Certificate**, you should also review §61.23 "Medical Certificates: Requirement and Duration" and §61.35 "Knowledge Test: Prerequisites and Passing Grades." Recreational and private pilot tests are comprehensive because they must test your knowledge in many subject areas. If you are pursuing a Recreational Pilot Certificate or added rating, you should closely examine and understand §61.97 "Aeronautical Knowledge" for the applicable knowledge areas. If you are pursuing a Private Pilot Certificate or added rating, you should closely examine and understand §61.105 "Aeronautical Knowledge" for the applicable knowledge areas.

Always check the current Part 61 for pilot certificate requirements. To be eligible for a Private Pilot certificate with an airplane, helicopter, or glider rating a person must:

1. Be at least 17 years old (16 for a glider or balloon rating).

2. Be able to read, speak, write, and understand English or have a limitation placed on the certificate.

3. Have at least a current Third Class Medical Certificate or a driver's license and compliance with Part 68 and §61.23.

4. Hold a U.S. Student Pilot, Sport Pilot, or Recreational Pilot Certificate.

5. Score at least 70 percent on the required FAA Knowledge Test on the appropriate subjects.

6. Pass an oral exam and flight check on the subjects and maneuvers outlined in the Private Pilot Airman Certification or Practical Test Standards (ACS-6, 8081-15, or 8081-3).

7. For an airplane or helicopter rating, have a total of 40 hours of instruction (for Part 61 programs) and solo flight time which must include the following:

   a. 20 hours of flight instruction, including at least—

      i. 3 hours cross-country,

      ii. 3 hours at night including 10 takeoffs and landings and one cross-country flight of over 100 nautical miles (NM) total distance for airplanes (50 NM for helicopters),

      iii. 3 hours of instrument flight training in a single-engine airplane for the airplane rating, and

      iv. 3 hours in an airplane or helicopter within the last 60 days in preparation for the flight test.

   b. 10 hours of solo flight time in airplanes or helicopters, including at least—

      i. 10 hours in airplanes or helicopters;

      ii. 5 hours cross-country in airplanes, each flight with a landing more than 50 NM from the point of departure and one flight of at least 150 NM with 3 landings, one of which must be least 50 NM from the departure point;

      iii. Or 3 hours of cross-country in helicopters with landings at three points at least 25 miles from each other and one cross-country flight of at least 75 NM total distance, with landings at a minimum of three points, and one segment of the flight being a straight-line distance of at least 25 NM between the takeoff and landing locations; and

iv. Three takeoffs and landings to a full stop at an airport with an operating control tower, each landing separated by an enroute phase of flight (and involving a flight in the traffic pattern in a helicopter).

8. For a glider rating, have at least one of the following:

a. If the applicant has not logged at least 40 hours of flight time as a pilot in a heavier-than-air aircraft: at least 10 hours of flight training in a glider, and 20 training flights performed on the appropriate areas, including—

i. 2 hours of solo flight in gliders in the areas of operation that apply to gliders, with not less than 10 launches and landings being performed; and

ii. Three training flights in a glider in preparation for the practical test within the 60-day period preceding the practical test.

b. If the applicant has logged at least 40 hours of flight time in heavier-than-air aircraft: at least 3 hours of flight training in a glider, and 10 training flights performed on the appropriate areas, including—

i. 10 solo flights in gliders on the areas of operation that apply to gliders, and

ii. Three training flights in preparation for the practical test within the 60-day waiting period preceding the test.

9. For a lighter-than-air rating, have at least one of the following:

a. For an airship rating:

i. 25 hours of flight training in airships, which consists of at least:

• 3 hours of cross-country flight training in an airship;

• 3 hours of night flight training in an airship that includes:

— A cross-country flight of over 25 NM total distance; and

— 5 takeoffs and 5 landings to a full stop (with each landing involving a flight in the traffic pattern) at an airport.

ii. 3 hours of instrument flight training in an airship;

iii. 3 hours of flight training in an airship in preparation for the practical test within the 60 days preceding the date of the test; and

iv. 5 hours performing the duties of PIC in an airship with an authorized instructor.

b. For a balloon rating, at least 10 hours of flight training that includes at least 6 training flights with an authorized instructor, that includes—

i. If the training is in a gas balloon, at least 2 flights of 2 hours each that consists of—

• At least one training flight with an authorized instructor within 60 days prior to application for the rating on the areas of operation for a gas balloon;

• At least one flight performing the duties of pilot in command in a gas balloon with an authorized instructor; and

• At least one flight involving a controlled ascent to 3,000 feet above the launch site.

ii. If the training is in a balloon with an airborne heater, at least—

• Two 1-hour flights within 60 days prior to application for the rating on the areas of operation appropriate to a balloon with an airborne heater;

• One solo flight in a balloon with an airborne heater; and

• At least one flight involving a controlled ascent to 2,000 feet above the launch site.

10. For a powered parachute rating, have at least 25 hours of flight time in a powered parachute that includes at least 10 hours of flight training with an authorized instructor, including 30 takeoffs and landings, and 10 hours of solo flight training, that includes—

    a. 1 hour of cross-country flight with a landing at an airport at least 25 NM from the airport of departure;

    b. 3 hours of night flight training in a powered parachute that includes 10 takeoffs and landings (with each landing involving a flight in the traffic pattern) at an airport;

    c. 3 hours of flight training within the last 60 days in preparation for the practical test in a powered parachute; and

    d. 3 hours of solo flight time in a powered parachute, consisting of at least—

        i. One solo cross-country flight with a landing at an airport at least 25 NM from the departure airport; and

        ii. 20 solo takeoffs and landings to a full stop (with each landing involving a flight in a traffic pattern) at an airport, with at least 3 takeoffs and landings at an airport with an operating control tower.

11. For a weight-shift control aircraft rating, have at least 40 hours of flight time that includes at least 20 hours of flight training with an authorized instructor and 10 hours of solo flight training that includes—

    a. 3 hours of cross-country flight training in a weight-shift control aircraft;

    b. 3 hours of night flight training in a weight-shift control aircraft that includes—

        i. One cross-country flight over 75 NM total distance; and

        ii. 10 takeoffs and landings (with each landing involving a flight in the traffic pattern) at an airport;

    c. 3 hours of flight training within the last 60 days in preparation for the practical test in a weight-shift control aircraft, and

    d. 10 hours of solo flight time in a weight-shift control aircraft, consisting of at least—

        i. 5 hours of solo cross-country time;

        ii. One solo cross-country flight over 100 NM total distance, with landings at a minimum of three points, and one segment of the flight being a straight line distance of at least 50 NM between takeoff and landing locations; and

        iii. Three takeoffs and landings (with each landing involving a flight in the traffic pattern) at an airport with an operating control tower.

Always check the current Part 61 for pilot certificate requirements. To be eligible for a Sport Pilot Certificate a person must:

1. Be at least 17 years old (16 if you are applying to operate a glider or balloon).

2. Be able to read, speak, write, and understand English or have a limitation placed on the certificate.

3. Score at least 70 percent on the required FAA Knowledge Test.

4. Pass a practical test on the subjects and maneuvers outlined in the Sport Pilot Practical Test Standards (#ASA-8081-SPORT Sport Pilot for Airplane, Weight-Shift Control, Powered Parachute, and Flight Instructor).

5. See §61.329 for the special provisions for obtaining a Sport Pilot certificate as a registered ultralight pilot with an FAA-recognized ultralight organization.

6. The table on the next page explains the aeronautical experience you must have to apply for a Sport Pilot Certificate.

| If you are applying for a sport pilot certificate with... | Then you must log at least... | Which must include at least... |
|---|---|---|
| **(a)** Airplane category and single-engine land or sea class privileges, | (1) 20 hours of flight time, including at least 15 hours of flight training from an authorized instructor in a single-engine airplane and at least 5 hours of solo flight training in the areas of operation listed in §61.311, | (i) 2 hours of cross-country flight training, <br>(ii) 10 takeoffs and landings to a full stop (with each landing involving a flight in the traffic pattern) at an airport; <br>(iii) One solo cross-country flight of at least 75 nautical miles total distance, with a full-stop landing at a minimum of two points and one segment of the flight consisting of a straight-line distance of at least 25 nautical miles between the takeoff and landing locations, and <br>(iv) 2 hours of flight training with an authorized instructor on those areas of operation specified in §61.311 in preparation for the practical test within the preceding 2 calendar months from the month of the test. |
| **(b)** Glider category privileges, and you have not logged at least 20 hours of flight time in a heavier-than-air aircraft, | (1) 10 hours of flight time in a glider, including 10 flights in a glider receiving flight training from an authorized instructor and at least 2 hours of solo flight training in the areas of operation listed in §61.311, | (i) Five solo launches and landings, and <br>(ii) at least 3 training flights with an authorized instructor on those areas of operation specified in §61.311 in preparation for the practical test within the preceding 2 calendar months from the month of the test. |
| **(c)** Glider category privileges, and you have logged 20 hours flight time in a heavier-than-air aircraft, | (1) 3 hours of flight time in a glider, including five flights in a glider while receiving flight training from an authorized instructor and at least 1 hour of solo flight training in the areas of operation listed in §61.311, | (i) Three solo launches and landings, and <br>(ii) at least 3 training flights with an authorized instructor on those areas of operation specified in §61.311 in preparation for the practical test within the preceding 2 calendar months from the month of the test. |
| **(d)** Rotorcraft category and gyroplane class privileges, | (1) 20 hours of flight time, including 15 hours of flight training from an authorized instructor in a gyroplane and at least 5 hours of solo flight training in the areas of operation listed in §61.311, | (i) 2 hours of cross-country flight training, <br>(ii) 10 takeoffs and landings to a full stop (with each landing involving a flight in the traffic pattern) at an airport, <br>(iii) One solo cross-country flight of at least 50 nautical miles total distance, with a full-stop landing at a minimum of two points, and one segment of the flight consisting of a straight-line distance of at least 25 nautical miles between the takeoff and landing locations, and <br>(iv) 2 hours of flight training with an authorized instructor on those areas of operation specified in §61.311 in preparation for the practical test within the preceding 2 calendar months from the month of the test. |
| **(e)** Lighter-than-air category and airship class privileges, | (1) 20 hours of flight time, including 15 hours of flight training from an authorized instructor in an airship and at least 3 hours performing the duties of pilot in command in an airship with an authorized instructor in the areas of operation listed in §61.311, | (i) 2 hours of cross-country flight training, <br>(ii) Three takeoffs and landings to a full stop (with each landing involving a flight in the traffic pattern) at an airport, <br>(iii) One cross-country flight of at least 25 nautical miles between the takeoff and landing locations, and <br>(iv) 2 hours of flight training with an authorized instructor on those areas of operation specified in §61.311 in preparation for the practical test within the preceding 2 calendar months from the month of the test. |
| **(f)** Lighter-than-air category and balloon class privileges, | (1) 7 hours of flight time in a balloon, including three flights with an authorized instructor and one flight performing the duties of pilot in command in a balloon with an authorized instructor in the areas of operation listed in §61.311, | (i) 2 hours of cross-country flight training and <br>(ii) 1 hour of flight training with an authorized instructor on those areas of operation specified in §61.311 in preparation for the practical test within the preceding 2 calendar months from the month of the test. |
| **(g)** Powered parachute category land or sea class privileges, | (1) 12 hours of flight time in a powered parachute, including 10 hours of flight training from an authorized instructor in a powered parachute, and at least 2 hours of solo flight training in the areas of operation listed in §61.311, | (i) 1 hour of cross-country flight training, <br>(ii) 20 takeoffs and landings to a full stop in a powered parachute with each landing involving flight in the traffic pattern at an airport, <br>(iii) 10 solo takeoffs and landings to a full stop (with each landing involving a flight in the traffic pattern) at an airport, <br>(iv) One solo flight with a landing at a different airport and one segment of the flight consisting of a straight-line distance of at least 10 nautical miles between takeoff and landing locations, and <br>(v) 1 hour of flight training with an authorized instructor on those areas of operation specified in §61.311 in preparation for the practical test within the preceding 2 calendar months from the month of the test. |
| **(h)** Weight-shift-control aircraft category land or sea class privileges, | (1) 20 hours of flight time, including 15 hours of flight training from an authorized instructor in a weight-shift-control aircraft and at least 5 hours of solo flight training in the areas of operation listed in §61.311, | (i) 2 hours of cross-country flight training; <br>(ii) 10 takeoffs and landings to a full stop (with each landing involving a flight in the traffic pattern) at an airport, <br>(iii) One solo cross-country flight of at least 50 nautical miles total distance, with a full-stop landing at a minimum of two points, and one segment of the flight consisting of a straight-line distance of at least 25 nautical miles between takeoff and landing locations, and <br>(iv) 2 hours of flight training with an authorized instructor on those areas of operation specified in §61.311 in preparation for the practical test within the preceding 2 calendar months from the month of the test. |

# Acronyms

For reference, acronyms appearing in this book are defined below.

| | | | | |
|---|---|---|---|---|
| AC | Advisory Circular | | FA | area forecast |
| ACS | Airman Certification Standard | | FAR | Federal Aviation Regulations |
| AD | Airworthiness Directive | | FB | winds and temperatures aloft forecast |
| ADM | aeronautical decision making | | FDC | Flight Data Center |
| ADS-B | Automatic Dependent Surveillance–Broadcast | | FL | flight level |
| AFM | aircraft flight manual | | FSDO | Flight Standards District Office |
| AGL | above ground level | | FSS | Flight Service Station |
| AIM | Aeronautical Information Manual | | GFA | Graphical Forecast for Aviation |
| AIRMET | airman's meteorological information | | GPO | Government Printing Office |
| AKTR | Airman Knowledge Test Report | | GPS | Global Positioning System |
| ALD | available landing distance | | GS | ground speed |
| AME | Aviation Medical Examiner | | IA | inspection authorization |
| ARTCC | Air Route Traffic Control Center | | IAS | indicated airspeed |
| ARTS | automated radar terminal system | | IFR | instrument flight rules |
| ASOS | Automated Surface Observing System | | IMC | instrument meteorological conditions |
| ATIS | Automatic Terminal Information Service | | KIAS | knots indicated airspeed |
| ATC | air traffic control | | LAHSO | land and hold short operations |
| ATCT | air traffic control tower | | LTE | loss of tail rotor effectiveness |
| AWC | Aviation Weather Center | | LSA | light sport aircraft |
| AWOS | Automated Surface Weather Observing System | | MC | magnetic course |
| CAMI | Civil Aeromedical Institute | | METAR | aviation routine weather report |
| CAS | calibrated airspeed | | MH | magnetic heading |
| CC | compass course | | MOA | Military Operations Area |
| CDI | course deviation indicator | | MSL | mean sea level |
| CG | center of gravity | | MTR | Military Training Route |
| CL | center of lift | | NAS | National Airspace System |
| CMEC | comprehensive medical examination checklist | | NAVAID | navigational aid |
| CONUS | continental United States | | NM | nautical mile |
| CTAF | Common Traffic Advisory Frequency | | NOTAM | Notice to Air Missions |
| DA | density altitude | | NTSB | National Transportation Safety Board |
| DAR | Designated Airworthiness Representative (FAA) | | OAT | outside air temperature |
| DEV | deviation (magnetic compass) | | OBS | omni bearing selector |
| DME | distance measuring equipment | | PAPI | precision approach path indicator |
| ELT | emergency locator transmitter | | PIC | pilot-in-command |
| E-LSA | experimental light sport aircraft | | PIREP | pilot report |
| | | | POH | pilot's operating handbook |
| | | | RAIM | receiver autonomous integrity monitoring |

| | |
|---|---|
| RCO | remote communication outlet |
| RPM | revolutions per minute |
| SAA | Special Activity Airspace |
| SIGMET | significant meteorological information |
| S-LSA | special light sport aircraft |
| SM | statute mile |
| TAF | terminal aerodrome forecast |
| TAS | true airspeed |
| TC | true course |
| TFR | temporary flight restriction |
| TH | true heading |
| TRSA | terminal radar service area |
| UAT | Universal Access Transceiver |
| UTC | Coordinated Universal Time |
| VAR | magnetic variation |
| VASI | visual approach slope indicator |
| VFR | visual flight rules |
| VIP | video integrator processor (weather radar) |
| VOR | VHF Omnidirectional Range |
| VOT | VOR Test Facility |
| WCA | wind correction angle |

# Knowledge Exam References

The FAA references the following documents to write the FAA Knowledge Exam questions. You should be familiar with all of these as part of your ground school studies, which you should complete before starting test preparation.

FAA-H-8083-1 *Aircraft Weight and Balance Handbook*

FAA-H-8083-2 *Risk Management Handbook*

FAA-H-8083-3 *Airplane Flying Handbook*

FAA-H-8083-5 *Weight-Shift Control Aircraft Flying Handbook*

FAA-H-8083-11 *Balloon Flying Handbook*

FAA-H-8083-13 *Glider Flying Handbook*

FAA-H-8083-21 *Helicopter Flying Handbook*

FAA-H-8083-25 *Pilot's Handbook of Aeronautical Knowledge*

FAA-H-8083-28 *Aviation Weather Handbook*

FAA-H-8083-29 *Powered Parachute Flying Handbook*

FAA-S-ACS-6 *Private Pilot Airplane Airman Certification Standards*

FAA-S-ACS-15 *Private Pilot Helicopter Airman Certification Standards*

FAA-S-8081-3 *Recreational Pilot Practical Test Standards*

FAA-S-8081-29 & FAA-S-8081-31 *Sport Pilot Practical Test Standards*

*Aeronautical Chart User's Guide*

*Chart Supplements U.S.*

Sectional Aeronautical Chart (SAC)

*Aeronautical Information Manual (AIM)*

14 CFR Parts 1, 21, 39, 43, 48, 61, 68, 71, 89, 91, 107

49 CFR Part 830 (NTSB)

49 CFR Part 1554 (TSA)

Visit **asa2fly.com** for these and many more titles and pilot supplies for your aviation endeavors.
Visit **asa2fly.com/TPP** for reader resources useful to private, recreational, and sport pilots.

# ASA Test Prep Layout

Sample FAA questions have been sorted into chapters according to subject matter. Within each chapter, similar questions are grouped together following introductory chapter text. Figures referenced in the chapter text are numbered with the appropriate chapter number, e.g., "Figure 1-1" is Chapter 1's first chapter text figure.

Some sample FAA questions refer to Figures or Legends immediately following the question number, e.g., "1201. (Refer to Figure 14.)." These are FAA Figures and Legends from the Airman Knowledge Testing Supplement (FAA-CT-8080-2H) that can be found at the back of this book. This supplement will be provided to you as a separate booklet when you take your FAA test.

Following each sample FAA test question is ASA's explanation in italics. The last line of the explanation contains a Learning Statement Code (LSC), for those tests referencing an FAA Practical Test Standard (PTS), or Airman Certification Standards (ACS) code, for those tests with an ACS, as well as a reference for further study. Some questions include an explanation for the incorrect answers for added clarity. When you encounter a difficult question, find the LSC or ACS code in Cross-Reference B, and then look for material relating to the subject description within the given reference(s). Refer to Cross-Reference B for more information on how to use LSCs or ACS codes for effective studying.

Answers to each question are found at the bottom of each page.

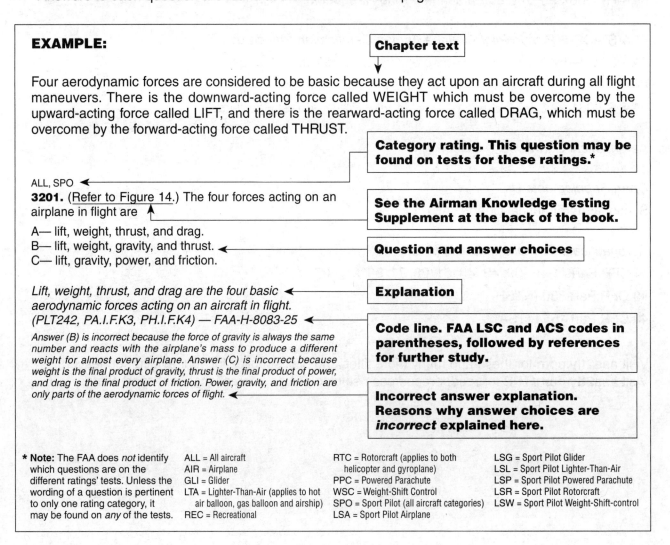

**EXAMPLE:**

Chapter text

Four aerodynamic forces are considered to be basic because they act upon an aircraft during all flight maneuvers. There is the downward-acting force called WEIGHT which must be overcome by the upward-acting force called LIFT, and there is the rearward-acting force called DRAG, which must be overcome by the forward-acting force called THRUST.

**Category rating. This question may be found on tests for these ratings.***

ALL, SPO

**3201.** (Refer to Figure 14.) The four forces acting on an airplane in flight are

**See the Airman Knowledge Testing Supplement at the back of the book.**

A— lift, weight, thrust, and drag.
B— lift, weight, gravity, and thrust.
C— lift, gravity, power, and friction.

**Question and answer choices**

*Lift, weight, thrust, and drag are the four basic aerodynamic forces acting on an aircraft in flight.*

**Explanation**

*(PLT242, PA.I.F.K3, PH.I.F.K4) — FAA-H-8083-25*

**Code line. FAA LSC and ACS codes in parentheses, followed by references for further study.**

*Answer (B) is incorrect because the force of gravity is always the same number and reacts with the airplane's mass to produce a different weight for almost every airplane. Answer (C) is incorrect because weight is the final product of gravity, thrust is the final product of power, and drag is the final product of friction. Power, gravity, and friction are only parts of the aerodynamic forces of flight.*

**Incorrect answer explanation. Reasons why answer choices are *incorrect* explained here.**

***\* Note:*** The FAA does *not* identify which questions are on the different ratings' tests. Unless the wording of a question is pertinent to only one rating category, it may be found on *any* of the tests.

ALL = All aircraft
AIR = Airplane
GLI = Glider
LTA = Lighter-Than-Air (applies to hot air balloon, gas balloon and airship)
REC = Recreational

RTC = Rotorcraft (applies to both helicopter and gyroplane)
PPC = Powered Parachute
WSC = Weight-Shift Control
SPO = Sport Pilot (all aircraft categories)
LSA = Sport Pilot Airplane

LSG = Sport Pilot Glider
LSL = Sport Pilot Lighter-Than-Air
LSP = Sport Pilot Powered Parachute
LSR = Sport Pilot Rotorcraft
LSW = Sport Pilot Weight-Shift-control

# Chapter 1
# Aerodynamics

# Aerodynamic Terms

An **airfoil** is a structure or body which produces a useful reaction to air movement. Airplane wings, helicopter rotor blades, and propellers are airfoils. See Figure 1-1.

The **chord line** is an imaginary straight line from the leading edge to the trailing edge of an airfoil. See Figure 1-2. Changing the shape of an airfoil (by lowering flaps, for example) will change the chord line. See Figure 1-3.

In aerodynamics, **relative wind** is the wind felt by an airfoil. It is created by the movement of air past an airfoil, by the motion of an airfoil through the air, or by a combination of the two. Relative wind is parallel to and travels in the opposite direction of the flight path of the airfoil. See Figure 1-4.

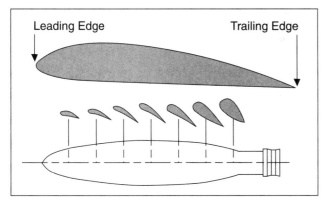

**Figure 1-1.** A typical airfoil cross-section

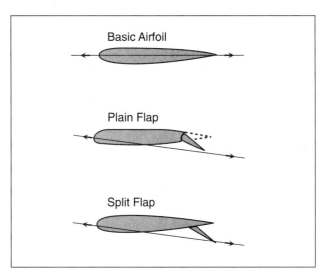

**Figure 1-3.** Changing shape of wing changes the chord line

**Figure 1-2.** Chord line

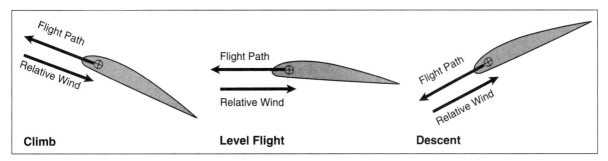

**Figure 1-4.** Relative wind

The **angle of attack** is the angle between the chord line of the airfoil and the relative wind. By manipulating the aircraft controls, the pilot can vary the angle of attack. See Figure 1-5.

The **angle of incidence** is the angle at which a wing is attached to the aircraft fuselage. The airplane pilot has no control over the angle of incidence. See Figure 1-6. The angle of incidence changes for a powered parachute based on the design, and is controlled by the pilot on a weight-shift control aircraft.

**Figure 1-5.** Angle of attack

**Figure 1-6.** Angle of incidence

ALL

**3203.** (Refer to Figure 1.) The acute angle A is the angle of

A—incidence.
B—attack.
C—dihedral.

*The angle of attack is the acute angle between the relative wind and the chord line of the wing. (PLT168, PA.I.F.K3, PH.I.F.K4) — FAA-H-8083-25*

Answer (A) is incorrect because the angle of incidence is the angle formed by the longitudinal axis of the airplane and the chord line. Answer (C) is incorrect because the dihedral is the upward angle of the airplane's wings with respect to the horizontal.

ALL, SPO

**3204.** The term "angle of attack" is defined as the angle

A—between the wing chord line and the relative wind.
B—between the airplane's climb angle and the horizon.
C—formed by the longitudinal axis of the airplane and the chord line of the wing.

*The angle of attack is the acute angle between the relative wind and the chord line of the wing. (PLT168, PA.I.F.K3, PH.I.F.K4) — FAA-H-8083-25*

Answer (B) is incorrect because there is no specific aviation term for this. Answer (C) is incorrect because this is the definition of the angle of incidence.

**Answers**

3203    [B]          3204    [A]

ALL

**3204-1.** The angle between the chord line of an airfoil and the relative wind is known as the angle of

A—lift.
B—attack.
C—incidence.

*The angle of attack is the acute angle between the chord line of the wing and the direction of the relative wind. (PLT168, PA.I.F.K3, PH.I.F.K4) — FAA-H-8083-25*

Answer (A) is incorrect because the angle of lift is not an aerodynamic term used in aviation. Answer (C) is incorrect because the angle between the chordline of an airfoil and the longitudinal axis of an aircraft is known as the angle of incidence.

ALL

**3317.** The term angle of attack is defined as the angle between the

A—chord line of the wing and the relative wind.
B—airplane's longitudinal axis and that of the air striking the airfoil.
C—airplane's center line and the relative wind.

*The angle of attack is the angle between the chord line of the airfoil and the direction of the relative wind. (PLT168, PA.I.F.K3, PH.I.F.K4) — FAA-H-8083-25*

SPO

**2225.** The angle of attack at which an airfoil stalls will

A—increase if the CG is moved forward.
B—remain the same regardless of gross weight.
C—change with an increase in gross weight.

*When the angle of attack is increased to between 18° and 20° (critical angle of attack) on most airfoils, the airstream can no longer follow the upper curvature of the wing because of the excessive change in direction. The airfoil will stall if the critical angle of attack is exceeded. The indicated airspeed at which stall occurs will be determined by weight and load factor, but the stall angle of attack is the same. (PLT477) — FAA-H-8083-25*

Answers (A) and (C) are incorrect because an airfoil will always stall at the same angle of attack, regardless of the CG position or gross weight.

SPO

**2225-1.** What is the effect of advancing the throttle in flight?

A—Both aircraft groundspeed and angle of attack will increase.
B—Airspeed will remain relatively constant but the aircraft will climb.
C—The aircraft will accelerate, which will cause a turn to the right.

*During straight-and-level flight, if the angle of attack is not coordinated (decreased) with an increase of thrust, the aircraft will climb. (PLT132) — FAA-H-8083-25*

**Answers**

3204-1 [B]          3317   [A]          2225   [B]          2225-1 [B]

# Axes of Rotation and the Four Forces

Aircraft have three axes of rotation: the lateral axis, longitudinal axis, and the vertical axis. See Figure 1-7.

The **lateral axis** is an imaginary line from wing tip to wing tip for an airplane. The rotation around this axis is called **pitch**. Pitch is controlled by the elevators, and this rotation is referred to as **longitudinal control** or **longitudinal stability**. See Figure 1-8.

The **longitudinal axis** is an imaginary line from the nose to the tail. Rotation around the longitudinal axis is called **roll**. Roll is controlled by the ailerons, and this rotation is referred to as **lateral control** or **lateral stability**. See Figure 1-9.

The **vertical axis** is an imaginary line extending vertically through the intersection of the lateral and longitudinal axes. Rotation about the vertical axis is called **yaw**. Yaw is controlled by the rudder, and this rotation is referred to as **directional control** or **directional stability**. See Figure 1-10.

The **center of gravity (CG)** (the imaginary point where all the weight is concentrated) is the point at which an airplane would balance if it were suspended at that point. The three axes intersect at the center of gravity. Weight-shift control and powered parachutes rotate around this center of gravity.

**Figure 1-7.** Axes of rotation

**Figure 1-8.** Effect of elevators

**Figure 1-9.** Effect of ailerons

**Figure 1-10.** Effect of rudder

Four aerodynamic forces are considered to be basic because they act upon an aircraft during all flight maneuvers: there is the downward-acting force called **weight** which must be overcome by the upward-acting force called **lift**; and there is the rearward-acting force called **drag**, which must be overcome by the forward-acting force called **thrust**. See Figure 1-11.

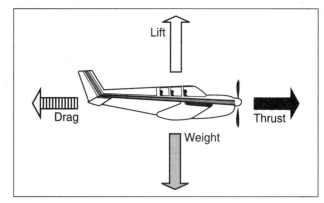

**Figure 1-11.** Relationship of forces in flight

## Lift

Air is a gas which can be compressed or expanded. When compressed, more air can occupy a given volume and air density is increased. When allowed to expand, air occupies a greater space and density is decreased. Temperature, atmospheric pressure, and humidity all affect air density. Air density has significant effects on an aircraft's performance.

As the velocity of a fluid (gas or liquid) increases, its pressure decreases. This is known as **Bernoulli's principle**. See Figure 1-12.

Lift is the result of a pressure difference between the top and the bottom of the wing. A wing is designed to accelerate air over the top camber of the wing, thereby decreasing the pressure on the top and producing lift. See Figure 1-13.

Several factors are involved in the creation of lift: angle of attack, wing area and shape (planform), air velocity, and air density. All of these factors have an effect on the amount of lift produced at any given moment. The pilot can actively control the angle of attack and the airspeed, and increasing either of these will result in an increase in lift.

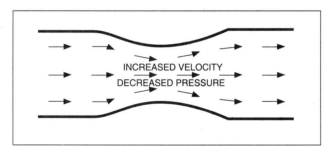

**Figure 1-12.** Flow of air through a constriction

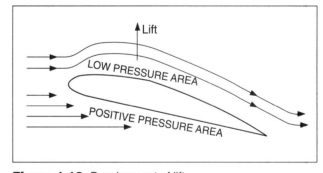

**Figure 1-13.** Development of lift

## Weight

Weight is the force with which gravity attracts all bodies vertically toward the center of the earth.

## Thrust

Thrust is the forward force which is produced by the propeller acting as an airfoil to displace a large mass of air to the rear.

# Drag

Drag is a rearward-acting force which resists the forward movement of an airplane through the air. Drag may be classified into two main types: parasite drag and induced drag.

**Parasite drag** is the resistance of the air produced by any part of an airplane that does not produce lift (antennae, landing gear, etc.). Parasite drag will increase as airspeed increases.

**Induced drag** is a by-product of lift. In other words, drag is induced as the wing develops lift. The high-pressure air beneath the wing, which is trying to flow around and over the wing tips into the area of low pressure, causes a vortex behind the wing tip. This vortex induces a spanwise flow and creates vortices all along the trailing edge of the wing. As the angle of attack is increased (up to the critical angle), lift will increase and so will the vortices and downwash. This downwash redirects the lift vector rearward, causing a rearward component of lift (induced drag). Induced drag will increase as airspeed decreases. See Figure 1-14.

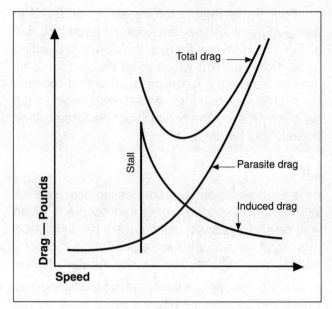

**Figure 1-14.** Drag curve diagram

During unaccelerated (straight-and-level) flight, the four aerodynamic forces which act on an airplane are said to be in equilibrium, or:

Lift = Weight

Thrust = Drag

---

ALL

**3201-1.** Which statement relates to Bernoulli's principle?

A—For every action there is an equal and opposite reaction.
B—An additional upward force is generated as the lower surface of the airfoil deflects air downward.
C—Air traveling faster over the curved upper surface of an airfoil causes lower pressure on the top surface.

*Bernoulli's principle states in part that the pressure of a fluid (liquid or gas) decreases at points where the speed of the fluid increases. In other words, high-speed flow is associated with low pressure, and low-speed flow with high pressure. Air traveling faster over the curved upper surface of an airfoil causes lower pressure on the top surface. (PLT025, PA.I.F.K3, PH.I.F.K4) — FAA-H-8083-25*

Answers (A) and (B) are incorrect because these refer to Newton's third law of motion.

ALL

**3201.** The four forces acting on an airplane in flight are

A—lift, weight, thrust, and drag.
B—lift, weight, gravity, and thrust.
C—lift, gravity, power, and friction.

*Lift, weight, thrust, and drag are the four basic aerodynamic forces acting on an aircraft in flight. (PLT242, PA.I.F.K3, PH.I.F.K4) — FAA-H-8083-25*

AIR

**3213.** What is the purpose of the rudder on an airplane?

A—To control yaw.
B—To control overbanking tendency.
C—To control roll.

*The purpose of the rudder is to control yaw. (PLT234, PA.I.G.K1a) — FAA-H-8083-25*

Answer (B) is incorrect because the ailerons control overbanking. Answer (C) is incorrect because roll is controlled by the ailerons.

---

**Answers**

3201-1 [C]        3201 [A]        3213 [A]

AIR, WSC, PPC, LSA, LSR, LSW, LSP

**3205.** What is the relationship of lift, drag, thrust, and weight when the airplane is in straight-and-level flight?

A—Lift equals weight and thrust equals drag.
B—Lift, drag, and weight equal thrust.
C—Lift and weight equal thrust and drag.

*Lift and thrust are considered positive forces, while weight and drag are considered negative forces and the sum of the opposing forces is zero. That is, lift = weight and thrust = drag. (PLT241, PA.I.F.K3) — FAA-H-8083-25*

AIR, GLI, WSC, PPC

**3202.** When are the four forces that act on an airplane in equilibrium?

A—During unaccelerated flight.
B—When the aircraft is accelerating.
C—When the aircraft is at rest on the ground.

*In unaccelerated (steady state) flight the opposing forces are in equilibrium. (PLT242, PA.I.F.K3) — FAA-H-8083-25*

Answer (B) is incorrect because thrust must exceed drag in order for the airplane to accelerate. Answer (C) is incorrect because when the airplane is at rest on the ground, the only aerodynamic force acting on it is weight.

LSA, LSG, LSW

**2239.** The best speed to use for a glide is one that will result in the greatest glide distance for a given amount of

A—altitude.
B—fuel.
C—drag.

*The best speed for the glide is one at which the airplane will travel the greatest forward distance for a given loss of altitude in still air. This best glide speed corresponds to an angle of attack resulting in the least drag on the airplane and giving the best lift-to-drag ratio (L/D_{MAX}). (PLT257) — FAA-H-8083-3*

LSA, LSR, LSW, LSP

**2229.** Climb performance depends upon the

A—reserve power or thrust.
B—maximum L/D ratio.
C—cruise power setting.

*Climb depends upon the reserve power or thrust. Reserve power is the available power over and above that required to maintain horizontal flight at a given speed. (PLT125) — FAA-H-8083-25*

LSA, LSG, LSW

**2215.** (Refer to Figure 72.) The horizontal dashed line from point C to point E represents the

A—ultimate load factor.
B—positive limit load factor.
C—airspeed range for normal operations.

*C to E is the maximum positive load limit. In this case it is 3.8 Gs, which is appropriate for normal category airplanes. (PLT074) — FAA-H-8083-25*

Answer (A) is incorrect because "ultimate load factor" is not a real term; it is not depicted in the figure. Answer (C) is incorrect because this is depicted by the vertical line from point A to point J, to the vertical line from point D to point G.

LSA, LSG, LSW

**2216.** (Refer to Figure 72.) The vertical dashed line from point E to point F is represented on the airspeed indicator by the

A—upper limit of the yellow arc.
B—upper limit of the green arc.
C—blue radial line.

*Never-exceed speed (V_{NE}), the vertical line from point E to F, is marked on airspeed indicators with a red radial line, the upper limit of the yellow arc. (PLT074) — FAA-H-8083-25*

# Stability

**Stability** is the inherent ability of an airplane to return, or not return, to its original flight condition after being disturbed by an outside force, such as rough air.

**Positive static stability** is the initial tendency of an aircraft to return or not return to its original position. See Figure 1-15.

**Positive dynamic stability** is the tendency of an oscillating airplane (with positive static stability) to return to its original position relative to time. See Figure 1-16.

Aircraft design normally ensures that the aircraft will be stable in pitch. The pilot can adversely affect this longitudinal stability by allowing the center of gravity (CG) to move forward or aft of specified CG limits through improper loading procedures. One undesirable flight characteristic a pilot might experience in an airplane loaded with the CG located aft of the aft CG limit would be the inability to recover from a stalled condition.

The location of the CG with respect to the center of lift (CL) will determine the longitudinal stability of an airplane. See Figure 1-17.

An airplane will be less stable at all airspeeds if it is loaded to the most aft CG. An advantage of an airplane said to be inherently stable is that it will require less effort to control.

Changes in pitch can also be experienced with changes in power settings (except in T-tail airplanes). When power is reduced, there is a corresponding reduction in downwash on the tail, which results in the nose "pitching" down.

A properly designed weight-shift control is stable because the center of lift is above the CG. Slower than trim, the center of lift moves aft. Faster than trim, the center of lift moves forward to make the aircraft stable.

Powered parachutes are stable because the center of gravity is well below the wing, creating pendulum stability.

**Figure 1-15.** Static stability

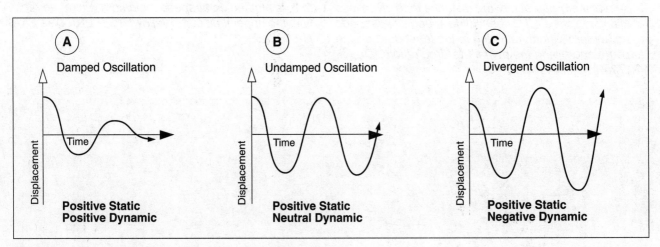

**Figure 1-16.** Positive static stability relative to dynamic stability

## Effects of Forward CG

1. Increased longitudinal stability.
2. Lower cruise speed. The wing flies at a higher angle of attack to create more lift to counter the added downward forces produced by the tail, therefore the wing also produces more induced drag.
3. Higher stall speed. The wing flies at a higher angle of attack to create more lift to counter the added downward forces produced by the tail, therefore the wing also produces more induced drag.

## Effects of Aft CG

1. Decreased longitudinal stability.
2. Higher cruise speed (for just the opposite reason listed above).
3. Lower stall speed.
4. Poor stall/spin recovery.

**Figure 1-17.** Effect of CG on airplane stability

AIR, GLI, LSA, LSR, LSG, LSW, LSP

**3210.** An airplane said to be inherently stable will

A—be difficult to stall.
B—require less effort to control.
C—not spin.

*A stable airplane will tend to return to the original condition of flight if disturbed by a force such as turbulent air. This means that a stable airplane is easy to fly. (PLT213, PA.I.F.K3) — FAA-H-8083-25*

Answer (A) is incorrect because stability of an airplane has an effect on its stall recovery, not the difficulty of stall entry. Answer (C) is incorrect because an inherently stable aircraft can still spin.

AIR, GLI

**3211.** What determines the longitudinal stability of an airplane?

A—The location of the CG with respect to the center of lift.
B—The effectiveness of the horizontal stabilizer, rudder, and rudder trim tab.
C—The relationship of thrust and lift to weight and drag.

*The location of the CG with respect to the center of lift determines to a great extent the longitudinal stability of an airplane. Center of gravity aft of the center of lift will result in an undesirable pitch-up moment during flight. An airplane with the CG forward of the center of lift will pitch down when power is reduced. This will increase the airspeed and the downward force on the elevators. This increased downward force on the elevators will bring the nose up, providing positive stability. The*

*farther forward the CG is, the more stable the airplane. (PLT213, PA.I.F.K3) — FAA-H-8083-25*

Answer (B) is incorrect because the rudder and rudder trim tab control the yaw. Answer (C) is incorrect because the relationship of thrust and lift to weight and drag affects speed and altitude.

AIR, GLI

**3212.** What causes an airplane (except a T-tail) to pitch nosedown when power is reduced and controls are not adjusted?

A—The CG shifts forward when thrust and drag are reduced.
B—The downwash on the elevators from the propeller slipstream is reduced and elevator effectiveness is reduced.
C—When thrust is reduced to less than weight, lift is also reduced and the wings can no longer support the weight.

*The location of the CG with respect to the center of lift determines to a great extent the longitudinal stability of an airplane. CG aft of the CL will result in an undesirable pitch-up moment during flight. An airplane with the CG forward of the CL will pitch down when power is reduced. This will increase the airspeed and the downward force on the elevators. This increased downward force on the elevators will bring the nose up, providing positive stability. The farther forward the CG is, the more stable the airplane. (PLT351, PA.I.F.K3) — FAA-H-8083-25*

Answer (A) is incorrect because the CG is not affected by changes in thrust or drag. Answer (C) is incorrect because thrust and weight have a small relationship to each other, unless thrust is opposite weight, as in the case of jet fighters and space shuttles.

AIR, GLI, WSC

**3287.** An airplane has been loaded in such a manner that the CG is located aft of the aft CG limit. One undesirable flight characteristic a pilot might experience with this airplane would be

A—a longer takeoff run.
B—difficulty in recovering from a stalled condition.
C—stalling at higher-than-normal airspeed.

*Loading in a tail-heavy condition can reduce the airplane's ability to recover from stalls and spins. Tail-heavy loading also produces very light stick forces, making it easy for the pilot to inadvertently overstress the airplane. (PLT003, PA.I.F.K2e) — FAA-H-8083-25*

Answer (A) is incorrect because an airplane with an aft CG has less drag from a reduction in horizontal stabilizer lift, resulting in a short takeoff run. Answer (C) is incorrect because an airplane with an aft CG flies at a lower angle of attack, resulting in a lower stall speed.

**Answers**

| 3210 | [B] | 3211 | [A] | 3212 | [B] | 3287 | [B] |

AIR, GLI

**3288.** Loading an airplane to the most aft CG will cause the airplane to be

A—less stable at all speeds.
B—less stable at slow speeds, but more stable at high speeds.
C—less stable at high speeds, but more stable at low speeds.

*Loading in a tail-heavy condition can reduce the airplane's ability to recover from stalls and spins. Tail-heavy loading also produces very light stick forces at all speeds, making it easy for the pilot to inadvertently overstress the airplane. (PLT328, PA.I.F.K2e) — FAA-H-8083-25*

Answers (B) and (C) are incorrect because an aft CG location causes an aircraft to be less stable at all airspeeds, due to less elevator effectiveness.

AIR, GLI, WSC

**3211-1.** Changes in the center of pressure of a wing affect the aircraft's

A—lift/drag ratio.
B—lifting capacity.
C—aerodynamic balance and controllability.

*The center of pressure of an asymmetrical airfoil moves forward as the angle of attack is increased, and backward as the angle of attack is decreased. This backward and forward movement of the point at which lift acts, affects the aerodynamic balance and the controllability of the aircraft. (PLT214, PA.I.F.K3) — FAA-H-8083-25*

Answer (A) is incorrect because the lift/drag ratio is determined by the angle of attack. Answer (B) is incorrect because lifting capacity is determined by angle of attack and airspeed.

# Turns, Loads, and Load Factors

When an airplane is banked into a turn, a portion of the vertical lift being developed is diverted into a **horizontal lift component**. It is this horizontal (sideward) force that forces the airplane from straight-and-level flight and causes it to turn. The reduced **vertical lift component** results in a loss of altitude unless total lift is increased by increasing angle of attack, increasing airspeed, or increasing both. See Figure 1-18.

In aerodynamics, **load** is the force (imposed stress) that must be supported by an airplane structure in flight. The loads imposed on the wings in flight are stated in terms of load factor.

In straight-and-level flight, the wings of an airplane support a load equal to the sum of the weight of the airplane plus its contents. This particular load factor is equal to "One G," where "**G**" refers to the pull of gravity.

However, a force called **centrifugal force** is generated which acts toward the outside of the curve any time an airplane is flying a curved path (turns, climbs, or descents).

Whenever the airplane is flying in a curved flight path with a positive load, the load that the wings must support will be equal to the weight of the airplane plus the load imposed by centrifugal force; therefore, it can be said that turns increase the load factor on an airplane.

As the angle of bank of a turn increases, the load factor increases, as is shown in Figure 1-19.

The amount of excess load that can be imposed on the wing of an airplane depends on the speed of the airplane. An example of this would be a change in direction made at high speed with forceful control movement, which results in a high load factor being imposed.

An increased **load factor** (weight) will cause an airplane to stall at a higher airspeed, as shown in Figure 1-20.

Some conditions that increase the weight (load) of an aircraft are: overloading the airplane, too steep an angle of bank, turbulence and abrupt movement of the controls.

Because different types of operations require different maneuvers (and therefore varying bank

**Answers**

3288    [A]          3211-1 [C]

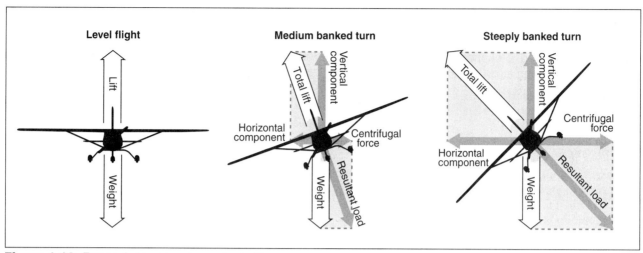

**Figure 1-18.** Forces during normal coordinated turn

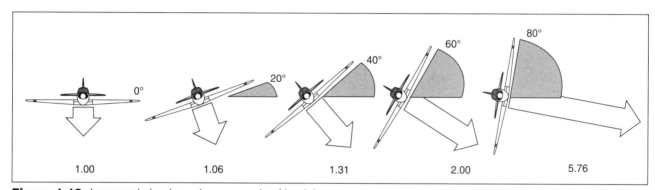

**Figure 1-19.** Increase in load on wings as angle of bank increases

angles and load factors), aircraft are separated into categories determined by the loads that their wing structures can support:

| Category | Positive Limit Load |
|---|---|
| *Normal*.................................. (nonacrobatic) (N) | 3.8 times gross wt. |
| *Utility* ..................................... (normal operations and limited acrobatic maneuvers) | 4.4 times gross wt. |
| *Acrobatic*................................ (A) | 6.0 times gross wt. |

The limit loads should not be exceeded in actual operation, even though a safety factor of 50% above limit loads is incorporated in the strength of the airplane.

**Figure 1-20.** Effect of angle of bank on stall speed

ASTM consensus standards determine similar load limits for light-sport aircraft.

AIR, WSC, PPC

**3214.** (Refer to Figure 2.) If an airplane weighs 2,300 pounds, what approximate weight would the airplane structure be required to support during a 60° banked turn while maintaining altitude?

A—2,300 pounds.
B—3,400 pounds.
C—4,600 pounds.

*Referencing FAA Figure 2, use the following steps:*

1. *Enter the chart at a 60° angle of bank and proceed upward to the curved reference line. From the point of intersection, move to the left side of the chart and read a load factor of 2 Gs.*

2. *Multiply the aircraft weight by the load factor:*

   *2,300 × 2 = 4,600 lbs*

*Or, working from the table:*

   *2,300 × 2.0 (load factor) = 4,600 lbs*

*(PLT309, PA.I.F.K3) — FAA-H-8083-25*

AIR, WSC, PPC

**3215.** (Refer to Figure 2.) If an airplane weighs 3,300 pounds, what approximate weight would the airplane structure be required to support during a 30° banked turn while maintaining altitude?

A—1,200 pounds.
B—3,100 pounds.
C—3,960 pounds.

*Referencing FAA Figure 2, use the following steps:*

1. *Enter the chart at a 30° angle of bank and proceed upward to the curved reference line. From the point of intersection, move to the left side of the chart and read an approximate load factor of 1.2 Gs.*

2. *Multiply the aircraft weight by the load factor:*

   *3,300 × 1.2 = 3,960 lbs*

*Or, working from the table:*

   *3,300 × 1.154 (load factor) = 3,808 lbs*

*Answer C is the closest.*

*(PLT309, PA.I.F.K3) — FAA-H-8083-25*

*Answers (A) and (B) are incorrect because they are less than 3,300 pounds; load factor increases with bank for level flight.*

AIR, WSC, PPC

**3216.** (Refer to Figure 2.) If an airplane weighs 4,500 pounds, what approximate weight would the airplane structure be required to support during a 45° banked turn while maintaining altitude?

A—4,500 pounds.
B—6,750 pounds.
C—7,200 pounds.

*Referencing FAA Figure 2, use the following steps:*

1. *Enter the chart at a 45° angle of bank and proceed upward to the curved reference line. From the point of intersection, move to the left side of the chart and read a load factor of 1.5 Gs.*

2. *Multiply the aircraft weight by the load factor.*

   *4,500 × 1.5 = 6,750 lbs*

*Or, working from the table:*

   *4,500 × 1.414 (load factor) = 6,363 lbs*

*Answer B is the closest.*

*(PLT309, PA.I.F.K3) — FAA-H-8083-25*

AIR, WSC

**3217.** The amount of excess load that can be imposed on the wing of an airplane depends upon the

A—position of the CG.
B—speed of the airplane.
C—abruptness at which the load is applied.

*At slow speeds, the maximum available lifting force of the wing is only slightly greater than the amount necessary to support the weight of the airplane. However, at high speeds, the capacity of the elevator controls, or a strong gust, may increase the load factor beyond safe limits. (PLT311, PA.VII.A.K1) — FAA-H-8083-25*

*Answer (A) is incorrect because the position of the CG affects the stability of the airplane, but not the total load the wings can support. Answer (C) is incorrect because abrupt control inputs do not limit load.*

**Answers**

| 3214 | [C] | 3215 | [C] | 3216 | [B] | 3217 | [B] |

AIR, WSC, PPC

**3218.** Which basic flight maneuver increases the load factor on an airplane as compared to straight-and-level flight?

A—Climbs.
B—Turns.
C—Stalls.

*A change in speed during straight flight will not produce any appreciable change in load, but when a change is made in the airplane's flight path, an additional load is imposed upon the airplane structure. This is particularly true if a change in direction is made at high speeds with rapid, forceful control movements. (PLT309, PA.I.F.K3) — FAA-H-8083-25*

Answer (A) is incorrect because the load increases only as the angle of attack is changed, momentarily. Once the climb attitude has been set, the wings only carry the load produced by the weight of the aircraft. Answer (C) is incorrect because in a stall, the wings are not producing lift.

AIR, GLI, WSC, PPC

**3301.** What force makes an airplane turn?

A—The horizontal component of lift.
B—The vertical component of lift.
C—Centrifugal force.

*As the airplane is banked, lift acts horizontally as well as vertically and the airplane is pulled around the turn. (PLT242, PA.I.F.K3) — FAA-H-8083-3*

Answer (B) is incorrect because the vertical component of lift has no horizontal force to make the airplane turn. Answer (C) is incorrect because the centrifugal force acts against the horizontal component of lift.

AIR, GLI, WSC

**3316.** During an approach to a stall, an increased load factor will cause the airplane to

A—stall at a higher airspeed.
B—have a tendency to spin.
C—be more difficult to control.

*Stall speed increases in proportion to the square root of the load factor. Thus, with a load factor of 4, an aircraft will stall at a speed which is double the normal stall speed. (PLT312, PA.I.F.K3) — FAA-H-8083-25*

Answer (B) is incorrect because an airplane's tendency to spin does not relate to an increase in load factors. Answer (C) is incorrect because an airplane's stability determines its controllability.

**Answers**

3218    [B]          3301    [A]          3316    [A]

# Maneuvers

## Rectangular Course

For best results when planning a **rectangular course**, the flight path should be positioned outside the field boundaries just far enough that they may be easily observed from either pilot seat by looking out the side of the airplane. The closer the track of the airplane is to the field boundaries, the steeper the bank necessary at the turning points. See Figure 1-21.

## Turns Around a Point

When flying **turns around a point**, the wings will be in alignment with the pylon only during the time the airplane is flying directly upwind or directly downwind. At all other points, a **wind correction angle** will keep the wings from pointing directly at the pylon.

If the student is instructed to not exceed a 45° bank in a turn around a point maneuver, the best place to start is the point where the bank angle will be steepest, which is when flying downwind. Throughout the remainder of the maneuver, the bank will be shallowing out.

The ground speed will be equal where the airplane is flying with the same headwind component. The angle of bank will be the same only where the airplane is flying directly crosswind. See Figure 1-22.

**Figure 1-21.** Rectangular Course

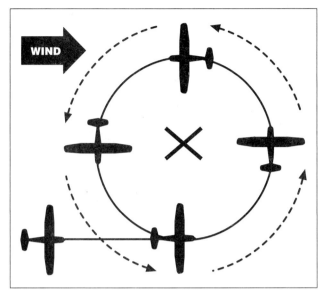

**Figure 1-22.** Turns around a point

## S-Turns

In a steep turn, the ground speed will be the same when the airplane has the same headwind component. The steepest angle of bank is required at the points where the airplane is flying downwind. The airplane will have to be crabbed into the wind the greatest amount where it is flying crosswind.

In the first half of an **S-turn**, the bank should begin shallow and increase in steepness as the airplane turns crosswind, and become steepest where the turn is downwind. If the turn is started with too steep a bank angle, the bank will increase too rapidly and the upwind half of the "S" will be smaller than the downwind half. The turn will not be completed by the time the airplane is over the reference line. See Figure 1-23.

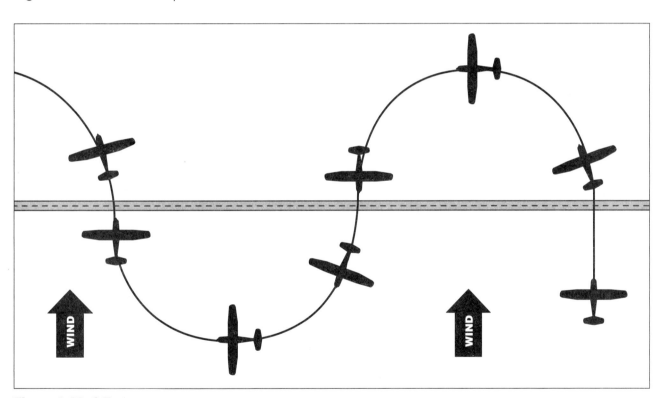

**Figure 1-23.** S-Turns

ALL, SPO

**3202-1.** Select the four flight fundamentals involved in maneuvering an aircraft.

A—Aircraft power, pitch, bank, and trim.
B—Starting, taxiing, takeoff, and landing.
C—Straight-and-level flight, turns, climbs, and descents.

*The four flight fundamentals involved in maneuvering an aircraft are: straight-and-level flight, turns, climbs, and descents. (PLT219, PA.I.F.K2, PH.I.F.K4) — FAA-H-8083-3*

ALL

**3202-2.** (Refer to Figure 62.) In flying the rectangular course, when would the aircraft be turned less than 90°?

A—Corners 1 and 4.
B—Corners 1 and 2.
C—Corners 2 and 4.

*The airplane will turn less than 90° at corners 1 and 4. At corner 1, the airplane turns to a heading that is crabbed into the wind, which makes the turn less than 90°. At corner 4, the airplane is crabbed into the wind when the turn is started, and the turn will be less than 90°. (PLT219, PA.V.B.K2) — FAA-H-8083-3*

ALL

**3202-3.** (Refer to Figure 66.) While practicing S-turns, a consistently smaller half-circle is made on one side of the road than on the other, and this turn is not completed before crossing the road or reference line. This would most likely occur in turn

A—1-2-3 because the bank is decreased too rapidly during the latter part of the turn.
B—4-5-6 because the bank is increased too rapidly during the early part of the turn.
C—4-5-6 because the bank is increased too slowly during the latter part of the turn.

*In the half of an S-turn labeled 4-5-6, the bank should begin shallow and increase in steepness as the airplane turns crosswind and become steepest at point 6 where the turn is downwind. If the turn at point 4 is started with too steep a bank angle, the bank will increase too rapidly, and the upwind half of the S will be smaller than the downwind half. The turn will not be completed by the time the airplane is over the reference line. (PLT219, PA.V.B.K2) — FAA-H-8083-3*

AIR, GLI, WSC, PPC

**3202-4.** If an emergency situation requires a downwind landing, pilots should expect a faster

A—airspeed at touchdown, a longer ground roll, and better control throughout the landing roll.
B—groundspeed at touchdown, a longer ground roll, and the likelihood of overshooting the desired touchdown point.
C—groundspeed at touchdown, a shorter ground roll, and the likelihood of undershooting the desired touchdown point.

*A downwind landing, using the same airspeed as is used on a normal upwind landing, will result in a higher approach ground speed, with the likelihood of overshooting the desired touchdown point. The ground speed at touchdown will be higher than normal, and the ground roll will be longer. (PLT208, PA.IX.B.K2c) — FAA-H-8083-3*

Answer (A) is incorrect because the airspeed will be the same, and the control throughout the landing roll will be less due to the higher ground speed. Answer (C) is incorrect because the ground roll will be longer, and there will be a greater likelihood of overshooting the touchdown point.

AIR

**3202-5.** When executing an emergency approach to land in a single-engine airplane, it is important to maintain a constant glide speed because variations in glide speed

A—increase the chances of shock cooling the engine.
B—assure the proper descent angle is maintained until entering the flare.
C—nullify all attempts at accuracy in judgment of gliding distance and landing spot.

*A constant gliding speed should be maintained because variations of gliding speed nullify all attempts at accuracy in judgment of gliding distance and the landing spot. (PLT208, PA.IX.B.K2a) — FAA-H-8083-3*

**Answers**

| 3202-1 [C] | 3202-2 [A] | 3202-3 [B] | 3202-4 [B] | 3202-5 [C] |
| --- | --- | --- | --- | --- |

# Stalls and Spins

As the angle of attack is increased (to increase lift), the air will no longer flow smoothly over the upper wing surface but instead will become turbulent or "burble" near the trailing edge. A further increase in the angle of attack will cause the turbulent area to expand forward. At an angle of attack of approximately 18° to 20° (for most wings), turbulence over the upper wing surface decreases lift so drastically that flight can not be sustained and the wing **stalls**. See Figure 1-24.

The angle at which a stall occurs is called the **critical angle of attack**. An airplane can stall at any airspeed or any attitude, but will always stall at the same critical angle of attack. The indicated airspeed at which a given airplane will stall in a particular configuration, however, will remain the same regardless of altitude. Because air density decreases with an increase in altitude, the airplane has to be flown faster at higher altitudes to cause the same pressure difference between pitot impact pressure and static pressure.

An aircraft will **spin** only after it has stalled, and will continue to spin as long as the outside wing continues to provide more lift than the inside wing and the aircraft remains stalled.

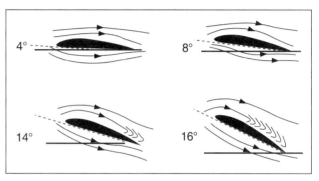

**Figure 1-24.** Flow of air over wing at various angles of attack

AIR, GLI, WSC, PPC

**3263.** As altitude increases, the indicated airspeed at which a given airplane stalls in a particular configuration will

A—decrease as the true airspeed decreases.
B—decrease as the true airspeed increases.
C—remain the same regardless of altitude.

*An increase in altitude has no effect on the indicated airspeed at which an airplane stalls at altitudes normally used by general aviation aircraft. This means that the same indicated airspeed should be maintained during the landing approach regardless of the elevation or the density altitude at the airport of landing. (PLT477, PA.IV.A.K1) — FAA-H-8083-25*

Answer (A) is incorrect because true airspeed does not decrease with increased altitude, and indicated airspeed at which an airplane stalls does not change. Answer (B) is incorrect because the indicated airspeed of the stall does not decrease with increased altitude.

SPO

**2233.** The direct cause of every stall is excessive

A—angle of attack.
B—density altitude.
C—upward vertical velocity.

*The direct cause of every stall is an excessive angle of attack. There are any number of flight maneuvers that may produce an increase in the angle of attack, but the stall does not occur until the angle of attack becomes excessive. (PLT477) — FAA-H-8083-25*

AIR, GLI

**3309.** In what flight condition must an aircraft be placed in order to spin?

A—Partially stalled with one wing low.
B—In a steep diving spiral.
C—Stalled.

*A spin results when a sufficient degree of rolling or yawing control input is imposed on an airplane in the stalled condition. If the wing is not stalled, a spin cannot occur. (PLT245, PA.VII.D.K2) — FAA-H-8083-3*

Answer (A) is incorrect because the aircraft must be at a full stall in order to spin. Answer (B) is incorrect because an airplane is not necessarily stalled when in a steep diving spiral.

**Answers**

| 3263 | [C] | 2233 | [A] | 3309 | [C] |
|------|-----|------|-----|------|-----|

AIR, GLI

**3310.** During a spin to the left, which wing(s) is/are stalled?

A—Both wings are stalled.
B—Neither wing is stalled.
C—Only the left wing is stalled.

*One wing is less stalled than the other, but both wings are stalled in a spin. (PLT245, PA.VII.D.K1) — FAA-H-8083-3*

Answer (B) is incorrect because both wings must be stalled through the spin. Answer (C) is incorrect because both wings are stalled; but the right wing is less fully stalled than the left.

AIR, GLI, WSC, PPC, LSA, LSG, LSW, LSP

**3311.** The angle of attack at which an airplane wing stalls will

A—increase if the CG is moved forward.
B—change with an increase in gross weight.
C—remain the same regardless of gross weight.

*When the angle of attack is increased to between 18° and 20° (critical angle of attack) on most airfoils, the airstream can no longer follow the upper curvature of the wing because of the excessive change in direction. The airplane will stall if the critical angle of attack is exceeded. The indicated airspeed at which stall occurs will be determined by weight and load factor, but the stall angle of attack is the same. (PLT168, PA.VII.D.K1) — FAA-H-8083-25*

Answers (A) and (B) are incorrect because an airplane will always stall at the same angle of attack, regardless of the CG position or gross weight.

# Flaps

Extending the flaps increases the wing camber and the angle of attack of a wing. This increases wing lift and also increases induced drag. See Figure 1-25.

The increased drag enables the pilot to make steeper approaches to a landing, without an increase in airspeed. VFR approaches to a landing at night should be made the same as during the daytime.

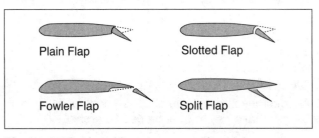

**Figure 1-25.** Use of flaps increases lift and drag

AIR, GLI

**3219.** One of the main functions of flaps during approach and landing is to

A—decrease the angle of descent without increasing the airspeed.
B—permit a touchdown at a higher indicated airspeed.
C—increase the angle of descent without increasing the airspeed.

*Flaps increase drag, allowing the pilot to make steeper approaches without increasing airspeed. (PLT473, PA.I.G.K1b) — FAA-H-8083-25*

Answer (A) is incorrect because extending the flaps increases drag, which enables the pilot to increase the angle of descent without increasing the airspeed. Answer (B) is incorrect because flaps increase lift at slow airspeed, which permits touchdown at a lower indicated airspeed.

AIR, GLI

**3220.** What is one purpose of wing flaps?

A—To enable the pilot to make steeper approaches to a landing without increasing the airspeed.
B—To relieve the pilot of maintaining continuous pressure on the controls.
C—To decrease wing area to vary the lift.

*Flaps increase drag, allowing the pilot to make steeper approaches without increasing airspeed. (PLT473, PA.I.G.K1b) — FAA-H-8083-25*

Answer (B) is incorrect because trim tabs help relieve control pressures. Answer (C) is incorrect because wing area usually remains the same, except for certain specialized flaps which increase the wing area.

**Answers**

3310    [A]           3311    [C]           3219    [C]           3220    [A]

# Chapter 2
# Aircraft Systems

# Aircraft Lighting

When an aircraft is being operated during the period from sunset to sunrise (except in Alaska), it must display lighted position lights and an anti-collision light. The anti-collision light may be either aviation red or aviation white. See Figure 2-1.

For collision avoidance, a pilot must know where each colored light is located on an aircraft. For example, if a pilot observes a steady red light and a flashing red light ahead and at the same altitude, the other aircraft is crossing to the left; a steady white and a flashing red light indicates that the other aircraft is headed away from the observer; and steady red and green lights at the same altitude as the observer indicates that the other aircraft is approaching head-on.

**Figure 2-1.** Aircraft lighting

ALL

**3162.** Except in Alaska, during what time period should lighted position lights be displayed on an aircraft?

A—End of evening civil twilight to the beginning of morning civil twilight.
B—1 hour after sunset to 1 hour before sunrise.
C—Sunset to sunrise.

*An aircraft must display lighted position lights from sunset to sunrise. (PLT119, PA.XI.A.K3, PH.IX.A.K4, PH.I.B.K3) — 14 CFR §91.209*

Answer (A) is incorrect because it applies to logging of night time. Answer (B) is incorrect because it applies to the night landing requirement.

ALL

**3916.** Pilots are encouraged to turn on their landing lights when operating below 10,000 feet, day or night, and when operating within

A—Class B airspace.
B—10 miles of any airport.
C—within 15 miles of a towered airport.

*Pilots are encouraged to turn on their landing lights when operating below 10,000 feet, day or night, especially when operating within 10 miles of any airport or in conditions of reduced visibility and in areas where flocks of birds may be expected. (PLT119, PA.XI.A.K3, PH.IX.A.K4, PH.I.B.K3) — AIM ¶4-3-23*

**Answers**

3162  [C]          3916  [B]

ALL

**3916-1.** The *Aeronautical Information Manual (AIM)* specifically encourages pilots to turn on their landing lights when operating below 10,000 feet, day or night, and especially when operating

A—in Class B airspace.
B—in conditions of reduced visibility.
C—within 15 miles of a towered airport.

*Pilots are encouraged to turn on their landing lights when operating below 10,000 feet, day or night, especially when operating within 10 miles of any airport or in conditions of reduced visibility and in areas where flocks of birds may be expected. (PLT119, PA.XI.A.K3, PH.IX.A.K4, PH.I.B.K3) — AIM ¶4-3-23*

AIR, RTC, LTA, WSC, PPC

**3715.** During a night flight, you observe a steady red light and a flashing red light ahead and at the same altitude. What is the general direction of movement of the other aircraft?

A—The other aircraft is crossing to the left.
B—The other aircraft is crossing to the right.
C—The other aircraft is approaching head-on.

*Airplanes have a red light on the left wing tip, a green light on the right wing tip and a white light on the tail. The flashing red light is the rotating beacon which can be seen from all directions around the aircraft. If the only steady light seen is red, then the airplane is crossing from right to left in relation to the observing pilot. (PLT119, PA.XI.A.K3, PH.IX.A.K4, PH.IX.A.K5) — FAA-H-8083-3*

AIR, RTC, LTA, WSC, PPC

**3716.** During a night flight, you observe a steady white light and a flashing red light ahead and at the same altitude. What is the general direction of movement of the other aircraft?

A—The other aircraft is flying away from you.
B—The other aircraft is crossing to the left.
C—The other aircraft is crossing to the right.

*Airplanes have a red light on the left wing tip, a green light on the right wing tip and a white light on the tail. The flashing red light is the rotating beacon which can be seen from all directions around the aircraft. When the only steady light seen is white, then the airplane is headed away from the observing pilot. (PLT119, PA.XI.A.K3, PH.IX.A.K4, PH.IX.A.K5) — FAA-H-8083-3*

AIR, RTC, LTA, WSC, PPC

**3717.** During a night flight, you observe steady red and green lights ahead and at the same altitude. What is the general direction of movement of the other aircraft?

A—The other aircraft is crossing to the left.
B—The other aircraft is flying away from you.
C—The other aircraft is approaching head-on.

*When both a red and green light of another airplane are observed, the airplane would be flying in a general direction toward you. Airplanes have a red light on the left wing tip, a green light on the right wing tip and a white light on the tail. (PLT119, PA.XI.A.K3, PH.IX.A.K4, PH.IX.A.K5) — FAA-H-8083-3*

SPO

**2020.** Pilots must operate the anti-collision lights

A—at night or in inclement weather.
B—at night when the visibility is less than three miles and flying in Class B airspace.
C—day and night, except when the pilot-in-command determines that they constitute a hazard to safety.

*Aircraft equipped with an anti-collision light system are required to operate that light system during all types of operations (day and night). However, the PIC may determine that the anti-collision lights should be turned off when their operation would constitute a hazard to safety. (PLT119) — 14 CFR §91.209*

**Answers**

3916-1 [B]        3715  [A]        3716  [A]        3717  [C]        2020  [C]

# Reciprocating Engines

Most small airplanes are powered by **reciprocating engines** made up, in part, of cylinders, pistons, connecting rods, and a crankshaft. The pistons move back and forth within the cylinders. Connecting rods connect the pistons to the crankshaft, which converts the back and forth movements of the pistons to a rotary motion. It is this rotary motion which drives the propeller.

One cycle of the engine consists of two revolutions of the crankshaft. These two crankshaft revolutions require four strokes of the piston; namely, the **intake**, **compression**, **power**, and **exhaust** strokes.

The top end of the cylinder houses an intake valve, an exhaust valve, and two spark plugs.

During the intake stroke, the intake valve is open and the piston moves away from the top of the cylinder and draws in a air-fuel mixture (Figure 2-2A).

At the completion of the intake stroke, the intake valve closes and the piston returns to the top of the cylinder and compresses the air-fuel mixture (Figure 2-2B).

When the piston reaches a precise point near the top of its stroke, the spark plugs ignite the compressed mixture and the rapid expansion of the burning mixture forces the piston downward (Figure 2-2C).

As the piston completes the downward movement of the power stroke, the exhaust valve opens and the piston rises to the top of the cylinder. This exhaust stroke forces out the burned gases and completes one cycle of the engine (Figure 2-2D).

Because of the many moving parts in a reciprocating engine, as soon as the engine is started, power should be set to the RPM recommended for engine warm-up and the engine gauges checked for the desired indications.

Should it be necessary to start the engine by **hand propping**, it is extremely important that a competent pilot be at the controls in the flight deck. In addition, the person turning the propeller should be thoroughly familiar with the procedure.

**A.** Intake  **B.** Compression  **C.** Power  **D.** Exhaust

**Figure 2-2.** Four strokes of an internal combustion engine

AIR

**3657.** Should it become necessary to handprop an airplane engine, it is extremely important that a competent pilot

A—call "contact" before touching the propeller.
B—be at the controls in the flight deck.
C—be in the flight deck and call out all commands.

*Because of the hazards involved in hand-starting airplane engines, it is extremely important that a competent pilot be at the controls in the flight deck and that all communications and procedures be agreed upon and rehearsed beforehand. (PLT479, PA.II.C.R1) — FAA-H-8083-25*

Answer (A) is incorrect because the person propping the engine is not required to be a pilot, and calling "contact" is not required. Answer (C) is incorrect because a pilot must be in control of the aircraft, not only in the flight deck. Also, the person propping the engine calls out the commands.

AIR, RTC, WSC, PPC

**3656.** What should be the first action after starting an aircraft engine?

A—Adjust for proper RPM and check for desired indications on the engine gauges.
B—Place the magneto or ignition switch momentarily in the OFF position to check for proper grounding.
C—Test each brake and the parking brake.

*As soon as the engine starts, check for unintentional movement of the aircraft and set power to the recommended warm-up RPM. The oil pressure should then be checked to determine that the oil system is functioning properly with pressure at recommended levels within the manufacturer's time limit. (PLT343, PA.I.G.K1c, PH.I.G.K1b) — FAA-H-8083-25*

Answer (B) is incorrect because this is usually done at the end of the flight. Answer (C) is incorrect because brakes are checked when beginning to taxi.

AIR, RTC, WSC, PPC

**3656-1.** What is one purpose for using reciprocating engines?

A—Heat is distributed better.
B—To preserve cylinder head duration and maintain lower temperatures.
C—They are relatively simple and inexpensive to operate.

*Most training aircraft use reciprocating engines because they are relatively simple and inexpensive to operate. (PLT343, PA.I.G.K1c, PH.I.G.K1b) — FAA-H-8083-25*

# Ignition and Electrical Systems

Most reciprocating engines used to power small aircraft incorporate two separate magneto ignition systems.

A **magneto** ("mag") is a self-contained source of electrical energy, so even if an aircraft loses total electrical power, the engine will continue to run.

When checking for magneto operation prior to flight, the engine should run smoothly when operating with the magneto selector set on "BOTH," and should experience a slight drop in revolutions per minute (RPM) when running on only one or the other magneto.

The main advantages of the dual ignition system are increased safety and improved engine performance.

AIR, WSC, PPC, LSA, LSR, LSW, LSP

**3223.** One purpose of the dual ignition system on an aircraft engine is to provide for

A—improved engine performance.
B—uniform heat distribution.
C—balanced cylinder head pressure.

*The dual ignition system has two magnetos to supply the electrical current to two spark plugs for each combustion chamber. This provides both a redundancy of ignition and an improvement of engine performance. (PLT478, PA.I.G.K1f) — FAA-H-8083-25*

Answer (B) is incorrect because heat distribution is not affected by the ignition system. Answer (C) is incorrect because cylinder head pressure in not affected by the ignition system.

**Answers**

| 3657 | [B] | 3656 | [A] | 3656-1 [C] | 3223 | [A] |

AIR, RTC, WSC, PPC, LSA, LSR, LSW, LSP

**3223-1.** An electrical system failure (battery and alternator) occurs during flight. In this situation, you would

A—experience avionics equipment failure.
B—probably experience failure of the engine ignition system, fuel gauges, aircraft lighting system, and avionics equipment.
C—probably experience engine failure due to the loss of the engine-driven fuel pump and also experience failure of the radio equipment, lights, and all instruments that require alternating current.

*If you experience an inflight electrical system failure, you have an avionics equipment failure and cannot use your electrical fuel boost pump. (PLT208, PA.I.G.K1f, PH.I.G.K1h) — FAA-H-8083-25*

*Answer (B) is incorrect because the ignition system of an aircraft reciprocating engine is powered by two self-contained magnetos that are not dependent upon the aircraft electrical system. Answer (C) is incorrect because the engine-driven fuel pumps are mechanical and not dependent on the electrical system.*

AIR, RTC, WSC, PPC

**3223-2.** If the ground wire between the magneto and the ignition switch becomes disconnected, the most noticeable result will be that the engine

A—will run very rough.
B—cannot be started with the switch in the ON position.
C—cannot be shut down by turning the switch to the OFF position.

*If the ground wire between a magneto and the ignition switch becomes disconnected, the primary current cannot be directed to ground, and the engine cannot be shut down by turning the switch to the OFF position. (PLT478, PA.I.G.K1f, PH.I.G.K1b) — FAA-H-8083-25*

LSA, LSR, LSW, LSP

**2242.** One purpose of the dual ignition system on a two-cycle engine is to provide for

A—system redundancy in the ignition system.
B—uniform heat distribution.
C—balanced cylinder head pressure.

*The dual ignition system has two magnetos to supply the electrical current to two spark plugs for each combustion chamber. This provides both a redundancy of ignition and an improvement of engine performance. (PLT478) — FAA-H-8083-25*

LSA, LSR, LSW, LSP

**2238.** An electrical system failure (battery and alternator) occurs in a magneto equipped aircraft during flight. In this situation, you would

A—probably experience engine failure due to the loss of the engine-driven fuel pump and also experience failure of the radio equipment, lights, and all instruments that require alternating current.
B—probably experience failure of the engine ignition system, fuel gauges, aircraft lighting system, and avionics equipment.
C—experience avionics equipment failure.

*If you experience an inflight electrical system failure, you have an avionics equipment failure and cannot use your electrical fuel boost pump. (PLT207) — FAA-H-8083-25*

*Answer (A) is incorrect because the engine-driven fuel pumps are mechanical and not dependent on the electrical system. Answer (B) is incorrect because the ignition system of an aircraft reciprocating engine is powered by two self-contained magnetos that are not dependent upon the aircraft electrical system.*

LSA, LSR, LSW, LSP

**2364.** Concerning the advantages of an aircraft generator or alternator, select the true statement.

A—A generator always provides more electrical current than an alternator.
B—An alternator provides more electrical power at lower engine RPM than a generator.
C—A generator charges the battery during low engine RPM; therefore, the battery has less chance to become fully discharged, as often occurs with an alternator.

*One of the basic differences between a generator and an alternator used on an aircraft engine is the number of magnetic poles used to produce the electricity. Generators normally have two or four poles, while alternators have between eight and 14 poles. Because of the greater number of poles, an alternator can provide more electrical power at a lower engine RPM than a generator. (PLT207) — FAA-H-8083-25*

**Answers**

3223-1 [A]        3223-2 [C]        2242    [A]        2238    [C]        2364    [B]

# Fuel Induction Systems

Most light airplane engines use either a carburetor or a fuel injection system to deliver a **air-fuel mixture** to the cylinders.

In a **carburetor induction system**, the float-type carburetor takes in air that flows through a restriction (venturi), which creates a low-pressure area. The pressure difference between the low-pressure area and outside air forces fuel into the airstream where it is mixed with the flowing air, drawn through an intake manifold, and delivered to the combustion chambers and ignited.

Carburetors are normally set to deliver the correct air-fuel mixture at sea level. Since air density decreases with altitude, a mixture control allows the pilot to decrease the fuel flow as altitude increases and thus maintain the correct mixture. Otherwise the mixture may become too "rich" at high altitudes.

When descending, air density increases. Unless fuel flow is increased, the mixture may become excessively "lean," i.e., the amount of fuel is too small for the amount of air reaching the cylinders. Modern four-stroke engines may automatically adjust the mixture control. Two-stroke engines typically require main jet changes for operations at different altitudes.

In a **fuel injection system** the fuel and air are mixed just prior to entering the combustion chamber. No carburetor is used.

AIR, RTC, WSC, PPC

**3225.** The operating principle of float-type carburetors is based on the

A—automatic metering of air at the venturi as the aircraft gains altitude.

B—difference in air pressure at the venturi throat and the air inlet.

C—increase in air velocity in the throat of a venturi causing an increase in air pressure.

*In a carburetor system, outside air flows into the carburetor and through a venturi (a narrow throat in the carburetor). When air flows rapidly through the venturi, a low pressure area is created. This low pressure allows the fuel to flow through the main fuel jet (located within the throat) and into the airstream where it mixes with the flowing air. (PLT191, PA.I.G.K1e, PH.I.G.K1e) — FAA-H-8083-25*

Answer (A) is incorrect because fuel, rather than air, is metered manually with the mixture control. Answer (C) is incorrect because there is a decrease in air pressure.

AIR, RTC, WSC, PPC

**3226.** The basic purpose of adjusting the air-fuel mixture at altitude is to

A—decrease the amount of fuel in the mixture in order to compensate for increased air density.

B—decrease the fuel flow in order to compensate for decreased air density.

C—increase the amount of fuel in the mixture to compensate for the decrease in pressure and density of the air.

*The mixture becomes richer as the airplane gains altitude, because the carburetor meters the same amount of fuel as at sea level. Leaning the mixture control prevents this by decreasing the rate of fuel discharge to compensate for the decrease in air density. (PLT191, PA.I.G.K1e, PH.I.G.K1e) — FAA-H-8083-25*

Answer (A) is incorrect because the pilot would increase the amount of fuel to compensate for increased air density. Answer (C) is incorrect because the pilot would decrease the amount of fuel to compensate for decreased air density.

AIR, RTC, WSC, PPC

**3228.** While cruising at 9,500 feet MSL, the air-fuel mixture is properly adjusted. What will occur if a descent to 4,500 feet MSL is made without readjusting the mixture?

A—The air-fuel mixture may become excessively lean.

B—There will be more fuel in the cylinders than is needed for normal combustion, and the excess fuel will absorb heat and cool the engine.

C—The excessively rich mixture will create higher cylinder head temperatures and may cause detonation.

*Air density increases in the descent, but the amount of fuel drawn into the carburetor remains the same. To re-establish a balanced air-fuel mixture in a descent, the mixture control must be adjusted toward rich. (PLT191, PA.I.G.K1e, PH.I.G.K1e) — FAA-H-8083-25*

Answer (B) is incorrect because the mixture will become too lean and the engine temperature will increase. Answer (C) is incorrect because an excessively lean mixture will result.

**Answers**

3225    [B]          3226    [B]          3228    [A]

# Carburetor Ice

As air flows through a carburetor it expands rapidly. At the same time, fuel forced into the airstream is vaporized. Expansion of the air and vaporization of the fuel causes a sudden cooling of the mixture which may cause ice to form inside the carburetor. The possibility of icing should always be considered when operating in conditions where the temperature is between 20°F and 70°F, and the relative humidity is high.

**Carburetor heat** preheats the air before it enters the carburetor and either prevents carburetor ice from forming or melts any ice which may have formed. When carburetor heat is applied, the heated air that enters the carburetor is less dense. This causes the air-fuel mixture to become enriched, and this in turn decreases engine output and increases engine operating temperatures.

During engine runup prior to departure from a high-altitude airport, the pilot may notice a slight engine roughness which is not affected by the magneto check, but grows worse during the carburetor heat check. In this case, the air-fuel mixture may be too rich due to the lower air density at the high altitude, and applying carburetor heat decreases the air density even more. A leaner setting of the mixture control may correct this problem.

In an airplane with a fixed-pitch propeller, the first indication of carburetor ice would likely be a decrease in RPM as the air supply is choked off. Application of carburetor heat will decrease air density, causing the RPM to drop even lower. Then, as the carburetor ice melts, the RPM will rise gradually.

Fuel injection systems do not utilize a carburetor and are generally considered to be less susceptible to icing than carburetor systems are.

AIR

**3227.** During the run-up at a high-elevation airport, a pilot notes a slight engine roughness that is not affected by the magneto check but grows worse during the carburetor heat check. Under these circumstances, what would be the most logical initial action?

A—Check the results obtained with a leaner setting of the mixture.
B—Taxi back to the flight line for a maintenance check.
C—Reduce manifold pressure to control detonation.

*When carburetor heat is applied, the air-fuel mixture of an engine will be enriched because any given volume of hot air is less dense than cold air of the same volume. This condition would be aggravated at high altitude where, because of decreased air density, the mixture is already richer than at sea level. (PLT253, PA.IX.C.K1) — FAA-H-8083-25*

*Answer (B) is incorrect because the pilot should taxi back only if positive results were not obtained by leaning the mixture. Answer (C) is incorrect because detonation would not occur if the mixture was too rich, and a rich fuel mixture was the condition described in the question.*

AIR, WSC, PPC

**3231.** If an aircraft is equipped with a fixed-pitch propeller and a float-type carburetor, the first indication of carburetor ice would most likely be

A—increase of RPM.
B—engine roughness.
C—loss of RPM.

*For airplanes with a fixed-pitch propeller, the first indication of carburetor ice is loss of RPM. (PLT190, PA.IX.C.K1) — FAA-H-8083-25*

*Answer (A) is incorrect because the RPM will decrease, not increase. Answer (B) is incorrect because this symptoms may develop, but only after a loss of RPM.*

**Answers**

3227    [A]          3231    [C]

AIR, WSC, PPC

**3235.** The presence of carburetor ice in an aircraft equipped with a fixed-pitch propeller can be verified by applying carburetor heat and noting

A—an increase in RPM and then a gradual decrease in RPM.
B—a decrease in RPM and then a constant RPM indication.
C—a decrease in RPM and then a gradual increase in RPM.

*When heat is applied there will be a drop in RPM in airplanes equipped with fixed-pitch propellers. If carburetor ice is present, there will normally be a rise in RPM after the initial drop. Then, when the carburetor heat is turned off, the RPM will rise to a setting greater than that before application of the heat. The engine should also run more smoothly after the ice has been removed. (PLT190, PA.IX.C.K1) — FAA-H-8083-25*

Answer (A) is incorrect because the warm air decreases engine RPM; melting ice also decreases RPM. Once the ice is gone, the RPM increases. Answer (B) is incorrect because this would happen if there was no carburetor ice to begin with.

AIR, RTC, WSC, PPC

**3229.** Which condition is most favorable to the development of carburetor icing?

A—Any temperature below freezing and a relative humidity of less than 50 percent.
B—Temperature between 32 and 50°F and low humidity.
C—Temperature between 20 and 70°F and high humidity.

*If the temperature is between -7°C (20°F) and 21°C (70°F) with visible moisture or high humidity, the pilot should be constantly on the alert for carburetor ice. (PLT190, PA.IX.C.K1, PH.I.G.K1k) — FAA-H-8083-25*

Answers (A) and (B) are incorrect because carburetor icing is more likely with high humidity.

AIR, RTC, WSC, PPC

**3230.** The possibility of carburetor icing exists even when the ambient air temperature is as

A—high as 70°F and the relative humidity is high.
B—high as 95°F and there is visible moisture.
C—low as 0°F and the relative humidity is high.

*If the temperature is between -7°C (20°F) and 21°C (70°F) with visible moisture or high humidity, the pilot should be constantly on the alert for carburetor ice. (PLT190, PA.IX.C.K1, PH.I.G.K1k) — FAA-H-8083-25*

Answer (B) is incorrect because icing is less likely to occur above 70°F. Answer (C) is incorrect because icing is less likely to occur below 20°F.

AIR, RTC, WSC, PPC

**3230-1.** Carburetor icing can occur with an OAT as high as

A—100°F and visible moisture.
B—20°C and high relative humidity.
C—75°F and low relative humidity.

*If the temperature is between -7°C (20°F) and 21°C (70°F), with visible moisture or high humidity, the pilot should constantly be on the alert for carburetor ice. (PLT190, PA.IX.C.K1, PH.I.G.K1k) — FAA-H-8083-25*

AIR, RTC, WSC, PPC

**3232.** Applying carburetor heat will

A—result in more air going through the carburetor.
B—enrich the air-fuel mixture.
C—not affect the air-fuel mixture.

*Carburetors are normally calibrated at sea level pressure to meter the correct air-fuel mixture. As altitude increases, air density decreases and the amount of fuel is too great for the amount of air—the mixture is too rich. This same result may be brought about by the application of carburetor heat. The heated air entering the carburetor has less density than unheated air and the air-fuel mixture is enriched. (PLT190, PA.IX.C.K1, PH.I.G.K1k) — FAA-H-8083-25*

Answer (A) is incorrect because applying carburetor heat decreases the density of air but does not affect the air going through the carburetor. Answer (C) is incorrect because the mixture is enriched by applying carburetor heat.

**Answers**

| | | | | |
|---|---|---|---|---|
| 3235 [C] | 3229 [C] | 3230 [A] | 3230-1 [B] | 3232 [B] |

AIR, RTC, WSC, PPC

**3233.** What change occurs in the air-fuel mixture when carburetor heat is applied?

A—A decrease in RPM results from the lean mixture.
B—The air-fuel mixture becomes richer.
C—The air-fuel mixture becomes leaner.

*Carburetors are normally calibrated at sea level pressure to meter the correct air-fuel mixture. As altitude increases, air density decreases and the amount of fuel is too great for the amount of air—the mixture is too rich. This same result may be brought about by the application of carburetor heat. The heated air entering the carburetor has less density than unheated air and the air-fuel mixture is enriched. (PLT190, PA.IX.C.K1, PH.I.G.K1k) — FAA-H-8083-25*

*Answers (A) and (C) are incorrect because the air-fuel mixture becomes richer.*

AIR, RTC, WSC, PPC

**3234.** Generally speaking, the use of carburetor heat tends to

A—decrease engine performance.
B—increase engine performance.
C—have no effect on engine performance.

*Use of carburetor heat tends to reduce the output of the engine and also to increase the operating temperature. (PLT190, PA.IX.C.K1, PH.I.G.K1k) — FAA-H-8083-25*

AIR, RTC, WSC, PPC

**3236.** With regard to carburetor ice, float-type carburetor systems in comparison to fuel injection systems are generally considered to be

A—more susceptible to icing.
B—equally susceptible to icing.
C—less susceptible to icing.

*Fuel injection systems are less susceptible to icing than carburetor systems because of the lack of the temperature drop caused by the venturi in a carburetor. Be aware that one can acquire carburetor ice even without easily visible moisture and, in the right circumstances, even at full power. (PLT190, PA.IX.C.K1, PH.I.G.K1k) — FAA-H-8083-25*

*Answers (B) and (C) are incorrect because the venturi throat of carburetors makes them more susceptible to icing than fuel injection systems.*

LSA, LSR, LSW, LSP

**2341.** Which condition is most favorable to the development of carburetor icing?

A—Any temperature below freezing and a relative humidity of less than 50 percent.
B—Temperature between 32 and 50°F and low humidity.
C—Temperature between 20 and 70°F and high humidity.

*If the temperature is between -7°C (20°F) and 21°C (70°F) with visible moisture or high humidity, the pilot should be constantly on the alert for carburetor ice. (PLT190) — FAA-H-8083-25*

*Answer (A) is incorrect because carburetor icing is more likely with high humidity. Answer (B) is incorrect because carburetor icing is more likely with high humidity.*

**Answers**

3233    [B]          3234    [A]          3236    [A]          2341    [C]

# Aviation Fuel

Fuel does two things for the engine; it acts both as an agent for combustion and as an agent for cooling (based on the mixture setting of the engine).

Aviation fuel is available in several grades. The proper grade for a specific engine will be listed in the aircraft flight manual. If the proper grade of fuel is not available, it is possible to use the next higher grade. A lower grade of fuel should never be used.

The use of low-grade fuel or a air-fuel mixture which is too lean may cause **detonation**, which is the uncontrolled spontaneous explosion of the mixture in the cylinder. Detonation produces extreme heat.

**Preignition** is the premature burning of the air-fuel mixture. It is caused by an incandescent area (such as a carbon or lead deposit heated to a red hot glow) which serves as an ignitor in advance of normal ignition.

Fuel can be contaminated by water and/or dirt. The air inside the aircraft fuel tanks can cool at night, and this cooling forms water droplets (through condensation) on the insides of the fuel tanks. These droplets then fall into the fuel. To avoid this problem, always fill the tanks completely when parking overnight.

Thoroughly drain all of the aircraft's sumps, drains, and strainers before a flight to get rid of all the water that might have collected.

Dirt can get into the fuel if refueling equipment is poorly maintained or if the refueling operation is sloppy. Use care when refueling an aircraft.

Two fuel pump systems are used on most airplanes. The main pump system is engine driven and an auxiliary electric driven pump is provided for use in the event the engine pump fails. The auxiliary pump, commonly known as the boost pump, provides added reliability to the fuel system, and is also used as an aid in engine starting. The electric auxiliary pump is controlled by a switch in the flight deck.

---

AIR, WSC, PPC, LSA, LSR, LSW, LSP

**3224.** On aircraft equipped with fuel pumps, when is the auxiliary electric driven pump used?

A—All the time, to aid the engine-driven fuel pump.
B—In the event engine-driven fuel pump fails.
C—Constantly, except in starting the engine.

*Two fuel pump systems are used on most airplanes. The main pump system is engine driven and an auxiliary electric driven pump is provided for use in the event the engine pump fails. The auxiliary pump, commonly known as the boost pump, provides added reliability to the fuel system, and is also used as an aid in engine starting. The electric auxiliary pump is controlled by a switch in the flight deck. (PLT253, PA.I.G.K1e) — FAA-H-8083-25*

AIR, RTC, WSC, PPC

**3237.** If the grade of fuel used in an aircraft engine is lower than specified for the engine, it will most likely cause

A—a mixture of fuel and air that is not uniform in all cylinders.
B—lower cylinder head temperatures.
C—detonation.

*Using fuel of a lower rating is harmful under any circumstances because it may cause loss of power, excessive heat, burned spark plugs, burned and sticky valves, high oil consumption, and detonation. (PLT250, PA.I.G.K1e, PH.I.G.K1e) — FAA-H-8083-25*

Answer (A) is incorrect because the carburetor will meter the lower-grade fuel the same as the proper fuel. Answer (B) is incorrect because lower-grade fuel raises cylinder head temperatures.

---

**Answers**

3224 [B]          3237 [C]

AIR, GLI, RTC, WSC

**3238.** Detonation may occur at high-power settings when

A—the fuel mixture ignites instantaneously instead of burning progressively and evenly.
B—an excessively rich fuel mixture causes an explosive gain in power.
C—the fuel mixture is ignited too early by hot carbon deposits in the cylinder.

*Detonation or knock is a sudden explosion or shock to a small area of the piston top, rather than the normal smooth burn in the combustion chamber. (PLT115, PA.I.G.K1e, PH.I.G.K1b) — FAA-H-8083-25*

Answer (B) is incorrect because detonation may occur with an excessively lean fuel mixture and a loss in power. Answer (C) is incorrect because this describes preignition.

AIR, RTC, WSC, PPC

**3238-1.** Detonation occurs in a reciprocating aircraft engine when

A—the spark plugs are fouled or shorted out or the wiring is defective.
B—hot spots in the combustion chamber ignite the air-fuel mixture in advance of normal ignition.
C—the unburned charge in the cylinders explodes instead of burning normally.

*Detonation is a sudden explosion, or instantaneous combustion, of the air-fuel mixture in the cylinders, producing extreme heat and severe structural stresses on the engine. (PLT115, PA.I.G.K1c, PH.I.G.K1b) — FAA-H-8083-25*

Answer (A) is incorrect because detonation does not have anything to do with the wiring. Answer (B) is incorrect because this describes preignition, not detonation.

AIR, RTC, WSC, PPC, LSA, LSR, LSW, LSP

**3240.** The uncontrolled firing of the air-fuel charge in advance of normal spark ignition is known as

A—combustion.
B—pre-ignition.
C—detonation.

*Preignition is defined as ignition of the fuel prior to normal ignition. (PLT478, PA.I.G.K1c, PH.I.G.K1b) — FAA-H-8083-25*

Answer (A) is incorrect because combustion is the normal engine process. Answer (C) is incorrect because detonation is the exploding of the air-fuel mixture.

AIR, RTC, WSC, PPC

**3242.** What type fuel can be substituted for an aircraft if the recommended octane is not available?

A—The next higher octane aviation gas.
B—The next lower octane aviation gas.
C—Unleaded automotive gas of the same octane rating.

*If the proper grade of fuel is not available, it is possible (but not desirable) to use the next higher (aviation) grade as a substitute. (PLT250, PA.I.G.K1e, PH.I.G.K1e) — FAA-H-8083-25*

Answer (B) is incorrect because burning lower octane fuel causes excessive engine temperatures. Answer (C) is incorrect because only aviation fuel should be used, except under special circumstances.

AIR, RTC, WSC, PPC, LSA, LSR, LSW, LSP

**3243.** Filling the fuel tanks after the last flight of the day is considered a good operating procedure because this will

A—force any existing water to the top of the tank away from the fuel lines to the engine.
B—prevent expansion of the fuel by eliminating airspace in the tanks.
C—prevent moisture condensation by eliminating airspace in the tanks.

*Water in the fuel system is dangerous and the pilot must prevent contamination. The fuel tanks should be filled after each flight, or at least after the last flight of the day. This will prevent moisture condensation within the tank, since no air space will be left inside. (PLT250, PA.I.G.K1e, PH.I.G.K1e) — FAA-H-8083-25*

Answer (A) is incorrect because water will settle to the bottom of a gas tank. Answer (B) is incorrect because fuel is allowed to expand by the fuel vent, whether the tanks are full or not.

AIR, RTC, LTA, WSC, PPC, LSA, LSR, LSW, LSP

**3243-1.** To properly purge water from the fuel system of an aircraft equipped with fuel tank sumps and a fuel strainer quick drain, it is necessary to drain fuel from the

A—fuel strainer drain.
B—lowest point in the fuel system.
C—fuel strainer drain and the fuel tank sumps.

*Many aircraft are equipped with fuel strainers located at the lowest point in the fuel lines and sump drains installed at the lowest point in each fuel tank. In order to completely purge all of the liquid water from the fuel system, the fuel strainer drain and the sumps in all of the tanks must be drained. (PLT253, PA.I.G.K1e, PH.I.G.K1e) — FAA-H-8083-25*

**Answers**

| 3238 | [A] | 3238-1 | [C] | 3240 | [B] | 3242 | [A] | 3243 | [C] | 3243-1 | [C] |

LSA, LSR
**2353.** During preflight in cold weather, crankcase breather lines should receive special attention because they are susceptible to being clogged by

A—congealed oil from the crankcase.
B—moisture from the outside air which has frozen.
C—ice from crankcase vapors that have condensed and subsequently frozen.

*The crankcase breather requires special consideration when preparing for cold weather. Frozen breather lines can create numerous problems. When crankcase vapors cool, they may condense in the breather line and subsequently freeze it closed. Special care is recommended during the preflight to ensure that the breather system is free of ice. (PLT126) — FAA-H-8083-25*

Answer (A) is incorrect because oil that lays in the bottom of the crankcase never gets into the breather lines. Answer (B) is incorrect because a low air temperature is usually associated with a low moisture content.

# Engine Temperatures

Engine lubricating **oil** not only prevents direct metal-to-metal contact of moving parts, it also absorbs and dissipates some of the engine heat produced by internal combustion. If the engine oil level should fall too low, an abnormally high engine oil temperature indication may result.

On the ground or in the air, excessively high engine temperatures can cause excessive oil consumption, loss of power, and possible permanent internal engine damage.

If the engine oil temperature and cylinder head temperature gauges have exceeded their normal operating range, or if the pilot suspects that the engine (with a fixed-pitch propeller) is detonating during climb-out, the pilot may have been operating with either too much power and the mixture set too lean, using fuel of too low a grade, or operating the engine with an insufficient amount of oil in it. Reducing the rate of climb and increasing airspeed, enriching the fuel mixture, or retarding the throttle will aid in cooling an engine that is overheating.

The most important rule to remember in the event of a power failure after becoming airborne is to maintain safe airspeed.

AIR, WSC, LSA, LSR, LSW
**3239.** If a pilot suspects that the engine (with a fixed-pitch propeller) is detonating during climb-out after takeoff, the initial corrective action to take would be to

A—lean the mixture.
B—lower the nose slightly to increase airspeed.
C—apply carburetor heat.

*To prevent detonation, the pilot should use the correct grade of fuel, maintain a sufficiently rich mixture, open the throttle smoothly, and keep the temperature of the engine within recommended operating limits. Some aircraft have an automatically enriched mixture for enhanced cooling in takeoff and climb-out at full throttle. Lowering the nose will allow the aircraft to gain airspeed, which eventually lowers the engine temperature. (PLT115, PA.I.G.K2) — FAA-H-8083-25*

Answer (A) is incorrect because leaning the mixture increases engine temperatures; detonation results from excessively high engine temperatures. Answer (C) is incorrect because although a richer fuel mixture results from applying carburetor heat, the heat may offset the cooling effect of the mixture change. The most efficient initial action would be to increase airspeed.

AIR, RTC, WSC, PPC
**3221.** Excessively high engine temperatures will

A—cause damage to heat-conducting hoses and warping of the cylinder cooling fins.
B—cause loss of power, excessive oil consumption, and possible permanent internal engine damage.
C—not appreciably affect an aircraft engine.

*Operating an engine at a higher temperature than it was designed for will cause loss of power, excessive oil consumption, and detonation. It will also lead to serious permanent injury to the engine including scoring of cylinder walls, damage to pistons and rings, and burning and warping of valves. (PLT342, PA.I.G.K1c, PH.I.G.K1b) — FAA-H-8083-25*

Answer (A) is incorrect because internal engine damage is more likely to result before external damage occurs. Answer (C) is incorrect because excessively high engine temperatures seriously affect an aircraft engine.

**Answers**

| | | |
|---|---|---|
| 2353 [C] | 3239 [B] | 3221 [B] |

AIR, RTC, WSC, PPC

**3221-1.** Excessively high engine temperatures, either in the air or on the ground, will

A—increase fuel consumption and may increase power due to the increased heat.
B—result in damage to heat-conducting hoses and warping of cylinder cooling fans.
C—cause loss of power, excessive oil consumption, and possible permanent internal engine damage.

*High engine temperatures can lead to loss of power, excessive oil consumption, detonation, and serious engine damage. (PLT253, PA.I.G.K1c, PH.I.G.K1b) — FAA-H-8083-25*

AIR, RTC, WSC, PPC

**3222.** If the engine oil temperature and cylinder head temperature gauges have exceeded their normal operating range, the pilot may have been operating with

A—the mixture set too rich.
B—higher-than-normal oil pressure.
C—too much power and with the mixture set too lean.

*Excessively high engine temperatures can result from insufficient cooling caused by too lean a mixture, too low a grade of fuel, low oil, or insufficient airflow over the engine. (PLT343, PA.I.G.K1c, PH.I.G.K1b) — FAA-H-8083-25*

Answer (A) is incorrect because a richer fuel mixture will normally cool an engine. Answer (B) is incorrect because high oil pressure does not cause high engine temperatures.

AIR, RTC, WSC, PPC

**3241.** Which would most likely cause the cylinder head temperature and engine oil temperature gauges to exceed their normal operating ranges?

A—Using fuel that has a lower-than-specified fuel rating.
B—Using fuel that has a higher-than-specified fuel rating.
C—Operating with higher-than-normal oil pressure.

*Excessively high engine temperatures result from insufficient cooling caused by too lean a mixture, too low a grade of fuel, low oil, or insufficient airflow over the engine. (PLT250, PA.I.G.K1c, PH.I.G.K1b) — FAA-H-8083-25*

Answer (B) is incorrect because higher octane fuel will burn at lower temperatures, keeping the engine cooler. Answer (C) is incorrect because high oil pressure does not cause high engine temperatures.

AIR, RTC, WSC, PPC

**3244.** For internal cooling, reciprocating aircraft engines are especially dependent on

A—a properly functioning thermostat.
B—air flowing over the exhaust manifold.
C—the circulation of lubricating oil.

*Oil, used primarily to lubricate the moving parts of the engine, also cools the internal parts of the engine as it circulates. (PLT342, PA.I.G.K1c, PH.I.G.K1b) — FAA-H-8083-25*

Answer (A) is incorrect because most air-cooled aircraft engines do not have thermostats. Answer (B) is incorrect because, although air-cooling is important, internal cooling is more reliant on oil circulation. Air cools the cylinders, not the exhaust manifold.

LSA, LSR

**2354.** Which is true regarding preheating an aircraft during cold weather operations?

A—The cabin area as well as the engine should be preheated.
B—The cabin area should not be preheated with portable heaters.
C—Hot air should be blown directly at the engine through the air intakes.

*Low temperatures may cause a change in the viscosity of engine oils, batteries may lose a high percentage of their effectiveness, and instruments may stick. Because of the above, preheating the engines as well as the cabin before starting is desirable in low temperatures. Extreme caution should be used in the preheat process to avoid fire. (PLT126) — FAA-H-8083-25*

AIR, RTC, WSC, PPC

**3245.** An abnormally high engine oil temperature indication may be caused by

A—the oil level being too low.
B—operating with a too high viscosity oil.
C—operating with an excessively rich mixture.

*Oil, used primarily to lubricate the moving parts of the engine, also helps reduce engine temperature by removing some of the heat from the cylinders. Therefore, if the oil level is too low, the transfer of heat to less oil would cause the oil temperature to rise. (PLT324, PA.I.G.K1e, PH.I.G.K1b) — FAA-H-8083-25*

Answer (B) is incorrect because the higher the viscosity, the better the lubricating and cooling capability of the oil. Answer (C) is incorrect because a rich air-fuel mixture usually decreases engine temperature.

**Answers**

| 3221-1 [C] | 3222 [C] | 3241 [A] | 3244 [C] | 2354 [A] | 3245 [A] |

AIR, RTC, WSC, PPC

**3651.** What action can a pilot take to aid in cooling an engine that is overheating during a climb?

A—Reduce rate of climb and increase airspeed.
B—Reduce climb speed and increase RPM.
C—Increase climb speed and increase RPM.

*To avoid excessive cylinder head temperatures, a pilot can open the cowl flaps, increase airspeed, enrich the mixture, or reduce power. Any of these procedures will aid in reducing the engine temperature. Establishing a shallower climb (increasing airspeed) increases the airflow through the cooling system, reducing high engine temperatures. (PLT342, PA.I.G.K2, PH.I.G.K1b) — FAA-H-8083-25*

Answer (B) is incorrect because reducing airspeed hinders cooling, and increasing RPM will further increase engine temperature. Answer (C) is incorrect because increasing RPM will increase engine temperature.

AIR, RTC, WSC, PPC

**3652.** What is one procedure to aid in cooling an engine that is overheating?

A—Enrichen the fuel mixture.
B—Increase the RPM.
C—Reduce the airspeed.

*To avoid excessive cylinder head temperatures, a pilot can open the cowl flaps, increase airspeed, enrich the mixture, or reduce power. Any of these procedures will aid in reducing the engine temperature. (PLT342, PA.I.G.K2, PH.I.G.K1b) — FAA-H-8083-25*

Answer (B) is incorrect because increasing the RPM increases the engine's internal heat. Answer (C) is incorrect because reducing the airspeed decreases the airflow needed for cooling, thus increasing the engine's temperature.

AIR, RTC, WSC

**3711.** The most important rule to remember in the event of a power failure after becoming airborne is to

A—immediately establish the proper gliding attitude and airspeed.
B—quickly check the fuel supply for possible fuel exhaustion.
C—determine the wind direction to plan for the forced landing.

*Maintaining the proper glide speed (safe airspeed) is the most important rule to remember in the event of a power failure. (PLT208, PA.IX.B.K2a, PH.V.A.R3b) — FAA-H-8083-3*

Answers (B) and (C) are incorrect because these steps should be taken only after establishing the proper glide speed.

**Answers**

3651 [A]          3652 [A]          3711 [A]

# Propellers

A propeller provides thrust to propel the airplane through the air. Some aircraft are equipped with a **constant-speed propeller**. This type of propeller allows the pilot to select the most efficient propeller blade angle for each phase of flight. In these aircraft, the throttle controls the power output as registered on the manifold pressure gauge, and the propeller control regulates the engine RPM.

A pilot should avoid a high manifold pressure setting with low RPM on engines equipped with a constant-speed propeller. To avoid high manifold pressure combined with low RPM, reduce the manifold pressure before reducing RPM when decreasing power settings (or increase the RPM before increasing the manifold pressure when increasing power settings).

AIR
**3653.** How is engine operation controlled on an engine equipped with a constant-speed propeller?

A—The throttle controls power output as registered on the manifold pressure gauge and the propeller control regulates engine RPM.
B—The throttle controls power output as registered on the manifold pressure gauge and the propeller control regulates a constant blade angle.
C—The throttle controls engine RPM as registered on the tachometer and the mixture control regulates the power output.

*On aircraft equipped with a constant-speed propeller, the throttle controls the engine power output which is registered on the manifold pressure gauge. The propeller control changes the pitch angle of the propeller and governs the RPM which is indicated on the tachometer. (PLT343, PA.I.G.K1c) — FAA-H-8083-25*

Answer (B) is incorrect because the propeller control does not maintain a constant pitch, it changes pitch in order to hold a constant RPM. Answer (C) is incorrect because the throttle does not directly control RPM, and mixture control does not regulate power.

AIR
**3654.** What is an advantage of a constant-speed propeller?

A—Permits the pilot to select and maintain a desired cruising speed.
B—Permits the pilot to select the blade angle for the most efficient performance.
C—Provides a smoother operation with stable RPM and eliminates vibrations.

*A constant-speed propeller permits the pilot to select the blade angle that will result in the most efficient performance for a particular flight condition. A low blade angle allows higher RPM and horsepower, desirable for takeoffs. An intermediate position can be used for subsequent climb. After airspeed is attained during cruising flight, the propeller blade may be changed to a higher angle for lower RPM, reduced engine noise, generally lower vibration, and greater fuel efficiency. (PLT351, PA.I.G.K1c) — FAA-H-8083-25*

Answer (A) is incorrect because a constant-speed propeller is not used to maintain airspeed, but rather constant engine RPM. Answer (C) is incorrect because a constant-speed propeller may not be smoother or operate with less vibration than a fixed-pitch propeller.

AIR
**3655.** A precaution for the operation of an engine equipped with a constant-speed propeller is to

A—avoid high RPM settings with high manifold pressure.
B—avoid high manifold pressure settings with low RPM.
C—always use a rich mixture with high RPM settings.

*On aircraft equipped with a constant-speed propeller, the throttle controls the engine power output which is registered on the manifold pressure gauge. The propeller control changes the pitch angle of the propeller and governs the RPM which is indicated on the tachometer. On most airplanes, for any given RPM, there is a manifold pressure that should not be exceeded. If an excessive amount of manifold pressure is carried for a given RPM, the maximum allowable pressure within the engine cylinders could be exceeded, thus putting undue strain on them. (PLT351, PA.I.G.K1c) — FAA-H-8083-25*

Answer (A) is incorrect because high manifold pressure is allowable with high RPM settings, within specification limits. Answer (C) is incorrect because the mixture should be leaned for best performance.

**Answers**

3653  [A]          3654  [B]          3655  [B]

# Torque

An airplane of standard configuration has an insistent tendency to turn to the left. This tendency is called torque, and is a combination of four forces: reactive force, spiraling slipstream, gyroscopic precession, and P-factor.

**Reactive force** is based on Newton's law of action and reaction. A propeller rotating in a clockwise direction (as seen from the rear) produces a force which tends to roll the airplane in a counterclockwise direction. See Figure 2-3.

The **spiraling slipstream** is the reaction of the air to a rotating propeller. (The propeller forces the air to spiral in a clockwise direction around the fuselage.) This spiraling slipstream strikes the airplane's vertical stabilizer on the left side. This pushes the tail of the airplane to the right and the nose of the airplane to the left. See Figure 2-4. Weight-shift control and powered parachutes do not have this effect.

**Gyroscopic precession** is the result of a deflective force applied to a rotating body (such as a propeller). The resultant action occurs 90° later in the direction of rotation. See Figure 2-5.

Asymmetric propeller loading, called **P-factor**, is caused by the downward moving blade on the right side of the propeller having a higher angle of attack, a greater action and reaction, and therefore a higher thrust than the upward moving opposite blade. This results in a tendency for the aircraft to yaw to the left around the vertical axis. Additional left-turning tendency from torque will be greatest when the aircraft is operating at low airspeed with a high power setting.

**Figure 2-3.** Reactive force

**Figure 2-4.** Spiraling slipstream

**Figure 2-5.** Gyroscopic precession

AIR, WSC, PPC

**3207.** In what flight condition are torque effects more pronounced in a single-engine airplane?

A—Low airspeed, high power, high angle of attack.
B—Low airspeed, low power, low angle of attack.
C—High airspeed, high power, high angle of attack.

*The effect of torque increases in direct proportion to the engine power, airspeed, and airplane attitude. If the power setting is high, the airspeed slow, and the angle of attack high (or a high deck angle for a PPC), the effect of torque is greater. (PLT243, PA.I.F.K3) — FAA-H-8083-25*

Answer (B) is incorrect because the least amount of torque effect is produced under these conditions. Answer (C) is incorrect because torque effect is negligible at higher airspeeds due to increased stability generated by more airflow moving over all airfoils.

AIR, WSC, PPC

**3208.** The left turning tendency of an airplane caused by P-factor is the result of the

A—clockwise rotation of the engine and the propeller turning the airplane counterclockwise.
B—propeller blade descending on the right, producing more thrust than the ascending blade on the left.
C—gyroscopic forces applied to the rotating propeller blades acting 90° in advance of the point the force was applied.

*The downward-moving blade on the right side of the propeller has a higher angle of attack and greater action and reaction than the upward moving blade on the left. This results in a tendency for the airplane to yaw around the vertical axis to the left. (PLT243, PA.I.F.K3) — FAA-H-8083-25*

Answer (A) is incorrect because it describes the characteristics involved with torque effect. Answer (C) is incorrect because it describes gyroscopic precession.

AIR, WSC, PPC

**3209.** When does P-factor cause the airplane to yaw to the left?

A—When at low angles of attack.
B—When at high angles of attack.
C—When at high airspeeds.

*The effects of P-factor, or asymmetric propeller loading, usually occur when the airplane is flown at high angles of attack (or a high deck angle for a PPC) and at high power settings. (PLT243, PA.I.F.K3) — FAA-H-8083-25*

Answer (A) is incorrect because the thrust differential between ascending and descending propeller blades at low angles of attack is slight. Answer (C) is incorrect because at higher airspeeds, an aircraft's angle of attack decreases in straight-and-level flight; therefore propeller-blade differential thrust becomes negligible.

**Answers**

3207  [A]        3208  [B]        3209  [B]

# Preflight Inspection Procedures

A thorough **preflight inspection** should be performed on an aircraft to help ensure that the aircraft is prepared for safe flight and should be a thorough and systematic means by which the pilot determines the airplane is ready for safe flight. Prior to every flight, a pilot should at least perform a walk-around inspection of the aircraft.

After an aircraft has been stored for an extended period of time, a special check should be made during preflight for damage or obstructions caused by animals, birds, or insects.

The use of a written checklist for preflight inspection and starting the engine is recommended to ensure that all necessary items are checked in a logical sequence.

Although 14 CFR Part 91 places primary responsibility on the owner or operator for maintaining an aircraft in an airworthy condition, the pilot-in-command is responsible for determining whether that aircraft is in condition for safe flight.

ALL, SPO

**3658.** During the preflight inspection who is responsible for determining the aircraft is safe for flight?

A—The pilot-in-command.
B—The owner or operator.
C—The certificated mechanic who performed the annual inspection.

*The pilot-in-command of an aircraft is responsible for determining whether that aircraft is in condition for safe flight. (PLT444, PA.II.A.K2, PH.II.A.K3d) — FAA-H-8083-25*

ALL

**3659.** How should an aircraft preflight inspection be accomplished for the first flight of the day?

A—Quick walk around with a check of gas and oil.
B—Thorough and systematic means recommended by the manufacturer.
C—Any sequence as determined by the pilot-in-command.

*The preflight inspection should be a thorough and systematic means by which the pilot determines that the airplane is ready for safe flight. Most AFM or POH contain a section devoted to a systematic method of performing a preflight inspection that should be used by the pilot for guidance. (PLT445, PA.II.A.K2, PH.II.A.K3a) — FAA-H-8083-25*

ALL, SPO

**3660.** Who is primarily responsible for maintaining an aircraft in airworthy condition?

A—Pilot-in-command.
B—Owner or operator.
C—Mechanic.

*14 CFR Part 91 places primary responsibility on the owner or operator for maintaining an aircraft in an airworthy condition. (PLT374, PA.II.A.K3d, PH.II.A.K2) — FAA-H-8083-25*

**Answers**

3658 [A]          3659 [B]          3660 [B]

# Helicopter Systems

RTC
**3318.** (Refer to Figure 10.) During flight, if cyclic control pressure is applied which results in a maximum increase in pitch angle of the rotor blade at position A, the rotor disc will tilt

A—forward.
B—aft.
C—left.

*Gyroscopic precession is the resultant action of a spinning object when a force is applied to the object. The action occurs approximately 90° later in the direction of rotation. Thus, if the maximum increase in angle of attack occurs at point A, maximum deflection takes place 90° later. This is maximum upward deflection at the rear, and the tip-path plane tips forward. (PH.I.F.K4) — FAA-H-8083-21*

RTC
**3319.** The lift differential that exists between the advancing main rotor blade and the retreating main rotor blade is known as

A—transverse flow effect.
B—dissymmetry of lift.
C—hunting tendency.

*The difference in lift that exists between the advancing blade half of the disc and retreating blade half, created by horizontal flight or by wind during hovering flight, is called dissymmetry of lift. (PH.I.F.K4) — FAA-H-8083-21*

RTC
**3320.** During forward cruising flight at constant airspeed and altitude, the individual rotor blades, when compared to each other, are operating

A—with increased lift on the retreating blade.
B—with a decreasing angle of attack on the advancing blade.
C—at unequal airspeed, unequal angles of attack, and equal lift moment.

*As the helicopter moves into forward flight, the relative wind moving over each rotor blade becomes a combination of the rotational speed of the rotor and the forward movement of the helicopter. Increased lift on the advancing blade will cause the blade to flap, decreasing the angle of attack. Decreased lift on the retreating blade will cause the blade to flap down, increasing the angle of attack. The combination of decreased angle of attack*

*on the advancing blade and increased angle of attack on the retreating blade through blade flapping action tends to equalize lift over the two halves of the rotor disc. (PH.I.F.K4) — FAA-H-8083-21*

RTC
**3321.** The upward bending of the rotor blades resulting from the combined forces of lift and centrifugal force is known as

A—coning.
B—blade slapping.
C—inertia.

*As a vertical takeoff is made, two major forces are acting at the same time—centrifugal force acting outward, perpendicular to the rotor mast, and lift, acting upward and parallel to the mast. The result of these two forces is that the blades assume a conical path instead of remaining in the plane perpendicular to the mast. (PH.I.F.K4) — FAA-H-8083-21*

RTC
**3322.** When a blade flaps up, the CG moves closer to its axis of rotation giving that blade a tendency to

A—decelerate.
B—accelerate.
C—stabilize its rotational velocity.

*When a rotor blade flaps up, the center of mass of that blade moves closer to the axis of rotation and blade acceleration takes place. (PH.I.F.K4) — FAA-H-8083-21*

RTC
**3323.** During a hover, a helicopter tends to drift to the right. To compensate for this, some helicopters have the

A—tail rotor tilted to the left.
B—tail rotor tilted to the right.
C—rotor mast rigged to the left side.

*To counteract drift, the rotor mast in some helicopters is rigged slightly to the left side so that the tip-path plane has a built-in tilt to the left, thus producing a small sideward thrust. (PH.IV.A.K3) — FAA-H-8083-21*

**Answers**

| | | | | | |
|---|---|---|---|---|---|
| 3318   [A] | 3319   [B] | 3320   [C] | 3321   [A] | 3322   [B] | 3323   [C] |

RTC
**3325.** Translational lift is the result of

A—decreased rotor efficiency.
B—airspeed.
C—both airspeed and groundspeed.

*Translational lift is that additional lift obtained when entering horizontal flight due to the increased efficiency of the rotor system. Translational lift depends upon airspeed rather than ground speed. (PH.V.I.K4) — FAA-H-8083-21*

RTC
**3326.** The primary purpose of the tail rotor system is to

A—assist in making a coordinated turn.
B—maintain heading during forward flight.
C—counteract the torque effect of the main rotor.

*The force that compensates for torque and keeps the fuselage from turning in the direction opposite to the main rotor is produced by means of an auxiliary rotor located on the end of the tail boom. (PH.I.G.K1a) — FAA-H-8083-21*

RTC
**3327.** If RPM is low and manifold pressure is high, what initial corrective action should be taken?

A—Increase the throttle.
B—Lower the collective pitch.
C—Raise the collective pitch.

*Lowering the collective pitch will reduce the manifold pressure, decrease drag on the rotor, and therefore increase the RPM. (PH.I.G.K1a) — FAA-H-8083-21*

RTC
**3328.** The purpose of the lead-lag (drag) hinge in a three-bladed, fully articulated helicopter rotor system is to compensate for

A—Coriolis effect.
B—coning.
C—geometric unbalance.

*In a fully articulated rotor system, each rotor blade is attached to the hub by a vertical hinge called a drag or lag hinge that permits each blade, independently of the others, to move back and forth in the plane of the rotor disc. This movement is called dragging, lead-lag, or hunting. The purpose of the drag hinge and dampers is to absorb the acceleration and deceleration of the rotor blades caused by Coriolis effect. (PH.I.G.K1c) — FAA-H-8083-21*

RTC
**3329.** High airspeeds, particularly in turbulent air, should be avoided primarily because of the possibility of

A—an abrupt pitchup.
B—retreating blade stall.
C—a low-frequency vibration developing.

*A tendency for the retreating blade to stall in forward flight is a major factor in limiting a helicopter's forward airspeed. When operating at high airspeeds, stalls are more liable to occur under conditions of high gross weight, low RPM, high density altitude, steep or abrupt turns, and/or turbulent flight. (PH.I.G.K1j) — FAA-H-8083-21*

RTC
**3330.** The maximum forward speed of a helicopter is limited by

A—retreating blade stall.
B—the rotor RPM red line.
C—solidity ratio.

*A tendency for the retreating blade to stall in forward flight is a major factor in limiting a helicopter's forward airspeed. When operating at high airspeeds, stalls are more liable to occur under conditions of high gross weight, low RPM, high density altitude, steep or abrupt turns, and/or turbulent flight. (PH.I.F.R7) — FAA-H-8083-21*

RTC
**3331.** When operating at high forward airspeeds, retreating blade stalls are more likely to occur under which condition?

A—Low gross weight and low density altitude.
B—High RPM and low density altitude.
C—Steep turns in turbulent air.

*A tendency for the retreating blade to stall in forward flight is a major factor in limiting a helicopter's forward airspeed. When operating at high airspeeds, stalls are more liable to occur under conditions of high gross weight, low RPM, high density altitude, steep or abrupt turns, and/or turbulent flight. (PH.I.F.R7) — FAA-H-8083-21*

**Answers**

3325 [B]     3326 [C]     3327 [B]     3328 [A]     3329 [B]     3330 [A]
3331 [C]

RTC

**3332.** Ground resonance is most likely to develop when

A—on the ground and harmonic vibrations develop between the main and tail rotors.
B—a series of shocks causes the rotor system to become unbalanced.
C—there is a combination of a decrease in the angle of attack on the advancing blade and an increase in the angle of attack on the retreating blade.

*When one landing gear of the helicopter strikes the surface first, a shock is transmitted through the fuselage to the rotor. This shock may cause the blades straddling the contact point to be forced closer together. When one of the other landing gears strikes, the unbalance could be aggravated. This sets up a resonance of the fuselage. (PH.VIII.I.K1) — FAA-H-8083-21*

RTC

**3333.** While in level cruising flight in a helicopter, a pilot experiences low-frequency vibrations (100 to 400 cycles per minute). These vibrations are normally associated with the

A—engine.
B—cooling fan.
C—main rotor.

*Low-frequency vibrations are always associated with the main rotor. (PH.I.G.K1c) — FAA-H-8083-21*

RTC

**3334.** Select the helicopter component that, if defective, would cause medium-frequency vibrations.

A—Tail rotor.
B—Main rotor.
C—Engine.

*Medium-frequency vibrations are a result of trouble with the tail rotor in most helicopters. (PH.I.G.K1c) — FAA-H-8083-21*

RTC

**3335.** The principal reason the shaded area of a Height vs. Velocity Chart should be avoided is

A—turbulence near the surface can dephase the blade dampers.
B—rotor RPM may decay before ground contact is made if an engine failure should occur.
C—insufficient airspeed would be available to ensure a safe landing in case of an engine failure.

*The chart can be used to determine those altitude-airspeed combinations from which it would be impossible to successfully complete an autorotative landing. The altitude-airspeed combinations that should be avoided are represented by the shaded areas of the chart. (PH. IV.B.R7) — FAA-H-8083-21*

RTC

**3336.** During surface taxiing, the collective pitch is used to control

A—drift during a crosswind.
B—rate of speed.
C—ground track.

*Collective pitch is used to control rate of speed during taxi. The higher the collective pitch, the faster will be the taxi speed. (PH.IV.D.R4) — FAA-H-8083-21*

RTC

**3337.** During surface taxiing, the cyclic pitch stick is used to control

A—forward movement.
B—heading.
C—ground track.

*Cyclic pitch is used to control ground track during surface taxi. (PH.I.G.K1a) — FAA-H-8083-21*

RTC, LSR

**3338.** If the pilot experiences ground resonance, and the rotor RPM is not sufficient for flight,

A—open the throttle full and liftoff.
B—apply the rotor brake and stop the rotor as soon as possible.
C—attempt to takeoff at that power setting.

*Ground resonance is an aerodynamic phenomenon associated with fully articulated rotor systems. It develops when the rotor blades move out of phase with each other and cause the rotor disc to become unbalanced. This condition can cause a helicopter to self-destruct in a matter of seconds. However, for this condition to occur, the helicopter must be in contact with the ground. If you experience ground resonance, and the rotor RPM is not yet sufficient for flight, apply the rotor brake to maximum and stop the rotor as soon as possible. If ground resonance occurs during takeoff, when rotor RPM is sufficient for flight, lift off immediately. (PH. VIII.I.K1b) — FAA-H-8083-21*

**Answers**

| 3332 | [B] | 3333 | [C] | 3334 | [A] | 3335 | [C] | 3336 | [B] | 3337 | [C] |
| 3338 | [B] | | | | | | | | | | |

LSR

**2329.** If ground resonance is experienced during rotor spin-up, what action should you take?

A—Taxi to a smooth area.
B—Make a normal takeoff immediately.
C—Close the throttle and slowly raise the spin-up lever.

*A corrective action for ground resonance is an immediate takeoff if RPM is in proper range (for helicopters) or an immediate closing of the throttle and placing the blades in low pitch if the RPM is low. "During spin-up" implies low RPM, so closing the throttle is appropriate. (PH.VIII.I.K1b) — FAA-H-8083-21*

RTC

**3733.** With calm wind conditions, which flight operation would require the most power?

A—A right-hovering turn.
B—A left-hovering turn.
C—Hovering out of ground effect.

*During a hovering turn to the left, the RPM will decrease if throttle is not added. In a hovering turn to the right, RPM will increase if throttle is not reduced slightly. (This is due to the amount of engine power that is being absorbed by the tail rotor, which is dependent upon the pitch angle at which the tail rotor blades are operating.) (PH.I.F.K2a) — FAA-H-8083-21*

RTC

**3734.** If the pilot were to make a near-vertical power approach into a confined area with the airspeed near zero, what hazardous condition may develop?

A—Ground resonance when ground contact is made.
B—A vortex ring state condition.
C—Blade stall vibration could develop.

*The following combination of conditions are likely to cause vortex ring state:*

1. *A vertical, or nearly vertical, descent of at least 300 fpm. (The actual critical rate depends on the gross weight, RPM, density altitude, and other pertinent factors.)*

2. *The rotor disc must be using some of the available engine power (20 to 100 percent).*

3. *The horizontal velocity must be slower than effective translational lift.*

*(PH.VIII.E.K5) — FAA-H-8083-21*

RTC

**3734-1.** A fully developed vortex ring state may reach a rate of descent that approaches

A—4,000 fpm.
B—6,000 fpm.
C—8,000 fpm.

*A fully developed vortex ring state is characterized by an unstable condition in which the helicopter experiences uncommanded pitch and roll oscillations, has little or no collective authority, and achieves a descent rate that may approach 6,000 fpm if allowed to develop. (PH.VIII.E.K4) — FAA-H-8083-21*

RTC

**3734-2.** An uncommanded, rapid yaw towards the advancing blade which does not subside of its own accord is known as

A—a loss of tail rotor effectiveness.
B—vortex ring state.
C—main rotor disc interference.

*Loss of tail rotor effectiveness (LTE), or an unanticipated yaw, is an uncommanded, rapid yaw towards the advancing blade which does not subside of its own accord. It can result in the loss of the aircraft if left unchecked. (PH.V.B.R6) — FAA-H-8083-21*

RTC

**3734-3.** What flight activity or condition would lend itself to a higher risk for loss of tail rotor effectiveness (LTE)?

A—While on short approach to landing at a heliport.
B—During departure from a heliport in a no-wind condition.
C—In a low-and-slow situation over a remote area.

*Low-and-slow situations over geographical areas where the exact wind speed and direction are hard to determine will typically lend the aircraft to be at higher risk for loss of tail rotor effectiveness. (PH.V.B.R6) — FAA-H-8083-21*

Answer (A) is incorrect because there will typically be a windsock available to determine wind direction and strength when landing at a heliport. Answer (B) is incorrect because in a no-wind condition the aircraft is less susceptible to LTE.

---

**Answers**

| | | | | | |
|---|---|---|---|---|---|
| 2329 [C] | 3733 [B] | 3734 [B] | 3734-1 [B] | 3734-2 [A] | 3734-3 [C] |

RTC
**3736.** (Refer to Figure 46.) Which airspeed/altitude combination should be avoided during helicopter operations?

A—30 mph/200 feet AGL.
B—50 mph/300 feet AGL.
C—60 mph/20 feet AGL.

*Use the following steps:*

1. *Note the shaded "avoid operation" areas of FAA Figure 46.*

2. *Locate each of the three height-above-terrain and airspeed points on the diagram.*

3. *The 60 mph/20 feet AGL point is located within the low-altitude high airspeed area.*

*(PH.VI.B.K5) — FAA-H-8083-21*

RTC
**3737.** (Refer to Figure 46.) Which airspeed/altitude combination should be avoided during helicopter operations?

A—20 mph/200 feet AGL.
B—35 mph/175 feet AGL.
C—40 mph/75 feet AGL.

*Use the following steps:*

1. *Note the shaded "avoid operation" areas of FAA Figure 46.*

2. *Locate each of the three height-above-terrain and airspeed points on the diagram.*

3. *The 20 mph/200 feet AGL point is located within the high-altitude low airspeed area.*

*(PH.VI.B.K5) — FAA-H-8083-21*

RTC
**3738.** If anti-torque failure occurred during the landing touchdown, what could be done to help straighten out a left yaw prior to touchdown?

A—A flare to zero airspeed and a vertical descent to touchdown should be made.
B—Apply available throttle to help swing the nose to the right just prior to touchdown.
C—A normal running landing should be made.

*If sufficient forward speed is maintained, the fuselage remains fairly well streamlined. However, if descent is attempted at slow speeds, a continuous turning movement to the left can be expected. (Know the manufacturer's recommendations in case of tail rotor failure for each particular helicopter you fly. This information will generally be found under Emergency Procedures in the*

*helicopter flight manual.) Directional control should be maintained primarily with cyclic control and, secondarily, by gently applying throttle momentarily, with needles joined, to swing the nose to the right. (PH.VIII.G.R3) — FAA-H-8083-21*

RTC
**3739.** Which flight technique is recommended for use during hot weather?

A—Use minimum allowable RPM and maximum allowable manifold pressure during all phases of flight.
B—During hovering flight, maintain minimum engine RPM during left pedal turns, and maximum engine RPM during right pedal turns.
C—During takeoff, accelerate slowly into forward flight.

*The following techniques should be used in hot weather:*

1. *Make full use of wind and translational lift.*

2. *Hover as low as possible and no longer than necessary.*

3. *Maintain maximum allowable engine RPM.*

4. *Accelerate very slowly into forward flight.*

5. *Employ running takeoffs and landings when necessary.*

6. *Use caution in maximum performance takeoffs and steep approaches.*

7. *Avoid high rates of descent in all approaches.*

*(PH.II.A.K4) — FAA-H-8083-21*

RTC
**3740.** Under what condition should a helicopter pilot consider using a running takeoff?

A—When gross weight or density altitude prevents a sustained hover at normal hovering altitude.
B—When a normal climb speed is assured between 10 and 20 feet.
C—When the additional airspeed can be quickly converted to altitude.

*A running takeoff is used when conditions of load and/ or density altitude prevent a sustained hover at normal hovering altitude. It is often referred to as a high-altitude takeoff. With insufficient power to hover at least momentarily or at a very low altitude, a running takeoff is not advisable. No takeoff should be attempted if the helicopter cannot be lifted off the surface momentarily at full power. (PH.V.B.K1) — FAA-H-8083-21*

**Answers**

3736   [C]          3737   [A]          3738   [B]          3739   [C]          3740   [A]

**RTC**
**3741.** What action should the pilot take if engine failure occurs at altitude?

A—Open the throttle as the collective pitch is raised.
B—Reduce cyclic back stick pressure during turns.
C—Lower the collective pitch control, as necessary, to maintain rotor RPM.

*By immediately lowering collective pitch (which must be done in case of engine failure), lift and drag will be reduced and the helicopter will begin an immediate descent, thus producing an upward flow of air through the rotor system. The impact of this upward flow of air provides sufficient thrust to maintain rotor RPM throughout the descent. (PH.VIII.B.K1) — FAA-H-8083-21*

**RTC**
**3742.** Which is a precaution to be observed during an autorotative descent?

A—Normally, the airspeed is controlled with the collective pitch.
B—Normally, only the cyclic control is used to make turns.
C—Do not allow the rate of descent to get too low at zero airspeed.

*When making turns during an autorotative descent, generally use cyclic control only. Use of antitorque pedals to assist or speed the turn causes loss of airspeed and downward pitching of the nose. This is especially true when the left pedal is used. When the autorotation is initiated, sufficient right pedal pressure should be used to maintain straight flight and prevent yawing to the left. This pressure should not be changed to assist the turn. (PH.I.G.K1a) — FAA-H-8083-21*

**RTC**
**3743.** The proper action to initiate a quick stop is to apply

A—forward cyclic and lower the collective pitch.
B—aft cyclic and raise the collective pitch.
C—aft cyclic and lower the collective pitch.

*A quick stop is initiated by applying aft cyclic to reduce forward speed. Simultaneously, the collective pitch should be lowered as necessary, to counteract any climbing tendency. The timing must be exact. If too little down collective is applied for the amount of aft cyclic applied, a climb will result. If too much down collective is applied for the amount of aft cyclic applied, a descent will result. A rapid application of aft cyclic requires an equally rapid application of down collective. As collective*

*pitch is lowered, the right pedal should be increased to maintain heading, and throttle should be adjusted to maintain RPM. (PH.VI.A.K1) — FAA-H-8083-21*

**RTC**
**3744.** What is the procedure for a slope landing?

A—When the downslope skid is on the ground, hold the collective pitch at the same position.
B—Minimum RPM shall be held until the full weight of the helicopter is on the skid.
C—When parallel to the slope, slowly lower the upslope skid to the ground prior to lowering the downslope skid.

*A downward pressure on the collective pitch will start the helicopter descending. As the upslope skid touches the ground, apply cyclic stick in the direction of the slope. This will hold the skid against the slope while the downslope skid is continuing to be let down with the collective pitch. (PH.IV.E.K1) — FAA-H-8083-21*

**RTC**
**3745.** Takeoff from a slope is normally accomplished by

A—moving the cyclic in a direction away from the slope.
B—bringing the helicopter to a level attitude before completely leaving the ground.
C—moving the cyclic stick to a full up position as the helicopter nears a level attitude.

*Recommended slope takeoff technique is to:*

1. *Adjust throttle to obtain takeoff RPM and move the cyclic stick in the direction of the slope so that the rotor rotation is parallel to the true horizontal rather than the slope.*

2. *Apply up-collective pitch. As the helicopter becomes light on the skids, apply the pedal as needed to maintain heading.*

3. *As the downslope skid is rising and the helicopter approaches a level attitude, move the cyclic stick back to the neutral position, keeping the rotor disc parallel to the true horizon. Continue to apply up-collective pitch and take the helicopter straight up to a hover before moving away from the slope. In moving away from the slope, the tail should not be turned upslope because of the danger of the tail rotor striking the surface.*

*(PH.IV.E.K1) — FAA-H-8083-21*

---

**Answers**

3741 [C]          3742 [B]          3743 [C]          3744 [C]          3745 [B]

RTC
**3746.** Which action would be appropriate for confined area operations?

A—Takeoffs and landings must be made into the wind.
B—Plan the flightpath over areas suitable for a forced landing.
C—A very steep angle of descent should be used to land on the selected spot.

*In any type of confined area operation, plan a flight path over areas suitable for forced landings if possible. (PH.V.F.K2) — FAA-H-8083-21*

RTC
**3747.** If possible, when departing a confined area, what type of takeoff is preferred?

A—A normal takeoff from a hover.
B—A vertical takeoff.
C—A normal takeoff from the surface.

*If possible, a normal takeoff from a hover should be made when departing a confined area. (PH.V.F.K3) — FAA-H-8083-21*

RTC
**3748.** Which is a correct general rule for pinnacle and ridgeline operations?

A—Gaining altitude on takeoff is more important than gaining airspeed.
B—The approach path to a ridgeline is usually perpendicular to the ridge.
C—A climb to a pinnacle or ridgeline should be performed on the upwind side.

*If necessary to climb to a pinnacle or ridgeline, the climb should be performed on the upwind side, when practicable, to take advantage of any updrafts. (PH.V.G.K1) — FAA-H-8083-21*

RTC
**3749.** Before beginning a confined area or pinnacle landing, the pilot should first

A—execute a high reconnaissance.
B—execute a low reconnaissance.
C—fly around the area to discover areas of turbulence.

*The purpose of the high reconnaissance is to determine the suitability of an area for landing. In a high reconnaissance, the following items should be accomplished:*

*1. Determine wind direction and speed.*

*2. Select the most suitable flight paths into and out of the area, with particular consideration being given to forced landing areas.*

*3. Plan the approach and select a point for touchdown.*

*4. Locate and determine the size of barriers, if any.*

*The approach path should be generally into the wind. The purpose of the low reconnaissance is to verify what was seen in the high reconnaissance.*

*(PH.V.G.K1) — FAA-H-8083-21*

**Answers**

3746　[B]　　　3747　[A]　　　3748　[C]　　　3749　[A]

# Glider Operations

GLI

**3174.** The minimum allowable strength of a towline used for an aerotow of a glider having a certified gross weight of 700 pounds is

A—560 pounds.
B—700 pounds.
C—1,000 pounds.

*No person may operate a civil aircraft towing a glider unless the towline used has a breaking strength not less than 80 percent of the maximum certificated operating weight of the glider, and not greater than twice this operating weight unless safety links are used.*

$$
\begin{array}{r}
700 \ lbs \\
\times\ 0.80 \\
\hline
560 \ lbs
\end{array}
$$

*(PLT496) — 14 CFR §91.309*

GLI

**3175.** The minimum allowable strength of a towline used for an aerotow of a glider having a certificated gross weight of 1,040 pounds is

A—502 pounds.
B—832 pounds.
C—1,040 pounds.

*No person may operate a civil aircraft towing a glider unless the towline used has a breaking strength not less than 80% of the maximum certificated operating weight of the glider, and not greater than twice this operating weight unless safety links are used.*

$$
\begin{array}{r}
1,040 \ lbs \\
\times\ 0.80 \\
\hline
832 \ lbs
\end{array}
$$

*(PLT496) — 14 CFR §91.309*

GLI

**3177.** When using a towline having a breaking strength more than twice the maximum certificated operating weight of the glider, an approved safety link must be installed at what point(s)?

A—Only the point where the towline is attached to the glider.
B—The point where the towline is attached to the glider and the point of attachment of the towline to the towplane.
C—Only the point where the towline is attached to the towplane.

*The towline may have a breaking strength of more than twice the maximum certificated operating weight of the glider if a safety link is installed at the point of attachment of the towline to the glider, and a safety link is installed at the point of attachment of the towline to the towing aircraft. (PLT496) — 14 CFR §91.309*

GLI

**3176.** For the aerotow of a glider that weighs 700 pounds, which towrope tensile strength would require the use of safety links at each end of the rope?

A—850 pounds.
B—1,040 pounds.
C—1,450 pounds.

*No person may operate a civil aircraft towing a glider unless the towline used has a breaking strength not less than 80 percent of the maximum certificated operating weight of the glider, and not greater than twice this operating weight unless safety links are used.*

$$
\begin{array}{r}
700 \ lbs \\
\times\ 2 \\
\hline
1,400 \ lbs
\end{array}
$$

*(PLT496) — 14 CFR §91.309*

GLI

**3340.** What force provides the forward motion necessary to move a glider through the air?

A—Lift.
B—Centripetal force.
C—Gravity.

*The pull of gravity provides the forward motion necessary to move the wings through the air. (PLT241) — FAA-H-8083-13*

**Answers**

3174　[A]　　　　3175　[B]　　　　3177　[B]　　　　3176　[C]　　　　3340　[C]

GLI

**3341.** To obtain maximum distance over the ground, the airspeed to use is the

A—minimum control speed.
B—best lift/drag speed.
C—minimum sink speed.

*If the maximum distance over the ground is desired, the airspeed for best L/D should be used. (PLT132) — FAA-H-8083-13*

GLI

**3342.** What effect would gusts and turbulence have on the load factor of a glider with changes in airspeed?

A—Load factor decreases as airspeed increases.
B—Load factor increases as airspeed increases.
C—Load factor increases as airspeed decreases.

*Both positive and negative gust load factors increase with increasing airspeed. (PLT132) — FAA-H-8083-13*

GLI

**3343.** (Refer to Figure 11.) Which yaw string and inclinometer illustrations indicate a slipping right turn?

A—3 and 6.
B—2 and 6.
C—2 and 4.

*In the case of a slipping right turn, the yaw string moves outside left and the ball moves inside, or right, as illustrated by 2 and 6 of FAA Figure 11. (PLT185) — FAA-H-8083-13*

GLI

**3344.** (Refer to Figure 11.) Which of the illustrations depicts the excessive use of right rudder during the entry of a right turn?

A—2 only.
B—2 and 4.
C—3 and 4.

*In the case of a skidding right turn, the yaw string moves inside right and the ball moves outside, or left, as illustrated by 3 and 4 of FAA Figure 11. (PLT185) — FAA-H-8083-13*

GLI

**3345.** A sailplane has a best glide ratio of 23:1. How many feet will the glider lose in 8 nautical miles?

A—1,840 feet.
B—2,100 feet.
C—2,750 feet.

*L/D is lift divided by drag. This significant ratio is numerically the same as glide ratio, the ratio of forward to downward motion. Hence, 23 to 1 glide ratio would indicate:*

1. $\dfrac{23}{1} = \dfrac{6,000 \ (feet/NM - forward)}{X \ (feet/NM - downward)}$

2. $\dfrac{23}{1} \times X = 6,000$

3. *X = 261 feet downward for each 6,000 feet (1 NM) forward.*

4. *The total sink is 8 NM × 261 feet/NM or about 2,100 feet in 8 NM in calm air.*

*(PLT006) — FAA-H-8083-13*

GLI

**3346.** A sailplane has a best glide ratio of 30:1. How many nautical miles will the glider travel while losing 2,000 feet?

A—10 nautical miles.
B—15 nautical miles.
C—21 nautical miles.

*L/D is lift divided by drag. This significant ratio is numerically the same as glide ratio, the ratio of forward to downward motion. Hence, 30 to 1 glide ratio would indicate:*

1. $\dfrac{30}{1} = \dfrac{X \ (feet/NM - forward)}{2,000 \ (feet/NM - downward)}$

2. $\dfrac{30}{1} \times 2,000 = X$

3. *X = 60,000 feet (10 NM) forward for each 2,000 feet downward.*

*(PLT006) — FAA-H-8083-13*

**Answers**

| | | | | | |
|---|---|---|---|---|---|
| 3341 [B] | 3342 [B] | 3343 [B] | 3344 [C] | 3345 [B] | 3346 [A] |

GLI
**3347.** A sailplane has lost 2,000 feet in 9 nautical miles. The best glide ratio for this sailplane is approximately

A—24:1.
B—27:1.
C—30:1.

*L/D is lift divided by drag. This significant ratio is numerically the same as glide ratio, the ratio of forward to downward motion. Assuming that 1 NM is approximately 6,000 feet, the glide ratio and L/D may be expressed as:*

$$\frac{9 \times 6,000 \text{ feet forward}}{2,000 \text{ feet downard}} = \frac{54,000}{2,000} = \frac{54}{2} = \frac{27}{1} \text{ or } 27{:}1$$

*(PLT006) — FAA-H-8083-13*

GLI
**3348.** How many feet will a sailplane sink in 15 nautical miles if its lift/drag ratio is 22:1?

A—2,700 feet.
B—3,600 feet.
C—4,100 feet.

*L/D is lift divided by drag. This significant ratio is numerically the same as glide ratio, the ratio of forward to downward motion. Hence, 22 to 1 glide ratio would indicate:*

1. $\dfrac{22}{1} = \dfrac{6,000 \text{ (feet/NM – forward)}}{X \text{ (feet/NM – downward)}}$

2. $\dfrac{22}{1} \times X = 6,000$

3. *X = 273 feet downward for each 6,000 feet (1 NM) forward.*

4. *The total sink is 15 NM × 273 feet/NM, or about 4,095 feet in 15 NM in calm air.*

*(PLT012) — FAA-H-8083-13*

GLI
**3349.** How many feet will a glider sink in 10 nautical miles if its lift/drag ratio is 23:1?

A—2,400 feet.
B—2,600 feet.
C—4,300 feet.

*L/D is lift divided by drag. This significant ratio is numerically the same as glide ratio, the ratio of forward to downward motion. Hence, 23 to 1 glide ratio would indicate:*

1. $\dfrac{23}{1} = \dfrac{6,000 \text{ (feet/NM – forward)}}{X \text{ (feet/NM – downward)}}$

2. $\dfrac{23}{1} \times X = 6,000$

3. *X = 261 feet downward for each 6,000 feet (1 NM) forward.*

4. *The total sink is 10 NM × 261 feet/NM, or about 2,610 feet in 10 NM in calm air.*

*(PLT012) — FAA-H-8083-13*

GLI
**3750.** What minimum upward current must a glider encounter to maintain altitude?

A—At least 2 feet per second.
B—The same as the glider's sink rate.
C—The same as the adjacent down currents.

*Zero sink occurs when upward currents are just strong enough to hold altitude. For a sink rate of about 2 feet per second, there must be an upward air current of at least 2 feet per second. (PLT516) — FAA-H-8083-28*

GLI
**3751.** On which side of a rocky knoll, that is surrounded by vegetation, should a pilot find the best thermals?

A—On the side facing the sun.
B—On the downwind side.
C—Exactly over the center.

*If a rocky knoll protrudes above a grassy plane, the most likely area for thermals to occur is over the eastern slope in the forenoon and over the western slope in the afternoon. (PLT494) — FAA-H-8083-28*

GLI
**3752.** What is one recommended method for locating thermals?

A—Fly an ever increasing circular path.
B—Maintain a straight track downwind.
C—Look for converging streamers of dust or smoke.

*Look for converging streamers of dust and smoke. (PLT494) — FAA-H-8083-28*

**Answers**

| | | | | | |
|---|---|---|---|---|---|
| 3347 [B] | 3348 [C] | 3349 [B] | 3750 [B] | 3751 [A] | 3752 [C] |

GLI
**3753.** What is a recommended procedure for entering a dust devil for soaring?

A—Enter above 500 feet and circle the edge in the same direction as the rotation.
B—Enter below 500 feet and circle the edge opposite the direction of rotation.
C—Enter at or above 500 feet and circle the edge opposite the direction of rotation.

*At around 500 feet, the pilot makes a circle on the outside of the dust devil against the direction of rotation. (PLT494) — FAA-H-8083-28*

GLI
**3754.** What is an important precaution when soaring in a dust devil?

A—Avoid the eye of the vortex.
B—Avoid the clear area at the outside edge of the dust.
C—Maintain the same direction as the rotation of the vortex.

*The rarefied air in the eye provides very little lift, and the wall of the hollow core is very turbulent. (PLT494) — FAA-H-8083-28*

GLI
**3755.** What is the best visual indication of a thermal?

A—Fragmented cumulus clouds with concave bases.
B—Smooth cumulus clouds with concave bases.
C—Scattered to broken sky with cumulus clouds.

*Look for a cumulus with a concave base, and with a firm, sharp, unfragmented outline. (PLT494) — FAA-H-8083-28*

GLI
**3756.** How can a pilot locate bubble thermals?

A—Look for wet areas where recent showers have occurred.
B—Look for birds that are soaring in areas of intermittent heating.
C—Fly the area just above the boundary of a temperature inversion.

*Birds may be soaring in a bubble thermal that has been pinched off and forced upward through intermittent shading. (PLT494) — FAA-H-8083-28*

GLI
**3757.** Where may the most favorable type thermals for cross-country soaring be found?

A—Just ahead of a warm front.
B—Along thermal streets.
C—Under mountain waves.

*Thermal streeting is a real boon to speed and distance. (PLT494) — FAA-H-8083-28*

GLI
**3758.** Where and under what condition can enough lift be found for soaring when the weather is generally stable?

A—On the upwind side of hills or ridges with moderate winds present.
B—In mountain waves that form on the upwind side of the mountains.
C—Over isolated peaks when strong winds are present.

*Stability affects the continuity and extent of lift over hills or ridges, allowing relatively streamlined upslope flow. An upslope wind of 15 knots creates lift of about 6 feet per second. (PLT173) — FAA-H-8083-28*

GLI
**3857.** Which is an advantage of using a CG hook for a winch tow rather than the nose hook?

A—A greater percent of the line length can be used to reach altitude.
B—Maximum release altitude is limited.
C—It is the safest method of launching.

*A distinct advantage of a CG hook is that the sailplane can gain a greater altitude with a given line length. (PLT304) — Soaring Flight Manual*

**Answers**

| | | | | | |
|---|---|---|---|---|---|
| 3753 [C] | 3754 [A] | 3755 [B] | 3756 [B] | 3757 [B] | 3758 [A] |
| 3857 [A] | | | | | |

GLI

**3858.** To stop pitch oscillation (porpoising) during a winch launch, the pilot should

A—release back pressure and then pull back against the cycle of pitching oscillation to get in phase with the undulations.
B—signal the ground crew to increase the speed of the tow.
C—relax the back pressure on the control stick and shallow the angle of climb.

*Porpoising is caused by the horizontal stabilizer oscillating in and out of a stalled condition during a winch tow. The cure is to relax back pressure on the stick and shallow the climb angle. (PLT304) — FAA-H-8083-13*

GLI

**3859.** A pilot plans to fly solo in the front seat of a two-place glider which displays the following placards on the instrument panel:

MINIMUM PILOT WEIGHT: 135 LBS
MAXIMUM PILOT WEIGHT: 220 LBS

NOTE: Seat ballast should be used as necessary.

The recommended towing speed for all tows is 55–65 knots. What action should be taken if the pilot's weight is 115 pounds?

A—Add 20 pounds of seat ballast to the rear seat.
B—Add 55 pounds of seat ballast to obtain the average pilot weight of 170 pounds.
C—Add 20 pounds of seat ballast.

*Two criteria must be satisfied in the loading of a glider:*

*1. The total weight must be within limits, and*

*2. Within those limits, placement of the weight with respect to the aerodynamic center of the wing must satisfy total moment conditions (Weight × Arm = Moment).*

*To satisfy the conditions specified in the question, first calculate the weight required:*

*135 – 115 = 20 lbs*

*In order for that weight to provide the same moment as the "pilot weight" it replaces, it will also need to be at the same (that is, the forward) seat location. (PLT328) — FAA-H-8083-13*

GLI

**3860.** A pilot plans to fly solo in the front seat of a two-place glider which displays the following placards on the instrument panel:

MINIMUM PILOT WEIGHT: 135 LB
MAXIMUM PILOT WEIGHT: 220 LB

NOTE: Seat ballast should be used as necessary.

The recommended towing speed for all tows is 55–65 knots. What action should be taken if the pilot's weight is 125 pounds?

A—Add 10 pounds of seat ballast to the rear seat.
B—Add 10 pounds of seat ballast.
C—Add 45 pounds of seat ballast to obtain the average pilot weight of 170 pounds.

*Two criteria must be satisfied in the loading of a glider:*

*1. The total weight must be within limits, and*

*2. Within those limits, placement of the weight with respect to the aerodynamic center of the wing must satisfy total moment conditions (Weight × Arm = Moment).*

*To satisfy the conditions specified in the question, first calculate the weight required:*

*135 – 125 = 10 lbs*

*In order for that weight to provide the same moment as the "pilot weight" it replaces, it will also need to be at the same (that is, the forward) seat location. (PLT328) — FAA-H-8083-13*

GLI

**3869.** (Refer to Figure 55.) Illustration 2 means

A—release towline.
B—ready to tow.
C—hold position.

*During all glider operations there should be a wing runner, if possible. Lowering the wing and raising the hands is the signal to hold position. (PLT502) — FAA-H-8083-13*

GLI

**3870.** (Refer to Figure 55.) Illustration 3 means

A—stop operations.
B—release towline or stop engine now.
C—take up slack.

*The wing runner moving a hand across the throat is the signal to release the towline or stop engine now. (PLT502) — FAA-H-8083-13*

**Answers**

| | | | | |
|---|---|---|---|---|
| 3858 [C] | 3859 [C] | 3860 [B] | 3869 [C] | 3870 [B] |

GLI
**3871.** (Refer to Figure 55.) Which illustration is a signal to stop operation?

A—2.
B—3.
C—7.

*Wing runners should use a paddle, flag, or some signaling device that is easily visible to the tow pilot. Moving the signaling device and free hand back and forth over the head is the signal to stop operation. (PLT502) — FAA-H-8083-13*

GLI
**3872.** (Refer to Figure 55.) Which illustration is a signal from the sailplane for the towplane to turn right?

A—5.
B—6.
C—11.

*To signal the towplane to turn, move the glider to the side opposite the direction of turn and gently pull the towplane's tail out. (PLT502) — FAA-H-8083-13*

GLI
**3873.** (Refer to Figure 55.) Which illustration is a signal that the glider is unable to release?

A—8.
B—10.
C—11.

*If the glider cannot release, the glider pilot should move to the left and rock the wings. (PLT502) — FAA-H-8083-13*

GLI
**3874.** (Refer to Figure 55.) Which illustration is a signal to the towplane to reduce airspeed?

A—7.
B—10.
C—12.

*To signal the towplane or ground launch crew to reduce airspeed or ground launch speed, the glider pilot should fishtail the glider. (PLT502) — FAA-H-8083-13*

GLI
**3875.** (Refer to Figure 55.) Which illustration means the towplane cannot release?

A—6.
B—8.
C—9.

*After the glider pilot has signaled that the glider cannot release, the towplane will attempt to release the glider. If the towplane cannot release, the tow pilot should fishtail the towplane. A landing on tow will then be necessary. (PLT502) — FAA-H-8083-13*

GLI, LSG
**3876.** What corrective action should the sailplane pilot take during takeoff if the towplane is still on the ground and the sailplane is airborne and drifting to the left?

A—Crab into the wind by holding upwind (right) rudder pressure.
B—Crab into the wind so as to maintain a position directly behind the towplane.
C—Establish a right wing low drift correction to remain in the flightpath of the towplane.

*Crab into the wind to maintain a position directly behind the towplane. (PLT304) — FAA-H-8083-13*

GLI
**3877.** An indication that the glider has begun a turn too soon on aerotow is that the

A—glider's nose is pulled to the outside of the turn.
B—towplane's nose is pulled to the outside of the turn.
C—towplane will pitch up.

*When a turn is begun too soon, the towplane's nose is pulled to the outside of the turn. (PLT221) — FAA-H-8083-13*

GLI
**3878.** The sailplane has become airborne and the towplane loses power before leaving the ground. The sailplane should release immediately,

A—and maneuver to the right of the runway.
B—extend the spoilers, and land straight ahead.
C—and maneuver to the left of the towplane.

*If the towplane loses power during the takeoff, the tow pilot should maneuver the towplane to the left side of the runway. The glider pilot should pull the towline release, land ahead, and be prepared to maneuver to the right side of the runway. (PLT221) — FAA-H-8083-13*

**Answers**

| 3871 | [C] | 3872 | [A] | 3873 | [B] | 3874 | [C] | 3875 | [C] | 3876 | [B] |
| 3877 | [B] | 3878 | [A] | | | | | | | | | | |

GLI

**3879.** What should a glider pilot do if a towline breaks below 200 feet AGL?

A—Turn into the wind, then back to the runway for a downwind landing.
B—Turn away from the wind, then back to the runway for a downwind landing.
C—Land straight ahead or make slight turns to reach a suitable landing area.

*At low altitude, the only alternative to landing straight ahead may be slight turns in order to reach a suitable landing area. (PLT221) — FAA-H-8083-13*

GLI

**3880.** A pilot unintentionally enters a steep diving spiral to the left. What is the proper way to recover from this attitude without overstressing the glider?

A—Apply up-elevator pressure to raise the nose.
B—Apply more up-elevator pressure and then use right aileron pressure to control the overbanking tendency.
C—Relax the back pressure and shallow the bank; then apply up-elevator pressure until the nose has been raised to the desired position.

*The correct recovery from a spiral dive is to relax back pressure on the stick and at the same time reduce the bank angle with coordinated aileron and rudder. When the bank is less than 45°, the stick may be moved back while continuing to decrease bank. (PLT219) — FAA-H-8083-13*

GLI

**3881.** What corrective action should be taken if, while thermalling at minimum sink speed in turbulent air, the left wing drops while turning to the left?

A—Apply more opposite (right) aileron pressure than opposite (right) rudder pressure to counteract the overbanking tendency.
B—Apply opposite (right) rudder pressure to slow the rate of turn.
C—Lower the nose before applying opposite (right) aileron pressure.

*If a wing begins to drop during a turn, it is an indication of a stall. The nose of the sailplane should be lowered before applying coordinated opposite aileron and rudder to break the stall. (PLT494) — FAA-H-8083-13*

GLI

**3882.** A sailplane pilot can differentiate between a spin and a spiral dive because in a spiral dive,

A—the speed remains constant.
B—the G loads increase.
C—there is a small loss of altitude in each rotation.

*A spiral dive, as contrasted to a spin, can be recognized by rapidly increasing speed and G loading. (PLT245) — FAA-H-8083-13*

GLI

**3883.** How are forward slips normally performed?

A—With the direction of the slip away from any crosswind that exists.
B—With dive brakes or spoilers fully open.
C—With rudder and aileron deflection on the same side.

*When using the forward slip to increase an angle of descent without acceleration, the dive brakes or spoilers are normally fully open. (PLT221) — FAA-H-8083-13*

GLI

**3884.** What would be a proper action or procedure to use if the pilot is getting too low on a cross-country flight in a sailplane?

A—Continue on course until descending to 1,000 feet above the ground and then plan the landing approach.
B—Fly directly into the wind and make a straight-in approach at the end of the glide.
C—Have a suitable landing area selected upon reaching 2,000 feet AGL, and a specific field chosen upon reaching 1,500 feet AGL.

*It is always necessary to have a suitable landing site in mind. As altitude decreases, plans have to get more specific. The area should be narrowed down at 2,000 feet and a specific field should be selected by 1,500 feet. (PLT221) — FAA-H-8083-13*

**Answers**

3879 [C]   3880 [C]   3881 [C]   3882 [B]   3883 [B]   3884 [C]

# Lighter-Than-Air Operations

LTA

**3351.** The part of a balloon that bears the entire load is the

A—envelope material.
B—envelope seams.
C—load tapes (or cords).

*The load tape supports the weight of the balloon and minimizes the strain on the envelope fabric. (PLT177) — FAA-H-8083-11*

LTA

**3352.** In hot air balloons, propane is preferred to butane or other hydrocarbons because it

A—is less volatile.
B—is slower to vaporize.
C—has a lower boiling point.

*Propane is preferred over butane and other hydrocarbons in balloon design because propane has a lower boiling point (-44°F). (PLT253) — FAA-H-8083-11*

LTA

**3353.** The initial temperature at which propane boils is

A—+32°F.
B—-44°F.
C—-60°F.

*Propane is preferred over butane and other hydrocarbons in balloon design because propane has a lower boiling point (-44°F). (PLT253) — FAA-H-8083-11*

LTA, LSL

**3354.** On cold days, it may be necessary to preheat the propane tanks because

A—the temperature of the liquid propane controls the burner pressure during combustion.
B—there may be ice in the lines to the burner.
C—the propane needs to be thawed from a solid to a liquid state.

*On very cold days, it may be necessary to preheat the propane tanks since the temperature of the liquid propane controls the burner pressure during combustion. (PLT254) — FAA-H-8083-11*

LTA

**3355.** When ample liquid propane is available, propane will vaporize sufficiently to provide proper operation between the temperatures of

A—+30 to +90°F.
B—-44 to +25°F.
C—-51 to +20°F.

*When ample liquid propane is available, propane will vaporize sufficiently to provide proper operation between 30°F and 90°F. (PLT250) — FAA-H-8083-11*

LTA, LSL

**3356.** If ample propane is available, within which temperature range will propane vaporize sufficiently to provide enough pressure for burner operation during flight?

A—0 to 30°F.
B—10 to 30°F.
C—30 to 90°F.

*When ample liquid propane is available, propane will vaporize sufficiently to provide proper operation between 30°F and 90°F. (PLT251) — FAA-H-8083-11*

LTA

**3357.** The valve located on the top of the propane tank which opens automatically when the pressure in the tank exceeds maximum allowable pressure is the

A—pressure relief valve.
B—metering valve.
C—blast valve.

*The pressure relief valve is located on top of the fuel tank and opens automatically when the pressure in the tank exceeds the maximum allowable pressure. (PLT254) — FAA-H-8083-11*

---

**Answers**

| 3351 | [C] | 3352 | [C] | 3353 | [B] | 3354 | [A] | 3355 | [A] | 3356 | [C] |
| 3357 | [A] | | | | | | | | | | |

LTA

**3358.** The valve located on each tank that indicates when the tank is filled to 80 percent capacity is the

A—main tank valve.
B—vapor-bleed valve.
C—pilot valve.

*A vapor-bleed valve, or "spit tube," is located on each tank and indicates when the tank is filled to 80% of capacity. (PLT254) — FAA-H-8083-11*

LTA, LSL

**3359.** The lifting forces which act on a hot air balloon are primarily the result of the interior air temperature being

A—greater than ambient temperature.
B—less than ambient temperature.
C—equal to ambient temperature.

*A hot air balloon derives lift from the fact that air inside the envelope is warmer and therefore, "lighter" than the air around the balloon. (PLT237) — FAA-H-8083-11*

LTA, LSL

**3360.** Burner efficiency of a hot air balloon decreases approximately what percent for each 1,000 feet above MSL?

A—4 percent.
B—8 percent.
C—15 percent.

*Burner efficiency of a hot air balloon system decreases at approximately 4 percent per 1,000 feet above MSL. (PLT177) — FAA-H-8083-11*

LTA, LSL

**3361.** While in flight, frost begins forming on the outside of the fuel tank in use. This would most likely be caused by

A—water in the fuel.
B—a leak in the fuel line.
C—vaporized fuel instead of liquid fuel being drawn from the tank into the main burner.

*If large quantities of vapor are withdrawn rapidly from a propane cylinder, the cooling effect of the vaporization in the tank cools the propane and lowers the vapor pressure and the rate of vaporization. (PLT254) — FAA-H-8083-11*

LTA

**3362.** For what reason is methanol added to the propane fuel of hot air balloons?

A—To check for fuel leaks.
B—As a fire retardant.
C—As an anti-icing additive.

*Since propane holds little water in solution, there is a tendency for free water to collect in the bottom of the tanks where it may reach the dip tube, be piped into the burner system, and freeze up the regulators. If water contamination is suspected, methyl alcohol (methanol) should be added to the system. (PLT251) — FAA-H-8083-11*

LTA, LSL

**3363.** On a balloon equipped with a blast valve, the blast valve is used for

A—climbs and descents only.
B—altitude control.
C—emergencies only.

*The blast valve is located on the burner and controls ascent or descent by use of short bursts of power. When reaching the desired altitude, the pilot should reduce the frequency of blasts. As the envelope cools, the desired altitude can be maintained by using short blasts of heat evenly spaced. (PLT177) — FAA-H-8083-11*

LTA, LSL

**3364.** The term "weigh-off" means to determine the

A—static equilibrium of the balloon as loaded for flight.
B—amount of gas required for an ascent to a preselected altitude.
C—standard weight and balance of the balloon.

*A weigh-off is used to determine the static equilibrium of the balloon. (PLT123) — FAA-H-8083-11*

**Answers**

| 3358 | [B] | 3359 | [A] | 3360 | [A] | 3361 | [C] | 3362 | [C] | 3363 | [B] |
| 3364 | [A] | | | | | | | | | | |

LTA, LSL

**3365.** What causes false lift which sometimes occurs during launch procedures?

A—Closing the maneuvering vent too rapidly.
B—Excessive temperature within the envelope.
C—Venturi effect of the wind on the envelope.

*False lift is caused by the venturi effect produced by the wind blowing across an inflated but stationary envelope. Dynamic lift is created by relative air movement. If the balloon is released, the relative wind decreases as the balloon accelerates to the speed of the wind and false lift decreases. (PLT237) — FAA-H-8083-11*

LTA

**3366.** What is the relationship of false lift with the wind?

A—False lift increases as the wind accelerates the balloon.
B—False lift does not exist if the surface winds are calm.
C—False lift decreases as the wind accelerates the balloon.

*False lift is caused by the venturi effect produced by the wind blowing across an inflated but stationary envelope. Dynamic lift is created by relative air movement. If the balloon is released, the relative wind decreases as the balloon accelerates to the speed of the wind and false lift decreases. (PLT237) — FAA-H-8083-11*

LTA

**3367.** What would cause a gas balloon to start a descent if a cold air mass is encountered and the envelope becomes cooled?

A—A density differential.
B—A barometric pressure differential.
C—The contraction of the gas.

*As the gas is cooled, it contracts and becomes more dense and displaces less air. (PLT183) — FAA-H-8083-11*

LTA, LSL

**3368.** Under which condition will an airship float in the air?

A—When buoyant force equals horizontal equilibrium existing between propeller thrust and airship drag.
B—When buoyant force is less than the difference between airship weight and the weight of the air volume being displaced.
C—When buoyant force equals the difference between airship weight and the weight of the air volume being displaced.

*A lighter-than-air craft is in equilibrium when buoyancy equals weight. The buoyant force is equal to the weight of the air volume displaced. (PLT153) — Goodyear Airship Operations Manual*

LTA, LSL

**3369.** During flight in an airship, when is vertical equilibrium established?

A—When buoyancy is greater than airship weight.
B—When buoyancy equals airship weight.
C—When buoyancy is less than airship weight.

*A lighter-than-air craft is in equilibrium when buoyancy equals weight. The buoyant force is equal to the weight of the air volume displaced. (PLT153) — Goodyear Airship Operations Manual*

LTA, LSL

**3370.** An airship descending through a steep temperature inversion will

A—show no change in superheat as altitude is lost.
B—show a decrease in superheat as altitude is lost.
C—become progressively lighter, thus becoming increasingly more difficult to drive down.

*As the airship descends into the colder temperature of the inversion, the weight of the displaced air volume increases, thereby increasing buoyancy. (PLT153) — Goodyear Airship Operations Manual*

**Answers**

| 3365 [C] | 3366 [C] | 3367 [C] | 3368 [C] | 3369 [B] | 3370 [C] |

LTA

**3371.** What is airship superheat?

A—A condition of excessive exterior temperature of the envelope.

B—The temperature of the lifting gas exceeding the red line.

C—The difference between outside air temperature and the temperature inside the envelope.

*Superheat is the difference between outside air temperature and the temperature in the airship envelope. (PLT153) — Goodyear Airship Operations Manual*

LTA

**3372.** In relation to the operation of an airship, what is the definition of aerostatics?

A—The gravitational factors involving equilibrium of a body freely suspended in the atmosphere.

B—The science of the dynamics involved in the expansion and contraction of hydrogen gas.

C—The expansion and contraction of the lifting gas helium.

*Aerostatics are the gravitational factors involving equilibrium of a body freely suspended in the atmosphere. (PLT124) — Goodyear Airship Operations Manual*

LTA

**3373.** Below pressure height, each 5°F of positive superheat amounts to approximately

A—1 percent of gross lift.

B—2 percent of net lift.

C—2 percent of total lift.

*Each 5°F amounts to about 1 percent of gross lift. (PLT153) — Goodyear Airship Operations Manual*

LTA

**3374.** When the airship is at pressure height and superheat increases, constant pressure must be maintained by valving

A—gas from the envelope.

B—air from the envelope.

C—gas from the ballonets.

*Expansion of the gas will cause the ballonets to completely deflate at pressure height. Gas must be valved from the envelope to maintain constant pressure. (PLT153) — Goodyear Airship Operations Manual*

LTA

**3375.** How does the pilot know when pressure height has been reached?

A—Liquid in the gas manometer will rise and the liquid in the air manometer will fall below normal levels.

B—Liquid in the gas and air manometers will fall below the normal level.

C—Liquid in the gas manometer will fall and the liquid in the air manometer will rise above normal levels.

*When pressure height has been reached, the liquid in the gas manometer will rise and the liquid in the air manometer will fall below normal levels. (PLT153) — Goodyear Airship Operations Manual*

LTA, LSL

**3376.** The pressure height of an airship is the altitude at which

A—the airship would be unable to gain more altitude.

B—gas pressure would reach 3 inches of water.

C—the ballonet(s) would be empty.

*Expansion of the gas will cause the ballonets to completely deflate at pressure height. Thus, no further increase in displaced air volume is possible. (PLT153) — Goodyear Airship Operations Manual*

LTA, LSL

**3377.** The maximum altitude that a rigid airship can reach (under a given atmospheric condition) and then return safely to the surface is determined by

A—the disposable load.

B—ballonet capacity.

C—pressure altitude.

*Expansion of the gas will cause the ballonets to completely deflate at pressure height. Thus, no further increase in displaced air volume is possible. (PLT153) — Goodyear Airship Operations Manual*

LTA, LSL

**3378.** An unbalanced condition of an airship in flight must be overcome by

A—valving air from the ballonets.

B—valving gas from the envelope.

C—a negative or a positive dynamic force.

*Dynamic force, created by movement through the air, must be used to overcome any out-of-equilibrium condition. (PLT153) — Goodyear Airship Operations Manual*

**Answers**

| | | | | | |
|---|---|---|---|---|---|
| 3371 [C] | 3372 [A] | 3373 [A] | 3374 [A] | 3375 [A] | 3376 [C] |
| 3377 [C] | 3378 [C] | | | | |

LTA

**3379.** Air damper valves should normally be kept closed during climbs because any air forced into the system would

A—increase the amount of gas that must be exhausted to prevent the airship from ascending at an excessively high rate.
B—increase the amount of air to be exhausted, resulting in a lower rate of ascent.
C—decrease the purity of the gas within the envelope.

*Any air entering the ballonets through the damper valves will have to be exhausted overboard as the gas expands. This will slow the rate of ascent. (PLT221) — Goodyear Airship Operations Manual*

LTA

**3380.** To check the gas pressures (pressure height) of an airship during a climb, the air damper valves should be

A—opened forward and closed aft.
B—opened aft and closed forward.
C—closed.

*If damper valves are open, ram air pressure will keep the ballonets inflated longer than they should be inflated. (PLT158) — Goodyear Airship Operations Manual*

LTA, LSL

**3396.** What condition does a rising barometer indicate for balloon operations?

A—Decreasing clouds and wind.
B—Chances of thunderstorms.
C—Approaching frontal activity.

*Within a high-pressure system, flying conditions are generally more favorable than in low-pressure areas because there are normally fewer clouds, better visibility, calm or light winds, and less turbulence. (PLT516) — FAA-H-8083-28*

LTA

**3885.** Why should propane tanks not be refueled in a closed trailer or truck?

A—Propane vapor is one and one-half times heavier than air and will linger in the floor of the truck or trailer.
B—The propane vapor is odorless and the refuelers may be overcome by the fumes.
C—Propane is very cold and could cause damage to the truck or trailer.

*Since propane vapor is 1-1/2 times heavier than air, it can linger on the floor. (PLT254) — FAA-H-8083-11*

LTA

**3886.** Why should special precautions be taken when filling the propane bottles?

A—Propane is transferred from the storage tanks to the propane bottles under high pressure.
B—During transfer, propane reaches a high temperature and can cause severe burns.
C—Propane vapor is super-cold and may cause severe freeze burns.

*Precautions, such as wearing gloves, should be taken when filling the propane bottles because propane is super-cold and may cause severe freeze burns. (PLT250) — FAA-H-8083-11*

LTA, LSL

**3895.** All fuel tanks should be fired during preflight to determine

A—the burner pressure and condition of the valves.
B—that the pilot light functions properly on each tank.
C—if there are any leaks in the tank.

*Burner output is dependent on fuel pressure. Proper valve operation is critical to safety and control. (PLT177) — FAA-H-8083-11*

**Answers**

3379 [B]     3380 [C]     3396 [A]     3885 [A]     3886 [C]     3895 [A]

LTA

**3896.** What is a recommended ascent upon initial launch?

A—Maximum ascent to altitude to avoid low-level thermals.
B—Shallow ascent to avoid flashbacks of flames as the envelope is cooled.
C—A moderate-rate ascent to determine wind directions at different levels.

*A moderate-rate ascent is recommended initially to accurately determine the wind direction at various altitudes. (PLT304) — FAA-H-8083-11*

LTA, LSL

**3897.** What is a potential hazard when climbing at maximum rate?

A—The envelope may collapse.
B—Deflation ports may be forced open.
C—The rapid flow of air may extinguish the burner and pilot light.

*The positive pressure on the top of the envelope could force the deflation ports open. (PLT219) — FAA-H-8083-11*

LTA

**3898.** How should a roundout from a moderate-rate ascent to level flight be made?

A—Reduce the amount of heat gradually as the balloon is approaching altitude.
B—Cool the envelope by venting and add heat just before arriving at altitude.
C—Vent at altitude and add heat upon settling back down to altitude.

*The most efficient roundout is to reduce the frequency of blasts so that the envelope cools to a level flight temperature just as the balloon reaches the desired altitude. (PLT219) — FAA-H-8083-11*

LTA

**3899.** What is one procedure for relighting the burner while in flight?

A—Open the regulator or blast valve full open and light the pilot light.
B—Close the tank valves, vent the fuel lines, reopen the tank valves, and light the pilot light.
C—Open another tank valve, open the regulator or blast valve, and light the main jets with reduced flow.

*The pilot should open another tank valve, open the regular or blast valve and light off the main jet with reduced flow. (PLT177) — FAA-H-8083-11*

LTA

**3900.** The windspeed is such that it is necessary to deflate the envelope as rapidly as possible during a landing. When should the deflation port (rip panel) be opened?

A—The instant the gondola contacts the surface.
B—As the balloon skips off the surface the first time and the last of the ballast has been discharged.
C—Just prior to ground contact.

*In a high-wind landing, the envelope should be ripped just prior to ground contact. (PLT184) — FAA-H-8083-11*

LTA, LSL

**3901.** When landing a free balloon, what should the occupants do to minimize landing shock?

A—Be seated on the floor of the basket.
B—Stand with knees slightly bent, in the center of the gondola, facing the direction of movement.
C—Stand back-to-back and hold onto the load ring.

*By facing forward with knees bent, the body is balanced and the legs act as springs, absorbing the landing shock. (PLT184) — FAA-H-8083-11*

**Answers**

| | | | | | |
|---|---|---|---|---|---|
| 3896 [C] | 3897 [B] | 3898 [A] | 3899 [C] | 3900 [C] | 3901 [B] |

LTA

**3902.** Prior to a high-wind landing, the pilot-in-command should brief the passengers to prepare for the landing by

A—kneeling on the floor and facing aft.
B—crouching on the floor and jumping out of the basket upon contact with the ground.
C—crouching while hanging on in two places, and remaining in the basket until advised otherwise.

*By facing forward with knees bent, the body is balanced and the legs act as springs absorbing the landing shock. It is important that everyone remain in the basket until the envelope cannot lift the balloon back into the air. (PLT208) — FAA-H-8083-11*

LTA

**3903.** Which precaution should be exercised if confronted with the necessity of having to land a balloon when the air is turbulent?

A—Land in any available lake close to the upwind shore.
B—Land in the center of the largest available field.
C—Land in the trees to absorb shock forces, thus cushioning the landing.

*At one time or another a balloonist will be faced with the necessity of having to land in turbulent air. When this happens, the landing should be attempted in the middle of the largest field available. (PLT486) — FAA-H-8083-11*

LTA

**3904.** What action is most appropriate when an envelope over-temperature condition occurs?

A—Throw all unnecessary equipment overboard.
B—Descend; hover in ground effect until the envelope cools.
C—Land as soon as practical.

*An envelope over-temperature can seriously degrade the strength of the envelope, so land as soon as is practical. (PLT208) — FAA-H-8083-11*

LTA, LSL

**3905.** In addition to the required documents, what carry-on equipment should be accounted for during preflight?

A—Flotation gear.
B—Emergency locator transmitter.
C—Two means of burner ignition.

*As a precaution against flameout, an ignitor must be carried to relight the burner. A second ignitor is necessary in case the first malfunctions or is lost overboard. (PLT473) — FAA-H-8083-11*

LTA, LSL

**3906.** How should a balloon fuel system be checked for leaks prior to flight?

A—Listen and smell.
B—Check all connections with a lighted match.
C—Cover all connections and tubing with soapy water.

*Propane is under pressure and has an artificial odor. If a leak exists, the fuel will hiss out and can be smelled. (PLT251) — FAA-H-8083-11*

LTA, LSL

**3907.** In a balloon, best fuel economy in level flight can be accomplished by

A—riding the haze line in a temperature inversion.
B—short blasts of heat at high frequency.
C—long blasts of heat at low frequency.

*The desired envelope temperature for level flight is best maintained by short blasts at high frequency. (PLT130) — FAA-H-8083-11*

LTA

**3908.** The minimum size a launch site should be is at least

A—twice the height of the balloon.
B—100 feet for every 1 knot of wind.
C—500 feet on the downwind side.

*A free balloon will move about 100 feet per minute for every knot of wind. A pilot should allow 100 feet of travel for each knot of wind speed. (PLT389) — Powerline Excerpts*

---

**Answers**

| | | | | | |
|---|---|---|---|---|---|
| 3902 [C] | 3903 [B] | 3904 [C] | 3905 [C] | 3906 [A] | 3907 [B] |
| 3908 [B] | | | | | |

LTA, LSL

**3909.** What is a hazard of rapid descents?

A—Wind shear can cavitate one side of the envelope, forcing air out of the mouth.
B—The pilot light cannot remain lit with the turbulent air over the basket.
C—Aerodynamic forces may collapse the envelope.

*Turbulent airflow may extinguish the pilot light. (PLT125) — FAA-H-8083-11*

LTA, LSL

**3910.** It may be possible to make changes in the direction of flight in a hot air balloon by

A—flying a constant atmospheric pressure gradient.
B—operating at different flight altitudes.
C—operating above the friction level, if there is no gradient wind.

*A free balloon has no propulsion and so must take advantage of differing wind directions at various altitudes. (PLT219) — FAA-H-8083-11*

LTA

**3911.** What action should be taken if a balloon encounters unforecast weather and shifts direction abruptly while in the vicinity of a thunderstorm?

A—Land immediately.
B—Descend to and maintain the lowest altitude possible.
C—Ascend to an altitude which will ensure adequate obstacle clearance in all directions.

*Weather conditions during flight may take a sudden and unpredictable change. When this occurs and if powerful wind gusts, thermals, wind shears, or precipitation and lightning, are encountered, the appropriate action is to land as soon as possible. (PLT208) — Goodyear Operations Manual*

LTA

**3912.** To land an airship that is 250 pounds heavy when the wind is calm, the best landing can usually be made if the airship is

A—in trim.
B—nose heavy approximately 20°.
C—tail heavy approximately 20°.

*A heavy airship should be trimmed tail heavy to provide dynamic lift during approach. (PLT221) — Goodyear Operations Manual*

LTA

**3913.** Which takeoff procedure is considered to be most hazardous for an airship?

A—Maintaining only 50 percent of the maximum permissible positive angle of inclination.
B—Failing to apply full engine power properly on all takeoffs, regardless of wind.
C—Maintaining a negative angle of inclination during takeoff after elevator response is adequate for controllability.

*The most hazardous takeoff condition would be maintaining a negative angle of inclination during takeoff, after elevator response is adequate for stability. (PLT221) — Goodyear Operations Manual*

LTA

**3914.** Which action is necessary in order to perform a normal descent in an airship?

A—Valve gas.
B—Valve air.
C—Take air into the aft ballonets.

*An airship is normally flown heavy, so a power reduction would cause a descent. Air should be taken into the forward ballonets. (PLT133) — Goodyear Operations Manual*

LTA, LSL

**3915.** If an airship should experience failure of both engines during flight and neither engine can be restarted, what initial immediate action must the pilot take?

A—The airship must be driven down to a landing before control and envelope shape are lost.
B—The emergency auxiliary power unit must be started for electrical power to the airscoop blowers so that ballonet inflation can be maintained.
C—Immediate preparations to operate the airship as a free balloon are necessary.

*An airship without power must be operated as a free balloon. (PLT208) — Goodyear Operations Manual*

**Answers**

| | | | | | |
|---|---|---|---|---|---|
| 3909 [B] | 3910 [B] | 3911 [A] | 3912 [C] | 3913 [C] | 3914 [A] |
| 3915 [C] | | | | | |

# Powered Parachute and Weight-Shift Control Operations

The explanations for the answers given describe the concepts that should be understood before taking the test. Many of these questions are based on older weight-shift and PPC designs and unique characteristics of specific designs. The correct answers to these questions are the best of the choices provided.

PPC, WSC, LSA, LSR, LSP, LSW

**3958.** The formation of ice in a carburetor's throat is indicated by

A—rough engine operation, followed by a decrease in oil pressure.
B—a rapid increase in RPM, followed by rough engine operation.
C—a drop in RPM, followed by rough engine operation.

*Carb ice restricts the airflow into the engine reducing its power and resultant RPM, which also results in rough engine operation. (PLT190) — FAA-H-8083-29*

Answers (A) and (B) are incorrect because oil pressure is not significantly affected by carb ice, and carb ice will not increase RPM.

PPC, WSC, LSA, LSR, LSP, LSW

**3959.** The purpose of the fuel tank vent system is to

A—remove dangerous vapors from the aircraft and prevent an explosion.
B—allow air to enter the tank as fuel is consumed.
C—ensure a proper fuel to air ratio.

*Fuel tanks are not normally sealed systems; they need air venting because the fuel level is falling, therefore no vacuum builds up in the fuel tank. (PLT253) — FAA-H-8083-29*

Answer (A) is incorrect because fuel tanks are isolated and fuel vapors are prevalent within the fuel tank confined area. Answer (C) relates to two-stroke engines only. It is incorrect because fuel and oil are mixed either before the mixture is poured into the fuel tank (pre-mix) or after when oil is injected into the air-fuel mixture oil before it goes into the combustion chamber.

PPC, WSC, LSA, LSR, LSP, LSW

**3960.** A standby source of fuel to an engine in a powered parachute is typically

A—from an electrically powered pump.
B—through gravity feed.
C—from a pressurized fuel tank.

*Some engines use an electric boost pump similar to an airplane to supply a back-up pump in case the engine-driven fuel pump fails when low to the ground. (PLT253) — FAA-H-8083-29*

Answer (B) is incorrect because if a gravity feed system was used, then this would supply fuel and no standby pump would be needed. Answer (C) is incorrect because pressurized fuel tanks are not normally used for light sport aircraft.

PPC, WSC, LSA, LSR, LSP, LSW

**3961.** The fuel vents on many powered parachutes and weight shift control aircraft are located

A—in the fuel cap.
B—adjacent to the crankcase breather.
C—in the fuel tank pressure relief valve.

*The fuel vent in many but not all fuel tanks is in the fuel cap. (PLT253) — FAA-H-8083-29*

Answer (B) is incorrect because the crankcase breather is used on a four-stroke engine and has nothing to do with the fuel supply system on a two-stroke engine. Answer (C) is incorrect because most PPCs do not have pressurized fuel tanks nor a fuel tank pressure relief valve.

PPC, WSC, LSA, LSR, LSP, LSW

**3962.** Combusted fuel is expelled from a two-cycle engine through an

A—exhaust valve and exhaust port.
B—exhaust valve.
C—exhaust port.

*All two-stroke engines expel exhaust through a passage called the exhaust port. (PLT253) — FAA-H-8083-29*

Answers (A) and (B) are incorrect because only some higher power engines use an exhaust valve, while all have an exhaust port.

**Answers**

| | | | | |
|---|---|---|---|---|
| 3958 [C] | 3959 [B] | 3960 [A] | 3961 [A] | 3962 [C] |

PPC, WSC, LSA, LSR, LSP, LSW

**3963.** Fuel enters a two-cycle engine through an

A—intake port and intake valve.
B—intake port and reed valve.
C—intake valve and reed valve.

*The air-fuel-oil mixture enters the crankcase through an intake port that some types of valve systems use to close off the crankcase and pressurize the mixture before it is ported to the top of the piston. Many engines use the positioning of the piston as the intake valve system and others use a rotary valve, while still others use a one-way flow reed or poppet valve. (PLT253) — FAA-H-8083-29*

Answer (B) is incorrect because not all two-stroke engines use a reed valve. Answer (C) is incorrect because you must have an intake port.

PPC, WSC, LSA, LSR, LSP, LSW

**3964.** The first indication of carburetor ice in an aircraft with a four-cycle engine and fixed-pitch propeller is

A—an increase in RPM.
B—a decrease in RPM.
C—a decrease in oil pressure.

*The first symptom of carb ice in a four-stroke engine is a reduction in engine RPM. (PLT190) — FAA-H-8083-29*

Answer (A) is incorrect because carb ice reduces RPM. Answer (C) is incorrect because carb ice has no noticeable effect on oil pressure.

PPC, WSC, LSA, LSR, LSP, LSW

**3965.** Air cooled engines dissipate heat

A—through cooling fins on the cylinder and head.
B—by air flowing through the radiator fins.
C—through the cylinder head temperature probe.

*Air cooled engines use fins on the cylinder and head, forcing air past them as the primary means to dissipate heat. (PLT342) — FAA-H-8083-29*

Answer (B) is incorrect because air cooled engines do not have separate radiators; only water and oil coolers need a radiator. Answer (C) is incorrect because the probe is not used to dissipate heat.

PPC, WSC, LSA, LSR, LSP, LSW

**3966.** Coolant in a liquid cooled engine is normally circulated by

A—capillary attraction.
B—an electric pump.
C—an engine driven pump.

*Most liquid-cooled systems are driven from some mechanical source or pump on the engine. (PLT342) — FAA-H-8083-29*

Answer (A) is incorrect because capillary attraction is not normally used for engine cooling. Answer (B) is incorrect because electric pumps are usually used as coolant pumps.

PPC, WSC, LSA, LSR, LSP, LSW

**3967.** In order to improve engine efficiency, two-cycle engine exhaust systems are tuned to

A—close the exhaust valve to stop the fuel mixture from exiting the cylinder.
B—stop the fuel mixture from exiting the cylinder before combustion.
C—use a reed valve to stop the fuel mixture from exiting the cylinder.

*If there is not an exhaust valve, tuned exhaust systems are designed to provide back pressure pulses at the exhaust port. The tuned exhaust bounces pressure back at the appropriate time, so the fuel mixture stays in the combustion chamber while both intake and exhaust ports are open. (PLT343) — FAA-H-8083-29*

Answer (A) is incorrect because if the exhaust port has a valve, it is not as critical to have a tuned exhaust to provide back pressure at the exhaust port. There are not usually exhaust valves in a two-stroke engine; however, some two-stroke engines do have them. An example of this is the RAVE exhaust valve on the ROTAX 618. Answer (C) is incorrect because the reed valve is typically used for the intake air-fuel mixture.

**Answers**

| | | | | |
|---|---|---|---|---|
| 3963 [A] | 3964 [B] | 3965 [A] | 3966 [C] | 3967 [B] |

PPC, WSC, LSA, LSR, LSP, LSW

**3968.** Two-cycle engine thrust and fuel efficiency can be greatly compromised when

A—exhaust systems are installed that are not specifically tuned for an engine.
B—carbon deposits build up on exhaust valves.
C—intake valve lifters fail to pressurize and provide adequate fuel to the combustion chamber.

*The exhaust systems should be tuned to the engine for maximum efficiency. (PLT343) — FAA-H-8083-29*

Answer (B) is incorrect because most two-stroke engines do not have exhaust valves. Answer (C) is incorrect because not all two-stroke engines have intake valve lifters.

PPC, WSC, LSA, LSR, LSP, LSW

**3969.** The purpose of a kill switch is to

A—shut off the fuel to the carburetor.
B—ground the lead wire to the ignition coil shutting down the powerplant.
C—ground the battery eliminating current for the ignition system.

*The kill switch shuts down the engine. (PLT207) — FAA-H-8083-29*

Answer (A) is incorrect because a fuel valve shuts off fuel. Answer (C) is incorrect because the battery should already be grounded.

PPC, WSC, LSA, LSR, LSP, LSW

**3970.** A typical two-cycle engine ignition coil is powered by

A—a battery.
B—a battery or an alternator.
C—a magneto.

*The magneto is an engine-driven generator that powers the ignition system and also supplies extra power to aircraft electrical system. (PLT478) — FAA-H-8083-29*

Answers (A) and (B) are incorrect because the battery is further down the line, and is also powered by the magneto.

PPC, WSC, LSA, LSR, LSP, LSW

**3971.** Many four-cycle engines utilize what type of lubrication system?

A—Forced.
B—Gravity.
C—Fuel/oil mixture.

*Most four-stroke engines have an oil pump that forces the oil through the system. (PLT343) — FAA-H-8083-29*

Answer (B) is incorrect because gravity systems are not a typical oil supply system. Answer (C) is incorrect because a fuel/oil mixture system is on two-stroke engines only.

PPC, WSC, LSA, LSR, LSP, LSW

**3972.** Adding more oil to the fuel than specified by the manufacturer of a two-cycle engine will result in

A—increased engine performance.
B—increased carbon buildup and engine fouling.
C—increased engine lubrication and optimal performance.

*Extra oil in the fuel would cause inefficient burning and more carbon buildup as a result. (PLT343) — FAA-H-8083-29*

Answers (A) and (C) are incorrect because oil does not increase performance.

PPC, WSC, LSA, LSR, LSP, LSW

**3973.** Pilots should refrain from revving an engine with a reduction drive because

A—the crankshaft counterbalances may be dislodged and cause extreme engine vibration.
B—the propeller blade tips may exceed their RPM limits.
C—the torque exerted on the gears during excessive acceleration and deceleration can cause the gear box to self-destruct.

*Revving the engine causes more stress than not revving it; it is good practice to not rev it unnecessarily. (PLT343) — FAA-H-8083-29*

Answer (A) is incorrect because not all engines have counterbalances. Answer (B) is incorrect because the propeller is designed to not exceed its maximum RPM at full power.

**Answers**

| | | | | | |
|---|---|---|---|---|---|
| 3968 [A] | 3969 [B] | 3970 [C] | 3971 [A] | 3972 [B] | 3973 [C] |

PPC, WSC, LSA, LSR, LSP, LSW

**3974.** During preflight, the fuel vent system should always be checked

A—to ensure the vent is closed.
B—to ensure the vent is open.
C—to ensure the vent system pressure is in the green range.

*The fuel vent needs to be open for flight for the air to fill the fuel tank as the fuel is consumed. (PLT253) — FAA-H-8083-29*

Answer (A) is incorrect because a closed fuel vent would cause a power loss in flight when air is unable to fill the tank as fuel is used. Answer (C) is incorrect because there is no pressure in the fuel tank since it is vented.

PPC, WSC, LSA, LSR, LSP, LSW

**3975.** Carburetor ice can form

A—only at temperatures near freezing and the humidity near the saturation point.
B—when the outside air temperature is as high as 100°F and the humidity is as low as 50 percent.
C—at any temperature or humidity level.

*Carburetor ice can form when the outside air temperature is as high as 100°F and the humidity is as low as 50 percent. This is not the optimum conditions for the ice to form, but it can form under these conditions. (PLT190) — FAA-H-8083-29*

Answer (A) is incorrect because carb ice can form when it is as high at 100°F. Answer (C) is incorrect because some moisture is needed to form the ice.

WSC, LSW

**3976.** As a weight shift aircraft wing approaches a stall, the wing tips

A—decrease the wing's angle of attack.
B—act in much the same way as ailerons on a three-axis aircraft.
C—increase the wing's angle of attack.

*As the angle of attack of the wing is increased, the nose is at a higher angle of attack and therefore stalls first while the tips keep flying. This drops the nose and as a result, decreases the wing's angle of attack. (PLT214) — FAA-H-8083-5*

Answer (B) is incorrect because the wing tips act the same way ailerons do while flying normally and while approaching a stall. Answer (C) is incorrect because the tips only increase the wing's angle of attack when the wing is at a low angle of attack, far from a stall.

WSC, LSW

**3977.** During a wing stall, the wing tips of a weight shift aircraft are

A—ineffective for stall recovery.
B—effective for stall recovery.
C—effective only when combined with maximum engine output.

*Since the wing tips are at a lower angle of attack, they do not normally stall when the rest of the wing is stalled. They keep flying, creating an up-force in back of the CG—causing the nose to rotate down and decrease the angle of attack of the wing—therefore they are very effective for stall recovery. (PLT214) — FAA-H-8083-5*

Answer (A) is incorrect because the tips are very effective for stall recovery, allowing the nose to fall through. Answer (C) is incorrect because the tips have more effect for stall recovery than the engine power.

WSC, LSW

**3978.** The crosstube is positioned by

A—a quick release pin.
B—self-locking bolts.
C—restraining cables attached to the rear of the keel.

*The crossbar is pulled back to tension the airframe into the sail with the crossbar cables. These are attached to a connection point on the rear of the keel. (PLT346) — FAA-H-8083-5*

Answers (A) and (B) are incorrect because these are fasteners and would only make smaller variations in the crossbar position if these fasteners were adjusted to different settings.

**Answers**

| 3974 | [B] | 3975 | [B] | 3976 | [A] | 3977 | [B] | 3978 | [C] |

WSC, LSW

**3979.** On some trikes, the hang point is part of

A—a variable trim arrangement that allows the pilot to adjust the aircraft center of gravity during flight to obtain the most favorable aircraft performance.

B—an adjustable trim arrangement that allows the pilot to adjust the aircraft center of gravity during flight to obtain the most favorable aircraft performance.

C—an adjustable trim arrangement that allows the center of gravity to shift fore and aft along the wing's keel.

*Most trikes have an adjustment to move the position on the keel fore and aft on the ground. This is a common way to adjust the trim speed and bar position of the wing. (PLT214) — FAA-H-8083-5*

*Answers (A) and (B) are incorrect because although this is a viable design concept that has been and may be used for trikes, not many incorporate the complexity of a variable CG during flight.*

WSC, LSW

**3980.** The keel pocket's purpose is to

A—act as a longitudinal stabilizer, keeping the wing from wandering left and right.

B—act as a roll stabilizer, keeping the wing from wandering left and right.

C—act as a yaw stabilizer, keeping the wing from wandering left and right.

*The most significant effect a keel pocket could have on stability would be for yaw. This was an early design concept used in the development of the flex wing. Today, the wing sweep, washout, and airfoil shape are designed to optimize the tracking (yaw) for the vertical axis. Keel pockets today are a fabric channel in the sail material the keel is inserted into, to hold the keel in place at the root of the wing. (PLT346) — FAA-H-8083-5*

*Answers (A) and (B) are incorrect because the keel pocket does not supply this stability.*

WSC, LSW

**3981.** How does the wing design feature "washout" affect the production of lift?

A—The wing tips continue producing lift when the main body of the wing is not producing lift.

B—The main body of the wing continues to produce lift when the wing tips are not producing lift.

C—The center of lift moves from the trailing edge of the wing, to the leading edge of the wing, as the wing begins to stall.

*The washout/twist in the wing starts with a high angle of attack at the root/nose and decreases the angle of attack as the you approach each tip. This washout/twist, sweep, and airfoil shape is designed to make the nose lose lift first while the tips keep flying at high angles of attack. (PLT214) — FAA-H-8083-5*

*Answer (B) is incorrect because this happens only when the wing is at very low angles of attack where the wing is not near the critical angle of attack to stall. Answer (C) is incorrect because this is not the design of any trike wing and would produce a wing that would be unstable near the stall.*

WSC, LSW

**3982.** The wing of a weight-shift aircraft twists so that the angle of attack

A—from the center of the wing to the wing tip is variable and can be adjusted by the pilot in flight to optimize performance.

B—changes from a low angle of attack at the center of the wing to a high angle of attack at the tips.

C—changes from a high angle of attack at the center of the wing to a low angle of attack at the tips.

*The fundamental design of the flex wing is for the wing to twist from a high angle of attack at the nose, to a lower angle of attack at the tips. (PLT214) — FAA-H-8083-5*

*Answer (A) is incorrect because this would provide a wing that would be unstable and dangerous. Flex wings are not designed this way. Answer (B) is incorrect because this only applies for some wing designs but not all. Varying the twist in the wing is common to most high performance hang gliders in flight and used as one method to trim weight-shift wings as well.*

**Answers**

| | | | |
|---|---|---|---|
| 3979 [C] | 3980 [C] | 3981 [A] | 3982 [C] |

PPC, LSP

**3983.** During flight, advancing thrust will

A—increase airspeed.
B—cause the aircraft to climb.
C—cause the aircraft to increase airspeed and climb.

*Throttle controls vertical speed in a PPC. Advancing the throttle will produce decreased descent rates or increased climb rates. Speed in a PPC is controlled by the weight and not the throttle. (PLT346) — FAA-H-8083-29*

*Answers (A) and (C) are incorrect because throttle does not affect airspeed.*

PPC, LSP

**3984.** The torque effect of an engine that rotates clockwise in a powered parachute is counteracted by

A—increasing the length of the right and decreasing the length of the left riser cables.
B—decreasing the length of the left riser cables.
C—decreasing the length of right riser cables.

*A clockwise or right-turning propeller when viewed from the rear creates an opposite reaction to turn the undercarriage aircraft to the left. Therefore, a slight right-hand turn needs to be built into the aircraft to accommodate for this torque. Many designs are used by manufacturers to accomplish this. Decreasing the length of the right-hand riser will accomplish this by bringing the right side of the wing down. (PLT346) — FAA-H-8083-29*

*Answers (A) and (B) are incorrect because they would create a turn in the wrong direction.*

PPC, LSP

**3985.** The steering bars

A—are used during taxi operations with the parachute stowed.
B—control the outboard trailing edge of the parachute.
C—control the main landing gear brakes.

*The steering bars are the main control to turning in flight. Pushing on the right-hand steering bar will pull the right control line, lower the trailing edge of the right wing, create more drag on the right side and turn the aircraft to the right. (PLT346) — FAA-H-8083-29*

*Answers (A) and (C) are incorrect because the steering bars control the wing and are not used for ground operations.*

PPC, LSP

**3986.** The center of gravity tube is

A—lengthened for heavier pilots.
B—shortened for lighter pilots.
C—lengthened for lighter pilots.

*The lighter the pilot, the more rearward the wing attachment should be for the hanging airframe to be balanced properly. Most modern designs have a number of wing attachment points fore and aft on the airframe. For the tube CG adjustment system, lengthening the CG tube moves the wing attachment point back to account for the lightweight person in the front. (PLT346) — FAA-H-8083-29*

*Answer (A) is incorrect because this would balance the airframe with the nose wheel too low. Answer (B) is incorrect because this would move the CG forward and the front wheel would be too high.*

PPC, LSP

**3987.** The fan guard surrounds the propeller and

A—increases aerodynamic efficiency.
B—reduces "P" factor.
C—protects the parachute suspension lines from damage.

*The purpose of the fan guard is to protect the parachute lines from hitting the prop. (PLT346) — FAA-H-8083-29*

*Answers (A) and (B) are incorrect because the fan guard reduces performance and has no effect on P factor.*

PPC, LSP

**3988.** Cross ports in the parachute ribs aid in

A—weight reduction of the canopy.
B—the pressurization of the neighboring cells.
C—drying of the canopy.

*Cross ports in the wing ribs allow air to flow sideways from cell to cell, called cross flow, in the wing. This causes the cells next to each other to transfer pressure inside the wing and cells to pressurize neighboring cells. (PLT346) — FAA-H-8083-29*

---

**Answers**

| 3983 | [B] | 3984 | [C] | 3985 | [B] | 3986 | [C] | 3987 | [C] | 3988 | [B] |

PPC, LSP

**3989.** Splicing severed suspension lines

A—is permissible if using the same size material as the original line.
B—is a very dangerous practice.
C—is an acceptable field repair.

*Splicing lines is dangerous because you can change the airfoil; the lines could come loose and go through the prop. (PLT346) — FAA-H-8083-29*

Answers (A) and (C) are incorrect because splicing is a dangerous practice.

PPC, LSP

**3990.** Tying a severed suspension line

A—will change the shape of the wing and is not permissible.
B—is permissible if it is shortened no more than six inches.
C—is an acceptable field repair.

*Tying a severed suspension line would shorten it and create a discontinuity in the wing shape and is not acceptable. (PLT346) — FAA-H-8083-29*

Answers (B) and (C) are incorrect because tying is a dangerous practice.

PPC, LSP

**3991.** What gives your powered parachute wing/canopy its airfoil shape?

A—The risers because, by decreasing the length of the right riser you will get the precise airfoil shape.
B—The suspension lines as they are precisely measured and fitted to a specific location.
C—The air as it enters the cell openings on the leading edge of the airfoil.

*The precise lengths of the suspension lines determine the bottom shape of the airfoil. Airfoil-shaped ribs attached to the bottom of the airfoil where the suspension lines are attached define the top shape of the airfoil. (PLT346) — FAA-H-8083-29*

Answer (A) is incorrect because the decreased length of the right riser is used to counteract torque on some designs, thus causing a turn. Answer (C) is incorrect because the air inflates the canopy to whatever airfoil shape the suspension lines and ribs define.

PPC, LSP

**3992.** Swapping wings from one brand or type of powered parachute to another is

A—permissible as long as the basic shape of the parachutes are similar.
B—dangerous since every wing is designed for a specific aircraft.
C—permissible if the overall area of the parachutes is the same.

*Every wing is designed for a specific airframe configuration, engine torque and weight. (PLT346) — FAA-H-8083-29*

Answers (A) and (C) are incorrect because there can be a different length in the lines between the right and left, which has nothing to do with the shape and area of the wing.

PPC, LSP

**3993.** Degradation of the parachute's protective polyurethane coating results in

A—increased takeoff distances, decreased maximum gross weight, and increased fuel consumption.
B—reduced takeoff distances, increased maximum gross weight, and reduced fuel consumption.
C—increased takeoff distances, increased maximum gross weight, and increased fuel consumption.

*A degradation of the fabric results in air leaking through the fabric and a loss in performance since this creates more drag. (PLT346) — FAA-H-8083-29*

Answers (B) and (C) are incorrect because there is no increased gross weight.

PPC, LSP

**3994.** Flaring allows the pilot to touchdown at a

A—higher rate of speed and a slower rate of descent.
B—lower rate of speed and a higher rate of descent.
C—lower rate of speed and a lower rate of descent.

*Flaring slows you down and decreases your descent rate for a soft and slow landing. (PLT221) — FAA-H-8083-29*

Answers (A) and (B) are incorrect because flaring does not produce a higher rate of speed or a higher rate of descent.

---

**Answers**

| | | | | | |
|---|---|---|---|---|---|
| 3989 [B] | 3990 [A] | 3991 [B] | 3992 [B] | 3993 [A] | 3994 [C] |

PPC, LSP

**3995.** Flaring during a landing

A—decreases the powered parachute's speed due to increased drag.

B—increases the powered parachute's speed due to reduced drag.

C—decreases the powered parachute's drag due to increased speed.

*Flaring or pulling down on the trailing edge creates more drag and slows the aircraft similar to a flap on an airplane. (PLT221) — FAA-H-8083-29*

Answers (B) and (C) are incorrect because flaring does not increase the speed of a PPC.

LSW

**2347.** One of the functions of the wing's crossbar is to

A—hold the wings open.

B—provide surface to grip and control the aircraft.

C—provide an attachment point for the carriage.

*The purpose of the crosstube is to hold the leading edges open and therefore the wing. (PLT114) — FAA-H-8083-5*

Answer (B) is incorrect because it is the control bar you grip to control the aircraft. Answer (C) is incorrect because the attachment point for the carriage is the keel, the carriage cannot be attached to the crossbar.

LSW

**2348.** Which aircraft component ensures the wing has a pitch-up tendency?

A—Keel pocket.

B—Luff lines.

C—Washout rod.

*The luff lines can be used for pitch up stability in level flight by pulling the trailing edge up, creating a reflex in the training edge of the wing from the root out towards the tips. The luff lines also provide a positive pitch up tendency in a steep dive or slight negative angles of attack by increasing reflex in the airfoil by keeping the trailing edge pulled up in this unusual situation. (PLT114) — FAA-H-8083-5*

Answer (A) is incorrect because the keel pocket simply holds the keel in place. Answer (C) is incorrect because the washout rods only provide a positive pitch-up moment when the aircraft is in a steep dive at zero angle of by holding the trailing edge up at the tips; the washout rods have no effect on the flight characteristics of the aircraft in normal flight conditions.

# Gyroplane

LSR

**2326.** Why should gyroplane operations within the cross-hatched portion of a height vs. velocity chart be avoided?

A—The rotor RPM may build excessively high if it is necessary to flare at such low altitudes.

B—Sufficient airspeed may not be available to ensure a safe landing in case of an engine failure.

C—Turbulence near the surface can dephase the blade dampers causing geometric unbalanced conditions on the rotor system.

*The chart can be used to determine those altitude-airspeed combinations from which it would be impossible to successfully complete an autorotative landing. The altitude-airspeed combinations that should be avoided are represented by the shaded areas of the chart. (PLT123) — FAA-H-8083-21*

LSR

**2327.** The principal factor limiting the never-exceed speed ($V_{NE}$) of a gyroplane is

A—turbulence and altitude.

B—blade-tip speed, which must remain below the speed of sound.

C—lack of sufficient cyclic stick control to compensate for dissymmetry of lift or retreating blade stall, depending on which occurs first.

*Retreating blade stall is the principal factor limiting the never-exceed speed. (PLT260) — FAA-H-8083-21*

**Answers**

| 3995 | [A] | 2347 | [A] | 2348 | [B] | 2326 | [B] | 2327 | [C] |

# Chapter 3
# Flight Instruments

# Pitot-Static Instruments

The pressure altimeter, vertical speed indicator, and airspeed indicator operate in response to pressures through the **pitot-static system**. See Figure 3-1.

**Static** (atmospheric) **pressure** is taken from the static vents and is provided to all three instruments. Clogging of the static vents or line will cause all three instruments to become inoperative or to display erroneous readings.

**Impact** (ram) **pressure** is taken from the pitot tube and furnished to the airspeed indicator only. Clogging of the pitot opening will not affect operation of the altimeter or vertical speed indicator.

**Figure 3-1.** Pitot-static system

ALL

**3248.** Which instrument will become inoperative if the pitot tube becomes clogged?

A—Altimeter.
B—Vertical speed.
C—Airspeed.

*The pitot tube provides input for the airspeed indicator only. (PLT337, PA.IX.C.K2c, PH.VIII.D.K2c) — FAA-H-8083-25*

Answers (A) and (B) are incorrect because the altimeter and vertical speed indicator operate off the static system and are not affected by a clogged pitot tube.

ALL

**3249.** Which instrument(s) will become inoperative if the static vents become clogged?

A—Airspeed only.
B—Altimeter only.
C—Airspeed, altimeter, and vertical speed.

*Airspeed, altimeter, and vertical speed all receive static input and would indicate inaccurately if the static sources became plugged. (PLT337, PA.IX.C.K2c, PH.VIII.D.K2c) — FAA-H-8083-25*

**Answers**

3248 [C]      3249 [C]

AIR, GLI, RTC, LSA, LSG, LSR, LSW

**3247.** If the pitot tube and outside static vents become clogged, which instruments would be affected?

A—The altimeter, airspeed indicator, and turn-and-slip indicator.

B—The altimeter, airspeed indicator, and vertical speed indicator.

C—The altimeter, attitude indicator, and turn-and-slip indicator.

*Airspeed, altimeter, and vertical speed all receive static input and would indicate inaccurately if the static sources became plugged. (PLT337, PA.IX.C.K2c, PH.VIII.D.K2c) — FAA-H-8083-25*

Answers (A) and (C) are incorrect because the turn-and-slip indicator and attitude indicator are gyroscopic instruments, and are not part of the pitot-static system.

AIR, GLI, RTC, LSA, LSG, LSR, LSW

**3262.** The pitot system provides impact pressure for which instrument?

A—Altimeter.

B—Vertical speed indicator.

C—Airspeed indicator.

*The pitot tube provides input for the airspeed indicator only. (PLT337, PA.I.G.K1h, PH.VIII.D.K2c) — FAA-H-8083-25*

Answers (A) and (B) are incorrect because the altimeter and vertical speed indicator operate off the static system.

# Airspeeds and the Airspeed Indicator

A pilot must be familiar with the following airspeed terms and abbreviations:

**Indicated airspeed (IAS)**—the uncorrected reading obtained from the airspeed indicator.

**Calibrated airspeed (CAS)**—indicated airspeed corrected for installation and instrument error.

**True airspeed (TAS)**—calibrated airspeed corrected for temperature and pressure variations.

A number of airspeed limitations, known as V-speeds, are indicated by color-coded marking on the airspeed indicator (see Figure 3-2):

$V_{S0}$—stall speed or minimum steady flight speed in the landing configuration (the lower limit of the white arc).

$V_{FE}$—maximum flap extended speed (the upper limit of the white arc). The entire white arc defines the flap operating range.

$V_{S1}$—the stall speed or minimum steady flight speed in a specified configuration (the lower limit of the green arc). The entire green arc defines the normal operating range.

$V_{NO}$—the maximum structural cruising speed (the upper limit of the green arc and lower limit of the yellow arc). The yellow arc defines the caution range, which should be avoided unless in smooth air.

$V_{NE}$—never-exceed speed (the upper limit of the yellow arc) marked in red.

There are other important airspeed limitations that are not color-coded on the airspeed indicator:

$V_{LE}$—the maximum landing gear extended speed.

$V_A$—the design maneuvering speed. If rough air or severe turbulence is encountered, airspeed should be reduced to maneuvering speed or less to minimize stress on the airplane structure.

$V_Y$—the best rate-of-climb speed (the airspeed that will result in the most altitude in a given period of time).

$V_X$—the best angle-of-climb speed (the airspeed that will result in the most altitude in a given distance).

**Answers**

3247  [B]          3262  [C]

**Figure 3-2.** Airspeed indicator

AIR, GLI, RTC, WSC
**3006.** Which V-speed represents maneuvering speed?

A—$V_A$.
B—$V_{LO}$.
C—$V_{NE}$.

*$V_A$ is design maneuvering speed. (PLT506, PA.I.F.R2, PH.I.G.K1i) — 14 CFR §1.2*

Answer (B) is incorrect because this is the maximum landing gear operating speed. Answer (C) is incorrect because this is the never-exceed speed.

AIR, GLI, RTC, WSC, LSA, LSG, LSR, LSW
**3264.** What does the red line on an airspeed indicator represent?

A—Maneuvering speed.
B—Turbulent or rough-air speed.
C—Never-exceed speed.

*The upper end of the arc is marked by a red radial line which is the never-exceed speed ($V_{NE}$). (PLT088, PA.I.F.R2, PH.I.G.K1i) — FAA-H-8083-25*

Answers (A) and (B) are incorrect because the maneuvering speed and turbulent or rough-air speed is not indicated on the airspeed indicator.

AIR, GLI, RTC, WSC
**3268.** (Refer to Figure 4.) Which color identifies the never-exceed speed?

A—Upper limit of the green arc.
B—Upper limit of the white arc.
C—The red radial line.

*The upper end of the arc is marked by a red radial line which is the never-exceed speed ($V_{NE}$). (PLT088, PA.I.F.R2, PH.I.G.K1i) — FAA-H-8083-25*

Answer (A) is incorrect because the upper limit of the green arc is the beginning of the caution range. Answer (B) is incorrect because the upper limit of the white arc is the maximum speed at which flaps may be extended.

AIR, WSC
**3269.** (Refer to Figure 4.) Which color identifies the power-off stalling speed in a specified configuration?

A—Upper limit of the green arc.
B—Upper limit of the white arc.
C—Lower limit of the green arc.

*The green arc is the normal operating range. The lower end of the arc ($V_{S1}$) is the stalling speed in a specified configuration. (PLT088, PA.VII.B.K2) — FAA-H-8083-25*

Answer (A) is incorrect because the upper limit of the green arc indicates the maximum structural cruising speed. Answer (B) is incorrect because the upper limit of the white arc is the maximum flap extended speed.

AIR, WSC, PPC
**3011.** Which would provide the greatest gain in altitude in the shortest distance during climb after takeoff?

A—$V_Y$.
B—$V_A$.
C—$V_X$.

*$V_X$ (best angle-of-climb speed) is the calibrated airspeed at which the aircraft will attain the highest altitude in a given horizontal distance. (PLT123, PA.IV.A.K2) — 14 CFR §1.2*

Answer (A) is incorrect because $V_Y$ is best rate-of-climb speed. Answer (B) is incorrect because $V_A$ is design maneuvering speed.

**Answers**

| | | | | |
|---|---|---|---|---|
| 3006 [A] | 3264 [C] | 3268 [C] | 3269 [C] | 3011 [C] |

AIR, WSC

**3012-1.** After takeoff, which airspeed would the pilot use to gain the most altitude in a given period of time?

A—$V_Y$.
B—$V_X$.
C—$V_A$.

$V_Y$ (best rate-of-climb speed) is the calibrated airspeed at which the airplane will obtain the maximum increase in altitude per unit of time (feet per minute) after takeoff. (PLT123, PA.IV.A.K2) — 14 CFR §1.2

Answer (B) is incorrect because $V_X$ is the best angle-of-climb speed. Answer (C) is incorrect because $V_A$ is the design maneuvering speed.

AIR

**3265.** (Refer to Figure 4.) What is the full flap operating range for the airplane?

A—55 to 100 knots.
B—55 to 208 knots.
C—55 to 165 knots.

The flap operating range is marked by the white arc. The low end is $V_{S0}$ (stall speed in a landing configuration), and the high end is $V_{FE}$ (maximum flap extended speed). (PLT088, PA.I.F.K2c) — FAA-H-8083-25

Answer (B) is incorrect because 55 to 208 knots is the entire operating range of this airplane, from the stall speed to the never-exceed speed. Answer (C) is incorrect because 55 to 165 knots is the normal operating range for this airplane (green arc).

AIR, WSC

**3267.** (Refer to Figure 4.) The maximum speed at which the airplane can be operated in smooth air is

A—100 knots.
B—165 knots.
C—208 knots.

The caution range (yellow arc) includes speeds which should only be flown in smooth air; the maximum speed in the caution range is 208 knots for this airplane. (PLT088, PA.I.F.R2) — FAA-H-8083-25

Answer (A) is incorrect because 100 knots is the upper limit of the white arc, which is the maximum flap extended speed. Answer (B) is incorrect because 165 knots is the upper limit of the green arc, which is the maximum structural cruising speed.

AIR

**3270.** (Refer to Figure 4.) What is the maximum flaps-extended speed?

A—65 knots.
B—100 knots.
C—165 knots.

The flap operating range is marked by the white arc. The high end is $V_{FE}$ (maximum flap extended speed), which is 100 knots for this airplane. (PLT088, PA.I.F.R2) — FAA-H-8083-25

Answer (A) is incorrect because 65 knots is the lower limit of the green arc, which is the power-off stall speed, $V_{S1}$. Answer (C) is incorrect because 165 knots is the upper limit of the green arc, which is $V_{NO}$.

AIR

**3271.** (Refer to Figure 4.) Which color identifies the normal flap operating range?

A—The yellow arc.
B—The green arc.
C—The white arc.

The flap operating range is marked by the white arc. The low end is $V_{S0}$ (stall speed in a landing configuration), and the high end is $V_{FE}$ (maximum flap extended speed). (PLT088, PA.I.F.K2c) — FAA-H-8083-25

Answer (A) is incorrect because the yellow arc is the caution range. Answer (B) is incorrect because the green arc indicates the normal operating range.

AIR

**3272.** (Refer to Figure 4.) Which color identifies the power-off stalling speed with wing flaps and landing gear in the landing configuration?

A—Upper limit of the green arc.
B—Upper limit of the white arc.
C—Lower limit of the white arc.

The flap operating range is marked by the white arc. The low end is $V_{S0}$ (stall speed in a landing configuration). (PLT088, PA.I.F.K2c) — FAA-H-8083-25

Answer (A) is incorrect because the upper limit of the green arc is $V_{NO}$. Answer (B) is incorrect because the upper limit of the white arc is $V_{FE}$.

**Answers**

| | | | | | |
|---|---|---|---|---|---|
| 3012-1 [A] | 3265 [A] | 3267 [C] | 3270 [B] | 3271 [C] | 3272 [C] |

AIR, WSC

**3273.** (Refer to Figure 4.) What is the maximum structural cruising speed?

A—100 knots.
B—165 knots.
C—208 knots.

*The green arc is the normal operating range. The upper end of the arc ($V_{NO}$) is the maximum structural cruising speed. (PLT088, PA.I.F.R2) — FAA-H-8083-25*

Answer (A) is incorrect because 100 knots is the upper limit of the white arc, which is the maximum flap extended speed. Answer (C) is incorrect because 208 knots is the never-exceed speed.

AIR, WSC

**3274.** What is an important airspeed limitation that is not color coded on airspeed indicators?

A—Never-exceed speed.
B—Maximum structural cruising speed.
C—Maneuvering speed.

*Maneuvering speed ($V_A$) is not displayed on the airspeed indicator. (PLT278, PA.I.F.R2) — FAA-H-8083-25*

Answer (A) is incorrect because the never-exceed speed is indicated by a red line on the airspeed indicator. Answer (B) is incorrect because the maximum structural cruising speed can be found on the airspeed indicator by the upper limit of the green arc.

AIR, GLI

**3007.** Which V-speed represents maximum flap extended speed?

A—$V_{FE}$.
B—$V_{LOF}$.
C—$V_{FC}$.

*$V_{FE}$ is the highest calibrated airspeed permissible with the wing flaps in a prescribed extended position. (PLT506, PA.I.F.R2) — 14 CFR §1.2*

Answer (B) is incorrect because this is the liftoff speed. Answer (C) is incorrect because this is the maximum speed for stability characteristics.

AIR, GLI

**3008.** Which V-speed represents maximum landing gear extended speed?

A—$V_{LE}$.
B—$V_{LO}$.
C—$V_{FE}$.

*$V_{LE}$ is the maximum calibrated airspeed at which the airplane can be safely flown with the landing gear extended. (PLT506, PA.I.F.R2) — 14 CFR §1.2*

Answer (B) is incorrect because $V_{LO}$ is maximum landing gear operating speed. Answer (C) is incorrect because $V_{FE}$ is maximum flap extended speed.

AIR, GLI, WSC

**3009.** $V_{NO}$ is defined as the

A—normal operating range.
B—never-exceed speed.
C—maximum structural cruising speed.

*$V_{NO}$ is the maximum calibrated airspeed for normal operation, or the maximum structural cruising speed. (PLT506, PA.I.F.R2) — 14 CFR §1.2*

Answer (A) is incorrect because this is not designated a V-speed, but rather it is the green arc on the airspeed indicator. Answer (B) is incorrect because this is $V_{NE}$.

AIR, GLI

**3010.** $V_{S0}$ is defined as the

A—stalling speed or minimum steady flight speed in the landing configuration.
B—stalling speed or minimum steady flight speed in a specified configuration.
C—stalling speed or minimum takeoff safety speed.

*$V_{S0}$ is the calibrated power-off stalling speed or the minimum steady-flight speed at which the aircraft is controllable in the landing configuration. (PLT506, PA.I.F.R2) — 14 CFR §1.2*

Answer (B) is incorrect because this is $V_{S1}$. Answer (C) is incorrect because $V_S$ is stalling speed, and $V_2$ is the minimum takeoff safety speed.

AIR, GLI, WSC

**3266.** (Refer to Figure 4.) What is the caution range of the airplane?

A—0 to 60 knots.
B—100 to 165 knots.
C—165 to 208 knots.

*The caution range (yellow arc) includes speeds which should only be flown in smooth air, and is 165 to 208 knots for this airplane. (PLT088, PA.I.F.K2c) — FAA-H-8083-25*

Answer (A) is incorrect because 0 to 60 knots is less than stall speed. Answer (B) is incorrect because 100 to 165 knots is the normal operating airspeed range from maximum flap extension speed to maximum structural cruising speed, the upper limit of the green arc and lower limit of the yellow arc.

---

**Answers**

| | | | | | |
|---|---|---|---|---|---|
| 3273 [B] | 3274 [C] | 3007 [A] | 3008 [A] | 3009 [C] | 3010 [A] |
| 3266 [C] | | | | | |

# Altitudes and the Altimeter

An **altimeter** is an instrument used to measure height (altitude) by responding to atmospheric pressure changes. See Figure 3-3.

Altitude is indicated by three hands on the face of the altimeter. The shortest hand indicates altitude in tens of thousands of feet; the intermediate hand, in thousands of feet; and the longest hand in hundreds of feet. The altimeter is subdivided into 20-foot increments.

**Altitude** means elevation with respect to any assumed reference level, and different terms identify the reference level used. See Figure 3-4.

**Indicated altitude**—the altitude read on the altimeter after it is set to the current local altimeter setting.

**Absolute altitude**—the height above the surface.

**True altitude**—the true height above mean sea level (MSL) normally measured in feet.

**Pressure altitude**—the altitude that is indicated whenever the altimeter setting dial (Kohlsman window) is adjusted to 29.92. This is the standard datum plane; a theoretical level where air pressure is equal to 29.92 inches of mercury ("Hg). The standard datum plane may be above, at, or below sea level.

**Density altitude**—the pressure altitude corrected for nonstandard temperature and/or pressure. Rotating the setting knob on the altimeter simultaneously rotates the setting dial and the altimeter hands at a rate of one inch per 1,000 feet of altitude. Thus, increasing the setting dial from 29.15 to 29.85 would cause the hands of the altimeter to show an increase of 700 feet.

Prior to takeoff, the altimeter should be set to the current local altimeter setting. This is the value to which the scale of the altimeter is set so that the altimeter indicates true altitude at field elevation. If the altimeter setting is not available, the altimeter should be set to the elevation of the departure airport.

After takeoff, the altimeter should remain set to the current local altimeter setting until climbing through 18,000 feet MSL. At that time, the altimeter should be set to 29.92.

On a standard day (29.92 "Hg and +15°C) at sea level, pressure altitude, true altitude, indicated altitude, and density altitude are all equal. Any variation from standard temperature or pressure will have an effect on the altimeter.

To compensate for the effect of nonstandard conditions, the altimeter must be set to the altimeter setting of a station within 100 NM of the aircraft (unless it is above 18,000 feet MSL).

If a flight is made from an area of low pressure/low temperature to an area of high pressure/high temperature without adjusting the altimeter setting, the altimeter will indicate *lower* than the actual altitude above ground level. If a flight is made from an area of high pressure/high temperature to an area of low pressure/low temperature without adjusting the altimeter setting, the altimeter will indicate *higher* than the actual altitude above mean sea level.

**Figure 3-3.** Altimeter components

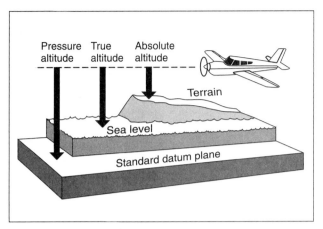

**Figure 3-4.** Types of altitude

ALL

**3105.** If an altimeter setting is not available before flight, to which altitude should the pilot adjust the altimeter?

A—The elevation of the nearest airport corrected to mean sea level.
B—The elevation of the departure area.
C—Pressure altitude corrected for nonstandard temperature.

*The altimeter should be set to the elevation of the departure airport for airplanes, and the departure area for other aircraft. (PLT381, PA.I.G.K1h, PH.I.G.K1i) — 14 CFR §91.121*

Answer (A) is incorrect because airport elevation is always expressed in feet above MSL. Answer (C) is incorrect because pressure altitude adjusted for nonstandard temperature is not true altitude, but density altitude.

ALL

**3106.** Prior to takeoff, the altimeter should be set to which altitude or altimeter setting?

A—The current local altimeter setting, if available, or the departure airport elevation.
B—The corrected density altitude of the departure airport.
C—The corrected pressure altitude for the departure airport.

*The altimeter should be set to the elevation of the departure airport for airplanes, and the departure area for other aircraft. (PLT381, PA.I.G.K1h, PH.I.G.K1i) — 14 CFR §91.121*

Answer (B) is incorrect because density altitude is pressure altitude corrected for nonstandard temperature variations and only concerns the performance of the aircraft. Answer (C) is incorrect because pressure altitude is the altitude indicated on the altimeter when the altimeter is set to 29.92.

ALL

**3107.** At what altitude shall the altimeter be set to 29.92, when climbing to cruising flight level?

A—14,500 feet MSL.
B—18,000 feet MSL.
C—24,000 feet MSL.

*The altimeter should be set to 29.92 "Hg at 18,000 feet MSL and above. Note: 18,000 feet is Class A airspace, which requires an instrument rating to operate in. (PLT381, PA.I.G.K1h, PH.I.G.K1i) — 14 CFR §91.121*

Answer (A) is incorrect because 14,500 feet is the base of Class E airspace, when not designated lower. Answer (C) is incorrect because 24,000 feet MSL is the altitude at which DME is required.

ALL

**3254.** Altimeter setting is the value to which the barometric pressure scale of the altimeter is set so the altimeter indicates

A—calibrated altitude at field elevation.
B—absolute altitude at field elevation.
C—true altitude at field elevation.

*The local altimeter setting corrects for the difference between existing pressure and standard atmospheric pressure. Whether local pressure is higher or lower than standard, it will indicate true altitude (MSL) at ground level, when the aircraft altimeter is set to the local altimeter setting (assuming no setting scale error). (PLT041, PA.I.G.K1h, PH.I.G.K1i) — FAA-H-8083-25*

Answer (A) is incorrect because "calibrated" does not apply to altitudes; it only applies to airspeeds. Answer (B) is incorrect because absolute altitude is the height above the ground.

**Answers**

3105 [B]     3106 [A]     3107 [B]     3254 [C]

ALL
**3255.** How do variations in temperature affect the altimeter?

A—Pressure levels are raised on warm days and the indicated altitude is lower than true altitude.
B—Higher temperatures expand the pressure levels and the indicated altitude is higher than true altitude.
C—Lower temperatures lower the pressure levels and the indicated altitude is lower than true altitude.

*On a warm day, the expanded air is lighter than on a cold day, and consequently the pressure levels are raised. For example, the pressure level where the altimeter indicates 10,000 feet will be higher on a warm day than under standard conditions. On a cold day the reverse is true. (PLT165, PA.I.G.K1h, PH.I.G.K1i) — FAA-H-8083-25*

Answer (B) is incorrect because raising the pressure levels would not cause the indicated altitude to be higher than the true altitude. Answer (C) is incorrect because lowering the pressure levels would not cause the indicated altitude to be lower than the true altitude.

ALL, SPO
**3256.** What is true altitude?

A—The vertical distance of the aircraft above sea level.
B—The vertical distance of the aircraft above the surface.
C—The height above the standard datum plane.

*True altitude is height above sea level. Airport terrain and obstacle elevations found on aeronautical charts are true altitudes. (PLT023, PA.I.G.K1h, PH.I.G.K1i) — FAA-H-8083-25*

Answer (B) is incorrect because the vertical distance above the surface is absolute altitude. Answer (C) is incorrect because the height above the standard datum plane is pressure altitude.

ALL
**3392.** Under what condition will true altitude be lower than indicated altitude?

A—In colder than standard air temperature.
B—In warmer than standard air temperature.
C—When density altitude is higher than indicated altitude.

*True altitude will be lower than indicated altitude in colder than standard air temperature, even with an accurate altimeter set to 29.92. (PLT023, PA.I.C.K3a, PH.I.G.K1i) — FAA-H-8083-28*

ALL, SPO
**3257.** What is absolute altitude?

A—The altitude read directly from the altimeter.
B—The vertical distance of the aircraft above the surface.
C—The height above the standard datum plane.

*Absolute altitude is height above the surface. This height may be indicated directly on a radar altimeter. Absolute altitude may be approximately computed from indicated altitude and chart elevation data. (PLT023, PA.I.G.K1h, PH.I.G.K1i) — FAA-H-8083-25*

Answer (A) is incorrect because the altitude read from the altimeter is indicated altitude. Answer (C) is incorrect because the height above the standard datum plane is pressure altitude.

ALL, SPO
**3258.** What is density altitude?

A—The height above the standard datum plane.
B—The pressure altitude corrected for nonstandard temperature.
C—The altitude read directly from the altimeter.

*Under standard atmospheric conditions, each level of air in the atmosphere has a specific density, and under standard conditions, pressure altitude and density altitude identify the same level. At temperatures higher or lower than standard, density altitude cannot be determined directly from the altimeter. (PLT023, PA.I.F.K2a, PH.I.G.K1i) — FAA-H-8083-25*

Answer (A) is incorrect because the height above the standard datum plane is pressure altitude. Answer (C) is incorrect because the altitude read from the altimeter is indicated altitude.

ALL, SPO
**3259.** What is pressure altitude?

A—The indicated altitude corrected for position and installation error.
B—The altitude indicated when the barometric pressure scale is set to 29.92.
C—The indicated altitude corrected for nonstandard temperature and pressure.

**Answers**

| | | | | | |
|---|---|---|---|---|---|
| 3255 [A] | 3256 [A] | 3392 [A] | 3257 [B] | 3258 [B] | 3259 [B] |

*The pressure altitude can be determined by either of two methods:*

1. *Setting the barometric scale of the altimeter to 29.92 and reading the indicated altitude, or*

2. *Applying a correction factor to the elevation (true altitude) according to the reported altimeter setting.*

*(PLT023, PA.I.G.K1h, PH.I.G.K1i) — FAA-H-8083-25*

Answer (A) is incorrect because the altimeter is not corrected for position and installation error. Answer (C) is incorrect because indicated altitude corrected for nonstandard temperature and pressure defines density altitude.

ALL, SPO

**3260.** Under what condition is indicated altitude the same as true altitude?

A—If the altimeter has no mechanical error.
B—When at sea level under standard conditions.
C—When at 18,000 feet MSL with the altimeter set at 29.92.

*On a standard day (29.92 "Hg and +15°C) at sea level, pressure altitude, indicated altitude, and density altitude are all equal. Any variation from standard temperature or pressure will have an effect on the altimeter. (PLT023, PA.I.C.K3a, PH.I.G.K1i) — FAA-H-8083-25*

Answer (A) is incorrect because mechanical error does not apply to true altitude. Answer (C) is incorrect because when the altimeter is set to 29.92, it indicates pressure altitude.

ALL, SPO

**3261.** If it is necessary to set the altimeter from 29.15 to 29.85, what change occurs?

A—70-foot increase in indicated altitude.
B—70-foot increase in density altitude.
C—700-foot increase in indicated altitude.

*When the knob on the altimeter is rotated, the pressure scale moves simultaneously with the altimeter pointers. The numerical values of pressure indicated in the window increase while the altimeter indicates an increase in altitude; or decrease while the altimeter indicates a decrease in altitude. This is contrary to the reaction on the pointers when air pressure changes, and is based solely on the mechanical makeup of the altimeter. The difference between the two settings is equal to 0.70 "Hg (29.85 – 29.15). At the standard pressure lapse rate of 1 "Hg = 1,000 feet in altitude, the amount of change equals 700 feet. (PLT166, PA.I.G.K1h, PH.I.G.K1i) — FAA-H-8083-25*

ALL

**3388.** Under which condition will pressure altitude be equal to true altitude?

A—When the atmospheric pressure is 29.92 "Hg.
B—When standard atmospheric conditions exist.
C—When indicated altitude is equal to the pressure altitude.

*Pressure altitude is equal to true altitude under standard atmospheric conditions. (PLT023, PA.I.C.K3a, PH.I.G.K1i) — FAA-H-8083-28*

ALL

**3389.** Under what condition is pressure altitude and density altitude the same value?

A—At sea level, when the temperature is 0°F.
B—When the altimeter has no installation error.
C—At standard temperature.

*When conditions are standard, pressure altitude and density altitude are the same. (PLT345, PA.I.C.K3a, PH.I.G.K1i) — FAA-H-8083-28*

Answer (A) is incorrect because standard temperature at sea level is 59°F. Answer (B) is incorrect because installation errors apply to airspeed indicators, not altimeters.

ALL

**3390.** If a flight is made from an area of low pressure into an area of high pressure without the altimeter setting being adjusted, the altimeter will indicate

A—the actual altitude above sea level.
B—higher than the actual altitude above sea level.
C—lower than the actual altitude above sea level.

*If a flight is made from a high-pressure area to a low-pressure area without adjusting the altimeter, the actual altitude of the airplane will be lower than the indicated altitude, and when flying from a low-pressure area to high-pressure area, the actual altitude of the airplane will be higher than the indicated altitude. (PLT167, PA.I.G.K1h, PH.I.G.K1i) — FAA-H-8083-28*

Answer (A) is incorrect because a correct altimeter setting must be used and/or standard atmospheric conditions must exist. Answer (B) is incorrect because the altimeter will indicate a lower altitude than actual.

**Answers**

| 3260 [B] | 3261 [C] | 3388 [B] | 3389 [C] | 3390 [C] |
|---|---|---|---|---|

**ALL**

**3391.** If a flight is made from an area of high pressure into an area of lower pressure without the altimeter setting being adjusted, the altimeter will indicate

A—lower than the actual altitude above sea level.
B—higher than the actual altitude above sea level.
C—the actual altitude above sea level.

*If a flight is made from a high-pressure area to a low-pressure area without adjusting the altimeter, the actual altitude of the airplane will be lower than the indicated altitude, and when flying from a low-pressure area to high-pressure area, the actual altitude of the airplane will be higher than the indicated altitude. (PLT167, PA.I.C.K3a, PH.I.G.K1i) — FAA-H-8083-28*

Answer (A) is incorrect because this change would indicate a flight into a high-pressure area from a low-pressure area. Answer (C) is incorrect because the lack of change would indicate constant pressure, thus actual altitude.

**ALL**

**3393.** Which condition would cause the altimeter to indicate a lower altitude than true altitude?

A—Air temperature lower than standard.
B—Atmospheric pressure lower than standard.
C—Air temperature warmer than standard.

*The altimeter will indicate a lower altitude than actually flown, in air temperature warmer than standard. (PLT023, PA.I.G.K1h, PH.I.G.K1i) — FAA-H-8083-28*

Answer (A) is incorrect because if the air temperature was lower, this would indicate a higher indicated altitude and a lower true altitude. Answer (B) is incorrect because when atmospheric pressure is lower than standard, the same conditions exist as described in Answer (A).

**ALL**

**3250.** (Refer to Figure 3.) Altimeter 1 indicates

A—500 feet.
B—1,500 feet.
C—10,500 feet.

*On altimeter #1 the 10,000-foot pointer (shortest hand) is just above 10,000 feet, the 1,000-foot pointer (fat hand) is between 0 and 1,000 feet, and the 100-foot pointer is on 500 feet. (PLT041, PA.I.G.K1h, PH.I.G.K1i) — FAA-H-8083-25*

**ALL**

**3251.** (Refer to Figure 3.) Altimeter 2 indicates

A—1,500 feet.
B—4,500 feet.
C—14,500 feet.

*On altimeter #2 the 10,000-foot pointer is between 10,000 feet and 20,000 feet. The 1,000-foot pointer is between 4,000 feet and 5,000 feet, and the 100-foot pointer is on 500 feet. (PLT041, PA.I.G.K1h, PH.I.G.K1i) — FAA-H-8083-25*

**ALL**

**3252.** (Refer to Figure 3.) Altimeter 3 indicates

A—9,500 feet.
B—10,950 feet.
C—15,940 feet.

*On altimeter #3 the 10,000-foot pointer is not quite to 10,000 feet. The 1,000-foot pointer is halfway between 9,000 and 10,000 feet, and the 100-foot pointer is on 500 feet. (PLT041, PA.I.G.K1h, PH.I.G.K1i) — FAA-H-8083-25*

**ALL**

**3253.** (Refer to Figure 3.) Which altimeter(s) indicate(s) more than 10,000 feet?

A—1, 2, and 3.
B—1 and 2 only.
C—1 only.

*The shortest hand (10,000 foot) in #1 is between 1 and 2, indicating 10,000 feet plus. The shortest hand in #2 also indicates 10,000 feet plus. The shortest hand in #3 indicates less than 10,000 feet. (PLT041, PA.I.G.K1h, PH.I.G.K1i) — FAA-H-8083-25*

**Answers**

| | | | | | |
|---|---|---|---|---|---|
| 3391 [B] | 3393 [C] | 3250 [C] | 3251 [C] | 3252 [A] | 3253 [B] |

ALL

**3253-1.** (Refer to Figure 82.) Altimeter 3 is indicating a VFR cruising altitude for which direction?

A—180°–359° magnetic.
B—179° true.
C—080° magnetic.

*On altimeter #3, the 10,000-foot pointer is just before 10,000 feet. The 1,000-foot pointer is between 9,000 feet and 10,000 feet, and the 100-foot pointer is on 500 feet. The aircraft is at an altitude of 9,500 feet. A magnetic course of 0° to 179° should be flown at a VFR cruising altitude of odd-thousands plus 500 feet. (PLT041, PA.I.G.K1h, PH.I.G.K1i) — AIM ¶3-1-5*

Answer (A) is incorrect because a VFR cruising altitude in a direction of 180°–359° should be flown at an even flight altitude plus 500 feet altitude. Answer (B) is incorrect because VFR cruising altitudes should be determined by magnetic direction, not true.

ALL

**3387.** If a pilot changes the altimeter setting from 30.11 to 29.96, what is the approximate change in indication?

A—Altimeter will indicate .15 "Hg higher.
B—Altimeter will indicate 150 feet higher.
C—Altimeter will indicate 150 feet lower.

*When the knob on the altimeter is rotated, the altimeter setting pressure scale moves simultaneously with the altimeter pointers. The numerical values of pressure indicated in the window increase while the altimeter indicates an increase in altitude, or decrease while the altimeter indicates a decrease in altitude. This is contrary to the reaction on the pointers when air pressure changes and is based solely on the mechanical makeup of the altimeter. The difference between the two settings is equal to .15 "Hg (30.11 − 29.96 = 0.15). At the standard pressure lapse rate of 1 "Hg = 1,000 feet in altitude, the amount of change equals 150 feet. (PLT167, PA.I.G.K1h, PH.I.G.K1i) — FAA-H-8083-28*

# Gyroscopic Instruments

Some aircraft instruments use gyroscopes. Simply stated, gyroscopes are rapidly spinning wheels or disks which resist any attempt to move them from their plane of rotation. This is called "rigidity in space." Three aircraft instruments which use gyroscopes are the **attitude indicator**, the **turn coordinator**, and the **heading indicator**.

## Attitude Indicator

The rigidity in space principle makes the gyroscope an excellent artificial horizon around which the attitude indicator (and the airplane) pivot.

When viewing the attitude indicator, the direction of bank is determined by the relationship of the miniature airplane to the horizon bar. The miniature airplane may be moved up or down from the horizon with an adjustment knob. Normally, the miniature airplane will be adjusted so that the wings overlap the horizon bar whenever the airplane is in straight-and-level flight.

## Turn Coordinator

The turn coordinator uses a miniature airplane to provide information concerning rate of roll and rate of turn. As the airplane enters a turn, movement of the miniature aircraft indicates rate of roll. When the bank is held constant, rate of turn is indicated. Simultaneously, the quality of turn, or movement about the yaw axis, is indicated by the ball of the inclinometer.

## Heading Indicator

The heading indicator is designed to avoid many of the errors inherent in a magnetic compass. However, the heading indicator does suffer from precession, caused mainly by bearing friction. Because of this precessional error, the heading indicator must periodically be realigned with the magnetic compass during straight-and-level, unaccelerated flight.

**Answers**

3253-1 [C]          3387   [C]

AIR, RTC

**3278.** (Refer to Figure 7.) How should a pilot determine the direction of bank from an attitude indicator such as the one illustrated?

A—By the direction of deflection of the banking scale (A).

B—By the direction of deflection of the horizon bar (B).

C—By the relationship of the miniature airplane (C) to the deflected horizon bar (B).

*The relationship of the miniature aircraft C to the horizon bar B is the same as the relationship of the real aircraft to the actual horizon. (PLT132, PA.I.G.K1h, PH.I.G.K1i) — FAA-H-8083-25*

Answer (A) is incorrect because the bank scale shows degrees, and not direction of bank. Answer (B) is incorrect because the horizon line deflects opposite the direction of turn, in order to correct horizon representation.

AIR

**3275.** (Refer to Figure 5.) A turn coordinator provides an indication of the

A—movement of the aircraft about the yaw and roll axis.

B—angle of bank up to but not exceeding 30°.

C—attitude of the aircraft with reference to the longitudinal axis.

*The movement of the miniature airplane on the instrument is proportional to the roll rate of the airplane. When the roll rate is reduced to zero, i.e., the bank is held constant, the instrument provides an indication of the rate of turn. This design features a realignment of the gyro in such a manner that it senses airplane movement about the yaw and roll axis. (PLT187, PA.I.G.K1h) — FAA-H-8083-25*

Answers (B) and (C) are incorrect because the miniature aircraft indicates rate of turn, not angle of bank or attitude.

AIR, RTC

**3277.** (Refer to Figure 7.) The proper adjustment to make on the attitude indicator during level flight is to align the

A—horizon bar to the level-flight indication.

B—horizon bar to the miniature airplane.

C—miniature airplane to the horizon bar.

*The miniature airplane C is adjusted so that the wings overlap the horizon bar B when the airplane is in straight-and-level cruising flight. (PLT166, PA.I.G.K1h, PH.I.G.K1i) — FAA-H-8083-25*

Answers (A) and (B) are incorrect because adjustment is only made to the miniature airplane.

AIR, RTC

**3276.** (Refer to Figure 6.) To receive accurate indications during flight from a heading indicator, the instrument must be

A—set prior to flight on a known heading.

B—calibrated on a compass rose at regular intervals.

C—periodically realigned with the magnetic compass as the gyro precesses.

*Because the heading indicator is run by a gyroscope instead of a magnetic source, precession will cause creep or drift from a heading to which it is set. It is important to check the indications frequently and reset the heading indicator to align it with the magnetic compass when required. (PLT118, PA.I.G.K1h, PH.I.G.K1i) — FAA-H-8083-25*

Answers (A) and (B) are incorrect because they don't do anything to correct for precession in flight.

**Answers**

3278　[C]　　　3275　[A]　　　3277　[C]　　　3276　[C]

# Magnetic Compass (Northern Hemisphere)

Deviation is a compass error caused by magnetic disturbances from electrical and metal components in the aircraft. The correction for this error is displayed on a compass correction card placed near the magnetic compass in the aircraft. Variation is the angular difference between the true, or geographic, poles and the magnetic poles at a given point. The compass magnet is aligned with the magnetic poles, while aeronautical charts are oriented to the geographic poles. This variation must be taken into consideration when determining an aircraft's actual geographic location. Indicated on charts by isogonic lines, it is not affected by the airplane's heading.

The magnetic compass, attracted to a magnetic field in the earth, points down as well as north. This downward pointing tendency, called **magnetic dip**, causes errors in compass indications.

When turning toward north from an easterly or westerly heading, the compass lags behind the actual aircraft heading. When a turn is initiated while on a northerly heading, the compass first indicates a turn in the opposite direction. The compass lags whenever turns are made to or from north.

When turning toward south from an easterly or westerly heading, the compass leads the actual aircraft heading. When a turn is initiated while on a southerly heading, the compass shows an immediate lead in the same direction as the turn. The compass leads whenever turns are made to or from south.

Accelerating or decelerating while heading either east or west will also cause compass errors. If acceleration occurs on a heading of east or west, the compass will indicate a turn to the north, while deceleration will cause an indication of a turn to the south. Therefore, it becomes apparent that the indications of a magnetic compass are accurate only during straight-and-level, unaccelerated flight.

The magnetic compass is also influenced by lines of force from magnetic fields within the aircraft. These errors are called deviations.

Some common mnemonics to help you remember compass errors in the northern hemisphere are UNOS (Undershoot North, Overshoot South) for turns and ANDS (Accelerate North, Decelerate South) for changes in velocity.

ALL

**3279.** Deviation in a magnetic compass is caused by the

A—presence of flaws in the permanent magnets of the compass.
B—difference in the location between true north and magnetic north.
C—magnetic fields within the aircraft distorting the lines of magnetic force.

*Magnetic disturbances from magnetic fields produced by metals and electrical accessories in an aircraft disturb the compass card and produce an additional error which is referred to as deviation. (PLT215, PA.VI.A.K2, PH.VII.A.K2) — FAA-H-8083-25*

Answer (A) is incorrect because deviation is not caused by magnet flaws. Answer (B) is incorrect because the difference between magnetic north and true north is called variation.

ALL

**3279-1.** The angular difference between true north and magnetic north is

A—magnetic deviation.
B—magnetic variation.
C—compass acceleration error.

*The angular difference between magnetic north, the reference for the magnetic compass, and true north is variation. (PLT320, PA.VI.A.K2, PH.VII.A.K2) — FAA-H-8083-25*

Answer (A) is incorrect because deviation is the error caused by magnetic fields produced by metal and electrical accessories within the airplane. Answer (C) is incorrect because compass acceleration errors are fluctuations in the compass during changes in speed.

**Answers**

3279   [C]          3279-1 [B]

ALL

**3279-2.** Deviation error of the magnetic compass is caused by

A—a northerly turning error.
B—certain metals and electrical systems within the aircraft.
C—the difference in location of true north and magnetic north.

*Magnetic disturbances from magnetic fields produced by metals and electrical accessories in an aircraft disturb the compass card and produce an additional error which is referred to as deviation. (PLT215, PA.VI.A.K2, PH.VII.A.K2) — FAA-H-8083-25*

Answer (A) is incorrect because this describes acceleration error. Answer (C) is incorrect because the difference between magnetic north and true north is called variation.

ALL

**3282.** In the Northern Hemisphere, a magnetic compass will normally indicate a turn toward the north if

A—an aircraft is decelerated while on an east or west heading.
B—a left turn is entered from a west heading.
C—an aircraft is accelerated while on an east or west heading.

*While on an east or west heading, an increase in airspeed or acceleration will cause the compass to indicate a turn toward the north and a deceleration will cause the compass to indicate a turn to the south. If on a north or south heading, no error will be apparent because of acceleration or deceleration. (Remember ANDS = Accelerate North Decelerate South). (PLT215, PA.VI.A.K2, PH.VII.A.K2) — FAA-H-8083-25*

ALL

**3283.** In the Northern Hemisphere, the magnetic compass will normally indicate a turn toward the south when

A—a left turn is entered from an east heading.
B—a right turn is entered from a west heading.
C—the aircraft is decelerated while on a west heading.

*While on an east or west heading, an increase in airspeed or acceleration will cause the compass to indicate a turn toward the north and a deceleration will cause the compass to indicate a turn to the south. If on a north or south heading, no error will be apparent because of acceleration or deceleration. (Remember ANDS = Accelerate North Decelerate South). (PLT215, PA.VI.A.K2, PH.VII.A.K2) — FAA-H-8083-25*

Answers (A) and (B) are incorrect because on east and west heading, turning error is negligible.

ALL

**3283-1.** What should be the indication on the magnetic compass as you roll into a standard rate turn to the right from a south heading in the Northern Hemisphere?

A—The compass will initially indicate a turn to the left.
B—The compass will indicate a turn to the right, but at a faster rate than is actually occurring.
C—The compass will remain on south for a short time, then gradually catch up to the magnetic heading of the airplane.

*If you are on a southerly heading and roll into a standard-rate turn to the right, the compass will immediately indicate a turn toward the west (to the right) because of the northerly turning error. During the first part of the turn, it will show a faster rate of turn than you are actually making. (PLT215, PA.VI.A.K2, PH.VII.A.K2) — FAA-H-8083-25*

Answer (A) is incorrect because the compass will initially indicate a turn to the left when rolling into a standard rate turn from a north heading in the Northern Hemisphere. Answer (C) is incorrect because the compass indication will lead the turn when rolling into a standard rate turn from a south heading in the Northern Hemisphere.

**Answers**

| 3279-2 [B] | 3282 [C] | 3283 [C] | 3283-1 [B] |

ALL

**3284.** In the Northern Hemisphere, if an aircraft is accelerated or decelerated, the magnetic compass will normally indicate

A—a turn momentarily.
B—correctly when on a north or south heading.
C—a turn toward the south.

*While on an east or west heading, an increase in airspeed or acceleration will cause the compass to indicate a turn toward the north and a deceleration will cause the compass to indicate a turn to the south. If on a north or south heading, no error will be apparent because of acceleration or deceleration. (Remember ANDS = Accelerate North Decelerate South). (PLT215, PA.VI.A.K2, PH.VII.A.K2) — FAA-H-8083-25*

Answers (A) and (C) are incorrect because acceleration error only occurs on an easterly/westerly heading; if accelerating, indicates a turn to the north and if decelerating, to the south.

ALL

**3280.** In the Northern Hemisphere, a magnetic compass will normally indicate initially a turn toward the west if

A—a left turn is entered from a north heading.
B—a right turn is entered from a north heading.
C—an aircraft is accelerated while on a north heading.

*If on a northerly heading and a turn is made toward east or west, the initial indication of the compass lags, or indicates a turn in the opposite direction. (PLT215, PA.VI.A.K2, PH.VII.A.K2) — FAA-H-8083-25*

Answer (A) is incorrect because a left turn would indicate a turn toward the east, while turning west. Answer (C) is incorrect because acceleration error does not occur on a north or south heading.

ALL

**3281.** In the Northern Hemisphere, a magnetic compass will normally indicate initially a turn toward the east if

A—an aircraft is decelerated while on a south heading.
B—an aircraft is accelerated while on a north heading.
C—a left turn is entered from a north heading.

*If on a northerly heading and a turn is made toward east or west, the initial indication of the compass lags, or indicates a turn in the opposite direction. (PLT215, PA.VI.A.K2, PH.VII.A.K2) — FAA-H-8083-25*

Answers (A) and (B) are incorrect because acceleration error does not occur on north or south headings.

ALL

**3286.** During flight, when are the indications of a magnetic compass accurate?

A—Only in straight-and-level unaccelerated flight.
B—As long as the airspeed is constant.
C—During turns if the bank does not exceed 18°.

*The magnetic compass should be read only when the aircraft is flying straight-and-level at a constant speed. This will help reduce errors to the minimum. (PLT215, PA.VI.A.K2, PH.VII.A.K2) — FAA-H-8083-25*

Answer (B) is incorrect because airspeed can remain constant in a turn, and the compass is subject to turning errors. Answer (C) is incorrect because no matter how steep the turn, the compass is still susceptible to turning errors.

GLI

**3285.** In the Northern Hemisphere, if a glider is accelerated or decelerated, the magnetic compass will normally indicate

A—a turn toward north while decelerating on an east heading.
B—correctly only when on a north or south heading.
C—a turn toward south while accelerating on a west heading.

*While on an east or west heading, an increase in airspeed or acceleration will cause the compass to indicate a turn toward the north and a deceleration will cause the compass to indicate a turn to the south. If on a north or south heading, no error will be apparent because of acceleration or deceleration. (Remember ANDS = Accelerate North Decelerate South). (PLT215) — FAA-H-8083-25*

**Answers**

| 3284 | [B] | 3280 | [B] | 3281 | [C] | 3286 | [A] | 3285 | [B] |
|------|-----|------|-----|------|-----|------|-----|------|-----|

# Chapter 4
# Aircraft Performance

# Density Altitude and Aircraft Performance

Aircraft performance charts show a pilot what can be expected of an airplane (rate of climb, takeoff roll, etc.) under stipulated conditions. Prediction of performance is based upon a sea level temperature of +15°C (+59°F) and atmospheric pressure of 29.92 "Hg (1013.2 mb). This combination of temperature and pressure is called a standard day. When the air is at a standard density, temperature and/or pressure deviations from standard will change the air density or the density altitude, which affects aircraft performance. Performance charts allow the pilot to predict how an aircraft will perform.

Relative humidity also affects density altitude, but is not considered when the performance charts are formulated. A combination of high temperature, high humidity, and high altitude result in a density altitude higher than the pressure altitude which, in turn, results in reduced aircraft performance.

## Problem:

Using the Density Altitude Chart shown in FAA Figure 8, and the following conditions, determine the density altitude.

## Conditions:

Altimeter setting ......................................... 30.35
Airport temperature.....................................+25°F
Airport elevation ................................. 3,894 feet

## Solution:

1. Determine the applicable altitude correction for the altimeter setting of 30.35 "Hg. See FAA Figure 8. That setting is not shown on the chart, so it is necessary to interpolate between the correction factors shown for 30.30 "Hg and 30.40 "Hg. To interpolate, add the two factors and divide by 2:

   -348 + (-440) = -788

   -788 ÷ 2 = -394

   Since the result is a negative number, subtract that value from the given airport elevation:

   3,894  feet
   − 394  feet
   ⎯⎯⎯⎯⎯⎯
   3,500  feet

2. Along the bottom of the chart, locate the given OAT (+25°F). From that point, proceed upward until intersecting the pressure altitude line that is equal to the corrected airport elevation (3,500 feet). From that point, proceed to the left and read the density altitude (2,000 feet).

   Note that high-density altitude reduces propeller efficiency as well as overall aircraft performance.

ALL, SPO

**3289.** If the outside air temperature (OAT) at a given altitude is warmer than standard, the density altitude is

A—equal to pressure altitude.
B—lower than pressure altitude.
C—higher than pressure altitude.

*If the temperature is above standard, the density altitude will be higher than pressure altitude. (PLT206, PA.I.F.K2a, PH.I.F.K2a) — FAA-H-8083-25*

ALL

**3294.** (Refer to Figure 8.) Determine the density altitude for these conditions:

Altimeter setting.................................................29.25
Runway temperature ........................................+81°F
Airport elevation ....................................5,250 ft MSL

A—4,600 feet MSL.
B—5,877 feet MSL.
C—8,500 feet MSL.

*Referencing FAA Figure 8, use the following steps:*

1. *Since the altimeter setting that is given is not shown in FAA Figure 8, interpolation is necessary. Locate the settings immediately above and below the given value of 29.25 "Hg:*

| Altimeter Setting | Conversion Factor |
|---|---|
| 29.20 | 673 feet |
| 29.30 | 579 feet |

2. *Determine the difference between the two conversion factors:*

   *673 – 579 = 94 feet*

3. *Determine the amount of difference to be added to the 29.30 "Hg conversion factor:*

   *94 × .5 = 47 feet*

4. *Add the amount of difference to the amount shown for the 29.30 "Hg conversion factor:*

   *579 + 47 = 626 feet*

5. *Add the correction factor to the airport elevation to find pressure altitude:*

   *5,250*
   *+ 626*
   *_____*
   *5,876 feet MSL (pressure altitude)*

6. *Determine the density altitude by entering the chart at +81°F; move upward to the 5,876 pressure altitude line; from the point of intersection, move to the left and read a density altitude of 8,500 feet.*

*(PLT005, PA.I.F.K2a, PH.I.F.K2a) — FAA-H-8083-25*

ALL

**3295.** (Refer to Figure 8.) Determine the pressure altitude at an airport that is 3,563 feet MSL with an altimeter setting of 29.96.

A—3,527 feet MSL.
B—3,556 feet MSL.
C—3,639 feet MSL.

*Referencing FAA Figure 8, use the following steps:*

1. *Since the altimeter setting that is given is not shown in FAA Figure 8, interpolation is necessary. Locate the settings immediately above and below the given value of 29.96 "Hg:*

| Altimeter Setting | Conversion Factor |
|---|---|
| 29.92 | 0 feet |
| 30.00 | -73 feet |

2. *Determine the difference between the two conversion factors:*

   *0 – 73 = -73 feet*

   *The setting 29.96 is halfway between the two values, so:*

   *-73 ÷ 2 = -36.5 feet*

3. *Determine the amount of difference to be subtracted from the 30.00 "Hg conversion factor.*

4. *Subtract the correction factor from the airport elevation to find pressure altitude:*

   *3,563.0*
   *– 36.5*
   *_____*
   *3,526.5 feet MSL (pressure altitude)*

*(PLT019, PA.I.F.K2a, PH.I.F.K2a) — FAA-H-8083-25*

**Answers**

3289   [C]          3294   [C]          3295   [A]

ALL
**3298.** (Refer to Figure 8.) Determine the density altitude for these conditions:

Altimeter setting.................................................30.35
Runway temperature ..........................................+25°F
Airport elevation .....................................3,894 ft MSL

A—2,000 feet MSL.
B—2,900 feet MSL.
C—3,500 feet MSL.

*Referencing FAA Figure 8, use the following steps:*

1. *Since the altimeter setting that is given is not shown in FAA Figure 8, interpolation is necessary. Locate the settings immediately above and below the given value of 30.35 "Hg:*

   | Altimeter Setting | Conversion Factor |
   |---|---|
   | 30.30 | -348 feet |
   | 30.40 | -440 feet |

2. *Determine the difference between the two factors:*

   *-440 + 348 = -92 feet*

3. *Determine amount of difference to be added to the 30.30 "Hg conversion factor:*

   *-92.0 × .5 = -46.0 feet*

4. *Add the amount of difference to the amount shown for the 30.30" Hg conversion factor:*

   *-348 + (-46) = -394 feet*

5. *Subtract the correction factor from the airport elevation to find pressure altitude:*

   3,894
   − 394
   ‾‾‾‾‾
   *3,500  feet MSL (pressure altitude)*

6. *Determine the density altitude by entering the chart at +25°F; proceed upward to the 3,500-foot pressure altitude line; from the point of intersection move to the left edge of the chart and read a density altitude of 2,000 feet.*

*(PLT019, PA.I.F.K2a, PH.I.F.K2a) — FAA-H-8083-25*

ALL
**3299.** (Refer to Figure 8.) What is the effect of a temperature decrease and a pressure altitude increase on the density altitude from 90°F and 1,250 feet pressure altitude to 55°F and 1,750 feet pressure altitude?

A—1,700-foot increase.
B—1,300-foot decrease.
C—1,700-foot decrease.

*Referencing FAA Figure 8, use the following steps:*

1. *Determine the density altitude when the temperature is +90°F and the pressure altitude is 1,250 feet. Enter the density altitude chart at +90°F and proceed upward to the 1,250-foot pressure altitude line. From the point of intersection move to the left edge of the chart and read a density altitude of 3,600 feet.*

2. *Determine the density altitude when the temperature is +55°F and the pressure altitude is 1,750 feet. Enter the density altitude chart at +55°F and proceed upward to the 1,750-foot pressure altitude line. From the point of intersection move to the left edge of the chart. Read a density altitude of 1,900 feet.*

3. *Determine the change in density altitude:*

   *3,600 – 1,900 = 1,700 foot (decrease)*

*(PLT124, PA.I.F.K2a, PH.I.F.K2a) — FAA-H-8083-25*

ALL, SPO
**3386.** What are the standard temperature and pressure values for sea level?

A—15°C and 29.92 "Hg.
B—59°C and 1013.2 millibars.
C—59°F and 29.92 millibars.

*Standard sea level pressure is 29.92 "Hg. Standard sea level temperature is 15°C. (PLT345, PA.I.F.K2a, PH.I.F.K2a) — FAA-H-8083-25*

ALL, SPO
**3394.** Which factor would tend to increase the density altitude at a given airport?

A—An increase in barometric pressure.
B—An increase in ambient temperature.
C—A decrease in relative humidity.

*On a hot day, the air becomes thinner, or lighter, and its density is equivalent to a higher altitude in the standard atmosphere, thus the term "high density altitude." (PLT206, PA.I.F.K2a, PH.I.F.K2a) — FAA-H-8083-28*

Answer (A) is incorrect because an increase in barometric pressure would decrease density altitude. Answer (C) is incorrect because a decrease in relative humidity would decrease density altitude.

**Answers**

| 3298 | [A] | 3299 | [C] | 3386 | [A] | 3394 | [B] |
|---|---|---|---|---|---|---|---|

AIR, RTC, WSC, PPC, SPO

**3290.** Which combination of atmospheric conditions will reduce aircraft takeoff and climb performance?

A—Low temperature, low relative humidity, and low density altitude.
B—High temperature, low relative humidity, and low density altitude.
C—High temperature, high relative humidity, and high density altitude.

*An increase in air temperature or humidity, or a decrease in air pressure (which results in a higher density altitude), will significantly decrease both power output and propeller efficiency. (PLT124, PA.I.F.K2a, PH.I.F.K2a) — FAA-H-8083-25*

Answer (A) is incorrect because all of these conditions improve performance. Answer (B) is incorrect because low humidity and low density altitude improve performance.

AIR, RTC, WSC, PPC, SPO

**3291.** What effect does high density altitude have on aircraft performance?

A—It increases engine performance.
B—It reduces climb performance.
C—It increases takeoff performance.

*An increase in air temperature or humidity, or a decrease in air pressure (which results in a higher density altitude), will significantly decrease both power output and propeller efficiency. (PLT127, PA.I.F.K2a, PH.I.F.K2a) — FAA-H-8083-25*

AIR, RTC, WSC, PPC

**3292.** (Refer to Figure 8.) What is the effect of a temperature increase from 25 to 50°F on the density altitude if the pressure altitude remains at 5,000 feet?

A—1,200-foot increase.
B—1,400-foot increase.
C—1,650-foot increase.

*Referencing FAA Figure 8, use the following steps:*

1. *Enter the density altitude chart at 25°F. Proceed upward to intersect the 5,000-foot pressure altitude line. From the point of intersection, move left to the edge of the chart and read a density altitude of 3,850 feet.*

2. *Enter the density altitude chart at 50°F. Proceed upward to the 5,000-foot pressure altitude line. From the point of intersection, move left to the edge of the chart and read a density altitude of 5,500 feet.*

3. *Determine the change in density altitude:*

   *5,500 – 3,850 = 1,650 feet (increase)*

*(PLT005, PA.I.F.K2a, PH.I.F.K2a) — FAA-H-8083-25*

AIR, RTC, WSC, PPC

**3293.** (Refer to Figure 8.) Determine the pressure altitude with an indicated altitude of 1,380 feet MSL with an altimeter setting of 28.22 at standard temperature.

A—2,991 feet MSL.
B—2,913 feet MSL.
C—3,010 feet MSL.

*Referencing FAA Figure 8, use the following steps:*

1. *Since the altimeter setting that is given is not shown in FAA Figure 8, interpolation is necessary. Locate the settings immediately above and below the given value of 28.22 "Hg:*

   | Altimeter Setting | Conversion Factor |
   | --- | --- |
   | 28.2 | 1,630 feet |
   | 28.3 | 1,533 feet |

2. *Determine the difference in the two conversion factors:*

   *1,630 – 1,533 = 97 feet*

3. *Determine the amount of the difference to be subtracted from the 28.20 "Hg conversion factor (2/10 of 97).*

   *97.0 × .2 = 19.4*

4. *Subtract the amount of difference from the amount shown for the 28.20 "Hg conversion factor:*

   *1,630.0 – 19.4 = 1,610.6*

5. *Add the correction factor to the indicated altitude to find the pressure altitude:*

   *1,610.6*
   *+ 1,380.0*
   *2,990.6 feet MSL (pressure altitude)*

*(PLT019, PA.I.F.K2a, PH.I.F.K2a) — FAA-H-8083-25*

**Answers**

| | | | |
| --- | --- | --- | --- |
| 3290 [C] | 3291 [B] | 3292 [C] | 3293 [A] |

AIR, RTC, WSC, PPC
**3296.** (Refer to Figure 8.) What is the effect of a temperature increase from 35 to 50°F on the density altitude if the pressure altitude remains at 3,000 feet MSL?

A—1,000-foot increase.
B—1,100-foot decrease.
C—1,300-foot increase.

*Referencing FAA Figure 8, use the following steps:*

1. *Enter the density altitude chart at 35°F. Proceed upward to the 3,000-foot pressure altitude line. From the point of intersection, move left to the edge of the chart and read a density altitude of 2,000 feet.*

2. *Enter the density altitude chart at 50°F. Proceed upward to the 3,000-foot pressure altitude line. From the point of intersection, move left to the edge of the chart and read a density altitude of 2,950 feet.*

3. *Find the difference between the two values: 2,950 – 2,000 = 950 foot (increase).*

*(PLT124, PA.I.F.K2a, PH.I.F.K2a) — FAA-H-8083-25*

SPO
**2356.** (Refer to Figure 8.) What is the effect of a temperature increase from 30 to 50°F on the density altitude if the pressure altitude remains at 3,000 feet MSL?

A—900-foot increase.
B—1,100-foot decrease.
C—1,300-foot increase.

*Referencing FAA Figure 24, use the following steps:*

1. *Enter the density altitude chart at 30°F. Proceed upward to the 3,000-foot pressure altitude line. From the point of intersection, move left to the edge of the chart and read a density altitude of 1,650 feet.*

2. *Enter the density altitude chart at 50°F. Proceed upward to the 3,000-foot pressure altitude line. From the point of intersection, move left to the edge of the chart and read a density altitude of 2,950 feet.*

3. *Find the difference between the two values: 2,950 – 1,650 = 1,300 foot (increase)*

*(PLT005) — FAA-H-8083-25*

AIR, RTC, WSC, PPC, SPO
**3297.** (Refer to Figure 8.) Determine the pressure altitude at an airport that is 1,386 feet MSL with an altimeter setting of 29.97.

A—1,341 feet MSL.
B—1,451 feet MSL.
C—1,562 feet MSL.

*Referencing FAA Figure 8, use the following steps:*

1. *Since the altimeter setting that is given is not shown in FAA Figure 8, interpolation is necessary. Locate the settings immediately above and below the given value of 29.97 "Hg:*

| Altimeter Setting | Conversion Factor |
|---|---|
| 29.92 | 0 feet |
| 30.00 | -73 feet |

2. *Determine the difference between the two conversion factors:*

   *0 – 73 = -73 feet*

3. *Determine the amount of the difference to be subtracted from the 29.92 "Hg conversion factor:*

   *(-73 ÷ 8) × 5 = -45.6 or 46 feet*

4. *Subtract the conversion factor from the airport elevation to determine the pressure altitude:*

   *1,386*
   *– 46*
   *1,340 feet MSL (pressure altitude)*

*(PLT019, PA.I.F.K2a, PH.I.F.K2a) — FAA-H-8083-25*

AIR, RTC, WSC, PPC, SPO
**3300.** What effect, if any, does high humidity have on aircraft performance?

A—It increases performance.
B—It decreases performance.
C—It has no effect on performance.

*An increase in air temperature or humidity, or a decrease in air pressure (which results in a higher density altitude) will significantly decrease both power output and propeller efficiency. If an air mass is humid, there is more water in it, therefore, less oxygen. (PLT124, PA.I.F.K2a, PH.I.F.K2a) — FAA-H-8083-25*

---

**Answers**

| | | | |
|---|---|---|---|
| 3296 [A] | 2356 [C] | 3297 [A] | 3300 [B] |

AIR, LTA, WSC, PPC, SPO

**3246.** What effect does high density altitude, as compared to low density altitude, have on propeller efficiency and why?

A—Efficiency is increased due to less friction on the propeller blades.
B—Efficiency is reduced because the propeller exerts less force at high density altitudes than at low density altitudes.
C—Efficiency is reduced due to the increased force of the propeller in the thinner air.

*The propeller produces thrust in proportion to the mass of air being accelerated through the rotating blades. If the air is less dense, propeller efficiency is decreased. (PLT351, PA.I.F.K2a) — FAA-H-8083-25*

RTC, LSR

**3702.** (Refer to Figure 39.) Determine the total takeoff distance required for a gyroplane to clear a 50-foot obstacle if the temperature is 95°F and the pressure altitude is 1,700 feet.

A—1,825 feet.
B—1,910 feet.
C—2,030 feet.

*Use the following steps:*

1. *Locate the 1,700-foot pressure altitude on the Take-Off Distance Graph (right).*

2. *Draw a horizontal line from the 1,700-foot position to the 95°F OAT point.*

3. *Draw a vertical line downward from the point of intersection to the total Take-Off Distance Scale. Note the distance 2,030 feet.*

*(PH.I.F.K2a) — FAA-H-8083-21*

SPO

**2067.** Density altitude, and its effect on landing performance, is defined by

A—pressure altitude and ambient temperature.
B—headwind and landing weight.
C—humidity and braking friction forces.

*The effect of pressure altitude and ambient temperature is to define density altitude and its effect on landing performance. (PLT127) — FAA-H-8083-25*

LTA

**3891.** (Refer to Figure 57.) What is the maximum altitude for the balloon if the gross weight is 1,100 pounds and standard temperature exists at all altitudes?

A—1,000 feet.
B—4,000 feet.
C—5,500 feet.

*Use FAA Figure 57, and the following steps:*

1. *Enter the graph at the 1,100-pound gross weight point and proceed to the right to intercept the standard temperature curve.*

2. *Note that the intercept is between sea level and the 5,000-foot limit lines, and is much closer to the 5,000-foot line (4,000 feet).*

*(PLT057) — FAA-H-8083-11*

LTA

**3892.** (Refer to Figure 57.) What is the maximum altitude for the balloon if the gross weight is 1,000 pounds and standard temperature exists at all altitudes?

A—4,000 feet.
B—5,500 feet.
C—11,000 feet.

*Use FAA Figure 57, and the following steps:*

1. *Enter the graph at the 1,000-pound gross weight point and proceed to the right to intercept the standard temperature curve.*

2. *Note that the intercept is just over 10,000 feet (11,000 feet).*

*(PLT057) — FAA-H-8083-11*

**Answers**

| 3246 | [B] | 3702 | [C] | 2067 | [A] | 3891 | [B] | 3892 | [C] |

# Takeoff Distance

The Takeoff Distance Graph, FAA Figure 40, allows the pilot to determine the ground roll required for takeoff under various conditions. It also shows the total distance required for a takeoff and climb to clear a 50-foot obstacle.

## Problem:

Using the Takeoff Distance Graph shown in FAA Figure 40, determine the approximate ground roll distance for takeoff and the total distance for a takeoff to clear a 50-foot obstacle under the following conditions:

OAT..............................................................90°F
Pressure altitude................................. 2,000 feet
Takeoff weight.........................................2,500 lbs
Headwind component.............................20 knots

## Solution:

1. Locate the OAT, 90°F, on the graph.
2. From that point, draw a line upward to the line representing the pressure altitude of 2,000 feet.
3. From the point of intersection, draw a line to the right to the reference line.
4. From that point, proceed downward and to the right (remaining proportionally between the existing guide lines) to the vertical line representing 2,500 pounds.
5. From there, draw a line to the right to the second reference line.
6. Then proceed down and to the right (remaining proportionally between the existing guide lines) to the line representing the 20-knot headwind component line.
7. From there, draw a line to the right to the third reference line.
8. From here, move to the right and read approximate ground roll for takeoff of 650 feet.
9. Proceed upward and to the right (remaining proportionately between the existing guide lines) to the vertical line representing a 50-foot obstacle and read the approximate total distance to clear a 50-foot obstacle (1,100 feet).

AIR
**3705.** (Refer to Figure 40.) Determine the total distance required for takeoff to clear a 50-foot obstacle.

OAT........................................................Std
Pressure altitude.............................. 4,000 ft
Takeoff weight ................................. 2,800 lb
Headwind component.........................Calm

A—1,500 feet.
B—1,750 feet.
C—2,000 feet.

*Use the following steps:*

1. *Locate the ISA curve on FAA Figure 40.*
2. *Note the intersection of the ISA curve with the pressure altitude, 4,000 feet.*
3. *From that point, draw a line to the right to the first reference line.*
4. *From there, proceed downward and to the right (remaining proportionally between the existing lines) to the vertical line representing 2,800 pounds.*
5. *Then proceed to the right to the second reference line.*
6. *In this case the reference line is also the vertical line representing the 0 mph wind component.*
7. *From that point, continue to the right to the third vertical reference line.*
8. *From there, proceed upward and to the right (remaining proportionally between the existing lines) to the vertical line representing the obstacle height, 50 feet.*
9. *Read the distance (approximately 1,750 feet).*
(PLT011, PA.I.F.K1) — FAA-H-8083-25

**Answers**

3705 [B]

AIR
**3706.** (Refer to Figure 40.) Determine the total distance required for takeoff to clear a 50-foot obstacle.

OAT..........................................................Std
Pressure altitude............................................. Sea level
Takeoff weight ................................................. 2,700 lb
Headwind component..........................................Calm

A—1,000 feet.
B—1,400 feet.
C—1,700 feet.

*Use the following steps:*

1. *Locate the OAT, 59°F, on FAA Figure 40.*

2. *From that point, draw a line upward to the line representing the pressure altitude, 0 feet (sea level).*

3. *From that point, draw a line to the right to the first reference line.*

4. *From there, proceed downward and to the right (remaining proportionally between the existing lines) to the vertical line representing 2,700 pounds.*

5. *Then draw a line to the right to the second reference line.*

6. *In this case, the reference line is also the vertical line representing the 0-knot wind component.*

7. *From that point, continue a horizontal line to the third vertical reference line.*

8. *Finally, proceed upward and to the right (remaining proportionally between the existing lines) to the vertical line representing the obstacle height, 50 feet and read the distance (approximately 1,400 feet).*

*(PLT011, PA.I.F.K1) — FAA-H-8083-25*

AIR
**3707.** (Refer to Figure 40.) Determine the approximate ground roll distance required for takeoff.

OAT....................................................100°F
Pressure altitude...............................................2,000 ft
Takeoff weight ..................................................2,750 lb
Headwind component..........................................Calm

A—1,150 feet.
B—1,300 feet.
C—1,800 feet.

*Use the following steps:*

1. *Locate the OAT, 100°F, on FAA Figure 40.*

2. *From that point, draw a line upward to the line representing the pressure altitude, 2,000 feet.*

3. *From that point, draw a line to the right to the first reference line.*

4. *From there, proceed downward and to the right (remaining proportionally between the existing lines) to the vertical line representing 2,750 pounds.*

5. *Then draw a line to the right to the second reference line.*

6. *In this case, the reference line is also the vertical line representing the 0-knot wind component.*

7. *Then draw a horizontal line to the third vertical reference line.*

8. *In this case, the reference line is also the vertical line representing the obstacle height, 0 feet.*

9. *From that point, draw a horizontal line to the right and read the distance (approximately 1,150 feet).*

*(PLT011, PA.I.F.K1) — FAA-H-8083-25*

AIR
**3708.** (Refer to Figure 40.) Determine the approximate ground roll distance required for takeoff.

OAT..................................................................95°F
Pressure altitude...............................................2,000 ft
Takeoff weight ..................................................2,500 lb
Headwind component......................................... 20 kts

A—650 feet.
B—850 feet.
C—1,000 feet.

*Use the following steps:*

1. *Locate the OAT, 95°F, on FAA Figure 40.*

2. *From that point, draw a line upward to the line representing the pressure altitude of 2,000 feet.*

3. *Form the point of intersection, draw a line to the right to the reference line and stop.*

4. *From that point, proceed downward and to the right (remaining proportionally between the existing guide lines) to the vertical line representing 2,500 pounds.*

5. *From there, draw a line to the right to the second reference line.*

6. *Then proceed down and to the right (remaining proportionally between the existing guide lines) to the line representing the 20-knot headwind component line.*

7. *From that point, draw a line to the right to the third reference line.*

8. *From there, move to the right and read an approximate ground roll for takeoff (650 feet).*

*(PLT011, PA.I.F.K1) — FAA-H-8083-25*

**Answers**

3706    [B]          3707    [A]          3708    [A]

RTC

**3703.** (Refer to Figure 39.) Determine the total takeoff distance required for a gyroplane to clear a 50-foot obstacle if the temperature is standard at sea level pressure altitude.

A—950 feet.
B—1,090 feet.
C—1,200 feet.

1. On the sea level line of FAA Figure 39 locate the intersection of the +59°F point.

2. Read takeoff distance of 1,200 feet.

(PH.I.F.K1) — FAA-H-8083-25

RTC

**3704.** (Refer to Figure 39.) Approximately how much additional takeoff distance will be required for a gyroplane to clear a 50-foot obstacle if the temperature increases from 75 to 90°F at a pressure altitude of 2,300 feet?

A—160 feet.
B—200 feet.
C—2,020 feet.

Use the following steps:

1. Locate the 2,300-foot pressure altitude on FAA Figure 39.

2. Draw a horizontal line from the 2,300-foot position to the 75°F and the 90°F OAT points.

3. From these points, draw vertical lines downward to the takeoff distance scale and note the distances (2,025 and 2,185, respectively).

4. The difference is the increase in takeoff distance.

    2,185 – 2,025 = 160 feet

(PH.I.F.K1) — FAA-H-8083-25

SPO

**2199.** What effect does an uphill runway slope have on takeoff performance?

A—Increases takeoff speed.
B—Increases takeoff distance.
C—Decreases takeoff distance.

The effect of runway slope on takeoff distance is due to the component of weight along the inclined path of the aircraft. An upslope would contribute a retarding force component, while a downslope would contribute an accelerating force component. In the case of an upslope, the retarding force component adds to drag and rolling friction to reduce the net accelerating force. (PLT129) — FAA-H-8083-25

Answer (A) is incorrect because runway slope has no effect on the takeoff speed. Answer (C) is incorrect because an upslope will increase the takeoff distance required.

LSA, LSG, LSR, LSW, LSP

**2283.** The most critical conditions of takeoff performance are the result of some combination of high gross weight, altitude, temperature, and

A—unfavorable wind.
B—obstacles surrounding the runway.
C—powerplant systems.

The most critical conditions of takeoff performance are the result of some combination of high gross weight, altitude, temperature, and unfavorable wind. In all cases, the pilot must make an accurate prediction of takeoff distance from the performance data of the AFM/POH, regardless of the runway available, and strive for a polished, professional takeoff procedure. (PLT134) — FAA-H-8083-25

SPO

**2234.** The most critical conditions of takeoff performance are the result of some combination of high gross weight, altitude, temperature, and

A—unfavorable wind.
B—obstacles surrounding the runway.
C—powerplant systems.

The most critical conditions for takeoff performance are the result of some combination of high gross weight, altitude, temperature, and unfavorable wind. In all cases, the pilot must make an accurate prediction of takeoff distance from the performance data of the AFM or POH, regardless of the runway available, and strive for a polished, professional takeoff procedure. (PLT134) — FAA-H-8083-25

**Answers**

3703  [C]          3704  [A]          2199  [B]          2283  [A]          2234  [A]

RTC
**3732.** (Refer to Figure 46.) What is the best rate-of-climb speed for the helicopter?

A—24 mph.
B—40 mph.
C—57 mph.

*Use the following steps:*

1. *Locate the recommended takeoff profile on FAA Figure 46.*

2. *Note that the best rate-of-climb speed at sea level is designated by the arrow pointing to the vertical line.*

3. *Interpret the diagram. The vertical line is most closely aligned with an IAS of about 57 mph.*

*(PH.I.F.K1) — FAA-H-8083-21*

# Landing Distance Graphs and Tables

Some landing distance graphs such as the one shown in FAA Figure 37, are used in the same manner as the takeoff distance graph.

Another type of landing distance table is shown in FAA Figure 38.

## Problem:

Using the Landing Distance Table shown in FAA Figure 38, determine the total distance required to land over a 50-foot obstacle.

Pressure altitude.................................. 5,000 feet
Headwind.................................................8 knots
Temperature ................................................ 41°F
Runway...........................................Hard surface

## Solution:

Enter FAA Figure 38 at 5,000 feet and 41°F to find 1,195 feet is required to clear a 50-foot obstacle. Note #1 states an additional correction is necessary for the headwind, 10% for each 4 knots. This would mean 20% for 8 knots. 20% of 1,195 feet is 239 feet, resulting in 956 feet—total distance required to land:

$1,195 \times .20 = 239$ feet

$1,195 - 239 = 956$ feet

AIR, WSC
**3698.** (Refer to Figure 38.) Determine the approximate landing ground roll distance.

Pressure altitude............................................ 1,250 ft
Headwind ........................................................ 8 kts
Temperature ..........................................................Std

A—275 feet.
B—366 feet.
C—470 feet.

*Use the following steps:*

1. *Locate the tables for sea level and 2,500 feet. Note that 1,250 feet is midway between sea level and 2,500 feet.*

2. *Interpolate between charts for 2,500 feet pressure altitude and sea level to find ground roll:*

    *(445 + 470) ÷ 2 = 457.5 ground roll*

3. *Apply Note 1 to account for the 8-knot headwind (a 20% decrease in distance):*

    *457.5 × .20 = 91.5 feet*
    *457.5 – 91.5 = 366 feet*

*(PLT008, PA.I.F.K1) — FAA-H-8083-25*

**Answers**

3732   [C]          3698   [B]

AIR, WSC

**3689.** (Refer to Figure 37.) Determine the total distance required to land.

OAT..................................................................... 32°F
Pressure altitude..........................................8,000 ft
Weight .......................................................... 2,600 lb
Headwind component...................................... 20 kts
Obstacle ........................................................... 50 ft

A—850 feet.
B—1,400 feet.
C—1,750 feet.

*Use the following steps:*

1. *Enter FAA Figure 37 at the point where the vertical 32°F temperature line intersects the 8,000-foot pressure altitude line.*

2. *From there, proceed to the right to the first vertical reference line.*

3. *From that point, proceed down and to the right (remaining proportionally between the existing lines) to the vertical line representing 2,600 pounds.*

4. *Then, proceed to the right to the second vertical reference line.*

5. *Then, proceed down and to the right (remaining proportionally between the existing headwind lines) to the vertical line representing 20 knots.*

6. *From that point, proceed to the right to the third reference line.*

7. *Finally, proceed up and to the right (remaining proportionally between the existing lines) to the 50-foot obstacle line at the end of the graph and read the landing distance (approximately 1,400 feet).*

*(PLT008, PA.I.F.K1) — FAA-H-8083-25*

AIR, WSC

**3690.** (Refer to Figure 37.) Determine the total distance required to land.

OAT.......................................................................Std
Pressure altitude.......................................... 10,000 ft
Weight .......................................................... 2,400 lb
Wind component ..............................................Calm
Obstacle ........................................................... 50 ft

A—750 feet.
B—1,925 feet.
C—1,450 feet.

*Use the following steps:*

1. *Enter the graph at the point where the ISA line intercepts the 10,000-foot pressure altitude line.*

2. *From that point, proceed to the right to the first vertical reference line.*

3. *From there, proceed down to the right (remaining proportionally between the existing lines), to the vertical line representing 2,400 pounds.*

4. *Then proceed to the right to the second vertical reference line.*

5. *Since the wind is calm, continue to the right to the third vertical reference line.*

6. *From there, proceed upward and to the right (remaining proportionally between the existing lines) to the vertical line representing the required 50-foot obstacle height. Read the landing distance from the vertical scale (approximately 1,900 feet).*

*(PLT008, PA.I.F.K1) — FAA-H-8083-25*

**Answers**

3689    [B]              3690    [B]

AIR, WSC
**3691.** (Refer to Figure 37.) Determine the total distance required to land.

OAT......................................................................90°F
Pressure altitude..........................................3,000 ft
Weight ....................................................... 2,900 lb
Headwind component...................................10 kts
Obstacle ..........................................................50 ft

A—1,450 feet.
B—1,550 feet.
C—1,725 feet.

*Use the following steps:*

1. *Enter FAA Figure 37 at the point where the vertical 90°F temperature line intersects the 3,000-foot pressure altitude line. (The point must be visualized midway between the 2,000- and 4,000-foot pressure altitude lines.)*

2. *From that point, proceed to the right to the first vertical reference line.*

3. *From there, proceed downward and to the right (remaining proportionally between the existing lines), to the vertical line representing 2,900 pounds.*

4. *Then proceed to the right to the second vertical reference line.*

5. *Since there is a 10-knot headwind, proceed downward and to the right (remaining proportionally between the existing lines) to the vertical line representing 10 knots.*

6. *From that point, proceed to the right to the third vertical reference line.*

7. *From there, proceed upward and to the right (remaining proportionally between the existing lines) to the vertical line representing the required 50-foot obstacle height. Read the landing distance from the vertical scale (approximately 1,725 feet).*

*(PLT008, PA.I.F.K1) — FAA-H-8083-25*

AIR, WSC
**3692.** (Refer to Figure 37.) Determine the approximate total distance required to land over a 50-foot obstacle.

OAT......................................................................90°F
Pressure altitude..........................................4,000 ft
Weight ....................................................... 2,800 lb
Headwind component...................................10 kts

A—1,525 feet.
B—1,775 feet.
C—1,950 feet.

*Use the following steps:*

1. *Enter FAA Figure 37 at the point where the vertical 90°F temperature line intersects the 4,000-foot pressure altitude line.*

2. *From that point, proceed to the right to the first vertical reference line.*

3. *From there, proceed downward and to the right (remaining proportionally between the existing lines), to the vertical line representing 2,800 pounds.*

4. *Then proceed to the right to the intersection with the second vertical reference line.*

5. *Since there is a 10-knot headwind component, proceed downward and to the right (remaining proportionally between the existing lines) to the vertical line representing 10 knots.*

6. *From that point, proceed to the right to the third vertical reference line.*

7. *Proceed upward to the right following the diagonal line for the 50-foot obstacle and then continue to read the landing distance (approximately 1,775 feet).*

*(PLT008, PA.I.F.K1) — FAA-H-8083-25*

AIR, WSC
**3693.** (Refer to Figure 38.) Determine the approximate landing ground roll distance.

Pressure altitude............................................ Sea level
Headwind ............................................................ 4 kts
Temperature ...........................................................Std

A—356 feet.
B—401 feet.
C—490 feet.

*Use the following steps:*

1. *Locate the sea level portion of FAA Figure 38.*

2. *Read the landing ground roll distance (445 feet).*

3. *Note 1 requires that the distances shown be decreased by 10% for each 4 knots of headwind.*

> *445 × .10 = 44.5 feet*
> *445.0 – 44.5 = 400.5 or 401 feet*

*(PLT008, PA.I.F.K1) — FAA-H-8083-25*

**Answers**

3691   [C]          3692   [B]          3693   [B]

AIR, WSC

**3694.** (Refer to Figure 38.) Determine the total distance required to land over a 50-foot obstacle.

Pressure altitude............................................. 7,500 ft
Headwind ......................................................... 8 kts
Temperature ...................................................... 32°F
Runway................................................. Hard surface

A—1,004 feet.
B—1,205 feet.
C—1,506 feet.

*Use the following steps:*

1. *Locate the portion of FAA Figure 38 that is applicable to a pressure altitude of 7,500 feet. The standard temperature at 7,500 feet is approximately 32°F, based on a temperature lapse rate of 3.5°F/1,000 feet.*

2. *Determine from the table that the basic distance to clear a 50-foot obstacle is 1,255 feet.*

3. *Apply Note 1 to account for an 8-knot headwind (a 20% decrease in distance):*

   *1,255 × .20 = 251 feet*
   *1,255 – 251 = 1,004 feet*

*(PLT008, PA.I.F.K1) — FAA-H-8083-25*

AIR, WSC

**3695.** (Refer to Figure 38.) Determine the total distance required to land over a 50-foot obstacle.

Pressure altitude............................................. 5,000 ft
Headwind ......................................................... 8 kts
Temperature ...................................................... 41°F
Runway................................................. Hard surface

A—837 feet.
B—956 feet.
C—1,076 feet.

*Use the following steps:*

1. *Locate the table applicable to a pressure altitude of 5,000 feet and ambient temperature of 41°F on FAA Figure 38.*

2. *Read the total distance required to clear a 50-foot obstacle (1,195 feet).*

3. *Apply Note 1 to account for an 8-knot headwind (a 20% decrease in distance):*

   *1,195 × .20 = 239 feet*
   *1,195 – 239 = 956 feet*

*(PLT008, PA.I.F.K1) — FAA-H-8083-25*

AIR, WSC

**3696.** (Refer to Figure 38.) Determine the approximate landing ground roll distance.

Pressure altitude............................................. 5,000 ft
Headwind ........................................................ Calm
Temperature ...................................................... 101°F

A—495 feet.
B—545 feet.
C—445 feet.

*Use the following steps:*

1. *Locate the table which applies to a pressure altitude of 5,000 feet on FAA Figure 38.*

2. *Read the ground roll of 495 feet.*

3. *Apply Note 2 to account for the temperature difference between 101°F ambient and the 41°F value on which the table is based.*

   *495 × .10 = 49.5 feet*
   *495 + 49.5 = 544.5 feet*

*(PLT008, PA.I.F.K1) — FAA-H-8083-25*

AIR, WSC

**3697.** (Refer to Figure 38.) Determine the total distance required to land over a 50-foot obstacle.

Pressure altitude............................................. 3,750 ft
Headwind ........................................................ 12 kts
Temperature ........................................................ Std

A—794 feet.
B—836 feet.
C—816 feet.

*Use the following steps:*

1. *Locate the 2,500-foot and 5,000-foot tables.*

2. *Interpolate (3,750 is midway between 2,500 feet and 5,000 feet) to obtain a landing distance:*

   *(1,135 + 1,195) ÷ 2 = 1,165 feet ground roll*

3. *Apply Note 1 to account for the 12-knot headwind.*

   *12 ÷ 4 = 3*
   *3.00 × .10 = .30*
   *1,165 × .30 = 349.5*
   *1,165 – 349.5 = 815.5 feet*

*(PLT008, PA.I.F.K1) — FAA-H-8083-25*

**Answers**

3694　[A]　　　　3695　[B]　　　　3696　[B]　　　　3697　[C]

RTC, LSR

**3699.** (Refer to Figure 39.) Determine the total landing distance to clear a 50-foot obstacle in a gyroplane. The outside air temperature (OAT) is 75°F and the pressure altitude at the airport is 2,500 feet.

A—521 feet.
B—525 feet.
C—529 feet.

*Use the following steps:*

1. *Locate the horizontal line corresponding to 2,500 feet pressure altitude on FAA Figure 39.*

2. *Draw vertical lines through the points of intersection of the 2,500-foot pressure altitude line with the 75°F point. Note the landing distance of 525 feet.*

*(PH.I.F.K1) — FAA-H-8083-21*

RTC

**3700.** (Refer to Figure 39.) Approximately how much additional landing distance will be required for a gyroplane to clear a 50-foot obstacle with an increase in temperature from 40 to 60°F at 3,200 feet pressure altitude?

A—4 feet.
B—8 feet.
C—12 feet.

*Use the following steps:*

1. *Locate the 3,200-foot pressure altitude point on FAA Figure 39.*

2. *Select any two adjacent temperature lines (which are separated by 20°F increments). Note the points of intersection of each line with the 3,200-foot pressure altitude.*

3. *Read downward from each of the two intersections to the distance scale.*

4. *Note the difference between the two distances (4 feet).*

*(PH.I.F.K1) — FAA-H-8083-25*

RTC

**3701.** (Refer to Figure 39.) Determine the total landing distance to clear a 50-foot obstacle in a gyroplane. The outside air temperature (OAT) is 80°F and the pressure altitude is 3,500 feet.

A—521 feet.
B—526 feet.
C—531 feet.

*Use the following steps:*

1. *Locate the horizontal line corresponding to 3,500 feet pressure altitude on FAA Figure 39.*

2. *Draw vertical lines through the points of intersection of the 3,500-foot pressure altitude line with the 80°F point. Note the landing distance of 531 feet.*

*(PH.I.F.K1) — FAA-H-8083-25*

GLI

**3864.** (Refer to Figure 54.) How many feet will the glider sink in 1 statute mile at 53 mph in still air?

A—144 feet.
B—171 feet.
C—211 feet.

*Use the following steps:*

1. *Read the L/D ratio (which is numerically the same as the glide ratio) for a speed of 53 mph from the graph (30.9:1).*

2. *Using the glide ratio of 30.9 feet forward for each foot of vertical sink, calculate the sink encountered in one statute mile (5,280 feet):*

$$\frac{Distance}{L/D\ Ratio} = Vertical\ Sink$$

$$\frac{5,280}{30.9} = 171\ feet\ vertical\ sink$$

*(PLT054) — FAA-H-8083-13*

GLI

**3865.** (Refer to Figure 54.) At what speed will the glider attain a sink rate of 5 feet per second in still air?

A—75 mph.
B—82 mph.
C—84 mph.

*Use the following steps:*

1. *Locate the sinking speed ($V_S$) curve and its associated scale (on the right side) of FAA Figure 54.*

2. *Read to the left from the 5 fps position to the sinking speed curved scale.*

3. *Interpreting the horizontal scale gives a speed of 82 mph forward.*

*(PLT054) — FAA-H-8083-13*

---

**Answers**

| 3699 | [B] | 3700 | [A] | 3701 | [C] | 3864 | [B] | 3865 | [B] |

GLI

**3866.** (Refer to Figure 54.) How many feet will the glider descend at minimum sink speed for 1 statute mile in still air?

A—132 feet.
B—170 feet.
C—180 feet.

*Use the following steps:*

1. *Locate the minimum sink speed (2.2 fps at 44 mph) on FAA Figure 54.*

2. *Determine the L/D (glide ratio) at 44 mph by reading up from 44 mph (on the $V_S$ coordinate) to the intersection with the L/D curve. Read from that intersection to the left (L/D) coordinate. At 44 mph the L/D ratio is 29.3:1.*

3. *Using the glide ratio of 29.3 feet forward for each foot of vertical sink, calculate the sink encountered in 5,280 feet (one statue mile):*

$$\frac{Distance}{L/D\ Ratio} = Vertical\ Sink$$

$$\frac{5,280}{29.3} = 180\ feet\ vertical\ sink$$

*(PLT054) — FAA-H-8083-13*

GLI

**3867.** (Refer to Figure 54.) At what speed will the glider gain the most distance while descending 1,000 feet in still air?

A—44 mph.
B—53 mph.
C—83 mph.

*The L/D ratio is numerically the same as the glide ratio. Hence, the best forward distance attained per foot of descent will be at the velocity which gives the maximum L/D. (PLT054) — FAA-H-8083-13*

GLI, LSG

**3868.** (Refer to Figure 54.) What approximate lift/drag ratio will the glider attain at 68 mph in still air?

A—10.5:1.
B—21.7:1.
C—28.5:1.

*Use the following steps:*

1. *Locate 68 mph on the V coordinate (at the bottom) on FAA Figure 54.*

2. *Read upward from the 68 mph point to the intersection with the L/D curve.*

3. *Read to the left, from the point of intersection, to the L/D scale and read L/D, 28.5:1.*

*(PLT054) — FAA-H-8083-13*

**Answers**

3866   [C]          3867   [B]          3868   [C]

# Headwind and Crosswind Component Graph

In general, taking off into a wind improves aircraft performance, and reduces the length of runway required to become airborne. The stronger the wind, the better the aircraft performs. Crosswinds, however, may make the aircraft difficult or impossible to control. The aircraft manufacturer determines the safe limit for taking off or landing with a crosswind and establishes the maximum allowable crosswind component. The graph shown in FAA Figure 36 is used to determine what extent a wind of a given direction and speed is felt as a headwind and/or crosswind.

## Problem:

The wind is reported to be from 085° at 30 knots, and you plan to land on Runway 11. What will the headwind and crosswind components be?

## Solution:

1. Determine the angular difference between the wind direction and the runway:

    110°  runway
    − 085°  wind
    _____
    25°  difference

2. Find the intersection of the 25°-angle radial line and the 30-knot wind speed arc on the graph shown in FAA Figure 36. From the intersection move straight down to the bottom of the chart and read that the crosswind component equals 13 knots. From the point of intersection move horizontally left and read that the headwind component equals 27 knots.

---

AIR, RTC, WSC, PPC

**3688.** (Refer to Figure 36.) What is the crosswind component for a landing on Runway 18 if the tower reports the wind as 220° at 30 knots?

A—19 knots.
B—23 knots.
C—30 knots.

*Use the following steps:*

1. *Determine the relative wind angle (WA) from the difference between the runway heading (RH) and the wind direction (WD).*

    *WA = WD − RH*
    *WA = 220° − 180°*
    *WA = 40°*

2. *Locate the arc corresponding to a 30-knot wind velocity.*

3. *Find the point of intersection of the 40° line with the 30-knot wind speed arc.*

4. *Draw a line downward from the intersection to the crosswind component scale and read the resulting velocity of 19 knots.*

*(PLT013, PA.I.F.K1, PH.I.F.K1) — FAA-H-8083-25*

Answer (B) is incorrect because this is the headwind component.
Answer (C) is incorrect because this is the wind speed.

AIR, RTC, WSC, PPC

**3683.** (Refer to Figure 36.) What is the headwind component for a landing on Runway 18 if the tower reports the wind as 220° at 30 knots?

A—19 knots.
B—23 knots.
C—26 knots.

*Use the following steps:*

1. *Determine the relative wind angle (WA) from the difference between the runway heading (RH) and the wind direction (WD):*

    *WA = WD − RH*
    *WA = 220° − 180°*
    *WA = 40°*

2. *Locate the arc corresponding to a 30-knot wind on FAA Figure 36.*

3. *Find the point of intersection of the 40° line with the 30-knot wind speed arc.*

4. *Draw a line to the left from the intersection to the headwind component scale and read the resulting velocity of 23 knots.*

*(PLT013, PA.I.F.K1, PH.I.F.K1) — FAA-H-8083-25*

---

**Answers**

3688  [A]          3683  [B]

AIR, RTC, WSC, PPC

**3684.** (Refer to Figure 36.) Determine the maximum wind velocity for a 45° crosswind if the maximum crosswind component for the airplane is 25 knots.

A—25 knots.
B—29 knots.
C—35 knots.

*Use the following steps:*

1. *Locate the 45° wind angle in FAA Figure 36.*

2. *Locate the vertical line representing a 25-knot crosswind component and its point of intersection with the 45° wind angle line.*

3. *Interpret the intersection point as lying on an arc midway between the 30- and 40-knot wind velocity arcs, or 35 knots.*

*(PLT013, PA.I.F.K1, PH.I.F.K1) — FAA-H-8083-25*

AIR, RTC, WSC, PPC

**3685.** (Refer to Figure 36.) What is the maximum wind velocity for a 30° crosswind if the maximum crosswind component for the airplane is 12 knots?

A—16 knots.
B—20 knots.
C—24 knots.

*Use the following steps:*

1. *Locate the 30° wind angle line on FAA Figure 36.*

2. *Locate the vertical line representing the maximum crosswind component of 12 knots and its point of intersection with the 30° wind angle line.*

3. *Interpret the point of intersection as lying on an arc slightly less than midway between the 20- and 30-knot wind velocity arcs or about 24 knots.*

*(PLT013, PA.I.F.K1, PH.I.F.K1) — FAA-H-8083-25*

AIR, RTC, WSC, PPC

**3686.** (Refer to Figure 36.) With a reported wind of north at 20 knots, which runway (6, 29, or 32) is acceptable for use for an airplane with a 13-knot maximum crosswind component?

A—Runway 6.
B—Runway 29.
C—Runway 32.

*Use the following steps:*

1. *Locate the 20-knot wind velocity arc on FAA Figure 36.*

2. *Draw a line upward from the 13-knot crosswind component (maximum crosswind).*

3. *Note that in this case, acceptable crosswind components will result anytime the relative wind angle is equal to or less than about 40° (the intersection of the 13-knot vertical line and the 20-knot wind arc).*

4. *Calculate the relative wind angle between the north wind (0°) and the runway headings:*

| RWY | Relative Angle | Landing |
|-----|----------------|---------|
| 6   | 60°            | Upwind  |
| 29  | 70°            | Upwind  |
| 32  | 40°            | Upwind  |

*Only Runway 32 provides a crosswind component that would be in acceptable limits for the airplane specified.*
*(PLT013, PA.I.F.K1, PH.I.F.K1) — FAA-H-8083-25*

AIR, RTC, WSC, PPC

**3687.** (Refer to Figure 36.) With a reported wind of south at 20 knots, which runway (10, 14, or 24) is appropriate for an airplane with a 13-knot maximum crosswind component?

A—Runway 10.
B—Runway 14.
C—Runway 24.

*Use the following steps:*

1. *Locate the 20-knot wind velocity arc on FAA Figure 36.*

2. *Draw a line upward from the 13-knot crosswind component (maximum crosswind).*

3. *Note that in this case, acceptable crosswind components will result anytime the relative wind angle is equal to or less than 40° (the intersection of the 13-knot vertical line and the 20-knot wind arc).*

4. *Calculate the relative wind angle between the south wind (180°) and the runway headings:*

| RWY | Relative Angle | Landing  |
|-----|----------------|----------|
| 10  | 80°            | Downwind |
| 14  | 40°            | Upwind   |
| 24  | 60°            | Upwind   |

*(PLT013, PA.I.F.K1, PH.I.F.K1) — FAA-H-8083-25*

**Answers**

3684   [C]          3685   [C]          3686   [C]          3687   [B]

# Wake Turbulence

All aircraft leave two types of **wake turbulence**: prop or jet blast, and wing-tip vortices.

The prop or jet blast could be hazardous to light aircraft on the ground behind large aircraft which are either taxiing or running-up their engines. In the air, jet or prop blast dissipates rapidly.

**Wing-tip vortices** are a by-product of lift. When a wing is flown at a positive angle of attack, a pressure differential is created between the upper and lower wing surfaces, and the pressure above the wing will be lower than the pressure below the wing. In attempting to equalize the pressure, air moves outward, upward, and around the wing tip, setting up a **vortex** which trails behind each wing. See Figure 4-1.

The strength of a vortex is governed by the weight, speed, and the shape of the wing of the generating aircraft. Maximum vortex strength occurs when the generating aircraft is heavy, clean, and slow.

Vortices generated by large aircraft in flight tend to sink below the flight path of the generating aircraft. A pilot should fly at or above the larger aircraft's flight path in order to avoid the wake turbulence created by the wing-tip vortices. See Figure 4-2.

Close to the ground, vortices tend to move laterally. A crosswind will tend to hold the upwind vortex over the landing runway, while a tailwind may move the vortices of a preceding aircraft forward into the touchdown zone.

To avoid wake turbulence when landing, a pilot should note the point where a preceding large aircraft touched down and then land past that point. See Figure 4-3.

On takeoff, lift off should be accomplished prior to reaching the rotation point of a preceding large aircraft; the flight path should then remain upwind and above the preceding aircraft's flight path. See Figure 4-4.

**Figure 4-2.** Vortices in cruise flight

**Figure 4-3.** Touchdown and wake end

**Figure 4-1.** Wing-tip vortices

**Figure 4-4.** Rotation and wake beginning

ALL

**3829-2.** When landing behind a large aircraft, which procedure should be followed for vortex avoidance?

A—Stay above its final approach flightpath all the way to touchdown.
B—Stay below and to one side of its final approach flightpath.
C—Stay well below its final approach flightpath and land at least 2,000 feet behind.

*When landing behind a large aircraft, stay at or above the large aircraft's final approach path. Note its touchdown point and land beyond it. (PLT509, PA.IV.B.R2d) — FAA-H-8083-25*

ALL

**3829-3.** How does the wake turbulence vortex circulate around each wingtip?

A—Inward, upward, and around each tip.
B—Inward, upward, and counterclockwise.
C—Outward, upward, and around each tip.

*The vortex circulation is outward, upward, and around the wing tips when viewed from either ahead or behind the aircraft. (PLT509, PA.II.F.R3) — AIM ¶7-3-4*

ALL

**3827.** When taking off or landing at an airport where heavy aircraft are operating, one should be particularly alert to the hazards of wingtip vortices because this turbulence tends to

A—rise from a crossing runway into the takeoff or landing path.
B—rise into the traffic pattern area surrounding the airport.
C—sink into the flightpath of aircraft operating below the aircraft generating the turbulence.

*Flight tests have shown that the vortices from large aircraft sink at a rate of about 400 to 500 feet per minute. They tend to level off at a distance about 900 feet below the path of the generating aircraft. (PLT509, PA.III.B.R3) — FAA-H-8083-25*

Answer (A) is incorrect because wing-tip vortices always trail behind an airplane and descend toward the ground; they will also drift with the wind. Answer (B) is incorrect because wing-tip vortices descend.

ALL, SPO

**3824.** Wingtip vortices are created only when an aircraft is

A—operating at high airspeeds.
B—heavily loaded.
C—developing lift.

*Lift is generated by the creation of a pressure differential over the wing surface. The lowest pressure occurs over the wing surface and the highest pressure occurs under the wing. This pressure differential triggers the roll up of the airflow aft of the wing, resulting in wing-tip vortices. Vortices are generated from the moment an aircraft leaves the ground, since trailing vortices are a by-product of wing lift. (PLT509, PA.II.F.R3) — FAA-H-8083-25*

Answer (A) is incorrect because the greatest turbulence is produced from an airplane developing lift at a slow airspeed. Answer (B) is incorrect because even though a heavily loaded airplane may produce greater turbulence, an airplane does not have to be heavily loaded in order to produce wing-tip vortices.

ALL, SPO

**3825.** The greatest vortex strength occurs when the generating aircraft is

A—light, dirty, and fast.
B—heavy, dirty, and fast.
C—heavy, clean, and slow.

*The strength of the vortex is governed by the weight, speed, and shape of the wing of the generating aircraft. The greatest vortex strength occurs when the generating aircraft is heavy, clean, and slow. (PLT509, PA.II.F.R3) — FAA-H-8083-25*

Answer (A) is incorrect because light aircraft produce less vortex turbulence than heavy aircraft. Answer (B) is incorrect because in order to be fast, the wing tip must be at a lower angle of attack, thus producing less lift than during climbout. Also, being dirty presents less of a danger than when clean and/or slow.

ALL, SPO

**3826.** Wingtip vortices created by large aircraft tend to

A—sink below the aircraft generating turbulence.
B—rise into the traffic pattern.
C—rise into the takeoff or landing path of a crossing runway.

*Flight tests have shown that the vortices from large aircraft sink at a rate of about 400 to 500 feet per minute. They tend to level off at a distance about 900 feet below the path of the generating aircraft. (PLT509, PA.II.F.R3) — FAA-H-8083-25*

Answers (B) and (C) are incorrect because wing-tip vortices sink toward the ground; however, they may move horizontally depending on crosswind conditions. •

**Answers**

| | | | | |
|---|---|---|---|---|
| 3829-2 [A] | 3829-3 [C] | 3827 [C] | 3824 [C] | 3825 [C] | 3826 [A] |

ALL

**3828.** The wind condition that requires maximum caution when avoiding wake turbulence on landing is a

A—light, quartering headwind.
B—light, quartering tailwind.
C—strong headwind.

*A tailwind condition can move the vortices of a preceding aircraft forward into the touchdown zone. A light quartering tailwind requires maximum caution. Pilots should be alert to large aircraft upwind from their approach and takeoff flight paths. (PLT509, PA.IV.B.R2d) — FAA-H-8083-25*

Answer (A) is incorrect because headwinds push the vortices out of the touchdown zone when landing beyond the touchdown point of the preceding aircraft. Answer (C) is incorrect because strong winds help diffuse wake turbulence vortices.

ALL, SPO

**3829.** When landing behind a large aircraft, the pilot should avoid wake turbulence by staying

A—above the large aircraft's final approach path and landing beyond the large aircraft's touchdown point.
B—below the large aircraft's final approach path and landing before the large aircraft's touchdown point.
C—above the large aircraft's final approach path and landing before the large aircraft's touchdown point.

*When landing behind a large aircraft, stay at or above the large aircraft's final approach path. Note its touchdown point and land beyond it. (PLT509, PA.IV.B.R2d) — FAA-H-8083-25*

Answer (B) is incorrect because below the flight path, you will fly into the sinking vortices generated by the large aircraft. Answer (C) is incorrect because by landing before the large aircraft's touchdown point, you will have to fly below the preceding aircraft's flight path and into the vortices.

ALL

**3830.** When departing behind a heavy aircraft, the pilot should avoid wake turbulence by maneuvering the aircraft

A—below and downwind from the heavy aircraft.
B—above and upwind from the heavy aircraft.
C—below and upwind from the heavy aircraft.

*When departing behind a large aircraft, note the large aircraft's rotation point, rotate prior to it, continue to climb above it, and request permission to deviate upwind of the large aircraft's climb path until turning clear of the aircraft's wake. (PLT509, PA.IV.A.R2d) — FAA-H-8083-25*

SPO

**2039.** What wind condition prolongs the hazards of wake turbulence on a landing runway for the longest period of time?

A—Light quartering headwind.
B—Direct tailwind.
C—Light quartering tailwind.

*A light wind with a cross runway component of 1 to 5 knots could result in the upwind vortex remaining in the touchdown zone for a period of time and hasten the drift of the downwind vortex toward another runway. Similarly, a tailwind condition can move the vortices of the preceding aircraft forward into the touchdown zone. The light quartering tailwind requires maximum caution. (PLT509) — AIM ¶7-3-4*

SPO

**2234-1.** A go-around from a poor landing approach

A—should not be attempted unless circumstances make it absolutely necessary.
B—is preferable to last minute attempts to prevent a bad landing.
C—should not be attempted after the landing flare has been initiated regardless of airspeed.

*It is safer to make a go-around than to touch down while drifting or while in a crab, or make a hard drop-in landing from a high round-out or a bounced landing. (PLT170) — FAA-H-8083-3*

Answer (A) is incorrect because a go-around should be executed whenever unfavorable conditions exist. Answer (C) is incorrect because the go-around can be started at any time in the landing process.

---

**Answers**

| | | | | |
|---|---|---|---|---|
| 3828 [B] | 3829 [A] | 3830 [B] | 2039 [C] | 2234-1 [B] |

# Ground Effect

**Ground effect** occurs when flying within one wingspan or less above the surface. The airflow around the wing and wing tips is modified and the resulting pattern reduces the downwash and the induced drag. These changes can result in an aircraft becoming airborne before reaching recommended takeoff speed or floating during an approach to land. See Figure 4-5.

An airplane leaving ground effect after takeoff will require an increase in angle of attack to maintain the same lift coefficient, which in turn will cause an increase in induced drag and, therefore, require increased thrust.

**Figure 4-5.** Ground effect phenomenon

ALL

**3315.** Ground effect is most likely to result in which problem?

A—Settling to the surface abruptly during landing.
B—Becoming airborne before reaching recommended takeoff speed.
C—Inability to get airborne even though airspeed is sufficient for normal takeoff needs.

*Due to the reduced drag in ground effect, the airplane may seem capable of takeoff well below the recommended speed. It is important that no attempt be made to force the airplane to become airborne with a deficiency of speed. The recommended takeoff speed is necessary to provide adequate initial climb performance. (PLT131, PA.IV.C.K4) — FAA-H-8083-25*

Answer (A) is incorrect because the airplane gains lift from a reduction in induced drag while entering ground effect; therefore, it does not cause the airplane to settle abruptly. Answer (C) is incorrect because ground effect helps the airplane become airborne before the airspeed is sufficient for a normal takeoff.

AIR, GLI, RTC, WSC, PPC, LSA, LSR, LSG, LSW

**3312.** What is ground effect?

A—The result of the interference of the surface of the Earth with the airflow patterns about an airplane.
B—The result of an alteration in airflow patterns increasing induced drag about the wings of an airplane.
C—The result of the disruption of the airflow patterns about the wings of an airplane to the point where the wings will no longer support the airplane in flight.

*Ground effect is the result of the interference of the surface of the Earth with the airflow patterns about an airplane. (PLT131, PA.IV.C.K4) — FAA-H-8083-25*

Answer (B) is incorrect because induced drag is decreased. Answer (C) is incorrect because the disruption of wing-tip vortices increases lift.

AIR, GLI, RTC, WSC, PPC

**3313.** Floating caused by the phenomenon of ground effect will be most realized during an approach to land when at

A—less than the length of the wingspan above the surface.
B—twice the length of the wingspan above the surface.
C—a higher-than-normal angle of attack.

*When the wing is at a height equal to its span, the reduction in induced drag is only 1.4%. However, when the wing is at a height equal to one-fourth its span, the reduction in induced drag is 23.5% and when the wing is at a height equal to one-tenth its span, the reduction in induced drag is 47.6%. (PLT131, PA.IV.C.K4) — FAA-H-8083-25*

Answer (B) is incorrect because ground effect extends up to one wingspan length. Answer (C) is incorrect because floating will result from higher-than-normal angle of attack.

AIR, GLI, RTC, WSC, LSA, LSG, LSR, LSW

**3314.** What must a pilot be aware of as a result of ground effect?

A—Wingtip vortices increase creating wake turbulence problems for arriving and departing aircraft.

B—Induced drag decreases; therefore, any excess speed at the point of flare may cause considerable floating.

C—A full stall landing will require less up elevator deflection than would a full stall when done free of ground effect.

*The reduction of the wing-tip vortices, due to ground effect, alters the spanwise lift distribution and reduces the induced angle of attack, and induced drag causing floating. (PLT131, PA.IV.C.K4) — FAA-H-8083-25*

Answer (A) is incorrect because wing-tip vortices are decreased. Answer (C) is incorrect because a full stall landing will require more up-elevator deflection, due to the increased lift in ground effect.

RTC

**3324.** Which is a result of the phenomenon of ground effect?

A—The induced angle of attack of each rotor blade is increased.

B—The lift vector becomes more horizontal.

C—The angle of attack generating lift is increased.

*In ground effect, as downwash velocity is reduced, the induced angle of attack is reduced and the lift vector becomes more vertical. Simultaneously, a reduction in induced drag occurs. In addition, as the induced angle of attack is reduced, the angle of attack generating lift is increased. The net result of these actions is a beneficial increase in lift and a lower power requirement to support a given weight. (PLT131) — FAA-H-8083-21*

Answer (A) is incorrect because the induced angle of attack isn't described in the first place so we can't assume a change. Answer (B) is incorrect because if lift vector became more horizontal, lift would decrease but thrust would increase in the lateral direction.

RTC

**3735.** (Refer to Figure 46.) The airspeed range to avoid while flying in ground effect is

A—25–40 mph.
B—25–57 mph.
C—40 mph and above.

*Use the following steps:*

1. *Locate the ground effect unsafe area on FAA Figure 46.*

2. *Note that the ground effect altitude in the forward flight region is 40 feet.*

3. *The diagram depicts that a pilot should avoid flight of 40 mph or greater at altitudes lower than 40 feet.*

*(PLT285) — FAA-H-8083-21*

LSA, LSR, LSG, LSW

**2223-2.** An aircraft leaving ground effect during takeoff will

A—experience a reduction in ground friction and require a slight power reduction.

B—experience an increase in induced drag and a decrease in performance.

C—require a lower angle of attack to maintain the same lift coefficient.

*An airplane leaving ground effect will:*

1. *Require an increase in angle of attack to maintain the same lift coefficient.*

2. *Experience an increase in induced drag and thrust required.*

3. *Experience a decrease in stability and a nose-up change in moments.*

4. *Produce a reduction in static source pressure and an increase in indicated airspeed.*

*(PLT131) — FAA-H-8083-25*

**Answers**

| | | | |
|---|---|---|---|
| 3314 [B] | 3324 [C] | 3735 [C] | 2223-2 [B] |

# Cruise Power Setting Table

The Cruise Power Setting Table (FAA Figure 35) may be used to forecast fuel flow and true airspeed and, therefore allow a pilot to determine the amount of fuel required and the estimated time en route.

## Problem:

Using the Cruise Power Setting Table shown in FAA Figure 35, determine the expected fuel consumption for a 1,000-statute-mile flight under the following conditions:

Pressure altitude.................................. 8,000 feet

Temperature ................................................-19°C

Manifold pressure ...................................19.5 "Hg

Wind ........................................................... Calm

## Solution:

1. Find the fuel flow and TAS. Enter the chart at the 8,000-foot pressure altitude line and proceed to the right and identify the chart which represents an indicated outside air temperature (IOAT) of -19°C at 8,000 feet (the chart for ISA -20°C). Continue reading to the right, noting the manifold pressure of 19.5 "Hg, the fuel flow per engine will be 6.6 pounds per square inch or 11.5 gallons per hour (GPH), and the TAS will be 157 knots or 181 mph.

2. Calculate the time flown. Using a flight computer, calculate the time en route:

    1,000 SM at 181 mph ≈ 5.52 hours

3. Calculate the fuel consumption. Using a flight computer, calculate the fuel burned in this time:

    5.52 hours × 11.5 GPH = 63.48 gallons consumed

AIR

**3678.** (Refer to Figure 35.) Approximately what true airspeed should a pilot expect with full throttle at 10,500 feet with a temperature of 36°F above standard?

A—190 kts.
B—159 kts.
C—165 kts.

*Use the following steps:*

1. *Locate +36°F (ISA +20°C) on FAA Figure 35. Notice that the stated altitude of 10,500 feet does not appear on the chart so it is necessary to interpolate.*

2. *Read across the 10,000-foot pressure altitude line and determine the TAS (166 knots).*

3. *Read across the 12,000-foot pressure altitude line and determine the TAS (163 knots).*

4. *Interpolate between the values for 10,000 feet and 12,000 feet to determine a TAS for 10,500 feet.*

    a. *166 knots (10,000 feet) – 163 knots (12,000 feet) = 3 knots difference in speed*

    b. *Interpolate to find one-quarter of difference for 10,500 feet: 3 × .25 = .75*

    c. *Subtract the difference to the speed for 10,000 feet to find TAS for 10,500 feet: 166 – .75 = 165.25*

*(PLT012, PA.I.F.K1) — FAA-H-8083-25*

**Answers**

3678   [C]

AIR

**3679.** (Refer to Figure 35.) What is the expected fuel consumption for a 1,000-nautical mile flight under the following conditions?

Pressure altitude.................................................8,000 ft
Temperature ...........................................................22°C
Manifold pressure.........................................20.8 "Hg
Wind ......................................................................Calm

A—60.2 gallons.
B—70.1 gallons.
C—73.2 gallons.

*Use the following steps:*

1. *Locate the pressure altitude of 8,000 feet on FAA Figure 35. Read to the right and identify the chart which presents an indicated outside temperature of 22°C at 8,000 feet (the chart for ISA +20°C).*

2. *On this chart, read across the 8,000-foot line, 22°C, 20.8 "Hg manifold pressure line. The fuel flow is 11.5 GPH and the TAS is 164 knots.*

3. *Using a flight computer, calculate the time en route (Ground Speed on FLT menu using CX-3):*

    *Distance is 1,000 NM*
    *TAS is 164 knots, with no wind*

    *Therefore, the time en route is 6 hours, 6 minutes.*

4. *Using a flight computer, calculate the fuel consumption (Fuel on FLT menu using CX-3):*

    *Time en route is 6 hours, 6 minutes*
    *Fuel burn is 11.5 GPH*

    *Therefore, the fuel consumption is 70.1 gallons.*

*(PLT012, PA.I.F.K1) — FAA-H-8083-25*

AIR

**3680.** (Refer to Figure 35.) What is the expected fuel consumption for a 500-nautical mile flight under the following conditions?

Pressure altitude.................................................4,000 ft
Temperature ........................................................+29°C
Manifold pressure..........................................21.3 "Hg
Wind ......................................................................Calm

A—31.4 gallons.
B—36.1 gallons.
C—40.1 gallons.

*Use the following steps:*

1. *Locate the pressure altitude of 4,000 feet on FAA Figure 35. Read to the right and identify the chart which presents an indicated outside temperature of +29°C at 4,000 feet (in this case, the chart for ISA +20°C).*

2. *On this chart, read across the 4,000-foot line, +29°C, 21.3 "Hg manifold pressure line. The fuel flow is 11.5 GPH and the TAS is 159 knots.*

3. *Using a flight computer, calculate the time en route (Ground Speed on FLT menu using CX-3):*

    *Distance is 500 NM*
    *TAS is 159 knots, with no wind*

    *Therefore, the time en route is 3 hours, 9 minutes.*

4. *Using a flight computer, calculate the fuel consumption (Fuel on FLT menu using CX-3):*

    *Time en route is 3 hours, 9 minutes*
    *Fuel burn is 11.5 GPH*

    *Therefore, the fuel consumption is 36.2 gallons.*

*(PLT012, PA.I.F.K1) — FAA-H-8083-25*

AIR

**3681.** (Refer to Figure 35.) What fuel flow should a pilot expect at 11,000 feet on a standard day with 65 percent maximum continuous power?

A—10.6 gallons per hour.
B—11.2 gallons per hour.
C—11.8 gallons per hour.

*Use the following steps:*

1. *Locate the Standard Day (ISA) Chart on FAA Figure 35. Notice that the stated altitude, 11,000 feet, does not appear on the chart, so it is necessary to interpolate.*

2. *Read across the 10,000-foot pressure altitude line and determine the fuel flow at that altitude (11.5 GPH).*

3. *Read across the 12,000-foot pressure altitude line and determine the fuel flow at that altitude (10.9 GPH).*

4. *To determine the flow at 11,000 feet, add the two flows and divide by two.*

$$Fuel\ Flow = \frac{(11.5 + 10.9)}{2} = \frac{22.4}{2} = 11.2\ GPH$$

*(PLT012, PA.I.F.K1) — FAA-H-8083-25*

---

**Answers**

3679 **[B]**        3680 **[B]**        3681 **[B]**

AIR

**3682.** (Refer to Figure 35.) Determine the approximate manifold pressure setting with 2,450 RPM to achieve 65 percent maximum continuous power at 6,500 feet with a temperature of 36°F higher than standard.

A—19.8 "Hg.
B—20.8 "Hg.
C—21.0 "Hg.

*Use the following steps:*

1. *Locate the +36°F (ISA + 20°C) Chart on FAA Figure 35. Notice that the stated altitude of 6,500 feet does not appear on the chart, so it is necessary to interpolate.*

2. *Read across the 6,000-foot pressure altitude line and determine the manifold pressure at that altitude (21.0 "Hg).*

3. *Read across the 8,000-foot pressure altitude line and determine the manifold pressure at that altitude (20.8 "Hg).*

4. *The altitude, 6,500 feet, is closer to the 6,000-foot value of 21.0 "Hg.*

*(PLT278, PA.I.F.K1) — FAA-H-8083-25*

# Maximum Range Performance

LSA, LSW, LSR

**2230.** Maximum endurance is obtained at the point of minimum power to maintain the aircraft

A—in steady, level flight.
B—in a long range descent.
C—at its slowest possible indicated airspeed.

*The maximum endurance condition is obtained at the point of minimum power required since this would require the lowest fuel flow to keep the airplane in steady, level flight. Maximum range condition occurs where the proportion between speed and power required is greatest. (PLT015) — FAA-H-8083-25*

LSA, LSW, LSR

**2236.** When range and economy of operation are the principal goals, the pilot must ensure that the airplane will be operated at the recommended

A—specific endurance.
B—long-range cruise performance.
C—equivalent airspeed.

*Total range is dependent on both fuel available and specific range. When range and economy of operation are the principal goals, the pilot must ensure that the airplane is operated at the recommended long-range cruise condition. By this procedure, the airplane will be capable of its maximum design operating radius, or can achieve lesser flight distances with a maximum of fuel reserve at the destination. (PLT501) — FAA-H-8083-25*

**Answers**

3682   [C]          2230   [A]          2236   [B]

# Weight and Balance

Even though an aircraft has been certificated for flight at a specified maximum gross weight, it may not be safe to take off with that load under all conditions. High altitude, high temperature, and high humidity are additional factors which may require limiting the load to some weight less than the maximum allowable.

Some of the problems caused by overloading an aircraft are:

- The aircraft will need a higher takeoff speed, which results in a longer takeoff run.
- Both the rate and angle of climb will be reduced.
- The service ceiling will be lowered.
- The cruising speed will be reduced.
- The cruising range will be shortened.
- Maneuverability will be decreased.
- A longer landing roll will be required because the landing speed will be higher.
- Excessive loads will be imposed on the structure, especially the landing gear.

The **empty weight** is obtained from appropriate charts. It includes the airframe, engine, all fixed equipment, and unusable fuel and oil. Some aircraft include all oil in the aircraft empty weight. The **useful load** includes the pilot, passengers, baggage, fuel and oil. The **takeoff weight** is the empty weight plus the useful load. The **landing weight** is the takeoff weight minus any fuel used.

The **arm** is the horizontal distance measured in inches from the datum line to a point on the aircraft. If measured aft, toward the tail, the arm is given a positive (+) value; if measured forward, toward the nose, the arm is given a negative (-) value. See Figure 4-6.

The **moment** is the product of the weight of an object multiplied by its arm and is expressed in pound-inches (lbs-in). A formula that is used to find moment is usually expressed as follows:

Weight × arm = moment

The **moment index** is a moment divided by a constant such as 100 or 1,000. It is used to simplify computations where heavy items and long arms result in large, unmanageable numbers. This is usually expressed as MOM/100 or MOM/1000, etc.

The center of gravity (CG) is the point about which an aircraft will balance, and it is expressed in inches from datum. The center of gravity is found by dividing the total moment by the total weight, and the formula is usually expressed as follows:

$$\frac{\text{Total moment}}{\text{Total weight}} = \text{CG (inches aft of datum)}$$

**Figure 4-6.** Positive and negative arm

**Standard weights** have been established for numerous items involved in weight and balance computations. These weights should not be used if actual weights are available. Some of the standard weights are:

| Item | Weight |
|---|---|
| General aviation crew and passenger | 190 lbs each |
| Gasoline | 6 lbs/U.S. gallon |
| Oil | 7.5 lbs/U.S. gallon |
| Water | 8.35 lbs/U.S. gallon |

# Airplane

In addition to considering the weight to be carried, the pilot must ensure that the load is arranged to keep the aircraft in balance. The balance point, or center of gravity (CG), is the point at which all of the weight of the airplane is considered to be concentrated. For an aircraft to be safe to fly, the center of gravity must fall between specified limits. All aircraft categories have unique balance requirements; some need to be balanced precisely while others are less sensitive to fore and aft weight distribution. The specific balance requirements for each aircraft category are covered in the pilot's operating handbook (POH) and will be tested on during the practical (checkride). To keep the CG within safe limits it may be necessary to move weight toward the nose of the aircraft (forward), which moves the CG forward, or toward the tail (aft) which moves the CG aft.

The specified forward and aft points within which the CG must be located for safe flight are called the center of gravity limits. These limits are specified by the manufacturer. The distance between the forward and aft CG limits is called the center of gravity range.

# Weight-Shift Control

Weight and loading is typically used for weight-shift control. The cart normally does not have balance requirements, but the attachment point to the cart is specified in the POH.

# Powered Parachute

Weight and loading is used for powered parachutes. The POH procedure for the fore and aft attachment points of the wing to the cart must be followed so that the cart will obtain the proper deck angle (the angle of the cart bottom with the horizontal plane).

ALL

**3663-1.** (Refer to Figure 61.) If 50 pounds of weight is located at point X and 100 pounds at point Z, how much weight must be located at point Y to balance the plank?

A—30 pounds.
B—50 pounds.
C—300 pounds.

*Find the moments left and right of the fulcrum, and set them equal to one another.*

> *Left = right*
>
> *50(50) + Y(25) = 100(100)*
>
> *2,500 + 25Y = 10,000*
>
> *Y = 300 pounds*

*(PLT021, PA.I.F.K2f, PH.I.F.K3) — FAA-H-8083-25*

ALL

**3663-2.** (Refer to Figure 60.) How should the 500-pound weight be shifted to balance the plank on the fulcrum?

A—1 inch to the left.
B—1 inch to the right.
C—4.5 inches to the right.

1. *Find the moments left and right of the fulcrum, and set them equal to one another.*

   > *left = right*
   >
   > *500(X) = 250(20) + 200(15)*
   >
   > *500X = 8,000*
   >
   > *X = 16 inches*

2. *The 500-pound weight must be 16 inches from the fulcrum to be in balance. It is currently located at 15 inches, therefore the weight should be shifted 1 inch to the left.*

*(PLT092, PA.I.F.K2f, PH.I.F.K3) — FAA-H-8083-25*

**Answers**

3663-1   [C]       3663-2   [A]

**AIR, REC**
**3815.** (Refer to Figure 67.) What effect does a 30-gallon fuel burn have on the weight and balance if the airplane weighed 2,784 pounds and the MOM/100 was 2,222 at takeoff?

A—No effect on CG.
B—Moment will increase to 2,357 in-lb.
C—Moment will decrease to 2,087 in-lb.

*The original CG is 2,222/2,784 = 79.8. Figure 67 includes a table summarizing fuel weights and moments. Burning 30 gallons of fuel will result in a 180-pound reduction, making the new airplane weigh 2,604 pounds (2,784 − 180). The moment is reduced by 135, making the new MOM/100 = 2,087 (2,222 − 135). The new CG is 2,087/2,604 = 80.1. (PLT021, PA.I.F.K2f, PH.I.F.K3) — FAA-H-8083-25*

Answer (A) is incorrect because the CG will increase from 79.8 to 80.1. Answer (B) is incorrect because 2,357 is an increase of 135 lbs-in.

**ALL, LSA, LSR, LSW, LSP**
**3661.** Which items are included in the empty weight of an aircraft?

A—Unusable fuel and undrainable oil.
B—Only the airframe, powerplant, and optional equipment.
C—Full fuel tanks and engine oil to capacity.

*Empty weight consists of the airframe, engines, and all items of operating equipment that have fixed locations and are permanently installed in the airplane. It includes optional and special equipment, fixed ballast, hydraulic fluid, unusable (residual) fuel, and undrainable (residual) oil. (PLT328, PA.I.F.K2f, PH.I.F.K3) — FAA-H-8083-25*

Answer (B) is incorrect because empty weight also includes operating fluids and unusable fuel. Answer (C) is incorrect because empty weight does not include full fuel.

**AIR, RTC, WSC, PPC**
**3662.** An aircraft is loaded 110 pounds over maximum certificated gross weight. If fuel (gasoline) is drained to bring the aircraft weight within limits, how much fuel should be drained?

A—15.7 gallons.
B—16.2 gallons.
C—18.4 gallons.

1. Determine the total weight to be removed (110 pounds) and the weight per gallon of gasoline (6 pounds).
2. Calculate the amount of gasoline to be drained using the formula:

$$Gallons = \frac{Pounds}{Pounds/Gallon}$$

*or:*

$$\frac{110}{6} = 18.33 \text{ gallons}$$

*When rounding an answer, do so in the sense that will provide the greater flight safety. In this case, round to 18.4. (PLT021, PA.I.F.K2f, PH.I.F.K3) — FAA-H-8083-25*

**AIR, RTC, WSC, PPC**
**3663.** If an aircraft is loaded 90 pounds over maximum certificated gross weight and fuel (gasoline) is drained to bring the aircraft weight within limits, how much fuel should be drained?

A—10 gallons.
B—12 gallons.
C—15 gallons.

1. Determine the total weight to be removed (90 pounds) and the weight per gallon of gasoline (6 pounds).
2. Calculate the amount of gasoline to be drained using the formula:

$$Gallons = \frac{Pounds}{Pounds/Gallon}$$

*or:*

$$\frac{90}{6} = 15 \text{ gallons}$$

*(PLT021, PA.I.F.K2f, PH.I.F.K3) — FAA-H-8083-25*

**SPO**
**2371.** (Refer to Figure 72.) The positive limit load factor is represented by the

A—vertical dashed line from E to F.
B—vertical solid line from D to G.
C—horizontal dashed line from C to point E.

*C to E is the maximum positive load limit. In this case it is 3.8 Gs, which is appropriate for normal category airplanes. (PLT074) — FAA-H-8083-25*

Answer (A) is incorrect because the vertical dashed line from E to F is the never-exceed airspeed (V$_{NE}$). Answer (B) is incorrect because the vertical solid line from D to G is the high end for normal operations.

**Answers**

3815 [C]   3661 [A]   3662 [C]   3663 [C]   2371 [C]

# Computing Weight and Balance Problems

## Using a Table

### Problem:

Determine if the airplane weight and balance is within limits.

Front seat occupants ............................. 340 lbs
Rear seat occupants.............................. 295 lbs
Fuel (main wing tanks) ............................. 44 gal
Baggage .................................................. 56 lbs

### Solution:

1. Determine the total weight. Using the information provided in the question, enter the items and the weights:

| Item | Weight (lbs) | Arm (in) | Moment (lbs-in) |
|------|------|------|------|
| Front seat occupants | 340 | | |
| Rear seat occupants | 295 | | |
| Fuel (main wing tanks) | 264 * | | |
| Baggage | 56 | | |
| Empty weight | + 2,015 ** | | |
| | 2,970 lbs | | |

*44 gal × 6 lbs/gal    **found in FAA Figure 33

2. Fill in the arms (found in FAA Figure 32) and calculate the moments. Moments are determined by multiplying in each row: weight × arm. Then divide that moment by 100 to keep the number a manageable size, and finally, total all moments.

| Item | Weight (lbs) | Arm (in) | Moment/100 (lbs-in) |
|------|------|------|------|
| Front seat occupants | 340 | 85 | 289.0 |
| Rear seat occupants | 295 | 121 | 357.0 |
| Fuel (main wing tanks) | 264 | 75 | 198.0 |
| Baggage | 56 | 140 | 78.4 |
| Empty weight | + 2,015 | | 1,554.0 |
| | 2,970 lbs | | 2,476.4 lbs-in |

3. Determine the balance conditions. Looking at FAA Figure 33, notice that the table stops at the maximum weight of 2,950. Even though the weight is off the scale, the Moment of 2,476.4 is between the minimum and maximum Moment limits given in the table. Therefore, we are 20 pounds overweight and within balance limits.

AIR
**3664.** GIVEN:

| | WEIGHT (LB) | ARM (IN) | MOMENT (LB-IN) |
|---|---|---|---|
| Empty weight | 1,495.0 | 101.4 | 151,593.0 |
| Pilot and passengers | 380.0 | 64.0 | — |
| Fuel (30 gal usable–no reserve) | — | 96.0 | — |

The CG is located how far aft of datum?

A—CG 92.44.
B—CG 94.01.
C—CG 119.8.

1. Compute the total weight and moment using the formula:

   Weight × arm = moment

   or:

| Item | Weight | Arm | Moment |
|---|---|---|---|
| Empty weight | 1,495.0 | 101.4 | 151,593.0 |
| Pilot & passenger | 380.0 | 64.0 | 24,320.0 |
| Fuel (30 × 6) | 180.0 | 96.0 | 17,280.0 |
| Total | 2,055.0 lbs | | 193,193.0 |

2. Compute the center of gravity using the formula:

$$CG = \frac{Total\ moment}{Total\ weight}$$

   or:

$$CG = \frac{193,193}{2,055} = 94.01\ inches\ aft\ of\ datum$$

(PLT021, PA.I.F.S1) — FAA-H-8083-25

AIR
**3665.** (Refer to Figures 32 and 33.) Determine if the airplane weight and balance is within limits.

Front seat occupants .........................................340 lb
Rear seat occupants .........................................295 lb
Fuel (main wing tanks).....................................44 gal
Baggage .............................................................56 lb

A—20 pounds overweight, CG aft of aft limits.
B—20 pounds overweight, CG within limits.
C—20 pounds overweight, CG forward of forward limits.

When multiplying a weight by its arm you must divide by 100 to get moment index (moment/100). Moments listed in FAA Figures 32 and 33 are already divided by 100, and are therefore moment indexes.

1. Calculate weight and moment index using the information from the question and from FAA Figures 32 and 33 and the formula:

   Weight × arm ÷ 100 = moment/index

| Item | Weight | Arm | Moment/100 |
|---|---|---|---|
| Empty weight | 2,015 lbs | | 1,554.0 lbs-in |
| Front seat | 340 lbs | 85 | 289.0 lbs-in |
| Rear seat | 295 lbs | 121 | 357.0 lbs-in |
| Fuel (44 × 6) | 264 lbs | 75 | 198.0 lbs-in |
| Baggage | 56 lbs | 140 | 78.4 lbs-in |
| Total | 2,970 lbs | | 2,476.4 lbs-in |

2. Consult the Moment Limits vs. Weight Table, FAA Figure 33. The aircraft weight is 2,970 pounds or 20 pounds in excess of the maximum weight on the chart. The moment of 2,476.4 lbs-in would be within limits if the chart went to 2,970 pounds gross weight.

(PLT121, PA.I.F.S1) — FAA-H-8083-25

AIR
**3666.** (Refer to Figures 32 and 33.) What is the maximum amount of baggage that can be carried when the airplane is loaded as follows?

Front seat occupants .........................................387 lb
Rear seat occupants .........................................293 lb
Fuel...................................................................35 gal

A—45 pounds.
B—63 pounds.
C—220 pounds.

1. When multiplying a weight times its arm you must divide by 100 to get moment index. Calculate total weight and total moment index using the information from the question and from FAA Figures 32 and 33 and the formula:

   Weight × arm ÷ 100 = moment/index

| Item | Weight | Arm | Moment/100 |
|---|---|---|---|
| Empty weight | 2,015 lbs | | 1,554.0 lbs-in |
| Front seat | 387 lbs | 85 | 329.0 lbs-in |
| Rear seat | 293 lbs | 121 | 354.5 lbs-in |
| Fuel (35 × 6) | 210 lbs | 75 | 157.5 lbs-in |
| Total | 2,905 lbs | | 2,395.0 lbs-in |

2. The maximum takeoff weight is 2,950 pounds. Calculate what the allowed baggage weight would be:

   2,950 – 2,905 = 45 pounds

3. Verify that the CG would remain within the allowable range with this much baggage by calculating the new weight and moment index.

**Answers**

| Item | Weight | Arm | Moment/100 |
|------|--------|-----|------------|
| Original total | 2,905 lbs | | 2,395.0 lbs-in |
| Baggage | + 45 lbs | 140 | + 63.0 lbs-in |
| New Total | 2,950 lbs | | 2,458.0 lbs-in |

4. Consult the Moment Limit vs. Weight Table, FAA Figure 33. For a weight of 2,950 pounds, the range of allowable moments is 2,422 to 2,499. The new total moment index of 2,458.0 is acceptable.

*(PLT021, PA.I.F.S1) — FAA-H-8083-25*

AIR

**3667.** (Refer to Figures 32 and 33.) Calculate the weight and balance and determine if the CG and the weight of the airplane are within limits.

Front seat occupants .........................................350 lb
Rear seat occupants ........................................325 lb
Baggage ............................................................27 lb
Fuel....................................................................35 gal

A—CG 81.7, out of limits forward.
B—CG 83.4, within limits.
C—CG 84.1, within limits.

*Use the following steps:*

1. Calculate weight and moment index using the information from the problem and from FAA Figures 32 and 33 and the formula:

   Weight × arm ÷ 100 = moment/index

| Item | Weight | Arm | Moment/100 |
|------|--------|-----|------------|
| Empty weight | 2,015 lbs | | 1,554.0 lbs-in |
| Front seat | 350 lbs | 85 | 297.5 lbs-in |
| Rear seat | 325 lbs | 121 | 393.3 lbs-in |
| Baggage | 27 lbs | 140 | 37.8 lbs-in |
| Fuel (35 × 6) | 210 lbs | 75 | 157.5 lbs-in |
| Total | 2,927 lbs | | 2,440.1 lbs-in |

2. Calculate the position of CG using the formula:

   $$CG = \frac{Total\ moment\ index}{Total\ weight} \times reduction\ factor$$

   or:

   $$CG = \frac{2,440.1}{2,927} \times 100 = 83.4\ inches\ aft\ of\ datum$$

*(PLT021, PA.I.F.S1) — FAA-H-8083-25*

AIR

**3668.** (Refer to Figures 32 and 33.) Determine if the airplane weight and balance is within limits.

Front seat occupants .........................................415 lb
Rear seat occupants ........................................110 lb
Fuel, main tanks ...............................................44 gal
Fuel, aux. tanks ................................................19 gal
Baggage ............................................................32 lb

A—19 pounds overweight, CG within limits.
B—19 pounds overweight, CG out of limits forward.
C—Weight within limits, CG out of limits.

*Use the following steps:*

1. Calculate weight and moment index using the information from the problem and from FAA Figures 32 and 33, and the formula:

   Weight × arm ÷ 100 = moment/index

| Item | Weight | Arm | Moment/100 |
|------|--------|-----|------------|
| Empty weight | 2,015 lbs | | 1,554.0 lbs-in |
| Front seat | 415 lbs | 85 | 352.8 lbs-in |
| Rear seat | 110 lbs | 121 | 133.1 lbs-in |
| Fuel main 44 × 6 | 264 lbs | 75 | 198.0 lbs-in |
| Fuel aux. 19 × 6 | 114 lbs | 94 | 107.2 lbs-in |
| Baggage | 32 lbs | 140 | 44.8 lbs-in |
| Total | 2,950 lbs | | 2,389.9 lbs-in |

2. Calculate the CG using the formula:

   $$CG = \frac{Total\ moment\ index}{Total\ weight} \times reduction\ factor$$

   or:

   $$CG = \frac{2,389.9}{2,950} \times 100 = 81.0\ inches\ aft\ of\ datum$$

3. Consult the Moment Limits vs. Weight Table (FAA Figure 33). A CG of 81 inches is 1.1 inches forward of the forward CG limit for a weight (allowed) of 2,950 pounds (2,422 ÷ 2,950 = 82.1); (82.1 – 81 = 1.1 inches forward).

*(PLT121, PA.I.F.S1) — FAA-H-8083-25*

**Answers**

3667    [B]          3668    [C]

AIR

**3674.** (Refer to Figures 32 and 33.) Upon landing, the front passenger (180 pounds) departs the airplane. A rear passenger (204 pounds) moves to the front passenger position. What effect does this have on the CG if the airplane weighed 2,690 pounds and the MOM/100 was 2,260 just prior to the passenger transfer?

A—The CG moves forward approximately 3 inches.
B—The weight changes, but the CG is not affected.
C—The CG moves forward approximately 0.1 inch.

*Use the following steps:*

1. Consider the effect on the total weight.

| Item | Weight |
|---|---|
| Original weight | 2,690 pounds |
| Deplaned passenger | – 180 pounds |
| New Weight | 2,510 pounds |

2. Consider the effect on the total moment index using the arms given in FAA Figure 32, and the formula:

   Weight × arm ÷ 100 = moment/index

| Item | Weight | Arm | Moment/100 |
|---|---|---|---|
| Original weight & Mom Ind | 2,690 | | 2,260.0 lbs-in |
| Passenger exiting, front | -180 | 85 | -153.0 lbs-in |
| Passenger exiting, rear | -204 | 121 | -246.8 lbs-in |
| Passenger into front | + 204 | 85 | + 173.4 lbs-in |
| New Total Weight & Moment | 2,510 | | 2,033.6 lbs-in |

3. Determine both the original and new CG using the formula:

$$CG = \frac{Total\ moment\ index}{Total\ weight} \times reduction\ factor$$

   or:

   a. Original CG =

   $$\frac{2,260}{2,690} \times 100 = 84.0\ inches\ aft\ of\ datum$$

   b. New CG =

   $$\frac{2,033.6}{2,510} \times 100 = 81.0\ inches\ aft\ of\ datum$$

4. Calculate the change in CG:

   84 – 81 = 3 inches (forward)

(PLT021, PA.I.F.S1) — FAA-H-8083-25

AIR

**3675.** (Refer to Figures 32 and 33.) Which action can adjust the airplane's weight to maximum gross weight and the CG within limits for takeoff?

Front seat occupants .......................................... 425 lb
Rear seat occupants ......................................... 300 lb
Fuel, main tanks ................................................ 44 gal

A—Drain 12 gallons of fuel.
B—Drain 9 gallons of fuel.
C—Transfer 12 gallons of fuel from the main tanks to the auxiliary tanks.

*Use the following steps:*

1. Calculate the original weights and moment index using the information from the problem and FAA Figures 32 and 33, and the formula:

   Weight × arm ÷ 100 = moment/index

| Item | Weight | Arm | Moment/100 |
|---|---|---|---|
| Empty weight | 2,015 lbs | | 1,554.0 lbs-in |
| Front seat | 425 lbs | 85 | 361.3 lbs-in |
| Rear seat | 300 lbs | 121 | 363.0 lbs-in |
| Fuel (44 × 6) | 264 lbs | 75 | 198.0 lbs-in |
| Total | 3,004 lbs | | 2,476.3 lbs-in |

2. If the aircraft has a maximum allowable takeoff weight of 2,950 lbs, compute the weight to be removed to reach an acceptable takeoff weight.

   3,004 – 2,950 = 54 pounds

3. Compute the amount of fuel (in gallons) that totals 54 lbs:

   54 ÷ 6 = 9 gallons

4. Compute the revised weight and moment index:

| Item | Weight | Arm | Moment/100 |
|---|---|---|---|
| Original totals | 3,004 lbs | | 2,476.3 lbs-in |
| Fuel | – 54 lbs | 75 | – 40.5 lbs-in |
| New Total | 2,950 lbs | | 2,435.8 lbs-in |

5. Consult the Moment Limits vs. Weight Chart. At 2,950 lbs takeoff weight, 2,435.8 is within the moments limits.

(PLT021, PA.I.F.S1) — FAA-H-8083-25

**Answers**

3674    [A]                3675    [B]

AIR

**3676.** (Refer to Figures 32 and 33.) What effect does a 35-gallon fuel burn (main tanks) have on the weight and balance if the airplane weighed 2,890 pounds and the MOM/100 was 2,452 at takeoff?

A—Weight is reduced by 210 pounds and the CG is aft of limits.
B—Weight is reduced by 210 pounds and the CG is unaffected.
C—Weight is reduced to 2,680 pounds and the CG moves forward.

*Use the following steps:*

1. *Calculate the change in both weight and moment index caused by a burn of 35 gallons, using the information from FAA Figures 32 and 33.*

   *Weight × arm ÷ 100 = moment/index*

   | Item | Weight | Arm | Moment |
   |------|--------|-----|--------|
   | Fuel (35 × 6) | 210 lbs | 75 | 158 lbs-in |

2. *Determine the effect of burn on total weight and moment index:*

   | Item | Weight | Arm | Moment/100 |
   |------|--------|-----|-----------|
   | Original total | 2,890 lbs | | 2,452.0 lbs-in |
   | Fuel burn | – 210 lbs | 75 | – 158.0 lbs-in |
   | New Total | 2,680 lbs | | 2,294.0 lbs-in |

3. *Consult the Moment Limits vs. Weight Table (FAA Figure 33). The allowed range of moment indexes for a weight of 2,680 lbs is 2,123 to 2,287 lbs-in/100. Hence the new moment index exceeds the maximum allowed and the CG is aft of limits.*

*(PLT021, PA.I.F.S1) — FAA-H-8083-25*

AIR

**3677.** (Refer to Figures 32 and 33.) With the airplane loaded as follows, what action can be taken to balance the airplane?

Front seat occupants .........................................411 lb
Rear seat occupants .......................................100 lb
Main wing tanks.................................................44 gal

A—Fill the auxiliary wing tanks.
B—Add a 100-pound weight to the baggage compartment.
C—Transfer 10 gallons of fuel from the main tanks to the auxiliary tanks.

*Use the following steps:*

1. *Calculate the weights and moments using the information from the problem and FAA Figures 32 and 33, and the formula:*

   *Weight × arm ÷ 100 = moment/index*

   | Item | Weight | Arm | Moment/100 |
   |------|--------|-----|-----------|
   | Empty weight | 2,015 lbs | | 1,554.0 lbs-in |
   | Front seat | 411 lbs | 85 | 349.4 lbs-in |
   | Rear seat | 100 lbs | 121 | 121.0 lbs-in |
   | Fuel 44 × 6 | 264 lbs | 75 | 198.0 lbs-in |
   | Total | 2,790 lbs | | 2,222.4 lbs-in |

2. *Consulting the Moment Limits vs. Weight Table (FAA Figure 33), the allowed range of moments for 2,790 lbs is between 2,243 and 2,374 lbs-in/100.*

3. *Since the moment index is too small, add weight, and for maximum increase in moment index with minimum weight penalty, as far aft as practical. Add 100 lbs in the baggage compartment and recompute weight and moment index:*

   | Item | Weight | Arm | Moment/100 |
   |------|--------|-----|-----------|
   | Original totals | 2,790 lbs | | 2,222.4 lbs-in |
   | Add weight | + 100 lbs | 140 | + 140.0 lbs-in |
   | New Totals | 2,890 lbs | | 2,362.4 lbs-in |

4. *Consult the Moment Limits vs. Weight Table. The allowed range of moments for 2,890 pounds is 2,354 to 2,452 lbs-in/100. The new moment is now within limits.*

*(PLT021, PA.I.F.S1) — FAA-H-8083-25*

**Answers**

3676   [A]            3677   [B]

# Using a Graph

## Problem:

Referring to FAA Figure 34, determine the maximum amount of baggage that may be loaded aboard the airplane for the CG to remain within the loading envelope.

| Item | Weight (lbs) | Moment/1,000 (lbs-in) |
|---|---|---|
| Empty weight | 1,350 | 51.5 |
| Pilot, front passenger | 250 | — |
| Rear passengers | 400 | — |
| Baggage | — | — |
| Fuel 30 gal. | — | — |
| Oil 8 qt. | — | — |

## Solution:

1. Determine the total weight. Using the information provided in the question, enter the items and the weights:

| Item | Weight (lbs) | Moment/1,000 (lbs-in) |
|---|---|---|
| Pilot, front passenger | 250 | |
| Rear passengers | 400 | |
| Fuel | 180 * | |
| Oil | 15 ** | |
| Baggage | — | |
| Empty weight | + 1,350 † | |
| | 2,195 lbs | |

*30 gal × 6 lbs/gal     **given in the note in the middle of FAA Figure 34     † given in problem

2. Determine the moments. Using FAA Figure 34, locate the moments for all the given weights:

| Item | Weight (lbs) | Moment/1,000 (lbs-in) |
|---|---|---|
| Pilot, front passenger | 250 | 9.3 |
| Rear passengers | 400 | 29.3 |
| Fuel | 180 | 8.7 |
| Oil | 15 | -0.2 * |
| Baggage | — | — |
| Empty weight | + 1,350 | 51.5 |
| | 2,195 lbs | 98.6 lbs-in |

*from note in center of FAA Figure 34

3. From the Center of Gravity Moment Envelope, at the bottom of FAA Figure 34, determine the maximum allowable gross weight of the aircraft, as indicated by the top of the "Normal Category" envelope (2,300 pounds). Comparing the total weight of this problem with the maximum allowable weight shows that 105 pounds of baggage could be carried:

$$\begin{array}{r} 2,300 \\ -\,2,195 \\ \hline 105 \end{array}$$

4. From the Loading Graph, determine the MOM/1000 of 105 pounds of baggage. Add that amount to the previous total MOM/1000:

| Item | Weight (lbs) | Moment/1,000 (lbs-in) |
|---|---|---|
| Totals | 2,195 | 98.6 |
| Baggage | + 105 | + 10.0 |
| New Totals | 2,300 lbs | 108.6 lbs-in |

5. Enter the Center of Gravity Moment Envelope Graph at the total Mom/1,000 (108.6) and the maximum allowable gross weight line at 2,300 pounds. The point of intersection falls within the "Normal Category" envelope and acceptable weight and balance conditions.

AIR
**3669.** (Refer to Figure 34.) What is the maximum amount of baggage that may be loaded aboard the airplane for the CG to remain within the moment envelope?

| | WEIGHT (LB) | MOM/1000 |
|---|---|---|
| Empty weight | 1,350 | 51.5 |
| Pilot and front passenger | 250 | — |
| Rear passengers | 400 | — |
| Baggage | — | — |
| Fuel, 30 gal | — | — |
| Oil, 8 qt | — | -0.2 |

A—105 pounds.
B—110 pounds.
C—120 pounds.

*Use the following steps:*

1. *Find total weight and moment index (except baggage) by using the loading graphs in FAA Figure 34. Note that the reduction factor is 1,000 in this problem. The standard weight for gasoline is 6 lbs/U.S. gallon, and for oil, 7.5 lbs/U.S. gallon.*

| Item | Weight | Moment/1,000 |
|---|---|---|
| Basic empty wt. | 1,350 lbs | 51.5 lbs-in |
| Pilot & pax (a) | 250 lbs | 9.3 lbs-in |
| Rear pax (b) | 400 lbs | 29.3 lbs-in |
| Fuel (30 × 6) (c) | 180 lbs | 8.7 lbs-in |
| Oil | 15 lbs | -0.2 lbs-in |
| Total | 2,195 lbs | 98.6 lbs-in |

2. *Calculate the maximum allowable weight for baggage:*

   *2,300 – 2,195 = 105 pounds*

3. *Add baggage and calculate the new totals for weight and moment index.*

| Weight | Moment/1,000 |
|---|---|
| 2,195 lbs | 98.6 lbs-in |
| + 105 lbs | 10.0 lbs-in |
| 2,300 lbs | 108.6 lbs-in |

4. *Plot the position of the point determined by 2,300 pounds and the moment of 108.6 lbs-in/1,000 on the center of gravity moment envelope graph. The point is in the normal category envelope.*

*(PLT092, PA.I.F.S1) — FAA-H-8083-25*

AIR
**3670.** (Refer to Figure 34.) Calculate the moment of the airplane and determine which category is applicable.

| | WEIGHT (LB) | MOM/1000 |
|---|---|---|
| Empty weight | 1,350 | 51.5 |
| Pilot and front passenger | 310 | — |
| Rear passengers | 96 | — |
| Fuel, 38 gal | — | — |
| Oil, 8 qt | — | -0.2 |

A—79.2, utility category.
B—80.8, utility category.
C—81.2, normal category.

*Use the following steps:*

1. *Find total weight and moment index by using the loading graph (FAA Figure 34). The standard weight for gasoline is 6 lbs/U.S. gallons and for oil, 7.5 lbs U.S. gallon.*

| Item | Weight | Moment/1,000 |
|---|---|---|
| Basic empty wt. | 1,350 lbs | 51.5 lbs-in |
| Pilot & pax (a) | 310 lbs | 11.5 lbs-in |
| Rear pax (b) | 96 lbs | 7.0 lbs-in |
| Fuel (38 × 6) (c) | 228 lbs | 11.0 lbs-in |
| Oil | 15 lbs | -0.2 lbs-in |
| Total | 1,999 lbs | 80.8 lbs-in |

2. *Plot the position of the point determined by 1,999 pounds and a moment of 80.8 lbs-in/1,000. The point is just inside the utility category envelope.*

*(PLT092, PA.I.F.S1) — FAA-H-8083-25*

*Answer (A) is incorrect because this answer choice doesn't have any significance. Answer (C) is incorrect because the oil moment needs to be subtracted.*

**Answers**

3669    [A]          3670    [B]

AIR
**3671.** (Refer to Figure 34.) What is the maximum amount of fuel that may be aboard the airplane on takeoff if loaded as follows?

|  | WEIGHT (LB) | MOM/1000 |
|---|---|---|
| Empty weight | 1,350 | 51.5 |
| Pilot and front passenger | 340 | — |
| Rear passengers | 310 | — |
| Baggage | 45 | — |
| Oil, 8 qt | — | — |

A—24 gallons.
B—32 gallons.
C—40 gallons.

1. Find the total weight and moment index (except fuel) by using the loading graph in FAA Figure 34.

| Item | Weight | Moment/1,000 |
|---|---|---|
| Basic empty wt. | 1,350 lbs | 51.5 lbs-in |
| Pilot & pax (a) | 340 lbs | 12.6 lbs-in |
| Rear pax (b) | 310 lbs | 22.6 lbs-in |
| Baggage (c) | 45 lbs | 4.2 lbs-in |
| Oil (d) | 15 lbs | -0.2 lbs-in |
| Total | 2,060 lbs | 90.7 lbs-in |

2. Calculate the additional fuel weight which can be added:

   2,300 – 2,060 = 240 lbs

3. Calculate the number of gallons of fuel at 6 lbs/gallon:

   240 ÷ 6 = 40 gallons

4. Calculate the added fuel moment index from the graph (40 gal fuel – 11.5 MOM/1,000).

5. Calculate the new total weight and moment index:

| Weight | Moment/1,000 |
|---|---|
| 2,060 lbs | 90.7 lbs-in |
| + 240 lbs | 11.5 lbs-in |
| 2,300 lbs | 102.2 lbs-in |

6. Plot the position of the point determined by 2,300 pounds and a moment index of 102.2 lbs-in/1,000. The point lies on the normal category envelope.

(PLT092, PA.I.F.S1) — FAA-H-8083-25

AIR
**3673.** (Refer to Figure 34.) Determine the aircraft loaded moment and the aircraft category.

|  | WEIGHT (LB) | MOM/1000 |
|---|---|---|
| Empty weight | 1,350 | 51.5 |
| Pilot and front passenger | 380 | — |
| Fuel, 48 gal | 288 | — |
| Oil, 8 qt | — | — |

A—78.2, normal category.
B—79.2, normal category.
C—80.4, utility category.

Use the following steps:

1. Find the total weight and moment index by using the loading graph from FAA Figure 34.

| Item | Weight | Moment/1,000 |
|---|---|---|
| Basic empty wt. | 1,350 lbs | 51.5 lbs-in |
| Pilot & pax (a) | 380 lbs | 14.0 lbs-in |
| Fuel (b) | 288 lbs | 13.8 lbs-in |
| Oil (c) | 15 lbs | -0.2 lbs-in |
| Total | 2,033 lbs | 79.1 lbs-in |

2. Plot the position of the point determined by 2,033 lbs. and a moment of 79.1 lbs-in/1,000. The point is within the normal category envelope.

(PLT092, PA.I.F.S1) — FAA-H-8083-25

AIR, WSC
**3672.** (Refer to Figure 34.) Determine the moment with the following data:

|  | WEIGHT (LB) | MOM/1000 |
|---|---|---|
| Empty weight | 1,350 | 51.5 |
| Pilot and front passenger | 340 | — |
| Fuel (std tanks) | Capacity | — |
| Oil, 8 qt | — | — |

A—69.9 pound-inches.
B—74.9 pound-inches.
C—77.6 pound-inches.

1. Find the total weight and moment index by using the loading graph from FAA Figure 34.

| Item | Weight | Moment/1,000 |
|---|---|---|
| Basic empty wt. | 1,350 lbs | 51.5 lbs-in |
| Pilot & pax (a) | 340 lbs | 12.6 lbs-in |
| Fuel (std. tanks) (b) | 228 lbs | 11.0 lbs-in |
| Oil (c) | 15 lbs | -0.2 lbs-in |
| Total | 1,933 lbs | 74.9 lbs-in |

(PLT003, PA.I.F.S1) — FAA-H-8083-25

**Answers**

3671  [C]          3673  [B]          3672  [B]

RTC
**3720.** (Refer to Figure 43.) What action, if any, should be taken for lateral balance if the helicopter is loaded as follows?

Gross weight ................................................. 1,800 lb
Pilot...................... 140 lb, 13.5 in. left of "0" MOM arm
Copilot ............... 180 lb, 13.5 in. right of "0" MOM arm

A—Add 10 pounds of weight to the pilot's side.
B—Decrease the gross weight 50 pounds.
C—No action is required.

*Use the following steps:*

1. *Compute the left and right moments using the formula:*

   *Weight × arm = moment*

   | *Item* | *Weight* | *Arm* | *Moment* |
   |--------|----------|-------|----------|
   | *Pilot* | *140 lbs* | *13.5* | *1,890 lbs-in (left)* |
   | *Copilot* | *180 lbs* | *13.5* | *2,430 lbs-in (right)* |

2. *Find the offset to the left or right:*

   $$\begin{array}{rl} 2,430.0 & \textit{lbs-in (right)} \\ -\ 1,890.0 & \textit{lbs-in (left)} \\ \hline 540.0 & \textit{lbs-in offset (right)} \end{array}$$

3. *Enter the bottom of the Lateral Offset Moment Graph at 540 lbs-in right of the zero point. Proceed upward until intercepting the 1,800-pound gross weight line. The point of intercept lies inside the envelope.*

*(PH.I.F.K3) — FAA-H-8083-21*

RTC
**3721.** (Refer to Figure 43.) What action should be taken for lateral balance if the helicopter is loaded as follows?

Gross weight ................................................. 1,800 lb
Pilot...................... 100 lb, 13.5 in. left of "0" MOM arm
Copilot ............... 200 lb, 13.5 in. right of "0" MOM arm

A—Add 50 pounds of weight to the pilot's side.
B—Decrease the gross weight 50 pounds.
C—No action is required.

*Use the following steps:*

1. *Compute the left and right moments using the formula:*

   *Weight × arm = moment*

   | *Item* | *Weight* | *Arm* | *Moment* |
   |--------|----------|-------|----------|
   | *Copilot* | *200 lbs* | *13.5* | *2,700 lbs-in (right)* |
   | *Pilot* | *100 lbs* | *13.5* | *1,350 lbs-in (left)* |

2. *Find the offset to the right or left:*

   $$\begin{array}{rl} 2,700.0 & \textit{lbs-in (right)} \\ -\ 1,350.0 & \textit{lbs-in (left)} \\ \hline 1,350.0 & \textit{lbs-in offset (right)} \end{array}$$

3. *Enter the bottom of the Lateral Offset Moment Envelope Graph of FAA Figure 43 at 1,350 right of the zero point. Proceed upward until intercepting the 1,800-pound gross weight line. The point of intercept falls outside the envelope to the right.*

4. *Try adding 50 pounds to the pilot's side and do the same computations:*

   *Copilot  200 × 13.5 = 2,700 (right)*
   *Pilot      150 × 13.5 = 2,025 (left)*

   $$\begin{array}{rl} 2,700 & \textit{(right)} \\ -\ 2,025 & \textit{(left)} \\ \hline 675 & \textit{(right)} \end{array}$$

*Plot the new values on the lateral offset envelope graph of FAA Figure 43.*

*(PH.I.F.K3) — FAA-H-8083-21*

---

**Answers**

3720   [C]                    3721   [A]

RTC
**3722.** (Refer to Figure 41.) Determine the weight and balance of the helicopter.

| | WEIGHT (LB) | ARM (IN) | MOMENT (LB-IN) |
|---|---|---|---|
| Empty weight | 1,495.0 | — | 151,593.0 |
| Pilot and one passenger | 350.0 | 64.0 | — |
| Fuel (40 gal usable) | — | 96.0 | — |

A—Over gross weight limit, but within CG limit.
B—Within gross weight limit and at the aft CG limit.
C—Over gross weight limit and exceeds the aft CG limit.

*Use the following steps:*

1. *Calculate the weight and moment using the information given in the problem and the formula:*

    *Weight × arm = moment*

    *Note: The standard weight of gasoline is 6 lbs/U.S. gallon.*

| Item | Weight | Arm | Moment |
|---|---|---|---|
| Empty weight | 1,495 lbs | | 151,593.0 lbs-in |
| Pilot & pax | 350 lbs | 64 | 22,400.0 lbs-in |
| Fuel 40 × 6 | 240 lbs | 96 | 23,040.0 lbs-in |
| Total | 2,085 lbs | | 197,033.0 lbs-in |

2. *Determine the position of the CG using the formula:*

$$CG = \frac{Total\ moment}{Total\ weight}$$

*or:*

$$CG = \frac{197,033}{2,085} = 94.5\ inches\ aft\ of\ datum$$

3. *Locate the point on FAA Figure 41 defined by a weight of 2,085 pounds and a CG of 94.5 inches, and find the aircraft within gross weight limit and at the aft CG limit.*

*(PH.I.F.K3) — FAA-H-8083-21*

RTC
**3723.** (Refer to Figure 42.) Determine if the helicopter's CG is within limits.

| | WEIGHT (LB) | MOMENT (lb-in) |
|---|---|---|
| Empty weight (including oil) | 1,025 | 102,705 |
| Pilot and passenger | 345 | — |
| Fuel, 35 gal | — | — |

A—Out of limits forward.
B—Within limits.
C—Out of limits aft.

*Use the following steps:*

1. *Calculate the weights and moments using the information from the problem and the Loading Chart of FAA Figure 42. Use the formula:*

    *Weight × arm = moment*

    *Note: The standard weight of gasoline is 6 lbs/U.S gallon.*

| Item | Weight | Arm | Moment |
|---|---|---|---|
| Empty weight | 1,025 lbs | | 102,705.0 lbs-in |
| Pilot & pax (a) | 345 lbs | 83.90 | 28,945.5 lbs-in |
| Fuel 35 × 6 (b) | 210 lbs | 107.0 | 22,470.0 lbs-in |
| Total | 1,580 lbs | | 154,120.5 lbs-in |

2. *Determine the position of the CG using the formula:*

$$CG = \frac{Total\ moment}{Total\ weight}$$

*or:*

$$CG = \frac{154,120.5}{1,580} = 97.54\ inches\ aft\ of\ datum$$

3. *Plot the point determined by a weight of 1,580 pounds and a moment of 154,120.5 lbs-in on the CG limit graph of FAA Figure 42. The point is within the forward and aft limits.*

*(PH.I.F.K3) — FAA-H-8083-21*

**Answers**

3722    [B]                3723    [B]

RTC

**3724.** (Refer to Figure 42.) What effect does adding a 185-pound passenger have on the CG, if prior to boarding the passenger, the helicopter weighed 1,380 pounds and the moment is 136,647.5 pound-inches?

A—The CG is moved forward 1.78 inches.
B—The CG is moved aft 1.78 inches.
C—The CG is moved forward 2.36 inches.

*Use the following steps:*

1. *Calculate the original position of the CG using the formula:*

$$CG = \frac{Total\ moment}{Total\ weight}$$

*or:*

$$CG = \frac{136,647.5}{1,380} = 99.02\ inches\ aft\ of\ datum$$

2. *Determine the revised weight and moment. The station for the passenger is 83.90 inches as shown on the Loading Chart of FAA Figure 42. Use the following formula:*

   *Weight × arm = moment*

| Item | Weight | Arm | Moment |
|------|--------|-----|--------|
| Original total | 1,380 lbs | | 136,647.5 lbs-in |
| Passenger | +185 lbs | 83.9 | 15,521.5 lbs-in |
| New Total | 1,565 lbs | | 152,169.0 lbs-in |

3. *Calculate the new CG:*

$$CG = \frac{152,169}{1,565} = 97.23\ inches\ aft\ of\ datum$$

4. *Compute the change in CG:*

   | | | |
   |---|---|---|
   | Original CG | 99.02 | inches aft of datum |
   | minus new CG | – 97.23 | inches aft of datum |
   | Movement | 1.79 | inches (forward) |

*(PH.I.F.K3) — FAA-H-8083-21*

RTC

**3725.** How is the CG of the helicopter affected after a fuel burn of 20 gallons?

Gross weight prior to fuel burn ...................... 2,050 lb
Moment .............................................. 195,365 lb-in
Fuel arm ............................................... 96.9 in

A—CG shifts forward 1.0 inch.
B—CG shifts forward 0.1 inch.
C—CG shifts aft 1.0 inch.

*Use the following steps:*

1. *Calculate the original position of the CG using the formula:*

$$CG = \frac{Total\ moment}{Total\ weight}$$

*or:*

$$CG = \frac{195,365}{2,050} = 95.3\ inches\ aft\ of\ datum$$

2. *Determine the revised weight and moment. The station for the fuel is 96.9 inches as shown on the question which contradicts FAA Figure 43. Use the following formula:*

   *Weight × arm = moment*

| Item | Weight | Arm | Moment |
|------|--------|-----|--------|
| Original total | 2,050 lbs | | 195,365 lbs-in |
| Fuel burn | – 120 lbs | 96.9 | 11,628 lbs-in |
| New Total | 1,930 lbs | | 183,737 lbs-in |

3. *Calculate the new CG:*

$$CG = \frac{183,737}{1,930} = 95.2\ inches\ aft\ of\ datum$$

4. *Compute the change in CG:*

   | | | |
   |---|---|---|
   | Original CG | 95.3 | inches aft of datum |
   | minus new CG | – 95.2 | inches aft of datum |
   | Movement | .1 | inch (forward) |

*(PH.I.F.K3) — FAA-H-8083-21*

**Answers**

3724   [A]          3725   [B]

RTC
**3726.** (Refer to Figure 42.) How is the CG of the helicopter affected when all of the auxiliary fuel is burned off?

Gross weight prior to fuel burn ...................... 1,660 lb
Moment ............................................... 159,898.5 lb-in

A—CG moves aft 0.12 inch.
B—CG moves forward 0.78 inch.
C—CG moves forward 1.07 inches.

*Use the following steps:*

1. *Calculate the original position of the CG using the formula:*

$$CG = \frac{Total\ moment}{Total\ weight}$$

   *or:*

$$CG = \frac{159,898.5}{1,660} = 96.32\ inches\ aft\ of\ datum$$

2. *Determine the revised weight and moment. The auxiliary fuel burn is 19 gallons (the dotted line goes from 44 to 25). 19 × 6 = 114 lbs. The station for the fuel is 107 inches as shown on the Loading Chart of FAA Figure 42. Use the following formula:*

   *Weight × arm = moment*

| Item | Weight | Arm | Moment |
|---|---|---|---|
| Original total | 1,660 lbs | | 159,898.5 lbs-in |
| Fuel burn | − 114 lbs | 107 | −12,198 lbs-in |
| New Total | 1,546 lbs | | 147,700.5 lbs-in |

3. *Calculate the new CG:*

   *147,700.5 ÷ 1,546 = 95.54 inches aft of datum*

4. *Compute the change in CG:*

| | | |
|---|---|---|
| Original CG | 96.32 | inches aft of datum |
| minus new CG | − 95.54 | inches aft of datum |
| Movement | .78 | inches (forward) |

*(PH.I.F.K3) — FAA-H-8083-21*

RTC
**3728.** (Refer to Figure 43.) Determine if the helicopter weight and balance is within limits.

| | WEIGHT (LB) | ARM (IN) | MOMENT (100) |
|---|---|---|---|
| Empty weight | 1,495.0 | 101.4 | 1,515.93 |
| Oil, 8 qt | — | 100.5 | — |
| Fuel, 40 gal | — | 96.0 | — |
| Pilot and copilot | 300.0 | 64.0 | — |

A—CG 95.2 inches, within limits.
B—CG 95.3 inches, weight and CG out of limits.
C—CG 95.4 inches, within limits.

*Use the following steps:*

1. *Calculate the weights and moment indexes using the information from the problem and the formula:*

   *Weight × arm ÷ reduction factor = moment/index*

   *Note: The standard weight for gasoline is 6 lbs/U.S. gallon and for oil, 7.5 lbs/U.S. gallon.*

| Item | Weight | Arm | Moment/100 |
|---|---|---|---|
| Empty weight | 1,495 lbs | 101.4 | 1,515.93 lbs-in |
| Oil, 8 qts (2 × 7.5) | 15 lbs | 100.5 | 15.08 lbs-in |
| Fuel (40 × 6) | 240 lbs | 96.0 | 230.40 lbs-in |
| Pilots | 300 lbs | 64.0 | 192 lbs-in |
| Total | 2,050 lbs | | 1,953.41 lbs-in |

2. *Determine the position of the CG using the formula:*

$$CG = \frac{Total\ moment\ index}{Total\ weight} \times reduction\ factor$$

   *or:*

$$\frac{1,953.41}{2,050} \times 100 = 95.29\ inches\ aft\ of\ datum$$

3. *Plot the point determined by a weight of 2,050 pounds and a CG of 95.29 inches on the longitudinal CG envelope of FAA Figure 43. The point is outside the allowable limits.*

*(PH.I.F.K3) — FAA-H-8083-21*

---

**Answers**

3726  [B]              3728  [B]

RTC

**3727.** (Refer to Figure 43.) Calculate the weight and balance of the helicopter, and determine if the CG is within limits.

| | WEIGHT (LB) | ARM (IN) | MOMENT (100) |
|---|---|---|---|
| Empty weight | 1,495.0 | 101.4 | 1,515.93 |
| Oil, 8 qt | — | 100.5 | — |
| Fuel, 40 gal | — | 96.0 | — |
| Pilot | 160.0 | 64.0 | — |

A—CG 90.48 inches, out of limits forward.
B—CG 95.32 inches, within limits.
C—CG 97.58 inches, within limits.

*This problem uses a reduction factor so we arrive at moment index instead of moment.*

*Use the following steps:*

1. *Calculate the weights and moment indexes using the information from the problem and the formula:*

    *Weight × arm ÷ reduction factor = moment/index*

    *Note: The standard weight for gasoline is 6 lbs/U.S. gallon and for oil, 7.5 lbs/U.S. gallon.*

| Item | Weight | Arm | Moment/100 |
|---|---|---|---|
| Empty weight | 1,495 lbs | 101.4 | 1,515.93 lbs-in |
| Oil, 8 qts (2 × 7.5) | 15 lbs | 100.5 | 15.08 lbs-in |
| Fuel (40 × 6) | 240 lbs | 96.0 | 230.40 lbs-in |
| Pilot | 160 lbs | 64.0 | 102.40 lbs-in |
| Total | 1,910 lbs | | 1,863.81 lbs-in |

2. *Determine the position of the CG using the formula:*

    $$CG = \frac{Total\ moment\ index}{Total\ weight} \times reduction\ factor$$

    *or:*

    $$\frac{1,863.81}{1,910} \times 100 = 97.58\ inches\ aft\ of\ datum$$

3. *Plot the point determined by a weight of 1,910 pounds and a CG of 97.58 inches on the longitudinal CG envelope of FAA Figure 43. The point is within the allowable limits.*

*(PH.I.F.K3) — FAA-H-8083-21*

RTC

**3729.** (Refer to Figures 44 and 45.) What is the new CG of the gyroplane after a 10-gallon fuel burn if the original weight was 1,450 pounds and the MOM/1000 was 108 pound-inches?

A—Out of limits forward.
B—Out of limits aft.
C—Within limits near the forward limit.

*Use the following steps:*

1. *Determine the change in load moment resulting from 10 gallons of fuel burned by entering the Loading Chart at the 10 gallon point on the fuel line, drawing a line downward and reading the moment for 10 gallons of fuel (5.3 × 1,000 lbs-in).*

2. *Calculate the new weight and moment:*

| Item | Weight | Moment/1,000 |
|---|---|---|
| Original total | 1,450.0 lbs | 108.0 lbs-in |
| Fuel (10 × 6) | – 60.0 lbs | – 5.3 lbs-in |
| New Total | 1,390.0 lbs | 102.7 lbs-in |

3. *Plot the point determined by 1,390 and 102.7 lbs-in/1,000 on the center of gravity moment envelope graph. The point is outside (to the left or forward) of the center of gravity moment envelope.*

*(PH.I.F.K3) — FAA-H-8083-21*

**Answers**

3727   [C]          3729   [A]

RTC
**3730.** (Refer to Figures 44 and 45.) What is the condition of the weight and balance of the gyroplane as loaded?

| | WEIGHT (LB) | MOMENT (1000) |
|---|---|---|
| Empty weight | 1,074 | 85.6 |
| Oil, 6 qt | — | 1.0 |
| Pilot and passenger | 247 | — |
| Fuel, 12 gal | — | — |
| Baggage | 95 | — |

A—Within limits.
B—Overweight.
C—Out of limits aft.

*Use the following steps:*

1. *Calculate the total weight and moments using the information in the problem and FAA Figure 45. The standard weight for oil is 7.5 lbs/U.S. gallon, and for gasoline it is 6 lbs/U.S. gallon.*

| *Item* | *Weight* | *Moment/1,000* |
|---|---|---|
| *Empty weight* | 1,074 *lbs* | 85.6 *lbs-in* |
| *Oil, 6 qts (1.5 × 7.5)* | 11.25 *lbs* | 1.0 *lbs-in* |
| *Pilot and pax (seat aft)* | 247 *lbs* | 14.1 *lbs-in* |
| *Fuel (12 × 6)* | 72 *lbs* | 6.3 *lbs-in* |
| *Baggage* | 95 *lbs* | 5.7 *lbs-in* |
| *Total* | 1,499 *lbs* | 112.7 *lbs-in* |

2. *Plot the point determined by 1,499 pounds and 112.7 × 1,000 lbs-in on FAA Figure 44. The point is within the envelope (Answer A).*

3. *Now, consider the effect of pilot and passenger in the forward position. The moment would now be 13.3 × 1,000 lbs-in and the resulting total moment would be reduced to 111.9 × 1,000 lbs-in. When plotted on the Center of Gravity Moment Envelope Graph SEAT FWD, the weight-moment is slightly outside the envelope. Note that the manufacturer uses an aft position in presenting sample weight and balance calculations for this aircraft.*

*(PH.I.F.K3) — FAA-H-8083-21*

RTC
**3731.** (Refer to Figures 44 and 45.) Approximately how much baggage, if any, may be carried in the gyroplane, without exceeding weight and balance limits?

| | WEIGHT (LB) | MOMENT (1000) |
|---|---|---|
| Empty weight | 1,074 | 85.6 |
| Oil, 6 qt | — | 1.0 |
| Fuel, Full | — | — |
| Pilot (FWD) | 224 | — |

A—None, overweight.
B—70 pounds.
C—100 pounds.

*Use the following steps:*

1. *Calculate the total weight and moment using the information in the problem and the Loading Chart. The standard weight for oil is 7.5 pounds per gallon and for gasoline is 6.0 pounds per gallon.*

| *Item* | *Weight* | *Moment/1,000* |
|---|---|---|
| *Empty weight* | 1,074 *lbs* | 85.6 *lbs-in* |
| *Oil, 6 qts. (1.5 × 7.5)* | 11.25 *lbs* | 1.0 *lbs-in* |
| *Pilot (a)* | 224 *lbs* | 12.1 *lbs-in* |
| *Fuel (full) (b)* | 119 *lbs* | 10.2 *lbs-in* |
| *Totals* | 1,428 *lbs* | 108.9 *lbs-in* |

2. *Consider adding enough baggage to approach the maximum takeoff weight 1,500 pounds.*

   *1,500 − 1,428 = 72 or about 70 pounds*
   *(Answer B)*
   *(This remains within the weight limit.)*

3. *Determine the moment of the 70 pounds of added baggage (4.2 × 1,000 lbs-in).*

4. *Compute the new weight and moment.*

| *Item* | *Weight* | *Moment* |
|---|---|---|
| *Original Total* | 1,428 | 108.9 |
| *Baggage* | + 70 | + 4.2 |
| *New Total* | 1,498 | 113.1 |

5. *Plot the point determined by 1,498 lbs and 113.1 × 1,000 lbs-in on the Center of Gravity Moment Envelope Graph of FAA Figure 44. The point is within the envelope.*

*(PH.I.F.K3) — FAA-H-8083-21*

**Answers**

3730 [A]        3731 [B]

GLI
**3861.** (Refer to Figure 53.) Calculate the weight and balance of the glider, and determine if the CG is within limits.

Pilot (fwd seat) .................................................. 160 lb
Passenger (aft seat) ......................................... 185 lb

A—CG 71.65 inches aft of datum–out of limits forward.
B—CG 79.67 inches aft of datum—within limits.
C—CG 83.43 inches aft of datum—within limits.

*Use the following steps:*

1. *Calculate the total weight and moment using the information in the question and in FAA Figure 53, and the formula:*

    *Weight × arm = moment*

    | Item | Weight | Arm | Moment |
    |------|--------|-----|--------|
    | Empty weight | 610 | 96.47 | 58,846.7 lbs-in |
    | Pilot (fwd seat) | 160 | 43.80 | 7,008.0 lbs-in |
    | Passenger (aft seat) | 185 | 74.70 | 13,819.5 lbs-in |
    | Totals | 955 | | 79,674.2 lbs-in |

2. *Calculate the position of the CG using the formula:*

    $$CG = \frac{Total\ moment}{Total\ weight}$$

    *or:*

    $$CG = \frac{79,674.2}{955} = 83.43\ inches\ aft\ of\ datum$$

3. *Compare the calculated value to the allowed range for the position of the CG, 78.20 to 86.10. The calculated position is within the allowed range of both maximum weight and CG.*

*(PLT021) — FAA-H-8083-13*

GLI
**3862.** (Refer to Figure 53.) How is the CG affected if radio and oxygen equipment weighing 35 pounds is added at station 43.8? The glider weighs 945 pounds with a moment of 78,000.2 pound-inches prior to adding the equipment.

A—CG shifts forward 0.79 inch—out of limits forward.
B—CG shifts forward 1.38 inches—within limits.
C—CG shifts aft 1.38 inches—out of limits aft.

*Use the following steps:*

1. *Calculate the weight and moment of the equipment to be added using the formula:*

    *Weight × arm = moment*

    | Item | Weight | Arm | Moment |
    |------|--------|-----|--------|
    | Added equip. | 35 lbs | 43.8 | 1,533.0 lbs-in |

2. *Calculate the new total weight and moment.*

    | Item | Weight | Moment |
    |------|--------|--------|
    | Old | 945 | 78,000.2 lbs-in |
    | Added | 35 | 1,533.0 lbs-in |
    | New Total | 980 | 79,533.2 lbs-in |

3. *Calculate the old and new positions of the center of gravity using the formula:*

    $$CG = \frac{Total\ moment}{Total\ weight}$$

    *Original CG =*
    $$\frac{78,000.2}{945} = 82.54\ inches\ aft\ of\ datum$$

    *New CG =* $\frac{79,533.2}{980} = 81.16\ inches\ aft\ of\ datum$

4. *Compute change and direction of change of the CG.*

    Original CG    82.54
    New CG        − 81.16
    _____
                  1.38 *inches closer to datum (forward)*

5. *Compare the calculated values of weight and CG position to the allowed range shown in FAA Figure 53. The allowed CG range is 78.20 to 86.10 and the calculated value is within these limits.*

*(PLT256) — FAA-H-8083-13*

**Answers**
3861    [C]            3862    [B]

**GLI**

**3863.** (Refer to Figure 53.) What is the CG of the glider if the pilot and passenger each weigh 215 pounds?

A—74.69 inches aft of datum—out of limits forward.
B—81.08 inches aft of datum—within limits.
C—81.08 inches aft of datum—over maximum gross weight.

*Use the following steps:*

1.  *Calculate the total weight and moment using the information in the question and in FAA Figure 53, and the formula:*

    *Weight × arm = moment*

    | Item | Weight | Arm | Moment |
    |---|---|---|---|
    | Empty weight | 610 | 96.47 | 58,846.7 lbs-in |
    | Pilot (fwd seat) | 215 | 43.80 | 9,417.0 lbs-in |
    | Passenger (aft seat) | 215 | 74.70 | 16,060.5 lbs-in |
    | Totals | 1,040 | | 84,324.2 lbs-in |

2.  *Calculate the position of the CG using the formula:*

    $$CG = \frac{Total\ moment}{Total\ weight}$$

    *or:*

    $$CG = \frac{84,324.2}{1,040} = 81.08\ inches\ aft\ of\ datum$$

3.  *Compare the calculated value to the allowed range for the position of the CG, 78.20 to 86.10. The calculated position is within the allowed range of both maximum weight and CG.*

*(PLT021) — FAA-H-8083-13*

**LTA, LSL**

**3887.** What constitutes the payload of a balloon?

A—Total gross weight.
B—Total weight of passengers, cargo, and fuel.
C—Weight of the aircraft and equipment.

*Payload is the total weight of passengers, cargo, and fuel an aircraft can legally carry on a given flight, excluding weight of the aircraft and equipment. (PLT177) — FAA-H-8083-11*

**LTA**

**3888.** (Refer to Figure 56.) The gross weight of the balloon is 1,350 pounds and the outside air temperature (OAT) is +51°F. The maximum height would be

A—5,000 feet.
B—8,000 feet.
C—10,000 feet.

*Use the following steps:*

1.  *Locate the gross weight, 1,350 pounds, on the bottom of the graph in FAA Figure 56.*

2.  *From that point, draw a line upward through the graph.*

3.  *Locate the OAT +51°F on the left side of the graph.*

4.  *From that point, draw a line to the right through the graph.*

5.  *Note the point of intersection of the two lines, which in this case falls on the 10,000-foot curve.*

*(PLT057) — FAA-H-8083-11*

**LTA**

**3889.** (Refer to Figure 56.) The gross weight of the balloon is 1,200 pounds and the maximum height the pilot needs to attain is 5,000 feet. The maximum temperature to achieve this performance is

A—+37°F.
B—+70°F.
C—+97°F.

*Use the following steps:*

1.  *Locate the gross weight, 1,200 pounds, on the bottom of the graph in FAA Figure 56.*

2.  *From that point, draw a line upward to the 5,000-foot pressure altitude line.*

3.  *From there, draw a line to the left to the air temperature scale and read the maximum temperature, 100°F.*

*(PLT057) — FAA-H-8083-11*

**LTA**

**3890.** (Refer to Figure 57.) Determine the maximum payload for a balloon flying at 2,500 feet at an ambient temperature of 91°F.

A—420 pounds.
B—465 pounds.
C—505 pounds.

*Payload is the total weight of passengers, cargo and fuel an aircraft can legally carry on a given flight, excluding weight of the aircraft and equipment. Using FAA Figure 57, perform the following steps:*

1.  *Enter the chart at an ambient temperature of 91°F. From that point, proceed upward to the 2,500-foot pressure altitude point (halfway between sea level and 5,000 feet).*

---

**Answers**

| 3863 [B] | 3887 [B] | 3888 [C] | 3889 [C] | 3890 [C] |
|---|---|---|---|---|

2. From the point of intersection, proceed to the left to determine the gross weight for 2,500 feet (840 pounds).

3. Note that the empty weight is 335 pounds. Compute the payload using the formula:

> Payload = gross weight – empty weight
> Payload = 840 lbs – 335 lbs
> Payload = 505 lbs

(PLT057) — FAA-H-8083-11

LTA
**3893.** (Refer to Figure 57.) Determine the maximum weight allowable for pilot and passenger for a flight at approximately 1,000 feet with a temperature of 68°F. Launch with 20 gallons of propane.

A—580 pounds.
B—620 pounds.
C—720 pounds.

Use FAA Figure 57, and the following steps:

(The standard weight of propane is 4.23 pounds per gallon.)

1. Enter the chart at the 68°F ambient temperature value. Move upward to a point about 1/5 of the distance between the sea level and 5,000-foot pressure altitude curves.

2. From that point, draw a line to the left and read the gross weight as 1,040 pounds.

3. Calculate the weight of 20 gallons of propane:

> 20 × 4.23 = 85 pounds

4. Compute the available lift:

| Item | Weight |
|---|---|
| Gross weight | 1,040 lbs |
| Empty weight | -335 lbs |
| Fuel weight | -85 lbs |
| Pilot and passengers | 620 lbs |

(PLT057) — FAA-H-8083-11

LTA
**3894.** (Refer to Figure 57.) What is the maximum weight allowed for pilot and passengers for a flight at 5,000 feet with a standard temperature? Launch with 20 gallons of propane.

A—670 pounds.
B—760 pounds.
C—1,095 pounds.

Use FAA Figure 57, and the following steps:

(The standard weight of propane is 4.23 pounds per gallon.)

1. Enter the chart where 5,000 feet and the standard temperature line intersect.

2. From that point, draw a line to the left and read the gross weight as 1,090 pounds.

3. Calculate the weight of 20 gallons of propane:

> 20 × 4.23 = 85 pounds

4. Compute the available lift:

| Item | Weight |
|---|---|
| Gross weight | 1,090 lbs |
| Empty weight | -335 lbs |
| Fuel weight | -85 lbs |
| Pilot and passengers | 670 lbs |

(PLT057) — FAA-H-8083-11

SPO
**2174.** Problems caused by overloading an aircraft include

A—reduced climb rate, excessive structural loads, and shortened cruising range.
B—increased service ceiling, increased angle of climb, and increased cruising speed.
C—slower takeoff speed, increased maneuverability, and shorter takeoff roll.

Some of the problems caused by overloading an aircraft are:

• The aircraft will need a higher takeoff speed, which results in a longer takeoff run.

• Both the rate and angle of climb will be reduced.

• The service ceiling will be lowered.

• The cruising speed will be reduced.

• The cruising range will be shortened.

• Maneuverability will be decreased.

• A longer landing roll will be required because the landing speed will be higher.

• Excessive loads will be imposed on the structure, especially the landing gear.

(PLT313) — FAA-H-8083-1

**Answers**

3893   [B]          3894   [A]          2174   [A]

**SPO**

**2182.** Most aircraft are so designed that if all seats are occupied, all baggage allowed by the baggage compartment structure is carried, and all the fuel tanks are full, the aircraft will be

A—grossly overloaded.
B—under maximum gross weight.
C—at maximum gross weight.

*The maximum allowable gross weight for an aircraft is determined by design considerations. However, the maximum operational weight may be less than the maximum allowable due to such considerations as high density altitude or high-drag field conditions caused by wet grass or water on the runway. The maximum gross weight may also be limited by the departure or arrival airport's runway length. One important preflight consideration is the distribution of the load in the aircraft. Loading an aircraft so the gross weight is less than the maximum allowable is not enough. This weight must be distributed to keep the CG within the limits specified in the POH or AFM. (PLT313) — FAA-H-8083-1*

**SPO**

**2183.** When operating an aircraft, the pilot-in-command is responsible for using

A—the most current weight and balance data.
B—weight and balance data from the factory.
C—recent weight and balance data.

*It is the responsibility of the PIC to use the most current weight and balance data when planning a flight and operating the aircraft. (PLT328) — FAA-H-8083-1*

**LSA, LSR**

**2350.** (Refer to Figures 44 and 45.) GIVEN:

| | Weight | Moment |
|---|---|---|
| Gyroplane basic weight | 1,150 | 92 |
| Pilot (seat forward) | 155 | ? |
| Passenger (seat forward) | 125 | ? |
| Fuel, 15 gallons | ? | ? |

The CG is located

A—outside the CG envelope; the maximum gross weight is exceeded.
B—outside the CG envelope; the maximum gross weight and the gross weight moment are exceeded.
C—within the CG envelope; neither maximum gross weight nor gross weight moment is exceeded.

*Total the weights and moments to determine if the CG is within limits.*

| Item | Weight | Moment |
|---|---|---|
| Gyroplane basic weight | 1,150 | 92 |
| Pilot (seat forward) | 155 | 8.4 |
| Passenger (seat forward) | 125 | 6.8 |
| Fuel, 15 gallons | + 100 | + 8.8 |
| Total | 1,530 | 116 |

*Weight exceeds the maximum gross weight by 30 pounds and the gross-weight moment is forward of limits. (PLT021) — FAA-H-8083-1*

**LSA, LSR**

**2351.** (Refer to Figures 44 and 45.) GIVEN:

| | Weight | Moment |
|---|---|---|
| Gyroplane basic weight | 1,150 | 92 |
| Pilot (seat forward) | 160 | ? |
| Passenger (seat forward) | 110 | ? |
| Fuel, 10 gallons | ? | ? |

The CG is located

A—outside the CG envelope; the maximum gross weight is exceeded.
B—outside the CG envelope; the maximum gross weight and the gross weight moment are exceeded.
C—within the CG envelope; neither maximum gross weight nor gross weight moment is exceeded.

*Total the weights and moments to determine if the CG is within limits.*

| Item | Weight | Moment |
|---|---|---|
| Gyroplane basic weight | 1,150 | 92 |
| Pilot (seat forward) | 160 | 8.6 |
| Passenger (seat forward) | 110 | 6 |
| Fuel, 10 gallons | + 70 | + 6 |
| Total | 1,490 | 112.6 |

*Both gross weight and moment are within limits. (PLT021) — FAA-H-8083-1*

---

**Answers**

| | | | |
|---|---|---|---|
| 2182 [A] | 2183 [A] | 2350 [B] | 2351 [C] |

# Chapter 5
# Regulations

# Introduction

Although FAR is used as the acronym for Federal Aviation Regulations, and found throughout the regulations themselves and hundreds of other publications, the FAA is now actively discouraging its use. FAR also means Federal Acquisition Regulations. To eliminate any possible confusion, the FAA cites the federal aviation regulations with reference to Title 14 of the Code of Federal Regulations. For example, "FAR Part 91.3" is referenced as "14 CFR Part 91 Section 3."

While **Federal Aviation Regulations** are many and varied, some are of particular interest to all pilots.

**14 CFR Part 1** contains definitions and abbreviations of many terms commonly used in aviation. For example, the term "night" means "the time between the end of evening civil twilight and the beginning of morning civil twilight, as published in the American Air Almanac, converted to local time" and is used for logging night time.

**14 CFR Part 61**, entitled "Certification: Pilots, Flight Instructors, and Ground Instructors," prescribes the requirements for issuing pilot and flight instructor certificates and ratings, the conditions of issue, and the privileges and limitations of those certificates and ratings.

**14 CFR Part 91**, entitled "General Operating and Flight Rules," describes rules governing the operation of aircraft (with certain exceptions) within the United States.

The **National Transportation Safety Board (NTSB)** has established rules and requirements for notification and reporting of aircraft accidents and incidents. These are contained in **NTSB Part 830**.

ALL, SPO
**3005.** The definition of nighttime is

A—sunset to sunrise.
B—1 hour after sunset to 1 hour before sunrise.
C—the time between the end of evening civil twilight and the beginning of morning civil twilight.

*Night is the time between the end of evening civil twilight and the beginning of morning civil twilight converted to local time, as published in the American Air Almanac. (PLT395, PA.XI.A.K3, PH.IX.A.K3) — 14 CFR §1.1*

Answer (A) is incorrect because it refers to the time when lighted position lights are required. Answer (B) is incorrect because it refers to the currency requirement to carry passengers.

# Pilot Certificate Privileges and Limitations

The types of pilot certificates and the attendant privileges are contained in 14 CFR Part 61 and are briefly stated as follows:

- The holder of a student pilot certificate is limited to solo flights or flights with an instructor.

- Recreational pilots may not carry more than one passenger, pay less than the pro rata share of the operating expenses of a flight with a passenger (provided the expenses involve only fuel, oil, airport expenses, or aircraft rental fees), fly an aircraft with more than four seats or high-performance characteristics, demonstrate an aircraft to a prospective buyer, fly between sunset and sunrise, or fly in airspace in which communication with air traffic control is required. Recreational pilots may fly beyond 50 NM from the departure airport with additional training and endorsements from an authorized instructor.

- A sport pilot may act as pilot-in-command of a light-sport aircraft, carry up to one passenger, during daylight hours, outside Class A, B, C, or D airspace (unless the sport pilot obtains further training and an endorsement), when visibilities are greater than 3 SM. Additional requirements are defined in 14 CFR §61.315

- A private pilot has unlimited solo privileges, and may carry passengers or cargo as long as the flying is for the pilots' pleasure or personal business and is not done for hire. A private pilot may fly in conjunction with his/her job as long as that flying is incidental to his/her employment.

- A private pilot may not pay less than the pro rata share of the operating expenses of a flight with passengers, provided the expenses involve only fuel, oil, airport expenditures, or rental fees. The only time passengers may pay for the entire flight is if a donation is made by the passengers to the charitable organization which is sponsoring the flight.

- Commercial pilots may fly for compensation or hire.

- An airline transport pilot may act as PIC of airline and scheduled commuter operations.

- All pilot certificates are valid indefinitely unless surrendered, superseded, or revoked.

ALL
**3064.** In regard to privileges and limitations, a private pilot may

A—not pay less than the pro rata share of the operating expenses of a flight with passengers provided the expenses involve only fuel, oil, airport expenditures, or rental fees.

B—act as pilot-in-command of an aircraft carrying a passenger for compensation if the flight is in connection with a business or employment.

C—not be paid in any manner for the operating expenses of a flight.

*A private pilot may not pay less than the pro rata share of the operating expenses of a flight with passengers, provided the expenses involve only fuel, oil, airport expenditures, or rental fees. (PLT448, PA.I.A.K2, PH.I.A.K2) — 14 CFR §61.113*

ALL
**3065.** According to regulations pertaining to privileges and limitations, a private pilot may

A—be paid for the operating expenses of a flight if at least three takeoffs and three landings were made by the pilot within the preceding 90 days.

B—not be paid in any manner for the operating expenses of a flight.

C—not pay less than the pro rata share of the operating expenses of a flight with passengers provided the expenses involve only fuel, oil, airport expenditures, or rental fees.

*A private pilot may not pay less than the pro rata share of the operating expenses of a flight with passengers, provided the expenses involve only fuel, oil, airport expenditures, or rental fees. (PLT448, PA.I.A.K2, PH.I.A.K2) — 14 CFR §61.113*

ALL
**3066.** What exception, if any, permits a private pilot to act as pilot-in-command of an aircraft carrying passengers who pay for the flight?

A—If the passengers pay all the operating expenses.

B—If a donation is made to a charitable organization for the flight.

C—There is no exception.

*A private pilot may act as PIC of an aircraft used in a passenger-carrying airlift sponsored by a charitable organization, and for which the passengers make a donation to the organization. This can be done if the sponsor of the airlift notifies the FSDO having jurisdiction over the area concerned, at least 7 days before the flight, and furnishes any essential information that the office requests. (PLT448, PA.I.A.K2, PH.I.A.K2) — 14 CFR §61.113*

ALL
**3067.** (Refer to Figure 74.) What minimum pilot certificate is required for a flight departing out of Hayward Executive (area 6)?

A—Student Pilot Certificate.

B—Private Pilot Certificate.

C—Sport Pilot Certificate.

*Hayward Executive is located in Class D airspace up to but not including 1,500 feet MSL as depicted by the blue segmented line surrounding it. No specific pilot certification is required for flight within Class D airspace. A student pilot may operate within Class D airspace with appropriate solo endorsements. (PLT448, PA.I.A.K2, PH.I.A.K2) — AIM ¶3-2-5*

Answer (B) and (C) are incorrect because no minimum pilot certificate is specified for operations in Class D airspace.

---

**Answers**

3064   [A]          3065   [C]          3066   [B]          3067   [A]

REC

**3044.** According to regulations pertaining to privileges and limitations, a recreational pilot may

A—be paid for the operating expenses of a flight.
B—not pay less than the pro rata share of the operating expenses of a flight with a passenger.
C—not be paid in any manner for the operating expenses of a flight.

*A recreational pilot may not pay less than the pro rata share of the operating expenses of a flight with a passenger, provided the expenses involve only fuel, oil, airport expenditures, or rental fees. (PLT448) — 14 CFR §61.101*

REC

**3045.** In regard to privileges and limitations, a recreational pilot may

A—fly for compensation or hire within 50 nautical miles from the departure airport with a logbook endorsement.
B—not be paid in any manner for the operating expenses of a flight from a passenger.
C—not pay less than the pro rata share of the operating expenses of a flight with a passenger.

*A recreational pilot may not pay less than the pro rata share of the operating expenses of a flight with a passenger, provided the expenses involve only fuel, oil, airport expenditures, or rental fees. (PLT448) — 14 CFR §61.101*

REC

**3046.** When may a recreational pilot act as pilot-in-command on a cross-country flight that exceeds 50 nautical miles from the departure airport?

A—After receiving ground and flight instructions on cross-country training and a logbook endorsement.
B—12 calendar months after receiving his or her recreational pilot certificate and a logbook endorsement.
C—After attaining 100 hours of pilot-in-command time and a logbook endorsement.

*A person who holds a recreational pilot certificate may act as PIC of an aircraft on a flight that exceeds 50 NM from the departure airport, provided that person has received ground and flight training from an authorized instructor, been found proficient in cross-country flying, and received an endorsement, which is carried in the person's possession in the aircraft. (PLT448) — 14 CFR §61.101*

REC

**3047.** A recreational pilot may act as pilot-in-command of an aircraft that is certificated for a maximum of how many occupants?

A—Two.
B—Three.
C—Four.

*A recreational pilot may not act as PIC of an aircraft that is certificated for more than four occupants. (PLT448) — 14 CFR §61.101*

REC

**3048.** A recreational pilot may act as pilot-in-command of an aircraft with a maximum engine horsepower of

A—160.
B—180.
C—200.

*A recreational pilot may not act as PIC of an aircraft that is certificated with a powerplant of more than 180 horsepower. (PLT448) — 14 CFR §61.101*

REC

**3049.** What exception, if any, permits a recreational pilot to act as pilot-in-command of an aircraft carrying a passenger for hire?

A—If the passenger pays no more than the operating expenses.
B—If a donation is made to a charitable organization for the flight.
C—There is no exception.

*A recreational pilot may not act as PIC of an aircraft that is carrying a passenger or property for compensation or hire, in furtherance of a business, or for a charitable organization. (PLT448) — 14 CFR §61.101*

Answer (A) is incorrect because the passenger may only pay an equal share of the operating expenses. Answer (B) is incorrect because a recreational pilot may not carry passengers for hire, even if the flight is a donation to a charitable organization.

**Answers**

| 3044 | [B] | 3045 | [C] | 3046 | [A] | 3047 | [C] | 3048 | [B] | 3049 | [C] |

REC

**3050.** May a recreational pilot act as pilot-in-command of an aircraft in furtherance of a business?

A—Yes, if the flight is only incidental to that business.
B—Yes, providing the aircraft does not carry a person or property for compensation or hire.
C—No, it is not allowed.

*A recreational pilot may not act as PIC of an aircraft in furtherance of a business. (PLT448) — 14 CFR §61.101*

REC

**3051.** With respect to daylight hours, what is the earliest time a recreational pilot may take off?

A—One hour before sunrise.
B—At sunrise.
C—At the beginning of morning civil twilight.

*A recreational pilot may not act as PIC of an aircraft between sunset and sunrise. The earliest a recreational pilot may takeoff is at sunrise. (PLT467) — 14 CFR §61.101*

REC

**3052.** If sunset is 2021 and the end of evening civil twilight is 2043, when must a recreational pilot terminate the flight?

A—2021.
B—2043.
C—2121.

*A recreational pilot may not act as PIC of an aircraft between sunset and sunrise. A recreational pilot must land by sunset. (PLT448) — 14 CFR §61.101*

SPO

**2130.** If sunset is 2021 and the end of evening civil twilight is 2043, when must a sport pilot terminate the flight?

A—2021.
B—2043.
C—2121.

*A sport pilot may not act as PIC of an aircraft at night. A sport pilot must land by the end of evening twilight. (PLT448) — 14 CFR §61.315*

REC

**3052-1.** When may a recreational pilot act as pilot-in-command of an aircraft at night?

A—When obtaining an additional certificate or rating under the supervision of an authorized instructor, provided the surface or flight visibility is at least 1 statute mile.
B—When obtaining an additional certificate or rating under the supervision of an authorized instructor, provided the surface or flight visibility is at least 3 statute miles.
C—When obtaining an additional certificate or rating under the supervision of an authorized instructor, provided the surface or flight visibility is at least 5 statute miles.

*For the purpose of obtaining additional certificates or ratings while under the supervision of an authorized instructor, a recreational pilot may fly as the sole occupant of an aircraft between sunset and sunrise, provided the flight or surface visibility is at least 5 SM. (PLT448) — 14 CFR §61.101*

REC

**3053.** When may a recreational pilot operate to or from an airport that lies within Class C airspace?

A—Anytime the control tower is in operation.
B—When the ceiling is at least 1,000 feet and the surface visibility is at least 2 miles.
C—After receiving training and a logbook endorsement from an authorized instructor.

*A recreational pilot may not operate in airspace where air traffic control is required until they receive and log ground and flight training and an endorsement from an authorized instructor. (PLT161) — 14 CFR §61.101*

REC

**3054.** Under what conditions may a recreational pilot operate at an airport that lies within Class D airspace and that has a part-time control tower in operation?

A—Between sunrise and sunset when the tower is in operation, the ceiling is at least 2,500 feet, and the visibility is at least 3 miles.
B—Any time when the tower is in operation, the ceiling is at least 3,000 feet, and the visibility is more than 1 mile.
C—Between sunrise and sunset when the tower is closed, the ceiling is at least 1,000 feet, and the visibility is at least 3 miles.

**Answers**

| | | | | | | | | | | |
|---|---|---|---|---|---|---|---|---|---|---|
| 3050 | [C] | | 3051 | [B] | | 3052 | [A] | | 2130 | [B] |
| 3054 | [C] | | | | | | | | | |

(with 3052-1 [C] and 3053 [C])

*A recreational pilot may not act as PIC of an aircraft in airspace in which communication with ATC is required. If the tower is closed, no communication is required and it reverts to Class E airspace. The visibility and cloud clearances for Class E airspace require a ceiling at least 1,000 feet and the visibility at least 3 miles. (PLT161) — 14 CFR §61.101*

*Answers (A) and (B) are incorrect because a recreational pilot may not operate in airspace that requires communication with ATC.*

REC
**3055.** When may a recreational pilot fly above 10,000 feet MSL?

A—When 2,000 feet AGL or below.
B—When 2,500 feet AGL or below.
C—When outside of controlled airspace.

*A recreational pilot may not act as PIC of an aircraft at an altitude of more than 10,000 feet MSL or 2,000 feet AGL, whichever is higher. (PLT448) — 14 CFR §61.101*

REC
**3056.** During daytime, what is the minimum flight or surface visibility required for recreational pilots in Class G airspace below 10,000 feet MSL?

A—1 mile.
B—3 miles.
C—5 miles.

*A recreational pilot may not act as PIC of an aircraft when the flight or surface visibility is less than 3 statute miles. (PLT163) — 14 CFR §61.101*

REC
**3057.** During daytime, what is the minimum flight visibility required for recreational pilots in controlled airspace below 10,000 feet MSL?

A—1 mile.
B—3 miles.
C—5 miles.

*A recreational pilot may not act as PIC of an aircraft when the flight or surface visibility is less than 3 statute miles. (PLT163) — 14 CFR §61.101*

REC
**3058.** Under what conditions, if any, may a recreational pilot demonstrate an aircraft in flight to a prospective buyer?

A—The buyer pays all the operating expenses.
B—The flight is not outside the United States.
C—None.

*A recreational pilot may not act as PIC of an aircraft to demonstrate that aircraft in flight to a prospective buyer. (PLT448) — 14 CFR §61.101*

REC
**3059.** When, if ever, may a recreational pilot act as pilot-in-command in an aircraft towing a banner?

A—If the pilot has logged 100 hours of flight time in powered aircraft.
B—If the pilot has an endorsement in his/her pilot logbook from an authorized flight instructor.
C—It is not allowed.

*A recreational pilot may not act as PIC of an aircraft that is towing any object. (PLT401) — 14 CFR §61.101*

REC
**3043.** How many passengers is a recreational pilot allowed to carry on board?

A—One.
B—Two.
C—Three.

*A recreational pilot may not carry more than one passenger. (PLT448) — 14 CFR §61.101*

SPO
**2123.** How many passengers is a sport pilot allowed to carry on board?

A—One.
B—Two.
C—Three.

*Sport Pilots may not act as PIC of a light-sport aircraft while carrying more than one passenger. (PLT448) — 14 CFR §61.315*

---

**Answers**

| | | | | | | | | | |
|---|---|---|---|---|---|---|---|---|---|
| 3055 | [A] | 3056 | [B] | 3057 | [B] | 3058 | [C] | 3059 | [C] | 3043 | [A] |
| 2123 | [A] | | | | | | | | |

REC

**3060.** When must a recreational pilot have a pilot-in-command flight check?

A—Every 400 hours.
B—Every 180 days.
C—If the pilot has less than 400 total flight hours and has not flown as pilot-in-command in an aircraft within the preceding 180 days.

*A recreational pilot who has logged fewer than 400 flight hours and who has not logged PIC time in an aircraft within the preceding 180 days may not act as PIC of an aircraft until flight instruction is received from an authorized flight instructor who certifies in the pilot's logbook that the pilot is competent to act as PIC of the aircraft. This requirement can be met in combination with the requirements of flight reviews, at the discretion of the instructor. (PLT448) — 14 CFR §61.101*

REC

**3061.** A recreational pilot may fly as sole occupant of an aircraft at night while under the supervision of a flight instructor provided the flight or surface visibility is at least

A—3 miles.
B—4 miles.
C—5 miles.

*For the purpose of obtaining additional certificates or ratings, while under the supervision of an authorized flight instructor, a recreational pilot may fly as sole occupant of an aircraft between sunset and sunrise, provided the flight or surface visibility is at least 5 SM. (PLT448) — 14 CFR §61.101*

REC

**3134.** What minimum visibility and clearance from clouds are required for a recreational pilot in Class G airspace at 1,200 feet AGL or below during daylight hours?

A—1 mile visibility and clear of clouds.
B—3 miles visibility and clear of clouds.
C—3 miles visibility, 500 feet below the clouds.

*Minimum flight or surface visibility for recreational pilots is 3 miles and minimum cloud clearance for all pilots in Class G airspace, below 1,200 AGL, is clear of clouds. (PLT163) — 14 CFR §61.101*

Answer (A) is incorrect because this would be for private pilots. Answer (C) is incorrect because this is for controlled airspace.

REC

**3135.** Outside controlled airspace, the minimum flight visibility requirement for a recreational pilot flying VFR above 1,200 feet AGL and below 10,000 feet MSL during daylight hours is

A—1 mile.
B—3 miles.
C—5 miles.

*Minimum flight or surface visibility for recreational pilots is 3 miles. (PLT163) — 14 CFR §61.101*

SPO

**2061.** Outside controlled airspace, the minimum flight visibility requirement for a sport pilot flying above 1,200 feet AGL and below 10,000 feet MSL during daylight hours is

A—1 statute mile.
B—3 statute miles.
C—5 statute miles.

*Minimum flight or surface visibility for sport pilots is 3 SM in all airspace at all times. (PLT467) — 14 CFR §61.315*

SPO

**2061-1.** The minimum flight visibility requirement for a sport pilot is

A—1 statute mile.
B—3 statute miles.
C—5 statute miles.

*Minimum flight or surface visibility for sport pilots is 3 SM. (PLT163) — 14 CFR §61.315*

**Answers**

| 3060 [C] | 3061 [C] | 3134 [B] | 3135 [B] | 2061 [B] | 2061-1 [B] |

# Pilot Ratings

When a pilot certificate is issued, it lists the category, class, and type (if appropriate) of aircraft in which the certificate holder is qualified. See Figure 5-1.

The term **category** means a broad classification of aircraft, such as airplane, rotorcraft, glider, and lighter-than-air. The term **class** means a classification within a category having similar operating characteristics, such as single-engine, multiengine, land, water, helicopter, and balloon. The term **type** means a specific make and basic model of aircraft, such as Cessna 172 or Gulfstream IV.

A type rating must be held by the pilot-in-command of a large aircraft. "Large aircraft" means aircraft of more than 12,500 pounds maximum certificated takeoff weight.

All turbojet-powered airplanes, regardless of weight, require the PIC to have a type rating.

In addition to the category, class, and type ratings, if a pilot wishes to fly IFR, an instrument rating is required.

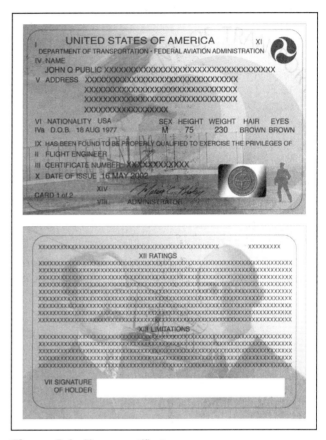

**Figure 5-1.** Airman certificate

ALL, SPO

**3001.** With respect to the certification of airmen, which are categories of aircraft?

A—Gyroplane, helicopter, airship, free balloon.
B—Airplane, rotorcraft, glider, lighter-than-air.
C—Single-engine land and sea, multiengine land and sea.

*With respect to the certification of airmen, category means a broad classification of aircraft such as airplane, rotorcraft, glider, lighter-than-air, weight-shift control, and powered parachute. (PLT371, PA.I.B.K1, PH.I.A.K1) — 14 CFR §1.1*

Answer (A) is incorrect because it refers to classes of rotorcraft and lighter-than-air craft. Answer (C) is incorrect because it refers to classes of airplanes.

ALL

**3002.** With respect to the certification of airmen, which are classes of aircraft?

A—Airplane, rotorcraft, glider, lighter-than-air.
B—Single-engine land and sea, multiengine land and sea.
C—Lighter-than-air, airship, hot air balloon, gas balloon.

*With respect to the certification of airmen, a class refers to aircraft with similar operating characteristics such as single-engine land/sea and multiengine land/sea, gyroplane, helicopter, airship, and free balloon. (PLT371, PA.I.B.K1, PH.I.A.K1) — 14 CFR §1.1*

Answer (A) is incorrect because it refers to categories of aircraft. Answer (C) is incorrect because it refers to lighter-than-air category. Airship and free balloon are lighter-than-air class ratings, but hot air balloon and gas balloon are not.

**Answers**

3001　[B]　　　3002　[B]

AIR, RTC
**3024.** The pilot-in-command is required to hold a type rating in which aircraft?

A—Aircraft operated under an authorization issued by the Administrator.
B—Aircraft having a gross weight of more than 12,500 pounds.
C—Aircraft involved in ferry flights, training flights, or test flights.

*A type rating is required in order for a pilot to act as PIC of a large aircraft (except lighter-than-air) which is further defined as more than 12,500 pounds maximum certificated takeoff weight or a turbojet-powered aircraft. (PLT451, PA.I.A.K1, PH.I.A.K1) — 14 CFR §61.31*

*Answers (A) and (C) are incorrect because they don't address the weight or type of propulsion.*

# Medical Certificates and BasicMed

Student pilot, recreational pilot, and private pilot operations (other than glider and balloon) require a Third Class Medical Certificate, or, if operating without a medical certificate, compliance with Part 68, referred to as BasicMed.

BasicMed privileges apply to persons exercising student, recreational, and private pilot privileges when acting as pilot-in-command and to persons exercising flight instructor privileges when acting as pilot-in-command. BasicMed privileges cannot be used to fly as a safety pilot, except when that pilot is acting as PIC. Pilots operating under BasicMed must hold a current and valid U.S. driver's license and comply with all medical requirements or restrictions associated with that license. Applicants operating under BasicMed regulations must also complete the comprehensive medical examination checklist (CMEC) in collaboration with a physical examination by a state-licensed physician. The physical must be completed within the last 48 months and the CMEC completed within the last 24 months. When operating under BasicMed, pilots are limited to:

1. Fly with no more than five passengers.

2. Fly an aircraft with a maximum certificated takeoff weight of no more than 6,000 pounds.

3. Fly an aircraft that is authorized to carry no more than six occupants.

4. Flights within the United States, at an indicated airspeed of 250 knots or less, and at an altitude at or below 18,000 feet MSL.

5. Prohibited from flying for compensation or hire.

If operating beyond these limitations, pilots must obtain an FAA Medical Certificate. A Third Class Medical Certificate expires at the end of:

1. The 60th month after the month of the date of the examination shown on the certificate if the person has not reached his or her 40th birthday on or before the date of examination; or

2. The 24th month after the month of the date of examination shown on the certificate if the person has reached his or her 40th birthday on or before the date of the examination.

The holder of a Second Class Medical Certificate may exercise commercial pilot privileges during the first 12 calendar months, but the certificate is valid only for private pilot privileges during the following (12 or 48) calendar months, depending on the applicant's age.

**Answers**

3024    [B]

The holder of a First Class Medical Certificate may exercise airline transport pilot privileges during the first 6 or 12 calendar months, commercial privileges during the following 6 or 0 calendar months, and private pilot privileges during the following 12 or 48 calendar months, depending on the applicant's age. To state another way, a medical certificate may last 6 months to a year with first-class privileges, 12 months (from the date of the examination) with second-class privileges, and 2 or 5 years with third-class privileges—depending on whether the applicant is above or below 40 years of age.

Each type of medical certificate is valid through the last day of the month (of the month it expires), regardless of the day the physical examination was given.

ALL
**3039.** A Third Class Medical Certificate was issued to a 19-year-old pilot on August 10, this year. To exercise the privileges of a Recreational or Private Pilot Certificate, the medical certificate will expire at midnight on

A—August 10, 2 years later.
B—August 31, 5 years later.
C—August 31, 2 years later.

*A Third Class Medical Certificate expires at the end of the last day of the 60th month after the month of the date of the examination shown on the certificate if the person has not reached his or her 40th birthday on or before the date of examination, for operations requiring a Recreational or Private Pilot Certificate. (PLT447, PA.I.A.K3, PH.I.A.K3) — 14 CFR §61.23*

ALL
**3020.** A Third Class Medical Certificate is issued to a 36-year-old pilot on August 10, this year. To exercise the privileges of a Private Pilot Certificate, the medical certificate will be valid until midnight on

A—August 10, 3 years later.
B—August 31, 5 years later.
C—August 31, 3 years later.

*A Third Class Medical Certificate expires at the end of the last day of the 60th month after the month of the date of the examination shown on the certificate if the person has not reached his or her 40th birthday on or before the date of examination, for operations requiring a Recreational or Private Pilot Certificate. (PLT447, PA.I.A.K3, PH.I.A.K3) — 14 CFR §61.23*

ALL
**3021.** A Third Class Medical Certificate is issued to a 51-year-old pilot on May 3, this year. To exercise the privileges of a Private Pilot Certificate, the medical certificate will be valid until midnight on

A—May 3, 1 year later.
B—May 31, 1 year later.
C—May 31, 2 years later.

*A Third Class Medical Certificate expires at the end of the last day of the 24th month after the month of the date of the examination shown on the certificate if the person has reached his or her 40th birthday on or before the date of examination, for operations requiring a Private Pilot Certificate. (PLT447, PA.I.A.K3, PH.I.A.K3) — 14 CFR §61.23*

ALL
**3022.** For private pilot operations, a Second Class Medical Certificate issued to a 42-year-old pilot on July 15, this year, will expire at midnight on

A—July 15, 2 years later.
B—July 31, 1 year later.
C—July 31, 2 years later.

*A Second Class Medical Certificate expires at the end of the last day of the 24th month after the month of the date of the examination shown on the certificate if the person has reached his or her 40th birthday on or before the date of examination, for operations requiring a Private Pilot Certificate. (PLT447, PA.I.A.K3, PH.I.A.K3) — 14 CFR §61.23*

**Answers**

3039 [B]         3020 [B]         3021 [C]         3022 [C]

ALL

**3023.** For private pilot operations, a First Class Medical Certificate issued to a 23-year-old pilot on October 21, this year, will expire at midnight on

A—October 21, 2 years later.
B—October 31, next year.
C—October 31, 5 years later.

*A First Class Medical Certificate expires at the end of the last day of the 60th month after the month of the date of the examination shown on the certificate if the person has not reached his or her 40th birthday on or before the date of examination, for operations requiring a Recreational or Private Pilot Certificate. (PLT447, PA.I.A.K3, PH.I.A.K3) — 14 CFR §61.23*

ALL

**3023-1.** To operate under BasicMed the pilot-in-command must have completed a physical examination by a state-licensed physician within the preceding

A—48 months.
B—24 months.
C—12 months.

*BasicMed regulations require you to complete the CMEC every 24 months while a physical examination by a state-licensed physician must be completed every 48 months. (PLT427, PA.I.A.K5, PH.I.A.K5) — AC 68-1*

ALL

**3023-2.** For private pilot operations under BasicMed, the pilot-in-command is allowed to fly with no more than

A—six passengers.
B—five passengers.
C—five occupants.

*As PIC during private pilot operations under BasicMed, the aircraft is restricted to fly with no more than five passengers and authorized to carry no more than six total occupants. (PLT427, PA.I.A.K5, PH.I.A.K5) — AC 68-1*

Answer (A) is incorrect because six passengers plus the PIC would equal seven total occupants. Answer (C) is incorrect because BasicMed allows for aircraft authorized to carry no more than six total occupants.

ALL

**3023-3.** To maintain BasicMed privileges you are required to complete the comprehensive medical examination checklist (CMEC) every

A—48 months.
B—24 months.
C—12 months.

*BasicMed regulations require you to complete a medical education course every 24 months and a medical examination checklist and physical examination with a state-licensed physician every 48 months. (PLT427, PA.I.A.K5, PH.I.A.K5) — AC 68-1*

GLI

**3062.** Prior to becoming certified as a private pilot with a glider rating, the pilot must have in his or her possession what type of medical certificate?

A—A statement from a designated medical examiner.
B—A Third Class Medical Certificate.
C—A medical certificate is not required.

*A person is not required to hold a medical certificate when exercising the privileges of a pilot certificate with a glider category rating. (PLT447) — 14 CFR §61.23*

LTA

**3063.** Prior to becoming certified as a private pilot with a balloon rating, the pilot must have in his or her possession what class of medical certificate?

A—A Third Class Medical Certificate.
B—A medical certificate is not required.
C—A statement from a designated medical examiner.

*A person is not required to hold a medical certificate when exercising the privileges of a pilot certificate with a balloon class rating. (PLT427) — 14 CFR §61.23*

**Answers**

| 3023 [C] | 3023-1 [A] | 3023-2 [B] | 3023-3 [A] | 3062 [C] | 3063 [B] |
|----------|------------|------------|------------|----------|----------|

# Required Certificates

When acting as pilot-in-command, a pilot must have a current pilot license, a photo ID, and a current medical certificate in their physical possession or readily accessible in the aircraft. Glider and balloon pilots do not need a medical certificate. A recreational pilot acting as PIC must have a current logbook endorsement in their personal possession within flights 50 NM from the departure airport.

A pilot must present their pilot license and medical certificate for inspection upon request of any FAA, NTSB, or federal, state, or local law enforcement officer.

ALL

**3016.** What document(s) must be in your personal possession or readily accessible in the aircraft while operating as pilot-in-command of an aircraft?

A—Certificates showing accomplishment of a checkout in the aircraft and a current flight review.

B—A pilot certificate with an endorsement showing accomplishment of an annual flight review and a pilot logbook showing recency of experience.

C—An appropriate pilot certificate and an appropriate current medical certificate if required.

*No person may act as PIC, or in any other capacity as a required pilot flight crewmember, of a civil aircraft of U.S. registry unless they have in possession or readily accessible in the aircraft a current pilot certificate and photo ID. Except for free balloon pilots piloting balloons and glider pilots piloting gliders, no person may act as PIC or in any other capacity as a required pilot flight crewmember of an aircraft unless they have in possession or readily accessible in the aircraft an appropriate current medical certificate or other documentation acceptable to the FAA. (PLT399, PA.I.A.K4, PH.I.A.K4) — 14 CFR §61.3*

*Answers (A) and (B) are incorrect because aircraft checkouts don't need to be recorded, and a flight review record and currency proof don't need to be in your possession.*

ALL

**3017.** When must a current pilot certificate be in the pilot's personal possession or readily accessible in the aircraft?

A—When acting as a crew chief during launch and recovery.

B—Only when passengers are carried.

C—Anytime when acting as pilot-in-command or as a required crewmember.

*No person may act as PIC, or in any other capacity as a required pilot flight crewmember, of a civil aircraft of U.S. registry unless they have in possession or readily accessible in the aircraft a current pilot certificate and a photo ID. (PLT399, PA.I.A.K4, PH.I.A.K4) — 14 CFR §61.3*

*Answers (A) and (B) are incorrect because a crew chief does not require a pilot certificate, and pilots must have certificates, regardless of whether carrying passengers or not.*

ALL

**3018.** A recreational or private pilot acting as pilot-in-command, or in any other capacity as a required pilot flight crewmember, must have in their personal possession or readily accessible in the aircraft a current

A—logbook endorsement to show that a flight review has been satisfactorily accomplished.

B—medical certificate if required and an appropriate pilot certificate.

C—endorsement on the pilot certificate to show that a flight review has been satisfactorily accomplished.

*No person may act as PIC, or in any other capacity as a required pilot flight crewmember, of a civil aircraft of U.S. registry unless they have in possession or readily accessible in the aircraft a current pilot certificate and a photo ID. Except for free balloon pilots piloting balloons and glider pilots piloting gliders, no person may act as PIC or in any other capacity as a required pilot flight crewmember of an aircraft unless they have in possession or readily accessible in the aircraft an appropriate current medical certificate or other documentation acceptable to the FAA. (PLT399, PA.I.A.K4, PH.I.A.K4) — 14 CFR §61.3*

*Answers (A) and (C) are incorrect because proof of a flight review does not need to be in your possession while acting as PIC.*

**Answers**

3016    [C]          3017    [C] *          3018    [B]

ALL
**3019.** Each person who holds a pilot certificate or a medical certificate shall present it for inspection upon the request of any

A—authorized representative of the Department of Transportation.
B—person in a position of authority.
C—local law enforcement officer.

*Each person who holds a pilot or medical certificate shall present it for inspection upon the request of the FAA Administrator, an NTSB representative, or any federal, state, or local law enforcement officer. (PLT399, PA.I.A.K4, PH.I.A.K4) — 14 CFR §61.3*

SPO
**2129.** Each person who holds a pilot certificate, a U.S. driver's license, or a medical certificate shall present it for inspection upon the request of the Administrator, the National Transportation Safety Board, or any

A—authorized representative of the Department of Transportation.
B—authorized representative of the Department of State.
C—federal, state, or local law enforcement officer.

*Each person who holds a pilot or medical certificate shall present it for inspection upon the request of the FAA Administrator, an NTSB representative, or any federal, state, or local law enforcement officer. (PLT399) — 14 CFR §61.3*

REC
**3038.** A recreational pilot acting as pilot-in-command must have in his or her personal possession while aboard the aircraft

A—a current logbook endorsement to show that a flight review has been satisfactorily accomplished.
B—a current logbook endorsement that permits flights within 50 NM from the departure airport.
C—the pilot logbook to show recent experience requirements to serve as pilot-in-command have been met.

*A recreational pilot may act as PIC on a flight within 50 NM from the departure airport, provided they receive from an authorized instructor a logbook endorsement, which is carried in the person's possession in the aircraft. (PLT448) — 14 CFR §61.101*

# Recent Flight Experience

No person may act as pilot-in-command of an aircraft unless within the preceding 24 calendar months they have accomplished a **flight review**. This review is given in an aircraft for which the pilot is rated by an appropriately rated instructor or other person designated by the FAA. A logbook entry will document satisfactory accomplishment of this requirement. If the pilot takes a proficiency check (as for a certificate or a new rating), it counts for the flight review.

No person may act as PIC of an aircraft carrying passengers unless, within the preceding 90 days, they have made three takeoffs and three landings as the sole manipulator of the controls in an aircraft of the same category, class, and, if a type rating is required, in the same type. Touch and go landings are acceptable unless the passengers are to be carried in a tailwheel airplane, in which case the landing must be to a full stop, and they must be in a tailwheel airplane.

If passengers are to be carried during the period from 1 hour after sunset to 1 hour before sunrise, the PIC must have made, within the preceding 90 days, at least three takeoffs and three landings during that period. The landings must have been to a full stop and in the same category and class of aircraft to be used.

**Answers**

3019  [C]       2129  [C]       3038  [B]

ALL
**3028.** To act as pilot-in-command of an aircraft carrying passengers, a pilot must show by logbook endorsement the satisfactory completion of a flight review or completion of a pilot proficiency check within the preceding

A—6 calendar months.
B—12 calendar months.
C—24 calendar months.

*Each pilot must complete a flight review every 24 calendar months. (PLT449, PA.I.A.K1, PH.I.A.K1) — 14 CFR §61.56*

ALL
**3029.** If recency of experience requirements for night flight are not met and official sunset is 1830, the latest time passengers may be carried is

A—1829.
B—1859.
C—1929.

*No person may act as PIC of an aircraft carrying passengers during the period beginning one hour after sunset and ending one hour before sunrise (as published in the American Air Almanac) unless, within the preceding 90 days, they have made at least three takeoffs and three landings to a full stop during that period in the category and class of aircraft to be used.*

*1830 + 59 minutes = 1929*

*(PLT442, PA.I.A.K1, PH.I.A.K1) — 14 CFR §61.57*

ALL
**3030.** To act as pilot-in-command of an aircraft carrying passengers, the pilot must have made at least three takeoffs and three landings in an aircraft of the same category, class, and if a type rating is required, of the same type, within the preceding

A—90 days.
B—12 calendar months.
C—24 calendar months.

*No person may act as PIC of an aircraft carrying passengers, unless, within the preceding 90 days, they have made three takeoffs and three landings as the sole manipulator of the flight controls in an aircraft of the same category and class and, if a type rating is required, of the same type. If the aircraft is a tailwheel airplane, the landings must have been made to a full stop. (PLT411, PA.I.A.K1, PH.I.A.K1) — 14 CFR §61.57*

ALL
**3030-1.** Your cousin wants you to take him flying. You must have made at least three takeoffs and three landings in your aircraft within the preceding

A—90 days.
B—60 days.
C—30 days.

*No person may act as PIC of an aircraft carrying passengers, unless, within the preceding 90 days, they have made three takeoffs and three landings as the sole manipulator of the flight controls in an aircraft of the same category and class and, if a type rating is required, of the same type. If the aircraft is a tailwheel airplane, the landings must have been made to a full stop. (PLT411, PA.I.A.K1, PH.I.A.K1) – 14 CFR §61.57*

ALL
**3031.** To act as pilot-in-command of an aircraft carrying passengers, the pilot must have made three takeoffs and three landings within the preceding 90 days in an aircraft of the same

A—make and model.
B—category and class, but not type.
C—category, class, and type, if a type rating is required.

*No person may act as PIC of an aircraft carrying passengers, unless, within the preceding 90 days, they have made three takeoffs and three landings as the sole manipulator of the flight controls in an aircraft of the same category and class and, if a type rating is required, of the same type. If the aircraft is a tailwheel airplane, the landings must have been made to a full stop. (PLT442, PA.I.A.K1, PH.I.A.K1) — 14 CFR §61.57*

ALL
**3034.** To meet the recency of experience requirements to act as pilot-in-command carrying passengers at night, a pilot must have made at least three takeoffs and three landings to a full stop within the preceding 90 days in

A—the same category and class of aircraft to be used.
B—the same type of aircraft to be used.
C—any aircraft.

*No person may act as PIC of an aircraft carrying passengers during the period beginning one hour after sunset and ending one hour before sunrise (as published in the American Air Almanac) unless, within the preceding 90 days, they have made at least three takeoffs and three landings to a full stop during that period in the category and class of aircraft to be used. (PLT442, PA.I.A.K1, PH.I.A.K1) — 14 CFR §61.57*

**Answers**

| | | | | | |
|---|---|---|---|---|---|
| 3028 [C] | 3029 [C] | 3030 [A] | 3030-1 [A] | 3031 [C] | 3034 [A] |

ALL

**3040.** If a recreational or private pilot had a flight review on August 8, this year, when is the next flight review required?

A—August 8, 2 years later.
B—August 31, next year.
C—August 31, 2 years later.

*Each pilot must have completed a biennial flight review since the beginning of the 24th calendar month before the month in which that pilot acts as PIC. A calendar month always ends at midnight of the last day of the month. If a pilot had a flight review on August 8, the next flight review would be due on August 31, two years later. (PLT442, PA.I.A.K1, PH.I.A.K1) — 14 CFR §61.56*

ALL

**3041.** Each recreational or private pilot is required to have

A—a biennial flight review.
B—an annual flight review.
C—a semiannual flight review.

*Each pilot must have completed a biennial flight review since the beginning of the 24th calendar month before the month in which that pilot acts as PIC. (PLT442, PA.I.A.K1, PH.I.A.K1) — 14 CFR §61.56*

AIR

**3032.** The takeoffs and landings required to meet the recency of experience requirements for carrying passengers in a tailwheel airplane

A—may be touch and go or full stop.
B—must be touch and go.
C—must be to a full stop.

*No person may act as PIC of an aircraft carrying passengers, unless, within the preceding 90 days, they have made three takeoffs and three landings as the sole manipulator of the flight controls in an aircraft of the same category and class and, if a type rating is required, of the same type. If the aircraft is a tailwheel airplane, the landings must have been made to a full stop. (PLT442, PA.I.A.K1) — 14 CFR §61.57*

AIR, RTC, WSC, PPC

**3033.** The three takeoffs and landings that are required to act as pilot-in-command at night must be done during the time period from

A—sunset to sunrise.
B—1 hour after sunset to 1 hour before sunrise.
C—the end of evening civil twilight to the beginning of morning civil twilight.

*No person may act as PIC of an aircraft carrying passengers during the period beginning one hour after sunset and ending one hour before sunrise (as published in the American Air Almanac) unless, within the preceding 90 days, they have made at least three takeoffs and three landings to a full stop during that period in the category and class of aircraft to be used. (PLT442, PA.I.A.K1, PH.I.A.K1) — 14 CFR §61.57*

Answer (A) is incorrect because this is the requirement for position lights. Answer (C) is incorrect because it refers to the time which may be logged as night flight.

# High-Performance Airplanes

No person holding a Private or Commercial Pilot Certificate may act as pilot-in-command of an airplane that has more than 200 horsepower unless they have received instruction from an authorized flight instructor who has certified in the pilot's log book that they are competent to pilot a high-performance airplane.

**Answers**

| 3040 | [C] | 3041 | [A] | 3032 | [C] | 3033 | [B] |

AIR
**3025.** What is the definition of a high-performance airplane?

A—An airplane with an engine of more than 200 horsepower.
B—An airplane with 180 horsepower, or retractable landing gear, flaps, and a fixed-pitch propeller.
C—An airplane with a normal cruise speed in excess of 200 knots.

*A high-performance airplane is one with an engine of more than 200 horsepower. (PLT395, PA.I.B.K1) — 14 CFR §61.31*

AIR
**3026.** Before a person holding a Private Pilot Certificate may act as pilot-in-command of a high-performance airplane, that person must have

A—passed a flight test in that airplane from an FAA inspector.
B—an endorsement in that person's logbook that he or she is competent to act as pilot-in-command.
C—received ground and flight instruction from an authorized flight instructor who then endorses that person's logbook.

*No person holding a Private or Commercial Pilot Certificate may pilot a high-performance aircraft unless they have received instruction and has been certified competent in their logbook. (PLT448, PA.I.A.K1) — 14 CFR §61.31*

Answer (A) is incorrect because a flight test is not required. Answer (B) is incorrect because instruction is required.

AIR
**3027.** In order to act as pilot-in-command of a high-performance airplane, a pilot must have

A—made and logged three solo takeoffs and landings in a high-performance airplane.
B—passed a flight test in a high-performance airplane.
C—received and logged ground and flight instruction in an airplane that has more than 200 horsepower.

*A high-performance airplane is one with more than 200 horsepower. No person holding a Private or Commercial Pilot Certificate may pilot a high-performance aircraft unless they have received ground and flight instruction and has been certified proficient in their logbook. (PLT448, PA.I.A.K1) — 14 CFR §61.31*

Answer (A) is incorrect because landings are only required in order to carry passengers, and they don't need to be solo. Answer (B) is incorrect because a flight test is not required.

# Glider Towing

A private pilot may not act as PIC of an aircraft towing a glider unless they have logged at least 100 hours of pilot flight time in the aircraft category, class, and type (if required), or 200 hours total pilot time. Within the preceding 24 months, the pilot must have made at least three actual or simulated glider tows while accompanied by a qualified pilot, or made three flights as PIC of a towed glider.

AIR, GLI, WSC
**3036.** A certificated private pilot may not act as pilot-in-command of an aircraft towing a glider unless there is entered in the pilot's logbook a minimum of

A—100 hours of pilot flight time in any aircraft, that the pilot is using to tow a glider.
B—100 hours of pilot-in-command time in the aircraft category, class, and type, if required, that the pilot is using to tow a glider.
C—200 hours of pilot-in-command time in the aircraft category, class, and type, if required, that the pilot is using to tow a glider.

*With a Private Pilot Certificate, no person may act as PIC of an aircraft towing a glider unless they have had, and entered in their logbook, at least:*

1. *100 hours of PIC time in the aircraft category, class, and type (if required), or*

2. *200 hours of PIC time in powered or other aircraft.*

*(PLT407, PA.I.A.K1) — 14 CFR §61.69*

Answer (A) is incorrect because the 100 hours must be as PIC and in the proper category, class, and type, if required. Answer (C) is incorrect because the 200 hours of flight time can be in a combination of powered and other-than-powered aircraft.

**Answers**

3025   [A]          3026   [C]          3027   [C]          3036   [B]

AIR, GLI, WSC

**3037.** To act as pilot-in-command of an aircraft towing a glider, a pilot is required to have made within the preceding 24 months.

A—at least three flights as observer in a glider being towed by an aircraft.
B—at least three flights in a powered glider.
C—at least three actual or simulated glider tows while accompanied by a qualified pilot.

*No person may act as a PIC of an aircraft towing a glider unless within the preceding 24 months they have:*

1. *Made at least three actual or simulated glider tows while accompanied by a qualified pilot who meets the requirements of 14 CFR §61.69; or*

2. *Made at least three flights as PIC of a glider towed by an aircraft.*

*(PLT407, PA.I.A.K1) — 14 CFR §61.69*

GLI, LSG

**3067-1.** (Refer to Figure 73.) These glider hand signals are examples of

A—aerotow visual signals.
B—aerotow prelaunch signals.
C—aerotow emergency signals.

*The glider hand signals displayed in the figure represent a few of the aerotow prelaunch signals used between pilots and launch crew members to facilitate a glider launch. (PLT407) – FAA-H-8083-13*

Answer (A) is incorrect because aerotow visual signals are displayed inflight by the use of aircraft movements. Answer (C) is incorrect because the figure does not depict an emergency signal used in glider operations.

# Change of Address

If a pilot changes their permanent mailing address without notifying the FAA Airmen's Certification Branch in writing within 30 days, they may not exercise the privileges of their certificate.

ALL, SPO

**3035.** If a certificated pilot changes permanent mailing address and fails to notify the FAA Airmen Certification Branch of the new address, the pilot is entitled to exercise the privileges of the pilot certificate for a period of only

A—30 days after the date of the move.
B—60 days after the date of the move.
C—90 days after the date of the move.

*The holder of a Pilot or Flight Instructor Certificate who has made a change in their permanent mailing address may not, after 30 days from the date moved, exercise the privileges of their certificate unless they have notified the FAA in writing. (PLT387, PA.I.A.K1, PH.I.A.K1) — 14 CFR §61.60*

# Pilot-in-Command Responsibility

The pilot-in-command of an aircraft is directly responsible, and is the final authority, for the safety and operation of that aircraft. Should an emergency require immediate action, the PIC may deviate from Part 91 to the extent necessary in the interest of safety. Upon request, a written report of any deviation from the rules must be sent to the Administrator.

If a pilot receives a clearance that would cause a deviation from a rule, they should query the controller and request that the clearance be amended.

---

**Answers**

3037   [C]          3067-1 [B]          3035   [A]

ALL
**3070.** The final authority as to the operation of an aircraft is the

A—Federal Aviation Administration.
B—pilot-in-command.
C—aircraft manufacturer.

*The PIC of an aircraft is directly responsible for and is the final authority as to the operation of that aircraft. (PLT444, PA.I.A.K2, PH.I.A.K1) — 14 CFR §91.3*

ALL, SPO
**3072.** If an in-flight emergency requires immediate action, the pilot-in-command may

A—deviate from any rule of 14 CFR Part 91 to the extent required to meet the emergency, but must submit a written report to the Administrator within 24 hours.
B—deviate from any rule of 14 CFR Part 91 to the extent required to meet that emergency.
C—not deviate from any rule of 14 CFR Part 91 unless prior to the deviation approval is granted by the Administrator.

*If an emergency requires immediate action, the PIC may deviate from the operating rules of Part 91 to the extent necessary to meet that emergency. No report of such deviation is required unless the FAA requests one. (PLT444, PA.I.A.K2, PH.I.A.K1) — 14 CFR §91.3*

ALL, SPO
**3073.** When must a pilot who deviates from a regulation during an emergency send a written report of that deviation to the Administrator?

A—Within 7 days.
B—Within 10 days.
C—Upon request.

*Each PIC who deviates from a rule in an emergency shall, upon request, send a written report of that deviation to the Administrator. (PLT440, PA.I.A.K2, PH.I.A.K1) — 14 CFR §91.3*

ALL, SPO
**3074.** Who is responsible for determining if an aircraft is in condition for safe flight?

A—A certificated aircraft mechanic.
B—The pilot-in-command.
C—The owner or operator.

*The PIC of an aircraft is responsible for determining whether that aircraft is in condition for safe flight. The pilot shall discontinue the flight when unairworthy mechanical, electrical, or structural conditions occur. (PLT444, PA.I.B.K1, PH.I.A.K1) — 14 CFR §91.7*

LTA
**3071.** Pre-takeoff briefing of passengers for a flight is the responsibility of

A—all passengers.
B—the pilot.
C—a crewmember.

*The PIC is responsible for briefing crewmembers and occupants in all areas of the flight, including inflation, tether, infight, landing, emergency, and recovery procedures. (PLT444) — 14 CFR §91.3*

LSL
**2308.** The person directly responsible for the pre-launch briefing of passengers for a flight is the

A—safety officer.
B—pilot-in-command.
C—ground crewmember.

*The PIC is responsible for briefing crewmembers and occupants in all areas of the flight, including inflation, tether, inflight, landing, emergency, and recovery procedures. (PLT444) — 14 CFR §91.3*

**Answers**

| | | | | | |
|---|---|---|---|---|---|
| 3070 [B] | 3072 [B] | 3073 [C] | 3074 [B] | 3071 [B] | 2308 [B] |

# Preflight Action

Before beginning a flight, the pilot-in-command is required to become familiar with all available information concerning that flight. This information must include the following:

1. Runway lengths; and

2. Takeoff and landing information for airports of intended use, including aircraft performance data.

If the flight will not be in the vicinity of the departure airport, the pilot must also consider the following:

1. Weather reports and forecasts;

2. Fuel requirements (enough fuel to fly to the first point of intended landing, and at normal cruising speed, to fly after that for at least 30 minutes if during the day, or for at least 45 minutes at night when in an airplane); and

3. Alternatives available if the flight cannot be completed as planned.

ALL, SPO

**3080.** Which preflight action is specifically required of the pilot prior to each flight?

A—Check the aircraft logbooks for appropriate entries.
B—Become familiar with all available information concerning the flight.
C—Review wake turbulence avoidance procedures.

*Each PIC shall, before each flight, become familiar with all available information concerning that flight. This information must include:*

*(a) For a flight under IFR or a flight not in the vicinity of an airport, weather reports and forecasts, fuel requirements, alternatives available if the planned flight cannot be completed, and any known traffic delays of which the pilot has been advised by ATC;*

*(b) For any flight, runway lengths of airports of intended use, and the following takeoff and landing distance information:*

*1. For civil aircraft for which an approved airplane or rotorcraft flight manual containing takeoff and landing distance data is required, the takeoff and landing distance data contained therein; and*

*2. For civil aircraft other than those specified in paragraph (b)(1) of this section, other reliable information appropriate to the aircraft, relating to aircraft performance under expected values of airport elevation and runway slope, aircraft gross weight, and wind and temperature.*

*(PLT445, PA.II.A.K3d, PH.II.A.K3) — 14 CFR §91.103*

ALL, SPO

**3081.** Preflight action, as required for all flights away from the vicinity of an airport, shall include

A—the designation of an alternate airport.
B—a study of arrival procedures at airports/ heliports of intended use.
C—an alternate course of action if the flight cannot be completed as planned.

*Each PIC shall, before each flight, become familiar with all available information concerning that flight. This information must include:*

*(a) For a flight under IFR or a flight not in the vicinity of an airport, weather reports and forecasts, fuel requirements, alternatives available if the planned flight cannot be completed, and any known traffic delays of which the pilot has been advised by ATC;*

*(b) For any flight, runway lengths of airports of intended use, and the following takeoff and landing distance information:*

*1. For civil aircraft for which an approved airplane or rotorcraft flight manual containing takeoff and landing distance data is required, the takeoff and landing distance data contained therein; and*

*2. For civil aircraft other than those specified in paragraph (b)(1) of this section, other reliable information appropriate to the aircraft, relating to aircraft performance under expected values of airport elevation and runway slope, aircraft gross weight, and wind and temperature.*

*(PLT445, PA.II.A.K3d, PH.II.A.K3) — 14 CFR §91.103*

**Answers**

3080   [B]          3081   [C]

ALL
**3082.** In addition to other preflight actions for a VFR flight away from the vicinity of the departure airport, regulations specifically require the pilot-in-command to

A—review traffic control light signal procedures.
B—check the accuracy of the navigation equipment and the emergency locator transmitter (ELT).
C—determine runway lengths at airports of intended use and the aircraft's takeoff and landing distance data.

*Each PIC shall, before each flight, become familiar with all available information concerning that flight. This information must include:*

*(a) For a flight under IFR or a flight not in the vicinity of an airport, weather reports and forecasts, fuel requirements, alternatives available if the planned flight cannot be completed, and any known traffic delays of which the pilot has been advised by ATC;*

*(b) For any flight, runway lengths of airports of intended use, and the following takeoff and landing distance information:*

*1. For civil aircraft for which an approved airplane or rotorcraft flight manual containing takeoff and landing distance data is required, the takeoff and landing distance data contained therein; and*

*2. For civil aircraft other than those specified in paragraph (b)(1) of this section, other reliable information appropriate to the aircraft, relating to aircraft performance under expected values of airport elevation and runway slope, aircraft gross weight, and wind and temperature.*

*(PLT444, PA.II.A.K3d, PH.II.A.K3) — 14 CFR §91.103*

AIR, WSC, PPC
**3132.** What is the specific fuel requirement for flight under VFR at night in an airplane?

A—Enough to complete the flight at normal cruising speed with adverse wind conditions.
B—Enough to fly to the first point of intended landing and to fly after that for 30 minutes at normal cruising speed.
C—Enough to fly to the first point of intended landing and to fly after that for 45 minutes at normal cruising speed.

*No person may begin a flight in an airplane under VFR unless (considering wind and forecast weather conditions) there is enough fuel to fly to the first point of intended landing and, assuming normal cruising speed, and night operations, to fly after that for at least 45 minutes. (PLT413, PA.II.A.K3d, PH.II.A.K3) — 14 CFR §91.151*

AIR, REC, WSC, PPC
**3131.** What is the specific fuel requirement for flight under VFR during daylight hours in an airplane?

A—Enough to complete the flight at normal cruising speed with adverse wind conditions.
B—Enough to fly to the first point of intended landing and to fly after that for 30 minutes at normal cruising speed.
C—Enough to fly to the first point of intended landing and to fly after that for 45 minutes at normal cruising speed.

*No person may begin a flight in an airplane under VFR unless (considering wind and forecast weather conditions) there is enough fuel to fly to the first point of intended landing and, assuming normal cruising speed, and day operations, to fly after that for at least 30 minutes. (PLT413, PA.II.A.K3d, PH.II.A.K3) — 14 CFR §91.151*

RTC
**3133.** No person may begin a flight in a rotorcraft under VFR unless there is enough fuel to fly to the first point of intended landing and, assuming normal cruising speed, to fly thereafter for at least

A—20 minutes.
B—30 minutes.
C—1 hour.

*No person may begin a flight in a rotorcraft under VFR unless (considering wind and forecast weather conditions) there is enough fuel to fly to the first point of intended landing and, assuming normal cruising speed, to fly after that for at least 20 minutes. (PH.II.A.K3) — 14 CFR §91.151*

**Answers**

| 3082 | [C] | 3132 | [C] | 3131 | [B] | 3133 | [A] |
|------|-----|------|-----|------|-----|------|-----|

SPO
**2033.** How should an aircraft preflight inspection be accomplished for the first flight of the day?

A—Quick walk around with a check of gas and oil.
B—Any sequence as determined by the pilot-in-command.
C—Thorough and systematic means recommended by the manufacturer.

*The preflight inspection should be a thorough and systematic means by which the pilot determines that the airplane is ready for safe flight. Most AFM/POH contain a section devoted to a systematic method of performing a preflight inspection that should be used by the pilot for guidance. (PLT444) — FAA-H-8083-25*

# Seatbelts

All required flight crewmembers must remain in their seats with seatbelts secured during the entire flight unless absent in connection with duties or physiological needs. When shoulder harnesses are installed they must be used during takeoffs and landings.

Prior to takeoff, the PIC must ensure that each person on board has been briefed on the use of seatbelts. In addition, the PIC must ensure that the passengers are notified to fasten their seatbelts during taxi, takeoffs, and landings. A child under two years of age may be held by an adult who is occupying a seat or berth.

ALL
**3083.** Flight crewmembers are required to keep their safety belts and shoulder harnesses fastened during

A—takeoffs and landings.
B—all flight conditions.
C—flight in turbulent air.

*During takeoff, landing, and while en route, each required flight crewmember shall keep their seatbelt fastened while at their station. During takeoff and landing, this includes wearing a shoulder harness (if installed) unless it interferes with required duties. (PLT440, PA.II.B.K1, PH.II.B.K1) — 14 CFR §91.105*

ALL, SPO
**3084.** Which best describes the flight conditions under which flight crewmembers are specifically required to keep their safety belts and shoulder harnesses fastened?

A—Safety belts during takeoff and landing; shoulder harnesses during takeoff and landing.
B—Safety belts during takeoff and landing; shoulder harnesses during takeoff and landing and while en route.
C—Safety belts during takeoff and landing and while en route; shoulder harnesses during takeoff and landing.

*During takeoff, landing, and while en route, each required flight crewmember shall keep their seatbelt fastened while at their station. During takeoff and landing, this includes wearing a shoulder harness (if installed) unless it interferes with required duties. (PLT464, PA.II.B.K1, PH.II.B.K1) — 14 CFR §91.105*

ALL
**3085.** With respect to passengers, what obligation, if any, does a pilot-in-command have concerning the use of safety belts?

A—The pilot-in-command must instruct the passengers to keep their safety belts fastened for the entire flight.
B—The pilot-in-command must brief the passengers on the use of safety belts and notify them to fasten their safety belts during taxi, takeoff, and landing.
C—The pilot-in-command has no obligation in regard to passengers' use of safety belts.

*Unless otherwise authorized by the Administrator, no pilot may takeoff in a civil aircraft unless the PIC of that aircraft ensures that each person on board is briefed on how to fasten and unfasten their seatbelt, and that each person has been notified to fasten the seatbelt during taxi, takeoff, and landing. (PLT465, PA.II.B.K1, PH.II.B.K1) — 14 CFR §91.107*

**Answers**

2033   [C]          3083   [A]          3084   [C]          3085   [B]

ALL

**3085-1.** Pre-takeoff briefing of passengers about the use of seat belts for a flight is the responsibility of

A—all passengers.
B—the pilot-in-command.
C—the right-seat pilot.

*Unless otherwise authorized by the Administrator, no pilot may takeoff in a civil aircraft unless the PIC of that aircraft ensures that each person on board is briefed on how to fasten and unfasten their seatbelt, and that each person has been notified to fasten the seatbelt during taxi, takeoff, and landing. (PLT384, PA.II.B.K1, PH.II.B.K1) — 14 CFR §91.107*

ALL

**3086.** With certain exceptions, safety belts are required to be secured about passengers during

A—taxi, takeoffs, and landings.
B—all flight conditions.
C—flight in turbulent air.

*During taxi, takeoff, and landing, each person on board the aircraft must occupy a seat or berth with a seatbelt and shoulder harness, properly secured if installed. (PLT465, PA.II.B.K1, PH.II.B.K1) — 14 CFR §91.107*

SPO

**2232.** The pilot-in-command is responsible for ensuring that each person on board applicable U.S. registered aircraft is briefed and instructed on how and when to

A—fasten and unfasten their seat belt and shoulder harness.
B—adjust their seat.
C—operate the fire extinguisher.

*Unless otherwise authorized by the FAA, no pilot may takeoff in a civil aircraft unless the PIC ensures that each person on board is briefed on how to fasten and unfasten their seatbelt, and that each person has been notified to fasten the seatbelt during taxi, takeoff, and landing. (PLT441) — 14 CFR §91.107*

ALL, SPO

**3087.** Safety belts are required to be properly secured about which persons in an aircraft and when?

A—Pilots only, during takeoffs and landings.
B—Passengers, during taxi, takeoffs, and landings only.
C—Each person on board the aircraft during the entire flight.

*During taxi, takeoff, and landing, each person on board the aircraft must occupy a seat or berth with a safety belt and shoulder harness, properly secured if installed. However, a child under two years of age may be held by an adult who is occupying a seat or a berth, and a person on board for the purpose of engaging in sport parachuting may use the floor of the aircraft as a seat. (PLT465, PA.II.B.K1, PH.II.B.K1) — 14 CFR §91.107*

**Answers**

3085-1 [B]          3086   [A]          2232   [A]          3087   [B]

# Alcohol and Drugs

No person may act as a crewmember on an aircraft under the following conditions:

1. Within 8 hours after the consumption of any alcoholic beverage;
2. While under the influence of alcohol (.04 percent by weight or more alcohol in the blood); and
3. While using any drug that affects their faculties in any way contrary to safety.

Except in an emergency, no pilot of an aircraft may allow a person who appears to be intoxicated or under the influence of drugs (except a medical patient under proper care) to be carried in that aircraft.

A conviction for the violation of any law relating to drugs or alcohol is grounds for: (1) Denial of an application for any certificate, rating, or authorization issued under Part 61 for a period of up to 1 year after the date of final conviction; or (2) suspension or revocation of any certificate, rating, or authorization issued under Part 61.

Pilots shall provide a written report of each alcohol- or drug-related motor vehicle action to the FAA Civil Aviation Security Division (AMC-700) not later than 60 days after the motor vehicle action.

ALL

**3077.** A person may not act as a crewmember of a civil aircraft if alcoholic beverages have been consumed by that person within the preceding

A—8 hours.
B—12 hours.
C—24 hours.

*No person may act or attempt to act as a crewmember of a civil aircraft within 8 hours after the consumption of any alcoholic beverage. Remember: "8 hours bottle to throttle." (PLT463, PA.I.H.K2, PH.I.H.K2) — 14 CFR §91.17*

ALL

**3078.** Under what condition, if any, may a pilot allow a person who is obviously under the influence of drugs to be carried aboard an aircraft?

A—In an emergency or if the person is a medical patient under proper care.
B—Only if the person does not have access to the flight deck or pilot's compartment.
C—Under no condition.

*Except in an emergency, or a medical patient under proper care, no pilot of a civil aircraft may allow a person who appears to be intoxicated, or who demonstrates by manner or physical indications that the individual is under the influence of drugs, to be carried in that aircraft. (PLT463, PA.I.H.K2, PH.I.H.K2) — 14 CFR §91.17*

ALL, SPO

**3079.** No person may attempt to act as a crewmember of a civil aircraft with

A—.008 percent by weight or more alcohol in the blood.
B—.004 percent by weight or more alcohol in the blood.
C—.04 percent by weight or more alcohol in the blood.

*No person may act, or attempt to act, as a crewmember of a civil aircraft while having .04 percent or more, by weight, alcohol in the blood. (PLT463, PA.I.H.K2, PH.I.H.K2) — 14 CFR §91.17*

SPO

**2087.** Which is true regarding the presence of alcohol within the human body?

A—A small amount of alcohol increases vision acuity.
B—An increase in altitude decreases the adverse effect of alcohol.
C—Judgment and decision-making abilities can be adversely affected by even small amounts of alcohol.

*As little as one ounce of liquor, one bottle of beer, or four ounces of wine can impair flying skills. (PLT205) — AIM ¶8-1-1*

*Answer (A) is incorrect because all mental and physical activities will be decreased with even small amounts of alcohol in the bloodstream. Answer (B) is incorrect because the adverse effects of alcohol are increased as altitude is increased.*

**Answers**

3077 [A]    3078 [A]    3079 [C]    2087 [C]

ALL

**3079-1.** How soon after the conviction for driving while intoxicated by alcohol or drugs shall it be reported to the FAA Civil Aviation Security Division?

A—No later than 60 days after the motor vehicle action.
B—No later than 30 working days after the motor vehicle action.
C—Required to be reported upon renewal of medical certificate.

*Each person holding a pilot certificate shall provide a written report of each drug or alcohol-related motor vehicle action to the AMC-700 not later than 60 days after the motor vehicle action. (PLT463, PA.I.H.K2, PH.I.H.K2) — 14 CFR §61.15*

SPO

**2126.** A pilot convicted of operating an aircraft under the influence of alcohol, or using drugs that affect the person's faculties, is grounds for a

A—denial of an application for an FAA certificate, rating, or authorization issued under 14 CFR Part 61.
B—written notification to the FAA Civil Aeromedical Institute (CAMI) within 60 days after the conviction.
C—written report to be filed with the FAA Civil Aviation Security Division (AMC-700) not later than 60 day after the conviction.

*A conviction for the violation of any federal or state statute relating to drugs or alcohol is grounds for: (1) Denial of an application for any certificate, rating, or authorization issued under Part 61 for a period of up to 1 year after the date of final conviction; or (2) suspension or revocation of any certificate, rating, or authorization issued under Part 61. (PLT463) — 14 CFR §61.15*

Answer (B) is incorrect because the report must be filed with AMC-700. Answer (C) is incorrect because this applies to automobile convictions, not aircraft convictions.

SPO

**2127.** A pilot convicted for the violation of any federal or state statute relating to the process, manufacture, transportation, distribution, or sale of narcotic drugs is grounds for

A—a written report to be filed with the FAA Civil Aviation Security Division (AMC-700) not later than 60 days after the conviction.
B—notification of this conviction to the FAA Civil Aeromedical Institute (CAMI) within 60 days after the conviction.
C—suspension or revocation of any certificate, rating, or authorization issued under 14 CFR Part 61.

*A conviction for the violation of any federal or state statute relating to the growing, processing, manufacture, sale, disposition, possession, transportation, or importation of narcotic drugs, marijuana, or depressant or stimulant drugs or substances is grounds for: (1) Denial of an application for any certificate, rating, or authorization for a period of up to 1 year after the date of final conviction; or (2) suspension or revocation of any certificate, rating, or authorization. (PLT463) — 14 CFR §61.15*

Answers (A) and (B) are incorrect because a written report to AMC-700 is only necessary for motor vehicle actions.

SPO

**2128.** A pilot convicted of operating a motor vehicle while either intoxicated by, impaired by, or under the influence of alcohol or a drug is required to provide a

A—written report to the FAA Civil Aeromedical Institute (CAMI) within 60 days after the motor vehicle action.
B—written report to the FAA Civil Aviation Security Division (AMC-700) not later than 60 days after the conviction.
C—notification of the conviction to an FAA Aviation Medical Examiner (AME) not later than 60 days after the motor vehicle action.

*Each person holding a pilot certificate shall provide a written report of each motor vehicle action to the FAA AMC-700 not later than 60 days after the motor vehicle action. (PLT463) — 14 CFR §61.15*

**Answers**

3079-1 [A]        2126    [A]        2127    [C]        2128    [B]

# Right-of-Way Rules

When weather conditions permit, vigilance must be maintained so as to see and avoid other aircraft.

An aircraft in distress has the right-of-way over all other air traffic. When aircraft of the same category are converging at approximately the same altitude (except head-on, or nearly so), the aircraft on the other's right has the right-of-way. See Figure 5-2.

If the aircraft are of different categories, the following applies:

1. A balloon has the right-of-way over any other category of aircraft;

2. A glider has the right-of-way over an airship, airplane, rotorcraft, weight-shift control, or powered parachute; and

3. An airship has the right-of-way over an airplane, rotorcraft, weight-shift control, or powered parachute.

An aircraft towing or refueling other aircraft has the right-of-way over all other engine driven aircraft.

When aircraft are approaching each other head-on, or nearly so, each pilot of each aircraft (regardless of category), shall alter course to the right. See Figure 5-3.

An aircraft being overtaken has the right-of-way. The overtaking aircraft shall alter course to the right to pass well clear. See Figure 5-4.

When two or more aircraft are approaching an airport for landing, the aircraft at the lower altitude has the right-of-way, but it shall not take advantage of this rule to cut in front of, or overtake another aircraft.

**Figure 5-2.** Aircraft on converging courses: Aircraft on the right has right-of-way—aircraft on the left must yield.

**Figure 5-3.** Aircraft approaching head-on

**Figure 5-4.** One aircraft overtaking another

ALL, SPO

**3089.** Which aircraft has the right-of-way over all other air traffic?

A—A balloon.
B—An aircraft in distress.
C—An aircraft on final approach to land.

*An aircraft in distress has the right-of-way over all other air traffic. (PLT414, PA.III.B.K3, PH.III.C.K3) — 14 CFR §91.113*

ALL, SPO

**3090.** What action is required when two aircraft of the same category converge, but not head-on?

A—The faster aircraft shall give way.
B—The aircraft on the left shall give way.
C—Each aircraft shall give way to the right.

*When two aircraft of the same "right-of-way" category converge at approximately the same altitude, the aircraft to the other's right has the right-of-way. (PLT414, PA.III.B.K3, PH.III.C.K3) — 14 CFR §91.113*

Answer (A) is incorrect because speed has nothing to do with right-of-way. Answer (C) is incorrect because "each aircraft giving way to the right" is the rule when approaching head-on.

ALL

**3093.** Which aircraft has the right-of-way over the other aircraft listed?

A—Glider.
B—Airship.
C—Aircraft refueling other aircraft.

*A glider has the right-of-way over an airship, airplane, or rotorcraft. (PLT414, PA.III.B.K3, PH.III.C.K3) — 14 CFR §91.113*

Answer (B) is incorrect because a glider has the right-of-way over powered aircraft. Answer (C) is incorrect because an aircraft refueling other aircraft only has right-of-way over other engine-driven aircraft.

ALL

**3092.** An airplane and an airship are converging. If the airship is left of the airplane's position, which aircraft has the right-of-way?

A—The airship.
B—The airplane.
C—Each pilot should alter course to the right.

*An airship has the right-of-way over an airplane or rotorcraft. (PLT414, PA.III.B.K3, PH.III.C.K3) — 14 CFR §91.113*

ALL

**3091.** Which aircraft has the right-of-way over the other aircraft listed?

A—Gyroplane.
B—Airship.
C—Aircraft towing other aircraft.

*An aircraft towing or refueling other aircraft has the right-of-way over all other engine-driven aircraft. (PLT414, PA.III.B.K3, PH.III.C.K3) — 14 CFR §91.113*

ALL

**3095.** When two or more aircraft are approaching an airport for the purpose of landing, the right-of-way belongs to the aircraft

A—that has the other to its right.
B—that is the least maneuverable.
C—at the lower altitude, but it shall not take advantage of this rule to cut in front of or to overtake another.

*When two aircraft are approaching an airport for landing, the lower aircraft has the right-of-way. A pilot shall not take advantage of that rule to overtake or cut in front of another aircraft. (PLT414, PA.III.B.K3, PH.III.C.K3) — 14 CFR §91.113*

AIR, WSC, PPC

**3096.** A seaplane and a motorboat are on crossing courses. If the motorboat is to the left of the seaplane, which has the right-of-way?

A—The motorboat.
B—The seaplane.
C—Both should alter course to the right.

*For water operation, when aircraft, or an aircraft and a vessel, are on crossing courses, the aircraft or vessel to the other's right has the right-of-way. (PLT414, PA.III.B.K3) — 14 CFR §91.115*

AIR, GLI, REC, WSC, PPC

**3094.** What action should the pilots of a glider and an airplane take if on a head-on collision course?

A—The airplane pilot should give way to the left.
B—The glider pilot should give way to the right.
C—Both pilots should give way to the right.

*When two aircraft are approaching each other from head-on, or nearly so, each pilot must alter course to the right. This rule does not give right-of-way by categories. (PLT414, PA.III.B.K3) — 14 CFR §91.113*

**Answers**

| 3089 | [B] | | 3090 | [B] | | 3093 | [A] | | 3092 | [A] | | 3091 | [C] | | 3095 | [C] |
| 3096 | [B] | | 3094 | [C] | | | | | | | | | | | | |

# Parachutes

If any passengers are carried, the pilot of an aircraft may not intentionally exceed 60° of bank or 30° of pitch unless each occupant is wearing an approved parachute. However, this requirement does not apply when a certified flight instructor is giving instruction in spins or any other flight maneuver required by regulations for a rating.

If the parachute is of the chair type, it must have been packed by a certificated and appropriately-rated parachute rigger within the preceding 180 days.

ALL

**3172.** An approved chair-type parachute may be carried in an aircraft for emergency use if it has been packed by an appropriately rated parachute rigger within the preceding

A—120 days.
B—180 days.
C—365 days.

*No pilot of a civil aircraft may allow a parachute that is available for emergency use to be carried in that aircraft unless, if a chair type, it has been packed by a certificated and appropriately-rated parachute rigger within the preceding 180 days. (PLT405, PA.I.A.K1, PH.I.A.K1) — 14 CFR §91.307*

ALL

**3173.** With certain exceptions, when must each occupant of an aircraft wear an approved parachute?

A—When a door is removed from the aircraft to facilitate parachute jumpers.
B—When intentionally pitching the nose of the aircraft up or down 30° or more.
C—When intentionally banking in excess of 30°.

*Unless each occupant of the aircraft is wearing an approved parachute, no pilot of a civil aircraft, carrying any person (other than a crewmember) may execute an intentional maneuver that exceeds 60° bank or 30° nose up or down, relative to the horizon. (PLT369, PA.I.A.K1, PH.I.A.K1) — 14 CFR §91.307*

# Deviation from Air Traffic Control Instructions

An ATC clearance is authorization for an aircraft to proceed under specified traffic conditions within controlled airspace. When an ATC clearance has been obtained, no PIC may deviate from that clearance, except in an emergency, unless the pilot obtains an amended clearance. If a pilot does deviate from a clearance or ATC instruction during an emergency, they must notify ATC of the deviation as soon as possible. If, in an emergency, a pilot is given priority over other aircraft by ATC, they may be requested to submit a detailed report even though no deviation from a rule occurred. The requested report shall be submitted within 48 hours to the chief of the ATC facility which granted the priority.

ALL

**3108.** When an ATC clearance has been obtained, no pilot-in-command may deviate from that clearance, unless that pilot obtains an amended clearance. The one exception to this regulation is

A—when the clearance states "at pilot's discretion."
B—an emergency.
C—if the clearance contains a restriction.

*Except in an emergency, no person may operate an aircraft contrary to an ATC clearance or instruction. (PLT444, PA.VIII.F.K1, PH.III.B.K2) — 14 CFR §91.123*

ALL

**3108-1.** As pilot-in-command of an aircraft, under which situation can you deviate from an ATC clearance?

A—When operating in Class A airspace at night.
B—If an ATC clearance is not understood and in VFR conditions.
C—In response to a traffic alert and collision avoidance system resolution advisory.

*The regulations authorize deviations from a clearance in response to a traffic alert and collision avoidance system resolution advisory. You must notify ATC as soon as possible following the deviation. (PLT444, PA.VIII.F.K1, PH.III.B.K2) — 14 CFR §91.123*

*Answers (A) and (B) are incorrect because neither of these are acceptable reasons to deviate from an ATC clearance.*

**Answers**

| | | | |
|---|---|---|---|
| 3172 [B] | 3173 [B] | 3108 [B] | 3108-1 [C] |

ALL, SPO

**3109.** When would a pilot be required to submit a detailed report of an emergency which caused the pilot to deviate from an ATC clearance?

A—Within 48 hours if requested by ATC.
B—Immediately.
C—Within 7 days.

*Each PIC who deviated from an ATC clearance during an emergency must submit a detailed report within 48 hours if requested by ATC. (PLT403, PA.VIII.F.K1, PH.III.B.K2) — 14 CFR §91.123*

ALL

**3110.** What action, if any, is appropriate if the pilot deviates from an ATC instruction during an emergency and is given priority?

A—Take no special action since you are pilot-in-command.
B—File a detailed report within 48 hours to the chief of the appropriate ATC facility, if requested.
C—File a report to the FAA Administrator, as soon as possible.

*Each PIC who (though not deviating from a rule of 14 CFR Part 91) is given priority by ATC in an emergency shall, if requested by ATC, submit a detailed report of that emergency within 48 hours to the chief of that ATC facility. (PLT444, PA.VIII.F.K1, PH.III.B.K2) — 14 CFR §91.123*

ALL

**3837.** An ATC clearance provides

A—priority over all other traffic.
B—adequate separation from all traffic.
C—authorization to proceed under specified traffic conditions in controlled airspace.

*An ATC clearance is an authorization by air traffic control, for the purpose of preventing collisions between known aircraft, for an aircraft to proceed under specified traffic conditions within controlled airspace. (PLT370, PA.VIII.F.K1, PH.III.B.K2) — Pilot/Controller Glossary*

Answer (A) is incorrect because a clearance does not provide priority. Answer (B) is incorrect because a clearance does not relieve the pilot of the responsibility for collision avoidance with aircraft not in instrument meteorological conditions (IMC).

SPO

**2003.** An ATC clearance means an authorization by ATC for an aircraft to proceed under specified conditions within

A—controlled airspace.
B—uncontrolled airspace.
C—published visual flight rules (VFR) routes.

*An ATC clearance means an authorization by air traffic control for the purpose of preventing collision between known aircraft, for an aircraft to proceed under specified traffic conditions within controlled airspace. (PLT044) — Pilot/Controller Glossary*

Answer (B) is incorrect because ATC does not provide clearances in uncontrolled airspace. Answer (C) is incorrect because an ATC clearance is not required to fly these routes.

ALL

**2004.** While on a VFR cross-country and not in contact with ATC, what frequency would you use in the event of an emergency?

A—121.5 MHz.
B—122.5 MHz.
C—128.725 MHz.

*Although the frequency in use or other frequencies assigned by ATC are preferable, the following emergency frequencies can be used for distress or urgency communications: 121.5 MHz, 243.0 MHz, or 406 MHz. (PLT391, PA.III.A.K1, PH.III.B.K2) — AIM ¶6-3-1*

**Answers**

| 3109 | [A] | 3110 | [B] | 3837 | [C] | 2003 | [A] | 2004 | [A] |

# Minimum Safe Altitudes

No minimum altitude applies during takeoff or landing. During other phases of flight, however, the following minimum altitudes apply:

**Anywhere**—The pilot must maintain an altitude which, in the event of engine failure, will allow an emergency landing without undue hazard to persons or property on the surface.

**Over congested areas**—An altitude of at least 1,000 feet above the highest obstacle within a horizontal radius of 2,000 feet of the aircraft must be maintained over any congested area of a city, town, or settlement or over any open-air assembly of people.

**Over other than congested areas**—An altitude of 500 feet above the surface must be maintained except over open water or sparsely populated areas. In that case, the aircraft may not be operated closer than 500 feet to any person, vessel, vehicle or structure.

ALL, SPO

**3101.** Except when necessary for takeoff or landing, what is the minimum safe altitude for a pilot to operate an aircraft anywhere?

A—An altitude allowing, if a power unit fails, an emergency landing without undue hazard to persons or property on the surface.

B—An altitude of 500 feet above the surface and no closer than 500 feet to any person, vessel, vehicle, or structure.

C—An altitude of 500 feet above the highest obstacle within a horizontal radius of 1,000 feet.

*Except when necessary for takeoff or landing, no person may operate an aircraft anywhere below an altitude allowing, if a power unit fails, an emergency landing without undue hazard to persons or property on the surface. (PLT430, PA.I.D.K2, PH.I.D.K2) — 14 CFR §91.119*

AIR, GLI, LTA, REC, WSC, PPC

**3102.** Except when necessary for takeoff or landing, what is the minimum safe altitude required for a pilot to operate an aircraft over congested areas?

A—An altitude of 1,000 feet above any person, vessel, vehicle, or structure.

B—An altitude of 500 feet above the highest obstacle within a horizontal radius of 1,000 feet of the aircraft.

C—An altitude of 1,000 feet above the highest obstacle within a horizontal radius of 2,000 feet of the aircraft.

*Except when necessary for takeoff or landing, no person may operate an aircraft over any congested area of a city, town, or settlement, or over any open air assembly of persons, below an altitude of 1,000 feet above the highest obstacle within a horizontal radius of 2,000 feet of the aircraft. (PLT430, PA.I.D.K2) — 14 CFR §91.119*

AIR, GLI, LTA, REC, WSC, PPC

**3103.** Except when necessary for takeoff or landing, what is the minimum safe altitude required for a pilot to operate an aircraft over other than a congested area?

A—An altitude allowing, if a power unit fails, an emergency landing without undue hazard to persons or property on the surface.

B—An altitude of 500 feet AGL, except over open water or a sparsely populated area, which requires 500 feet from any person, vessel, vehicle, or structure.

C—An altitude of 500 feet above the highest obstacle within a horizontal radius of 1,000 feet.

*Except when necessary for takeoff or landing, no person may operate an aircraft over other than congested areas below an altitude of 500 feet above the surface except over open water or sparsely populated areas. In that case, the aircraft may not be operated closer than 500 feet to any person, vessel, vehicle, or structure. (PLT430, PA.I.D.K2) — 14 CFR §91.119*

AIR, GLI, LTA, REC, WSC, PPC

**3104.** Except when necessary for takeoff or landing, an aircraft may not be operated closer than what distance from any person, vessel, vehicle, or structure?

A—500 feet.

B—700 feet.

C—1,000 feet.

*Except when necessary for takeoff or landing, no person may operate an aircraft closer than 500 feet to any person, vessel, vehicle, or structure. (PLT430, PA.I.D.K2) — 14 CFR §91.119*

**Answers**

3101    [A]          3102    [C]          3103    [B]          3104    [A]

# VFR Weather Minimums

Rules governing flight under **visual flight rules (VFR)** have been adopted to assist the pilot in meeting their responsibility to see and avoid other aircraft. See Figure 5-5.

In addition, when operating within the lateral boundaries of the surface area of Class B, C, D or E airspace designated for an airport, the ceiling must not be less than 1,000 feet. If the pilot intends to land, take off, or enter a traffic pattern within such airspace, the ground visibility must be at least 3 miles at that airport. If ground visibility is not reported, 3 miles flight visibility is required in the pattern.

| Airspace | Flight Visibility | Distance from Clouds |
|---|---|---|
| Class A | Not Applicable | Not Applicable |
| Class B | 3 statute miles | Clear of clouds |
| Class C | 3 statute miles | 500 feet below<br>1,000 feet above<br>2,000 feet horizontal |
| Class D | 3 statute miles | 500 feet below<br>1,000 feet above<br>2,000 feet horizontal |
| Class E<br>Less than<br>  10,000 feet MSL | 3 statute miles | 500 feet below<br>1,000 feet above<br>2,000 feet horizontal |
| At or above<br>  10,000 feet MSL | 5 statute miles | 1,000 feet below<br>1,000 feet above<br>1 statute mile horizontal |
| Class G<br>1,200 feet or less<br>  above the surface<br>  (regardless of<br>  MSL altitude)<br>Day, except as provided<br>  in §91.155(b) | 1 statute mile | Clear of clouds |
| Night, except as pro-<br>  vided in §91.155(b) | 3 statute miles | 500 feet below<br>1,000 feet above<br>2,000 feet horizontal |
| More than 1,200 feet<br>  above the surface<br>  but less than<br>  10,000 feet MSL<br>Day | 1 statute mile | 500 feet below<br>1,000 feet above<br>2,000 feet horizontal |
| Night | 3 statute miles | 500 feet below<br>1,000 feet above<br>2,000 feet horizontal |
| More than 1,200 feet<br>  above the surface<br>  and at or above<br>  10,000 feet MSL | 5 statute miles | 1,000 feet below<br>1,000 feet above<br>1 statute mile horizontal |

**Figure 5-5**

ALL
**3136.** During operations within controlled airspace at altitudes of less than 1,200 feet AGL, the minimum horizontal distance from clouds requirement for VFR flight is

A—1,000 feet.
B—1,500 feet.
C—2,000 feet.

*Minimum horizontal distance from clouds within Class C, D, or E airspace below 10,000 feet MSL is 2,000 feet. (PLT163, PA.I.E.S1, PH.I.E.S1) — 14 CFR §91.155*

ALL
**3138.** What minimum flight visibility is required for VFR flight operations on an airway below 10,000 feet MSL?

A—1 mile.
B—3 miles.
C—4 miles.

*An airway below 10,000 feet MSL is in either Class B, C, or D, or E airspace, and requires 3 miles flight visibility. (PLT467, PA.I.E.S1, PH.I.E.S1) — 14 CFR §91.155*

ALL
**3139.** The minimum distance from clouds required for VFR operations on an airway below 10,000 feet MSL is

A—remain clear of clouds.
B—500 feet below, 1,000 feet above, and 2,000 feet horizontally.
C—500 feet above, 1,000 feet below, and 2,000 feet horizontally.

*An airway below 10,000 feet MSL is in either Class B, C, or D, or E airspace, and requires a cloud clearance of 500 feet below, 1,000 feet above, and 2,000 feet horizontally. (PLT468, PA.I.E.S1, PH.I.E.S1) — 14 CFR §91.155*

**Answers**

3136    [C]            3138    [B]            3139    [B]

ALL
**3140.** During operations within controlled airspace at altitudes of more than 1,200 feet AGL, but less than 10,000 feet MSL, the minimum distance above clouds requirement for VFR flight is

A—500 feet.
B—1,000 feet.
C—1,500 feet.

*Class B, C, D, and E airspace are all controlled airspace in which VFR flight is allowed, and requires a cloud clearance of 1,000 feet above at altitudes of more than 1,200 feet AGL, but less than 10,000 feet MSL. (PLT468, PA.I.E.S1, PH.I.E.S1) — 14 CFR §91.155*

ALL
**3141.** VFR flight in controlled airspace above 1,200 feet AGL and below 10,000 feet MSL requires a minimum visibility and vertical cloud clearance of

A—3 miles, and 500 feet below or 1,000 feet above the clouds in controlled airspace.
B—5 miles, and 1,000 feet below or 1,000 feet above the clouds at all altitudes.
C—5 miles, and 1,000 feet below or 1,000 feet above the clouds only in Class A airspace.

*With the exception of Class B airspace, VFR flight into controlled airspace requires 3 statute miles visibility and cloud clearance of 500 feet below and 1,000 feet above when operating above 1,200 feet AGL and below 10,000 feet MSL. (PLT468, PA.I.E.S1, PH.I.E.S1) — 14 CFR §91.155*

ALL
**3145.** The minimum flight visibility required for VFR flights above 10,000 feet MSL and more than 1,200 feet AGL in controlled airspace is

A—1 mile.
B—3 miles.
C—5 miles.

*Controlled airspace above 10,000 feet which allows VFR is Class E airspace, and requires 5 statute miles visibility above 10,000 feet MSL and more than 1,200 feet AGL. (PLT163, PA.I.E.S1, PH.I.E.S1) — 14 CFR §91.155*

ALL
**3146.** For VFR flight operations above 10,000 feet MSL and more than 1,200 feet AGL, the minimum horizontal distance from clouds required is

A—1,000 feet.
B—2,000 feet.
C—1 mile.

*Controlled airspace above 10,000 feet which allows VFR is Class E airspace, and requires cloud clearance of 1,000 feet below, 1,000 feet above, and 1 SM horizontal during operations above 10,000 feet MSL and more than 1,200 feet AGL. (PLT163, PA.I.E.S1, PH.I.E.S1) — 14 CFR §91.155*

ALL
**3147.** During operations at altitudes of more than 1,200 feet AGL and at or above 10,000 feet MSL, the minimum distance above clouds requirement for VFR flight is

A—500 feet.
B—1,000 feet.
C—1,500 feet.

*Controlled airspace above 10,000 feet which allows VFR is Class E airspace, and requires cloud clearance of 1,000 feet below, 1,000 feet above, and 1 SM horizontal during operations above 10,000 feet MSL and more than 1,200 feet AGL. (PLT163, PA.I.E.S1, PH.I.E.S1) — 14 CFR §91.155*

ALL
**3620-1.** (Refer to Figure 22, area 1.) The visibility and cloud clearance requirements to operate VFR during daylight hours over Sandpoint Airport at 1,200 feet AGL are

A—1 mile and 1,000 feet above, 500 feet below, and 2,000 feet horizontally from each cloud.
B—1 mile and clear of clouds.
C—3 miles and 1,000 feet above, 500 feet below, and 2,000 feet horizontally from each cloud.

*The Sandpoint Airport Class E airspace starts at 700 feet AGL. The visibility and cloud clearance requirements to operate VFR during daylight hours over Sandpoint Airport at 1,200 feet AGL are 3 SM, 500 feet below, 1,000 feet above, and 2,000 feet horizontal. (PLT064, PA.I.E.S1, PH.I.E.S1) — AIM ¶3-1-4*

**Answers**

| | | | | | |
|---|---|---|---|---|---|
| 3140 [B] | 3141 [A] | 3145 [C] | 3146 [C] | 3147 [B] | 3620-1 [C] |

ALL
**3620-2.** (Refer to Figure 22, area 1.) The visibility and cloud clearance requirements to operate at night over Sandpoint Airport at less than 700 feet AGL are

A—3 miles and 1,000 feet above, 500 feet below, and 2,000 feet horizontally from each cloud.
B—3 miles and clear of clouds.
C—1 mile and 1,000 feet above, 500 feet below, and 2,000 feet horizontally from each cloud.

*The Sandpoint Airport Class E airspace starts at 700 feet AGL. Below 700 feet AGL, the visibility and cloud clearance requirements to operate VFR during daylight hours is 1 mile visibility and clear of clouds. At night, the requirements are 3 SM, 500 feet below, 1,000 feet above, and 2,000 feet horizontal. (PLT064, PA.I.E.S1, PH.I.E.S1) — AIM ¶3-1-4*

ALL
**3621-1.** (Refer to Figure 26, area 2.) The visibility and cloud clearance requirements to operate VFR during daylight hours over the town of Cooperstown between 1,200 feet AGL and 10,000 feet MSL are

A—1 mile and clear of clouds.
B—1 mile and 1,000 feet above, 500 feet below, and 2,000 feet horizontally from clouds.
C—3 miles and 1,000 feet above, 500 feet below, and 2,000 feet horizontally from clouds.

*For VFR flight during daylight hours, between 1,200 feet AGL and 10,000 feet MSL, in Class E airspace, visibility and cloud clearances require 3 miles and 1,000 feet above, 500 feet below, and 2,000 feet horizontally. (PLT101, PA.I.E.S1, PH.I.E.S1) — AIM ¶3-1-4*

ALL
**3621-2.** (Refer to Figure 26, area 2.) The day VFR visibility and cloud clearance requirements to operate over the town of Cooperstown after departing and climbing out of Cooperstown Airport at or below 700 feet AGL are

A—3 miles and clear of clouds.
B—1 mile and 1,000 feet above, 500 feet below, and 2,000 feet horizontally from clouds.
C—1 mile and clear of clouds.

*Cooperstown is in Class G airspace from the surface to 700 feet AGL. Therefore, the visibility and cloud clearance requirements are 1 mile and clear of clouds. (PLT064, PA.I.E.S1, PH.I.E.S1) — AIM ¶3-1-4*

ALL
**3621-3.** (Refer to Figure 78.) What are the basic VFR weather minima required to takeoff from the Onawa (K36) airport during the day?

A—3 statute miles visibility, 500 feet below the clouds, 1,000 feet above the clouds and 2,000 feet horizontally from the clouds.
B—0 statute miles, clear of clouds.
C—1 statute mile, clear of clouds.

*Onawa (K36) is in the bottom right quadrant of the sectional excerpt. It is outside any shading or lines, indicating the airport is in Class G airspace. The basic VFR weather minima for a daytime departure from a Class G airport is 1 statute mile and clear of clouds. (PLT064, PA.I.E.S1, PH.I.E.S1) — AIM ¶3-1-4*

ALL, SPO
**3520.** (Refer to Figure 26, area 2.) Inflight and approaching the Bryn (Pvt) Airstrip, the weather minimums are

A—1 statute mile visibility.
B—3 statute miles in all airspace.
C—no visibility, remain clear of clouds.

*Bryn (Pvt) Airstrip is located in Class G airspace. Therefore, the visibility and cloud clear requirements are 1 SM and clear of clouds. (PLT064, PA.I.E.S1, PH.I.E.S1) — AIM ¶3-1-4*

ALL
**3137.** What minimum visibility and clearance from clouds are required for VFR operations in Class G airspace at 700 feet AGL or below during daylight hours?

A—1 mile visibility and clear of clouds.
B—1 mile visibility, 500 feet below, 1,000 feet above, and 2,000 feet horizontal clearance from clouds.
C—3 miles visibility and clear of clouds.

*Minimum visibility and cloud clearance for Class G airspace at 700 feet AGL or below during daylight hours is 1 mile visibility and clear of clouds. (PLT163, PA.I.E.S1, PH.I.E.S1) — 14 CFR §91.155*

Answer (B) is incorrect because this is for Class C, D, or E airspace.
Answer (C) is incorrect because this is for Class B airspace.

---

**Answers**

| | | | | | |
|---|---|---|---|---|---|
| 3620-2 [A] | 3621-1 [C] | 3621-2 [C] | 3621-3 [C] | 3520  [A] | 3137  [A] |

ALL

**3142.** During operations outside controlled airspace at altitudes of more than 1,200 feet AGL, but less than 10,000 feet MSL, the minimum flight visibility for VFR flight at night is

A—1 mile.
B—3 miles.
C—5 miles.

*At altitudes of more than 1,200 feet AGL but less than 10,000 feet MSL, Class G airspace requires 3 miles visibility at night. (PLT163, PA.I.E.S1, PH.I.E.S1) — 14 CFR §91.155*

ALL

**3143.** During operations outside controlled airspace at altitudes of more than 1,200 feet AGL, but less than 10,000 feet MSL, the minimum flight visibility for day VFR flight is

A—1 mile.
B—3 miles.
C—5 miles.

*At altitudes of more than 1,200 feet AGL but less than 10,000 feet MSL, Class G airspace requires 1 mile visibility during the day. (PLT163, PA.I.E.S1, PH.I.E.S1) — 14 CFR §91.155*

ALL

**3144.** During operations outside controlled airspace at altitudes of more than 1,200 feet AGL, but less than 10,000 feet MSL, the minimum distance below clouds requirement for VFR flight at night is

A—500 feet.
B—1,000 feet.
C—1,500 feet.

*At altitudes of more than 1,200 feet AGL but less than 10,000 feet MSL, Class G airspace requires a cloud clearance of 500 feet below, 1,000 feet above, and 2,000 feet horizontal, during both day and night flights. (PLT163, PA.I.E.S1, PH.I.E.S1) — 14 CFR §91.155*

ALL, SPO

**3148.** No person may take off or land an aircraft under basic VFR at an airport that lies within Class D airspace unless the

A—flight visibility at that airport is at least 1 mile.
B—ground visibility at that airport is at least 1 mile.
C—ground visibility at that airport is at least 3 miles.

*Except for Special VFR procedures, no person may operate an aircraft under VFR within Class D airspace, beneath the ceiling when the ceiling is less than 1,000 feet. No person may takeoff or land an aircraft, or enter the traffic pattern of an airport under VFR, within Class D airspace unless ground visibility at that airport is at least 3 statute miles. (PLT163, PA.I.E.S1, PH.I.E.S1) — 14 CFR §91.155*

ALL, SPO

**3149.** The basic VFR weather minimums for operating an aircraft within Class D airspace are

A—500-foot ceiling and 1 mile visibility.
B—1,000-foot ceiling and 3 miles visibility.
C—clear of clouds and 2 miles visibility.

*Except for Special VFR procedures, no person may operate an aircraft under VFR within Class D airspace, beneath the ceiling when the ceiling is less than 1,000 feet. No person may takeoff or land an aircraft, or enter the traffic pattern of an airport under VFR, within Class D airspace unless ground visibility at that airport is at least 3 statute miles. (PLT163, PA.I.E.S1, PH.I.E.S1) — 14 CFR §91.155*

SPO

**2137.** During operations within Class E airspace at altitudes of less than 1,200 feet AGL, the minimum horizontal distance from clouds requirement for flight is

A—500 feet.
B—1,000 feet.
C—2,000 feet.

*Minimum horizontal distance from clouds within Class C, D, or E airspace below 10,000 feet is 2,000 feet. (PLT163) — 14 CFR §91.155*

SPO

**2040.** Sport Pilot minimum flight visibility for Class E airspace less than 10,000 feet MSL is

A—2,000 feet horizontal.
B—3 statute miles.
C—3 nautical miles.

*The minimum flight visibility for Class E airspace less than 10,000 feet MSL is 3 SM. (PLT163) — FAA-H-8083-25*

Answer (A) is incorrect because this is the required distance from clouds, not flight visibility. Answer (C) is incorrect because flight visibility is based on statute miles, not nautical.

**Answers**

| | | | | | |
|---|---|---|---|---|---|
| 3142 [B] | 3143 [A] | 3144 [A] | 3148 [C] | 3149 [B] | 2137 [C] |
| 2040 [B] | | | | | |

SPO
**2203.** You need to maintain this distance below clouds:

A—500 feet.
B—1,000 feet.
C—2,000 feet.

*Sport pilots need to maintain this distance from clouds: 500 feet below, 1,000 feet above, and 2,000 feet horizontal in all controlled airspace. (PLT163) — 14 CFR §91.155*

Answer (B) is incorrect because this is the distance you must maintain above clouds. Answer (C) is incorrect because this is the distance you must maintain horizontally from clouds.

SPO
**2186-1.** (Refer to Figure 26, area 2.) As a Sport Pilot, in flight and approaching the Bryne Airstrip, the weather minimums are

A—1 statute mile visibility.
B—3 statute miles in all airspace.
C—no visibility, remain clear of clouds.

*This airport lies in Class G airspace. You must have 3 miles of visibility and be clear of clouds to operate when operating as a Sport Pilot. (PLT163) — 14 CFR §91.155*

## Special VFR

When ATC issues a **Special VFR** clearance, an aircraft may be operated within the lateral boundaries of the surface area of Class B, C, D, or E airspace designated for an airport when the ceiling is less than 1,000 feet and/or the visibility is less than 3 miles.

Special VFR requires the aircraft to be operated clear of clouds with flight visibility of at least 1 statute mile.

For Special VFR operation between sunset and sunrise, the pilot must hold an Instrument Rating and the airplane must be equipped for instrument flight.

Requests for Special VFR arrival or departure clearance should be directed to the airport traffic control tower if one is in operation.

AIR, RTC, WSC, PPC
**3150.** A Special VFR clearance authorizes the pilot of an aircraft to operate VFR while within Class D airspace when the visibility is

A—less than 1 mile and the ceiling is less than 1,000 feet.
B—at least 1 mile and the aircraft can remain clear of clouds.
C—at least 3 miles and the aircraft can remain clear of clouds.

*No person may operate an aircraft (other than a helicopter) in a Class D airspace under Special VFR unless clear of clouds and flight visibility is at least 1 statute mile. (PLT376, PA.I.E.S1, PH.I.E.K4) — 14 CFR §91.157*

AIR, RTC, WSC, PPC
**3151.** What is the minimum weather condition required for airplanes operating under Special VFR in Class D airspace?

A—1 mile flight visibility.
B—1 mile flight visibility and 1,000-foot ceiling.
C—3 miles flight visibility and 1,000-foot ceiling.

*No person may operate an aircraft (other than a helicopter) in a Class D airspace under special VFR unless clear of clouds and flight visibility is at least 1 statute mile. (PLT376, PA.I.E.S1, PH.I.E.K4) — 14 CFR §91.157*

**Answers**

| | | | |
|---|---|---|---|
| 2203 [A] | 2186-1 [B] | 3150 [B] | 3151 [A] |

RTC
**3152.** Under what conditions, if any, may a private pilot operate a helicopter under Special VFR at night within Class D airspace?

A—The helicopter must be fully instrument equipped and the pilot must be instrument rated.
B—The flight visibility must be at least 1 mile.
C—There are no conditions; regulations permit this.

*There are no restrictions on helicopters for Special VFR operations within Class D airspace. (PH.I.E.K4) — 14 CFR §91.157*

AIR, WSC, PPC
**3153.** What are the minimum requirements for airplane operations under Special VFR in Class D airspace at night?

A—The airplane must be under radar surveillance at all times while in Class D airspace.
B—The airplane must be equipped for IFR with an altitude reporting transponder.
C—The pilot must be instrument rated, and the airplane must be IFR equipped.

*No person may operate an aircraft (other than a helicopter) in a Class D airspace under special weather minimums between sunset and sunrise unless the pilot and airplane are certified for instrument flight. (PLT161, PA.I.E.S1) — 14 CFR §91.157, §91.205*

Answers (A) and (B) are incorrect because radar and transponder are not required in Class D airspace.

AIR
**3154.** No person may operate an airplane within Class D airspace at night under Special VFR unless the

A—flight can be conducted 500 feet below the clouds.
B—airplane is equipped for instrument flight.
C—flight visibility is at least 3 miles.

*No person may operate an aircraft (other than a helicopter) in a Class D airspace under special weather minimums between sunset and sunrise unless the airplane and pilot are certified for instrument flight. (PLT161, PA.I.E.S1) — 14 CFR §91.155*

AIR, RTC, WSC, PPC
**3813.** What ATC facility should the pilot contact to receive a special VFR departure clearance in Class D airspace?

A—Automated Flight Service Station.
B—Air traffic control tower.
C—Air Route Traffic Control Center.

*When a control tower is in operation, requests for Special VFR clearances should be to the tower. (PLT161, PA.I.E.S1, PH.I.E.K4) — AIM ¶4-4-6*

## VFR Cruising Altitudes

When operating an aircraft under VFR in level cruising flight more than 3,000 feet above the surface and below 18,000 feet MSL, a pilot is required to maintain an appropriate altitude in accordance with certain rules. This requirement is sometimes called the hemispherical cruising rule, and is based on magnetic course, not magnetic heading. See Figure 5-6.

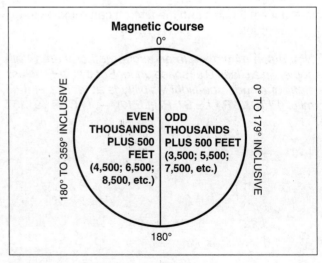

**Figure 5-6.** VFR cruising altitudes

**Answers**

| | | | |
|---|---|---|---|
| 3152 [C] | 3153 [C] | 3154 [B] | 3813 [B] |

AIR, RTC, WSC, PPC

**3155.** Which cruising altitude is appropriate for a VFR flight on a magnetic course of 135°?

A—Even thousandths.
B—Even thousandths plus 500 feet.
C—Odd thousandths plus 500 feet.

*When operating below 18,000 feet MSL in VFR cruising flight more than 3,000 feet above the surface and on a magnetic course of 0° through 179°, any odd thousand-foot MSL altitude plus 500 feet (i.e., 3,500, 5,500, etc.) is appropriate. On a course of 180° through 359°, even thousands plus 500 feet (4,500, 6,500, etc.) is appropriate. (PLT467, PA.I.D.K2, PH.I.D.K2) — 14 CFR §91.159*

AIR, RTC, WSC, PPC

**3156.** Which VFR cruising altitude is acceptable for a flight on a victor airway with a magnetic course of 175°? The terrain is less than 1,000 feet.

A—4,500 feet.
B—5,000 feet.
C—5,500 feet.

*When operating below 18,000 feet MSL in VFR cruising flight more than 3,000 feet above the surface and on a magnetic course of 0° through 179°, any odd thousand-foot MSL altitude plus 500 feet (i.e., 3,500, 5,500, etc.) is appropriate. On a course of 180° through 359°, even thousands plus 500 feet (4,500, 6,500, etc.) is appropriate. (PLT467, PA.I.D.K2, PH.I.D.K2) — 14 CFR §91.159*

AIR, RTC, WSC, PPC

**3157.** Which VFR cruising altitude is appropriate when flying above 3,000 feet AGL on a magnetic course of 185°?

A—4,000 feet.
B—4,500 feet.
C—5,000 feet.

*When operating below 18,000 feet MSL in VFR cruising flight more than 3,000 feet above the surface and on a magnetic course of 0° through 179°, any odd thousand-foot MSL altitude plus 500 feet (i.e., 3,500, 5,500, etc.) is appropriate. On a course of 180° through 359°, even thousands plus 500 feet (4,500, 6,500, etc.) is appropriate. (PLT467, PA.I.D.K2, PH.I.D.K2) — 14 CFR §91.159*

AIR, RTC, WSC, PPC

**3158.** Each person operating an aircraft at a VFR cruising altitude shall maintain an odd-thousand plus 500-foot altitude while on a

A—magnetic heading of 0° through 179°.
B—magnetic course of 0° through 179°.
C—true course of 0° through 179°.

*When operating below 18,000 feet MSL in VFR cruising flight more than 3,000 feet above the surface and on a magnetic course of 0° through 179°, any odd thousand-foot MSL altitude plus 500 feet (i.e., 3,500, 5,500, etc.) is appropriate. On a course of 180° through 359°, even thousands plus 500 feet (4,500, 6,500, etc.) is appropriate. (PLT467, PA.I.D.K2, PH.I.D.K2) — 14 CFR §91.159*

*Answers (A) and (C) are incorrect because VFR altitudes are based on a magnetic course.*

# Transponder and ADS-B Requirements

A transponder is an airborne radar beacon transmitter-receiver that automatically receives signals from a ground-based radar beacon transmitter-receiver (interrogator). The transponder selectively replies (with a specific code) only to interrogations received on the mode to which it is set. Civil Mode A transponders have 4,096 discrete four-digit codes. This return signal is displayed on a radarscope on the ground, which a controller can then identify and pinpoint the position of each aircraft (target) under his or her control.

Additionally, some Mode A transponders are equipped with an automatic altitude reporting capability. This system converts aircraft altitude (in 100-foot increments) to coded digital information which is transmitted back to the interrogating radar system. Mode C transponders have this same altitude reporting capability, giving the controller information on the aircraft's altitude as well as its position. The transponder "Ident" feature should not be activated unless requested by ATC. Activating it will show a blip on a radar screen allowing the controller to quickly locate your position. Mode C, which should be operated at all times, unless ATC requests otherwise, is also required for all flights above 10,000 feet MSL.

**Answers**

| | | | | | | | |
|---|---|---|---|---|---|---|---|
| 3155 | [C] | 3156 | [C] | 3157 | [B] | 3158 | [B] |

The transponder code for VFR flight is 1200. When changing transponder codes, avoid inadvertent selection of codes 7500 (hijack), 7600 (lost communications), 7700 (emergency), and 7777 (military interceptor operations).

If ATC advises that radar service is being terminated, the transponder should be set to code 1200 for VFR flight.

Aircraft operating in airspace previously requiring the use of a transponder are required to have an Automatic Dependent Surveillance–Broadcast (ADS-B) system that includes a certified position source capable of meeting requirements defined in 14 CFR §91.227. For altitudes below FL180, this system can be either a 1090-ES or Universal Access Transceiver (UAT).

ADS-B Out is a function of an aircraft's avionics that periodically broadcasts the aircraft's three-dimnesional position and velocity along with additional identifying information prescribed by §91.227. If the aircraft is equipped with ADS-B Out, it must be operated in transmit mode at all time. The following airspace requires the use of ADS-B Out:

- Class A;
- Class B, from the surface to 10,000 feet MSL including the airspace from portions of Class B that extend beyond the Mode C Veil up to 10,000 feet MSL;
- Class C, from the surface up to 4,000 feet MSL including the airspace above the horizontal boundary up to 10,000 feet MSL;
- Class E, above 10,000 feet MSL over the 48 states and Washington, D.C., excluding airspace at and below 2,500 feet AGL, and over the Gulf of Mexico at and above 3,000 feet MSL within 12 NM of the coastline of the United States; and
- Within a Mode C Veil, the airspace within a 30 NM radius of any airport listed in Part 91, Appendix D, Section 1, from the surface up to 10,000 feet MSL.

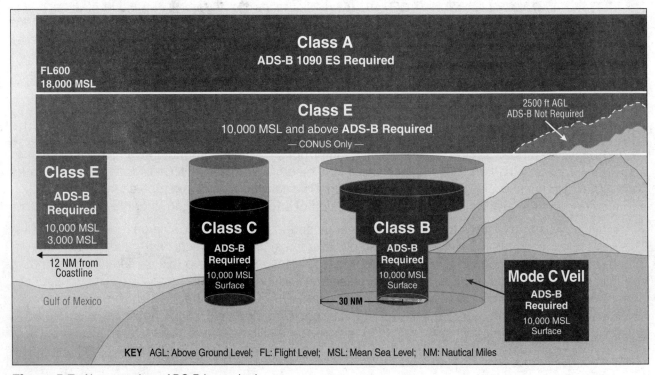

**Figure 5-7.** Airspace where ADS-B is required

Aircraft that were not originally certificated with an electrical system, such as balloons and gliders, are exempt from operations requiring ADS-B Out in certain specified airspace:

- Outside any Class B or Class C airspace area; and
- Below the altitude of the ceiling of a Class B or Class C airspace area designated for an airport, or 10,000 feet MSL—whichever is lower.

Operations of aircraft with inoperable ADS-B equipment are allowed as long as an ATC authorized deviation has been approved by the ATC facility that has jurisdiction over the airspace. These requests can be made at any time.

ALL
**3165.** An operable 4096-code transponder with an encoding altimeter is required in which airspace?

A—Class A, Class B (and within 30 miles of the Class B primary airport), and Class C.
B—Class D and Class E (below 10,000 feet MSL).
C—Class D and Class G (below 10,000 feet MSL).

*Class A, B (and within 30 miles of the Class B primary airport), and C airspace require a Mode C transponder. (PLT161, PA.III.A.K4, PH.III.B.K4) — 14 CFR §91.215*

ALL
**3129.** An operable 4096-code transponder and Mode C encoding altimeter are required in

A—Class B airspace and within 30 miles of the Class B primary airport.
B—Class D airspace.
C—Class E airspace below 10,000 feet MSL.

*Encoding transponders are required within all Class B airspace and within 30 miles of the primary airport even if you are below a Class B airspace layer. (PLT497, PA.III.A.K4, PH.III.B.K4) — 14 CFR §91.131, §91.215*

Answers (B) and (C) are incorrect because transponders are not required in Class D airspace, or below 10,000 feet unless in Class B or C airspace.

ALL
**3801.** When operating under VFR below 18,000 feet MSL, unless otherwise authorized, what transponder code should be selected?

A—1200.
B—7600.
C—7700.

*Unless otherwise instructed by an ATC facility, adjust the transponder to reply on Mode 3/A, code 1200, regardless of altitude. (PLT497, PA.III.A.K4, PH.III.B.K4) — AIM ¶4-1-20*

ALL
**3996.** When operating the transponder on the VFR code (1200), what is the minimum mode the transponder must be in?

A—Mode A.
B—Mode C.
C—Mode F.

*When operating on the VFR code 1200, adjust the transponder to reply on Mode A unless otherwise instructed by an ATC facility. (PLT497, PA.III.A.K4, PH.III.B.K4) — AIM ¶4-1-20*

Answer (B) is incorrect because while altitude-reporting Mode C should be used if it is installed, it is not required to squawk 1200. Answer (C) is incorrect because F is not a transponder mode.

ALL
**3803.** If Air Traffic Control advises that radar service is terminated when the pilot is departing Class C airspace, the transponder should be set to code

A—0000.
B—1200.
C—4096.

*When VFR, unless otherwise instructed by an ATC facility, adjust transponder to reply code 1200 regardless of altitude. (PLT161, PA.III.A.K4, PH.III.B.K4) — AIM ¶4-1-20*

ALL
**3166.** With certain exceptions, all aircraft within 30 miles of a Class B primary airport from the surface upward to 10,000 feet MSL must be equipped with

A—an operable VOR or TACAN receiver and an ADF receiver.
B—instruments and equipment required for IFR operations.
C—ADS-B Out equipment.

---

**Answers**

| 3165 [A] | 3129 [A] | 3801 [A] | 3996 [A] | 3803 [B] | 3166 [C] |

*With certain exceptions, all aircraft operating within 30 miles of Class B airspace will require ADS-B equipment to be installed and in transmit mode. (PLT161, PA.III.A.K4, PH.III.B.K4) — 14 CFR §91.225*

Answers (A) and (B) are incorrect because they apply to IFR flight.

ALL

**3166-1.** Each person operating an aircraft equipped with ADS-B Out must operate this equipment

A—in transit mode at all times.
B—when flying in controlled airspace.
C—at all times at and above 10,000 feet MSL.

*Each person operating an aircraft equipped with ADS-B Out must operate this equipment in transit mode at all times, regardless of the airspace or altitude. (PLT161, PA.III.A.K4, PH.III.B.K4) — 14 CFR §91.225*

ALL

**3166-2.** What type of ADS-B Out equipment is required for aircraft operating below 18,000 feet MSL when flying in class C airspace?

A—1090-ES.
B—Universal Access Transceiver.
C—1090-ES or Universal Access Transceiver.

*For flights below 18,000 feet MSL either 1090-ES or UAT ADS-B Out equipment can be used. For flights above 18,000 feet MSL in Class A airspace, the aircraft must be equipped with 1090-ES. (PLT161, PA.III.A.K4, PH.III.B.K4) — 14 CFR §91.225*

ALL

**3166-3.** For operations of an aircraft in class C airspace with inoperative ADS-B Out equipment, a request must be made to the ATC facility having jurisdiction over the airspace

A—at least 1 hour before the operation.
B—at any time.
C—24 hours before the proposed operation.

*For operations of an aircraft with inoperative ADS-B Out, the request may be made to ATC at any time. (PLT161, PA.III.A.K4, PH.III.B.K4) — 14 CFR §91.225*

Answer (A) is incorrect because a request to operate an aircraft without ADS-B equipment must be made 1 hour before the operation. Answer (C) is incorrect because the request may be made at any time.

ALL

**3166-4.** ADS-B Out equipment broadcasts the aircraft's

A—three-dimensional position.
B—three-dimensional velocity.
C—three-dimensional position and velocity.

*ADS-B Out broadcasts the aircraft's state vector (three-dimensional position and velocity) as well as additional required information. (PLT161, PA.III.A.K4, PH.III.B.K4) — 14 CFR §91.227*

ALL

**3166-5.** Unless otherwise authorized, which situation requires ADS-B?

A—Landing at an airport with an operating control tower.
B—Overflying Class C airspace below 10,000 ft MSL.
C—Flying under the shelf of Class C airspace.

*Aircraft are required to use ADS-B when operating in Class C airspace from the surface up to 4,000 feet MSL including the airspace above the horizontal boundary up to 10,000 feet MSL, as well as when operating within a Mode C Veil, the airspace within a 30 NM radius of any airport listed in Part 91, Appendix D, Section 1, from the surface up to 10,000 feet MSL. (PLT497, PA.I.E.K1, PH.III.B.K4) — 14 CFR §91.225*

Answer (A) is incorrect because ADS-B is not required in Class D airspace—ADS-B would not be required to land at an airport with an operating control tower in Class D airspace. Answer (C) is incorrect because ADS-B is not required if flying under the shelf of Class C airspace under 3,000 feet MSL.

ALL

**3800.** When making routine transponder code changes, pilots should avoid inadvertent selection of which codes?

A—0700, 1700, 7000.
B—1200, 1500, 7000.
C—7500, 7600, 7700.

*When making routine code changes, pilots should avoid selecting codes 7500, 7600, or 7700, thereby preventing false alarms at automated ground facilities. (PLT497, PA.I.E.K1, PH.III.B.K4) — AIM ¶4-1-20*

**Answers**

| 3166-1 [A] | 3166-2 [C] | 3166-3 [B] | 3166-4 [C] | 3166-5 [B] | 3800 [C] |

ALL

**3800-1.** When making routine transponder code changes, pilots should avoid inadvertent selection of which code?

A—7200.
B—7000.
C—7500.

*When making routine code changes, pilots should avoid selecting codes 7500, 7600, or 7700, thereby preventing false alarms at automated ground facilities. (PLT497, PA.I.E.K1, PH.III.B.K4) — AIM ¶4-1-20*

ALL

**3802.** Unless otherwise authorized, if flying a transponder equipped aircraft, a pilot should squawk which VFR code?

A—1200.
B—7600.
C—7700.

*It is important for pilots to operate the transponder and encoder so radar controllers will know the aircraft's position and altitude—even if not in communication with ATC. (PLT497, PA.I.E.K1, PH.III.B.K4) — AIM ¶4-1-20*

GLI

**3802-1.** If you are operating a glider equipped with a 4096 code radar beacon transponder and not in contact with an ATC facility, what is the transponder code you should be operating on (squawking)?

A—1202.
B—1200.
C—7700.

*Gliders not in contact with an ATC facility should squawk 1202 in lieu of 1200. (PLT161) — AIM ¶4-1-20*

SPO

**2005.** When a distress or urgency condition is encountered, the pilot of an aircraft with a coded radar beacon transponder, who desires to alert a ground radar facility, should squawk code

A—7700
B—7600
C—7500

*When a distress or urgency condition is encountered, the pilot of an aircraft with a coded radar beacon transponder, who desires to alert a ground radar facility, should squawk Code 7700 and then immediately establish communications with the ATC facility. (PLT497) — AIM ¶6-2-2*

Answer (B) is incorrect because 7600 is used for lost communications. Answer (C) is incorrect because 7500 is used to indicate a hijack situation.

**Answers**

3800-1 [C]          3802    [A]          3802-1 [A]          2005    [A]

# Emergency Locator Transmitter (ELT)

ELTs have been developed as a means of locating downed aircraft. Transmitting on 406 MHz, the ELT will operate continuously for at least 48 hours.

To prevent false alarms, the ELT should be tested only during the first 5 minutes after any hour and only for one to three sweeps. False alarms can also be minimized by monitoring 406 MHz prior to engine shutdown at the end of each flight.

Non-rechargeable batteries used in ELTs must be replaced when 50 percent of their useful life has expired, or when the transmitter has been in use for more than 1 cumulative hour.

ALL

**3819.** When activated, an emergency locator transmitter (ELT) transmits on

A—118.0 MHz.
B—406 MHz.
C—123.0 MHz.

*ELTs transmit an audio tone on 406 MHz. (PLT402, PA.IX.D.K1, PH.VIII.K.K1) — AIM ¶6-2-4*

ALL

**3160.** When must batteries in an emergency locator transmitter (ELT) be replaced or recharged, if rechargeable?

A—After any inadvertent activation of the ELT.
B—When the ELT has been in use for more than 1 cumulative hour.
C—When the ELT can no longer be heard over the airplane's communication radio receiver.

*ELT batteries must be replaced after 1 hour of cumulative use or when 50 percent of their useful life has expired, whichever comes first. (PLT402, PA.IX.D.K1, PH.VIII.K.K1) — 14 CFR §91.207*

ALL

**3161.** When are non-rechargeable batteries of an emergency locator transmitter (ELT) required to be replaced?

A—Every 24 months.
B—When 50 percent of their useful life expires.
C—At the time of each 100-hour or annual inspection.

*ELT batteries must be replaced after 1 hour of cumulative use or when 50 percent of their useful life has expired, whichever comes first. (PLT402, PA.IX.D.K1, PH.VIII.K.K1) — 14 CFR §91.207*

ALL

**3820.** When must the battery in an emergency locator transmitter (ELT) be replaced (or recharged if the battery is rechargeable)?

A—After one-half the battery's useful life.
B—During each annual and 100-hour inspection.
C—Every 24 calendar months.

*ELT batteries must be replaced after 1 hour of cumulative use or when 50 percent of their useful life has expired, whichever comes first. (PLT402, PA.IX.D.K1, PH.VIII.K.K1) — AIM ¶6-2-4*

ALL

**3821.** When may an emergency locator transmitter (ELT) be tested?

A—Anytime.
B—At 15 and 45 minutes past the hour.
C—During the first 5 minutes after the hour.

*An ELT test should be conducted only during the first 5 minutes after any hour and then only for three audible sweeps. (PLT402, PA.IX.D.K1, PH.VIII.K.K1) — AIM ¶6-2-4*

ALL

**3822.** Which procedure is recommended to ensure that the emergency locator transmitter (ELT) has not been activated?

A—Turn off the aircraft ELT after landing.
B—Ask the airport tower if they are receiving an ELT signal.
C—Monitor 121.5 before engine shutdown.

*Immediately after hard landings and before parking, check radio frequency 121.5 MHz. (PLT402, PA.IX.D.K1, PH.VIII.K.K1) — AIM ¶6-2-4*

---

**Answers**

3819 [B]    3160 [B]    3161 [B]    3820 [A]    3821 [C]    3822 [C]

# Categories of Aircraft

The term **category**, when used with respect to the certification of aircraft, means a grouping of aircraft based upon intended use or operating limitations. Examples include normal, utility, aerobatic, restricted, experimental, transport, limited, and provisional categories.

Both restricted and experimental category aircraft are prohibited from carrying persons or property for compensation or hire. In addition, both categories are normally prohibited from flying over densely populated areas or in congested airways.

ALL
**3003.** With respect to the certification of aircraft, which is a category of aircraft?

A—Normal, utility, acrobatic.
B—Airplane, rotorcraft, glider.
C—Landplane, seaplane.

*With respect to the certification of aircraft, a category of aircraft means a grouping of aircraft based upon intended use or operating limitations. Examples include normal, utility, acrobatic, transport, limited, restricted, and provisional. (PLT371, PA.I.B.K1, PH.I.B.K1) — 14 CFR §1.1*

Answer (B) is incorrect because it refers to the certification of air-men, not aircraft. Answer (C) is incorrect because it is not any kind of category.

ALL
**3004.** With respect to the certification of aircraft, which is a class of aircraft?

A—Airplane, rotorcraft, glider, balloon.
B—Normal, utility, acrobatic, limited.
C—Transport, restricted, provisional.

*With respect to the certification of aircraft, class is a broad grouping of aircraft having similar means of propulsion, flight, or landing. Examples include airplane, rotorcraft, glider, balloon, landplane, and seaplane. (PLT371, PA.I.B.K1, PH.I.B.K1) — 14 CFR §1.1*

Answers (B) and (C) are incorrect because they refer to category of aircraft rather than class.

ALL
**3179.** Unless otherwise specifically authorized, no person may operate an aircraft that has an experimental certificate

A—beneath the floor of Class B airspace.
B—over a densely populated area or in a congested airway.
C—from the primary airport within Class D airspace.

*Unless otherwise authorized by the Administrator in special operating limitations, no person may operate an aircraft that has an experimental certificate over a densely populated area or in a congested airway. (PLT383, PA.I.B.K1, PH.I.B.K1) — 14 CFR §91.319*

AIR, GLI, RTC, WSC, PPC
**3178.** Which is normally prohibited when operating a restricted category civil aircraft?

A—Flight under instrument flight rules.
B—Flight over a densely populated area.
C—Flight within Class D airspace.

*No person may operate a restricted category civil aircraft within the United States:*

1. *Over a densely populated area.*

2. *In a congested airway.*

3. *Near a busy airport where passenger transport operations are conducted.*

*(PLT373, PA.I.B.K1, PH.I.B.K1) — 14 CFR §91.313*

**Answers**

| 3003 | [A] | 3004 | [A] | 3179 | [B] | 3178 | [B] |

# Formation Flight and Dropping Objects

Flying so close to another aircraft as to create a collision hazard is prohibited. If the intent is to fly formation, prior arrangement with the pilot-in-command of each aircraft is required. In any case, no person may operate an aircraft carrying passengers for hire in formation flight.

The PIC of an aircraft may not allow any object to be dropped while in flight unless reasonable precautions are taken to avoid injury or damage to persons or property on the surface.

ALL, SPO
**3088.** No person may operate an aircraft in formation flight

A—over a densely populated area.
B—in Class D airspace under special VFR.
C—except by prior arrangement with the pilot-in-command of each aircraft.

*No person may operate an aircraft in formation flight except by arrangement with the PIC of each aircraft in the formation. The only restriction to formation flight is when carrying passengers for hire. (PLT431, PA.I.A.K2, PH.I.A.K2) — 14 CFR §91.111*

ALL
**3076.** Under what conditions may objects be dropped from an aircraft?

A—Only in an emergency.
B—If precautions are taken to avoid injury or damage to persons or property on the surface.
C—If prior permission is received from the FAA.

*No PIC of a civil aircraft may allow any object to be dropped from an aircraft in flight that creates a hazard to persons or property. However, this does not prohibit the dropping of any object if reasonable precautions are taken to avoid injury or damage to persons or property. (PLT401, PA.I.A.K2, PH.I.A.K2) — 14 CFR §91.15*

SPO
**2133-1.** Which is true with respect to formation flights? Formation flights are

A—authorized when carrying passengers for hire, with prior arrangement with the pilot-in-command of each aircraft in the formation.
B—not authorized, except by arrangement with the pilot-in-command of each aircraft.
C—not authorized, unless the pilot-in-command of each aircraft is trained and found competent in formation.

*No person may operate an aircraft so close to another aircraft as to create a collision hazard. No person may operate an aircraft in formation flight except by arrangement with the PIC of each aircraft in the formation. No person may operate an aircraft, carrying passengers for hire, in formation flight. (PLT431) — 14 CFR §91.111*

**Answers**

3088　[C]　　　　3076　[B]　　　　2133-1 [B]

# Speed Limits

The following maximum speed limits for aircraft have been established in the interest of safety:

1. Below 10,000 feet MSL, the speed limit is 250 knots indicated air speed (KIAS). See Figure 5-8A.
2. The speed limit within Class B airspace (Figure 5-8B) is also 250 KIAS.
3. The maximum speed authorized in a VFR corridor through Class B airspace (Figure 5-8C) or in airspace underlying Class B airspace (Figure 5-8D) is 200 KIAS.
4. In Class D airspace, aircraft are restricted to a maximum of 200 KIAS (Figure 5-8E).
5. Unless otherwise authorized or required by ATC, no person may operate an aircraft at or below 2,500 feet AGL within 4 NM of the primary airport of a Class C or Class D airspace area at an indicated airspeed of more than 200 knots.

**Figure 5-8.** Maximum speed limits

AIR, RTC

**3097.** Unless otherwise authorized, what is the maximum indicated airspeed at which a person may operate an aircraft below 10,000 feet MSL?

A—200 knots.
B—250 knots.
C—288 knots.

*Maximum speed below 10,000 feet MSL is 250 knots. (PLT383, PA.I.E.K1, PH.I.E.K1) — 14 CFR §91.117*

AIR, RTC

**3098.** Unless otherwise authorized, the maximum indicated airspeed at which aircraft may be flown when at or below 2,500 feet AGL and within 4 nautical miles of the primary airport of Class C airspace is

A—200 knots.
B—230 knots.
C—250 knots.

*Unless otherwise authorized or required by ATC, no person may operate an aircraft at or below 2,500 feet AGL within 4 NM of the primary airport of a Class C or Class D airspace area at an indicated airspeed of more than 200 knots. (PLT383, PA.I.E.K1, PH.I.E.K1) — 14 CFR §91.117*

AIR, RTC

**3099.** When flying in the airspace underlying Class B airspace, the maximum speed authorized is

A—200 knots.
B—230 knots.
C—250 knots.

*No person may operate an aircraft in the airspace underlying Class B airspace at a speed of more than 200 knots. (PLT161, PA.I.E.K1, PH.I.E.K1) — 14 CFR §91.117*

AIR, RTC

**3100.** When flying in a VFR corridor designated through Class B airspace, the maximum speed authorized is

A—180 knots.
B—200 knots.
C—250 knots.

*Maximum speed in a VFR corridor through Class B airspace is 200 KIAS. (PLT161, PA.I.E.K1, PH.I.E.K1) — 14 CFR §91.117*

# Airworthiness

Each aircraft is issued an airworthiness certificate, which remains valid as long as the aircraft is maintained and operated as required by regulations. This airworthiness certificate, along with the aircraft registration certificate, operating limitations, and weight and balance must be aboard the aircraft during flight. Remember:

- **A**irworthiness
- **R**egistration
- **O**perating limitations
- **W**eight and balance

The aircraft's operating limitations may be found in the airplane flight manual, approved manual material, markings, and placards, or any combination thereof.

Summarized below are important points in understanding the definition of light-sport aircraft and the privileges associated with the Sport Pilot Certificate:

- Two-place maximum (pilot and one passenger).
- Maximum gross takeoff weight 1,320 lbs (599 kg); 1,430 lbs for seaplanes.
- Lighter-than-air light-sport aircraft maximum gross weight 660 lbs (300 kg).
- Maximum stall speed 51.8 mph (45 knots).
- Maximum speed in level flight with maximum continuous power 138 mph (120 knots).

**Answers**

| 3097 [B] | 3098 [A] | 3099 [A] | 3100 [B] |
|----------|----------|----------|----------|

- All LSA aircraft logbook signoffs are based on a specific make and model, allowing you to fly a similar "set" of performance and handling aircraft. Aircraft are organized by the FAA from classes to sets in the following order:
  - **Category and class**—fixed wing/airplane category (land and sea classes), weight-shift control/trike category (land and sea classes), powered parachute category (land and sea classes), glider, rotorcraft category (gyroplane class), lighter-than-air category (balloon and airship classes).
  - **Set**—a more detailed breakdown of similar performance and handling.
  - **Make and model**—manufacturer specific that define/specify a set.
  - **Type**—special light-sport aircraft (S-LSA) or experimental light-sport aircraft (E-LSA).
- Single, non-turbine engine only, includes rotary or diesel engines.
- Fixed or ground-adjustable propeller.
- Unpressurized cabin with fixed landing gear.
- Seaplanes with landing gear that can be configured so the wheels rotate for amphibious operation.
- Will have FAA registration N number.
- U.S. or foreign manufacture of light-sport aircraft is authorized.
- S-LSA are manufactured and sold ready-to-fly under a new certification without 14 CFR Part 23 compliance, but must meet ASTM consensus standards. Aircraft under this certification may be used for sport and recreation, flight training, and aircraft rental.
- E-LSA are a kit built from an S-LSA design. May be used for sport and recreation and flight instruction for the owner of the aircraft.
- Aircraft with a standard airworthiness certificate (vintage production aircraft) that meet LSA specifications may be flown by sport pilots. However, that airworthiness certification category will not be changed to a light-sport aircraft. Maintenance must therefore be done by an A&P as it has in the past.
- Holders of a Sport Pilot Certificate may fly an aircraft with a standard airworthiness certificate if it meets the definition of a light-sport aircraft.
- May be operated at night if the aircraft is equipped per 14 CFR §91.209 and the pilot holds at least a Private Pilot certificate and a minimum of a third-class medical.
- May operate an amateur-built E-LSA in which the amateur-builder completes 51% of the building of the aircraft.

ALL
**3075.** Where may an aircraft's operating limitations be found?

A—On the airworthiness certificate.
B—In the current, FAA-approved flight manual, approved manual material, markings, and placards, or any combination thereof.
C—In the aircraft airframe and engine logbooks.

*No person may operate a civil aircraft without complying with the limitations found in the approved flight manual, markings, and placards. (PLT373, PA.I.B.K1, PH.I.B.K1) — 14 CFR §91.9*

ALL
**3075-1.** Where may an aircraft's operating limitations be found if the aircraft has an experimental or special light-sport airworthiness certificate?

A—Attached to the Airworthiness Certificate.
B—In the current, FAA-approved flight manual.
C—In the aircraft airframe and engine logbooks.

*Operating limitations for experimental and special light-sport aircraft are attached to the airworthiness certificate. 14 CFR §21.190 and §91.319 describe the qualification for issuance and operating limitations. FAA Order 8130.2G specifically states that the operating limitations will be attached to FAA Form 8130-7. (PLT400, PA.I.B.K1, PH.I.B.K1) — 14 CFR §21.190, §91.319*

**Answers**

3075    [B]                 3075-1 [A]

ALL, SPO

**3159.** In addition to a valid airworthiness certificate, what documents or records must be aboard an aircraft during flight?

A—Aircraft engine and airframe logbooks, and owner's manual.
B—Radio operator's permit, and repair and alteration forms.
C—Operating limitations and registration certificate.

*No person may operate an aircraft unless it has within it:*

1. *An appropriate and current airworthiness certificate, displayed at the cabin or flight deck entrance so that it is legible to passengers or crew.*

2. *A registration certificate issued to its owner.*

3. *An approved flight manual, manual material, markings and placards or any combination thereof, which show the operating limitations of the aircraft.*

*(PLT400, PA.I.B.K1, PH.I.B.K1) — 14 CFR §91.203*

ALL, SPO

**3187.** How long does the airworthiness certificate of an aircraft remain valid?

A—As long as the aircraft has a current registration certificate.
B—Indefinitely, unless the aircraft suffers major damage.
C—As long as the aircraft is maintained and operated as required by Federal Aviation Regulations.

*Unless sooner surrendered, suspended, revoked, or a termination date is otherwise established by the Administrator, standard airworthiness certificates and airworthiness certificates issued for restricted or limited category aircraft are effective as long as the maintenance, preventive maintenance, and alterations are performed in accordance with Parts 43 and 91 and the aircraft are registered in the United States. (PLT377, PA.I.B.K1a, PH.I.B.K1) — 14 CFR §21.181*

# Maintenance and Inspections

The owner or operator of an aircraft is primarily responsible for maintaining that aircraft in an airworthy condition, including compliance with Airworthiness Directives. The owner is also responsible for all records of maintenance, repairs, and alterations. (The pilot-in-command is responsible for determining that the aircraft is in an airworthy condition prior to flight.) The airworthiness of an aircraft can be determined by a preflight inspection and a review of the maintenance records.

The holder of a pilot certificate is allowed (within certain limits) to perform preventive maintenance on any aircraft they own and operate. Preventive maintenance is limited to tasks such as replacing defective safety wire, servicing landing gear wheel bearings, replacing safety belts, and other tasks listed in 14 CFR Part 43, Appendix A. After preventive maintenance has been performed on an aircraft, the signature, certificate type and certificate number of the person approving the aircraft for return to service, and a description of the work must be entered in the aircraft maintenance records.

An aircraft may not be operated unless, within the preceding 12 calendar months, it has had an annual inspection and has been approved for return to service. This will be indicated by the appropriate notation in the aircraft maintenance records. To determine the expiration date of the last annual inspection, refer to the aircraft maintenance records. For example, if the aircraft's last annual inspection was performed on July 12, 2023, the next annual inspection will be due no later than midnight, July 31, 2024.

If an aircraft is used to carry passengers for hire or used for flight instruction for hire, it must have, in addition to the annual inspection, an inspection following each 100 hours of flight time. (An annual inspection may be substituted for the 100-hour inspection, but a 100-hour inspection may not be substituted for an annual inspection.) The 100-hour limitation may be exceeded by not more than 10 hours if necessary to reach a place at which the inspection can be done. The excess time should not be used in computing the next 100 hours of time in service. The next 100-hour inspection should be performed 100 hours after the previous inspection was due, not after the time the inspection was actually completed. For example: a 100-hour inspection was due at 3,302.5 hours on the hobbs meter. The 100-hour inspection was actually done at 3,309.5 hours. The next 100-hour inspection is due at 3,402.5 hours.

**Answers**

3159  [C]          3187  [C]

The transponder cannot be operated unless within the preceding 24 calendar months, it has been inspected and found satisfactory.

If an aircraft has been maintained, rebuilt, or altered in any manner that may have appreciably changed its flight characteristics or operation in flight, no passengers may be carried until it has been flight tested by an appropriately rated pilot (with at least a Private Pilot Certificate) and approved for return to service.

## Light-Sport Repair Certificates

Two additional repairman certificates are available for working on light-sport aircraft: the Maintenance and Inspection Ratings.

The **Maintenance Rating** allows repairmen to do maintenance, preventative maintenance, and alterations to E-LSA and S-LSA. The course is 120 hours (airplane category); 104 hours (weight-shift or powered parachute); 80 hours (glider or lighter-than-air). An A&P certificate counts towards these hour requirements for light-sport aircraft qualifications, but additional training on specific category of aircraft will be required.

The **Inspection Rating** allows E-LSA repairmen and owners the ability to perform the annual inspection on their own aircraft. This course is 16 hours on the specific aircraft category and class. The 100-hour inspection required for training and hire for all E-LSA and S-LSA must be done by an appropriately-rated A&P mechanic or an LSA repairman with a Maintenance Rating.

Light-sport aircraft FAA Designated Airworthiness Representatives (DAR) must attend a three-day FAA course to inspect and issue E-LSA and S-LSA airworthiness certificates.

### S-LSA Maintenance

A certificated pilot (Sport Pilot rating or higher) can perform preventive maintenance as specified by the manufacturer (typically similar to 14 CFR Part 43, Appendix A) and return to service on his own aircraft with no Sport Pilot Repairman Certificate. However, the annual and 100-hour condition inspection must be completed by:

- An appropriately rated A&P mechanic;
- An appropriately rated repair station; or
- A light-sport repairman with a Maintenance Rating.

### E-LSA Maintenance

No rating is required to perform maintenance on E-LSA. The annual condition inspection can be completed by:

- An appropriately-rated A&P mechanic;
- An appropriately-rated repair station;
- A light-sport repairman with a Maintenance Rating; or
- A light-sport repairman with an Inspection Rating (16 hour course) on their own aircraft.

ALL

**3180-1.** The responsibility for ensuring that an aircraft is maintained in an airworthy condition is primarily that of the

A—pilot-in-command.
B—owner or operator.
C—mechanic who performs the work.

*The owner or operator of an aircraft is primarily responsible for maintaining the aircraft in an airworthy condition. The PIC of a civil aircraft is responsible for determining whether that aircraft is in condition for safe flight. (PLT374, PA.I.B.K1, PH.I.B.K1) — 14 CFR §91.403*

ALL

**3180-2.** The airworthiness of an aircraft can be determined by a preflight inspection and a

A—statement from the owner or operator that the aircraft is airworthy.
B—log book endorsement from a flight instructor.
C—review of the maintenance records.

*The airworthiness of an aircraft can be determined by a preflight inspection and a review of the maintenance records. Each owner or operator shall ensure that maintenance personnel make appropriate entries in the aircraft maintenance records indicating maintenance done and the aircraft has been approved for return to service. (PLT377, PA.I.B.K1, PH.I.B.K1) — 14 CFR §91.405*

ALL

**3181-1.** The responsibility for ensuring that maintenance personnel make the appropriate entries in the aircraft maintenance records indicating the aircraft has been approved for return to service lies with the

A—owner or operator.
B—pilot-in-command.
C—mechanic who performed the work.

*The registered owner or operator shall ensure that the aircraft maintenance records include the signature and the certificate number of the person approving the aircraft for return to service. (PLT374, PA.I.B.K1b, PH.I.B.K1) — 14 CFR §91.417*

ALL

**3181-2.** Who is responsible for ensuring appropriate entries are made in maintenance records indicating the aircraft has been approved for return to service?

A—Owner or operator.
B—Certified mechanic.
C—Repair station.

*Each owner or operator shall ensure that maintenance personnel make appropriate entries in the aircraft maintenance records indicating maintenance done and the aircraft has been approved for return to service. (PLT374, PA.I.B.K1b, PH.I.B.K1) — 14 CFR §91.405*

ALL

**3182.** Completion of an annual condition inspection and the return of the aircraft to service should always be indicated by

A—the relicensing date on the registration certificate.
B—an appropriate notation in the aircraft maintenance records.
C—an inspection sticker placed on the instrument panel that lists the annual inspection completion date.

*Each registered owner or operator shall keep records of the maintenance and alteration, and records of the 100-hour, annual, progressive, and other required or approved inspections, as appropriate, for each aircraft (including the airframe) and each engine, propeller, rotor, and appliance of an aircraft. The records must include:*

*1. A description (or reference to data acceptable to the Administrator) of the work performed;*

*2. The date of completion of the work performed; and*

*3. The signature and certificate number of the person approving the aircraft for return to service.*

*(PLT372, PA.I.B.K1b, PH.I.B.K1) — 14 CFR §91.417*

ALL

**3185.** An aircraft's annual condition inspection was performed on July 12, this year. The next annual inspection will be due no later than

A—July 1, next year.
B—July 13, next year.
C—July 31, next year.

*No person may operate an aircraft unless, within the preceding 12 calendar months, it has had an annual inspection in accordance with Part 43 and has been approved for return to service by an authorized person. (PLT372, PA.I.B.K1b, PH.I.B.K1) — 14 CFR §91.409*

**Answers**

3180-1 [B]          3180-2 [C]          3181-1 [A]          3181-2 [A]          3182  [B]          3185  [C]

ALL
**3186.** To determine the expiration date of the last annual aircraft inspection, a person should refer to the

A—airworthiness certificate.
B—registration certificate.
C—aircraft maintenance records.

*Each registered owner or operator shall keep records of the maintenance and alteration, and records of the 100-hour, annual, progressive, and other required or approved inspections, as appropriate, for each aircraft (including the airframe) and each engine, propeller, rotor, and appliance of an aircraft. (PLT372, PA.I.B.K1, PH.I.B.K1) — 14 CFR §91.417*

ALL
**3188.** What aircraft inspections are required for rental aircraft that are also used for flight instruction?

A—Annual condition and 100-hour inspections.
B—Biannual condition and 100-hour inspections.
C—Annual condition and 50-hour inspections.

*No person may operate an aircraft carrying any person for hire, and no person may give flight instruction for hire in an aircraft which that person provides, unless within the preceding 100 hours of time in service it has received an annual or 100-hour inspection and been approved for return to service. (PLT426, PA.I.B.K1b, PH.I.B.K1) — 14 CFR §91.409*

ALL
**3191.** No person may use an ATC transponder unless it has been tested and inspected within at least the preceding

A—6 calendar months.
B—12 calendar months.
C—24 calendar months.

*No person may use an ATC transponder unless within the preceding 24 calendar months, the ATC transponder has been tested and inspected and found to comply with Appendix F of Part 43. (PLT426, PA.I.B.K1b, PH.I.B.K1) — 14 CFR §91.413*

ALL
**3192.** Maintenance records show the last transponder inspection was performed on September 1, 2014. The next inspection will be due no later than

A—September 30, 2015.
B—September 1, 2016.
C—September 30, 2016.

*No person may use an ATC transponder unless within the preceding 24 calendar months, the ATC transponder has been tested and inspected and found to comply with Appendix F of Part 43. (PLT508, PA.I.B.K1b, PH.I.B.K1) — 14 CFR §91.413*

ALL
**3013-1.** Preventive maintenance has been performed on an aircraft. What paperwork is required?

A—A full, detailed description of the work done must be entered in the airframe logbook.
B—The date the work was completed, and the name of the person who did the work must be entered in the airframe and engine logbook.
C—The signature, certificate number, and kind of certificate held by the person approving the work and a description of the work must be entered in the aircraft maintenance records.

*Each registered owner or operator shall keep records of preventative maintenance. The records must include:*

1. *A description of the work performed;*

2. *The date of completion of the work performed; and*

3. *The signature and certificate number of the person approving the aircraft for return to service (could be pilot certificate number for Part 43 when you are doing your own preventative maintenance).*

*(PLT446, PA.I.B.K2, PH.I.B.K1) — 14 CFR §91.417*

Answer (A) is incorrect because it is incomplete. Answer (B) is incorrect because it refers to who performed the work rather than who approved it.

ALL
**3013-2.** What regulation allows a private pilot to perform preventive maintenance?

A—14 CFR §91.403.
B—14 CFR §43.7.
C—14 CFR §61.113.

*14 CFR §43.7, "Persons authorized to approve aircraft, airframes, aircraft engines, propellers, appliances, or component parts for return to service after maintenance, preventive maintenance, rebuilding, or alteration," says a person holding at least a private pilot certificate may approve an aircraft for return to service after performing preventive maintenance under the provisions of §43.3(g). (PLT375, PA.I.B.K2, PH.I.B.K2) — 14 CFR §43.7*

Answer (A) is incorrect because 14 CFR §91.403 explains that the owner or operator must maintain the aircraft in airworthy condition. Answer (C) is incorrect because 14 CFR §61.113 details the private pilot privileges and limitations while operating as pilot-in-command.

ALL
**3013-3.** Who may perform preventive maintenance on an aircraft and approve it for service?

A—Student or recreational pilot.
B—Private or commercial pilot.
C—None of the above.

*A person holding at least a Private Pilot Certificate may approve an aircraft for return to service after performing preventive maintenance. (PLT375, PA.I.B.K2, PH.I.B.K2) — 14 CFR §43.7*

ALL
**3014.** Which operation would be described as preventive maintenance?

A—Replenishing hydraulic fluid.
B—Repair of portions of skin sheets by making additional seams.
C—Repair of landing gear brace struts.

*Preventative maintenance items which can be performed by the pilot are listed in Part 43 and include such basic items as oil changes, wheel bearing lubrication, and hydraulic fluid (brakes, landing gear system) refills. (PLT446, PA.I.B.K2, PH.I.B.K2) — 14 CFR Part 43*

Answers (B) and (C) are incorrect because they both list major maintenance.

ALL
**3183.** If an alteration or repair substantially affects an aircraft's operation in flight, that aircraft must be test flown by an appropriately-rated pilot and approved for return to service prior to being operated

A—by any private pilot.
B—with passengers aboard.
C—for compensation or hire.

*No person may carry any person (other than crewmembers) in an aircraft that has been maintained, rebuilt, or altered in a manner that may have appreciably changed its flight characteristics or substantially affected its operation in flight until an appropriately rated pilot with at least a Private Pilot Certificate flies the aircraft, makes an operational check of the maintenance performed or alteration made, and logs the flight in the aircraft records. (PLT375, PA.I.B.K1b, PH.I.B.K1) — 14 CFR §91.407*

ALL
**3184.** Before passengers can be carried in an aircraft that has been altered in a manner that may have appreciably changed its flight characteristics, it must be flight tested by an appropriately-rated pilot who holds at least a

A—Commercial Pilot Certificate with an Instrument Rating.
B—Private Pilot Certificate.
C—Commercial Pilot Certificate and a mechanic's certificate.

*No person may carry any person (other than crewmembers) in an aircraft that has been maintained, rebuilt, or altered in a manner that may have appreciably changed its flight characteristics or substantially affected its operation in flight until an appropriately rated pilot with at least a Private Pilot Certificate flies the aircraft, makes an operational check of the maintenance performed or alteration made, and logs the flight in the aircraft records. (PLT375, PA.I.B.K1b, PH.I.B.K1) — 14 CFR §91.407*

**Answers**

3013-2 [B]        3013-3 [B]        3014   [A]        3183   [B]        3184   [B]

AIR, RTC, WSC, PPC

**3189.** An aircraft had a 100-hour inspection when the tachometer read 1259.6. When is the next 100-hour inspection due?

A—1349.6 hours.
B—1359.6 hours.
C—1369.6 hours.

*The 100-hour limitation may be exceeded by not more than 10 hours if necessary to reach a place at which the inspection can be done. The excess time, however, is included in computing the next 100 hours in service.*

   1259.6  *time at 100-hour inspection*
+ *100.0  time in service*
   1359.6  *time next inspection due*

*(PLT372, PA.I.B.K1b, PH.I.B.K1) — 14 CFR §91.409*

AIR, RTC, WSC, PPC

**3190.** A 100-hour inspection was due at 3302.5 hours. The 100-hour inspection was actually done at 3309.5 hours. When is the next 100-hour inspection due?

A—3312.5 hours.
B—3402.5 hours.
C—3395.5 hours.

*The 100-hour limitation may be exceeded by not more than 10 hours if necessary to reach a place at which the inspection can be done. The excess time, however, is included in computing the next 100 hours in service.*

   3302.5  *time inspection was due*
+ *100.0  time in service*
   3402.5  *time next inspection due*

*(PLT372, PA.I.B.K1b, PH.I.B.K1) — 14 CFR §91.409*

# ADs, ACs, and NOTAMs

**Airworthiness Directives (ADs)** identify unsafe aircraft conditions and prescribe regulatory actions (such as inspections or modifications) or limitations under which the affected aircraft may continue to be operated and are mandatory. Compliance with an applicable AD must be entered in the appropriate aircraft maintenance records. The owner or operator is responsible for ensuring ADs are complied with. Pilots may operate an aircraft not in compliance with an AD, if the AD allows for this.

In addition to ADs, light-sport aircraft must comply with manufacturers' safety directives.

**Advisory Circulars (ACs)** are issued by the FAA to inform the aviation community in a systematic way of non-regulatory material of interest. In many cases, they are the result of a need to fully explain a particular subject (wake turbulence, for example). They are issued in a numbered-subject system corresponding to the subject areas of the Federal Aviation Regulations. Advisory Circulars (some free, others at cost) may be obtained by ordering from the Government Printing Office (GPO).

The *Aeronautical Information Manual (AIM)* is the official guide to basic flight information and ATC procedures. It is updated every 180 days and is available from the FAA website.

**Notices to Air Missions (NOTAMs)** provide the most current information available. They provide time-critical information on airports and changes that affect the national airspace system and are of concern to IFR operations. NOTAM information is classified into five categories: NOTAM (D) or distant, Flight Data Center (FDC) NOTAMs, pointer NOTAMs, Special Activity Airspace (SAA) NOTAMs, and military NOTAMs.

NOTAM (D)s are attached to hourly weather reports and are available at Flight Service Stations (AFSS/FSS). FDC NOTAMs are issued by the National Flight Data Center and contain regulatory information, such as temporary flight restrictions or an amendment to instrument approach procedures.

Pointer NOTAMs highlight or point out another NOTAM, such as an FDC or NOTAM (D). This type of NOTAM will assist pilots in cross-referencing important information that may not be found under an airport or NAVAID identifier. Military NOTAMs pertain to U.S. Air Force, Army, Marine, and Navy NAVAIDs/airports that are part of the NAS.

---

**Answers**

3189   [B]        3190   [B]

SAA NOTAMs are issued when Special Activity Airspace will be active outside the published schedule times and when required by the published schedule. Pilots and other users are still responsible to check published schedule times for Special Activity Airspace as well as any NOTAMs for that airspace.

NOTAM (D)s and FDC NOTAMs are contained in the Notices to Air Missions publication, which is issued every 28 days. Prior to any flight, pilots should check for any NOTAMs that could affect their intended flight.

An FDC NOTAM will be issued to designate a temporary flight restriction (TFR). The NOTAM will begin with the phrase "FLIGHT RESTRICTIONS" followed by the location of the temporary restriction, effective time period, area defined in statute miles, and altitudes affected. The NOTAM will also contain the FAA coordination facility and telephone number, the reason for the restriction, and any other information deemed appropriate. The pilot should check the NOTAMs as part of flight planning. Some of the purposes for establishing a temporary restriction are: protect persons and property in the air or on the surface from an existing or imminent hazard, provide a safe environment for the operation of disaster relief aircraft, prevent an unsafe congestion of sightseeing aircraft above an incident or event, which may generate a high degree of public interest, protect declared national disasters for humanitarian reasons in the State of Hawaii, protect the President, Vice President, or other public figures, provide a safe environment for space agency operations.

ALL

**3193.** Which records or documents shall the owner or operator of an aircraft keep to show compliance with an applicable Airworthiness Directive?

A—Aircraft maintenance records.
B—Airworthiness Certificate and Pilot's Operating Handbook.
C—Airworthiness and Registration Certificates.

*Each registered owner or operator shall keep records of the maintenance and alteration, and records of the 100-hour, annual, progressive, and other required or approved inspections, as appropriate, for each aircraft (including the airframe) and each engine, propeller, rotor, and appliance of an aircraft. (PLT425, PA.I.B.K1c, PH.I.B.K1c) — 14 CFR §91.417*

ALL

**3012-2.** What should an owner or operator know about Airworthiness Directives (ADs)?

A—For Informational purposes only.
B—They are mandatory.
C—They are voluntary.

*ADs are mandatory. No person may operate a product to which an airworthiness directive applies except in accordance with the requirements of that airworthiness directive. (PLT426, PA.I.B.K1c, PH.I.B.K1c) — 14 CFR §39.3*

ALL, SPO

**3012-3.** May a pilot operate an aircraft that is not in compliance with an Airworthiness Directive (AD)?

A—Yes, under VFR conditions only.
B—Yes, ADs are only voluntary.
C—Yes, if allowed by the AD.

*No person may operate a product to which an airworthiness directive applies except in accordance with the requirements of that airworthiness directive. (PLT378, PA.I.B.K1c, PH.I.B.K1c) — 14 CFR §39.3*

ALL

**3181-3.** Who is responsible for ensuring Airworthiness Directives (ADs) are complied with?

A—Owner or operator.
B—Repair station.
C—Mechanic with inspection authorization (IA).

*The owner or operator of an aircraft is primarily responsible for maintaining that aircraft in an airworthy condition, including compliance with the ADs found in 14 CFR Part 39. (PLT374, PA.I.B.K1c, PH.I.B.K1c) — 14 CFR §91.403*

**Answers**

3193    [A]          3012-2 [B]          3012-3 [C]          3181-3 [A]

ALL
**3709.** FAA Advisory Circulars (some free, others at cost) are available to all pilots and are obtained by

A—distribution from the nearest FAA district office.
B—ordering those desired from the Government Printing Office.
C—subscribing to the Federal Register.

*Advisory circulars which are offered for sale or free may be ordered from the Superintendent of Documents, U.S. Government Printing Office. (PLT116, PA.I.B.K1c, PH.I.B.K1c) — AC 00-2*

ALL
**3854.** FAA Advisory Circulars containing subject matter specifically related to Airmen are issued under which subject number?

A—60.
B—70.
C—90.

*Appendix II of the Advisory Circular Checklist contains the Circular Numbering System wherein advisory circular numbers relate to Federal Aviation Regulations subchapter titles and correspond to the parts and/or sections of the regulations. The four to remember are:*
    *20 — Aircraft;*
    *60 — Airmen;*
    *70 — Airspace; and*
    *90 — Air Traffic and General Operating Rules*

*(PLT116, PA.I.A.K1, PH.I.B.K1c) — AC 00-2*

ALL
**3855.** FAA Advisory Circulars containing subject matter specifically related to Airspace are issued under which subject number?

A—60.
B—70.
C—90.

*Appendix II of the Advisory Circular Checklist contains the Circular Numbering System wherein advisory circular numbers relate to Federal Aviation Regulations subchapter titles and correspond to the parts and/or sections of the regulations. The four to remember are:*
    *20 — Aircraft;*
    *60 — Airmen;*
    *70 — Airspace; and*
    *90 — Air Traffic and General Operating Rules*

*(PLT116, PA.I.E.K1, PH.I.B.K1c) — AC 00-2*

ALL, SPO
**3856.** FAA Advisory Circulars containing subject matter specifically related to Air Traffic Control and General Operations are issued under which subject number?

A—60.
B—70.
C—90.

*Appendix II of the Advisory Circular Checklist contains the Circular Numbering System wherein advisory circular numbers relate to Federal Aviation Regulations subchapter titles and correspond to the parts and/or sections of the regulations. The four to remember are:*
    *20 — Aircraft;*
    *60 — Airmen;*
    *70 — Airspace; and*
    *90 — Air Traffic and General Operating Rules*

*(PLT116, PA.III.A.K1, PH.I.B.K1c) — AC 00-2*

SPO
**2109.** Unless incorporated into a regulation by reference, Advisory Circulars (ACs) are issued to inform the public of nonregulatory material

A—and are not binding.
B—but are binding.
C—and self-cancel after 1 year.

*The FAA issues ACs to inform the aviation public in a systematic way of nonregulatory material. Unless incorporated into a regulation by reference, the contents of an AC are not binding on the public. (PLT116) — AC 00-2*

SPO
**2110.** Some Advisory Circulars (ACs) are available free of charge while the remaining ACs must be purchased. All aviation safety ACs may be obtained by following the procedures in the AC Checklist (AC 00-2) or by

A—referring to the FAA internet home page and following the links to ACs.
B—contacting the local airport Fixed Base Operator and requesting the desired AC.
C—reading the ACs in the *Aeronautical Information Manual (AIM)*.

*A number of FAA organizations have made their ACs available on the Internet. These ACs may be found through the FAA home page at: faa.gov located under Regulatory/Advisory, select Advisory Circulars. (PLT116) — AC 00-2*

*Answers (B) and (C) are incorrect because FBOs are not responsible for distributing ACs, nor are they included as part of the AIM.*

**Answers**

3709 [B]    3854 [A]    3855 [B]    3856 [C]    2109 [A]    2110 [A]

SPO

**2117.** The FAA publication that provides the aviation community with basic flight information and ATC procedures for use in the National Airspace System of the United States is the

A—*Aeronautical Information Manual (AIM).*
B—Chart Supplements U.S.
C—Advisory Circular Checklist (AC 00-2).

*The AIM is the official guide to basic flight information and ATC procedures. (PLT116) — AIM*

Answer (B) is incorrect because the Chart Supplements U.S. contains information on airports, communications, NAVAIDs, instrument landing systems, VOR receiver check points, preferred routes, Flight Service Station/weather service telephone numbers, ARTCC frequencies, part-time surface areas, and various other pertinent special notices essential to air navigation. Answer (C) is incorrect because AC 00-2 is the Advisory Circular Checklist and status of other FAA publications, contains advisory circulars that are for sale as well as those distributed free-of-charge by the FAA.

SPO

**2120.** Flight Data Center (FDC) NOTAMs are issued by the National Flight Data Center and contain regulatory information, such as

A—temporary flight restrictions.
B—markings and signs used at airports.
C—standard communication procedures at uncontrolled airports.

*FDC NOTAMs are issued by the National Flight Data Center and contain regulatory information, such as temporary flight restrictions. (PLT323) — FAA-H-8083-25*

SPO

**2121.** Time-critical information on airports and changes that affect the national airspace system are provided by

A—Notices to Air Missions (NOTAMs).
B—the Chart Supplements U.S.
C—Advisory Circulars (ACs).

*Notices to Air Missions provide the most current information available. They provide time-critical information on airports and changes that affect the national airspace system. (PLT323) — FAA-H-8083-25*

Answer (B) is incorrect because Chart Supplements U.S. are only revised every 8 weeks. Answer (C) is incorrect because the FAA issues ACs to inform the aviation public in a systematic way of nonregulatory material.

SPO

**2053.** One of the purposes for issuing a Temporary Flight Restriction (TFR) is to

A—announce parachute jump areas.
B—protect public figures.
C—identify airport advisory areas.

*TFRs are imposed in order to:*

1. *Protect persons and property in the air or on the surface from an existing or imminent flight associated hazard;*

2. *Provide a safe environment for the operation of disaster relief aircraft;*

3. *Prevent an unsafe congestion of sightseeing aircraft above an incident;*

4. *Protect the President, Vice President, or other public figures; and,*

5. *Provide a safe environment for space agency operations.*

*Pilots are expected to check appropriate NOTAMs during flight planning when conducting flight in an area where a temporary flight restriction is in effect. (PLT376) — FAA-H-8083-15, Glossary*

Answer (A) is incorrect because this is done through NOTAMs. Answer (C) is incorrect because these are identified through the Sectional and Chart Supplements U.S.

**Answers**

| 2117 | [A] | 2120 | [A] | 2121 | [A] | 2053 | [B] |

# Accident Reporting Requirements

The National Transportation Safety Board (NTSB) Part 830 contains rules pertaining to notification and reporting of aircraft accidents and incidents. It also addresses preservation of aircraft wreckage, mail, cargo, and records.

The term **accident** means "an occurrence in which any person suffers death or serious injury, or in which the aircraft receives substantial damage."

**Serious injury** means any injury which: (1) requires hospitalization for more than 48 hours, commencing within 7 days from the date the injury was received; (2) results in a fracture of any bone (except simple fractures of fingers, toes, or nose); (3) causes severe hemorrhages, nerve, muscle, or tendon damage; (4) involves any internal organ; or (5) involves second or third degree burns, or any burns affecting more than 5 percent of the body surface.

**Substantial damage** means damage or failure which adversely affects the structural strength, performance, or flight characteristics of the aircraft, and which would normally require major repair or replacement of the affected component. The following are *not* considered substantial damage: engine failure, bent fairings or cowling, dented skin, small punctured holes in the skin or fabric, ground damage to rotor or propeller blades, and damage to landing gear, wheels, tires, flaps, engine accessories, brakes, or wingtips.

The term **incident** means "an occurrence other than an accident, which affects or could affect the safety of operations."

Immediate notification of the NTSB is required when an aircraft accident occurs, and any of a specified list of incidents, which include:

1. Inability of a flight crewmember to perform their duties due to illness or injury;
2. Infight fire;
3. An aircraft is overdue and believed to have been involved in an accident;
4. Flight control system malfunction or failure; or
5. When aircraft collide in flight or damage of more than $25,000 occurs to property other than the aircraft.

The operator of an aircraft involved in an accident or incident which requires notification of the NTSB is responsible for preserving the wreckage, mail, or cargo until the NTSB takes custody. These items may be moved to protect the wreckage from further damage.

The operator of an aircraft involved in an accident is required to file an accident report within 10 days. A report of an incident must be reported only upon request.

---

ALL, SPO

**3194.** If an aircraft is involved in an accident which results in substantial damage to the aircraft, the nearest NTSB field office should be notified

A—immediately.
B—within 48 hours.
C—within 7 days.

*The operator of an aircraft shall immediately, and by the most expeditious means available, notify the nearest NTSB field office when an aircraft accident occurs. (PLT366, PA.III.A.K8, PH.III.B.K8) — 49 CFR §830.5*

ALL

**3195.** Which incident requires an immediate notification to the nearest NTSB field office?

A—A forced landing due to engine failure.
B—Landing gear damage due to a hard landing.
C—Flight control system malfunction or failure.

*A flight control system malfunction or failure requires immediate NTSB notification. (PLT366, PA.III.A.K8, PH.III.B.K8) — 49 CFR §830.5*

**Answers**

3194　[A]　　　　3195　[C]

ALL
**3196.** Which incident would necessitate an immediate notification to the nearest NTSB field office?

A—An inflight generator/alternator failure.
B—An inflight fire.
C—An inflight loss of VOR receiver capability.

*Immediate notification of the NTSB is necessary if an inflight fire occurs. (PLT366, PA.III.A.K8, PH.III.B.K8) — 49 CFR §830.5*

ALL
**3197.** Which incident requires an immediate notification be made to the nearest NTSB field office?

A—An overdue aircraft that is believed to be involved in an accident.
B—An inflight radio communications failure.
C—An inflight generator or alternator failure.

*When an aircraft is overdue and believed to have been involved in an accident, the NTSB must be notified immediately. (PLT366, PA.III.A.K8, PH.III.B.K8) — 49 CFR §830.5*

ALL, SPO
**3198.** May aircraft wreckage be moved prior to the time the NTSB takes custody?

A—Yes, but only if moved by a federal, state, or local law enforcement officer.
B—Yes, but only to protect the wreckage from further damage.
C—No, it may not be moved under any circumstances.

*Prior to the time the Board and its authorized representative takes custody of aircraft wreckage, it may not be disturbed or moved except to remove persons injured or trapped, to protect the wreckage from further damage, or to protect the public from injury. (PLT366, PA.III.A.K8, PH.III.B.K8) — 49 CFR §830.10*

ALL, SPO
**3199.** The pilot of an aircraft that has been involved in an accident is required to file an NTSB accident report within how many days?

A—5.
B—7.
C—10.

*The operator of an aircraft shall file a report on Board Form 6120.1 or 6120.2 within 10 days of an accident. (PLT366, PA.III.A.K8, PH.III.B.K8) — 49 CFR §830.15*

ALL, SPO
**3200.** The operator of an aircraft that has been involved in an incident is required to submit a report to the nearest field office of the NTSB

A—within 7 days.
B—within 10 days.
C—when requested.

*A report on an incident for which notification is required shall be filed only as requested by an authorized representative of the Board. (PLT366, PA.III.A.K8, PH.III.B.K8) — 49 CFR §830.15*

SPO
**2189.** While taxiing on the parking ramp, the landing gear, wheel, and tire are damaged by striking ground equipment. What action would be required to comply with 49 CFR Part 830?

A—A report must be filed with the nearest FAA field office within 7 days.
B—An immediate notification must be filed by the operator of the aircraft with the nearest NTSB field office.
C—No notification or report is required.

*This unfortunate event would not require notification or a report with the NTSB, as it is not an accident or considered substantial damage per the regulations. (PLT366) — 49 CFR §830.2*

Answer (A) is incorrect because a report must be filed within 7 days for certain accidents or injuries, of which the taxiing incident described here does not qualify. Answer (B) is incorrect because an immediate notification must be filed only when an aircraft accident occurs, of which the taxiing incident described here does not qualify.

**Answers**

| 3196 [B] | 3197 [A] | 3198 [B] | 3199 [C] | 3200 [C] | 2189 [C] |

SPO

**2211.** Which publication covers the procedures required for aircraft accident and incident reporting responsibilities for pilots?

A—14 CFR Part 61.
B—14 CFR Part 91.
C—49 CFR Part 830.

*49 CFR Part 830 contains regulations pertaining to notification and reporting of aircraft accidents or incidents and overdue aircraft, and preservation of aircraft wreckage, mail, cargo, and records. (PLT366) — 49 CFR Part 830*

Answer (A) is incorrect because 14 CFR Part 61 contains regulations on certification of pilots. Answer (B) is incorrect because 14 CFR Part 91 contains regulations on general operating and flight rules.

SPO

**2212.** Notification to the NTSB is required when there has been substantial damage

A—which requires repairs to landing gear.
B—to an engine caused by engine failure in flight.
C—which adversely affects structural strength or flight characteristics.

*The operator of an aircraft shall immediately, and by the most expeditious means available, notify the nearest NTSB field office when an aircraft accident occurs. An aircraft accident is an occurrence associated with the operation of an aircraft which takes place between the time any person boards the aircraft with the intention of flight and all such persons have disembarked, and in which any person suffers death or serious injury, or in which the aircraft receives substantial damage which adversely affects the structural strength, performance, or flight characteristics of the aircraft. (PLT366) — 49 CFR §830.2, §830.5*

SPO

**2213.** What period of time must a person be hospitalized before an injury may be defined by the NTSB as a "serious injury"?

A—10 days, with no other extenuating circumstances.
B—48 hours; commencing within 7 days after date of the injury.
C—72 hours; commencing within 10 days after date of the injury.

*Serious injury means any injury requiring hospitalization for more than 48 hours, commencing within 7 days from the date the injury was received. (PLT395) — 49 CFR §830.2*

SPO

**2214.** Which incident would require that the nearest NTSB field office be notified immediately?

A—Inflight fire.
B—Ground fire resulting in fire equipment dispatch.
C—Fire of the primary aircraft while in a hangar which results in damage to other property of more than $25,000.

*The operator of an aircraft shall immediately and by the most expeditious means available notify the nearest NTSB field office of any infight fire. (PLT416) — 49 CFR §830.5*

Answers (B) and (C) are incorrect because the regulation specifies "infight" fires only.

**Answers**

2211   [C]          2212   [C]          2213   [B]          2214   [A]

# Chapter 6
# Airspace and Airport Operations

# Airspace

Controlled airspace, that is, airspace within which some or all aircraft may be subject to air traffic control, consists of those areas designated as Class A, Class B, Class C, Class D, and Class E airspace.

Much of the controlled airspace begins at either 700 feet or 1,200 feet above the ground. The lateral limits and floors of Class E airspace of 700 feet are defined by a magenta vignette; while the lateral limits and floors of 1,200 feet are defined by a blue vignette if it abuts uncontrolled airspace. Floors other than 700 feet or 1,200 feet are indicated by a number indicating the floor.

**Class A**—Class A airspace extends from 18,000 feet MSL up to and including FL600 and is not depicted on VFR sectional charts. No flight under visual flight rules (VFR), including VFR-on-top, is authorized in Class A airspace.

**Class B**—Class B airspace consists of controlled airspace extending upward from the surface or higher to specified altitudes. Each Class B airspace sector, outlined in blue on the sectional aeronautical chart, is labeled with its delimiting altitudes. On the Terminal Area Chart, each Class B airspace sector is, again, outlined in blue and is labeled with its delimiting arcs, radials, and altitudes. Each Class B airspace location will contain at least one primary airport. An ATC clearance is required prior to operating within Class B airspace. A pilot landing or taking off from one of a group of twelve specific, busy airports must hold at least a Private Pilot Certificate. At other airports, a student pilot may not operate an aircraft on a solo flight within Class B airspace or to, from, or at an airport located within Class B airspace unless both ground and flight instruction has been received from an authorized instructor to operate within that Class B airspace or at that airport, and the flight and ground instruction has been received within that Class B airspace or at the specific airport for which the solo flight is authorized. The student's logbook must be endorsed within the preceding 90 days by the instructor who gave the flight training and the endorsement must specify that the student has been found competent to conduct solo flight operations in that Class B airspace or at that specific airport. Each airplane operating within Class B airspace must be equipped with a two-way radio with appropriate ATC frequencies, and a 4096 code transponder with Mode C automatic altitude-reporting capability.

**Class C**—All Class C airspace has the same dimensions with minor site variations. They are composed of two circles both centered on the primary airport. The inner circle (now called surface area) has a radius of 5 NM and extends from the surface up to 4,000 feet above the airport. The outer circle (now called shelf area) has a radius of 10 nautical miles and extends vertically from 1,200 feet AGL up to 4,000 feet above the primary airport. In addition to the Class C airspace proper, there is an outer area with a radius of 20 NM and vertical coverage from the lower limits of the radio/radar coverage up to the top of the approach control facility's delegated airspace. Within the outer area, pilots are encouraged to participate but it is not a VFR requirement. Class C airspace service to aircraft proceeding to a satellite airport will be terminated at a sufficient distance to allow time to change to the appropriate tower or advisory frequency. Aircraft departing satellite airports within Class C airspace shall establish two-way communication with ATC as soon as practicable after takeoff. On aeronautical charts, Class C airspace is depicted by solid magenta lines.

**Class D**—Class D airspace extends upward from the surface to approximately 2,500 feet AGL (the actual height is as needed). Class D airspace may include one or more airports and is normally 4 NM in radius. The actual size and shape is depicted by a blue dashed line and numbers showing the top. When the ceiling of Class D airspace is less than 1,000 feet and/or the visibility is less than 3 SM, pilots wishing to take off or land must hold an instrument rating, must have filed an instrument flight plan, and must have received an appropriate clearance from ATC. In addition, the aircraft must be equipped for instrument flight. At some locations, a pilot who does not hold an instrument rating may be authorized to take off or land when the weather is less than that required for visual flight rules. When special VFR flight is prohibited, it will be depicted by "No SVFR" above the airport information on the chart.

**Class E**—Magenta shading identifies Class E airspace starting at 700 feet AGL, and no shading (or blue if next to Class G airspace) identifies Class E airspace starting at 1,200 feet AGL. It may also start at other altitudes. All airspace from 14,500 feet to 17,999 feet and airspace above 60,000 feet is Class E airspace. It also includes the surface area of some airports with an instrument approach but no control tower.

An **airway** is a corridor of controlled airspace extending from 1,200 feet above the surface (or as designated) up to and including 17,999 feet MSL, and 4 NM either side of the centerline. The airway is indicated by a centerline, shown in blue.

**Class G**—Class G airspace is airspace within which ATC has neither the authority nor responsibility to exercise any control over air traffic. Class G airspace typically extends from the surface to the base of the overlying controlled (Class E) airspace which is normally 700 or 1,200 feet AGL. In some areas of the western United States and Alaska, Class G airspace may extend from the surface to 14,500 feet MSL. An exception to this rule occurs when 14,500 feet MSL is lower than 1,500 feet AGL.

**Prohibited Areas** are blocks of airspace within which the flight of aircraft is prohibited.

**Restricted Areas** denote the presence of unusual, often invisible, hazards to aircraft such as artillery firing, aerial gunnery, or guided missiles. Penetration of Restricted Areas without authorization of the using or controlling agency may be extremely hazardous to the aircraft and its occupants.

**Warning Areas** contain the same hazardous activities as those found in Restricted Areas, but are located in international airspace. Prohibited, restricted, or warning areas are depicted as shown in FAA Legend 1.

**Military Operations Areas (MOAs)** consist of airspace established for the purpose of separating certain military training activities from instrument flight rules (IFR) traffic. Pilots operating under VFR should exercise extreme caution while flying within an active MOA. Any FSS within 100 miles of the area will provide information concerning MOA hours of operation. Prior to entering an active MOA, pilots should contact the controlling agency for traffic advisories.

**Figure 6-1.** Airspace

**Alert Areas** may contain a high volume of pilot training activities or an unusual type of aerial activity, neither of which is hazardous to aircraft. Pilots of participating aircraft as well as pilots transiting the area are equally responsible for collision avoidance.

Aircraft are requested to remain at least 2,000 feet above the surface of National Parks, National Monuments, Wilderness and Primitive Areas, and National Wildlife Refuges.

**Military Training Routes (MTRs)** have been developed for use by the military for the purpose of conducting low-altitude, high-speed training. Generally, MTRs are established below 10,000 feet MSL for operations at speeds in excess of 250 knots.

**IFR Military Training Routes (IR)** operations are conducted in accordance with IFR, regardless of weather conditions. **VFR Military Training Routes (VR)** operations are conducted in accordance with VFR. IR and VR at and below 1,500 feet AGL (with no segment above 1,500) will be identified by four digit numbers, e.g., VR1351, IR1007. IR and VR above and below 1,500 feet AGL (segments of these routes may be below 1,500) will be identified by three digit numbers, e.g., IR341, VR426.

ALL, SPO

**3599.** (Refer to Figure 25, area 4.) The floor of Class B airspace overlying Hicks Airport (T67) north-northwest of Fort Worth Meacham Field is

A—at the surface.
B—3,200 feet MSL.
C—4,000 feet MSL.

*The thick blue lines on the sectional chart indicate the boundaries of the overlying Class B airspace. Within each segment, the floor and ceiling are denoted by one number over a second number or the letters SFC. The floor of the Class B airspace is 4,000 feet MSL. (PLT040, PA.I.E.K2, PH.I.E.K2) — AIM ¶3-2-3*

ALL, SPO

**3600.** (Refer to Figure 25, area 2.) The floor of Class B airspace at Addison Airport is

A—at the surface.
B—3,000 feet MSL.
C—3,100 feet MSL.

*The thick blue lines on the sectional chart indicate the boundaries of the overlying Class B airspace. Within each segment, the floor and ceiling are denoted by one number over a second number or the letters SFC. The floor of the Class B airspace is 3,000 feet MSL. (PLT040, PA.I.E.K2, PH.I.E.K2) — AIM ¶3-2-3*

ALL

**3126.** What minimum pilot certification is required for operation within Class B airspace?

A—Commercial Pilot Certificate.
B—Private Pilot Certificate or Student Pilot Certificate with appropriate logbook endorsements.
C—Private Pilot Certificate with an Instrument Rating.

*It is generally true that no person may operate a civil aircraft within Class B airspace unless the pilot-in-command holds at least a Private Pilot Certificate or is a student pilot that has the proper logbook endorsements. However, there are certain Class B airports which never permit students, even if they have the proper endorsements. (PLT161, PA.I.E.K1, PH.I.E.K1) — 14 CFR §91.131*

Answer (A) is incorrect because Private pilots may operate in Class B airspace. Answer (C) is incorrect because only some airports restrict student pilots, and none require an Instrument Rating.

ALL

**3127.** What minimum pilot certification is required for operation within Class B airspace?

A—Private Pilot Certificate or Student Pilot Certificate with appropriate logbook endorsements.
B—Recreational Pilot Certificate.
C—Private Pilot Certificate with an Instrument Rating.

*It is generally true that no person may operate a civil aircraft within Class B airspace unless the pilot-in-command holds at least a Private Pilot Certificate or a student pilot has the proper logbook endorsements. However, there are some Class B airports which never permit students, even if they have the proper endorsements. (PLT161, PA.I.E.K1, PH.I.E.K1) — 14 CFR §61.95, §91.131*

Answer (B) is incorrect because the PIC must hold at least a Private Pilot Certificate. Answer (C) is incorrect because an Instrument Rating is not required to operate within Class B airspace.

**Answers**

| 3599 | [C] | 3600 | [B] | 3126 | [B] | 3127 | [A] |
|------|-----|------|-----|------|-----|------|-----|

ALL

**3128.** What minimum radio equipment is required for VFR operation within Class B airspace?

A—Two-way radio communications equipment and a 4096-code transponder.

B—Two-way radio communications equipment, a 4096-code transponder, and an encoding altimeter.

C—Two-way radio communications equipment, a 4096-code transponder, an encoding altimeter, and a VOR or TACAN receiver.

*Unless otherwise authorized by ATC, no person may operate an aircraft within Class B airspace unless that aircraft is equipped with an operable two-way radio capable of communications with ATC, a transponder with applicable altitude reporting equipment, and an encoding altimeter. (PLT161, PA.I.E.K1, PH.I.E.K1) — 14 CFR §91.131*

ALL

**3628.** (Refer to Figure 25.) At which airports is fixed-wing Special VFR not authorized?

A—Fort Worth Meacham and Fort Worth Spinks.

B—Dallas-Fort Worth International and Dallas Love Field.

C—Addison and Dallas Executive.

*Special VFR operations by fixed-wing aircraft are prohibited in some Class B, C, and D airspaces due to the volume of IFR traffic. These airspaces are depicted by the notation "No SVFR" over the airport information. (PLT064, PA.I.E.K2, PH.I.E.K2) — AIM ¶4-4-6*

ALL, SPO

**3117.** A blue segmented circle on a Sectional Chart depicts which class airspace?

A—Class B.

B—Class C.

C—Class D.

*A blue segmented circle on a sectional chart depicts Class D airspace which means a control tower is in operation. (PLT101, PA.I.E.K2, PH.I.E.K2) — 14 CFR §1.1*

Answer (A) is incorrect because Class B airspace is depicted by a solid blue line. Answer (B) is incorrect because Class C airspace is depicted by a solid magenta line.

ALL, SPO

**3118.** Airspace at an airport with a part-time control tower is classified as Class D airspace only

A—when the weather minimums are below basic VFR.

B—when the associated control tower is in operation.

C—when the associated Flight Service Station is in operation.

*Class D airspace means a control tower is in operation. If the tower closes, it reverts to Class E airspace. (PLT161, PA.I.E.K1, PH.I.E.K1) — 14 CFR §1.1*

Answer (A) is incorrect because weather minimums have nothing to do with airspace classifications. Answer (C) is incorrect because an FSS has nothing to do with the class of airspace.

ALL

**3787.** The lateral dimensions of Class D airspace are based on

A—the number of airports that lie within the Class D airspace.

B—5 statute miles from the geographical center of the primary airport.

C—the instrument procedures for which the controlled airspace is established.

*The dimensions of Class D airspace are as needed for each individual circumstance. The airspace may include extensions necessary for IFR arrival and departure paths. (PLT161, PA.I.E.K1, PH.I.E.K1) — AIM ¶3-2-5*

ALL

**3787-1.** When a control tower, located on an airport within Class D airspace, ceases operation for the day, what happens to the airspace designation?

A—The airspace designation normally will not change.

B—The airspace remains Class D airspace as long as a weather observer or automated weather system is available.

C—The airspace reverts to Class E or a combination of Class E and G airspace during the hours the tower is not in operation.

*By definition, Class D airspace surrounds airports that have an operational control tower. Class D airspace reverts to Class E airspace (if the weather observer is present or the weather system is automated) or Class G airspace (at the airports where the tower controllers are also the weather observers). (PLT162, PA.I.E.K1, PH.I.E.K2) — AIM ¶3-2-5*

Answer (A) is incorrect because the tower must be operational

---

**Answers**

3128 [B]     3628 [B]     3117 [C]     3118 [B]     3787 [C]     3787-1 [C]

*for the airspace to be designated Class D. Answer (B) is incorrect because the airspace will revert to Class E if the tower is closed but the weather observer is present or an automated weather system is available.*

ALL

**3788.** A non-tower satellite airport, within the same Class D airspace as that designated for the primary airport, requires radio communications be established and maintained with the

A—satellite airport's UNICOM.
B—associated Flight Service Station.
C—primary airport's control tower.

*Radio communications must be established and maintained with the primary control tower even when operating to and from a non-tower airport located within the lateral limits of Class D airspace. On takeoff from a satellite airport, communication must be established as soon as practicable after takeoff. (PLT162, PA.I.E.K1, PH.I.E.K1) — AIM ¶3-2-5*

ALL

**3124.** Two-way radio communication must be established with the Air Traffic Control facility having jurisdiction over the area prior to entering which class airspace?

A—Class C.
B—Class E.
C—Class G.

*Two-way radio communication must be established with the ATC facility having jurisdiction over the Class C airspace prior to entry and thereafter as instructed by ATC. (PLT434, PA.I.E.K1, PH.I.E.K1) — 14 CFR §91.130*

*Answers (B) and (C) are incorrect because airports within Class E and G airspace only require two-way radio communication when a control tower is present.*

ALL, SPO

**3799.** Which initial action should a pilot take prior to entering Class C airspace?

A—Contact approach control on the appropriate frequency.
B—Contact the tower and request permission to enter.
C—Contact the FSS for traffic advisories.

*Radio contact is required to operate in Class C airspace, but permission is not required. (PLT161, PA.I.E.K1, PH.I.E.K1) — AIM ¶3-2-4*

ALL, SPO

**3779.** The vertical limit of Class C airspace above the primary airport is normally

A—1,200 feet AGL.
B—3,000 feet AGL.
C—4,000 feet AGL.

*Class C airspace consists of two circles, both centered on the primary/Class C airspace airport. The surface area has a radius of 5 NM. The shelf area usually has a radius of 10 NM. The airspace of the surface area usually extends from the surface of the Class C airspace airport up to 4,000 feet above that airport. The airspace area between the 5 and 10 NM rings usually begins at a height of 1,200 feet AGL and extends to the same altitude cap as the inner circle. These dimensions may be varied to meet individual situations. (PLT161, PA.I.E.K1, PH.I.E.K1) — AIM ¶3-2-4*

ALL, SPO

**3780.** The radius of the procedural Outer Area of Class C airspace is normally

A—10 NM.
B—20 NM.
C—30 NM.

*The normal radius of the outer area will be 20 NM. (PLT161, PA.I.E.K1, PH.I.E.K1) — AIM ¶3-2-4*

ALL

**3781.** All operations within Class C airspace must be in

A—accordance with instrument flight rules.
B—compliance with ATC clearances and instructions.
C—an aircraft equipped with a 4096-code transponder with Mode C encoding capability.

*Aircraft operating in Class C airspace must have a Mode C transponder. (PLT161, PA.I.E.K1, PH.I.E.K1) — AIM ¶3-2-4*

*Answer (A) is incorrect because visual flight rules are also used within Class C airspace. Answer (B) is incorrect because an ATC clearance is not required to operate within Class C airspace.*

**Answers**

| | | | | | |
|---|---|---|---|---|---|
| 3788 [C] | 3124 [A] | 3799 [A] | 3779 [C] | 3780 [B] | 3781 [C] |

ALL

**3782.** Under what condition may an aircraft operate from a satellite airport within Class C airspace?

A—The pilot must file a flight plan prior to departure.
B—The pilot must monitor ATC until clear of the Class C airspace.
C—The pilot must contact ATC as soon as practicable after takeoff.

*For aircraft departing a satellite airport, two-way radio communication must be established as soon as practicable and thereafter maintained with ATC while within the area. (PLT161, PA.I.E.K1, PH.I.E.K1) — AIM ¶3-2-4*

Answers (A) and (B) are incorrect because Class C airspace does not require flight plans, and a pilot must maintain contact with ATC in Class C airspace.

ALL

**2122.** (Refer to Figure 69.) What minimum equipment is required for a flight from Kleberg Co. Airport (area 7) to Corpus Christi Intl. Airport (area 3)?

A—ADS-B.
B—Two-way radio equipment.
C—Two-way radio and Mode C transponder with altitude reporting equipment.

*A flight from Kleberg County Airport to Corpus Christi International requires flight into Class C airspace. This is shown by the magenta circle around Corpus Christi International Airport. Minimum required equipment for flight into Class C airspace is two-way radio and Mode C transponder with automatic altitude reporting equipment. (PLT393, PA.I.E.K2, PH.I.E.K1) — AIM ¶3-2-4*

Answer (A) is incorrect because ADS-B is not required equipment for flight into Class C airspace. Answer (B) is incorrect because besides a two-way radio, a Mode C transponder with altitude reporting equipment is also required.

ALL, SPO

**3626.** (Refer to Figure 23, area 3.) What is the floor of the Savannah Class C airspace at the shelf area (outer circle)?

A—1,300 feet AGL.
B—1,300 feet MSL.
C—1,700 feet MSL.

*Within the outer magenta circle of Savannah Class C airspace, there is a number 41 directly above the number 13. These depict the floor and ceiling of the Class C airspace; the floor being 1,300 feet MSL and the ceiling being 4,100 feet MSL. (PLT161, PA.I.E.K2, PH.I.E.K1) — AIM ¶3-2-4*

ALL

**3627.** (Refer to Figure 20, area 1.) What minimum radio equipment is required to land and take off at Norfolk International?

A—Mode C transponder and omnireceiver.
B—Mode C transponder and two-way radio.
C—Mode C transponder, omnireceiver, and DME.

*Norfolk International is in Class C airspace. To operate within Class C airspace, an aircraft must have two-way communications capability and a Mode C transponder. (PLT064, PA.I.E.K2, PH.I.E.K2) — AIM ¶3-2-4*

ALL

**3125.** What minimum radio equipment is required for operation within Class C airspace?

A—Two-way radio communications equipment and a 4096-code transponder.
B—Two-way radio communications equipment, a 4096-code transponder, and DME.
C—Two-way radio communications equipment, a 4096-code transponder, and an encoding altimeter.

*Class C requires two-way radio communications equipment, a transponder, and an encoding altimeter. (PLT393, PA.I.E.K1, PH.I.E.K1) — 14 CFR §91.130 and §91.215*

ALL

**3069.** Normal VFR operations in Class D airspace with an operating control tower require the ceiling and visibility to be at least

A—1,000 feet and 1 mile.
B—1,000 feet and 3 miles.
C—2,500 feet and 3 miles.

*Except as provided in 14 CFR §91.157, no person may operate an aircraft, under VFR, within the lateral boundaries of the surface areas of Class B, Class C, Class D, or Class E airspace designated for an airport when the ceiling is less than 1,000 feet. The flight visibility and cloud clearance for VFR operations in Class D airspace is 3 SM visibility, and 500 feet below, 1,000 feet above, 2,000 feet horizontal from all clouds. (PLT163, PA.I.E.K1, PH.I.E.K1) — 14 CFR §91.155*

---

**Answers**

| 3782 | [C] | 2122 | [C] | 3626 | [B] | 3627 | [B] | 3125 | [C] | 3069 | [B] |

ALL

**3119.** Unless otherwise authorized, two-way radio communications with Air Traffic Control are required for landings or takeoffs

A—at all tower controlled airports regardless of weather conditions.

B—at all tower controlled airports only when weather conditions are less than VFR.

C—at all tower controlled airports within Class D airspace only when weather conditions are less than VFR.

*No person may operate an aircraft to, from, or on an airport having a control tower operated by the United States unless two-way radio communications are maintained between that aircraft and the control tower. (PLT044, PA.I.E.K1, PH.I.E.K1) —14 CFR §91.126, §91.127, and §91.129*

ALL, SPO

**3625.** (Refer to Figure 25, area 4.) The airspace directly overlying Fort Worth Meacham is

A—Class B airspace to 10,000 feet MSL.

B—Class C airspace to 5,000 feet MSL.

C—Class D airspace to 3,200 feet MSL.

*A blue segmented circle depicts Class D airspace which extends from the surface to 3,200 feet MSL, in this case as shown by the blue number 32 surrounded by the blue segmented box. (PLT101, PA.I.E.K2, PH.I.E.K2) — AIM ¶3-2-5*

Answer (A) is incorrect because although Class B airspace does overlie Fort Worth Meacham to 10,000 feet MSL, its base is 4,000 feet MSL. Answer (B) is incorrect because Class C airspace does not exist around Fort Worth Meacham.

ALL, SPO

**3421.** (Refer to Figure 59, area 3.) The airspace directly overlying the town of Findlay is

A—Class E airspace from 700 feet AGL.

B—surface area Class E airspace.

C—Class E airspace from 1,200 feet AGL.

*The town of Findlay is outlined in yellow just north of Findlay (FDY) Airport. Findlay's magenta segmented line depicts surface area Class E airspace. (PLT101, PA.I.E.K2, PH.I.E.K2) — FAA-H-8083-25*

ALL, SPO

**3068.** Unless otherwise specified, Federal Airways include that Class E airspace extending upward from

A—700 feet above the surface up to and including 17,999 feet MSL.

B—1,200 feet above the surface up to and including 17,999 feet MSL.

C—the surface up to and including 18,000 feet MSL.

*Federal airways are part of Class B, C, D, or E airspace. They are 8 miles wide, 4 miles either side of centerline. They usually begin at 1,200 AGL and continue up to but not including 18,000 feet MSL, or FL180. (PLT161, PA.I.E.K1, PH.I.E.K1) — 14 CFR §71.71*

ALL

**3068-1.** With certain exceptions, Class E airspace extends upward from either 700 feet or 1,200 feet AGL to, but does not include,

A—10,000 feet MSL.

B—14,500 feet MSL.

C—18,000 feet MSL.

*Class E airspace extends upward to (but not including) 18,000 feet MSL. (PLT161, PA.I.E.K1, PH.I.E.K1) — 14 CFR §71.71*

ALL, SPO

**3068-2.** (Refer to Figure 20, area 1.) The NALF Fentress (NFE) Airport is in what type of airspace?

A—Class C.

B—Class E.

C—Class G.

*The Nalf Fentress (NFE) airport is halfway between areas 1 and 2 in Figure 20. It is inside a magenta dashed line indicating Class E airspace starts at the surface. (PLT064, PA.I.E.K2, PH.I.E.K2) — AIM ¶3-2-6*

Answer (A) is incorrect because Class C airspace is indicated with a solid magenta line. Answer (C) is incorrect because Class G airspace would be indicated with solid (shaded) magenta or blue lines.

**Answers**

| 3119 [A] | 3625 [C] | 3421 [B] | 3068 [B] | 3068-1 [C] | 3068-2 [B] |
|---|---|---|---|---|---|

ALL, SPO
**3629.** (Refer to Figure 22, area 3.) The vertical limits of that portion of Class E airspace designated as a Federal Airway over Magee Airport are

A—700 feet MSL to 12,500 feet MSL.
B—7,500 feet MSL to 17,999 feet MSL.
C—1,200 feet AGL to 17,999 feet MSL.

*The VOR and L/MF Airway System consists of airways designated from 1,200 feet above the surface (in some instances higher) up to, but not including, 18,000 feet MSL. (PLT064, PA.I.E.K2, PH.I.E.K2) — AIM ¶3-2-6*

ALL, SPO
**3622.** (Refer to Figure 26, area 1.) Identify the airspace over Tomlinson Airport.

A—Class G airspace—surface up to but not including 18,000 feet MSL.
B—Class G airspace—surface up to but not including 1,200 feet AGL, Class E airspace—1,200 feet AGL up to but not including 18,000 feet MSL.
C—Class G airspace—surface up to but not including 700 feet MSL, Class E airspace—700 feet to 14,500 feet MSL.

*The blue shading in the bottom left corner of Figure 26 indicates Tomlinson Airport lies in Class G airspace from the surface to 1,200 feet AGL, and Class E airspace from 1,200 feet AGL to 18,000 feet MSL. The blue shading of the Victor airways indicates Class E airspace from 1,200 feet AGL. (PLT161, PA.I.E.K2, PH.I.E.K2) — AIM ¶3-2-1*

ALL, SPO
**3623.** (Refer to Figure 26, area 5.) The airspace overlying and within 5 miles of Barnes County Airport is

A—Class D airspace from the surface to the floor of the overlying Class E airspace.
B—Class E airspace from the surface to 1,200 feet MSL.
C—Class G airspace from the surface to 700 feet AGL.

*The Barnes County Airport is depicted inside the magenta shading, which is controlled airspace from 700 feet AGL up to but not including 18,000 feet. Therefore, the airspace below 700 feet AGL is Class G. (PLT040, PA.I.E.K2, PH.I.E.K2) — AIM ¶3-2-1*

ALL, SPO
**3624.** (Refer to Figure 25, area 7.) The airspace overlying Collin Co RGL McKinney (TKI) is controlled from the surface to

A—2,500 feet MSL.
B—2,900 feet MSL.
C—700 feet AGL.

*The [29] indicates the Class D airspace around McKinney (TKI) goes from the surface to 2,900 feet MSL. (PLT101, PA.I.E.K2, PH.I.E.K2) — AIM ¶3-2-1*

ALL, SPO
**3601.** (Refer to Figure 20, area 4.) What hazards to aircraft may exist in restricted areas such as R-5302B?

A—Military training activities that necessitate acrobatic or abrupt flight maneuvers.
B—Unusual, often invisible, hazards such as aerial gunnery or guided missiles.
C—High volume of pilot training or an unusual type of aerial activity.

*Restricted areas denote the presence of unusual, often invisible, hazards to aircraft such as artillery firing, aerial gunnery, or guided missiles. Penetration of restricted areas without authorization of the using or controlling agency may be extremely hazardous to the aircraft and its occupants. (PLT064, PA.I.E.K3, PH.I.E.K2) — AIM ¶3-4-3*

Answer (A) is incorrect because this defines a military operations area. Answer (C) is incorrect because this defines an alert area.

ALL, SPO
**3601-1.** (Refer to Figure 75, Area 6.) During preflight planning, your course is plotted to fly through R-2305. Where would you find additional information regarding this airspace?

A—In the *Aeronautical Information Manual.*
B—In the Chart Supplements U.S.
C—On the Sectional Chart in the Special Use Airspace area.

*Area 6 is within Restricted Airspace. Restricted Areas denote the presence of unusual, often invisible, hazards to aircraft such as artillery firing, aerial gunnery, or guided missiles. Penetration of Restricted Areas without authorization of the using or controlling agency may be extremely hazardous to the aircraft and its occupants. Special Use Airspace, such as Restricted Airspace, is charted on IFR or visual charts and include the hours of operation, altitudes, and the controlling agency. (PLT064, PA.I.E.K3, PH.I.E.K2) — AIM ¶3-4-3*

---

**Answers**

| 3629 | [C] | 3622 | [B] | 3623 | [C] | 3624 | [B] | 3601 | [B] | 3601-1 [C] |

ALL, SPO

**3602.** (Refer to Figure 26, area 2.) What hazards to aircraft may exist in areas such as Devils Lake East MOA?

A—Unusual, often invisible, hazards to aircraft such as artillery firing, aerial gunnery, or guided missiles.
B—High volume of pilot training or an unusual type of aerial activity.
C—Military training activities that necessitate acrobatic or abrupt flight maneuvers.

*An MOA contains military training activities such as aerobatics, and calls for extreme caution. (PLT393, PA.I.E.K3, PH.I.E.K3) — AIM ¶3-4-5*

ALL

**3783.** Under what condition, if any, may pilots fly through a restricted area?

A—When flying on airways with an ATC clearance.
B—With the controlling agency's authorization.
C—Regulations do not allow this.

*Restricted Areas can be penetrated but only with the permission of the controlling agency. No person may operate an aircraft within a restricted area contrary to the restrictions imposed unless they have the permission of the using or controlling agency as appropriate. Penetration of Restricted Areas without authorization from the using or controlling agency may be fatal to the aircraft and its occupants. (PLT393, PA.I.E.K3, PH.I.E.K3) — AIM ¶3-4-3*

ALL

**3783-1.** Flight through a restricted area should not be accomplished unless the pilot has

A—filed an IFR flight plan.
B—received prior authorization from the controlling agency.
C—received prior permission from the commanding officer of the nearest military base.

*Restricted Areas denote the existence of unusual, often invisible hazards to aircraft such as artillery firing, aerial gunnery, or guided missiles. Authorization must be received prior to entering any Restricted Areas. (PLT393, PA.I.E.K3, PH.I.E.K3) — AIM ¶3-4-3*

ALL

**3785.** What action should a pilot take when operating under VFR in a Military Operations Area (MOA)?

A—Obtain a clearance from the controlling agency prior to entering the MOA.
B—Operate only on the airways that transverse the MOA.
C—Exercise extreme caution when military activity is being conducted.

*Pilots operating under VFR should exercise extreme caution while flying within a MOA when military activity is being conducted. No clearance is necessary to enter a MOA. (PLT393, PA.I.E.K3, PH.I.E.K3) — AIM ¶3-4-5*

ALL

**3786.** Responsibility for collision avoidance in an alert area rests with

A—the controlling agency.
B—all pilots.
C—Air Traffic Control.

*All activity within an Alert Area shall be conducted in accordance with FAA regulations, without waiver, and pilots of participating aircraft, as well as pilots transiting the area, shall be equally responsible for collision avoidance. (PLT444, PA.I.E.K3, PH.I.E.K3) — AIM ¶3-4-6*

ALL

**3603.** (Refer to Figure 21, area 3.) What type military flight operations should a pilot expect along IR 644?

A—IFR training flights above 1,500 feet AGL at speeds in excess of 250 knots.
B—VFR training flights above 1,500 feet AGL at speeds less than 250 knots.
C—Instrument training flights below 1,500 feet AGL at speeds in excess of 150 knots.

*IR644 begins at the lower left (eastbound) and turns northeast as a thin gray line. IR644 has three digits, which mean: generally above 1,500 feet AGL (but some segments below), operations under IFR, and (as with all MTRs) may be over 250 knots. (PLT064, PA.I.E.K3, PH.I.E.K3) — AIM ¶3-5-2*

**Answers**

| 3602 [C] | 3783 [B] | 3783-1 [B] | 3785 [C] | 3786 [B] | 3603 [A] |

ALL, SPO

**3618.** (Refer to Figure 26, area 3.) When flying over Arrowwood National Wildlife Refuge, a pilot should fly no lower than

A—2,000 feet AGL.
B—2,500 feet AGL.
C—3,000 feet AGL.

*All aircraft are requested to maintain a minimum altitude of 2,000 feet above the surface of National Parks, monuments, seashores, lakeshores, recreation areas, and scenic riverways administered by the National Park Service, National Wildlife Refuges, Big Game Refuges, Game Ranges and Wildlife Ranges administered by the U.S. Fish and Wildlife Service, and Wilderness and Primitive areas administered by the U.S. Forest Service. (PLT376, PA.I.E.K3, PH.I.E.K3) — AIM ¶7-5-6*

ALL

**3831.** Pilots flying over a national wildlife refuge are requested to fly no lower than

A—1,000 feet AGL.
B—2,000 feet AGL.
C—3,000 feet AGL.

*All aircraft are requested to maintain a minimum altitude of 2,000 feet above the surface of the following: National Parks, monuments, seashores, lakeshores, recreation areas and scenic riverways administered by the National Park Service, National Wildlife Refuges, Big Game Refuges, Game Ranges and Wildlife Ranges administered by the U.S. Fish and Wildlife Service, and Wilderness and Primitive areas administered by the U.S. Forest Service. (PLT064, PA.I.E.K3, PH.I.E.K3) — AIM ¶7-5-6*

AIR, GLI, WSC, PPC

**3130.** In which type of airspace are VFR flights prohibited?

A—Class A.
B—Class B.
C—Class C.

*No person may operate an aircraft within Class A airspace unless that aircraft is operated under IFR at a specific flight level assigned by ATC. (PLT161, PA.I.E.K1) — 14 CFR §91.135*

LTA, LSL

**3784.** A balloon flight through a restricted area is

A—permitted at certain times, but only with prior permission by the appropriate authority.
B—permitted anytime, but caution should be exercised because of high-speed military aircraft.
C—never permitted.

*Restricted Areas can be penetrated but only with the permission of the controlling agency. No person may operate an aircraft within a Restricted Area contrary to the restrictions imposed unless they have the permission of the using or controlling agency as appropriate. Penetration of Restricted Areas without authorization from the using or controlling agency may be fatal to the aircraft and its occupants. (PLT393) — AIM ¶3-4-3*

SPO

**2192.** Which is true regarding flight operations in Class B airspace?

A—The pilot must receive an ATC clearance before operating an aircraft in that area.
B—Flight under VFR is not authorized unless the pilot-in-command is instrument rated.
C—Solo student pilot operations are not authorized.

*No person may operate an aircraft within Class B airspace unless the operator first receives an ATC clearance from the ATC facility having jurisdiction for that area. (PLT162) — 14 CFR §91.131*

Answer (B) is incorrect because a Private Pilot Certificate without an Instrument Rating is sufficient to operate in Class B airspace. Answer (C) is incorrect because with the proper training and endorsements, a student pilot may operate in Class B airspace.

SPO

**2193.** Which is true regarding flight operations in Class B airspace?

A—The pilot-in-command must hold at least a Private Pilot Certificate with an Instrument Rating.
B—The pilot-in-command must hold at least a Student Pilot Certificate.
C—The aircraft must be equipped with an ATC transponder and altitude reporting equipment.

---

**Answers**

| | | | | | |
|---|---|---|---|---|---|
| 3618 [A] | 3831 [B] | 3130 [A] | 3784 [A] | 2192 [A] | 2193 [C] |

*You may not operate an aircraft in Class B airspace unless the aircraft is equipped with an operating transponder and automatic altitude reporting equipment or you have requested a waiver at least one hour before the proposed operation. Both 14 CFR §§91.130 and 91.131 have provisions to allow any aircraft to operate in the airspace without transponders. (PLT162) — 14 CFR §91.131*

Answer (A) is incorrect because a Private Pilot Certificate without an Instrument Rating is sufficient to operate in Class B airspace. Answer (B) is incorrect because Class B airspace requires the PIC hold a Private Pilot Certificate or have a logbook endorsement confirming that the necessary training was received.

SPO
**2043.** Which is true regarding flight operations to a satellite airport, without an operating control tower, within Class C airspace?

A—Prior to entering that airspace, a sport pilot must contact the FSS.
B—Prior to entering that airspace, a sport pilot must contact the primary airport tower.
C—Prior to entering that airspace, a sport pilot must receive the appropriate logbook endorsement.

*A sport pilot must receive ground training and a logbook endorsement to operate in Class B, C, and D airspace. (PLT162) — 14 CFR §61.94*

Answer (A) is incorrect because airports in Class C airspace have a control tower; all communications must be established with this facility, not FSS. Answer (B) is incorrect because the sport pilot must first have specific ground training and a logbook endorsement before attempting to enter Class C airspace.

SPO
**2049.** What designated airspace associated with an airport becomes inactive when the control tower at that airport is not in operation?

A—Class D, which then becomes Class C.
B—Class D, which then becomes Class E.
C—Class B.

*Class D airspace means a control tower is in operation. If the tower closes, it reverts to Class E airspace. (PLT161) — 14 CFR §1.1*

SPO
**2050.** (Refer to Figure 70, point 5) What minimum altitude is required to avoid the Livermore Airport (LVK) Class D airspace?

A—2,503 feet MSL.
B—2,901 feet MSL.
C—3,297 feet MSL.

*The Class D airspace at Livermore has a top of 2,900 feet MSL, indicated by the [29] within the blue segmented circle. Therefore, the minimum altitude to fly over and avoid the Class D airspace is 2,901 feet MSL. (PLT040) — AIM ¶3-2-5*

Answer (A) is incorrect because 2,503 feet MSL would place you within the Class D airspace. Answer (C) is incorrect because although 3,297 feet MSL would keep you outside the Class D airspace, it is not the minimum altitude required to avoid it.

SPO
**2052.** The purpose of Military Training Routes, charted as VFR Military Training Routes (VR) and IFR Military Training Routes (IR) on sectional charts, is to ensure the greatest practical level of safety for all flight operations and to allow the military to conduct

A—low altitude, high-speed training.
B—radar instrument training.
C—air-to-air refueling training.

*The military services must train in a wide range of airborne tactics. One phase of this training involves "low level" combat tactics. The required maneuvers and high speeds are such that they may occasionally make the see-and-avoid aspect of VFR flight more difficult without increased vigilance in areas containing such operations. In an effort to ensure the greatest practical level of safety for all flight operations, the MTR program was conceived. (PLT116) — AIM ¶3-5-2*

SPO
**2056.** Who is responsible for collision avoidance in a Military Operations Area (MOA)?

A—Each pilot.
B—ATC controllers.
C—Military controllers.

*Pilots operating under VFR should exercise extreme caution while flying within a MOA when military activity is being conducted. No clearance is necessary to enter a MOA. (PLT162) — AIM ¶3-4-5*

---

**Answers**

| | | | | |
|---|---|---|---|---|
| 2043 [C] | 2049 [B] | 2050 [B] | 2052 [A] | 2056 [A] |

SPO

**2059.** (Refer to Figure 24, point 6) The floor of the Class E airspace over the town of Commerce is

A—1,200 feet MSL.
B—700 feet AGL.
C—1,200 feet AGL.

*The magenta shading around Commerce indicates the floor of the Class E airspace starts 700 feet above the surface. (PLT064) — Sectional Chart*

*Answers (A) and (C) are incorrect because 1,200 feet AGL (not MSL) is indicated with blue shading.*

SPO

**2198.** Which is true concerning the colors used to depict airports on Sectional Aeronautical Charts?

A—Airports with control towers underlying Class D and E airspace are magenta.
B—Airports with control towers are shown in magenta.
C—Airports with control towers are shown in blue.

*Reference FAA Legend 1 in the Computer Testing Supplement. Airports having control towers are shown in blue, all others in magenta. (PLT064) — Sectional Chart*

SPO

**2115.** (Refer to Figure 71, point 6) Sky Way Airport is

A—an airport restricted to use by private and recreational pilots.
B—a restricted military stage field within restricted airspace.
C—a nonpublic use airport.

*The "Pvt" after the airport names indicates Sky Way airport is a restricted or non-public use airport. (PLT064) — Sectional Chart*

*Answer (A) is incorrect because the R in the circle indicates the airport is a nonpublic-use airport. Answer (B) is incorrect because the blue box near Sky Way airport indicates an alert area.*

SPO

**2204.** (Refer to Figure 71, point 1.) The floor of the Class E airspace above Georgetown Airport (E36) is at

A—the surface.
B—700 feet AGL.
C—3,823 feet MSL.

*Georgetown Airport is outside the magenta shaded area, which indicates the floor of Class E airspace is at 1,200 feet AGL. The airport elevation is given in the airport data as 2,623 feet MSL. Therefore, the Class E airspace above Georgetown Airport is 3,823 feet MSL (2,623 + 1,200). (PLT064) — Sectional Chart*

*Answer (A) is incorrect because Class E airspace begins at the surface only when surrounded by a magenta segmented circle. Answer (B) is incorrect because Class E airspace begins at 700 feet AGL inside the magenta shaded areas.*

SPO

**2138.** (Refer to Figure 22, area 1.) The visibility and cloud clearance requirements for a sport pilot to operate over Sandpoint Airport at less than 700 feet AGL are

A—3 miles and clear of clouds.
B—1 mile and 1,000 feet above, 500 feet below, and 2,000 feet horizontally from each cloud.
C—3 miles and 1,000 feet above, 500 feet below, and 2,000 feet horizontally from each cloud.

*The Sandpoint Airport Class E airspace starts at 700 feet AGL (indicated by the magenta shading). Class G airspace exists below this. The sport pilot clearance requirements are 3 miles visibility and clear of clouds. (PLT163) — 14 CFR §61.315*

SPO

**2179.** Airports with control towers are shown in

A—magenta.
B—blue.
C—brown.

*Reference FAA Legend 1. Airports having control towers are shown in blue, all others in magenta. (PLT064) — Sectional Chart*

SPO

**2055-1.** (Refer to Figure 26.) The Devils Lake East MOA (area 1) is a

A—meteorological observation area.
B—military observation area.
C—military operations area.

*An MOA contains military training activities such as aerobatics, and calls for extreme caution. (PLT064) — AIM ¶3-4-5*

**Answers**

| | | | | | |
|---|---|---|---|---|---|
| 2059 [B] | 2198 [C] | 2115 [C] | 2204 [C] | 2138 [A] | 2179 [B] |
| 2055-1 [C] | | | | | |

SPO
**2367.** (Refer to Figure 26.) The floor of the Class E airspace over the Jamestown airport is

A—surface.
B—700 feet AGL.
C—1,200 feet AGL.

*The magenta shading around Jamestown indicates the floor of the Class E airspace starts 700 feet above the surface. The dashed area means the Class E goes all the way to the surface (PLT064) — Sectional Chart*

Answer (B) is incorrect because 700 feet AGL is indicated with magenta shading; however, there is a dashed line as well near the airport bringing Class E to the surface. Answer (C) is incorrect because 1,200 feet AGL would require blue shading around the airport.

SPO
**2113-1.** (Refer to Figure 25, area 7.) What is the base of Class B airspace at Air Park-Dallas (F69)?

A—3000.
B—4000.
C—1700.

*The thick blue lines on the sectional chart indicate the boundaries of the overlying Class B airspace. Within each segment, the floor and ceiling are denoted by one number over a second number or the letters SFC. The floor of the Class B airspace at F69 airport is 3,000 feet MSL. (PLT011) — AIM ¶3-2-3*

SPO
**2138-1.** (Refer to Figure 75.) The airspace surrounding the Gila Bend AF AUX Airport (GXF) (area 6) is classified as Class

A—B.
B—C.
C—D.

*The GXF airport is surrounded by a dashed blue line which indicates it is within Class D airspace. (PLT040) — Sectional Chart*

SPO
**2138-2.** (Refer to Figure 22.) Weather information is available at the Coeur d'Alene (COE) Airport (area 2)

A—over the nearest VOR.
B—from AWOS 3 135.075.
C—from UNICOM (CTAF) on 122.8.

*AWOS is available on 135.075. (PLT116) — Sectional Chart Legend*

**Answers**

2367   [A]          2113-1 [A]          2138-1 [C]          2138-2 [B]

# Uncontrolled and Tower-Controlled Airports

Airport traffic control towers are established to promote the safe, orderly, and expeditious flow of air traffic. The tower controller will issue instructions for aircraft to follow the desired flight path while in the airport traffic area whenever necessary by using terminology as shown in Figure 6-2.

**Figure 6-2**

The tower controller will also direct aircraft taxiing on the surface movement area of the airport. In all instances, an appropriate clearance must be received from the tower before taking off or landing.

At airports without an operating control tower, pilots of fixed-wing and weight-shift control aircraft must circle the airport to the left ("left traffic") unless visual indicators indicate right traffic.

A common visual indicator is the segmented circle system, which consists of the following components (see Figure 6-3):

- The **segmented circle** is located in a position readily visible to pilots in the air and on the ground.

- A **tetrahedron** may be used to indicate the direction of landings and takeoffs. The small end of the tetrahedron points in the direction of landing. Pilots are cautioned against using the tetrahedron to determine wind direction, because it may not indicate the correct direction in light winds.

- A **wind cone**, **wind sock**, or **wind tee** may be installed near the operational runway to indicate wind direction. The large end of the wind cone or sock points into the wind as does the cross bar of the wind tee. See Figure 6-4.

**Figure 6-3.** Segmented circle and landing direction indicator

**Figure 6-4.** Wind/landing direction indicators

The tetrahedron, wind cone, wind sock, or wind tee may be located in the center of the segmented circle and may be lit for night operations.

Landing runway (landing strip) indicators are installed in pairs and used to show alignment of runways. See Figure 6-5(a). Traffic pattern indicators are installed in pairs in conjunction with landing strip indicators, and are used to indicate the direction of turns. See Figure 6-5(b).

Approaching to land at an airport without a control tower, or when the control tower is not in operation, the pilot should observe the indicator for the approach end of the runway to be used. VFR landings at night should be made the same as during daytime.

Aircraft departing an uncontrolled airport must comply with any FAA traffic pattern established for that airport.

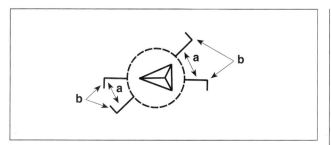

**Figure 6-5.** Landing runway and traffic pattern indicators

ALL, SPO

**3123.** Which is the correct traffic pattern departure procedure to use at a noncontrolled airport?

A—Depart in any direction consistent with safety, after crossing the airport boundary.
B—Make all turns to the left.
C—Comply with any FAA traffic pattern established for the airport.

*In the case of an aircraft departing an airport without an operating control tower, comply with any FAA traffic pattern for that airport. (PLT201, PA.III.B.K1, PH.III.C.K2) — 14 CFR §91.127*

ALL

**3123-1.** The recommended entry position to an airport traffic pattern is

A—45° to the base leg just below traffic pattern altitude.
B—to enter 45° at the midpoint of the downwind leg at traffic pattern altitude.
C—to cross directly over the airport at traffic pattern altitude and join the downwind leg.

*The recommended entry position for an airport traffic pattern is 45° to the midpoint of the downwind leg at traffic pattern altitude. (PLT150, PA.III.B.K1, PH.III.C.K2) — AIM ¶4-3-3*

ALL

**3807.** (Refer to Figure 50.) The segmented circle indicates that the airport traffic is

A—left-hand for Runway 36 and right-hand for Runway 18.
B—left-hand for Runway 18 and right-hand for Runway 36.
C—right-hand for Runway 9 and left-hand for Runway 27.

*The traffic pattern indicators on a segmented circle are used to indicate the direction of turns. The traffic pattern indicators, shown as extensions from the segmented circle, represent the base and final approach legs. (PLT039, PA.III.B.K4, PH.III.C.K2) — AIM ¶4-3-3*

ALL, LSA, LSR, LSW, LSP

**3808.** (Refer to Figure 50.) The traffic patterns indicated in the segmented circle have been arranged to avoid flights over an area to the

A—south of the airport.
B—north of the airport.
C—southeast of the airport.

*The segmented circle depicts the direction of landing for each airport; the long part of the "L" depicts the runway, and the short part depicts the airport traffic pattern for that runway. This figure indicates there are no flights that cross the southeast area of the airport. (PLT039, PA.III.B.K4, PH.III.C.K2) — AIM ¶4-3-3*

**Answers**

3123   [C]          3123-1 [B]          3807   [A]          3808   [C]

ALL
**3809.** (Refer to Figure 50.) The segmented circle indicates that a landing on Runway 26 will be with a

A—right-quartering headwind.
B—left-quartering headwind.
C—right-quartering tailwind.

*The large end of the wind cone (wind sock) points into the wind. The wind cone in FAA Figure 50 indicates a wind from the northwest. When landing on Runway 26, this would be a right quartering headwind. (PLT039, PA.III.B.K4, PH.III.C.K2) — AIM ¶4-3-3*

ALL, SPO
**3810.** (Refer to Figure 50.) Which runway and traffic pattern should be used as indicated by the wind cone in the segmented circle?

A—Right-hand traffic on Runway 9.
B—Right-hand traffic on Runway 18.
C—Left-hand traffic on Runway 36.

*The large end of the wind cone (wind sock) points into the wind. The wind cone in FAA Figure 50 indicates a wind from the northwest. Landing into the wind can be accomplished on either Runway 27 or Runway 36. The traffic pattern indicators require right traffic to Runway 27 and left traffic to Runway 36. (PLT039, PA.III.B.K4, PH.III.C.K2) — AIM ¶4-3-3*

AIR, RTC, WSC, PPC
**3719.** VFR approaches to land at night should be accomplished

A—at a higher airspeed.
B—with a steeper descent.
C—the same as during daytime.

*Inexperienced pilots often have a tendency to make approaches and landings at night with excessive airspeed. Every effort should be made to execute the approach and landing in the same manner as during the day. (PLT221, PA.IV.B.K1, PH.III.C.K2) — FAA-H-8083-3*

RTC, PPC
**3122.** Which is appropriate for a helicopter approaching an airport for landing?

A—Remain below the airplane traffic pattern altitude.
B—Avoid the flow of fixed-wing traffic.
C—Fly right-hand traffic.

*Helicopters and powered parachutes must avoid the flow of fixed-wing aircraft. (PLT170, PH.III.C.K2) — 14 CFR §91.127, §91.129*

SPO
**2060.** When approaching to land at an airport in Class G airspace that does not have light signals or other visual markings, an airplane pilot must make

A—a straight-in approach.
B—all turns to the right.
C—all turns to the left.

*When approaching to land at an airport without an operating control tower in a Class G airspace area, each pilot of an airplane must make all turns of that airplane to the left unless the airport displays approved light signals or visual markings indicate otherwise. (PLT435) — 14 CFR §91.126*

SPO
**2194.** When approaching to land at an airport, without an operating control tower, in Class G airspace, the pilot should

A—enter and fly a traffic pattern at 800 feet AGL.
B—make all turns to the left, unless otherwise indicated.
C—fly a left-hand traffic pattern at 800 feet AGL.

*When approaching to land at an airport without an operating control tower in Class G airspace, each pilot of an airplane must make all turns to the left unless the airport displays approved light signals or visual markings indicating that turns should be made to the right. (PLT435) — 14 CFR §91.126*

Answers (A) and (C) are incorrect because the traffic pattern altitude will vary for each airport and aircraft; however, all turns should be to the left unless otherwise indicated.

SPO
**2002.** Entries into traffic patterns while descending create specific collision hazards and

A—should be avoided.
B—should be used whenever possible.
C—are illegal.

*Entries into traffic patterns while descending create specific collision hazards and should be avoided. (PLT170) — AIM ¶4-4-15*

**Answers**

| | | | | | |
|---|---|---|---|---|---|
| 3809 [A] | 3810 [C] | 3719 [C] | 3122 [B] | 2060 [C] | 2194 [B] |
| 2002 [A] | | | | | |

SPO

**2007-1.** Inbound to an airport with no tower, FSS, or UNICOM in operation, a pilot should self-announce on MULTICOM frequency

A—123.0.
B—122.9.
C—122.7.

*Where there is no tower, FSS, or UNICOM station on the airport, use MULTICOM frequency 122.9 for self-announce procedures. (PLT204) — AIM ¶4-1-9*

SPO

**2007-2.** Inbound to an airport with no tower, FSS, or UNICOM in operation, a pilot should self-announce on MULTICOM frequency

A—20 miles out.
B—10 miles out.
C—5 miles out.

*Pilots of inbound traffic should monitor and communicate as appropriate on the designated frequency from 10 miles to landing. (PLT204) — AIM ¶4-1-9*

SPO

**2034-1.** (Refer to Figure 20.) What is the recommended communications procedure for departure at Currituck County Airport (area 3)?

A—Broadcast intentions prior to taxi and announcing runway of departure.
B—Calling the Elizabeth City tower on 120.5.
C—Radio need not be used.

*Pilots of departing aircraft should monitor/communicate on the appropriate frequency from start-up, during taxi, and until 10 miles from the airport unless regulations or local procedures require otherwise. (PLT435) — AIM ¶4-1-9*

Answer (B) is incorrect because this is a nontowered airport; 120.5 is the CTAF. Answer (C) is incorrect because pilots should use the radio to announce intentions.

# Airport Markings and Signs

Runway numbers and letters are determined from the approach direction. The number is the magnetic heading of the runway rounded to the nearest 10°. For example, an azimuth of 183° would result in a runway number of 18; a magnetic azimuth of 076° would result in a runway numbered 8. Runway letters differentiate between left (L), right (R), or center (C). See Figure 6-6.

The designated beginning of the runway that is available and suitable for the landing of aircraft is called the **threshold** (Figure 5-6a). A threshold that is not at the beginning of the full-strength runway pavement is a **displaced threshold**. The paved area behind the displaced threshold is marked by arrows (Figure 5-6b) and is available for taxiing, takeoff, and landing rollout, but is not to be used for landing, usually because of an obstruction in the approach path. See Figure 6-7.

Stopways are found extending beyond some usable runways. These areas are marked by chevrons, and while they appear usable, they are suitable only as overrun areas. See Figure 6-8.

A closed runway which is unusable and may be hazardous, even though it may appear usable, will be marked by an "X."

LAHSO stands for land and hold short operations. These operations include landing and holding short of an intersecting runway, an intersecting taxiway, or some other designated point on a runway other than an intersecting runway or taxiway. LAHSO is an air traffic control procedure that requires pilot participation to balance the needs for increased airport capacity and system efficiency, consistent with safety. Student pilots or pilots not familiar with LAHSO should not participate in the program. The pilot-in-command has the final authority to accept or decline any land and hold short clearance. The safety and operation of the aircraft remain the responsibility of the pilot. Pilots are expected to decline a LAHSO clearance if they determine it will compromise safety. Available landing distance (ALD) data is

**Answers**

2007-1 [B]        2007-2 [B]        2034-1 [A]

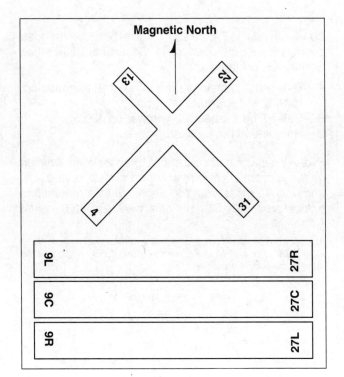

**Figure 6-6.** Runway numbers and letters

**Figure 6-7.** Threshold marking

published in the special notices section of the Chart Supplements U.S. and in the U.S. Terminal Procedures Publications. Pilots should only receive a LAHSO clearance when there is a minimum ceiling of 1,000 feet and 3 statute miles visibility. The intent of having "basic" VFR weather conditions is to allow pilots to maintain visual contact with other aircraft and ground vehicle operations.

**Figure 6-8.** Stopway marking

Looking at FAA Figure 64 in the Airman Knowledge Testing Supplement:

**A** is a surface painted runway marking

**B** is a stop bar/ILS hold

**C** is vehicle lanes

**D** is hold marking for land and hold short operations

**E** is taxiway/taxiway hold marking

**F** is taxiway edge marking (do not cross)

Looking at FAA Figure 65 in the Airman Knowledge Testing Supplement:

**A** is a taxiway/runway hold position sign.

**B** is a runway approach hold position sign.

**C** is an ILS critical area hold position sign.

**D** is a no entry sign.

**E** is a taxiway location sign.

**F** is a runway location sign.

**G** is a runway safety area/obstacle free zone boundary.

**H** is an ILS critical area boundary.

**I** is an inbound destination sign.

**J** is an outbound destination sign.

**K** is a taxiway direction sign.

**L** is a runway distance remaining (in 1,000 foot increments).

**M** is a runway/runway hold position sign.

**N** is a taxiway ending marker.

A closed runway which is unusable and may be hazardous, even though it may appear usable, will be marked by an "X."

ALL

**3778.** The numbers 9 and 27 on a runway indicate that the runway is oriented approximately

A—009° and 027° true.
B—090° and 270° true.
C—090° and 270° magnetic.

*The runway number is the whole number nearest one-tenth the magnetic azimuth of the centerline of the runway, measured clockwise from magnetic north. For example: 272° = Runway 27; 087° = Runway 9. (PLT141, PA.II.D.K3, PH.III.A.K1) — AIM ¶2-3-3*

ALL

**3778-1.** The numbers 8 and 26 on the approach ends of the runway indicate that the runway is orientated approximately

A—008° and 026° true.
B—080° and 260° true.
C—080° and 260° magnetic.

*The runway number is the whole number nearest one-tenth the magnetic azimuth of the centerline of the runway, measured clockwise from magnetic north. (PLT141, PA.II.D.K3, PH.III.A.K1) — AIM ¶2-3-3*

SPO

**2024.** The numbers 35 and 17 on a runway indicate that the runway is oriented approximately

A—035°; and 017°; magnetic heading.
B—350°; and 170°; magnetic heading.
C—350°; and 170°; true heading.

*The runway number is the whole number nearest one-tenth the magnetic azimuth of the centerline of the runway, measured clockwise from magnetic north. For example: 352° = Runway 35; 172° = Runway 17. (PLT141) — AIM ¶2-3-3*

Answer (A) is incorrect because runway numbers drop the last digit from the heading. Answer (C) is incorrect because runway numbers are based on magnetic direction.

ALL

**3778-2.** When turning onto a taxiway from another taxiway, what is the purpose of the taxiway directional sign?

A—Indicates direction to take-off runway.
B—Indicates designation and direction of exit taxiway from runway.
C—Indicates designation and direction of taxiway leading out of an intersection.

*The taxiway directional sign identifies the designation(s) of the intersecting taxiway(s) leading out of the intersection that a pilot would normally be expected to turn onto or hold short of. (PLT141, PA.II.D.K3, PH.III.A.K1) — AIM ¶2-3-10*

Answer (A) is incorrect because this is the purpose of the runway location sign. Answer (B) is incorrect because this is the purpose of the destination sign.

**Answers**

| | | | |
|---|---|---|---|
| 3778 [C] | 2024 [B] | 3778-1 [C] | 3778-2 [C] |

ALL, SPO

**3778-3.** (Refer to Figure 64.) Which symbol indicates a taxiway/taxiway intersection hold position marking?

A—B.
B—D.
C—E.

*Symbol "E" indicates a taxiway/taxiway hold marking. (PLT141, PA.II.D.K3, PH.III.A.K1) — AIM ¶2-3-4*

Answer (A) is incorrect because "B" is a stop bar/ILS hold marking. Answer (B) is incorrect because "D" is a hold marking for land and hold short operations.

ALL, SPO

**3778-4.** (Refer to Figure 64.) Which marking indicates a vehicle lane?

A—A.
B—C.
C—E.

*The vehicle roadway markings are used when necessary to define a pathway for vehicle operations on or crossing areas that are also intended for aircraft. These markings consist of a white solid line to delineate each edge of the roadway and a dashed line to separate lanes within the edges of the roadway. In lieu of the solid lines, zipper markings may be used to delineate the edges of the vehicle roadway. (PLT141, PA.II.D.K3, PH.III.A.K1) — AIM ¶2-3-6*

ALL

**3778-5.** The yellow demarcation bar marking indicates

A—a runway with a displaced threshold that precedes the runway.
B—a hold line from a taxiway to a runway.
C—the beginning of available runway for landing on the approach side.

*A demarcation bar delineates a runway with a displaced threshold from a blast pad, stopway or taxiway that precedes the runway. A demarcation bar is 3 feet (1 m) wide and yellow, since it is not located on the runway. (PLT141, PA.II.D.K3, PH.III.A.K1) — AIM ¶2-3-3*

ALL

**3957.** (Refer to the Runway Incursion Figure.) You have requested taxi instructions for takeoff using Runway 16. The controller issues the following taxi instructions: "N123, Taxi to Runway 16." Where are you required to stop in order to be in compliance with the controller's insructions?

**Runway Incursion**

A—5 (Five).
B—6 (Six).
C—9 (Nine).

*When ATC clears an aircraft to "taxi to" an assigned takeoff runway, the absence of holding instructions does not authorize the aircraft to "cross" all runways which the taxi route intersects except the assigned takeoff runway. A clearance must be obtained prior to crossing any runway. It does not include authorization to "taxi onto" or "cross" the assigned takeoff runway at any point. You should taxi and hold short of Runway 16, which is position 5. (PLT141, PA.II.D.K3, PH.III.A.K1) — AIM ¶4-3-18*

Answer (B) is incorrect because "taxi to" does not authorize the aircraft to "taxi onto" the assigned takeoff runway. Answer (C) is incorrect because the airplane should taxi the most direct route to the assigned runway unless instructed otherwise; position 9 would not be encountered for the airplane at the west ramp to taxi to Runway 16.

**Answers**

3778-3 [C]        3778-4 [B]        3778-5 [A]        3957   [A]

ALL

**3951.** Who should not participate in the Land and Hold Short Operations (LAHSO) program?

A—Recreational pilots only.
B—Military pilots.
C—Student pilots.

*Student pilots or pilots not familiar with LAHSO should not participate in the program. (PLT140, PA.IV.B.R3b, PH.III.A.K2) — AIM ¶4-3-11*

ALL

**3952.** Who has final authority to accept or decline any land and hold short (LAHSO) clearance?

A—Pilot-in-command.
B—Air traffic controller.
C—Second-in-command.

*The PIC has the final authority to accept or decline any land and hold short clearance. The safety and operation of the aircraft remain the responsibility of the pilot. (PLT444, PA.IV.B.R3b, PH.III.A.K2) — AIM ¶4-3-11*

ALL

**3953.** When should pilots decline a land and hold short (LAHSO) clearance?

A—When it will compromise safety.
B—Only when the tower operator concurs.
C—Pilots can not decline clearance.

*Pilots are expected to decline a LAHSO clearance if they determine it will compromise safety. (PLT140, PA.IV.B.R3b, PH.III.A.K2) — AIM ¶4-3-11*

ALL

**3954.** Where is the Available Landing Distance (ALD) data published for an airport that utilizes Land and Hold Short Operations (LAHSO)?

A—Special Notices Section of the Chart Supplement U.S.
B—14 CFR Part 91, General Operating and Flight Rules.
C—*Aeronautical Information Manual (AIM).*

*ALD data is published in the special notices section of the Chart Supplements U.S. and in the U.S. Terminal Procedures Publications. (PLT140, PA.IV.B.R3b, PH.III.A.K2) — AIM ¶4-3-11*

ALL

**3955.** What is the minimum visibility for a pilot to receive a land and hold short (LAHSO) clearance?

A—3 nautical miles.
B—3 statute miles.
C—1 statute mile.

*Pilots should only receive a LAHSO clearance when there is a minimum ceiling of 1,000 feet and 3 statute miles visibility. The intent of having basic VFR weather conditions is to allow pilots to maintain visual contact with other aircraft and ground vehicle operations. (PLT141, PA.IV.B.R3b, PH.III.A.K2) — AIM ¶4-3-11*

ALL

**3955-1.** When approaching taxiway holding lines from the side with the continuous lines, the pilot

A—may continue taxiing.
B—should not cross the lines without ATC clearance.
C—should continue taxiing until all parts of the aircraft have crossed the lines.

*When approaching the holding line from the side with the continuous lines, a pilot should not cross the holding line without ATC clearance at a controlled airport, or without making sure of adequate separation from other aircraft at uncontrolled airports. (PLT141, PA.II.D.K3, PH.III.A.K1) — AIM ¶2-3-5*

*Answers (A) and (C) are incorrect because no part of the aircraft may cross the hold line without ATC clearance.*

ALL, SPO

**3955-2.** What is the purpose of the runway/runway hold position sign?

A—Denotes entrance to runway from a taxiway.
B—Denotes area protected for an aircraft approaching or departing a runway.
C—Denotes intersecting runways.

*Mandatory instruction signs are used to denote an entrance to a runway or critical area and areas where an aircraft is prohibited from entering. The runway holding position sign is located at the holding position on taxiways that intersect a runway or on runways that intersect other runways. (PLT141, PA.II.D.K3, PH.III.A.K1) — AIM ¶2-3-8*

---

**Answers**

| | | | | | |
|---|---|---|---|---|---|
| 3951 [C] | 3952 [A] | 3953 [A] | 3954 [A] | 3955 [B] | 3955-1 [B] |
| 3955-2 [C] | | | | | |

ALL
**3955-3.** What does the outbound destination sign identify?

A—Identifies entrance to the runway from a taxiway.
B—Identifies direction to take-off runways.
C—Identifies runway on which an aircraft is located.

*Outbound destination signs provide information for locating the departure runway. (PLT141, PA.II.D.K3, PH.III.A.K1) — AIM ¶2-3-11*

Answer (A) is incorrect because this is a runway marking. Answer (C) is incorrect because this is a runway location sign.

ALL, SPO
**3955-4.** What is the purpose of the no entry sign?

A—Identifies a paved area where aircraft are prohibited from entering.
B—Identifies area that does not continue beyond intersection.
C—Identifies the exit boundary for the runway protected area.

*The no entry sign prohibits an aircraft from entering an area. Typically, this sign would be located on a taxiway intended to be used in only one direction or at the intersection of vehicle roadways with runways, taxiways or aprons where the roadway may be mistaken as a taxiway or other aircraft movement surface. (PLT141, PA.II.D.K3, PH.III.A.K1) — AIM ¶2-3-8*

Answer (B) is incorrect because this is the purpose of a hold position sign. Answer (C) is incorrect because this is the purpose of the runway boundary sign.

ALL
**3955-5.** (Refer to Figure 65.) Which airport marking is a runway safety area/obstacle free zone boundary?

A—G.
B—H.
C—N.

*The runway boundary sign has a yellow background and a black inscription, with a graphic that depicts the pavement holding-position marking. This sign, which faces the runway and is visible to the pilot exiting the runway, is located adjacent to the holding position marking on the pavement. The sign is intended to provide pilots with another visual cue they can use as a guide in deciding when they are clear of the runway. (PLT141, PA.II.D.K3, PH.III.A.K1) — AIM ¶2-3-9*

Answer (B) is incorrect because this is an ILS critical area boundary sign. Answer (C) is incorrect because this is a taxiway-ending marker.

ALL, SPO
**3955-6.** (Refer to Figure 65.) From the flight deck, marking G confirms the aircraft to be

A—on a taxiway, about to enter runway zone.
B—on a runway, about to clear.
C—near an instrument approach clearance zone.

*Illustration G is a runway boundary sign, which has a yellow background and a black inscription with a graphic that depicts the pavement holding position marking. This sign, which faces the runway and is visible to the pilot exiting the runway, is located adjacent to the holding position marking on the pavement. It is intended to provide pilots with another visual cue they can use in deciding if they are clear of the runway. (PLT141, PA.II.D.K3, PH.III.A.K1) — AIM ¶2-3-9*

SPO
**2026.** The runway hold position sign denotes

A—an entrance to a runway from a taxiway.
B—an area protected for an aircraft approaching a runway.
C—an entrance to a taxiway from a runway.

*Mandatory instruction signs are used to denote an entrance to a runway or critical area and areas where an aircraft is prohibited from entering. The runway holding position sign is located at the holding position on taxiways that intersect a runway or on runways that intersect other runways. (PLT141) — AIM ¶2-3-8*

SPO
**2028.** What is the purpose for the runway hold position markings on the taxiway?

A—Holds aircraft short of the runway.
B—Allows an aircraft permission onto the runway.
C—Identifies area where aircraft are prohibited.

*Runway holding position markings on taxiways identify the locations on a taxiway where an aircraft is supposed to stop when it does not have clearance to proceed onto the runway. (PLT141) — AIM ¶2-3-5*

**Answers**

3955-3 [B]  3955-4 [A]  3955-5 [A]  3955-6 [B]  2026 [A]  2028 [A]

SPO
**2030.** Holding position signs have

A—red inscriptions on white background.
B—white inscriptions on red background.
C—yellow inscriptions on red background.

*Hold position signs have white inscriptions on red background. (PLT141) — AIM ¶2-3-5*

Answers (A) and (C) are incorrect because these color combination are not used in airport signs.

SPO
**2031.** Runway hold position markings on the taxiway

A—identifies where aircraft hold short of the runway.
B—identifies an area where aircraft are prohibited.
C—allows an aircraft permission onto the runway.

*Runway holding position markings on taxiways identify the locations on a taxiway where an aircraft is supposed to stop when it does not have clearance to proceed onto the runway. (PLT141) — AIM ¶2-3-5*

SPO
**2025.** Runway hold position markings on the taxiway

A—identify areas where aircraft are prohibited.
B—identify where aircraft hold short of the runway.
C—allow an aircraft permission onto the runway.

*Runway holding position markings on taxiways identify the locations on a taxiway where an aircraft is supposed to stop when it does not have clearance to proceed onto the runway. (PLT141) — AIM ¶2-3-5*

ALL, SPO
**3773.** (Refer to Figure 48.) The portion of the runway identified by the letter A may be used for

A—landing.
B—taxiing and takeoff.
C—taxiing and landing.

*Thresholds are marked at the beginning of a full-strength runway surface able to endure landing impacts or at a point on the runway which will encourage pilots to avoid short approaches due to hidden noise or obstacle problems. Area A of Figure 48 is marked with arrows which point towards a displaced threshold. Thus, the paved surface prior to the threshold is available for taxi, takeoff and landing rollout, but not for touchdown. (PLT077, PA.II.D.K3, PH.III.A.K1) — AIM ¶2-3-3*

ALL
**3774.** (Refer to Figure 48.) According to the airport diagram, which statement is true?

A—Runway 30 is equipped at position E with emergency arresting gear to provide a means of stopping military aircraft.
B—Takeoffs may be started at position A on Runway 12, and the landing portion of this runway begins at position B.
C—The takeoff and landing portion of Runway 30 begins at position E.

*Thresholds are marked at the beginning of a full-strength runway surface able to endure landing impacts or at a point on the runway which will encourage pilots to avoid short approaches due to hidden noise or obstacle problems. Area A of Figure 48 is marked with arrows which point towards a displaced threshold. Thus, the paved surface prior to the threshold is available for taxi, takeoff, and landing rollout, but not for touchdown. (PLT077, PA.II.D.K3, PH.III.A.K1) — AIM ¶2-3-3*

ALL
**3776.** (Refer to Figure 48.) Area C on the airport depicted is classified as a

A—stabilized area.
B—multiple heliport.
C—closed runway.

*An "X" painted on the end of runway means it is closed. (PLT077, PA.II.D.K3, PH.III.A.K1) — AIM ¶2-3-3*

ALL, SPO
**3777.** (Refer to Figure 49.) The arrows that appear on the end of the north/south runway indicate that the area

A—may be used only for taxiing.
B—is usable for taxiing, takeoff, and landing.
C—cannot be used for landing, but may be used for taxiing and takeoff.

*The paved area behind the displaced runway threshold is available for taxiing, landing rollout, and the takeoff of aircraft. (PLT077, PA.II.D.K3, PH.III.A.K1) — AIM ¶2-3-3*

**Answers**

| | | | | | |
|---|---|---|---|---|---|
| 2030 [B] | 2031 [A] | 2025 [B] | 3773 [B] | 3774 [B] | 3776 [C] |
| 3777 [C] | | | | | |

SPO

**2206.** Which publication contains an explanation of airport signs and markings?

A—*Aeronautical Information Manual (AIM)*.
B—Advisory Circulars (AC).
C—Chart Supplements U.S.

*Both the AIM and the Pilot's Handbook of Aeronautical Knowledge (FAA-H-8083-25) contain explanations of airport signs and markings. (PLT141) — AIM Chapter 2, Section 3*

Answer (B) is incorrect because ACs provide information on non-regulatory material of interest. Answer (C) is incorrect because the Chart Supplements U.S. provide only comprehensive information on a given airport (such as runway lengths, available services, lighting, etc.).

ALL

**3805.** (Refer to Figure 49.) Select the proper traffic pattern and runway for landing.

A—Left-hand traffic and Runway 18.
B—Right-hand traffic and Runway 18.
C—Left-hand traffic and Runway 22.

*The small end of the tetrahedron points into the wind, indicating the direction of landing. The wind is coming from the southwest. However, the runway most nearly aligned into the wind is closed (X), leaving Runway 18 as the most suitable runway. The traffic pattern indicators on a segmented circle are used to indicate the direction of turns. The traffic pattern indicators, shown as extensions from the segmented circle, represent the base and final approach legs. The traffic pattern indicator shows right traffic for Runway 18. (PLT039, PA.II.D.K4, PH.III.A.K1) — AIM ¶4-3-3*

ALL, SPO

**3806.** (Refer to Figure 49.) If the wind is as shown by the landing direction indicator, the pilot should land on

A—Runway 18 and expect a crosswind from the right.
B—Runway 22 directly into the wind.
C—Runway 36 and expect a crosswind from the right.

*The small end of the tetrahedron points into the wind indicating the direction of landing. Landing to the south on Runway 18, the pilot could expect a right crosswind. (PLT077, PA.II.D.K4, PH.III.A.K1) — AIM ¶4-3-3*

ALL, SPO

**3806-1.** (Refer to Figure 65.) Sign F confirms your position on

A—Runway 22.
B—routing to Runway 22.
C—taxiway 22.

*F is a runway location sign, which identifies the runway on which the aircraft is located. (PLT141, PA.II.D.K3, PH.III.A.K1) — AIM ¶2-3-9*

ALL, SPO

**3806-2.** (Refer to Figure 65.) Sign E is a visual clue that

A—confirms the aircraft's location to be on taxiway B.
B—warns the pilot of approaching taxiway B.
C—indicates B holding area is ahead.

*E is a taxiway location sign, which identifies the taxiway upon which the aircraft is located. (PLT141, PA.II.D.K3, PH.III.A.K1) — AIM ¶2-3-9*

ALL, SPO

**3806-3.** (Refer to Figure 65.) A left turn at the intersection depicting sign A would place the aircraft

A—ready for a Runway 4 intersection takeoff.
B—on the taxiway leading to Runway 4.
C—ready for a Runway 22 intersection takeoff.

*Sign A is a runway holding position sign. The inscription on the sign contains the designation of the intersecting runway. The runway numbers on the sign are arranged to correspond to the respective runway threshold. "4-22" indicates that the threshold for Runway 4 is to the left and the threshold for Runway 22 is to the right. Making a left turn at the sign would put you ready for a Runway 22 intersection takeoff. (PLT141, PA.II.D.K3, PH.III.A.K1) — AIM ¶2-3-8*

SPO

**2029.** (Refer to Figure 65.) Which sign indicates the runway on which the aircraft is located?

A—E
B—F
C—L

*F is a runway location sign, which identifies the runway on which the aircraft is located. (PLT141) — AIM ¶2-3-9*

Answer (A) is incorrect because E is a taxiway location sign, which identifies the taxiway on which the aircraft is located. Answer (C) is incorrect because this is a runway distance remaining sign, which identifies the runway length remaining.

**Answers**

| | | | | | |
|---|---|---|---|---|---|
| 2206 [A] | 3805 [B] | 3806 [A] | 3806-1 [A] | 3806-2 [A] | 3806-3 [C] |
| 2029 [B] | | | | | |

SPO
**2218.** The taxiway ending marker

A—indicates taxiway does not continue.
B—identifies area where aircraft are prohibited.
C—provides general taxiing direction to named taxiway.

*Taxiway ending markers are used to indicate that the taxiway does not continue. (PLT141) — AIM ¶2-3-4*

# Airport Lighting

At night, the location of an airport can be determined by the presence of an airport **rotating beacon** light. The colors and color combinations that denote the type of airports are:

White and green .................... Lighted land airport

Green alone* .......................... Lighted land airport

White and yellow.................... Lighted water airport

Yellow alone* ......................... Lighted water airport

Green, yellow, white............... Lighted heliport

*Note:* Green alone or yellow alone is used only in connection with a white-and-green or white-and-yellow beacon display, respectively.

A civil lighted land airport beacon will show alternating white and green flashes. A military airfield will be identified by dual-peaked (two quick) white flashes between green flashes.

In Class B, C, D, or E airspace, operation of the airport beacon during the hours of daylight often indicates the ceiling is less than 1,000 feet and/or the visibility is less than 3 miles. However, pilots should not rely solely on the operation of the airport beacon to indicate if weather conditions are IFR or VFR.

**Runway edge lights** are used to outline the runway at night or during periods of low visibility. For the most part, runway edge lights are white, and may be high-, medium-, or low-intensity, while taxiways are outlined by blue omnidirectional lights.

**Radio control of lighting** is available at some airports, providing airborne control of lights by keying the aircraft's microphone. The control system is responsive to 7, 5, or 3 microphone clicks. Keying the microphone seven times within 5 seconds will turn the lighting to its highest intensity; five times in 5 seconds will set the lights to medium intensity; low intensity is set by keying three times in 5 seconds.

ALL, SPO
**3769.** An airport's rotating beacon operated during daylight hours indicates

A—there are obstructions on the airport.
B—that weather at the airport located in Class D airspace is below basic VFR weather minimums.
C—the Air Traffic Control tower is not in operation.

*In Class B, C, D or E airspace, operation of the airport beacon during the hours of daylight often indicates that the weather in the airspace is below basic VFR weather minimums (ground visibility is less than 3 miles and/or the ceiling is less than 1,000 feet). (PLT141, PA.II.D.K3, PH.III.A.K1) — AIM ¶2-1-9*

AIR, RTC, WSC, PPC
**3718.** Airport taxiway edge lights are identified at night by

A—white directional lights.
B—blue omnidirectional lights.
C—alternate red and green lights.

*A taxiway edge lighting system consists of omnidirectional blue lights which outline the usable limits of taxi paths. (PLT141, PA.II.D.K3, PH.III.A.K1) — FAA-H-8083-3*

**Answers**

2218 [A]    3769 [B]    3718 [B]

AIR, RTC, WSC, PPC
**3768.** To set the high intensity runway lights on medium intensity, the pilot should click the microphone seven times, and then click it

A—one time within four seconds.
B—three times within three seconds.
C—five times within five seconds.

*To save money at low-usage airports, pilot-controlled lighting is installed. Key the mic seven times to set the highest level, then adjust to medium with five clicks. (PLT462, PA.II.D.K3, PH.III.A.K1) — AIM ¶2-1-8*

AIR, RTC, LTA, WSC, PPC
**3770.** A lighted heliport may be identified by a

A—green, yellow, and white rotating beacon.
B—flashing yellow light.
C—blue lighted square landing area.

*A lighted heliport has a green, yellow, and white beacon flashing 30 to 60 times per minute. A flashing yellow light identifies a lighted water port. (PLT141, PA.II.D.K3, PH.III.A.K1) — AIM ¶2-1-9*

AIR, RTC, LTA, WSC, PPC
**3771.** A military air station can be identified by a rotating beacon that emits

A—white and green alternating flashes.
B—two quick white flashes between green flashes.
C—green, yellow, and white flashes.

*Military airport beacons flash alternately white and green, but are differentiated from civil beacons by dual-peaked (two quick) white flashes between the green flashes. (PLT141, PA.II.D.K3, PH.III.A.K1) — AIM ¶2-1-9*

AIR, RTC, LTA, WSC, PPC
**3772.** How can a military airport be identified at night?

A—Alternate white and green light flashes.
B—Dual peaked (two quick) white flashes between green flashes.
C—White flashing lights with steady green at the same location.

*Military airport beacons flash alternately white and green, but are differentiated from civil beacons by dual-peaked (two quick) white flashes between the green flashes. (PLT141, PA.II.D.K3, PH.III.A.K1) — AIM ¶2-1-9*

# Visual Approach Slope Indicator (VASI)

The **visual approach slope indicator (VASI)** is a lighting system arranged so as to provide visual-descent guidance information during approach to a runway. The lights are visible for up to 5 miles during the day. The VASI glide path provides obstruction clearance, while lateral guidance is provided by the runway or runway lights. When operating to an airport with an operating control tower, the pilot of an airplane approaching to land on a runway served by a VASI is required to maintain an altitude at or above the glide slope until a lower altitude is necessary for landing.

Most VASI installations consist of two bars, near and far, which provide one visual glide path. On final approach flying toward the runway of intended landing, if the pilot sees both bars as red, the aircraft is below the glide path (Figure 6-9A). Maintaining altitude, the pilot will see the near bar turn pink and then white, while the far bar remains red, indicating the glide path is being intercepted (Figure 6-9B). If the aircraft is above the glide path, the pilot will see both near and far bars as white (Figure 6-9C).

Pulsating VASIs normally consist of a single light unit projecting a two-color visual approach path. The below-glide-path indication is normally

**Figure 6-9.** A 2-bar VASI

**Answers**

3768   [C]       3770   [A]       3771   [B]       3772   [B]

red or pulsating red, and the above-glide-path indication is normally pulsating white. The on-glide-path indication is usually steady white. See Figure 6-10.

The **precision approach path indicator (PAPI)** uses a single row of lights. Four white lights means "too high." One red light and three white lights means "slightly high," etc. See Figure 6-11.

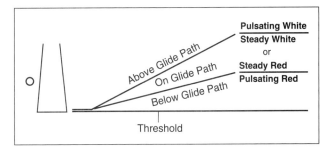

**Figure 6-10.** Pulsating VASI system

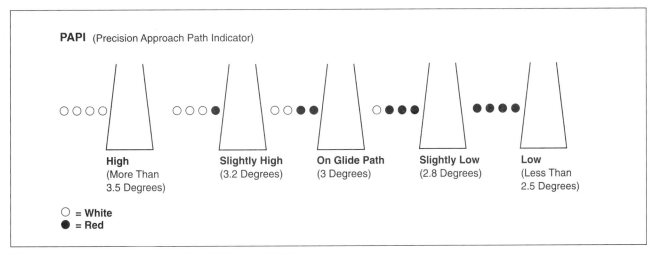

**Figure 6-11.** Precision approach path indicator (PAPI)

ALL

**3762-1.** Which approach and landing objective is assured when the pilot remains on the proper glidepath of the VASI?

A—Runway identification and course guidance.
B—Safe obstruction clearance in the approach area.
C—Lateral course guidance to the runway.

*The VASI is a system of lights arranged to provide visual descent guidance information during the approach to a runway. These lights are visible from 3 to 5 miles during the day, and up to 20 miles or more at night. The visual glidepath of the VASI provides safe obstruction clearance within ±10° of the extended runway centerline, and to 4 NM from the runway threshold. (PLT147, PA.III.B.S1, PH.III.A.K1) — AIM ¶2-1-2*

ALL, SPO

**3764.** A below glide slope indication from a pulsating approach slope indicator is a

A—pulsating white light.
B—steady white light.
C—pulsating red light.

*Pulsating visual approach slope indicators normally consist of a single light unit projecting a two-color visual approach path. The below-glide-path indication is red or pulsating red. The on-glide-path indication is a steady white light for one type of system, while for another system it is an alternating red and white light. (PLT147, PA.III.B.S1, PH.III.A.K1) — AIM ¶2-1-2*

ALL

**3120.** While operating in Class D airspace, each pilot of an aircraft approaching to land on a runway served by a visual approach slope indicator (VASI) shall

A—maintain a 3° glide until approximately 1/2 mile to the runway before going below the VASI.
B—maintain an altitude at or above the glide slope until a lower altitude is necessary for a safe landing.
C—stay high until the runway can be reached in a power-off landing.

*An airplane approaching to land on a runway served by a VASI shall maintain an altitude at or above the glide slope until a lower altitude is necessary for a safe landing. (PLT170, PA.III.B.K2, PH.III.A.K1) — 14 CFR §91.129*

ALL

**3121.** When approaching to land on a runway served by a visual approach slope indicator (VASI), the pilot shall

A—maintain an altitude that captures the glide slope at least 2 miles downwind from the runway threshold.
B—maintain an altitude at or above the glide slope.
C—remain on the glide slope and land between the two-light bar.

*An airplane approaching to land on a runway served by a VASI shall maintain an altitude at or above the glide slope until a lower altitude is necessary for a safe landing. (PLT147, PA.III.B.K2, PH.III.A.K1) — 14 CFR §91.129*

ALL

**3760.** A slightly high glide slope indication from a precision approach path indicator is

A—four white lights.
B—three white lights and one red light.
C—two white lights and two red lights.

*The PAPI uses light units similar to the VASI but are installed in a single row of either two or four light units. Four white lights means you are above the glide slope, three white lights and one red light means you are slightly high, two red and two white lights means you are on the glide slope, three reds and one white light means you are slightly low and four red lights means you are below the glide slope. (PLT147, PA.III.B.S1, PH.III.A.K1) — AIM ¶2-1-2*

ALL

**3765.** (Refer to Figure 47.) Illustration A indicates that the aircraft is

A—below the glide slope.
B—on the glide slope.
C—above the glide slope.

*The two-bar VASI on-glide-slope indication is red over white lights. (PLT147, PA.III.B.S1, PH.III.A.K1) — AIM ¶2-1-2*

ALL

**3766.** (Refer to Figure 47.) VASI lights as shown by illustration C indicate that the airplane is

A—off course to the left.
B—above the glide slope.
C—below the glide slope.

*The two-bar VASI above-glide-slope indication is white over white lights. VASI lights do not give horizontal direction. (PLT147, PA.III.B.S1, PH.III.A.K1) — AIM ¶2-1-2*

ALL, LSA, LSR, LSW, LSP

**3767.** (Refer to Figure 47.) While on final approach to a runway equipped with a standard 2-bar VASI, the lights appear as shown by illustration D. This means that the aircraft is

A—above the glide path.
B—below the glide path.
C—on the glide path.

*The below-glide-slope indication from a two-bar VASI is red over red lights. (PLT147, PA.III.B.S1, PH.III.A.K1) — AIM ¶2-1-2*

**Answers**

| | | | | | |
|---|---|---|---|---|---|
| 3120 [B] | 3121 [B] | 3760 [B] | 3765 [B] | 3766 [B] | 3767 [B] |

# Surface Operations

Taxiing to or from the runway generally presents no problems during calm or light wind conditions. However, when taxiing in moderate to strong wind conditions, the airplane's control surfaces must be used to counteract the effects of wind. In airplanes equipped with a nose wheel (tricycle-gear), use the following taxi procedures:

1. The elevator should be in the neutral position when taxiing into a headwind.

2. The upwind aileron should be held in the up position when taxiing in a crosswind (or the upwind wing will tend to be lifted).

3. The elevator should be held in the down position and the upwind aileron down when taxiing with a quartering tailwind (the most critical condition for a nosewheel-type airplane). See Figure 6-12.

When an airplane equipped with a tailwheel is taxied into a headwind, the elevator should be held in the up position to hold the tail down. In a quartering tailwind, both the upwind aileron and the elevator should be in the down position.

**Figure 6-12.** Control position while taxiing

AIR, REC, LSA

**3302.** When taxiing with strong quartering tailwinds, which aileron positions should be used?

A—Aileron down on the downwind side.
B—Ailerons neutral.
C—Aileron down on the side from which the wind is blowing.

*Taxiing with a quartering tailwind provides the most hazardous conditions. In this case, the elevator should be in the down position and the aileron on the upwind side should also be in the down position to keep the wing from lifting. (PLT486, PA.II.D.S3) — FAA-H-8083-3*

AIR, REC

**3303.** Which aileron positions should a pilot generally use when taxiing in strong quartering headwinds?

A—Aileron up on the side from which the wind is blowing.
B—Aileron down on the side from which the wind is blowing.
C—Ailerons neutral.

*When taxiing a nosewheel aircraft in the presence of moderate to strong winds, extra caution should be taken. For a quartering headwind, the elevator should be held in the neutral position, and the aileron on the upwind side should be in the up position. (PLT486, PA.II.D.S3) — FAA-H-8083-3*

**Answers**

3302    [C]          3303    [A]

AIR, REC

**3304.** Which wind condition would be most critical when taxiing a nosewheel equipped high-wing airplane?

A—Quartering tailwind.
B—Direct crosswind.
C—Quartering headwind.

*When taxiing a nosewheel aircraft in the presence of moderate to strong winds, extra caution should be taken. Taxiing with a quartering tailwind produces the most hazardous conditions. (PLT486, PA.II.D.S3) — FAA-H-8083-3*

AIR, REC

**3305.** (Refer to Figure 9, area A.) How should the flight controls be held while taxiing a tricycle-gear equipped airplane into a left quartering headwind?

A—Left aileron up, elevator neutral.
B—Left aileron down, elevator neutral.
C—Left aileron up, elevator down.

*When taxiing a nosewheel aircraft in the presence of moderate to strong winds, extra caution should be taken. For a quartering headwind, the elevator should be held in the neutral position, and the aileron on the upwind side should be in the up position. (PLT112, PA.II.D.S3) — FAA-H-8083-3*

AIR, REC

**3306.** (Refer to Figure 9, area B.) How should the flight controls be held while taxiing a tailwheel airplane into a right quartering headwind?

A—Right aileron up, elevator up.
B—Right aileron down, elevator neutral.
C—Right aileron up, elevator down.

*When taxiing a tailwheel airplane with a quartering headwind, the aileron on the upwind side should be up, and the elevator held in the up position to hold the tail down. (PLT112, PA.II.D.S3) — FAA-H-8083-3*

AIR, REC

**3307.** (Refer to Figure 9, area C.) How should the flight controls be held while taxiing a tailwheel airplane with a left quartering tailwind?

A—Left aileron up, elevator neutral.
B—Left aileron down, elevator neutral.
C—Left aileron down, elevator down.

*When taxiing a tailwheel aircraft with a quartering tailwind, the upwind aileron should be down to keep that wing from lifting, and the elevator should also be down. (PLT112, PA.II.D.S3) — FAA-H-8083-3*

AIR, REC

**3308.** (Refer to Figure 9, area C.) How should the flight controls be held while taxiing a tricycle-gear equipped airplane with a left quartering tailwind?

A—Left aileron up, elevator neutral.
B—Left aileron down, elevator down.
C—Left aileron up, elevator down.

*Taxiing with a quartering tailwind produces the most hazardous conditions. In this case, the elevator should be in the down position, and the aileron on the upwind side should also be in the down position to keep the wing from lifting. (PLT112, PA.II.D.S3) — FAA-H-8083-3*

AIR, GLI, REC

**3308-1.** To minimize the side loads placed on the landing gear during touchdown, the pilot should keep the

A—direction of motion of the aircraft parallel to the runway.
B—longitudinal axis of the aircraft parallel to the direction of its motion.
C—downwind wing lowered sufficiently to eliminate the tendency for the aircraft to drift.

*It is extremely important that the touchdown occur with the airplane's longitudinal axis exactly parallel to the direction in which the airplane is moving along the runway. Failure to accomplish this imposes severe side loads on the landing gear. To avoid these side stresses, the pilot should not allow the airplane to touch down while turned into the wind or drifting. (PLT170, PA.II.D.S3) — FAA-H-8083-3*

Answer (A) is incorrect because moving alongside the runway is not sufficient to reduce or eliminate side loads on the landing gear; the aircraft must be heading straight down the runway. Answer (C) is incorrect because this describes what happens on final approach, but the aircraft must be heading straight before it touches down.

**Answers**

| 3304 [A] | 3305 [A] | 3306 [A] | 3307 [C] | 3308 [B] | 3308-1 [B] |
|----------|----------|----------|----------|----------|------------|

LSR

**2328.** Select the true statement concerning gyroplane taxi procedures.

A—Taxi speed should be limited to no faster than a brisk walk in ideal conditions.
B—The cyclic stick should be held in the neutral position at all times.
C—The cyclic stick should be held slightly aft of neutral at all times.

*A gyroplane should not be taxied in close proximity to people or obstructions while the rotor is turning. In addition, taxi speed should be limited to no faster than a brisk walk in ideal conditions, and adjusted appropriately according to the circumstances. (PLT149) — FAA-H-8083-21*

LSR

**2331.** Select the true statement concerning gyroplane taxi procedures.

A—Avoid abrupt control movements when blades are turning.
B—The cyclic stick should be held in the neutral position at all times.
C—The cyclic stick should be held slightly aft of neutral at all times.

*A gyroplane should not be taxied in close proximity to people or obstructions while the rotor is turning. In addition, taxi speed should be limited to no faster than a brisk walk in ideal conditions, and adjusted appropriately according to the circumstances. Avoid abrupt control motions while taxiing. (PLT149) — FAA-H-8083-21*

LSR

**2332.** During the transition from pre-rotation to flight, all rotor blades change pitch

A—simultaneously to the same angle of incidence.
B—simultaneously but to different angles of incidence.
C—in sequence to the same angle of incidence.

*Compensation for dissymmetry of lift requires constant change in the blade angle of incidence, with one increasing as another simultaneously decreases. During the transition from pre-rotation to flight (or any time there is dissymmetry of lift) all rotor blades change pitch simultaneously, but to different angles of incidence. (PLT260) — FAA-H-8083-21*

RTC

**3339.** What precaution should be taken while taxiing a gyroplane?

A—The cyclic stick should be held in the neutral position at all times.
B—Avoid abrupt control movements when blades are turning.
C—The cyclic stick should be held slightly aft of neutral at all times.

*Avoid abrupt control motions while taxiing. (PLT170) — FAA-H-8083-21*

**Answers**

2328    [A]          2331    [A]          2332    [B]          3339    [B]

# Chart Supplement U.S.

The Chart Supplements U.S. is a publication designed primarily as a pilot's operational manual containing all airports, seaplane bases, and heliports open to the public including communications data, navigational facilities, and certain special notices and procedures. Directories are reissued in their entirety every 56 days.

Because of the wealth of information provided, an extensive legend is required for the Chart Supplements Airport/Facility section. See FAA Legends 2–19.

ALL, SPO

**3619.** (Refer to Figure 71, area 4 and Legend 1.) For information about the parachute jumping operations at Lincoln Regional/Harder (LHM) Airport, refer to

A—notes on the border of the chart.
B—the Chart Supplements U.S.
C—the Notices to Air Missions (NOTAM) publication.

*Tabulations of parachute jump areas in the U.S. are contained in the Chart Supplements U.S. (PLT064, PA.II.D.K1, PH.IV.B.K1) — AIM ¶3-5-4*

ALL

**3619-1.** Information concerning parachute jumping sites may be found in the

A—NOTAMs.
B—Chart Supplements U.S.
C—Graphic Notices and Supplemental Data.

*Tabulations of parachute jump areas in the U.S. are contained in the Chart Supplements U.S. (PLT281, PA.II.D.K1, PH.IV.B.K1) — AIM ¶3-5-4*

ALL

**3841.** (Refer to Figure 52.) Where is Loup City Municipal located in relation to the city?

A—Northeast approximately 3 miles.
B—Northwest approximately 1 mile.
C—East approximately 7 miles.

*Airport location is expressed as distance and direction from the center of the associated city in NM and cardinal points. The first item in parentheses is the airport identifier and the second item is the relation from the city. In this case, "1 NW." (PLT078, PA.II.D.K1, PH.IV.B.K1) — Chart Supplements U.S. Legend*

ALL

**3842.** (Refer to Figure 52.) Traffic patterns in effect at Lincoln Municipal are

A—to the right on Runway 18 and Runway 36.
B—to the right on Runway 18 and Runway 35; to the left on Runway 36.
C—to the right on Runways 14–32.

*Traffic is to the left unless otherwise stated in the Chart Supplements U.S. as "Rgt tfc." (PLT078, PA.II.D.K1, PH.IV.B.K1) — Chart Supplements U.S. Legend*

ALL, SPO

**3513.** (Refer to Figure 63.) What is the length of the displaced threshold for runway 22 at Toledo (TDZ)?

A—25 feet.
B—100 feet.
C—380 feet.

*The Chart Supplements U.S. for Toledo Executive (TDZ) shows a displaced threshold (Thld dsplcd) of 380 feet for Runway 22. (PLT078, PA.II.D.K1, PH.IV.B.K1) — Chart Supplements U.S. Legend*

Answer (A) is incorrect because 25 feet is the touchdown zone height for runway 22. Answer (B) is incorrect because 100 feet is the displaced threshold for runway 4.

ALL

**3838-1.** (Refer to Figures 76 and 77.) Inbound to Pierre Regional (PIR) from the southwest, with wind 240 at 12 knots, expect to make

A—left traffic for Runway 25.
B—right traffic for Runway 25.
C—left traffic for Runway 07.

*Unless otherwise noted in the Chart Supplements U.S. airport traffic patterns are left traffic for the stated runway. Wind is 240 at 12 knots resulting in a landing into the wind on runway 25. (PLT078, PA.II.D.K1, PH.IV.B.K1) — 14 CFR §91.127, Chart Supplements U.S. Legend*

Answer (B) is incorrect because the Chart Supplements U.S. does not list or specify right traffic for Runway 25. Answer (C) is incorrect because landing on Runway 07 would result in a significant tailwind landing.

**Answers**

| | | | | | |
|---|---|---|---|---|---|
| 3619 [B] | 3619-1 [B] | 3841 [B] | 3842 [B] | 3513 [C] | 3838-1 [A] |

ALL

**3841-1.** (Refer to Figure 78, 79 and Legend 3.) Where in relation to the airfield is the airport beacon located for Sioux City (SUX) airport?

A — West of runway 17-35.
B — East of runway 17-35.
C — Approach end of runway 31.

*Using Legend 3, you can determine that an airport beacon is depicted by a star feature. In both Figure 78 and on the airport diagram of Figure 79, locate the star feature on the east side of the airport or east of runway 17-35. (PLT064, PA.II.D.K1, PH.IV.B.K1) – Chart Supplements U.S. Legend*

AIR, RTC, WSC, PPC

**3838.** (Refer to Figure 52.) When approaching Lincoln Municipal from the west at noon for the purpose of landing, initial communications should be with

A—Lincoln Approach Control on 124.0 MHz.
B—Minneapolis Center on 128.75 MHz.
C—Lincoln Tower on 118.5 MHz.

*Arriving aircraft landing at airports within Class C airspace should contact approach control from outside the Class C airspace on the specified frequency.*

1. *Figure 52 shows UTC-6 (-5DT). This means that local time is 6 hours behind UTC time, and 5 hours behind during daylight saving time. In order to convert local time to UTC time, add this difference to local time:*
   1200 *local*
   + 0600 *UTC conversion*
   ―――――
   1800 *Z*

   *Lincoln Municipal approach should be contacted since its hours of operation are 1130 – 0630Z.*

2. *Identify the appropriate frequency for the aircraft's arrival from the west, 270°. Two frequencies are available. Aircraft approaching from any direction between 180° and 359° should make contact on 124.0 MHz.*

*(PLT078, PA.II.D.K1, PH.IV.B.K1) — AIM ¶3-2-4*

AIR, RTC, WSC, PPC

**3839.** (Refer to Figure 52.) Which type radar service is provided to VFR aircraft at Lincoln Municipal?

A—Sequencing to the primary Class C airport and standard separation.
B—Sequencing to the primary Class C airport and conflict resolution so that radar targets do not touch, or 1,000 feet vertical separation.
C—Sequencing to the primary Class C airport, traffic advisories, conflict resolution, and safety alerts.

*Radar service in Class C airspace consists of sequencing to the primary airport, standard IFR/IFR separation, IFR/VFR separation (so that targets do not touch or have less than 500-foot separation), and providing traffic advisories and safety alerts. (PLT078, PA.II.D.K1, PH.IV.B.K1) — AIM ¶3-2-4*

AIR, RTC, REC, WSC, PPC

**3840.** (Refer to Figure 52.) What is the recommended communications procedure for landing at Lincoln Municipal during the hours when the tower is not in operation?

A—Monitor airport traffic and announce your position and intentions on 118.5 MHz.
B—Contact UNICOM on 122.95 MHz for traffic advisories.
C—Monitor ATIS for airport conditions, then announce your position on 122.95 MHz.

*At an airport where the tower is operated on a part-time basis, a pilot should self-announce on the CTAF. (PLT078, PA.II.D.K1, PH.IV.B.K1) — AIM ¶4-1-9*

SPO

**2107.** The Chart Supplements U.S. will generally have the latest information pertaining to airport elevation, runway facilities, and control tower frequencies. If there are differences, it should be used in preference to the information

A—on the sectional chart.
B—in the Pilot's Handbook of Aeronautical Knowledge.
C—in the *Aeronautical Information Manual (AIM)*.

*Chart Supplements U.S. are revised every 8 weeks; sectional charts are revised semiannually. If there are differences, the Chart Supplements U.S. should be relied upon since they are more current. (PLT078) — FAA-H-8083-25*

*Answers (B) and (C) are incorrect because these publications do not have airport specific information.*

---

**Answers**

3841-1 [B]       3838   [A]       3839   [C]       3840   [A]       2107   [A]

SPO
**2118.** The most comprehensive information on a given airport is provided by

A—the Chart Supplements U.S.
B—Notices to Air Missions (NOTAMs).
C—sectional charts.

*The Chart Supplements U.S. provides the most comprehensive information on a given airport. (PLT281) — FAA-H-8083-25*

Answer (B) is incorrect because NOTAMs provide time-critical information on airports and changes that affect the national airspace system. Answer (C) is incorrect because sectional charts provide broad information on airport services and airspace.

SPO
**2119.** For a complete listing of information provided in Chart Supplements U.S. and how the information may be decoded, refer to the

A—Directory Legend Sample located in the front of each Chart Supplements U.S.
B—*Aeronautical Information Manual (AIM).*
C—legend on sectional and VFR terminal area charts.

*For a complete listing of information provided in Chart Supplements U.S. and how the information may be decoded, refer to the Directory Legend Sample located in the front of each Chart Supplements U.S. (PLT078) — FAA-H-8083-25*

# Airport Traffic Area Communications and Light Signals

Unless otherwise authorized, aircraft are required to maintain two-way radio communication with the ATC towers when operating to, from, or on the controlled airport, regardless of the weather. If radio contact cannot be maintained, ATC will direct traffic by means of light gun signals as shown in Figure 6-13.

If the aircraft radios fail while inbound to a tower-controlled airport, the pilot should remain outside or above the airport traffic area until the direction and flow of traffic has been determined and then join the airport traffic pattern and watch the tower for light signals.

The general warning signal (alternating red and green) may be followed by any other signal. For example, while on final approach for landing, an alternating red and green light followed by a flashing red light is received from the control tower. Under these circumstances, the pilot should abandon the approach, realizing the airport is unsafe for landing.

| Color & Type of Signal | Movement of Vehicles, Equipment & Personnel | Aircraft on the Ground | Aircraft in Flight |
|---|---|---|---|
| Steady green | Cleared to cross, proceed or go | Cleared for takeoff | Cleared to land |
| Flashing green | Not applicable | Cleared for taxi | Return for landing (to be followed by steady green at the proper time) |
| Steady red | STOP | STOP | Give way to other aircraft and continue circling |
| Flashing red | Clear the taxiway/runway | Taxi clear of the runway in use | Airport unsafe, do not land |
| Flashing white | Return to starting point on airport | Return to starting point on airport | Not applicable |
| Alternating red and green | Exercise extreme caution | Exercise extreme caution | Exercise extreme caution |

**Figure 6-13.** ATC light gun signals

**Answers**

2118 [A]          2119 [A]

ALL, SPO

**3111.** A steady green light signal directed from the control tower to an aircraft in flight is a signal that the pilot

A—is cleared to land.
B—should give way to other aircraft and continue circling.
C—should return for landing.

*A steady green light signal directed to an aircraft in flight means that the pilot is cleared to land. (PLT141, PA.III.A.K3, PH.III.B.K3) — 14 CFR §91.125*

Answer (B) is incorrect because this would be a steady red signal. Answer (C) is incorrect because this would be a flashing green signal.

ALL

**3115.** An alternating red and green light signal directed from the control tower to an aircraft in flight is a signal to

A—hold position.
B—exercise extreme caution.
C—not land; the airport is unsafe.

*An alternating red and green light signal means to exercise extreme caution. (PLT141, PA.III.A.K3, PH.III.B.K3) — 14 CFR §91.125*

Answer (A) is incorrect because you can't hold position in flight. Answer (C) is incorrect because this would be a flashing red signal.

AIR, RTC, WSC, PPC

**3112.** Which light signal from the control tower clears a pilot to taxi?

A—Flashing green.
B—Steady green.
C—Flashing white.

*A flashing green light signal clears a pilot to taxi. (PLT141, PA.III.A.K3, PH.III.B.K3) — 14 CFR §91.125*

Answer (B) is incorrect because this means cleared to takeoff/land. Answer (C) is incorrect because this means return to starting point on airport.

AIR, RTC, WSC, PPC

**3113.** If the control tower uses a light signal to direct a pilot to give way to other aircraft and continue circling, the light will be

A—flashing red.
B—steady red.
C—alternating red and green.

*A steady red signal directed to an aircraft in flight indicates the pilot should give way to other aircraft and continue circling. (PLT141, PA.III.A.K3, PH.III.B.K3) — 14 CFR §91.125*

Answer (A) is incorrect because this means the airport is unsafe. Answer (C) is incorrect because this means the pilot should exercise extreme caution.

AIR, RTC, WSC, PPC

**3114.** A flashing white light signal from the control tower to a taxiing aircraft is an indication to

A—taxi at a faster speed.
B—taxi only on taxiways and not cross runways.
C—return to the starting point on the airport.

*A flashing white light signal to a taxiing aircraft is an indication to return to the starting point on the airport. (PLT141, PA.III.A.K3, PH.III.B.K3) — 14 CFR §91.125*

Answers (A) and (B) are incorrect because there are no light signals for these instructions.

AIR, RTC, WSC, PPC

**3116.** While on final approach for landing, an alternating green and red light followed by a flashing red light is received from the control tower. Under these circumstances, the pilot should

A—discontinue the approach, fly the same traffic pattern and approach again, and land.
B—exercise extreme caution and abandon the approach, realizing the airport is unsafe for landing.
C—abandon the approach, circle the airport to the right, and expect a flashing white light when the airport is safe for landing.

*An alternating red and green light means to exercise extreme caution. A flashing red light means the airport is unsafe, do not land. (PLT141, PA.III.A.K3, PH.III.B.K3) — 14 CFR §91.125*

Answer (A) is incorrect because the flashing red light indicates the airport is unsafe for landing. Answer (C) is incorrect because a flashing white is not applicable in flight.

**Answers**

| 3111 | [A] | | 3115 | [B] | | 3112 | [A] | | 3113 | [B] | | 3114 | [C] | | 3116 | [B] |

AIR, RTC, WSC, PPC

**3804.** If the aircraft's radio fails, what is the recommended procedure when landing at a controlled airport?

A—Observe the traffic flow, enter the pattern, and look for a light signal from the tower.
B—Enter a crosswind leg and rock the wings.
C—Flash the landing lights and cycle the landing gear while circling the airport.

*When a transmitter, receiver, or both have become inoperative, an aircraft should observe the traffic flow, enter the pattern, and look for a light signal from the tower, when landing at a controlled airport. (PLT150, PA.III.A.K3, PH.III.B.K3) — AIM ¶4-2-13*

Answers (B) and (C) are incorrect because entering on the crosswind is not required and rocking the wings is used to acknowledge light signals during the day. Flashing the lights is used to acknowledge light signals during night, and a fixed gear airplane would not be able to cycle the gear.

SPO

**2012.** A steady red light from the tower, for an aircraft on the ground indicates

A—Give way to other aircraft and continue circling.
B—Stop.
C—Taxi clear of the runway in use.

*A steady red light from the tower, for an aircraft on the ground indicates the aircraft should stop. (PLT044) — 14 CFR §91.125*

Answer (A) is incorrect because this would be issued to an aircraft in flight. Answer (C) is incorrect because this would be a flashing red light.

# Communication Phraseology, Techniques, and Procedures

**Automatic Terminal Information Service (ATIS)** is a continuous broadcast of non-control information in selected high-activity terminal areas. To relieve frequency congestion, pilots are urged to listen to ATIS, and on initial contact, to advise controllers that the information has been received by repeating the alphabetical code word appended to the broadcast. For example: "information Sierra received." The phrase "have numbers" does not indicate receipt of the ATIS broadcast.

When transmitting an altitude to ATC (up to but not including 18,000 feet MSL), state the separate digits of the thousands, plus the hundreds. For example, 13,500 is "one three thousand five hundred" and 4,500 is "four thousand five hundred."

At airports with operating air traffic control towers (ATCT), approval must be obtained prior to moving an aircraft onto the movement area. Ground control frequencies are provided to reduce congestion on the tower frequency. They are used for issuance of taxi information, clearances and other necessary contacts. If instructed by ground control to "taxi to" a particular runway, the pilot must stop prior to crossing any runway. A clearance must be obtained prior to crossing any runway.

Aircraft arriving at an airport where a control tower is in operation should not change to ground control frequency until directed to do so by ATC.

The key to operating at an airport without an operating control tower is selection of the correct **Common Traffic Advisory Frequency (CTAF)**. The CTAF is identified in appropriate aeronautical publications and on the sectional chart. If the airport has a part-time air traffic control tower, the CTAF is usually a tower frequency. If a Flight Service Station (FSS) is located on the airport, they will usually monitor that frequency and provide advisories when the tower is closed. Where there is no tower or FSS, UNICOM, (if available) is usually the CTAF. UNICOM is limited to the necessities of safe and expeditious operation of private aircraft pertaining to runways and wind conditions, types of fuel available, weather, and dispatching. Secondarily, communications may be transmitted concerning ground transportation, food, lodging and services available during transit. When no tower, FSS, or UNICOM is available, use MULTICOM frequency 122.9 for self-announce procedures. See Figure 6-14.

**Answers**

3804   [A]          2012   [B]

| Facility at Airport | Frequency Use | Communication/Broadcast Procedures | | |
|---|---|---|---|---|
| | | *Outbound* | *Inbound* | *Practice Instrument Approach* |
| 1 UNICOM (No Tower or FSS) | Communicate with UNICOM station on published CTAF frequency (122.7, 122.8, 122.725, 122.975, or 123.0). If unable to contact UNICOM station, use self-announce procedures on CTAF. | Before taxiing and before taxiing on the runway for departure. | 10 miles out. Entering downwind, base, and final. Leaving the runway. | |
| 2 No Tower, FSS, or UNICOM | Self-announce on MULTICOM frequency 122.9. | Before taxiing and before taxiing on the runway for departure. | 10 miles out. Entering downwind, base, and final. Leaving the runway. | Departing final approach fix (name) or on final approach segment inbound. |
| 3 No Tower in operation, FSS open | Communicate with FSS on CTAF frequency. | Before taxiing and before taxiing on the runway for departure. | 10 miles out. Entering downwind, base, and final. Leaving the runway. | Approach completed/terminated. |
| 4 FSS closed (No Tower) | Self-announce on CTAF. | Before taxiing and before taxiing on the runway for departure. | 10 miles out. Entering downwind, base, and final. Leaving the runway. | |
| 5 Tower or FSS not in operation | Self-announce on CTAF. | Before taxiing and before taxiing on the runway for departure. | 10 miles out. Entering downwind, base, and final. Leaving the runway. | |

**Figure 6-14.** Summary of recommended communications procedures

ALL

**3613.** When flying HAWK N666CB, the proper phraseology for initial contact with McAlester Flight Service is

A—"MC ALESTER RADIO, HAWK SIX SIX SIX CHARLIE BRAVO, RECEIVING ARDMORE VORTAC, OVER."
B—"MC ALESTER STATION, HAWK SIX SIX SIX CEE BEE, RECEIVING ARDMORE VORTAC, OVER."
C—"MC ALESTER FLIGHT SERVICE STATION, HAWK NOVEMBER SIX CHARLIE BRAVO, RECEIVING ARDMORE VORTAC, OVER."

*The term "initial radio contact," or "initial callup," means the first radio call you make to a given facility, or the first call to a different controller or Flight Service specialist within a facility. Use the following format:*

*1. Name of facility being called;*

*2. Your full aircraft identification as filed in the flight plan;*

*3. Type of message to follow or your request if it is short, and*

*4. The word "over," if required.*

*Example: "New York Radio, Mooney Three One One Echo."*

*When the aircraft manufacturer's name or model is stated, the prefix "N" is dropped. The first two characters of the call sign may be dropped only after ATC calls you by your last three letters/numbers. (PLT204, PA.III.A.K2, PH.III.B.K2) — AIM ¶4-2-3*

ALL

**3614.** The correct method of stating 4,500 feet MSL to ATC is

A—"FOUR THOUSAND FIVE HUNDRED."
B—"FOUR POINT FIVE."
C—"FORTY-FIVE HUNDRED FEET MSL."

*Up to but not including 18,000 feet MSL, state the separate digits of the thousands, plus the hundreds, if appropriate. Example: "4,500—four thousand, five hundred." (PLT204, PA.III.A.K2, PH.III.B.K2) — AIM ¶4-2-9*

ALL

**3615.** The correct method of stating 10,500 feet MSL to ATC is

A—"TEN THOUSAND, FIVE HUNDRED FEET."
B—"TEN POINT FIVE."
C—"ONE ZERO THOUSAND, FIVE HUNDRED."

**Answers**

3613  [A]          3614  [A]          3615  [C]

*Up to but not including 18,000 feet MSL, state the separate digits of the thousands, plus the hundreds, if appropriate. Example: "10,500—one zero thousand, five hundred." (PLT204, PA.III.A.K2, PH.III.B.K2) — AIM ¶4-2-9*

ALL, SPO

**3604.** (Refer to Figure 20, area 3.) What is the recommended communications procedure for a landing at Currituck County Airport?

A—Transmit intentions on 122.9 MHz when 10 miles out and give position reports in the traffic pattern.
B—Contact Elizabeth City FSS for airport advisory service.
C—Contact New Bern FSS for area traffic information.

*Where there is no tower, Flight Service, or UNICOM station on the airport, use MULTICOM frequency 122.9 for self-announce procedures. Such airports will be identified in the appropriate aeronautical information publications. (PLT435, PA.III.A.K2, PH.III.B.K2) — AIM ¶4-1-9*

ALL

**3605.** (Refer to Figure 21, area 2.) The CTAF/MULTICOM frequency for Garrison Airport is

A—122.8 MHz.
B—122.9 MHz.
C—123.0 MHz.

*Where there is no tower, Flight Service, or UNICOM station on the airport, use MULTICOM frequency 122.9 for self-announce procedures. Such airports will be identified in the appropriate aeronautical information publications. (PLT435, PA.III.A.K2, PH.III.B.K2) — AIM ¶4-1-9*

ALL

**3998.** When should pilots state their position on the airport when calling the tower for takeoff?

A—When visibility is less than 1 mile.
B—When parallel runways are in use.
C—When departing from a runway intersection.

*Pilots should state their position on the airport when calling the tower for takeoff from a runway intersection. (PLT222, PA.III.A.K2, PH.III.B.K2) — AIM ¶4-3-10*

ALL

**3605-1.** As standard operating practice, all inbound traffic to an airport without a control tower should continuously monitor the appropriate facility from a distance of

A—25 miles.
B—20 miles.
C—10 miles.

*Pilots of inbound traffic should monitor and communicate as appropriate on the designated CTAF from 10 miles to landing. Pilots of departing aircraft should monitor/communicate on the appropriate frequency from start-up, during taxi, and until 10 miles from the airport unless the CFRs or local procedures require otherwise. (PLT435, PA.III.A.K2, PH.III.B.K2) — AIM ¶4-1-9*

ALL

**3605-2.** Absence of the sky condition and visibility on an ATIS broadcast indicates that

A—weather conditions are at or above VFR minimums.
B—the sky condition is clear and visibility is unrestricted.
C—the ceiling is at least 5,000 feet and visibility is 5 miles or more.

*The absence of a sky condition or ceiling and/or visibility on ATIS indicates a ceiling of 5,000 feet or above and visibility of 5 miles or more. (PLT196, PA.III.A.K2, PH.III.B.K2) — AIM ¶4-1-13*

ALL

**3606.** (Refer to Figure 22, area 2; and Figure 31.) At Coeur D'Alene, which frequency should be used as a Common Traffic Advisory Frequency (CTAF) to self-announce position and intentions?

A—122.05 MHz.
B—122.1/108.8 MHz.
C—122.8 MHz.

*CTAF is a frequency designed for the purpose of carrying out airport advisory practices and/or position reporting at an uncontrolled airport (which may also occur during hours when a tower is closed). The CTAF may be a UNICOM, MULTICOM, FSS, or tower frequency and is identified in the appropriate aeronautical publications. A solid dot with the letter "C" inside indicates the CTAF. When the control tower operates part time and a UNICOM frequency is provided, use the UNICOM frequency. (PLT064, PA.III.A.K1, PH.III.B.K2) — AIM ¶4-1-9*

---

**Answers**

| 3604 [A] | 3605 [B] | 3998 [C] | 3605-1 [C] | 3605-2 [C] | 3606 [C] |
|----------|----------|----------|------------|------------|----------|

ALL, SPO

**3607.** (Refer to Figure 22, area 2; and Figure 31.) At Coeur D'Alene, which frequency should be used as a Common Traffic Advisory Frequency (CTAF) to monitor airport traffic?

A—122.05 MHz.
B—135.075 MHz.
C—122.8 MHz.

*CTAF is a frequency designed for the purpose of carrying out airport advisory practices and/or position reporting at an uncontrolled airport (which may also occur during hours when a tower is closed). The CTAF may be a UNICOM, MULTICOM, FSS, or tower frequency and is identified in the appropriate aeronautical publications. A solid dot with the letter "C" inside indicates the CTAF. When the control tower operates part time and a UNICOM frequency is provided, use the UNICOM frequency. (PLT064, PA.III.A.K1, PH.III.B.K2) — AIM ¶4-1-9*

SPO

**2014.** (Refer to Figure 22, area 2; and Figure 31.) What is the correct UNICOM frequency to be used at Coeur D'Alene?

A—135.075 MHz.
B—122.05 MHz.
C—122.8 MHz.

*The sectional chart and Chart Supplements U.S. both list the UNICOM frequency as 122.8. The UNICOM frequency is depicted in the airport information in the lower right-hand corner. (PLT064) — AIM ¶4-1-11*

Answer (A) is incorrect because 135.075 is used to listen to AWOS. Answer (B) is incorrect because 122.05 is the remote communication outlet (RCO) frequency to contact Boise FSS in the Coeur D'Alene vicinity.

ALL

**3608.** (Refer to Figure 22, area 2; and Figure 31.) What is the correct UNICOM frequency to be used at Coeur D'Alene to request fuel?

A—135.075 MHz.
B—122.1/108.8 MHz.
C—122.8 MHz.

*The sectional chart and Chart Supplements U.S. both list the UNICOM frequency as 122.8. This is the appropriate frequency to use to contact UNICOM. The UNICOM frequency is depicted in the airport information in the lower right-hand corner. (PLT064, PA.III.A.K1, PH.III.B.K2) — AIM ¶4-1-11*

ALL

**3609.** (Refer to Figure 25, area 3.) If Dallas Executive (RBD) Tower is not in operation, which frequency should be used as a Common Traffic Advisory Frequency (CTAF) to monitor airport traffic?

A—127.25 MHz.
B—122.95 MHz.
C—126.35 MHz.

*A solid dot with the letter "C" inside indicates the CTAF. (PLT064, PA.III.A.K1, PH.III.B.K2) — AIM ¶4-1-9*

ALL

**3641.** (Refer to Figure 25, area 2.) The control tower frequency for Addison Airport is

A—122.95 MHz.
B—126.0 MHz.
C—133.4 MHz.

*The correct answer is found in the explanatory box for Addison airport in area 2: 126.0 MHz. (PLT101, PA.III.A.K1, PH.III.B.K2) — Sectional Chart Legend*

ALL

**3610.** (Refer to Figure 26, area 2.) What is the recommended communication procedure when inbound to land at Cooperstown Airport?

A—Broadcast intentions when 10 miles out on the CTAF/MULTICOM frequency, 122.9 MHz.
B—Contact UNICOM when 10 miles out on 122.8 MHz.
C—Circle the airport in a left turn prior to entering traffic.

*MULTICOM frequency is always 122.9 MHz, and the correct procedure is to broadcast intentions when 10 miles from the airport. (PLT064, PA.III.A.K2, PH.III.B.K2) — AIM ¶4-1-9*

**Answers**

| | | | | | |
|---|---|---|---|---|---|
| 3607 [C] | 2014 [C] | 3608 [C] | 3609 [A] | 3641 [B] | 3610 [A] |

ALL
**3611.** (Refer to Figure 26, area 4.) The CTAF/UNICOM frequency at Jamestown Airport is

A—122.0 MHz.
B—123.0 MHz.
C—123.6 MHz.

*CTAF is a frequency designed for the purpose of carrying out airport advisory practices and/or position reporting at an uncontrolled airport (which may also occur during hours when a tower is closed). The CTAF may be a UNICOM, MULTICOM, FSS, or tower frequency and is identified in the appropriate aeronautical publications. A solid dot with the letter "C" inside indicates the CTAF; it may be a UNICOM, MULTICOM, FSS, or tower frequency. (PLT064, PA.III.A.K1, PH.III.B.K2) — AIM ¶4-1-9*

ALL
**3612.** (Refer to Figure 26, area 5.) What is the CTAF/UNICOM frequency at Barnes County Airport?

A—122.0 MHz.
B—122.8 MHz.
C—123.6 MHz.

*CTAF is a frequency designed for the purpose of carrying out airport advisory practices and/or position reporting at an uncontrolled airport (which may also occur during hours when a tower is closed). The CTAF may be a UNICOM, MULTICOM, FSS, or tower frequency and is identified in the appropriate aeronautical publications. A solid dot with the letter "C" inside indicates the CTAF. (PLT064, PA.III.A.K1, PH.III.B.K2) — AIM ¶4-1-9*

ALL
**3791.** Automatic Terminal Information Service (ATIS) is the continuous broadcast of recorded information concerning

A—pilots of radar-identified aircraft whose aircraft is in dangerous proximity to terrain or to an obstruction.
B—nonessential information to reduce frequency congestion.
C—noncontrol information in selected high-activity terminal areas.

*ATIS is the continuous broadcast of recorded non-control information in selected high-activity terminal areas. (PLT196, PA.III.A.K1, PH.III.B.K2) — AIM ¶4-1-13*

ALL
**3790.** Select the UNICOM frequencies normally assigned to stations at landing areas used exclusively as heliports.

A—122.75 and 123.65 MHz.
B—123.0 and 122.95 MHz.
C—123.05 and 123.075 MHz.

*Frequencies used solely for heliports are 123.050 and 123.075. (PLT204, PA.III.A.K1, PH.III.B.K2) — AIM ¶4-1-11*

AIR, RTC, WSC, PPC
**3811.** After landing at a tower-controlled airport, when should the pilot contact ground control?

A—When advised by the tower to do so.
B—Prior to turning off the runway.
C—After reaching a taxiway that leads directly to the parking area.

*A pilot who has just landed should not change from tower to ground frequency until advised to do so by the controller. (PLT044, PA.III.A.K2, PH.III.B.K2) — AIM ¶4-3-14*

AIR, RTC, WSC, PPC
**3812.** If instructed by ground control to taxi to Runway 9, the pilot may proceed

A—via taxiways and across runways to, but not onto, Runway 9.
B—to the next intersecting runway where further clearance is required.
C—via taxiways and across runways to Runway 9, where an immediate takeoff may be made.

*When ATC clears an aircraft to "taxi to" an assigned takeoff runway, the absence of holding instructions does not authorize the aircraft to "cross" all runway which the taxi route intersects except the assigned takeoff runway. A clearance must be obtained prior to crossing any runway. It does not include authorization to "taxi on to" or "cross" the assigned takeoff runway at any point. (PLT502, PA.III.A.K2, PH.III.B.K2) — AIM ¶4-3-18*

**Answers**

| | | | | | |
|---|---|---|---|---|---|
| 3611 [B] | 3612 [B] | 3791 [C] | 3790 [C] | 3811 [A] | 3812 [B] |

SPO
**2205.** What services will a FSS provide?

A—Fuel pricing.
B—Assistance during an emergency.
C—Clearance to taxi for takeoff.

*FSSs are air traffic facilities that provide pilot briefings, enroute communications and VFR search-and-rescue services, assist lost aircraft and aircraft in emergency situations, relay ATC clearances, originate Notices to Air Missions, broadcast aviation weather and NAS information, receive and process IFR flight plans, and monitor navigational aids (NAVAIDs). In addition, at selected locations FSSs provide En Route Flight Advisory Service (Flight Watch), take weather observations, issue airport advisories, and advise Customs and Immigration of transborder flights. (PLT172) — AIM ¶4-1-3*

Answer (A) is incorrect because this is done by UNICOM. Answer (C) is incorrect because this is done by ground control or tower control.

SPO
**2006.** When outbound from an airport with a UNICOM station on the published common traffic advisory frequency (CTAF) and there is no tower or Flight Service Station (FSS), the pilot should contact UNICOM or use self-announce procedures on CTAF before

A—engine start.
B—taxiing and before taxiing on the runway.
C—the preflight inspection.

*Pilots should contact UNICOM before taxiing, crossing any runway, and again before taxiing on the runway for departure. (PLT435) — AIM ¶4-1-9*

SPO
**2007.** When outbound from an airport without a UNICOM station, tower or Flight Service Station (FSS), the pilot should self-announce on frequency

A—122.7
B—122.9
C—122.8

*Where there is no tower, FSS, or UNICOM station on the airport, use MULTICOM frequency 122.9 for self-announce procedures. (PLT435) — AIM ¶4-1-9*

Answers (A) and (C) are incorrect because these are both CTAF frequencies used to communicate with a UNICOM station.

SPO
**2015.** You have just landed at a towered airport and the tower tells you to contact ground control when clear of the runway. You are considered clear of the runway when

A—all parts of the aircraft have crossed the hold line.
B—the aircraft flight deck is clear of the hold line.
C—the tail of the aircraft is clear of the runway edge.

*An aircraft exiting a runway is not clear of the runway until all parts of the aircraft have crossed the applicable holding position marking. (PLT112) — AIM ¶2-3-5*

SPO
**2016.** Pilots should state their position on the airport when calling the tower for takeoff

A—from a runway intersection, during instrument conditions.
B—from a runway intersection or the end of the runway.
C—from a runway intersection, only at night.

*Pilots should state their position on the airport when calling the tower for takeoff from a runway intersection. Example: "Cleveland Tower, Apache Three Seven Two Two Papa, at the intersection of taxiway Oscar and runway two three right, ready for departure." (PLT486) — AIM ¶4-3-10*

Answers (A) and (C) are incorrect because this rule applies to all operations.

SPO
**2017.** After landing at a tower controlled airport a pilot should contact ground control

A—when advised by the tower.
B—prior to turning off the runway.
C—after reaching a taxiway that leads directly to the parking area.

*A pilot who has just landed should not change from the tower frequency to the ground control frequency until directed to do so by the controller. (PLT170) — AIM ¶4-3-14*

---

**Answers**

2205 [B]  2006 [B]  2007 [B]  2015 [A]  2016 [B]  2017 [A]

# Radar Assistance to VFR Aircraft

Radar-equipped ATC facilities provide traffic advisories and limited vectoring (called basic radar service) to VFR aircraft, provided the aircraft can communicate with the facility, is within radar coverage, and can be radar-identified.

Stage II service provides radar advisories and sequencing for VFR aircraft. Arriving aircraft should initiate contact with approach control. Approach control will assume Stage II service is requested, unless the pilot states that the service is not wanted. Pilots of departing VFR aircraft should request Stage II terminal radar advisory service from ground control on initial contact.

At some locations Stage III service has been established to provide separation between all participating VFR aircraft and all IFR aircraft in the terminal radar service area (TRSA). Unless the pilot states "negative Stage III" on initial contact with approach control, the service will be provided.

Traffic advisories given by a radar service will refer to the other aircraft by azimuth in terms of the 12-hour clock, with twelve o'clock being the direction of flight (track), not aircraft heading. Each hour is equal to 30°. For example, an aircraft heading 090° is advised of traffic at the three o'clock position. The pilot should look 90° to the right of the direction of flight, or to the south. In Figure 6-15, traffic information would be issued to the pilot of aircraft A as twelve o'clock. The actual position of the traffic as seen by the pilot of aircraft A would be two o'clock. Traffic information issued to aircraft B would also be given as twelve o'clock, but in this case, the pilot of B would see traffic at ten o'clock.

These radar programs are not to be interpreted as relieving pilots of their responsibilities to see and avoid other traffic operating in basic VFR weather conditions, to maintain appropriate terrain and obstruction clearance, or to remain in weather conditions equal to or better than the minimum required by FAA regulations. Whenever compliance with an assigned route, heading, and/or altitude is likely to compromise pilot responsibilities respecting terrain, obstruction clearance, and weather minimums, the controller should be so advised and a revised clearance or instruction obtained.

**Figure 6-15.** Traffic advisory

ALL
**3792-1.** When an air traffic controller issues radar traffic information in relation to the 12-hour clock, the reference the controller uses is the aircraft's

A—true course.
B—ground track.
C—magnetic heading.

*Azimuth information given by ATC is based on the ground track of an aircraft as it is observed. The pilot must apply a correction to the reported azimuth using a drift-correction angle in order to maintain the track. (PLT044, PA.III.A.K7, PH.III.B.K7) — AIM ¶4-1-15*

ALL
**3792.** An ATC radar facility issues the following advisory to a pilot flying on a heading of 090°:

"TRAFFIC THREE O'CLOCK, 2 MILES, WEST-BOUND..."

Where should the pilot look for this traffic?

A—East.
B—South.
C—West.

*Traffic information will be given in azimuth from the aircraft in terms of the 12-hour clock. Thus, each hour would constitute an angle of 30°. Picture a clock in your lap; three o'clock is to your right, nine o'clock is to your left, twelve o'clock is straight ahead, and six o'clock is*

**Answers**

3792-1 [B]          3792   [B]

behind you. If an aircraft is proceeding on a heading of 090° (east), traffic located at the three o'clock position would be 90° right of the nose, south of the aircraft. (PLT194, PA.III.A.K7, PH.III.B.K7) — AIM ¶4-1-15

ALL

**3793.** An ATC radar facility issues the following advisory to a pilot flying on a heading of 360°:

"TRAFFIC 10 O'CLOCK, 2 MILES, SOUTHBOUND..."

Where should the pilot look for this traffic?

A—Northwest.
B—Northeast.
C—Southwest.

If an aircraft is proceeding on a heading of 360° (north), traffic located at the ten o'clock position would be 60° (left) of the nose, or to the northwest. (PLT194, PA.III.A.K7, PH.III.B.K7) — AIM ¶4-1-15

ALL

**3798.** TRSA Service in the terminal radar program provides

A—IFR separation (1,000 feet vertical and 3 miles lateral) between all aircraft.
B—warning to pilots when their aircraft are in unsafe proximity to terrain, obstructions, or other aircraft.
C—sequencing and separation for participating VFR aircraft.

TRSA Service provides separation of participating VFR aircraft and all IFR aircraft operating within the airspace. (PLT370, PA.III.A.K7, PH.III.B.K7) — AIM ¶4-1-18

ALL

**3794.** An ATC radar facility issues the following advisory to a pilot during a local flight:

"TRAFFIC 2 O'CLOCK, 5 MILES, NORTHBOUND..."

Where should the pilot look for this traffic?

A—Between directly ahead and 90° to the left.
B—Between directly behind and 90° to the right.
C—Between directly ahead and 90° to the right.

Traffic information issued to the pilot as "two o'clock" would mean approximately 60° right. (PLT194, PA.III.A.K7, PH.III.B.K7) — AIM ¶4-1-15

SPO

**2054.** An ATC radar facility issues the following advisory to a pilot flying on a heading of 270°: "TRAFFIC 3 O'CLOCK, 2 MILES, EASTBOUND..." Where should the pilot look for this traffic?

A—North.
B—South.
C—West.

Traffic information will be given in azimuth from the aircraft in terms of the 12-hour clock. Thus, each hour would constitute an angle of 30°. Picture a clock in your lap; three o'clock is to your right, nine o'clock is to your left, twelve o'clock is straight ahead, and six o'clock is behind you. If an aircraft is proceeding on a heading of 270° (west), traffic located at the three o'clock position would be 90° right of the nose, north of the aircraft. (PLT194) — AIM ¶4-1-15

ALL

**3795.** An ATC radar facility issues the following advisory to a pilot flying north in a calm wind:

"TRAFFIC 9 O'CLOCK, 2 MILES, SOUTHBOUND..."

Where should the pilot look for this traffic?

A—South.
B—North.
C—West.

An aircraft flying north in calm wind would be heading 360°. When advised of traffic at the nine o'clock position, the pilot should look 90° left of the nose, to the west. (PLT194, PA.III.A.K7, PH.III.B.K7) — AIM ¶4-1-15

ALL

**3796.** Basic radar service in the terminal radar program is best described as

A—safety alerts, traffic advisories and limited vectoring to VFR aircraft.
B—mandatory radar service provided by the Automated Radar Terminal System (ARTS) program.
C—wind shear warning at participating airports.

In addition to the use of radar for the control of IFR aircraft, all commissioned radar facilities provide safety alerts, traffic advisories and limited vectoring (on a workload-permitting basis) to VFR aircraft. Radar facilities are not responsible for weather information and the service is not mandatory. (PLT172, PA.III.A.K7, PH.III.B.K7) — AIM ¶4-1-18

---

**Answers**

| 3793 [A] | 3798 [C] | 3794 [C] | 2054 [A] | 3795 [C] | 3796 [A] |

ALL

**3797.** From whom should a departing VFR aircraft request radar traffic information during ground operations?

A—Clearance delivery.
B—Tower, just before takeoff.
C—Ground control, on initial contact.

*Pilots of departing VFR aircraft are encouraged to request radar traffic information by notifying ground control on initial contact with their request and proposed direction of flight. (PLT204, PA.III.A.K7, PH.III.B.K7) — AIM ¶4-1-18*

SPO

**2226.** During departure, when visual separation is employed by Air Traffic Control (ATC), traffic is no longer a factor when

A—the other aircraft turns away or is on a diverging course.
B—visual contact with the other aircraft is lost.
C—the other aircraft is passed.

*Traffic is no longer a factor when during approach phase the other aircraft is in the landing phase of flight or executes a missed approach; and during departure or en route, when the other aircraft turns away or is on a diverging course. (PLT116) — AIM ¶4-4-14*

**Answers**

3797    [C]          2226    [A]

# Chapter 7
# Enroute Flight and Navigation

# Pilotage

Air navigation is the art of directing an aircraft along a desired course and being able to determine its geographical position at any time. Such navigation may be accomplished by pilotage, dead reckoning, or using radio navigational aids.

**Pilotage** is the use of visible landmarks to maintain a desired course, and is the basic form of navigation for the beginning pilot operating under visual flight rules (VFR). Visible landmarks which can be identified on aeronautical charts allow the pilot to proceed from one check point to the next.

The aeronautical charts most commonly used by VFR pilots are the **VFR Sectional Aeronautical Chart**, the **VFR Terminal Area Chart**, and the **World Aeronautical Chart**. All three charts include aeronautical information such as airports, airways, special use airspace, and other pertinent data.

The scale of the VFR Sectional Aeronautical Chart is 1:500,000 (1 inch = 6.86 NM). Designed for visual navigation of slow speed aircraft in VFR conditions, this chart portrays terrain relief and checkpoints such as populated places, roads, railroads, and other distinctive landmarks. These charts have the best detail and are revised every 6 months.

Information found on the VFR Terminal Area Chart is similar to that found on the VFR Sectional Chart, but the scale on this chart is 1:250,000 (1 inch = 3.43 NM). These charts are for a specific city with Class B airspace. They show much detail, but have small coverage.

The World Aeronautical Chart has a scale of 1:1,000,000, which is more convenient for use in navigation by moderate speed aircraft. It depicts cities, railroads, and distinctive landmarks, etc. These charts have less detail and are revised no more than once a year.

To identify a point on the surface of the earth, a geographic coordinate, or grid, system was devised. By reference to meridians of **longitude** and parallels of **latitude**, any position may be accurately located when using the grid system.

Equidistant from the poles is an imaginary circle called the **equator**. The lines running east and west, parallel to the equator are called parallels of latitude, and are used to measure angular distance north or south of the equator. From the equator to either pole is 90°, with 0° being at the equator; while 90° north latitude describes the location of the North Pole. See Figure 7-1.

Lines called meridians of longitude are drawn from pole to pole at right angles to the equator. The **prime meridian**, used as the zero degree line, passes through Greenwich, England. From this line, measurements are made in degrees both easterly and westerly up to 180°.

Any specific geographical point can be located by reference to its longitude and latitude. For example, Washington, DC is approximately 39° north of the equator and 77° west of the prime meridian and would be stated as 39°N 77°W. Note that latitude is stated first.

In order to describe a location more precisely, each degree (°) is subdivided into 60 minutes (') and each minute further divided into 60 seconds ("), although seconds are not shown. Thus, the location of the airport at Elk City, Oklahoma is described as being at 35°25'55"N 99°23'15"W (35 degrees, 25 minutes, 55 seconds north latitude; 99 degrees, 23 minutes, 15 seconds west longitude). Degrees of west longitude increase from east to west. Degrees of north latitude increase from south to north.

**Figure 7-1.** Meridians of longitude and parallels of latitude

ALL
**3530-1.** Which statement about longitude and latitude is true?

A—Lines of longitude are parallel to the equator.
B—Lines of longitude cross the equator at right angles.
C—The 0° line of latitude passes through Greenwich, England.

*Meridians of longitude encircle the earth from pole to pole, and all meridians cross the equator at right angles. (PLT101, PA.VI.A.K1, PH.VII.A.K1) — FAA-H-8083-25*

Answer (A) is incorrect because lines of latitude are parallel to the equator. Answer (C) is incorrect because the 0° line of longitude passes through Greenwich, England.

ALL
**3530.** (Refer to Figure 20, area 3.) Determine the approximate latitude and longitude of Currituck County Airport.

A—36°24'N – 76°01'W.
B—36°48'N – 76°01'W.
C—47°24'N – 75°58'W.

*Graticules on Sectional Aeronautical Charts are the lines dividing each 30 minutes of latitude and each 30 minutes of longitude. Each tick mark represents one minute of latitude or longitude. Latitude increases northward, west longitude increases going westward. The approximate latitude and longitude of Currituck County Airport is 36°24'N, 76°01'W. (PLT064, PA.VI.A.K1, PH.VII.A.K1) — FAA-H-8083-25*

ALL, SPO
**3535.** (Refer to Figure 21, area 2.) Which airport is located at approximately 47°35'30"N latitude and 100°43'00"W longitude?

A—Turtle Lake.
B—Makeeff.
C—Johnson.

*Graticules on Sectional Aeronautical Charts are the lines dividing each 30 minutes of latitude and each 30 minutes of longitude. Each tick mark represents one minute of latitude or longitude. Latitude increases northward, west longitude increases going westward. The Makeeff (Pvt) airport is located at approximately 47°35'30"N latitude and 100°43'00"W longitude. (PLT064, PA.VI.A.K1, PH.VII.A.K1) — FAA-H-8083-25*

ALL
**3536.** (Refer to Figure 21, area 3.) Which airport is located at approximately 47°21'N latitude and 101°01'W longitude?

A—Lorentzen.
B—Johnson.
C—Washburn.

*Graticules on Sectional Aeronautical Charts are the lines dividing each 30 minutes of latitude and each 30 minutes of longitude. Each tick mark represents one minute of latitude or longitude. Latitude increases northward, west longitude increases going westward. Washburn is located at approximately 47°21'N latitude and 101°01'W longitude. (PLT064, PA.VI.A.K1, PH.VII.A.K1) — FAA-H-8083-25*

ALL
**3543.** (Refer to Figure 22, area 3.) Determine the approximate latitude and longitude of Shoshone County Airport.

A—47°02'N – 116°11'W
B—47°33'N – 116°11'W
C—47°32'N – 116°41'W

*Graticules on Sectional Aeronautical Charts are the lines dividing each 30 minutes of latitude and each 30 minutes of longitude. Each tick mark represents one minute of latitude or longitude. Latitude increases northward, west longitude increases going westward. The approximate latitude and longitude of Shoshone County Airport is 47°33'N, 116°11'W. (PLT064, PA.VI.A.K1, PH.VII.A.K1) — FAA-H-8083-25*

ALL
**3567.** (Refer to Figure 26, area 2.) What is the approximate latitude and longitude of Cooperstown Airport?

A—47°25'N – 98°06'W.
B—47°25'N – 99°54'W.
C—47°55'N – 98°06'W.

*Graticules on Sectional Aeronautical Charts are the lines dividing each 30 minutes of latitude and each 30 minutes of longitude. Each tick mark represents one minute of latitude or longitude. Latitude increases northward, west longitude increases going westward. Cooperstown airport is approximately at 47°25'N latitude, and 98°06'W longitude. (PLT064, PA.VI.A.K1, PH.VII.A.K1) — FAA-H-8083-25*

**Answers**

3530-1 [B]   3530 [A]   3535 [B]   3536 [C]   3543 [B]   3567 [A]

SPO

**2106.** During VFR navigation without radio instruments, heading and groundspeed, as calculated by dead reckoning, should be constantly monitored and corrected by

A—pilotage as observed from checkpoints.
B—the wind triangle.
C—wet compass and the groundspeed indicator.

*Except for flights over water, dead reckoning is usually used with pilotage. The heading and ground speed as calculated is constantly monitored and corrected by pilotage as observed from checkpoints. (PLT116) — FAA-H-8083-25*

SPO

**2108.** For cross-country flights over land, navigation without radio instruments is usually accomplished using dead reckoning and

A—pilotage.
B—the wind triangle.
C—compass heading.

*Except for flights over water, dead reckoning is usually used with pilotage. The heading and ground speed as calculated is constantly monitored and corrected by pilotage as observed from checkpoints. (PLT116) — FAA-H-8083-25*

SPO

**2178.** Using pilotage, a pilot can keep from drifting too far off course by

A—flying the flight plan heading.
B—filing a flight plan.
C—referring to selected features or checkpoints.

*Pilotage is navigation by reference to landmarks or checkpoints. The checkpoints selected should be prominent features common to the area of the flight and be readily identified by other features such as roads, rivers, and power lines. Select features that will make useful boundaries or brackets on each side of the course, such as highways, rivers, railroads, and mountains. (PLT335) — FAA-H-8083-25*

# Time .

Time is measured in relation to the rotation of the earth. A day is defined as the time required for the earth to make one complete revolution of 360°. Since the day is divided into 24 hours, it follows that the earth revolves at the rate of 15° each hour. Thus, longitude may be expressed as either 90° or 6 hours west of Greenwich.

Twenty-four time zones have been established. Each time zone is 15° of longitude in width, with the first zone centered on the meridian of Greenwich. Each zone uses the local time of its central meridian as shown in FAA Figure 27.

For example, when the sun is above the 90th meridian, it is noon central standard time (CST). At the same time it is 6 p.m. Greenwich, 11 a.m. mountain standard time (MST), and 1 p.m. eastern standard time (EST). When daylight saving time (DST) is in effect, the sun is over the 75th meridian at noon CST.

Most aviation operations time is expressed in terms of the 24-hour clock, (for example, 8 a.m. is expressed as 0800; 2 p.m. is 1400; 11 p.m. is 2300) and may be either local or **Coordinated Universal Time (UTC)**. UTC is the time at the prime meridian and is represented in aviation operations by the letter "Z," referred to as **Zulu time**. For example, 1500Z would be read as "one five zero zero Zulu."

In the United States, conversion from local time to UTC is made in accordance with the table in the lower left corner of FAA Figure 27.

**Answers**

2106   [A]          2108   [A]          2178   [C]

**Problem:** An aircraft departs an airport in the Pacific standard time zone at 1030 PST for a 4-hour flight to an airport located in the central standard time zone. The landing should be at what coordinated universal time (UTC)?

**Solution:** Use the conversion table in FAA Figure 27 and the following steps:

1. Convert 1030 PST to UTC:

    ```
      1030    PST (takeoff time)
    + 0800    (conversion)
    ──────
      1830    (UTC)
    ```

2. Add the flight time.

    ```
      1830    (UTC)
    + 0400    (flight time)
    ──────
      2230    UTC (time the aircraft should land)
    ```

ALL

**3571.** (Refer to Figure 27.) An aircraft departs an airport in the eastern daylight time zone at 0945 EDT for a 2-hour flight to an airport located in the central daylight time zone. The landing should be at what coordinated universal time?

A—1345Z.
B—1445Z.
C—1545Z.

*Use the following steps:*

1. *Convert the EDT takeoff time to UTC:*

    ```
      0945    EDT takeoff time
    + 0400    conversion
    ──────
      1345 Z  UTC (also called "ZULU" time)
    ```

2. *Add the flight time to the ZULU time of takeoff:*

    ```
      1345 Z  takeoff time
    + 0200
    ──────
      1545 Z  time of landing
    ```

*(PLT012, PA.I.D.K3b, PH.VII.A.K5c) — FAA-H-8083-25*

ALL

**3572.** (Refer to Figure 27.) An aircraft departs an airport in the central standard time zone at 0930 CST for a 2-hour flight to an airport located in the mountain standard time zone. The landing should be at what time?

A—0930 MST.
B—1030 MST.
C—1130 MST.

*Use the following steps:*

1. *Change the CST takeoff time to UTC:*

    ```
      0930    CST takeoff time
    + 0600    conversion
    ──────
      1530 Z  UTC (also called "ZULU" time)
    ```

2. *Add the flight time to the time of takeoff:*

    ```
      1530 Z  takeoff time
    + 0200    flight time
    ──────
      1730 Z  time of landing
    ```

3. *Convert UTC to MST:*

    ```
      1730 Z  UTC
    − 0700    conversion
    ──────
      1030    MST time of landing
    ```

*(PLT012, PA.I.D.K3b, PH.VII.A.K5c) — FAA-H-8083-25*

**Answers**

3571  [C]          3572  [B]

ALL
**3573.** (Refer to Figure 27.) An aircraft departs an airport in the central standard time zone at 0845 CST for a 2-hour flight to an airport located in the mountain standard time zone. The landing should be at what coordinated universal time?

A—1345Z.
B—1445Z.
C—1645Z.

*Use the following steps:*

*1. Convert the CST takeoff time to UTC:*

| 0845 | CST takeoff time |
|---|---|
| + 0600 | conversion |
| 1445 Z | UTC (also called "ZULU" time) |

*2. Add the flight time to the ZULU time of takeoff:*

| 1445 Z | takeoff time |
|---|---|
| + 0200 | flight time |
| 1645 Z | the time of landing |

*(PLT012, PA.I.D.K3b, PH.VII.A.K5c) — FAA-H-8083-25*

ALL
**3574.** (Refer to Figure 27.) An aircraft departs an airport in the mountain standard time zone at 1615 MST for a 2-hour 15-minute flight to an airport located in the Pacific standard time zone. The estimated time of arrival at the destination airport should be

A—1630 PST.
B—1730 PST.
C—1830 PST.

*Use the following steps:*

*1. Convert the MST takeoff time to UTC:*

| 1615 | MST takeoff time |
|---|---|
| + 0700 | conversion |
| 2315 Z | UTC (also called "ZULU" time) |

*2. Add the flight time to the ZULU time of takeoff:*

| 2315 Z | takeoff time |
|---|---|
| + 0215 | flight time |
| 0130 Z | time of landing |

*3. Convert UTC to PST:*

| 0130 Z | UTC |
|---|---|
| − 0800 | conversion |
| 1730 | PST time of landing |

*(PLT012, PA.I.D.K3b, PH.VII.A.K5c) — FAA-H-8083-25*

ALL
**3575.** (Refer to Figure 27.) An aircraft departs an airport in the Pacific standard time zone at 1030 PST for a 4-hour flight to an airport located in the central standard time zone. The landing should be at what coordinated universal time?

A—2030Z.
B—2130Z.
C—2230Z.

*Use the following steps:*

*1. Convert the PST takeoff time to UTC:*

| 1030 | PST takeoff time |
|---|---|
| + 0800 | conversion |
| 1830 Z | UTC (also called "ZULU" time) |

*2. Add the flight time to the ZULU takeoff time:*

| 1830 Z | takeoff time |
|---|---|
| + 0400 | flight time |
| 2230 Z | time of landing |

*(PLT012, PA.I.D.K3b, PH.VII.A.K5c) — FAA-H-8083-25*

ALL
**3576.** (Refer to Figure 27.) An aircraft departs an airport in the mountain standard time zone at 1515 MST for a 2-hour 30-minute flight to an airport located in the Pacific standard time zone. What is the estimated time of arrival at the destination airport?

A—1645 PST.
B—1745 PST.
C—1845 PST.

*Use the following steps:*

*1. Convert the MST takeoff time to UTC:*

| 1515 | MST takeoff time |
|---|---|
| + 0700 | conversion |
| 2215 Z | UTC (also called "ZULU" time) |

*2. Add the flight time to the ZULU takeoff time:*

| 2215 Z | takeoff time |
|---|---|
| + 0230 | flight time |
| 2445 Z | (0045) Z time of landing |

*3. Convert UTC to PST:*

| 2445 Z | (0045) Z |
|---|---|
| − 0800 | conversion |
| 1645 | PST time of landing |

*(PLT012, PA.I.D.K3b, PH.VII.A.K5c) — FAA-H-8083-25*

---

**Answers**

| 3573 | [C] | 3574 | [B] | 3575 | [C] | 3576 | [A] |
|---|---|---|---|---|---|---|---|

# Topography

A VFR Sectional Aeronautical Chart is a pictorial representation of a portion of the Earth's surface upon which lines and symbols in a variety of colors represent features and/or details that can be seen on the Earth's surface. Contour lines, shaded relief, color tints, obstruction symbols, and maximum elevation figures are all used to show topographical information. Explanations and examples may be found in the chart legend. Pilots should become familiar with all of the information provided in each Sectional Chart Legend, found in FAA Legend 1.

ALL, SPO

**3637-1.** Which is true concerning the blue and magenta colors used to depict airports on Sectional Aeronautical Charts?

A—Airports with control towers underlying Class A, B, and C airspace are shown in blue, Class D and E airspace are magenta.

B—Airports with control towers underlying Class C, D, and E airspace are shown in magenta.

C—Airports with control towers underlying Class B, C, D, and E airspace are shown in blue.

*Reference FAA Legend 1. Airports having control towers are shown in blue, all others in magenta. (PLT101, PA.I.E.K2, PH.VII.A.K3) — Sectional Chart Legend*

Answer (A) is incorrect because Class A airspace is not depicted on a Sectional; Class C airspace is magenta; and Class E airspace is both blue and magenta depending on where the floor of the airspace starts. Answer (B) is incorrect because airports with control towers are shown in blue.

ALL

**3637.** (Refer to Figure 23, area 3.) What is the height of the lighted obstacle approximately 6 nautical miles southwest of Savannah International?

A—1,500 feet MSL.
B—1,531 feet AGL.
C—1,548 feet MSL.

*Reference FAA Legend 1. The top number, printed in bold, is the height of the obstruction above mean sea level. The second number, printed in parentheses, is the height of the obstruction above ground level. The obstruction is shown as 1,548 feet MSL and 1,534 feet AGL. (PLT064, PA.I.E.K2, PH.VII.A.K3) — Sectional Chart Legend*

ALL

**3638.** (Refer to Figure 23, area 3.) The top of the group obstruction approximately 11 nautical miles from the Savannah VORTAC on the 009° radial is

A—400 feet AGL.
B—454 feet MSL.
C—432 feet MSL.

*Reference FAA Legend 1. On Figure 24, area 3, the group obstruction near the 009° radial has the word "stacks" below **454**. The bold number (**454**) indicates the height of the obstruction above mean sea level. (PLT064, PA.I.E.K2, PH.VII.A.K3) — Sectional Chart Legend*

ALL

**3639.** (Refer to Figure 24, area 1.) What minimum altitude is necessary to vertically clear the obstacle on the northeast side of Airpark East Airport by 500 feet?

A—1,010 feet MSL.
B—1,273 feet MSL.
C—1,283 feet MSL.

*The elevation of the top of the obstacle is shown as 773 feet MSL. Add the 500-foot vertical clearance specified by the question to the height (MSL) of the obstacle:*

```
   773  feet MSL
 + 500
 1,273  feet MSL minimum altitude
```

*(PLT064, PA.I.E.K2, PH.VII.A.K3) — Sectional Chart Legend*

ALL, SPO

**3640.** (Refer to Figure 24, area 2.) What minimum altitude is necessary to vertically clear the obstacle on the southeast side of Winnsboro Airport by 500 feet?

A—823 feet MSL.
B—1,013 feet MSL.
C—1,403 feet MSL.

*The elevation of the top of the obstacle is shown as 903 feet MSL. Add the 500-foot vertical clearance specified by the question to the height (MSL) of the obstacle:*

$$\begin{array}{r} 903 \ \ feet \ MSL \\ +\ 500 \quad\quad\quad \\ \hline 1,403 \ \ feet \ MSL \end{array}$$

*(PLT064, PA.I.E.K2, PH.VII.A.K3) — Sectional Chart Legend*

ALL

**3631.** (Refer to Figure 20, area 5.) The CAUTION box denotes what hazard to aircraft?

A—Unmarked balloon on cable to 3,008 feet MSL.
B—Unmarked balloon on cable to 3,008 feet AGL.
C—Unmarked blimp hangers at 308 feet MSL.

*Reference FAA Legend 1. The boxed caution reads, "CAUTION: UNMARKED BALLOON ON CABLE TO 3,008 MSL." (PLT064, PA.I.E.K2, PH.VII.A.K3) — Sectional Chart Legend*

ALL, SPO

**3632.** (Refer to Figure 20, area 2.) The flag symbol at Lake Drummond represents a

A—compulsory reporting point for Norfolk Class C airspace.
B—compulsory reporting point for Hampton Roads Airport.
C—visual checkpoint used to identify position for initial callup to Norfolk Approach Control.

*Reference FAA Legend 1. The flag symbol represents a visual checkpoint used to identify position for initial call-up to Norfolk Approach Control. (PLT064, PA.I.E.K2, PH.VII.A.K3) — Sectional Chart Legend*

ALL

**3633.** (Refer to Figure 20, area 2.) The elevation of the Chesapeake Regional Airport is

A—19 feet.
B—55 feet.
C—230 feet.

*Reference FAA Legend 1. The airport elevation is noted in the airport information, beneath the airport symbol. The elevation of Chesapeake Regional Airport is 19 feet. (PLT064, PA.I.E.K2, PH.VII.A.K3) — Sectional Chart Legend*

ALL

**3634.** (Refer to Figure 21.) The terrain elevation of the light tan area between Minot (area 1) and Audubon Lake (area 2) varies from

A—sea level to 2,000 feet MSL.
B—2,000 feet to 2,500 feet MSL.
C—2,000 feet to 2,700 feet MSL.

*Reference FAA Legend 1. The contour line which borders the tan area is labeled 2,000 feet. There are no higher contour levels depicted inside the tan area. (PLT012, PA.I.E.K2, PH.VII.A.K3) — Sectional Chart Legend*

Answer (A) is incorrect because the light tan area indicates terrain between 2,000–3,000 feet MSL. Answer (C) is incorrect because contour intervals are 500 feet, not 700.

ALL

**3635.** (Refer to Figure 21.) Which public use airports depicted are indicated as having fuel?

A—Minot Intl. (area 1) and Garrison (area 2).
B—Minot Intl. (area 1).
C—Mercer County Regional Airport (area 3) and Garrison (area 2).

*Reference FAA Legend 1. Minot International is depicted as having fuel, as indicated by the ticks around the basic airport symbol. (PLT064, PA.I.E.K2, PH.VII.A.K3) — Sectional Chart Legend*

**Answers**

| 3640 | [C] | 3631 | [A] | 3632 | [C] | 3633 | [A] | 3634 | [B] | 3635 | [B] |

**ALL**

**3636.** (Refer to Figure 23.) The flag symbols at Statesboro Bullock County Airport, Claxton-Evans County Airport, and Ridgeland Airport are

A—outer boundaries of Savannah Class C airspace.
B—airports with special traffic patterns.
C—visual checkpoints to identify position for initial callup prior to entering Savannah Class C airspace.

*Reference FAA Legend 1. "Visual check point" is the name for the flag symbol. (PLT064, PA.I.E.K2, PH.VII.A.K3) — Sectional Chart Legend*

**ALL, SPO**

**3642.** (Refer to Figure 25, area 8.) What minimum altitude is required to fly over the Cedar Hill TV towers in the congested area south of Dallas Executive (RBD)?

A—2,655 feet MSL.
B—3,549 feet MSL.
C—3,449 feet MSL.

*The height of the tower is 2,549 MSL. A 1,000-foot clearance is required between obstructions and aircraft over a congested area.*

$$\begin{array}{r} 2{,}549 \ \ MSL \\ + \ 1{,}000 \ \ \\ \hline 3{,}549 \ \ MSL \end{array}$$

*(PLT101, PA.I.E.K2, PH.VII.A.K3) — 14 CFR §91.119*

**LTA, LSL**

**3644.** (Refer to Figure 20, area 4.) A balloon launched at the town of Edenton drifts northeasterly along the railroad. What minimum altitude must it maintain to clear all of the obstacles in the vicinity of Hertford by at least 500 feet?

A—805 feet MSL.
B—1,000 feet MSL.
C—1,014 feet MSL.

*Use the following steps:*

*1. Locate the towns of Edenton and Hertford.*

*2. Note the highest obstruction in the vicinity of Hertford (514 feet MSL).*

*3. Calculate the minimum altitude (MSL) by adding the required 500-foot clearance to the obstacle height.*

$$\begin{array}{r} 514 \ \ feet \\ + \ 500 \ \ feet \\ \hline 1{,}014 \ \ feet \ MSL \end{array}$$

*(PLT064) — Sectional Chart Legend*

**LTA, LSL**

**3645.** (Refer to Figure 21, area 1.) A balloon launched at Flying S Airport drifts southward towards the lighted obstacle. If the altimeter was set to the current altimeter setting upon launch, what should it indicate if the balloon is to clear the obstacle at 500 feet above the top?

A—1,531 feet MSL.
B—1,809 feet MSL.
C—3,649 feet MSL.

*The height of the lit obstacle is 3,149 feet MSL. The altimeter will indicate 3,649 (3,149 + 500) if set to the current altimeter setting upon launch. (PLT064) — Sectional Chart Legend*

**LTA**

**3646.** (Refer to Figure 22, area 1.) A balloon, launched at Delta Shores Airport located near the east end of Lake Pend Oreille, drifts south-southwest. What is the approximate elevation of the highest terrain for 20 miles along its path?

A—2,000 – 4,000 feet MSL.
B—4,000 – 6,000 feet MSL.
C—6,000 – 7,000 feet MSL.

*On Sectional Aeronautical Charts, color tints are used to depict bands of elevation. These colors range from light green for the lowest elevations to brown for the higher elevations. Note the terrain height of 6,405 feet MSL within the tan shading south-southwest of Delta Shores Airport. (PLT064) — Sectional Chart Legend*

---

**Answers**

| | | | | |
|---|---|---|---|---|
| 3636　[C] | 3642　[B] | 3644　[C] | 3645　[C] | 3646　[C] |

# Dead Reckoning

Dead reckoning is the method used for determining position with a heading indicator and calculations based on speed, elapsed time, and wind effect from a known position. The instruments used for dead reckoning navigation include the outside air temperature gauge, the airspeed indicator, the altimeter, the clock, and the magnetic compass system or slaved gyro system. These instruments provide information concerning direction, airspeed, altitude, and time, and must be correctly interpreted for successful navigation.

## Plotting Courses

A course is the direction of flight measured in degrees clockwise from north. Meridians of longitude run from the south pole to the north pole. This alignment is called true north. When a course is plotted on a chart in relation to the lines of longitude and/or latitude it is called a **true course (TC)**, and will be expressed in three digits. North may be either 360° or 000°; east is 090°; south is 180°; and west is 270°. Any attempt to project lines of latitude and longitude onto a flat surface such as a chart results in a certain amount of distortion. When plotting a course on a sectional aeronautical chart, this distortion may be minimized by measuring true course in reference to the meridian nearest to the halfway point between the departure point and the destination.

A common type of plotter that is used to plot a course is shown in Figure 7-2 on the next page. This plotter is a semi-circular protractor with a straight edge attached to it. The straight edge has distance scales that match various charts and these scales may depict both statute and nautical miles. A small hole at the base of the protractor portion indicates the center of the arc of the angular scale. Two complete scales cover the outer edge of the protractor, and they are graduated in degrees. An inner scale measures the angle from the vertical.

To determine true course, use the plotter in the following manner:

1. Using the straight edge of the plotter as a guide, draw a line from the point of departure to the destination.

2. Place the top straight edge of the plotter parallel to the plotted course and move the plotter along the course line as necessary to place the small center hole over a meridian as near to the halfway point of the course as possible. See Figure 7-2a.

3. The true course is the angle measured between the meridian and the course line. See Figure 7-2b. The outer scale is used to read all angles between north through east to south, and the inner scale is used to read all angles between south through west to north. In Figure 7-2 the true course from point (a) to point (b) is 115° as read at point (c).

4. Course lines which fall within 30° of true north or south can be more easily measured by sliding the plotter along the course line until the hole falls over a horizontal latitude line; use the partial protractor scale for these measurements.

*(continued)*

**Figure 7-2.** Placing the plotter on the course line

## Magnetic Variation

The north pole where all meridians converge is **true north**. The north pole which attracts the needle of a compass is **magnetic north**. These two poles are not in the same place. At any point where magnetic north and true north are in line with each other, the compass needle points both to magnetic north, and coincidentally, true north. The line along which this occurs is known as the **agonic line**. When positioned west of the agonic line, a compass will point right (east) of true north. When positioned east of the agonic line, a compass will point left (west) of true north. This angular difference between true north and magnetic north is called **magnetic variation (VAR)**. West of the agonic line, variation is "easterly." East of the agonic line, variation is "westerly."

The amount and direction of variation is depicted on sectional charts as dashed magenta colored lines connecting points of equal variation, called isogonic lines.

A course measured on a sectional chart is a true course: it is measured from a meridian, which runs from the south pole to the north pole. Since a magnetic compass is used to maintain a course while flying, this true course must now be converted to a **magnetic course (MC)**. This conversion is made by either adding or subtracting the variation. To convert a TC to an MC, subtract easterly variation and add westerly variation: "East is least, west is best."

TC ± VAR = MC

ALL
**3531.** (Refer to Figure 20.) Determine the magnetic course from First Flight Airport (area 5) to Hampton Roads Airport (area 2).

A—141°.
B—321°.
C—332°.

*Use the following steps:*

1. *Plot the course from First Flight Airport to Hampton Roads Airport.*

2. *Measure the true course angle at the approximate midpoint of the route. The true course is 321°.*

3. *Note that the variation is 11°W as shown on the isogonic line.*

4. *Using the formula:*

$$MC = TC \pm VAR$$
$$MC = 321° + 11°W$$
$$MC = 332°$$

*(PLT064, PA.VI.A.K5a, PH.VII.A.K5a) — FAA-H-8083-25*

ALL
**3556.** (Refer to Figure 24.) Determine the magnetic course from Airpark East Airport (area 1) to Winnsboro Airport (area 2). Magnetic variation is 6°30'E.

A—075°.
B—082°.
C—091°.

*Use the following steps:*

1. *Plot the course from Airpark East Airport to Winns-boro Airport.*

2. *Measure the true course angle at the approximate midpoint of the route (082°).*

3. *Calculate the magnetic course by subtracting the magnetic variation (6°30') from the true course (082°).*

$$MC = TC \pm VAR$$
$$MC = 082° - 6°30'E$$
$$MC = 75°30' \ (075° \ is \ the \ closest \ answer)$$

*(PLT012, PA.VI.A.K5a, PH.VII.A.K5a) — FAA-H-8083-25*

ALL
**3568.** (Refer to Figure 26.) Determine the magnetic course from Tomlinson Airport (area 1) to Jamestown Airport (area 4).

A—153°.
B—154°.
C—159°.

*Use the following steps:*

1. *Plot the course from Tomlinson Airport to Jamestown Airport.*

2. *Measure the true course angle at the approximate midpoint of the route (158°).*

3. *Note that the variation is 5° E as shown on the dashed isogonic line.*

4. *Using the formula:*

$$MC = TC \pm VAR$$
$$MC = 158 - 5° \ East$$
$$MC = 153°$$

*(PLT012, PA.VI.A.K5a, PH.VII.A.K5a) — FAA-H-8083-25*

SPO
**2201.** Heading and groundspeed are calculated using dead reckoning procedures. In flight, they are constantly monitored and corrected by

A—pilotage as observed from checkpoints.
B—the wind triangle.
C—the wet compass and the groundspeed indicator.

*Dead reckoning is navigation solely by means of computations based on time, airspeed, distance, and direction. The products derived from these variables, when adjusted by windspeed and velocity, are heading and ground speed. Except for flights over water, dead reckoning is usually used with pilotage for cross-country flying. The heading and ground speed as calculated is constantly monitored and corrected by pilotage as observed from checkpoints. (PLT335) — FAA-H-8083-25*

SPO
**2102.** The course measured on a sectional chart by reference to a meridian is known as the

A—true course.
B—magnetic course.
C—true heading.

*The course measured on the chart is known as the true course. (PLT320) — FAA-H-8083-25*

Answer (B) is incorrect because magnetic course adds variation to the course measured on the chart. Answer (C) is incorrect because true heading accounts for wind.

**Answers**

| | | | | |
|---|---|---|---|---|
| 3531 [C] | 3556 [A] | 3568 [A] | 2201 [A] | 2102 [A] |

## Magnetic Deviation

The magnetic compass is affected by influences within the aircraft such as electrical circuits, radios, engines, magnetized metal parts, etc., which cause the compass needle to be deflected from its normal reading. This deflection is known as **deviation (DEV)**, and it must be applied to convert a magnetic course to a **compass course (CC)** to make it usable in flight.

Deviation, which is different for each aircraft, may also vary for different courses in the same airplane. To let the pilot know the appropriate correction, a correction card is mounted near the compass.

To determine the actual compass reading to be followed during flight, it is necessary to apply the corrections for both variation and deviation:

True course ± variation = magnetic course ± deviation = compass course

or,

TC ± VAR = MC ± DEV = CC.

# Wind and Its Effects

An additional computation, common to both pilotage and dead reckoning, is necessary to compensate for the effect of wind.

Wind direction is reported as the direction from which the wind blows, i.e., wind blowing from the west to the east is a west wind. Wind speed is the rate of motion without regard to direction. In the United States, wind speed is usually expressed in knots. Wind velocity includes both direction and speed of the wind; for example, a west wind of 25 knots.

Downwind movement is with the wind; upwind movement is against the wind. Moving air exerts a force in the direction of its motion on any object within it. Objects that are free to move in air will move in a downwind direction at the speed of the wind.

If a powered aircraft is flying in a 20-knot wind, it will move 20 nautical miles downwind in 1 hour in addition to its forward movement through the air. The path of an aircraft over the earth is determined both by the motion of the aircraft through the air and by the motion of the air over the earth's surface. Direction and movement through the air is governed both by the direction that the aircraft nose is pointing and by aircraft speed.

The sideward displacement of an aircraft caused by wind is called drift. Drift can be determined by measuring the angle between the heading (the direction in which the nose is pointing) and the track (the actual path of the aircraft over the earth). See Figure 7-3.

For example, Figure 7-3 shows an aircraft which departs point A on a heading of 360° and flies for 1 hour in a wind of 270° at 20 knots. Under a no-wind condition the aircraft would arrive at point B at the end of 1 hour. However, this example has a wind of 20 knots, and the aircraft moves with the wind; so at the end of 1 hour, the aircraft is at point C, 20 nautical miles downwind from B. From A to B is the intended path of the aircraft, from B to C is the motion of the body of air, and from A to C is the actual path of the aircraft over the earth (the track).

A given wind will cause a different drift on each aircraft heading and it will also affect the distance traveled over the ground in a given time. With a given wind, the ground speed varies with each different aircraft heading. Figure 7-4 illustrates how a wind of 270° at 20 knots would affect the ground speed and track of an aircraft on various headings. In this particular illustration, on a heading of 360°, drift would be to the right; on a heading of 180°, drift would be to the left. With a 90° crosswind and no heading

**Figure 7-3.** Drift

**Figure 7-4.** Different effects of wind on track and ground speed

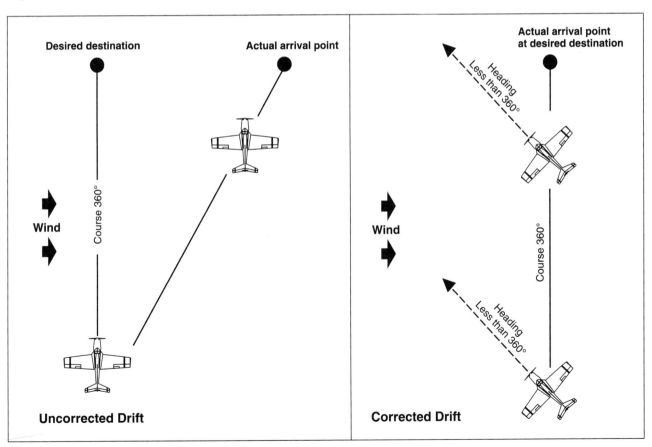

**Figure 7-5.** Compensating for wind drift

correction applied, there would be little effect on ground speed. On a heading of 090°, no left or right drift would be experienced; instead, the ground speed would be increased by the tailwind. On a 270° heading, the ground speed would be reduced by the headwind.

By determining the amount of drift, a pilot can counteract the effect of wind and make the track of the aircraft coincide with the desired course. For example, if the wind is from the left, the correction would be made by pointing the aircraft to the left a certain number of degrees, thereby compensating for wind drift. This is the wind correction angle (WCA), and it is expressed as degrees left or right of the course. See Figure 7-5.

Any course, true, magnetic, or compass, becomes a heading when it is corrected for wind. See Figure 7-6.

| Course | | | | Heading |
|---|---|---|---|---|
| True | ± | WCA | = | True |
| ± | | | | ± |
| Variation | | | | Variation |
| = | | | | = |
| Magnetic | ± | WCA | = | Magnetic |
| ± | | | | ± |
| Deviation | | | | Deviation |
| = | | | | = |
| Compass | ± | WCA | = | Compass |

**Figure 7-6**

SPO
**2177.** If proper correction has been made for the wind, ground track will be identical with

A—drift angle.
B—course.
C—heading.

*If proper correction has been made for the wind, track and course will be identical. (PLT198) — FAA-H-8083-25*

SPO
**2103.** Motion of the air affects the speed with which aircraft move

A—over the Earth's surface.
B—through the air.
C—in a turn.

*Motion of the air affects the speed with which airplanes move over the Earth's surface. (PLT198) — FAA-H-8083-25*

SPO
**2104.** If a flight is to be made on a course to the east, with a wind blowing from northeast, the aircraft must be headed

A—somewhat to the north of east to counteract drift.
B—south of east to counteract drift.
C—north to counteract torque.

*If the mass of air is moving across the course from the left, the airplane will drift to the right, and a correction must be made by heading the airplane sufficiently to the left to offset this drift. (PLT198) — FAA-H-8083-25*

**Answers**
2177 [B]          2103 [A]          2104 [A]

# The Wind Triangle

True course is determined by measuring the course on an aeronautical chart. **True airspeed** is known by applying the appropriate correction to the indication of the airspeed indicator. The wind direction and velocity are known from reports or forecasts from Flight Service Stations.

The true heading and the ground speed can be found by drawing a wind triangle of vectors. One side of the triangle is the wind direction and velocity, one side is the true heading and true airspeed, the final side is the track, or true course, and the ground speed. Each side of a wind triangle is the vector sum of the other two sides.

ALL

**3816.** (Refer to Figure 68.) The line from point A to point B of the wind triangle represents

A—true heading and airspeed.
B—true course and ground speed.
C—ground speed and true heading.

*The line A to B of the wind triangle represents true heading and the true airspeed. It is the vector sum of the lines C to B (the true course and ground speed) and C to A (the wind direction and speed). (PLT012, PA.VI.A.K5b, PH.VII.A.K5b) — FAA-H-8083-25*

Answer (B) is incorrect because this is represented by the line from point C to B. Answer (C) is incorrect because these values are defined by separate lines of the wind triangle.

ALL

**3817.** (Refer to Figure 68.) The line from point C to point B of the wind triangle represents

A—airspeed and heading.
B—ground speed and true course.
C—true heading and ground speed.

*The line from point C to B of the wind triangle represents the ground speed and true course. (PLT012, PA.VI.A.K5b, PH.VII.A.K5b) — FAA-H-8083-25*

Answer (A) is incorrect because this is represented by the line from point A to B. Answer (C) is incorrect because these values are defined by separate lines of the wind triangle.

ALL

**2001.** (Refer to Figure 68.) The line from point C to point A of the wind triangle represents

A—wind direction and velocity.
B—true course and ground speed.
C—true heading and ground speed.

*The line from point C to A of the wind triangle represents the wind direction and speed (velocity). (PLT012, PA.VI.A.K5b, PH.VII.A.K5b) — FAA-H-8083-25*

Answer (B) is incorrect because this is represented by the line from point C to B. Answer (C) is incorrect because these are the values found by using the wind triangle.

**Answers**

3816  [A]          3817  [B]          2001  [A]

# The Flight Computer (E6-B)

*Note:* ASA's CX-3 is an electronic flight computer and can be used in place of the E6-B. This aviation computer can solve all flight planning problems, as well as perform standard mathematical calculations.

## Finding Wind Correction Angle (WCA) and Ground Speed (GS)

The WCA required to change a course to a heading can be found by using the wind face of the E6-B. Ground speed can also be determined as a part of this procedure.

The wind face of the E6-B consists of a transparent, rotatable plotting disk mounted in a frame as shown in Figure 7-7. A compass rose is located around the plotting disk (Figure 7-7a). A correction scale on the top of the frame is graduated in degrees left and right of the true index (Figure 7-7b), and it is used for calculating drift correction. A small reference circle, called a grommet, is located at the center of the plotting disk (Figure 7-7c).

A sliding grid (Figure 7-7d) inserted behind the plotting disk is used for wind computations. The slide has converging lines (track or drift lines) which indicate degrees left or right of center (Figure 7-7e). Concentric arcs (speed circles) on the slide are used for calculations of speed (Figure 7-7f). The wind correction angle and ground speed may be found when true course, true airspeed, wind speed and wind direction (relative to true north) are known.

**Problem:** Using a flight computer and the following conditions, find the WCA, the true heading (TH), and the ground speed (GS).

## Conditions:

True course (TC) .................................................. 090°

True airspeed (TAS) .................................... 120 knots

True wind direction ............................................ 160°

Wind speed ................................................. 30 knots

**Solution:**

1. Using the wind face side of the E6-B, set the true wind direction (160°) under the true index (Figure 7-8a).

2. Plot the wind speed above the grommet 30 units (wind speed). *Note:* The sliding grid can be at any value for this step. Place a wind dot within a circle at this point (Figure 7-8b).

3. Rotate the plotting disk and set the true course (090°) under the true index (Figure 7-9a).

4. Adjust the sliding grid so that the TAS arc (120 knots) is at the wind dot (Figure 7-9b). Note the wind dot is 14° right of centerline (Figure 7-9c), so the WCA = 14°R.

5. Under the grommet, read the ground speed of 106 knots (Figure 7-9d).

**Figure 7-7.** Wind face of E6-B computer

**Figure 7-8.** Plotting wind speed and wind direction

6. Determine the true heading by applying the formula:

TC + WCA = TH

In this case the wind correction is to the right, so it will be added to the true course:

$$\begin{array}{ll} 090° & \text{(TC)} \\ + 14° & \text{(WCA)} \\ \hline 104° & \text{(TH)} \end{array}$$

## Flight Computer Calculator Face

Opposite the windface of the flight computer is a circular slide rule or calculator face. The outer scale, called the miles scale, is stationary (Figure 7-10a). The inner circle rotates and is called the minutes scale (Figure 7-10b).

The numbers on the computer scale represent multiples of 10, of the values shown. For example, the number 24 on either scale may be 0.24, 2.4, 24, 240, etc. On the inner scale, minutes may be converted to hours by reference to the adjacent hours scale. In Figure 7-10c, for example, 4 hours is found adjacent to 24, meaning 240 minutes.

Relative values must be kept in mind. For example, the numbers 21 and 22 are separated by divisions, each space representing 2 units. Thus, the second division past 21 will be read as 21.4, 214, or 2,140. Between 80 and 90 are 10 divisions, each space representing 1 unit. Thus, the second division past 80 will be read as 8.2, 82 or 820.

There are three index marks on the miles (outer) scale which are used for converting statute miles (SM), nautical miles (NM) and kilometers (KM). The E6-B computer has a scale for converting statute

**Figure 7-9.** Determining the wind correction angle and ground speed

**Figure 7-10.** Slide rule (calculator) face

miles, nautical miles, and kilometers. Place the known figure on the inner scale under "naut," "stat," or "KM," as appropriate, and read the equivalent value under the other indexes. For example, to convert 85 statute miles to kilometers and nautical miles, place 85 on the inner scale under the "stat" index. Under the "KM" index, read 137; under the "naut" index read 74.

Each scale has a 10-index used as a reference mark for multiplication and division. The 10-index on the inner scale can also be used as a rate index representing 1 hour. Also on the inner scale is a 60-index, representing 60 minutes and usually used for computation instead of the 10 or 1 hour index (Figure 7-10d) and a 36 or "seconds" index (3,600 seconds = 1 hour) (Figure 7-10e).

## Finding Time, Rate, and Distance

The flight computer will commonly be used to solve problems of time, rate, and distance. When two factors are known, the third can be found using the proportion:

$$\text{Rate (speed)} = \frac{\text{Distance}}{\text{Time}}$$

**Problem:** How far does an aircraft travel in 2 hours and 15 minutes at a ground speed of 138 knots?

**Solution:** Use the formula: *distance = ground speed × time*

Or use the flight computer in the following manner:

1. Place the 60 (speed) index (inner scale) under 138 (outer scale).

2. Over the time of 135 minutes or 2 hours +15 minutes (inner scale), read 310 NM (on the outer scale). See Figure 7-11.

**Figure 7-11.** Computing distance on the E6-B

**Figure 7-12.** Determining time required on the E6-B

**Problem:** How much time is required to fly 320 NM at a ground speed of 174 knots?

**Solution:** Use the formula: *time = distance ÷ ground speed*

Or use the flight computer in the following manner:

1. Set the 60 (speed) index under 174 (outer scale).

2. Under 320 (outer scale), read 110 minutes or 1 hour 50 minutes (inner scale). See Figure 7-12.

**Problem:** What is the ground speed if it takes 40 minutes to fly 96 NM?

**Solution:** Use the formula: *ground speed = distance ÷ time*

Or use the flight computer in the following manner:

1. Place 40 minutes (inner scale) under 96 (outer scale).

2. Over the 60 (speed) index, read 144 knots (outer scale). See Figure 7-13.

**Problem:** If 50 minutes are required to fly 120 NM, how many minutes are required to fly 86 NM at the same rate?

**Solution:**

1. Set 50 (inner scale) under 120 (outer scale).

2. Under 86 (outer scale), read 36 minutes required (inner scale). See Figure 7-14.

**Figure 7-13.** Determining groundspeed on the E6-B

**Figure 7-14.** Determining time-rate-distance on the E6-B

# Calculating Fuel Consumption

Fuel consumption problems are solved in the same manner as time-rate-distance problems.

**Problem:** If 18 gallons of fuel are consumed in 1 hour, how much fuel will be used in 2 hours 20 minutes?

**Solution:**

1. Set the 60-index (inner scale) under 18 (outer scale).
2. Over 2 hour 20 minute (inner scale), read 42 gallons (outer scale). See Figure 7-15.

**Problem:** What is the rate of fuel consumption if 30 gallons of fuel are consumed in 111 minutes?

**Solution:**

1. Set 111 (inner scale) under 30 (outer scale).
2. Over the 60-index (inner scale), read 16.2 gallons per hour (outer scale). See Figure 7-16.

**Problem:** Forty gallons of fuel have been consumed in 135 minutes (2 hours and 15 minutes) flying time. How much longer can the aircraft continue to fly if 25 gallons of available fuel remain and the rate of consumption remains the same?

**Solution:**

1. Set 135 (inner scale) under 40 (outer scale).
2. Under 25 (outer scale), read 84.5 minutes of fuel remaining. See Figure 7-17.

**Figure 7-15.** Determining total fuel consumed on the E6-B

**Figure 7-16.** Determining rate of consumption on the E6-B

# Finding True Airspeed and Density Altitude

The calculator (slide rule) side of the computer may also be used to determine true airspeed by correcting calibrated airspeed for temperature and pressure altitude. Density altitude is computed simultaneously.

**Problem:** Using a flight computer and the following conditions, find the true airspeed and the density altitude (DA).

**Conditions:**

True air temperature ........................................ +10°C

Pressure altitude (PA) .............................. 10,000 feet

Calibrated airspeed (CAS) .......................... 140 knots

**Solution:**

1. Using the window marked "for airspeed and density altitude computations," place the true air temperature over the pressure altitude (Figure 7-18a).

2. In the density altitude window read the density altitude of 11,800 feet. (Figure 7-18b).

3. Over 140 knots CAS (inner scale) read the TAS of 167 knots (outer scale). See Figure 7-18c.

**Figure 7-17.** Determining flight time remaining on the E6-B

**Figure 7-18.** Determining true airspeed and density altitude on the E6-B

AIR, RTC, GLI, WSC, PPC

**3529-1.** If a true heading of 135° results in a ground track of 130° and a true airspeed of 135 knots results in a groundspeed of 140 knots, the wind would be from

A—019° and 12 knots.
B—200° and 13 knots.
C—246° and 13 knots.

*You are heading to the southeast (135°) at 135 knots. The wind is blowing you left of course (130°) and giving you a faster ground speed which means the wind is blowing from the southwest. Use your manual or electronic flight computer to determine the wind direction and speed at 246° and 13 knots. (PLT012, PA.VI.A.K5b, PH.VII.A.K5b) — FAA-H-8083-25*

Answer (A) is incorrect because a wind from 019° would blow you right of course (resulting in a ground track of 140°). Answer (B) is incorrect because a wind from 200° would be a right quartering headwind which wouldn't increase your ground speed.

AIR, RTC, GLI, WSC, PPC, SPO

**3529-2.** When converting from true course to magnetic heading, a pilot should

A—subtract easterly variation and right wind correction angle.
B—add westerly variation and subtract left wind correction angle.
C—subtract westerly variation and add right wind correction angle.

*When converting a true course to a true heading, subtract a left wind correction angle or add a right wind correction angle. When converting from a true heading to a magnetic heading, add westerly variation or subtract easterly variation. (PLT198, PA.VI.A.K5b, PH.VII.A.K5b) — FAA-H-8083-25*

Answer (A) is incorrect because right wind correction is added. Answer (C) is incorrect because westerly variation is added.

AIR, RTC, GLI, WSC, PPC

**3529-3.** How far will an aircraft travel in 2-1/2 minutes with a groundspeed of 98 knots?

A—2.45 NM.
B—3.35 NM.
C—4.08 NM.

*To find the distance flown in a given time, multiply ground speed by time. The distance flown in 2-1/2 minutes (convert to hours by dividing by 60) at a ground speed of 98 knots is .04 × 98 = 4.08 NM. (PLT012, PA.VI.A.K5c, PH.VII.A.K5c) — FAA-H-8083-25*

ALL

**3529-4.** How far will an aircraft travel in 7.5 minutes with a ground speed of 114 knots?

A—14.25 NM.
B—15.00 NM.
C—14.50 NM.

*To find the distance flown in a given time, multiply ground speed by time. The distance flown in 7.5 minutes (convert to hours by dividing by 60) at a ground speed of 114 knots is .125 × 114 = 14.25 NM. (PLT012, PA.VI.A.K5c, PH.VII.A.K5c) — FAA-H-8083-25*

AIR, RTC, WSC, PPC

**3565.** (Refer to Figure 25.) Determine the magnetic heading for a flight from Fort Worth Meacham (area 4) to Denton Muni (area 1). The wind is from 330° at 25 knots, the true airspeed is 110 knots, and the magnetic variation is 7° east.

A—004°.
B—017°.
C—023°.

*Use the following steps:*

1. *Plot a course from Meacham to Denton, and measure the course (021°).*

2. *Using the wind obtained, calculate a correction angle. This angle will be the difference between the course bearing and the heading required to maintain that course. Wind correction angle is 10° to the left.*

3. *Add course bearing and wind correction angle to obtain true heading.*

   *021 + -010 = 011° (TH)*

4. *Find the magnetic heading by adding the variation to the true heading.*

   *011 + -7 = 004° (MH)*

*(PLT012, PA.VI.A.K5a, PH.VII.A.K5a) — FAA-H-8083-25*

AIR, RTC, WSC, PPC

**3551.** (Refer to Figures 23 and 58.) Determine the compass heading for a flight from Claxton-Evans County Airport (area 2) to Hampton Varnville Airport (area 1). The wind is from 280° at 08 knots, the true airspeed is 85 knots, and the magnetic variation is 5° west.

A—033°.
B—042°.
C—038°.

---

**Answers**

| | | | | | |
|---|---|---|---|---|---|
| 3529-1 [C] | 3529-2 [B] | 3529-3 [C] | 3529-4 [A] | 3565 [A] | 3551 [B] |

Use the following steps:

1. Plot the course from Claxton-Evans County Airport to Hampton Varnville Airport.

2. Measure the true course angle at the approximate midpoint of the route (044°).

3. Use a flight computer to find the true heading (Wind Correction on FLT menu using CX-3):

   Wind direction is 280° (given in question)
   Wind speed is 8 knots (given in question)
   True course is 044° (found in Step 2)
   True airspeed is 85 knots (given in question)

   Therefore, the true heading is 40°.

4. Calculate the magnetic heading by adding the westerly variation (5°W) to the true heading (40°).

   MH = TH ± VAR
   MH = 40° + 5°W
   MH = 045°

5. Note the compass deviation card in Figure 58 indicates that in order to fly a magnetic course of 030°, the pilot must steer a compass heading of 027° or a 3° compass deviation. To fly a magnetic course of 060°, the pilot must steer a compass heading of 056° or a 4° compass deviation. Interpolate between these to find the compass correction for 045° (3.5°). Calculate the compass heading (CH) by subtracting the compass deviation (3.5°) from the magnetic heading (045°).

   CH = MH ± DEV
   CH = 045° − 3.5°
   CH = 41.5°

(PLT012, PA.VI.A.K5a, PH.VII.A.K5a) — FAA-H-8083-25

---

AIR, RTC, WSC, PPC

**3538.** (Refer to Figure 21.) Determine the magnetic heading for a flight from Mercer County Regional Airport (area 3) to Minot International (area 1). The wind is from 330° at 25 knots, the true airspeed is 100 knots, and the magnetic variation is 10° east.

A—002°
B—012°.
C—352°.

Use the following steps:

1. Plot the course from Mercer County Regional Airport to Minot Airport.

2. Measure the true course angle at the approximate midpoint of the route. The true course is 011°.

3. Find the true heading using a flight computer (Wind Correction on FLT menu using CX-3):

   Wind direction is 330° (given in question)
   Wind speed is 25 knots (given in question)
   True course is 011° (found in Step 2)
   True airspeed is 100 knots (given in question)

   Therefore, the true heading is 002°.

4. Calculate the magnetic heading by subtracting the easterly variation (10°) from the true heading (002°).

   MH = TH ± VAR
   MH = 002° − 10°E
   MH = 352°

(PLT012, PA.VI.A.K5a, PH.VII.A.K5a) — FAA-H-8083-25

---

AIR, RTC, WSC, PPC

**3545.** (Refer to Figure 22.) Determine the magnetic heading for a flight from Sandpoint Airport (area 1) to St. Maries Airport (area 4). The wind is from 215° at 25 knots and the true airspeed is 125 knots.

A—172°.
B—349°.
C—187°.

Use the following steps:

1. Plot the course from Sandpoint Airport to St. Maries Airport.

2. Measure the true course angle at the approximate midpoint of the route (181°).

3. Find the true heading using a flight computer (Wind Correction on FLT menu using CX-3):

   Wind direction is 215° (given in question)
   Wind speed is 25 knots (given in question)
   True course is 181° (found in Step 2)
   True airspeed is 125 knots (given in question)

   Therefore, the true heading is 187°.

4. Calculate the magnetic heading by subtracting the easterly variation (15°) from the true heading (187°).

   MH = TH ± VAR
   MH = 187° − 15°E
   MH = 172°

(PLT012, PA.VI.A.K5a, PH.VII.A.K5a) — FAA-H-8083-25

---

**Answers**

3538    [C]                3545    [A]

AIR, RTC, WSC, PPC

**3546.** (Refer to Figure 22.) What is the magnetic heading for a flight from Priest River Airport (area 1) to Shoshone County Airport (area 3)? The wind is from 030° at 12 knots and the true airspeed is 95 knots.

A—121°.
B—143°.
C—136°.

Use the following steps:

1. Plot the course from Priest River to Shoshone County Airport.

2. Measure the true course angle at the approximate midpoint of the route (143°).

3. Find the true heading using a flight computer (Wind Correction on FLT menu using CX-3):

Wind direction is 030° (given in question)
Wind speed is 12 knots (given in question)
True course is 143° (found in Step 2)
True airspeed is 95 knots (given in question)

Therefore, the true heading is 136°.

4. Calculate the magnetic heading by subtracting the easterly variation (15°E, as shown on the dashed isogonic line) from the true heading (136°).

$MH = TH \pm VAR$
$MH = 136° - 15°E$
$MH = 121°$

(PLT012, PA.VI.A.K5a, PH.VII.A.K5a) — FAA-H-8083-25

AIR, RTC, WSC, PPC

**3547.** (Refer to Figure 22.) Determine the magnetic heading for a flight from St. Maries Airport (area 4) to Priest River Airport (area 1). The wind is from 340° at 10 knots, and the true airspeed is 90 knots.

A—345°.
B—329°.
C—327°.

Use the following steps:

1. Plot the course from St. Maries Airport to Priest River Airport.

2. Measure the true course angle at the approximate midpoint of the route (345°).

3. Find the true heading using a flight computer (Wind Correction on FLT menu using CX-3):

Wind direction is 340° (given in question)
Wind speed is 10 knots (given in question)
True course is 345° (found in Step 2)
True airspeed is 90 knots (given in question)

Therefore, the true heading is 344°.

4. Calculate the magnetic heading by subtracting the easterly variation (15°E, as shown on the dashed isogonic line) from the true heading (344°).

$MH = TH \pm VAR$
$MH = 344° - 15°E$
$MH = 329°$

(PLT012, PA.VI.A.K5a, PH.VII.A.K5a) — FAA-H-8083-25

AIR, RTC, WSC, PPC

**3550.** (Refer to Figure 23.) Determine the magnetic heading for a flight from Allendale County Airport (area 1) to Claxton-Evans County Airport (area 2). The wind is from 090° at 16 knots, the true airspeed is 90 knots, and the magnetic variation is 6° west.

A—209°.
B—230°.
C—212°.

Use the following steps:

1. Plot the course from Allendale County Airport to Claxton-Evans County Airport.

2. Measure the true course angle at the approximate midpoint of the route (212°).

3. Find the true heading using a flight computer (Wind Correction on FLT menu using CX-3):

Wind direction is 090° (given in question)
Wind speed is 16 knots (given in question)
True course is 212° (found in Step 2)
True airspeed is 90 knots (given in question)

Therefore, the true heading is 203°.

4. Calculate the magnetic heading by adding the westerly variation (6°W, as shown on the dashed isogonic line) from the true heading (203°).

$MH = TH \pm VAR$
$MH = 203° + 6°W$
$MH = 209°$

(PLT012, PA.VI.A.K5a, PH.VII.A.K5a) — FAA-H-8083-25

**Answers**

3546   [A]        3547   [B]        3550   [A]

AIR, RTC, WSC, PPC

**3550-1.** On a cross-country flight, point A is crossed at 1500 hours and the plan is to reach point B at 1530 hours. Use the following information to determine the indicated airspeed required to reach point B on schedule.

Distance between A and B .............................70 NM
Forecast wind ......................................... 310° at 15 kts
Pressure altitude.............................................8,000 ft
Ambient temperature .........................................-10°C
True course..........................................................270°

The required indicated airspeed would be approximately

A—126 knots.
B—137 knots.
C—152 knots.

*Use your CX-3 electronic flight computer to find the answer:*

1. *Find the ground speed that must be made between points A and B (Ground Speed on FLT menu)*

   Distance .......................................................70 NM
   Time to travel................................................ 30 min
   Ground speed................................................ 140 kts

2. *Find the true airspeed (Wind Correction on FLT menu)*

   Wind direction.................................................. 310°
   Wind speed ...................................................... 15 kts
   Course................................................................270°
   Ground speed................................................... 140 kts
   True airspeed ................................................ 151.8 kts
   True heading .................................................... 274°

3. *Find the required indicated (or calibrated) airspeed (Airspeed on FLT menu).*

   Pressure altitude ......................................... 8,000 ft
   Temperature .................................................... -10°C
   True airspeed ............................................... 151.8 kts
   Indicated airspeed.......................................137.1 kts
   *(same as calibrated)*

*(PLT012, PA.VI.A.K5c, PH.VII.A.K5c) — FAA-H-8083-25*

---

AIR, RTC, GLI, WSC, PPC

**3564.** (Refer to Figure 25.) Determine the magnetic heading for a flight from Dallas Executive (area 3) to Fort Worth Meacham (area 4). The wind is from 030° at 10 knots, the true airspeed is 135 knots, and the magnetic variation is 7° east.

A—266°.
B—286°.
C—312°.

*Use the following steps:*

1. *Plot a course from Dallas Executive to Meacham, and measure the course (289°).*

2. *Using the wind obtained, calculate a correction angle. This angle will be the difference between the course bearing and the heading required to maintain that course. Wind correction angle is 4° to the right.*

3. *Add true course and wind correction angle to obtain true heading.*

   289° TC
   + 4° WCA
   ―――――
   293° TH

4. *Find the magnetic heading by adding the variation to the true heading.*

   293° TH
   − 007° VAR (E)
   ―――――
   286° MH

*(PLT012, PA.VI.A.K5a, PH.VII.A.K5a) — FAA-H-8083-25*

---

AIR, RTC, LSA

**3564-1.** (Refer to Figure 75.) What is the time en route from the Gila Bend VORTAC to Buckeye VOR along V461 at a TAS of 125 knots with forecasted winds from 180 at 17 knots?

A—Approximately 14 minutes.
B—Approximately 15 minutes.
C—Approximately 13 minutes.

*Use your CX-3 electronic flight computer to find the answer:*

1. *Your course along V461 can be determined by using Figure 75 and identifying the 332° to Buckeye.*

2. *Next determine your ground speed using your CX-3 and the following information: course 332°, TAS 125 knots, wind direction 180, and wind speed of 17 knots. This results in a GS of 140 knots (Wind Correction on FLT menu).*

3. *The distance along V461 is determined by the number 31.*

4. *Determine your time en route using your CX-2: 31 NM at 140 knots results in 13 minutes and 18 seconds (Ground Speed on FLT menu).*

*(PLT012, PA.VI.A.K5c, PH.VII.A.K5c) — FAA-H-8083-25*

---

**Answers**

3550-1 [B]          3564    [B]          3564-1 [C]

ALL
**3564-2.** (Refer to Figure 21.) What is the estimated time en route from Mercer County Regional Airport (area 3) to Minot International (area 1)? The wind is from 330° at 25 knots and the true airspeed is 100 knots. Add 3-1/2 minutes for departure and climb-out.

A—47 minutes.
B—44 minutes.
C—52 minutes.

*Use your CX-3 electronic flight computer to find the answer:*

1. *Use your plotter on Figure 21 to identifying the distance (58 NM) and course (12°) between Mercer and Minot airports.*

2. *Next determine your ground speed using your CX-3 and the following information: distance 58 NM, TAS 100 knots, course 15°, wind direction 330, and wind speed 25 knots. This results in a GS of 80 knots (Wind Correction on FLT menu).*

3. *Determine your time enroute using your CX-3, 43 minutes (Ground Speed on FLT menu).*

4. *Add 3-1/2 minutes per the question requirements, 46-1/2 minutes.*

*(PLT012, PA.VI.A.K5c, PH.VII.A.K5c) — FAA-H-8083-25*

---

GLI
**3650.** (Refer to Figure 26, areas 5 and 6.) What minimum altitude should be used for a go-ahead point at Eckelson in order to arrive at Barnes County Airport at 1,000 feet AGL if the glide ratio is 22:1 in no wind conditions? Use the recommended safety factor.

A—5,959 feet MSL.
B—7,960 feet MSL.
C—9,359 feet MSL.

*Use the following steps:*

1. *A safety margin is provided to allow for any performance degradation. Use one-half the published L/D ratio for planning purposes. In this case use 11 to 1 (no wind).*

2. *Determine the distance from Eckelson to Barnes County Airport (14.5 SM).*

3. *If 1 SM = 5,280 feet, calculate the total sink in 14.5 SM at a glide ratio of 11:1.*

> *5,280 ÷11= 480 feet sink per SM*
> *480.0 × 14.5 = 6,960.0 feet total sink*

4. *Calculate the arrival altitude (MSL) by adding 1,000 feet AGL to the Barnes County elevation of 1,400 feet.*

> *1,400  Barnes County elevation*
> *+ 1,000  arrival (AGL)*
> *2,400  arrival (MSL)*

5. *Determine the go-ahead minimum by adding total sink to the required.arrival altitude.*

> *6,960  feet total sink*
> *+ 2,400  feet MSL arrival altitude*
> *9,360  feet MSL go-ahead minimum altitude*

*(PLT303) — Soaring Flight Manual*

---

LTA, LSL
**3537.** (Refer to Figure 21.) An airship crosses over Minot VORTAC (area 1) at 1056 and over the creek 8 nautical miles south-southeast on Victor 15 at 1108. What should be the approximate position on Victor 15 at 1211?

A—Over Lake Nettie National Wildlife Refuge.
B—Crossing the road east of Underwood.
C—Over the powerlines east of Washburn Airport.

*This is a time/speed/distance problem.*

1. *The distance is 8 NM (given in the question).*

2. *The time is:*

> *11:08 – 10:56 = 12 minutes*

3. *Use:* $\dfrac{Distance}{Time} \times 60 = Ground\ speed$

> $\dfrac{8\ NM}{12\ min} \times 60 = 40\ knots$

4. *Calculate the distance traveled on the next leg at this speed by 12:11.*

> *12:11 – 11:08 = :63 minutes*

5. *Use:* $\dfrac{Speed}{60} \times Time = Distance$

> $\dfrac{40\ kts}{60\ min} \times 63\ min = 42\ NM$

6. *Locate the 8 NM creek and measure an additional 42 NM along V15. You are east of Underwood; it is west of your position. The legs were 8 NM and 42 NM, total 50 NM.*

*(PLT012) — FAA-H-8083-25*

---

**Answers**

3564-2 [A]        3650   [C]        3537   [B]

**LTA**
**3558.** (Refer to Figure 24.) Determine the magnetic heading for a flight from Majors Airport (area 1) to Winnsboro Airport (area 2). The wind is from 340° at 12 knots, the true airspeed is 36 knots, and the magnetic variation is 6°30'E.

A—078°.
B—091°.
C—101°.

*Use the following steps:*

1. *Plot the course from Majors Airport to Winnsboro Airport.*

2. *Measure the true course angle at the approximate midpoint of the route (100°).*

3. *Find true heading, using a flight computer (Wind Correction on FLT menu using CX-3):*

   *Wind direction is 340° (given in question)*
   *Wind speed is 12 knots (given in question)*
   *True course is 100° (found in Step 2)*
   *True airspeed is 36 knots (given in question)*

   *Therefore, the true heading is 083°.*

4. *Calculate the magnetic heading by subtracting the easterly variation (6°30'E) from the true heading (084°).*

   *MH = TH ± VAR*
   *MH = 084° – 6°30'E*
   *MH = 78°*

*(PLT012) — FAA-H-8083-25*

**LTA**
**3569.** (Refer to Figure 26, area 5.) A balloon drifts over the town of Eckelson on a magnetic course of 014° at 10 mph. If wind conditions remain constant, where will the balloon be after 2 hours 30 minutes?

A—Cooperstown airport.
B—West of Dazey.
C—Hannaford.

*Use the following steps:*

1. *Calculate the distance traveled at 10 mph during 2-1/2 hours.*

   *Distance = Speed × Time*
   *Distance = 10 mph × 2.5 H = 25 SM*

2. *Locate Eckelson in FAA Figure 27.*

3. *Note that the magnetic variation near Eckelson, as shown on the dashed isogonic line, is 5°E.*

4. *Calculate the true course from the magnetic course:*

   *TC ± VAR = MC*
   *TC – 5° = 14°*
   *TC = 019°*

5. *Plot a true course of 019° from Eckelson extending 25 SM. The balloon would be over the town of Hannaford.*

*(PLT012) — FAA-H-8083-25*

**SPO**
**2099.** If an aircraft is consuming 3 gallons of fuel per hour at a cruising altitude of 500 feet and the groundspeed is 45 mph, how much fuel is required to travel 75 SM?

A—6 gallons.
B—5 gallons.
C—3 gallons.

*To determine the fuel required for a given flight, the time required for the flight must be known. Time in flight multiplied by rate of consumption gives the quantity of fuel required. For example, a flight of 75 SM at a ground speed of 45 mph requires 1.67 hours (distance divided by ground speed = time). If the plane consumes 3 gallons an hour, the total consumption will be 1.67 × 3, or 5 gallons. (PLT012) — FAA-H-8083-25*

**SPO**
**2105.** To find the distance flown in a given time, multiply time by

A—groundspeed.
B—indicated airspeed.
C—equivalent airspeed.

*Distance D = GS × T: To find the distance flown in a given time, multiply ground speed by time. (PLT012) — FAA-H-8083-25*

**SPO**
**2101.** Given:

True course............050
True Heading...........040
True airspeed..........75 kts
Groundspeed............65 kts

Determine the wind direction and speed.

A—105°; and 16 knots
B—355°; and 16 knots
C—355°; and 10 knots

**Answers**

3558 [A]    3569 [C]    2099 [B]    2105 [A]    2101 [B]

*Using an E6-B computer:*

1. *Turn compass azimuth so 050° is at the true index.*

2. *Slide board so grommet is on the ground speed arc, 65 knots.*

3. *Determine the WCA by comparing course to heading.*
   *050° – 040° = 10° left*

4. *Plot WCA at TAS arc with a pencil dot, 75 knots.*

5. *Rotate compass azimuth so pencil dot is on the centerline.*

6. *Read wind direction under true index and wind speed as number of units between grommet and pencil dot, 354° and 16 knots.*

*Alternate method, using a CX-3 Flight Computer:*

1. *Press FLT and select Wind Correction.*

2. *Enter the given ground speed (GS) 65 kts, true airspeed (TAS) 75 kts, true course (TCrs) 050°, and true heading (THdg) 040°.*

3. *Press enter to find a wind speed (WSpd) of 15.75 kts and a wind direction (WDir) of 354°.*

*Alternate method, using logic to find answer.*

1. *Picture your true course flying northeast.*

2. *Picture your heading 10° to the north.*

3. *This indicates a crosswind from your left.*

4. *Note your ground speed is lower than your airspeed. This indicates a headwind rather than a tailwind.*

5. *From items 3 and 4 above, the wind can be determined from the northwest.*

6. *Your true airspeed and ground speed are exactly 10 knots apart; since you are crabbed, the wind must be stronger than 10 knots overall.*

7. *You pick answer B because the wind is from the estimated direction, and the speed is above 10 knots.*

8. *Looking at the answer and determining direction and speed, this confirms your assumptions and the correct answer.*

*(PLT012) — FAA-H-8083-25*

LSL
**2222.** (Refer to Figure 71, point 1.)

Given:
Departure point...................Georgetown Airport (E36)
Departure time.......................................................0637
Winds aloft forecast (FD) at your altitude ............ 1008
Airspeed ............................................................ 8 kts

At 0755, the aircraft should be

A—over Auburn Airport (AUN).
B—over the town of Auburn.
C—slightly west of the town of Garden Valley.

1. *Calculate time en route:*
   *0755 – 0637 = 1:18 = 1.3 hours*

2. *Compute distance traveled:*
   *Distance = Speed × Time*
   *8 × 1.3 = 10.4 NM*

3. *Plot course of 100° + 180° = 280° out to a distance of 10.4 NM from Georgetown Airport (E36), point 1. The aircraft should be just south of there.*

*(PLT012) — FAA-H-8083-25*

**Answers**

2222 [A]

# VHF Omnidirectional Range (VOR)

The **VHF Omnidirectional Range (VOR)** is the backbone of the National Airway System, and this radio aid to navigation (**NAVAID**) provides guidance to pilots operating under visual flight rules as well as those flying instruments.

On Sectional Aeronautical Charts, VOR locations are shown by blue symbols centered in a blue compass rose which is oriented to Magnetic North. A blue identification box adjacent to the VOR symbol lists the name and frequency of the facility, its three-letter identifier and Morse Code equivalent, and other information as appropriate. See the "Radio Aids to Navigation and Communications Box" information in FAA Legend 1.

Some VORs have a voice identification alternating with the Morse code identifier. Absence of the identifier indicates the facility is unreliable or undergoing routine maintenance; in either case, it should not be used for navigation. Some VORs also transmit a T-E-S-T code when undergoing maintenance.

The VOR station continuously transmits navigation signals, providing 360 magnetic courses to or radials from the station. Courses are TO the station and radials are FROM the station.

TACAN, a military system which provides directional guidance, also informs the pilot of the aircraft's distance from the TACAN Station. When a VOR and a TACAN are co-located, the facility is called a VORTAC. Civil pilots may receive both azimuth and distance information from a VORTAC.

At some VOR sites, additional equipment has been installed to provide pilots with distance information. Such an installation is termed a VOR/DME (for distance measuring equipment).

Flight deck display of VOR information is by means of an indicator as shown in Figure 7-19.

The **omni bearing selector (OBS)** is an azimuth dial which can be rotated to select a course or to determine which radial the aircraft is on. The **TO/FROM indicator** shows whether flying the selected course would take the aircraft to or from the VOR station. A TO indication shows the radial selected is on the far side of the VOR station, while a FROM indication means the aircraft and the selected course are on the same side.

The **course deviation indicator (CDI)**, when centered, indicates the aircraft is on the selected course, or, when not centered, whether that course is to the left or right of the aircraft. For example, Figure 7-20 is indicating that a course of 030° would take the aircraft to the selected station, and to get on that course, the aircraft would have to fly to the left of 030°.

To determine position in relation to one or more VOR stations, first tune and identify the selected station. Next, rotate the OBS until the CDI centers with a FROM indication. The OBS reading is the magnetic course from the VOR station to the aircraft. With reference to Figure 7-21, the line of position is established on the 265° radial of the XYZ VOR.

Repeat the procedure using a second VOR. The aircraft is located at the point where the two lines of position cross. See Figure 7-22.

**Figure 7-19.** The VOR indicator

**Figure 7-20.** Interpreting the OBS and CDI indications

**Figure 7-21.** Aircraft on the 265° radial of a VOR

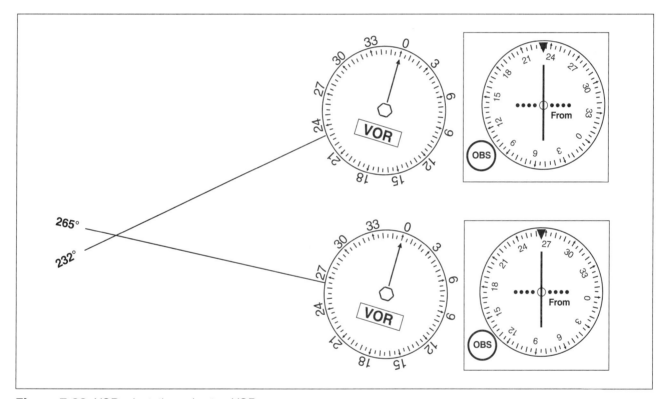

**Figure 7-22.** VOR orientation using two VORs

To determine the course to be flown to a VOR station on the sectional aeronautical chart, first draw a line from the starting point to the VOR symbol in the center of the compass rose. At the point where the course line crosses the compass rose, read the radial. The course to the station is the reciprocal of that radial. See Figure 7-23.

The routes established between VORs are depicted by blue-tinted bands showing the airway number following the letter "V," and are called Victor airways. See Figure 7-24.

When approaching a VOR where airways converge, a pilot must exercise extreme vigilance for other aircraft. In addition, when climbing or descending VFR on an airway, it is considered good operating practice to execute gentle banks left and right for continuous visual scanning of the airspace.

VOR receiver accuracy may be checked by means of a VOR Test Facility (VOT), ground check points, or airborne check points.

VOTs transmit only the 360° radial signal. Thus, when the OBS is set to 360°, the CDI will center with a FROM indication; while the reciprocal, 180°, will cause the CDI to center with a TO indication. An accuracy factor of plus or minus 4° is allowed when using a VOT facility.

**Figure 7-23.** Determining course to a VOR station

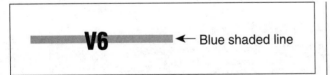

**Figure 7-24**

AIR, RTC
**3643.** (Refer to Figure 25, area 5.) The navigation facility at Dallas-Ft. Worth International (DFW) is a

A—VOR.
B—VORTAC.
C—VOR/DME.

*Reference FAA Legend 1. There is a VOR/DME at DFW. (PLT101, PA.I.E.K2, PH.VII.B.K1) — Sectional Chart Legend*

AIR, RTC
**3552.** (Refer to Figure 23.) What is the approximate position of the aircraft if the VOR receivers indicate the 320° radial of Savannah VORTAC (area 3) and the 184° radial of Allendale VOR (area 1)?

A—Southeast of Guyton.
B—Town of Springfield.
C—Over Briggs Airport.

*Use the following steps:*

1. *Plot the 320° radial (magnetic course FROM) of the Savannah VORTAC.*

2. *Plot the 184° radial of the Allendale VOR.*

3. *Note the intersection of the two plotted radials southeast of the town of Guyton.*

*(PLT335, PA.VI.B.K1, PH.VII.B.K1) — FAA-H-8083-25*

**Answers**

3643  [C]          3552  [A]

AIR, RTC

**3559.** (Refer to Figure 24.) What is the approximate position of the aircraft if the VOR receivers indicate the 245° radial of Sulphur Springs VOR/DME (area 5) and the 140° radial of Bonham VORTAC (area 3)?

A—Weese Intl. Airport.
B—Glenmar Airport.
C—Majors Airport.

*Use the following steps:*

1. *Plot the 245° radial (magnetic course FROM) of the Sulphur Springs VOR/DME.*

2. *Plot the 140° radial (magnetic course FROM) of the Bonham VORTAC.*

3. *Note the intersection of the two plotted radials over the Glenmar Airport (Pvt).*

*(PLT101, PA.VI.B.K1, PH.VII.B.K1) — FAA-H-8083-25*

AIR, RTC

**3566.** (Refer to Figure 25, area 5.) The VOR is tuned to the VOR-DME at the Dallas-Fort Worth airport. The omnibearing selector (OBS) is set on 253°, with a TO indication, and a right course deviation indicator (CDI) deflection. What is the aircraft's position from the VOR-DME?

A—East–northeast.
B—North–northeast.
C—West–southwest.

*The course selected is 253° and the TO/FROM indicator has a TO flag, which means the aircraft is south of the course but north of the VOR. The CDI needle is deflected to the right, which means the aircraft is left (or east) of the course. Therefore, the aircraft must be to the east northeast of the station to satisfy the VOR indications. (PLT101, PA.VI.B.K1, PH.VII.B.K1) — FAA-H-8083-25*

AIR, RTC

**3577.** (Refer to Figure 28, illustration 4.) The VOR receiver has the indications shown. What is the aircraft's position relative to the station?

A—North.
B—East.
C—South.

*The course selected is 210° and the TO/FROM indicator is showing TO with a left deflection. This means the aircraft is right of the course and north of the station. (PLT090, PA.VI.B.K1, PH.VII.B.K1) — FAA-H-8083-25*

AIR, RTC

**3578.** (Refer to Figure 28, illustration 7.) The VOR receiver has the indications shown. What is the aircraft's position relative to the station?

A—East.
B—Southeast.
C—West.

*Observe from illustration #7 of FAA Figure 28, that there is no TO/FROM indication and the CDI is deflected left with an OBS set on 030°. The aircraft is somewhere along the perpendicular line (120/300°). The CDI left means the 030° radial is to the left, or west, of the aircraft position. Answer B is the only one placing the aircraft on the 120° radial, or southeast of the station. (PLT090, PA.VI.B.K1, PH.VII.B.K1) — FAA-H-8083-25*

AIR, RTC

**3579.** (Refer to Figure 28, illustration 5.) The VOR receiver has the indications shown. What radial is the aircraft crossing?

A—030°.
B—210°.
C—300°.

*The CDI is centered with the OBS set to 210° with a TO indication. Therefore, the aircraft is located on the 030° radial. (PLT090, PA.VI.B.K1, PH.VII.B.K1) — FAA-H-8083-25*

AIR, RTC

**3553.** (Refer to Figure 23.) On what course should the VOR receiver (OBS) be set to navigate direct from Hampton Varnville Airport (area 1) to Savannah VORTAC (area 3)?

A—003°.
B—195°.
C—200°.

*Use the following steps:*

1. *Plot the course direct from Hampton Varnville Airport to the Savannah VORTAC.*

2. *Note the radial (magnetic course from Savannah) on which the plotted course lies (015°).*

3. *Determine the course TO the VORTAC by finding the reciprocal:*

    *TO = FROM + 180°*
    *TO = 015° + 180°*
    *TO = 195°*

*(PLT064, PA.VI.B.K1, PH.VII.B.K1) — FAA-H-8083-25*

**Answers**

| | | | | | |
|---|---|---|---|---|---|
| 3559 [B] | 3566 [A] | 3577 [A] | 3578 [B] | 3579 [A] | 3553 [B] |

AIR, RTC

**3560.** (Refer to Figure 24.) On what course should the VOR receiver (OBS) be set in order to navigate direct from Majors Airport (area 1) to Quitman VOR/DME (area 2)?

A—101°.
B—108°.
C—281°.

*Use the following steps:*

1. *Plot the course direct from Majors Airport to Quitman VOR/DME.*

2. *Note the radial (magnetic course FROM) of Quitman VOR/DME on which the plotted course lies (281°).*

3. *Determine the course TO the VOR/DME by finding the reciprocal:*

> *TO = FROM + 180°*
> *TO = 281° + 180°*
> *TO = 461° − 360° = 101°*

*(PLT090, PA.VI.B.K1, PH.VII.B.K1) — FAA-H-8083-25*

AIR, RTC

**3533.** (Refer to Figure 20, area 3; and Figure 28.) The VOR is tuned to Elizabeth City VOR/DME, and the aircraft is positioned over Shawboro, a small town 3 NM west of Currituck County Regional (ONX). Which VOR indication is correct?

A—2.
B—5.
C—8.

1. *Locate the Shawboro Airport and the Elizabeth City VOR in FAA Figure 20. Draw the radial (magnetic course FROM) of the Elizabeth City VOR on which Shawboro lies (030°).*

2. *When over Shawboro on the 030 radial, the CDI should be centered with a 030 FROM indication or a 210 TO indication (the reciprocal). Dials 5 and 9 satisfy these conditions.*

*(PLT090, PA.VI.B.K1, PH.VII.B.K1) — FAA-H-8083-25*

AIR, RTC

**3561.** (Refer to Figure 24 and Figure 28.) The VOR is tuned to Bonham VORTAC (area 3), and the aircraft is positioned over the town of Sulphur Springs (area 5). Which VOR indication is correct?

A—1.
B—7.
C—8.

*Use the following steps:*

1. *Locate and draw the magnetic course from Bonham VORTAC to Sulphur Springs (120°).*

2. *Notice that the OBS selections of all the dials in FAA Figure 28 are 030° or 210°, both of which are at 90° with respect to the 120° radial. Therefore, when over Sulphur Springs, the flag should indicate neither TO nor FROM and the course needle should have a full deflection either side.*

3. *Both dials 3 and 7 of FAA Figure 28 are at 90° from the correct radial of 120°. However, only dial 7 is a valid answer option.*

*(PLT090, PA.VI.B.K1, PH.VII.B.K1) — FAA-H-8083-25*

AIR, RTC

**3570.** (Refer to Figure 26, areas 4 and 2; and Figure 28.) The VOR is tuned to Jamestown VOR, and the aircraft is positioned over Cooperstown Airport. Which VOR indication is correct?

A—2.
B—5.
C—8.

1. *Locate the Cooperstown Airport and the Jamestown VOR in FAA Figure 26. Draw the radial (magnetic course FROM) of the Jamestown VOR on which Cooperstown Airport lies (030°).*

2. *When over Cooperstown Airport on the 030 radial, the CDI should have a 030 FROM indication or a 210 TO indication (the reciprocal). Dial 5 satisfies these conditions.*

*(PLT090, PA.VI.B.K1, PH.VII.B.K1) — FAA-H-8083-25*

**Answers**

| | | | |
|---|---|---|---|
| 3560 [A] | 3533 [B] | 3561 [B] | 3570 [B] |

AIR, RTC

**3539.** (Refer to Figure 21.) What course should be selected on the omnibearing selector (OBS) to make a direct flight from Mercer County Regional Airport (area 3) to the Minot VORTAC (area 1) with a TO indication?

A—001°.
B—359°.
C—179°.

*Use the following steps:*

1. *Plot a direct course from Mercer Airport to the Minot Airport VORTAC.*

2. *Note the radial (magnetic course FROM Minot VOR-TAC) on which the plotted course lies (179°).*

3. *Determine the course TO Minot VORTAC by finding the reciprocal:*

   $$TO = FROM + 180°$$
   $$TO = 179° + 180°$$
   $$TO = 359°$$

*(PLT012, PA.VI.B.K1, PH.VII.B.K1) — FAA-H-8083-25*

SPO

**2100.** True course measurements on a Sectional Aeronautical Chart should be made at a meridian near the midpoint of the course because the

A—values of isogonic lines change from point to point.
B—angles formed by isogonic lines and lines of latitude vary from point to point.
C—angles formed by lines of longitude and the course line vary from point to point.

*Sectional Aeronautical Charts are made on grid in which the meridians of longitude are nonparallel straight lines that all meet at the earth's poles. When planning a flight, measure the true course from the mid-meridian to get an average true course. (PLT200) — FAA-H-8083-25*

ALL

**3814.** What procedure is recommended when climbing or descending VFR on an airway?

A—Execute gentle banks, left and right for continuous visual scanning of the airspace.
B—Advise the nearest FSS of the altitude changes.
C—Fly away from the centerline of the airway before changing altitude.

*During climbs and descents in flight conditions which permit visual detection of other traffic, pilots should execute gentle banks, left and right, at a frequency which permits continuous visual scanning of the airspace about them. (PLT125, PA.VI.B.K1, PH.VII.B.K1) — AIM ¶4-4-15*

AIR, RTC

**3598-1.** When the course deviation indicator (CDI) needle is centered during an omnireceiver check using a VOR test signal (VOT), the omnibearing selector (OBS) and the TO/FROM indicator should read

A—180° FROM, only if the pilot is due north of the VOT.
B—0° TO or 180° FROM, regardless of the pilot's position from the VOT.
C—0° FROM or 180° TO, regardless of the pilot's position from the VOT.

*To use the VOT service, tune in the VOT frequency on the VOR receiver. With the CDI centered, the OBS should read 0° with the TO/FROM indication showing "FROM" or the OBS should read 180° with the TO/FROM indication showing "TO." (PLT300, PA.VI.B.K1, PH.VII.B.K1) — AIM ¶1-1-4*

**Answers**

3539  [B]       2100  [C]       3814  [A]       3598-1 [C]

# Global Positioning System (GPS)

GPS is a United States satellite-based radio navigational, positioning, and time transfer system operated by the Department of Defense. The system provides highly accurate position and velocity information and precise time on a continuous global basis to an unlimited number of properly equipped users. The GPS constellation of satellites is designed so that a minimum of five are always observable by a user anywhere on earth. The GPS receiver uses data from a minimum of four satellites to yield a three dimensional position (latitude, longitude, and altitude) and time solution.

The GPS receiver verifies the integrity (usability) of the signals received from the GPS satellites through receiver autonomous integrity monitoring (RAIM) to determine if a satellite is providing corrupted information. Without RAIM capability, the pilot has no assurance of the accuracy of the GPS position. If RAIM is not available, another type of navigation and approach system must be used, another destination selected, or the trip delayed until RAIM is predicted to be available on arrival.

ALL

**3598-3.** If receiver autonomous integrity monitoring (RAIM) capability is lost in flight,

A—the pilot may still rely on GPS derived altitude for vertical information.

B—the pilot has no assurance of the accuracy of the GPS position.

C—GPS position is reliable provided at least 3 GPS satellites are available.

*The GPS receiver verifies the integrity (usability) of the signals received from the GPS constellation through RAIM to determine if a satellite is providing corrupted information. At least one satellite, in addition to those required for navigation, must be in view for the receiver to perform the RAIM function; thus, RAIM needs a minimum of 5 satellites in view, or 4 satellites and a barometric altimeter (baro-aiding) to detect an integrity anomaly. For receivers capable of doing so, RAIM needs 6 satellites in view (or 5 satellites with baro-aiding) to isolate the corrupt satellite signal and remove it from the navigation solution. GPS derived altitude should not be relied upon to determine aircraft altitude since the vertical error can be quite large and no integrity is provided. (PLT354, PA.VI.B.K2, PH.VII.B.K2) — AIM ¶1-1-17*

ALL

**3598-4.** How many Global Positioning System (GPS) satellites are required to yield a three dimensional position (latitude, longitude, and altitude) and time solution?

A—5.

B—6.

C—4.

*The GPS receiver uses data from a minimum of four satellites to yield a three-dimensional position (latitude, longitude, and altitude) and time solution. (PLT354, PA.VI.B.K2, PH.VII.B.K2) — FAA-H-8083-25*

**Answers**

3598-3 [B]          3598-4 [C]

# Flight Plan Form

Filing a flight plan is not required by regulations; however, it is a good operating practice, since the information contained in the flight plan can be used in search and rescue in the event of an emergency. When completing a flight plan, use the planned cruising altitude in hundreds of feet for the first or the whole portion of the route to be flown expressed as "A" followed by three figures: A075 for 7,500 feet MSL.

Although filing a VFR flight plan is not mandatory (except under certain circumstances), it is considered good operating practice.

The pilot must close a VFR flight plan at the completion of a flight. This can be done by contacting the FAA upon landing.

ALL, SPO

**2175.** Why should you file a VFR flight plan with the FAA?

A—You are required to do so when flying beyond 25 NM from an airport.
B—To provide traffic reports with Flight Service.
C—To provide search and rescue in the event of an emergency.

*Filing a flight plan is not required by regulations; however, it is a good operating practice, since the information contained in the flight plan can be used in search and rescue in the event of an emergency. (PLT225, PA.I.D.K4, PH.I.D.K5) — FAA-H-8083-25*

ALL, SPO

**2175-1.** (Refer to Figure 51.) What information should be entered for Item 15, level, on the flight plan form?

A—VFR cruising altitude.
B—Aircraft service ceiling.
C—Aircraft center of gravity.

*Insert the planned cruising altitude in hundreds of feet for the first or the whole portion of the route to be flown expressed as "A" followed by three figures: A075 for 7,500 feet MSL. (PLT225, PA.I.D.K4, PH.I.D.K5) — AIM ¶5-1-9*

ALL

**3818.** How should a VFR flight plan be closed at the completion of the flight at a controlled airport?

A—The tower will automatically close the flight plan when the aircraft turns off the runway.
B—The pilot must close the flight plan with the FAA upon landing.
C—The tower will relay the instructions to the nearest FSS when the aircraft contacts the tower for landing.

*The PIC, upon canceling or completing the flight under the flight plan, shall notify an FAA Flight Service Station or ATC facility. (PLT225, PA.I.D.K5, PH.I.D.K5) — AIM ¶5-1-14*

**Answers**

2175　[C]　　　　2175-1 [A]　　　　3818　[B]

# Chapter 8
# **Weather**

# The Heating of the Earth

The major source of all weather is the sun. Changes or variations of weather patterns are caused by the unequal heating of the Earth's surface.

Every physical process of weather is accompanied by or is a result of unequal heating of the Earth's surface. The heating of the Earth (and therefore the heating of the air surrounding the Earth) is unequal around the entire planet. Both north or south of the equator, one square foot of sunrays is not concentrated over one square foot of the surface, but over a larger area. This lower concentration of sunrays produces less radiation of heat over a given surface area; therefore, less atmospheric heating takes place in that area.

The unequal heating of the Earth's atmosphere creates a large air cell circulation pattern (wind) because the warmer air has a tendency to rise (low pressure) and the colder air has a tendency to settle or descend (high pressure) and replace the rising warmer air. This unequal heating, which causes pressure variations, will also cause variations in altimeter settings between weather reporting points.

Because the Earth rotates, this large, simple air cell circulation pattern is greatly distorted by a phenomenon known as the **Coriolis force**. When the wind (which is created by high pressure trying to flow into low pressure) first begins to move at higher altitudes, the Coriolis force deflects it to the right (in the Northern Hemisphere) causing it to flow parallel to the isobars (lines of equal pressure). These deflections of the large-cell circulation pattern create general wind patterns as depicted in Figure 8-1.

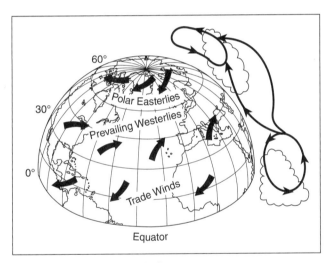

**Figure 8-1.** Prevailing wind systems

ALL, SPO

**3381.** Every physical process of weather is accompanied by, or is the result of, a

A—movement of air.
B—pressure differential.
C—heat exchange.

*Every physical process of weather is accompanied by, or is a result of, unequal heating of the Earth's surface. (PLT512, PA.I.C.K3a, PH.I.C.K3c) — FAA-H-8083-28*

ALL, SPO

**3382.** What causes variations in altimeter settings between weather reporting points?

A—Unequal heating of the Earth's surface.
B—Variation of terrain elevation.
C—Coriolis force.

*All altimeter settings are corrected to sea level. Unequal heating of the Earth's surface causes pressure differences. (PLT165, PA.I.C.K3, PH.I.C.K3) — FAA-H-8083-28*

GLI

**3448.** The development of thermals depends upon

A—a counterclockwise circulation of air.
B—temperature inversions.
C—solar heating.

*Thermals are updrafts in convective currents dependent on solar heating. A temperature inversion would result in stable air with very little, if any, convective activity. (PLT494) — FAA-H-8083-28*

**Answers**

3381  [C]          3382  [A]          3448  [C]

GLI
**3647.** (Refer to Figure 20.) Over which area should a glider pilot expect to find the best lift under normal conditions?

A—2.
B—7.
C—5.

*Dry areas get hotter than moist areas. Dry fields or dry ground of any nature are better thermal sources than moist areas. This applies to woods or forests, which are poor sources of thermals because of the large amount of moisture given off by foliage. (PLT064) — FAA-H-8083-13*

# Circulation and Wind

The general circulation and wind rules in the Northern Hemisphere are as follows:

1. Air circulates in a clockwise direction around a high;

2. Air circulates in a counterclockwise direction around a low;

3. The closer the isobars are together, the stronger the wind speed; and

4. Due to surface friction (up to about 2,000 feet AGL), surface winds do not exactly parallel the isobars, but move outward from the center of the high toward lower pressure. See Figure 8-2.

Knowing that air flows out of the high in a clockwise direction and into the low in a counterclockwise direction is useful in preflight planning. Assume a flight from point A to point B as shown in Figure 8-3. Going direct would involve fighting the wind flowing around the low. However, by traveling south of the low-pressure area, the circulation pattern could help instead of hinder. Generally speaking, in the Northern Hemisphere, when traveling west to east, the most favorable winds can be found by flying north of high-pressure areas and south of low-pressure areas. Conversely, when flying east to west, the most favorable winds can be found south of high-pressure areas and north of low-pressure areas.

**Figure 8-2.** Gradient and surface wind

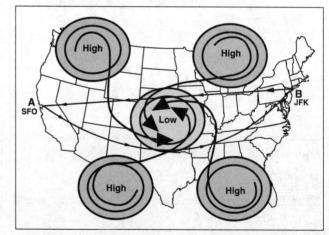

**Figure 8-3.** Circulation and wind

**Answers**

3647 [A]

ALL

**3395.** The wind at 5,000 feet AGL is southwesterly while the surface wind is southerly. This difference in direction is primarily due to

A—stronger pressure gradient at higher altitudes.
B—friction between the wind and the surface.
C—stronger Coriolis force at the surface.

*Friction between the wind and the surface slows the wind. The Coriolis force has less affect on slower winds, therefore there will be less deflection with surface winds than with winds at 5,000 feet AGL. (PLT516, PA.I.C.K3b, PH.I.C.K3b) — FAA-H-8083-28*

Answer (A) is incorrect because pressure gradient is not the reason for wind direction differences; it is the force which causes wind. Answer (C) is incorrect because slower wind speed results in weaker Coriolis force at the surface.

ALL

**3450.** Convective circulation patterns associated with sea breezes are caused by

A—warm, dense air moving inland from over the water.
B—water absorbing and radiating heat faster than the land.
C—cool, dense air moving inland from over the water.

*Caused by the heating of land on warm, sunny days, the sea breeze usually begins during early morning, reaches a maximum during the afternoon, and subsides around dusk after the land has cooled. The leading edge of the cool sea breeze forces warmer air inland to rise. Rising air from over land returns seaward at higher altitude to complete the convective cell. (PLT516, PA.I.C.K3b, PH.I.C.K3b) — FAA-H-8083-28*

Answer (A) is incorrect because there will be cooler air over the water. Answer (B) is incorrect because land absorbs and radiates heat faster.

GLI

**3350.** What is the proper airspeed to use when flying between thermals on a cross-country flight against a headwind?

A—The best lift/drag speed increased by one-half the estimated wind velocity.
B—The minimum sink speed increased by one-half the estimated wind velocity.
C—The best lift/drag speed decreased by one-half the estimated wind velocity.

*When gliding into a headwind, maximum distance will be achieved by adding approximately one-half the estimated headwind velocity to the best L/D speed. (PLT303) — FAA-H-8083-13*

# Temperature

In aviation, temperature is measured in degrees Celsius (°C). The standard temperature at sea level is 59°F (15°C). The average decrease in temperature with altitude (standard lapse rate) is 2°C (3.5°F) per 1,000 feet. Since this is an average, the exact value seldom exists; in fact, temperature sometimes increases with altitude (an inversion). The most frequent type of ground- or surface-based **temperature inversion** is one that is produced by terrestrial radiation on a clear, relatively still night.

ALL

**3383.** When there is a temperature inversion, you would expect to experience

A—clouds with extensive vertical development above an inversion aloft.
B—good visibility in the lower levels of the atmosphere and poor visibility above an inversion aloft.
C—an increase in temperature as altitude increases.

*An increase in temperature with altitude is defined as an inversion. An inversion often develops near the ground on clear, cool nights when wind is light. The ground radiates heat and cools much faster than the overlying air. Air in contact with the ground becomes cold while the temperature a few hundred feet above changes very little. Thus, the temperature increases with height. A ground-based inversion usually means poor visibility. (PLT301, PA.I.C.K3a, PH.I.C.K3c) — FAA-H-8083-28*

Answer (A) is incorrect because a temperature inversion will not result in vertical development, since warm air will not rise if the air above is warmer. Answer (B) is incorrect because a temperature inversion will trap dust, smoke, and other particles, thus causing reduced visibilities.

**Answers**

| 3395 | [B] | 3450 | [C] | 3350 | [A] | 3383 | [C] |

ALL

**3384.** The most frequent type of ground or surface-based temperature inversion is that which is produced by

A—terrestrial radiation on a clear, relatively still night.
B—warm air being lifted rapidly aloft in the vicinity of mountainous terrain.
C—the movement of colder air under warm air, or the movement of warm air over cold air.

*An inversion often develops near the ground on clear, cool nights when wind is light. The ground radiates heat and cools much faster than the overlying air. Air in contact with the ground becomes cold while the temperature a few hundred feet above changes very little. Thus, the temperature increases with height. (PLT301, PA.I.C.K3a, PH.I.C.K3c) — FAA-H-8083-28*

*Answer (B) is incorrect because this is an example of convective activity. Answer (C) is incorrect because this describes a cold front and a warm front.*

# Moisture

Air has moisture (water vapor) in it. The water vapor content of air can be expressed in two different ways. The two commonly used terms are relative humidity and dew point.

**Relative humidity** relates the actual water vapor present in the air to that which could be present in the air. Temperature largely determines the maximum amount of water vapor that air can hold. Warm air can hold more water vapor than can cold air. See Figure 8-4.

Air with 100% relative humidity is said to be saturated, and less than 100% is unsaturated.

**Dew point** is the temperature to which air must be cooled to become saturated by the water already present in the air. See Figure 8-5.

**Moisture** can be added to the air by either evaporation or sublimation. Moisture is removed from the air by either condensation or sublimation.

When water vapor condenses on large objects such as leaves, windshields, or airplanes, it will form **dew**; and when it condenses on microscopic particles such as salt, dust, or combustion by-products (condensation nuclei), it will form clouds or fog.

**Figure 8-4.** Capacity of air to hold water

**Figure 8-5.** Relative humidity and dew point

**Answers**

3384 [A]

To summarize, relative humidity can be increased either by lowering the air temperature or by increasing the amount of moisture in the air. If the temperature and dew point spread is small and decreasing, condensation is about to occur. If the temperature is above freezing, the weather most likely to develop will be fog or low clouds.

ALL, SPO

**3397.** What is meant by the term dew point?

A—The temperature at which condensation and evaporation are equal.
B—The temperature at which dew will always form.
C—The temperature to which air must be cooled to become saturated.

*Dew point is the temperature to which air must be cooled to become saturated by the water vapor already present in the air. (PLT512, PA.I.C.K3d, PH.I.C.K3d) — FAA-H-8083-28*

Answer (A) is incorrect because evaporation is not directly related to the dew point. Answer (B) is incorrect because dew will form only when an object cools below the dew point of the surrounding air.

ALL

**3398.** The amount of water vapor which air can hold depends on the

A—dew point.
B—air temperature.
C—stability of the air.

*Temperature largely determines the maximum amount of water vapor air can hold. (PLT512, PA.I.C.K3d, PH.I.C.K3d) — FAA-H-8083-28*

ALL, SPO

**3399.** Clouds, fog, or dew will always form when

A—water vapor condenses.
B—water vapor is present.
C—relative humidity reaches 100 percent.

*As water vapor condenses or sublimates on condensation nuclei, liquid or ice particles begin to grow. Some condensation nuclei have an affinity for water and can induce condensation or sublimation even when air is almost, but not completely, saturated. (PLT512, PA.I.C.K3d, PH.I.C.K3d) — FAA-H-8083-28*

Answer (B) is incorrect because the presence of water vapor does not result in clouds, fog, or dew unless condensation occurs. Answer (C) is incorrect because it is possible to have 100% humidity without the occurrence of condensation, which is necessary for clouds, fog, or dew to form.

ALL

**3400.** What are the processes by which moisture is added to unsaturated air?

A—Evaporation and sublimation.
B—Heating and condensation.
C—Supersaturation and evaporation.

*Evaporation is the changing of liquid water to invisible water vapor. Sublimation is the changing of solid water directly to the vapor phase or water vapor to ice, by passing the liquid state in each process. (PLT512, PA.I.C.K3d, PH.I.C.K3d) — FAA-H-8083-28*

Answer (B) is incorrect because heating and condensation alone do not add moisture to unsaturated air. Answer (C) is incorrect because "supersaturation" does not fit the context of the question.

SPO

**2369.** Moisture is added to air by

A—sublimation and condensation.
B—evaporation and condensation.
C—evaporation and sublimation.

*Evaporation is the changing of liquid water to invisible water vapor. Sublimation is the changing of ice directly to water vapor. (PLT512) — FAA-H-8083-28*

Answers (A) and (B) are incorrect because condensation removes moisture from the air.

ALL

**3444.** If the temperature/dew point spread is small and decreasing, and the temperature is 62°F, what type weather is most likely to develop?

A—Freezing precipitation.
B—Thunderstorms.
C—Fog or low clouds.

*With a small temperature/dew point spread, the air is close to saturation. This will usually result in fog or low clouds. Anticipate fog when the temperature/dew point spread is 5°F or less and decreasing. (PLT512, PA.I.C.K3d, PH.I.C.K3d) — FAA-H-8083-28*

Answer (A) is incorrect because precipitation will not freeze at a temperature of 62°F. Answer (B) is incorrect because temperature/dew point spread does not relate to the development of thunderstorms.

**Answers**

| 3397 | [C] | 3398 | [B] | 3399 | [A] | 3400 | [A] | 2369 | [C] | 3444 | [C] |

# Air Masses and Fronts

When a body of air comes to rest on, or moves slowly over, an extensive area having fairly uniform properties of temperature and moisture, the air takes on these properties. The area over which the air mass acquires its identifying distribution of temperature and moisture is its source region. As this air mass moves from its source region, it tends to take on the properties of the new underlying surface. The trend toward change is called air mass modification.

A **ridge** is an elongated area of high pressure. A **trough** is an elongated area of low pressure. All fronts lie in troughs. A **cold front** is the leading edge of an advancing cold air mass. A **warm front** is the leading edge of an advancing warm air mass. Warm fronts move about half as fast as cold fronts. **Frontal waves** and **cyclones** (areas of low pressure) usually form on slow-moving cold fronts or stationary fronts. Figure 8-6 shows the symbols that would appear on a weather map.

The physical manifestations of a warm or cold front can be different with each front. They vary with the speed of the air mass on the move and the degree of stability of the air mass being overtaken. A stable air mass forced aloft will continue to exhibit stable characteristics, while an unstable air mass forced to ascend will continue to be characterized by cumulus clouds, turbulence, showery precipitation, and good visibility.

Frontal passage will be indicated by the following discontinuities:

1. A temperature change (the most easily recognizable discontinuity);

2. A continuous decrease in pressure followed by an increase as the front passes; and

3. A shift in the wind direction, speed, or both.

**Figure 8-6.** Weather map symbols

ALL

**3422.** One of the most easily recognized discontinuities across a front is

A—a change in temperature.
B—an increase in cloud coverage.
C—an increase in relative humidity.

*Temperature is one of the most easily recognized discontinuities across a front. (PLT511, PA.I.C.K3e, PH.I.C.K3e) — FAA-H-8083-28*

*Answer (B) is incorrect because cloud coverage is not always present across a front. Answer (C) is incorrect because relative humidity is not an easily recognized discontinuity across a front.*

ALL

**3423.** One weather phenomenon which will always occur when flying across a front is a change in the

A—wind direction.
B—type of precipitation.
C—stability of the air mass.

*Wind direction always changes across a front. (PLT511, PA.I.C.K3e, PH.I.C.K3e) — FAA-H-8083-28*

*Answer (B) is incorrect because precipitation does not always exist with a front. Answer (C) is incorrect because the stability on both sides of the front may be the same.*

**Answers**

3422  [A]          3423  [A]

GLI

**3451.** During which period is a sea breeze front most suitable for soaring flight?

A—Shortly after sunrise.
B—During the early forenoon.
C—During the afternoon.

*A sea breeze begins during early afternoon and reaches a maximum in the afternoon, subsiding around dusk. (PLT516) — FAA-H-8083-28*

# Stability of the Atmosphere

**Atmospheric stability** is defined as the resistance of the atmosphere to vertical motion. A stable atmosphere resists any upward or downward movement. An unstable atmosphere allows an upward or downward disturbance to grow into a vertical (convective) current.

Determining the stability of the atmosphere requires measuring the difference between the actual existing (ambient) temperature lapse rate of a given parcel of air and the dry adiabatic (3°C per 1,000 feet) lapse rate.

A stable layer of air would be associated with a temperature inversion. Warming from below, on the other hand, would decrease the stability of an air mass.

The conditions shown in Figure 8-7 can be characteristic of stable or unstable air masses.

| Unstable Air | Stable Air |
|---|---|
| Cumuliform clouds | Stratiform clouds and fog |
| Showery precipitation | Continuous precipitation |
| Rough air (turbulence) | Smooth air |
| Good visibility except in blowing obstructions | Fair to poor visibility in haze and smoke |

**Figure 8-7**

ALL

**3385.** Which weather conditions should be expected beneath a low-level temperature inversion layer when the relative humidity is high?

A—Smooth air, poor visibility, fog, haze, or low clouds.
B—Light wind shear, poor visibility, haze, and light rain.
C—Turbulent air, poor visibility, fog, low stratus type clouds, and showery precipitation.

*A ground-based inversion leads to poor visibility by trapping fog, smoke, and other restrictions into low levels of the atmosphere. The layer is stable and convection is suppressed. (PLT301, PA.I.C.K3a, PH.I.C.K3a) — FAA-H-8083-28*

*Answer (B) is incorrect because wind shear would occur above the inversion. Answer (C) is incorrect because showery precipitation and turbulent air are not associated with the presence of a low-level temperature inversion.*

ALL

**3403.** What measurement can be used to determine the stability of the atmosphere?

A—Atmospheric pressure.
B—Actual lapse rate.
C—Surface temperature.

*The difference between the existing lapse rate of a given mass of air and the adiabatic rates of cooling in upward moving air determines if the air is stable or unstable. (PLT173, PA.I.C.K3a, PH.I.C.K3a) — FAA-H-8083-28*

ALL

**3404.** What would decrease the stability of an air mass?

A—Warming from below.
B—Cooling from below.
C—Decrease in water vapor.

*When air near the surface is warm and moist, suspect instability. Surface heating, cooling aloft, converging or upslope winds, or an invading mass of colder air may lead to instability and cumuliform clouds. (PLT173, PA.I.C.K3a, PH.I.C.K3a) — FAA-H-8083-28*

*Answer (B) is incorrect because cooling from the air below would increase the stability of the air. Answer (C) is incorrect because an increase in water vapor will result in a decrease in stability.*

**Answers**

| | | | | | | | |
|---|---|---|---|---|---|---|---|
| 3451 | [C] | 3385 | [A] | 3403 | [B] | 3404 | [A] |

ALL, SPO

**3405.** What is a characteristic of stable air?

A—Stratiform clouds.
B—Unlimited visibility.
C—Cumulus clouds.

*Since stable air resists convection, clouds in stable air form in horizontal, sheet-like layers or "strata." (PLT173, PA.I.C.K3a, PH.I.C.K3a) — FAA-H-8083-28*

Answers (B) and (C) are incorrect because unlimited visibility and cumulus clouds are characteristics of unstable air.

ALL

**3408.** What feature is associated with a temperature inversion?

A—A stable layer of air.
B—An unstable layer of air.
C—Chinook winds on mountain slopes.

*If the temperature increases with altitude through a layer (an inversion), the layer is stable and convection is suppressed. (PLT492, PA.I.C.K3a, PH.I.C.K3a) — FAA-H-8083-28*

ALL, SPO

**3412.** What are characteristics of a moist, unstable air mass?

A—Cumuliform clouds and showery precipitation.
B—Poor visibility and smooth air.
C—Stratiform clouds and showery precipitation.

*Characteristics of a moist, unstable air mass include cumuliform clouds, showery precipitation, rough air (turbulence), and good visibility (except in blowing obstructions). (PLT511, PA.I.C.K3a, PH.I.C.K3a) — FAA-H-8083-28*

ALL

**3413.** What are characteristics of unstable air?

A—Turbulence and good surface visibility.
B—Turbulence and poor surface visibility.
C—Nimbostratus clouds and good surface visibility.

*Characteristics of an unstable air mass include cumuliform clouds, showery precipitation, rough air (turbulence), and good visibility (except in blowing obstructions). (PLT511, PA.I.C.K3a, PH.I.C.K3a) — FAA-H-8083-28*

ALL

**3414.** A stable air mass is most likely to have which characteristic?

A—Showery precipitation.
B—Turbulent air.
C—Poor surface visibility.

*Characteristics of a stable air mass include stratiform clouds and fog, continuous precipitation, smooth air, and fair to poor visibility in haze and smoke. (PLT511, PA.I.C.K3a, PH.I.C.K3a) — FAA-H-8083-25*

# Clouds

Stability determines which of two types of clouds will be formed: cumuliform or stratiform.

**Cumuliform** clouds are the billowy-type clouds having considerable vertical development, which enhances the growth rate of precipitation. They are formed in unstable conditions, and they produce showery precipitation made up of large water droplets. See Figure 8-8.

**Stratiform** clouds are the flat, more evenly based clouds formed in stable conditions. They produce steady, continuous light rain and drizzle made up of much smaller raindrops. See Figure 8-9.

Steady precipitation (in contrast to showery) preceding a front is an indication of stratiform clouds with little or no turbulence.

Clouds are divided into four families according to their height range: low, middle, high, and clouds with extensive vertical development. See Figure 8-10.

The first three families—low, middle, and high—are further classified according to the way they are formed. Clouds formed by vertical currents (unstable) are cumulus (heap) and are billowy in appearance. Clouds formed by the cooling of a stable layer are stratus (layered) and are flat and sheet-like in appearance. A further classification is the prefix "nimbo-" or suffix "-nimbus," which means raincloud.

**Answers**

| | | | | |
|---|---|---|---|---|
| 3405 [A] | 3408 [A] | 3412 [A] | 3413 [A] | 3414 [C] |

**Figure 8-8.** Cumulus clouds

**Figure 8-9.** Stratiform clouds

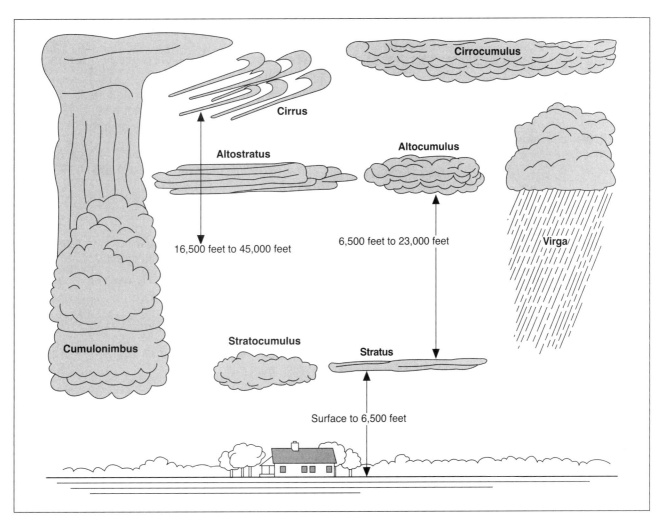

**Figure 8-10.** Cloud families

High clouds, called **cirrus**, are composed mainly of ice crystals; therefore, they are least likely to contribute to structural icing (since it requires water droplets).

The base of a cloud (AGL) that is formed by vertical currents (cumuliform clouds) can be roughly calculated by dividing the difference between the surface temperature and dew point by 4.4 and multiplying the rounded result by 1,000. The convergence of the temperature and the dew point lapse rate is 4.4°F per 1,000 feet.

**Problem:** What is the approximate base of the cumulus clouds if the surface air temperature is 70°F and the dew point is 61°F?

**Solution:**

Use the following steps:

1.   70°F  (Temperature)
   − 61°F  (Dew point)
      9°F

2. 9 ÷ 4.4 = 2.05 or 2

3. 2 × 1,000 = 2,000 feet AGL (base of cloud)

ALL

**3406.** When warm, moist, stable air flows upslope, it

A—produces stratus type clouds.
B—causes showers and thunderstorms.
C—develops convective turbulence.

*When stable air is forced upward the air tends to retain horizontal flow and any cloudiness is flat and stratified. (PLT192, PA.I.C.K3f, PH.I.C.K3f) — FAA-H-8083-28*

ALL, SPO

**3407.** If an unstable air mass is forced upward, what type clouds can be expected?

A—Stratus clouds with little vertical development.
B—Stratus clouds with considerable associated turbulence.
C—Clouds with considerable vertical development and associated turbulence.

*When unstable air is forced upward, the disturbance grows. Any resulting cloudiness shows extensive vertical development. (PLT192, PA.I.C.K3f, PH.I.C.K3f) — FAA-H-8083-28*

ALL

**3424.** Steady precipitation preceding a front is an indication of

A—stratiform clouds with moderate turbulence.
B—cumuliform clouds with little or no turbulence.
C—stratiform clouds with little or no turbulence.

*Precipitation from stratiform clouds is usually steady and there is little or no turbulence. (PLT511, PA.I.C.K3f, PH.I.C.K3f) — FAA-H-8083-28*

ALL

**3433.** The conditions necessary for the formation of cumulonimbus clouds are a lifting action and

A—unstable air containing an excess of condensation nuclei.
B—unstable, moist air.
C—either stable or unstable air.

*For a cumulonimbus cloud or thunderstorm to form, the air must have:*

1. *Sufficient water vapor,*

2. *An unstable lapse rate, and*

3. *An initial upward boost (lifting) to start the storm process in motion.*

*(PLT192, PA.I.C.K3f, PH.I.C.K3f) — FAA-H-8083-28*

**Answers**

3406   [A]         3407   [C]         3424   [C]         3433   [B]

ALL
**3409.** What is the approximate base of the cumulus clouds if the surface air temperature at 1,000 feet MSL is 70°F and the dew point is 48°F?

A—4,000 feet MSL.
B—5,000 feet MSL.
C—6,000 feet MSL.

*When lifted, unsaturated air cools at approximately 5.4°F per 1,000 feet. The dew point cools at approximately 1°F per 1,000 feet. Therefore, the convergence of the temperature and dew point lapse rates is 4.4°F per 1,000 feet. The base of a cloud (AGL) that is formed by vertical currents can be roughly calculated by dividing the difference between the surface temperature and the dew point by 4.4 and multiplying the rounded result by 1,000.*

1.  70°F surface temperature
    – 48°F dew point
    —————
    22°F

2.  22 ÷ 4.4 = 5

3.  5 × 1,000 = 5,000 feet AGL

4.   5,000 feet AGL
    + 1,000 feet field elevation
    ——————
     6,000 feet MSL

*(PLT512, PA.I.C.K3f, PH.I.C.K3f) — FAA-H-8083-28*


ALL
**3410.** At approximately what altitude above the surface would the pilot expect the base of cumuliform clouds if the surface air temperature is 82°F and the dew point is 38°F?

A—9,000 feet AGL.
B—10,000 feet AGL.
C—11,000 feet AGL.

*When lifted, unsaturated air cools at approximately 5.4°F per 1,000 feet. The dew point cools at approximately 1°F per 1,000 feet. Therefore, the convergence of the temperature and dew point lapse rates is 4.4°F per 1,000 feet. The base of a cloud (AGL) that is formed by vertical currents can be roughly calculated by dividing the difference between the surface temperature and the dew point by 4.4 and multiplying the rounded result by 1,000.*

1.  82°F surface temperature
    – 38°F dew point
    —————
    44°F

2.  44 ÷ 4.4 = 10

3.  10 × 1,000 = 10,000 feet AGL

*(PLT512, PA.I.C.K3f, PH.I.C.K3f) — FAA-H-8083-28*


ALL, SPO
**3415.** The suffix "nimbus," used in naming clouds, means

A—a cloud with extensive vertical development.
B—a rain cloud.
C—a middle cloud containing ice pellets.

*The prefix "nimbo-" or suffix "-nimbus" means rain cloud. (PLT192, PA.I.C.K3f, PH.I.C.K3f) — FAA-H-8083-28*


ALL
**3416.** Clouds are divided into four families according to their

A—outward shape.
B—height range.
C—composition.

*For identification purposes, clouds are divided into four families: high clouds, middle clouds, low clouds, and clouds with extensive vertical development. (PLT192, PA.I.C.K3f, PH.I.C.K3f) — FAA-H-8083-28*


**Answers**

3409   [C]          3410   [B]          3415   [B]          3416   [B]

# Turbulence

Cumulus clouds are formed by convective currents (heating from below); therefore, a pilot can expect turbulence below or inside cumulus clouds, especially towering cumulus clouds. The greatest turbulence could be expected inside cumulonimbus clouds.

If severe turbulence is encountered either inside or outside of clouds, the airplane's airspeed should be reduced to maneuvering speed and the pilot should attempt to maintain a level flight attitude because the amount of excess load that can be imposed on the wing will be decreased. Any attempt to maintain a constant altitude will greatly increase the stresses that are applied to the aircraft.

ALL

**3419.** What clouds have the greatest turbulence?

A—Towering cumulus.
B—Cumulonimbus.
C—Nimbostratus.

*Cumulonimbus are the ultimate manifestation of instability. They are vertically developed clouds of large dimensions with dense boiling tops, often crowned with thick veils of dense cirrus (the anvil). Nearly the entire spectrum of flying hazards are contained in these clouds including violent turbulence. (PLT192, PA.I.C.K3g, PH.I.C.K3g) — FAA-H-8083-28*

ALL

**3417.** An almond or lens-shaped cloud which appears stationary, but which may contain winds of 50 knots or more, is referred to as

A—an inactive frontal cloud.
B—a funnel cloud.
C—a lenticular cloud.

*Crests of standing waves may be marked by stationary, lens-shaped clouds known as standing lenticular clouds. (PLT192, PA.I.C.K3g, PH.I.C.K3g) — FAA-H-8083-28*

ALL

**3418.** Crests of standing mountain waves may be marked by stationary, lens-shaped clouds known as

A—mammatocumulus clouds.
B—standing lenticular clouds.
C—roll clouds.

*Crests of standing waves may be marked by stationary, lens-shaped clouds known as standing lenticular clouds. (PLT192, PA.I.C.K3g, PH.I.C.K3g) — FAA-H-8083-28*

ALL, SPO

**3420.** What cloud types would indicate convective turbulence?

A—Cirrus clouds.
B—Nimbostratus clouds.
C—Towering cumulus clouds.

*Towering cumulus signifies a relatively deep layer of unstable air. They show considerable vertical development and have billowing cauliflower tops. Showers can result from these clouds. Expect very strong turbulence, and perhaps some clear icing above the freezing level. (PLT192, PA.I.C.K3g, PH.I.C.K3g) — FAA-H-8083-28*

ALL

**3425.** Possible mountain wave turbulence could be anticipated when winds of 40 knots or greater blow

A—across a mountain ridge, and the air is stable.
B—down a mountain valley, and the air is unstable.
C—parallel to a mountain peak, and the air is stable.

*Always anticipate possible mountain wave turbulence when strong winds of 40 knots or greater blow across a mountain or ridge and the air is stable. (PLT263, PA.I.C.K3g, PH.I.C.K3g) — FAA-H-8083-28*

SPO

**2159.** One of the most dangerous features of mountain waves is the turbulent areas in and

A—below rotor clouds.
B—above rotor clouds.
C—below lenticular clouds.

*Rotor clouds appear to remain stationary, parallel the range, and stand a few miles leeward of the mountains. Turbulence is most frequent and most severe in and below the standing rotors just beneath the wave crests at or below mountaintop levels. (PLT501) — FAA-H-8083-28*

**Answers**

| | | | | | |
|---|---|---|---|---|---|
| 3419 [B] | 3417 [C] | 3418 [B] | 3420 [C] | 3425 [A] | 2159 [A] |

ALL
**3442.** Upon encountering severe turbulence, which flight condition should the pilot attempt to maintain?

A—Constant altitude and airspeed.
B—Constant angle of attack.
C—Level flight attitude.

*The primary concern is to avoid undue stress on the airframe. This can best be done by attempting to maintain a constant attitude while keeping the airspeed below design maneuvering speed (V$_A$). (PLT263, PA.I.C.K3g, PH.I.C.K3g) — FAA-H-8083-28*

Answer (A) is incorrect because attempting to maintain a constant altitude or airspeed may result in overstressing the aircraft. Answer (B) is incorrect because a constant angle of attack would be impossible to maintain with the wind shear and shifts encountered in severe turbulence.

# Thunderstorms

Thunderstorms present many hazards to flying. Three conditions necessary to the formation of a thunderstorm are:

1. Sufficient water vapor;
2. An unstable lapse rate; and
3. An initial upward boost (lifting).

The initial upward boost can be caused by heating from below, frontal lifting, or by mechanical lifting (wind blowing air upslope on a mountain).

There are three stages of a thunderstorm: the cumulus, mature, and dissipating stages. See Figure 8-11.

The **cumulus stage** is characterized by continuous updrafts, and these updrafts create low-pressure areas. Thunderstorms reach their greatest intensity during the **mature stage**, which is characterized by updrafts and downdrafts inside the cloud. Precipitation inside the cloud aids in the development of these downdrafts, and the start of rain from the base of the cloud signals the beginning of the mature stage. The precipitation that evaporates before it reaches the ground is called **virga**. The **dissipating stage** of a thunderstorm is characterized predominantly by downdrafts.

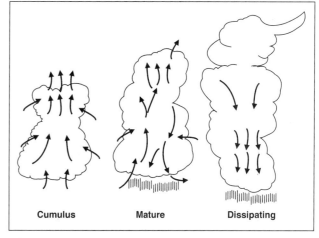

**Figure 8-11.** Stages of thunderstorms

**Lightning** is always associated with a thunderstorm.

**Hail** is formed inside thunderstorms by the constant freezing, melting, and refreezing of water as it is carried about by up- and downdrafts.

A pilot should always expect the hazardous and invisible atmospheric phenomena called **wind shear turbulence** when operating anywhere near a thunderstorm (within 20 NM).

Thunderstorms that generally produce the most intense hazard to aircraft are called **squall line thunderstorms**. These non-frontal, narrow bands of thunderstorms often develop ahead of a cold front.

**Embedded thunderstorms** are those that are obscured by massive cloud layers and cannot be seen.

**Answers**

3442   [C]

ALL

**3434.** What feature is normally associated with the cumulus stage of a thunderstorm?

A—Roll cloud.
B—Continuous updraft.
C—Frequent lightning.

*The key feature of the cumulus stage is an updraft. Precipitation beginning to fall from the cloudbase is the signal that a downdraft has developed also and a cell has entered the mature stage. (PLT495, PA.I.C.K3h, PH.I.C.K3h) — FAA-H-8083-28*

Answer (A) is incorrect because a roll cloud is associated with a mountain wave. Answer (C) is incorrect because frequent lightning may be present in any stage.

ALL

**3435.** Which weather phenomenon signals the beginning of the mature stage of a thunderstorm?

A—The appearance of an anvil top.
B—Precipitation beginning to fall.
C—Maximum growth rate of the clouds.

*The key feature of the cumulus stage is an updraft. Precipitation beginning to fall from the cloudbase is the signal that a downdraft has developed also and the cell has entered the mature stage. (PLT495, PA.I.C.K3h, PH.I.C.K3h) — FAA-H-8083-28*

Answer (A) is incorrect because the appearance of an anvil top is characteristic of the dissipating stage. Answer (C) is incorrect because the maximum growth rate of the clouds is during the mature stage of a thunderstorm, but it does not signal the beginning of that stage.

ALL, SPO

**3436.** What conditions are necessary for the formation of thunderstorms?

A—High humidity, lifting force, and unstable conditions.
B—High humidity, high temperature, and cumulus clouds.
C—Lifting force, moist air, and extensive cloud cover.

*For a cumulonimbus cloud or thunderstorm to form, the air must have:*

*1. Sufficient water vapor;*

*2. An unstable lapse rate; and*

*3. An initial upward boost (lifting) to start the storm process in motion.*

*(PLT495, PA.I.C.K3h, PH.I.C.K3h) — FAA-H-8083-28*

ALL

**3437.** During the life cycle of a thunderstorm, which stage is characterized predominately by downdrafts?

A—Cumulus.
B—Dissipating.
C—Mature.

*Downdrafts characterize the dissipating stage of the thunderstorm cell and the storm dies rapidly. (PLT495, PA.I.C.K3h, PH.I.C.K3h) — FAA-H-8083-28*

Answer (A) is incorrect because updrafts occur during the cumulus stage. Answer (C) is incorrect because both updrafts and downdrafts occur during the mature stage.

ALL, SPO

**3438.** Thunderstorms reach their greatest intensity during the

A—mature stage.
B—downdraft stage.
C—cumulus stage.

*All thunderstorm hazards reach their greatest intensity during the mature stage. (PLT495, PA.I.C.K3h, PH.I.C.K3h) — FAA-H-8083-28*

ALL, SPO

**3439.** Thunderstorms which generally produce the most intense hazard to aircraft are

A—squall line thunderstorms.
B—steady-state thunderstorms.
C—warm front thunderstorms.

*A squall line is a non-frontal, narrow band of active thunderstorms. The line may be too long to easily detour and too wide and severe to penetrate. It often contains severe steady-state thunderstorms and presents the single, most intense weather hazard to aircraft. (PLT495, PA.I.C.K3h, PH.I.C.K3h) — FAA-H-8083-28*

ALL, SPO

**3521.** The mature stage of a thunderstorm begins with

A—formation of the anvil top.
B—the start of precipitation.
C—continuous downdrafts.

*The mature stage of a thunderstorm is characterized by updrafts and downdrafts inside the cloud and the start of rain. (PLT495, PA.I.C.K3h, PH.I.C.K3h) — FAA-H-8083-28*

Answer (A) is incorrect because this represents the cumulus stage. Answer (C) is incorrect because this represents the dissipating stage.

**Answers**

| 3434 | [B] | 3435 | [B] | 3436 | [A] | 3437 | [B] | 3438 | [A] | 3439 | [A] |
| 3521 | [B] | | | | | | | | | | |

ALL

**3440.** A nonfrontal, narrow band of active thunderstorms that often develop ahead of a cold front is known as a

A—prefrontal system.
B—squall line.
C—dry line.

*A squall line is a nonfrontal, narrow band of active thunderstorms. The line may be too long to easily detour and too wide and severe to penetrate. It often contains severe steady-state thunderstorms and presents the single, most intense weather hazard to aircraft. (PLT495, PA.I.C.K3h, PH.I.C.K3h) — FAA-H-8083-28*

ALL

**3441.** If there is thunderstorm activity in the vicinity of an airport at which you plan to land, which hazardous atmospheric phenomenon might be expected on the landing approach?

A—Precipitation static.
B—Wind shear turbulence.
C—Steady rain.

*Wind shear is an invisible hazard associated with all thunderstorms. Shear turbulence has been encountered 20 miles laterally from a severe storm. (PLT495, PA.I.C.K3h, PH.I.C.K3h) — FAA-H-8083-28*

Answer (A) is incorrect because precipitation static is not considered a hazardous atmospheric phenomenon. Answer (C) is incorrect because showery precipitation is a characteristic of thunderstorm activity.

ALL

**3452.** Which weather phenomenon is always associated with a thunderstorm?

A—Lightning.
B—Heavy rain.
C—Hail.

*A thunderstorm is, in general, a local storm invariably produced by a cumulonimbus cloud, and is always accompanied by lightning and thunder. (PLT495, PA.I.C.K3h, PH.I.C.K3h) — FAA-H-8083-28*

GLI, LSG

**3449.** Which is considered to be the most hazardous condition when soaring in the vicinity of thunderstorms?

A—Static electricity.
B—Lightning.
C—Wind shear and turbulence.

*During the mature stage of a thunderstorm, updrafts and downdrafts in close proximity create strong vertical shears and a very turbulent environment. A lightning strike can puncture the skin of an aircraft and damage communication and navigation equipment. (PLT120) — FAA-H-8083-28*

**Answers**

| 3440 | [B] | 3441 | [B] | 3452 | [A] | 3449 | [C] |

# Wind Shear

Wind shear is defined as a change in wind direction and/or speed over a very short distance in the atmosphere. This can occur at any level of the atmosphere and can be detected by the pilot as a sudden change in airspeed.

**Low-level** (low-altitude) **wind shear** can be expected during strong temperature inversions, on all sides of a thunderstorm and directly below the cell. A pilot can expect a wind shear zone in a temperature inversion whenever the wind speed at 2,000 feet to 4,000 feet above the surface is at least 25 knots.

Low-level wind shear can also be found near frontal activity because winds can be significantly different in the two air masses which meet to form the front.

In warm front conditions, the most critical period is before the front passes. Warm front shear may exist below 5,000 feet for about 6 hours before surface passage of the front. The wind shear associated with a warm front is usually more extreme than that found in cold fronts.

The shear associated with cold fronts is usually found behind the front. If the front is moving at 30 knots or more, the shear zone will be 5,000 feet above the surface 3 hours after frontal passage.

Basically, there are two potentially hazardous shear situations—the loss of a tailwind or the loss of a headwind.

A tailwind may shear to either a calm or headwind component. The airspeed initially increases, the aircraft pitches up, and altitude increases. Lower than normal power would be required initially, followed by a further decrease as the shear is encountered, and then an increase as the glide slope is regained. See Figure 8-12.

A headwind may shear to a calm or tailwind component. Initially, the airspeed decreases, the aircraft pitches down, and altitude decreases. See Figure 8-13.

Some airports can report boundary winds as well as the wind at the tower. When a tower reports a boundary wind which is significantly different from the airport wind, there is a possibility of hazardous wind shear.

**Figure 8-12.** Tailwind shearing to headwind or calm

**Figure 8-13.** Headwind shearing to tailwind or calm

ALL, SPO

**3426.** Where does wind shear occur?

A—Only at higher altitudes.
B—Only at lower altitudes.
C—At all altitudes, in all directions.

*Wind shear may be associated with either a wind shift or a wind speed gradient at any level in the atmosphere. (PLT518, PA.I.C.K3b, PH.I.C.K3b) — FAA-H-8083-28*

ALL, SPO

**3427.** When may hazardous wind shear be expected?

A—When stable air crosses a mountain barrier where it tends to flow in layers forming lenticular clouds.
B—In areas of low-level temperature inversion, frontal zones, and clear air turbulence.
C—Following frontal passage when stratocumulus clouds form indicating mechanical mixing.

*Hazardous wind shear can occur near the ground with either thunderstorms or a strong temperature inversion. (PLT518, PA.I.C.K3b, PH.I.C.K3b) — FAA-H-8083-28*

*Answer (A) is incorrect because turbulence can be expected when stable air crosses a mountain barrier. Answer (C) is incorrect because turbulence can be expected following frontal passage when stratocumulus clouds form, indicating mechanical mixing.*

ALL, SPO

**3428.** A pilot can expect a wind shear zone in a temperature inversion whenever the windspeed at 2,000 to 4,000 feet above the surface is at least

A—10 knots.
B—15 knots.
C—25 knots.

*An increase in temperature with altitude is defined as a temperature inversion. A pilot can be relatively certain of a shear zone in the inversion if the pilot knows the wind at 2,000 to 4,000 feet is 25 knots or more. (PLT518, PA.I.C.K3b, PH.I.C.K3b) — FAA-H-8083-28*

SPO

**2163.** If a temperature inversion is encountered immediately after takeoff or during an approach to a landing, a potential hazard exists due to

A—wind shear.
B—strong surface winds.
C—strong convective currents.

*When taking off or landing in calm wind under clear skies within a few hours before or after sunrise, be prepared for a temperature inversion near the ground. You can be relatively certain of a shear zone in the inversion if you know the wind at 2,000 to 4,000 feet is 25 knots or more. Allow a margin of airspeed above normal climb or approach speed to alleviate danger of stall in event of turbulence or sudden change in wind velocity. (PLT518) — FAA-H-8083-28*

# Icing

Structural icing occurs on an aircraft whenever supercooled condensed droplets of water make contact with any part of the aircraft that is also at a temperature below freezing. An inflight condition necessary for structural icing to form is visible moisture (clouds or raindrops).

Icing in precipitation (rain) is of concern to the VFR pilot because it can occur outside of clouds. Aircraft structural ice will most likely have the highest accumulation in freezing rain which indicates warmer temperature at a higher altitude. See Figure 8-14 on the next page. The effects of structural icing on an aircraft may be seen in Figure 8-15.

The presence of ice pellets at the surface is evidence that there is freezing rain at a higher altitude, while wet snow indicates that the temperature at your altitude is above freezing. A situation conducive to any icing would be flying in the vicinity of a front.

**Answers**

| | | | | | | | |
|---|---|---|---|---|---|---|---|
| 3426 | [C] | 3427 | [B] | 3428 | [C] | 2163 | [A] |

**Clear – Hard and Glossy**
Temperature 0° to -15°C
Large water droplets
Cumuliform clouds

**Rime – Brittle and Frost-like**
Temperature 0° to -10°C
Small water droplets
Stratiform clouds

**Figure 8-14.** Clear and rime ice

Lift lessens

Drag increases

Thrust falls off

Weight grows
Stalling speed increases

**Effects of icing are cumulative**

**Figure 8-15.** Effects of structural icing

ALL
**3402.** The presence of ice pellets at the surface is evidence that there

A—are thunderstorms in the area.
B—has been cold frontal passage.
C—is a temperature inversion with freezing rain at a higher altitude.

*Ice pellets always indicate freezing rain at higher altitude. (PLT301, PA.I.C.K3i, PH.I.C.K3i) — FAA-H-8083-28*

AIR, GLI, RTC, WSC, PPC
**3429.** One inflight condition necessary for structural icing to form is

A—small temperature/dew point spread.
B—stratiform clouds.
C—visible moisture.

*Two conditions are necessary for structural icing in flight:*

1. *The aircraft must be flying through visible water such as rain or cloud droplets; and*

2. *The temperature at the point where the moisture strikes the aircraft must be 0°C (32°F) or colder.*

*(PLT274, PA.I.C.K3i, PH.I.C.K3i) — FAA-H-8083-28*

AIR, GLI, RTC, WSC, PPC
**3430.** In which environment is aircraft structural ice most likely to have the highest accumulation rate?

A—Cumulus clouds with below freezing temperatures.
B—Freezing drizzle.
C—Freezing rain.

*A condition favorable for rapid accumulation of clear icing is freezing rain below a frontal surface. (PLT274, PA.I.C.K3i, PH.I.C.K3i) — FAA-H-8083-28*

Answers (A) and (B) are incorrect because although cumulus clouds with below-freezing temperatures and freezing drizzle are conducive to structural icing, they will not have as high an accumulation rate as freezing rain.

ALL
**3956.** During a cross-country flight you picked up rime icing which you estimate is 1/2" thick on the leading edge of the wings. You are now below the clouds at 2,000 feet AGL and are approaching your destination airport under VFR. Visibility under the clouds is more than 10 miles, winds at the destination airport are 8 knots right down the runway, and the surface temperature is 3°C. You decide to:

A—use a faster than normal approach and landing speed.
B—approach and land at your normal speed since the ice is not thick enough to have any noticeable effect.
C—fly your approach slower than normal to lessen the wind chill effect and break up the ice.

*Ice will accumulate unevenly on the airplane. It will add weight and drag, and decrease thrust and lift. With ice accumulations, landing approaches should be made with a minimum wing flap setting and with an added margin of airspeed. Sudden and large configuration and airspeed changes should be avoided. (PLT128, PA.I.C.K3i, PH.I.C.K3i) — FAA-H-8083-3*

Answer (B) is incorrect because ice having a thickness similar to sandpaper on the leading edge and upper surface of a wing can reduce wing lift by as much as 30 percent and increase drag by 40 percent. Answer (C) is incorrect because ice will increase drag, requiring additional lift (airspeed); wind chill effect cannot be relied upon to melt/remove the ice that has already accumulated; flying slower than normal increases the possibility of a stall due to the decreased lift.

**Answers**

3402   [C]      3429   [C]      3430   [C]      3956   [A]

# Fog

Fog is a surface-based cloud (restricting visibility) composed of either water droplets or ice crystals. Fog may form by cooling the air to its dew point or by adding moisture to the air near the ground. A small temperature/dew point spread is essential to the formation of fog. An abundance of condensation nuclei from combustion products makes fog prevalent in industrial areas.

Fog is classified by the way it is formed.

**Radiation fog (ground fog)** is formed when terrestrial radiation cools the ground, which in turn cools the air in contact with it. When the air is cooled to its dew point (or within a few degrees), fog will form. This fog will form most readily in warm, moist air over low, flatland areas on clear, calm (no wind) nights.

**Advection fog (sea fog)** is formed when warm, moist air moves (wind is required) over colder ground or water (e.g., an air mass moving inland from the coast in winter).

**Upslope fog** is formed when moist, stable air is cooled to its dew point as it moves (wind is required) up sloping terrain. Cooling will be at the dry adiabatic lapse rate of approximately 3°C per 1,000 feet.

**Precipitation (rain or drizzle) induced fog** is most commonly associated with frontal activity and is formed by relatively warm drizzle or rain falling through cooler air. Evaporation from the precipitation saturates the cool air and fog forms. This fog is especially critical because it occurs in the proximity of precipitation and other possible hazards such as icing, turbulence, and thunderstorms.

**Steam fog** forms in the winter when cold, dry air passes from land areas over comparatively warm ocean waters. Low-level turbulence can occur and icing can become hazardous in a steam fog.

ALL
**3443.** What situation is most conducive to the formation of radiation fog?

A—Warm, moist air over low, flatland areas on clear, calm nights.
B—Moist, tropical air moving over cold, offshore water.
C—The movement of cold air over much warmer water.

*Conditions favorable for radiation fog are clear sky, little or no wind, and small temperature/dew point spread (high relative humidity). Radiation fog is restricted to land because water surfaces cool little from nighttime radiation. (PLT226, PA.I.C.K3j, PH.I.C.K3j) — FAA-H-8083-28*

*Answers (B) and (C) are incorrect because radiation fog will not form over water since water surfaces cool little from nighttime radiation.*

ALL
**3445.** In which situation is advection fog most likely to form?

A—A warm, moist air mass on the windward side of mountains.
B—An air mass moving inland from the coast in winter.
C—A light breeze blowing colder air out to sea.

*Advection fog forms when moist air moves over colder ground or water. It is most common along coastal areas. This fog frequently forms offshore as a result of cold water, then is carried inland by the wind. (PLT226, PA.I.C.K3j, PH.I.C.K3j) — FAA-H-8083-28*

*Answer (A) is incorrect because a warm, moist air mass on the windward side of mountains will form upslope fog and/or rain. Answer (C) is incorrect because a light breeze blowing colder air out to sea will form steam fog.*

**Answers**

3443   [A]          3445   [B]

ALL

**3446.** What types of fog depend upon wind in order to exist?

A—Radiation fog and ice fog.
B—Steam fog and ground fog.
C—Advection fog and upslope fog.

*Advection fog forms when moist air moves over colder ground or water. It is most common along coastal areas, but often develops deep in continental areas. Advection fog deepens as wind speed increases up to about 15 knots. Wind much stronger than 15 knots lifts the fog into a layer of low stratus or stratocumulus. Upslope fog forms as a result of moist, stable air being cooled adiabatically as it moves up sloping terrain. Once upslope wind ceases, the fog dissipates. (PLT226, PA.I.C.K3j, PH.I.C.K3j) — FAA-H-8083-28*

*Answer (A) is incorrect because radiation fog and ice fog do not depend upon wind in order to exist. Answer (B) is incorrect because ground fog does not depend on wind in order to exist.*

ALL

**3447.** Low-level turbulence can occur and icing can become hazardous in which type of fog?

A—Rain-induced fog.
B—Upslope fog.
C—Steam fog.

*Steam fog forms in the winter when cold, dry air passes from land areas over comparatively warm ocean waters. Low-level turbulence can occur and icing can become hazardous in a steam fog. (PLT226, PA.I.C.K3j, PH.I.C.K3j) — FAA-H-8083-28*

# Frost

Frost is described as ice deposits formed by sublimation on a surface when the temperature of the collecting surface is at or below the dew point of the adjacent air and the dew point is below freezing.

Frost causes early airflow separation on an airfoil resulting in a loss of lift. Therefore, all frost should be removed from the lifting surfaces of an airplane before flight or it may prevent the airplane from becoming airborne.

ALL

**3401.** Which conditions result in the formation of frost?

A—The temperature of the collecting surface is at or below freezing when small droplets of moisture fall on the surface.
B—The temperature of the collecting surface is at or below the dew point of the adjacent air and the dew point is below freezing.
C—The temperature of the surrounding air is at or below freezing when small drops of moisture fall on the collecting surface.

*Frost forms in much the same way as dew. The difference is that the dew point of surrounding air must be colder than freezing. (PLT493, PA.I.C.K3k, PH.I.C.K3k) — FAA-H-8083-28*

*Answers (A) and (C) are incorrect because ice will form in these situations.*

AIR

**3432.** How does frost affect the lifting surfaces of an airplane on takeoff?

A—Frost may prevent the airplane from becoming airborne at normal takeoff speed.
B—Frost will change the camber of the wing, increasing lift during takeoff.
C—Frost may cause the airplane to become airborne with a lower angle of attack at a lower indicated airspeed.

*The roughness of the surface of frost spoils the smooth flow of air, thus causing a slowing of the airflow. This slowing of the air causes early air flow separation over the affected airfoil, resulting in a loss of lift. Even a small amount of frost on airfoils may prevent an aircraft from becoming airborne at normal takeoff speed. (PLT128, PA.I.C.K3k, PH.I.C.K3k) — FAA-H-8083-28*

*Answer (B) is incorrect because frost does not change the basic aerodynamic shape of the airfoil. Answer (C) is incorrect because frost may prevent the aircraft from becoming airborne at normal takeoff speed and will not lower the angle of attack.*

**Answers**

3446 [C]        3447 [C]        3401 [B]        3432 [A]

AIR, GLI

**3206.** How will frost on the wings of an airplane affect takeoff performance?

A—Frost will disrupt the smooth flow of air over the wing, adversely affecting its lifting capability.

B—Frost will change the camber of the wing, increasing its lifting capability.

C—Frost will cause the airplane to become airborne with a higher angle of attack, decreasing the stall speed.

*The roughness of the surface of frost spoils the smooth flow of air, thus causing a slowing of the airflow. This slowing of the air causes early air flow separation over the affected airfoil, resulting in a loss of lift. Even a small amount of frost on airfoils may prevent an aircraft from becoming airborne at normal takeoff speed. (PLT134, PA.I.C.K3k, PH.I.C.K3k) — FAA-H-8083-25*

Answer (B) is incorrect because frost will not change the shape of the wing. Answer (C) is incorrect because frost on the wings of an airplane will increase the stall speed.

AIR, GLI, RTC, WSC, PPC

**3431.** Why is frost considered hazardous to flight?

A—Frost changes the basic aerodynamic shape of the airfoils, thereby increasing lift.

B—Frost slows the airflow over the airfoils, thereby increasing control effectiveness.

C—Frost spoils the smooth flow of air over the wings, thereby decreasing lifting capability.

*The roughness of the surface of frost spoils the smooth flow of air, thus causing a slowing of the airflow. This slowing of the air causes early air flow separation over the affected airfoil, resulting in a loss of lift. Even a small amount of frost on airfoils may prevent an aircraft from becoming airborne at normal takeoff speed. (PLT128, PA.I.C.K3k, PH.I.C.K3k) — FAA-H-8083-28*

Answer (A) is incorrect because frost does not change the basic aerodynamic shape of the airfoil, nor does it increase lift. Answer (B) is incorrect because frost does not have an effect on the control effectiveness.

SPO

**2170.** Which is true with respect to a high- or low-pressure system?

A—A high-pressure area or ridge is an area of rising air.

B—A low-pressure area or trough is an area of descending air.

C—A high-pressure area or ridge is an area of descending air.

*Highs and ridges are areas of descending air. (PLT517) — FAA-H-8083-28*

Answer (A) is incorrect because a high or ridge is an area of descending air. Answer (B) is incorrect because a low or trough is an area of rising air.

LSG

**2312.** During which period is a sea breeze front most suitable for soaring flight?

A—Shortly after sunrise.

B—During the middle of the morning.

C—During the afternoon.

*A sea breeze begins during early afternoon and reaches a maximum in the afternoon, subsiding around dusk. (PLT511) — FAA-H-8083-28*

**Answers**

| 3206 | [A] | 3431 | [C] | 2170 | [C] | 2312 | [C] |

# Chapter 9
# Weather Services

# Aviation Routine Weather Report (METAR)

An international weather reporting code is used for weather reports (METAR) and forecasts (TAFs) worldwide. The reports follow the format shown in Figure 9-1.

For aviation purposes, the ceiling is the lowest broken or overcast layer, or vertical visibility into an obscuration.

**Figure 9-1.** TAF/METAR weather card

ALL, SPO

**3462.** (Refer to Figure 12.) Which of the reporting stations have VFR weather?

A—All.
B—KINK, KBOI, and KJFK.
C—KINK, KBOI, and KLAX.

*IFR conditions are a ceiling less than 1,000 feet and/or visibility less than 3 miles.*

*KINK: Visibility is 15 statute miles and the sky is clear: VFR.*

*KBOI: Visibility is 30 statute miles and sky is scattered at 15,000 feet: VFR.*

*KLAX: Visibility is 6 statute miles with mist and the sky is scattered at 700 feet (SCT does not constitute a ceiling): VFR.*

*KMDW: Visibility is 1-1/2 statute miles with rain and the ceiling is overcast at 700 feet: IFR.*

*KJFK: Visibility is 1/2 statute mile with fog and the ceiling is overcast at 500 feet: IFR.*

*(PLT059, PA.I.C.K2, PH.I.C.K2a) — FAA-H-8083-28*

ALL, SPO

**3463.** For aviation purposes, ceiling is defined as the height above the Earth's surface of the

A—lowest reported obscuration and the highest layer of clouds reported as overcast.
B—lowest broken or overcast layer or vertical visibility into an obscuration.
C—lowest layer of clouds reported as scattered, broken, or thin.

*For aviation purposes, the ceiling is the lowest broken or overcast layer, or vertical visibility into an obscuration. (PLT026, PA.I.C.K2, PH.I.C.K2a) — FAA-H-8083-28*

ALL, SPO

**3464.** (Refer to Figure 12.) The wind direction and velocity at KJFK is from

A—180° true at 4 knots.
B—180° magnetic at 4 knots.
C—040° true at 18 knots.

*The wind is reported as a five-digit group (six digits if speed is over 99 knots). The first three digits is the direction the wind is blowing from rounded to the nearest tens of degrees relative to true north, or "VRB" if the direction is variable. The next two digits is the speed in knots, or if over 99 knots, the next three digits. If the wind is gusty, it is reported as a "G" after the speed followed by the highest gust reported. The abbreviation "KT" is appended to denote the use of knots for wind speed. The wind group for KJFK is 18004KT which means the wind is from 180° at 4 knots. (PLT059, PA.I.C.K2, PH.I.C.K2a) — FAA-H-8083-28*

ALL

**3465.** (Refer to Figure 12.) What are the wind conditions at Wink, Texas (KINK)?

A—Calm.
B—110° at 12 knots, gusts 18 knots.
C—111° at 2 knots, gusts 18 knots.

*The wind is reported as a five-digit group (six digits if speed is over 99 knots). The first three digits is the direction the wind is blowing from rounded to the nearest tens of degrees relative to true north, or "VRB" if the direction is variable. The next two digits is the speed in knots, or if over 99 knots, the next three digits. If the wind is gusty, it is reported as a "G" after the speed followed by the highest gust reported. The abbreviation "KT" is appended to denote the use of knots for wind speed. The wind group for KINK is 11012G18KT which means the wind is from 110° at 12 knots, with gusts to 18 knots. (PLT059, PA.I.C.K2, PH.I.C.K2a) — FAA-H-8083-28*

ALL

**3466.** (Refer to Figure 12.) The remarks section for KMDW has RAB35 listed. This entry means

A—blowing mist has reduced the visibility to 1-1/2 SM.
B—rain began at 1835Z.
C—the barometer has risen .35 "Hg.

*The entry RAB35 means that rain began 35 minutes past the hour. (PLT059, PA.I.C.K2, PH.I.C.K2a) — FAA-H-8083-28*

Answer (A) is incorrect because mist is reported as BR. Answer (C) is incorrect because there is no format for reporting a change in altimeter in a METAR.

**Answers**

| 3462 | [C] | 3463 | [B] | 3464 | [A] | 3465 | [B] | 3466 | [B] |

ALL

**3467.** (Refer to Figure 12.) What are the current conditions depicted for Chicago Midway Airport (KMDW)?

A—Sky 700 feet overcast, visibility 1-1/2 SM, rain

B—Sky 7000 feet overcast, visibility 1-1/2 SM, heavy rain

C—Sky 700 feet overcast, visibility 11, occasionally 2 SM, with rain.

*The current conditions at KMDW are 1-1/2 SM visibility (1-1/2 SM) with rain (RA), ceiling overcast at 700 feet (OVC007). (PLT059, PA.I.C.K2, PH.I.C.K2a) — FAA-H-8083-28*

# Pilot Weather Reports (PIREPs) (UA)

Aircraft in flight are the only means of directly observing cloud tops, icing, and turbulence; therefore, no observation is more timely than one made from the flight deck. While the FAA encourages pilots to report inflight weather, a report of any unforecast weather is required by regulation. A **PIREP** (identified by the letters "UA") is usually transmitted in a prescribed format. See Figure 9-2.

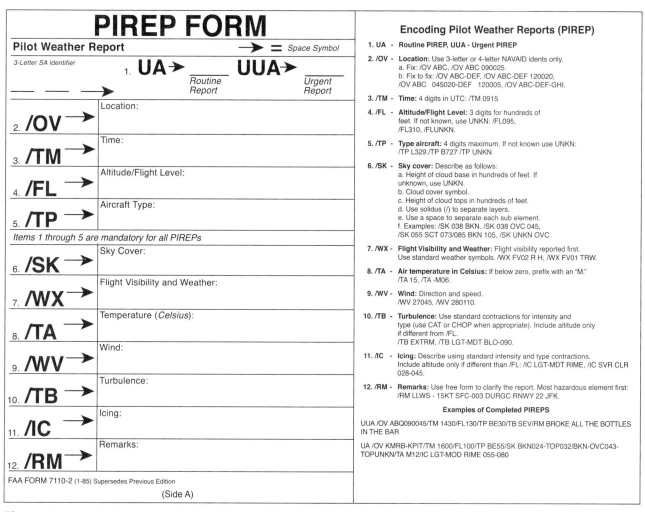

**Figure 9-2**

*(continued)*

UA/OV KOKC-KTUL/TM 1800/FL120/TP BE90/SK BKN018-TOP055/OVC072-TOP089/CLR ABV/TA M7/ WV 08021/TB LGT 055-072/IC LGT-MOD RIME 072-089.

Decodes as follows:

Pilot report, Oklahoma City to Tulsa at 1800Z at 12,000 feet.

Type of aircraft is a Beech King Air 90.

The first cloud layer has a base of 1,800 feet broken, with tops at 5,500 feet.

The second cloud layer base is 7,200 feet overcast with tops at 8,900 feet.

It is clear above.

Outside air temperature is -7° Celsius.

The wind is 080° at 21 knots.

There is light turbulence between 5,500 feet and 7,200 feet.

There is light to moderate rime icing reported between 7,200 feet and 8,900 feet.

ALL

**3472.** (Refer to Figure 14.) The base and tops of the overcast layer reported by a pilot are

A—1,800 feet MSL and 5,500 feet MSL.
B—5,500 feet AGL and 7,200 feet MSL.
C—7,200 feet MSL and 8,900 feet MSL.

*Cloud layers in a PIREP are found after the "SK" heading. Height of the cloud base is given in hundreds of feet, then the cloud cover symbol (SCT, BKN, etc.) is given, followed by the height of cloud tops in hundreds of feet. A diagonal slash is used to separate cloud layers.*

*The base of the broken (BKN) layer was reported to be 1,800 feet and tops at 5,500 feet (BKN018-TOP055).*

*The question is asking for the overcast (OVC) layer that has a reported base at 7,200 feet and tops at 8,900 feet. All cloud heights in a PIREP are MSL (OVC072-TOP089). (PLT061, PA.I.C.K2, PH.I.C.K2a) — FAA-H-8083-28*

ALL

**3473.** (Refer to Figure 14.) The wind and temperature at 12,000 feet MSL as reported by a pilot are

A—090° at 21 mph and -9°F.
B—090° at 21 knots and -9°C.
C—080° at 21 knots and -7°C.

*Winds are given after the "WV" heading. Wind direction is listed first, followed by wind speed in knots. WV 08021/ means wind from 080° at 21 knots. Air temperature is given in 2 digits, (in degrees Celsius), after the "TA" heading. If below zero, it will be prefixed with an "M." Therefore, /TA M7/ means that the outside air temperature is -7°C. (PLT061, PA.I.C.K2, PH.I.C.K2a) — FAA-H-8083-28*

ALL

**3474.** (Refer to Figure 14.) If the terrain elevation is 1,295 feet MSL, what is the height above ground level of the base of the ceiling?

A—505 feet AGL.
B—1,295 feet AGL.
C—6,586 feet AGL.

*Cloud layers in a PIREP are found after the "SK" heading. Height of the cloud base is given in hundreds of feet, then the cloud cover symbol (SCT, BKN, etc.) is given, followed by the height of the cloud tops in hundreds of feet. All cloud heights in a PIREP are MSL.*

*The first cloud layer was reported by a pilot to have bases at 1,800 feet and tops at 5,500 feet with broken (BKN) cloud cover (a broken cloud layer does constitute a ceiling).*

*If the field elevation is 1,295 feet MSL and the base of the first cloud layer (BKN) is 1,800 feet MSL, then the base of the ceiling is 505 feet AGL.*

$$\begin{array}{r} 1,800 \text{ MSL} \\ - 1,295 \text{ MSL} \\ \hline 505 \text{ AGL} \end{array}$$

*(PLT061, PA.I.C.K2, PH.I.C.K2a) — FAA-H-8083-28*

**Answers**

3472 [C]        3473 [C]        3474 [A]

ALL

**3475.** (Refer to Figure 14.) The intensity of the turbulence reported at a specific altitude is

A—moderate from 5,500 feet to 7,200 feet.
B—moderate at 5,500 feet and at 7,200 feet.
C—light from 5,500 feet to 7,200 feet.

*Turbulence in a PIREP is found after the "TB" heading. /TB LGT 055-072/ means light turbulence between 5,500 feet MSL and 7,200 feet MSL. (PLT061, PA.I.C.K2, PH.I.C.K2a) — FAA-H-8083-28*

ALL

**3476.** (Refer to Figure 14.) The intensity and type of icing reported by a pilot is

A—light to moderate.
B—light to moderate rime.
C—light to moderate clear.

*The intensity and type of icing is listed in a PIREP after the "IC" heading. /IC LGT-MOD RIME 072-089 means light (LGT) to moderate (MOD) rime icing from 7,200 feet MSL to 8,900 feet MSL. (PLT061, PA.I.C.K2, PH.I.C.K2a) — FAA-H-8083-28*

# Terminal Aerodrome Forecast (TAF)

A Terminal Aerodrome Forecast (TAF) is a concise statement of the expected meteorological conditions at an airport during a specified period (usually 24 hours). TAFs use the same code used in the METAR weather reports (See Figure 7-1).

TAFs are issued in the following format:

TYPE / LOCATION / ISSUANCE TIME / VALID TIME / FORECAST

*Note:* The "/" above are for separation purposes and do not appear in the actual TAFs.

ALL, SPO

**3479.** (Refer to Figure 15.) What is the valid period for the TAF for KMEM?

A—12th 1800Z to 13th 2400Z.
B—12th at 1700Z.
C—1218Z to 1324Z.

*The valid period of the TAF is 1218/1324. The first two numbers in each four number grouping identify the date followed by the time in Zulu. It reads as 12th at 1800Z to the 13th at 2400Z. (PLT072, PA.I.C.K2, PH.I.C.K2c) — FAA-H-8083-28*

ALL

**3480.** (Refer to Figure 15.) In the TAF for KMEM, what does "SHRA" stand for?

A—Rain showers.
B—A shift in wind direction is expected.
C—A significant change in precipitation is possible.

*"SH" stands for showers, and "RA" stands for rain. (PLT072, PA.I.C.K2, PH.I.C.K2c) — FAA-H-8083-28*

Answers (B) and (C) are incorrect because a permanent change in existing conditions during the valid period of the TAF is indicated by the change groups FMHH (FroM) and BECMG (BECoMinG) HHhh.

ALL

**3481.** (Refer to Figure 15.) Between 1000Z and 1200Z the visibility at KMEM is forecast to be

A—1/2 statute mile.
B—3 statute miles.
C—6 statute miles.

*Between 1000Z and 1200Z, the visibility at KMEM is forecast to be 3 SM (BECMG 1310/1312 00000KT…3SM). (PLT072, PA.I.C.K2, PH.I.C.K2c) — FAA-H-8083-28*

ALL

**3482.** (Refer to Figure 15.) What is the forecast wind for KMEM from 1600Z until the end of the forecast?

A—No significant wind.
B—Variable in direction at 4 knots.
C—Variable in direction at 6 knots.

*From 1600Z until the end of the forecast, wind will be variable in direction at 6 knots (VRB06KT). (PLT072, PA.I.C.K2, PH.I.C.K2c) — FAA-H-8083-28*

**Answers**

| | | | | | |
|---|---|---|---|---|---|
| 3475 [C] | 3476 [B] | 3479 [A] | 3480 [A] | 3481 [B] | 3482 [C] |

ALL

**3483.** (Refer to Figure 15.) In the TAF from KOKC, the "FM (FROM) Group" is forecast for the hours from 1600Z to 2200Z with the wind from

A—160° at 10 knots.
B—180° at 10 knots, becoming 200° at 13 knots.
C—180° at 10 knots.

*The FROM group is forecast for the hours from 1600 (051600) to 2200Z (BECMG 0522/0524) with the wind from 180 degrees at 10 knots (18010KT). (PLT072, PA.I.C.K2, PH.I.C.K2c) — FAA-H-8083-28*

Answer (A) is incorrect because 18010 indicates the wind will be from 180. Answer (B) is incorrect because "BECMG" indicates another change group; the wind will change from 200 at 13 knots between 2200 and 2400Z.

ALL

**3484.** (Refer to Figure 15.) In the TAF from KOKC, the clear sky becomes

A—overcast at 2,000 feet during the forecast period between 2200Z and 2400Z.
B—overcast at 200 feet with a 40% probability of becoming overcast at 600 feet during the forecast period between 2200Z and 2400Z.
C—overcast at 200 feet with the probability of becoming overcast at 400 feet during the forecast period between 2200Z and 2400Z.

*Between 2200Z and 2400Z (BECMG 0522/0524), the sky will be overcast at 2,000 feet (OVC020). (PLT072, PA.I.C.K2, PH.I.C.K2c) — FAA-H-8083-28*

ALL

**3485.** (Refer to Figure 15.) During the time period from 0600Z to 0800Z, what visibility is forecast for KOKC?

A—Greater than 6 statute miles.
B—Not forecasted.
C—Possibly 6 statute miles.

*During the period from 0600Z to 0800Z (0606/0608), the visibilities are forecast to be greater than 6 SM (P6SM). (PLT072, PA.I.C.K2, PH.I.C.K2c) — FAA-H-8083-28*

ALL

**3486.** (Refer to Figure 15.) The only cloud type forecast in TAF reports is

A—nimbostratus.
B—cumulonimbus.
C—scattered cumulus.

*Cumulonimbus clouds are the only cloud types forecast in TAFs. (PLT072, PA.I.C.K2, PH.I.C.K2c) — FAA-H-8083-28*

# Graphical Forecasts for Aviation (GFA)

The GFA at the Aviation Weather Center (AWC) website is an interactive display providing continuously updated observed and forecast weather information over the continental United States (CONUS). It is intended to give users a complete picture of weather critical to aviation safety. The GFA display shows user-selected weather categories, each containing multiple fields of interest at altitudes from the surface up to FL480. Depending on the field of interest chosen, weather information is available from -14 hours in the past (observed) to +18 hours in the future (forecast).

The GFA is not considered a weather product but an aggregate of several existing weather products. The information and data from the various weather products are overlaid on a high-resolution basemap of the United States: **aviationweather.gov/gfa**. The user selects flight levels and current time period for either observed or forecast weather information. Mouse-clicking or hovering over the map provides additional information in textual format, such as current METAR or TAF for a selected airport. The GFA replaces the textual area forecast (FA) for the CONUS and Hawaii with a more modern digital solution for obtaining weather information. The Aviation Surface Forecast and Aviation Cloud Forecast graphics are snapshot images derived from a subset of the aviation weather forecasts.

**Answers**

| | | | |
|---|---|---|---|
| 3483 [C] | 3484 [A] | 3485 [A] | 3486 [B] |

ALL, SPO
**3487.** To best determine general forecast weather conditions covering a flight information region, the pilot should refer to

A—Graphical Forecasts for Aviation (GFA).
B—Weather Depiction Charts.
C—Satellite Maps.

*The GFA is intended to provide the necessary aviation weather information to give users a complete picture of the weather that may impact flight in the continental U.S. (CONUS). (PLT514, PA.I.C.K2, PH.I.C.K2d) — FAA-H-8083-28*

# Winds and Temperatures Aloft Forecast (FB)

The winds and temperatures aloft forecast is displayed in a 6-digit format (DDffTT). It shows wind direction (DD), wind velocity (ff), and the temperature (TT) that is forecast to exist at specified levels. For example, "234502" decodes as: winds from 230 degrees true north, at 45 knots, temperatures 02°C.

When the wind speed (ff) is between 100 and 199 knots, the wind direction (DD) portion of the code will be greater than 50. In cases such as this, you will need to subtract 50 from the coded wind direction, and add 100 to the coded wind speed in order to decipher the code. For example, "734502" decodes as: winds from 230 degrees true north at 145 knots, temperature 02 degrees C.

Temperatures with a negative symbol in front of them (DDff-37) are negative. For flight levels above 24,000, temperatures are always negative and will not have a negative symbol. Light and variable winds or wind speeds below 5 knots are indicated by 9900, followed by the forecast temperature. For example, the coded winds aloft forecast for flight level FL270 (flight level 27,000) is "990017" and decodes as: winds are light and variable, temperature negative 17.

The observed winds aloft chart shows temperature, wind direction, and speed at selected stations. Arrows with pennants and barbs indicate wind direction and speed. Each pennant is 50 knots, each barb is 10 knots, and each half barb is 5 knots. Wind direction is shown by an arrow drawn to the nearest 10 degrees, with the second digit of the coded direction entered at the outer end of the arrow. Thus, a wind in the northwest quadrant with the digit 3 indicates 330 degrees, and a wind in the southwest quadrant with the digit 3 indicates 230 degrees.

ALL, SPO
**3500.** (Refer to Figure 17.) What wind is forecast for STL at 9,000 feet?

A—230° true at 32 knots.
B—230° magnetic at 25 knots.
C—230° true at 25 knots.

*A six-digit group shows wind directions (in reference to true north) in the first two digits, wind speed (in knots) in the second two digits, and temperature (in Celsius) in the last two digits. In this case, 2332+02 means 230° at 32 knots, and the temperature is 2°C. (PLT076, PA.I.C.K2, PH.I.C.K2e) — FAA-H-8083-28*

ALL
**3501.** (Refer to Figure 17.) What wind is forecast for STL at 12,000 feet?

A—230° true at 56 knots.
B—230° magnetic at 56 knots.
C—230° true at 39 knots.

*A six-digit group shows wind directions (in reference to true north) in the first two digits, wind speed (in knots) in the second two digits, and temperature (in Celsius) in the last two digits. In this case, 2339-04 means 230° at 39 knots, and the temperature is -4°C. (PLT076, PA.I.C.K2, PH.I.C.K2e) — FAA-H-8083-28*

**Answers**

3487    [A]                3500    [A]                3501    [C]

ALL

**3502.** (Refer to Figure 17.) Determine the wind and temperature aloft forecast for DEN at 9,000 feet.

A—230° magnetic at 53 knots, temperature 47°C.
B—230° true at 53 knots, temperature -47°C.
C—230° true at 21 knots, temperature -4°C.

*A six-digit group shows wind directions (in reference to true north) in the first two digits, wind speed (in knots) in the second two digits, and temperature (in Celsius) in the last two digits. In this case, 2321-04 means 230° at 21 knots, and the temperature is -4°C. (PLT076, PA.I.C.K2, PH.I.C.K2e) — FAA-H-8083-28*

ALL

**3503.** (Refer to Figure 17.) Determine the wind and temperature aloft forecast for MKC at 6,000 feet.

A—200° true at 6 knots, temperature +3°C.
B—050° true at 7 knots, temperature missing.
C—200° magnetic at 6 knots, temperature +3°C.

*A six-digit group shows wind directions (in reference to true north) in the first two digits, wind speed (in knots) in the second two digits, and temperature (in Celsius) in the last two digits. In this case, 2006+03 means 200° at 6 knots, and the temperature is 3°C. (PLT076, PA.I.C.K2, PH.I.C.K2e) — FAA-H-8083-28*

ALL

**3505.** What values are used for winds aloft forecasts?

A—Magnetic direction and knots.
B—Magnetic direction and miles per hour.
C—True direction and knots.

*A six-digit group shows wind directions (in reference to true north) in the first two digits, wind speed (in knots) in the second two digits, and temperature (in Celsius) in the last two digits. (PLT284, PA.I.C.K2, PH.I.C.K2e) — FAA-H-8083-28*

ALL

**3506.** When the term "light and variable" is used in reference to a winds aloft forecast, the coded group and windspeed is

A—0000 and less than 7 knots.
B—9900 and less than 5 knots.
C—9999 and less than 10 knots.

*When the forecast speed is less than 5 knots, the coded group is "9900" and reads "light and variable" on the winds aloft forecast. (PLT284, PA.I.C.K2, PH.I.C.K2e) — FAA-H-8083-28*

# Inflight Weather Advisories (WA, WS, WST)

Inflight Weather Advisories advise enroute pilots of the possibility of encountering hazardous flying conditions that may not have been forecast at the time of the preflight weather briefing.

**AIRMETs (WA)** contain information on weather that may be hazardous to single-engine and other light aircraft and VFR pilots. The items covered are moderate icing or turbulence, sustained winds of 30 knots or more at the surface, widespread areas of IFR conditions, and extensive mountain obscurement.

**SIGMETs (WS)** advise of weather potentially hazardous to all aircraft. The items covered are severe icing, severe or extreme turbulence, and widespread sandstorms, dust storms, or volcanic ash lowering visibility to less than 3 miles.

SIGMETs and AIRMETs are broadcast upon receipt and at 30-minute intervals (H + 15 and H + 45) during the first hour. If the advisory is still in effect after the first hour, an alert notice will be broadcast. Pilots may contact the nearest FSS to ascertain whether the advisory is pertinent to their flights.

**Convective SIGMETs (WST)** cover weather developments such as tornadoes, lines of thunderstorms, and embedded thunderstorms, and they also imply severe or greater turbulence, severe icing, and low-level wind shear. When a SIGMET forecasts embedded thunderstorms, it indicates that the thunderstorms are obscured by massive cloud layers and cannot be seen. Convective SIGMET bulletins are issued hourly at H + 55. Unscheduled convective SIGMETs are broadcast upon receipt and at 15-minute intervals for the first hour (H + 15; H + 30; H + 45).

**Answers**

| | | | |
|---|---|---|---|
| 3502 [C] | 3503 [A] | 3505 [C] | 3506 [B] |

ALL

**3495.** What is indicated when a current Convective SIGMET forecasts thunderstorms?

A—Moderate thunderstorms covering 30 percent of the area.
B—Moderate or severe turbulence.
C—Thunderstorms obscured by massive cloud layers.

*Convective SIGMETs include: severe thunderstorms, embedded thunderstorms, line of thunderstorms, thunderstorms greater than or equal to VIP level "A" affecting 40 percent or more of an area of 3,000 square miles. (PLT290, PA.I.C.K2, PH.I.C.K2g) — FAA-H-8083-28*

ALL

**3496.** What information is contained in a Convective SIGMET?

A—Tornadoes, embedded thunderstorms, and hail 3/4 inch or greater in diameter.
B—Severe icing, severe turbulence, or widespread dust storms lowering visibility to less than 3 miles.
C—Surface winds greater than 40 knots or thunderstorms equal to or greater than video integrator processor (VIP) level 4.

*Any convective SIGMET implies severe or greater turbulence, severe icing, and low-level wind shear. The forecast may be issued for severe thunderstorms due to:*

1. *Surface winds greater than or equal to 50 knots;*

2. *Hail at the surface greater than or equal to 3/4 inch in diameter; or*

3. *Tornadoes, embedded thunderstorms, lines of thunderstorms.*

*(PLT290, PA.I.C.K2, PH.I.C.K2g) — FAA-H-8083-28*

ALL, SPO

**3497.** SIGMETs are issued as a warning of weather conditions hazardous to which aircraft?

A—Small aircraft only.
B—Large aircraft only.
C—All aircraft.

*A SIGMET advises of weather potentially hazardous to all aircraft. (PLT290, PA.I.C.K2, PH.I.C.K2g) — FAA-H-8083-28*

ALL

**3498.** Which inflight advisory would contain information on severe icing not associated with thunderstorms?

A—Convective SIGMET.
B—SIGMET.
C—AIRMET.

*A SIGMET advises of weather potentially hazardous to all aircraft other than convective activity. Some items included are severe icing, and severe or extreme turbulence. (PLT290, PA.I.C.K2, PH.I.C.K2g) — FAA-H-8083-28*

ALL

**3499.** AIRMETs are advisories of significant weather phenomena but of lower intensities than SIGMETs and are intended for dissemination to

A—only IFR pilots.
B—all pilots.
C—only VFR pilots.

*AIRMETs are intended for dissemination to all pilots in the preflight and enroute phase of flight to enhance safety. (PLT290, PA.I.C.K2, PH.I.C.K2g) — FAA-H-8083-28*

**Answers**

| | | | | |
|---|---|---|---|---|
| 3495 [C] | 3496 [A] | 3497 [C] | 3498 [B] | 3499 [B] |

# 1-800-WX-BRIEF (Telephone and Self-Briefing)

When telephoning a weather briefing facility for preflight weather information, pilots should:

- Identify themselves as pilots;
- State whether they intend to fly VFR or IFR;
- State the intended route, destination, and type of aircraft;
- Request a standard briefing to get a "complete" weather briefing;
- Request an abbreviated briefing to supplement mass disseminated data or when only one or two items are needed; and
- Request an outlook briefing whenever the proposed departure time is 6 or more hours from the time of briefing.

ALL

**3455.** When telephoning Flight Service for preflight weather information, pilots should state

A—whether they intend to fly VFR only.
B—that they possess a current pilot certificate.
C—the full name and address of the formation commander.

*When requesting a preflight weather briefing, identify yourself as a pilot or the tail number of the aircraft to be flown and provide the type of flight planned (e.g., VFR or IFR). (PLT514, PA.I.C.K1, PH.I.C.K1) — FAA-H-8083-25*

ALL

**3456.** To get a complete weather briefing for the planned flight, the pilot should request

A—a general briefing.
B—an abbreviated briefing.
C—a standard briefing.

*You should request a standard briefing any time you are planning a flight and you have not received a previous briefing. (PLT514, PA.I.C.K1, PH.I.C.K1) — FAA-H-8083-28*

ALL, SPO

**3457.** Which type weather briefing should a pilot request, when departing within the hour, if no preliminary weather information has been received?

A—Outlook briefing.
B—Abbreviated briefing.
C—Standard briefing.

*You should request a standard briefing any time you are planning a flight and you have not received a previous briefing. (PLT514, PA.I.C.K1, PH.I.C.K1) — FAA-H-8083-28*

ALL, SPO

**3458.** Which type of weather briefing should a pilot request to supplement mass disseminated data?

A—An outlook briefing.
B—A supplemental briefing.
C—An abbreviated briefing.

*Request an abbreviated briefing when you need information to supplement mass disseminated data, update a previous briefing, or when you need only one or two specific items. (PLT514, PA.I.C.K1, PH.I.C.K1) — FAA-H-8083-28*

ALL, SPO

**3459.** To update a previous weather briefing, a pilot should request

A—an abbreviated briefing.
B—a standard briefing.
C—an outlook briefing.

*Request an abbreviated briefing when you need information to supplement mass disseminated data, update a previous briefing, or when you need only one or two specific items. (PLT514, PA.I.C.K1, PH.I.C.K1) — FAA-H-8083-28*

ALL

**3460.** A weather briefing that is provided when the information requested is 6 or more hours in advance of the proposed departure time is

A—an outlook briefing.
B—a forecast briefing.
C—a prognostic briefing.

*You should request an outlook briefing whenever your proposed time of departure is 6 or more hours from the time of the briefing. This type of briefing is provided for*

**Answers**

| 3455 [A] | 3456 [C] | 3457 [C] | 3458 [C] | 3459 [A] | 3460 [A] |
|----------|----------|----------|----------|----------|----------|

*planning purposes only. You should obtain a standard or abbreviated briefing prior to departure in order to obtain such items as current conditions, updated forecasts, winds aloft, and NOTAMs. (PLT514, PA.I.C.K1, PH.I.C.K1) — FAA-H-8083-28*

ALL
**3461.** When requesting weather information for the following morning, a pilot should request

A—an outlook briefing.
B—a standard briefing.
C—an abbreviated briefing.

*You should request an outlook briefing whenever your proposed time of departure is 6 or more hours from the time of the briefing. This type of briefing is provided for planning purposes only. You should obtain a standard or abbreviated briefing prior to departure in order to obtain such items as current conditions, updated forecasts, winds aloft, and NOTAMs. (PLT514, PA.I.C.K1, PH.I.C.K1) — FAA-H-8083-28*

ALL
**3526.** What should pilots state initially when telephoning Flight Service for preflight weather information?

A—The intended route of flight radio frequencies.
B—The address of the pilot-in-command.
C—The intended route of flight and destination.

*When requesting a briefing, pilots should identify themselves and provide as much information regarding the proposed flight as possible. (PLT514, PA.I.C.K1, PH.I.C.K1) — FAA-H-8083-25*

Answer (A) is incorrect because the pilot only needs to identify the route of flight. Answer (B) is incorrect because the caller only needs to provide an aircraft number or pilot's name.

ALL, SPO
**3527.** What should pilots state initially when telephoning Flight Service for preflight weather information?

A—Tell the number of occupants on board.
B—Identify themselves as pilots.
C—State their total flight time.

*When requesting a briefing, pilots should identify themselves and provide as much information regarding the proposed flight as possible. The information received*

*will depend on the type of briefing requested. The following would be helpful to the briefer.*

1. *Type of flight: VFR or IFR*
2. *Aircraft number or pilot's name*
3. *Aircraft type*
4. *Departure point*
5. *Route of flight*
6. *Destination*
7. *Flight altitude(s)*
8. *Estimated time of departure*
9. *Estimated time en route or estimated time of arrival*

*(PLT514, PA.I.C.K1, PH.I.C.K1) — FAA-H-8083-25*

ALL
**3528.** When telephoning Flight Service for preflight weather information, pilots should state

A—the aircraft identification or the pilot's name.
B—true airspeed.
C—fuel on board.

*When requesting a briefing, make known you are a pilot. Give clear and concise facts about your flight:*

1. *Type of flight: VFR or IFR*
2. *Aircraft identification or pilot's name*
3. *Aircraft type*
4. *Departure point*
5. *Route of flight*
6. *Destination*
7. *Altitude*
8. *Estimated time of departure*
9. *Estimated time en route or estimated time of arrival*

*(PLT514, PA.I.C.K1, PH.I.C.K1) — FAA-H-8083-25*

Answers (B) and (C) are incorrect because these are necessary when filing a flight plan, but not when obtaining a weather briefing.

**Answers**

| | | | |
|---|---|---|---|
| 3461　[A] | 3526　[C] | 3527　[B] | 3528　[A] |

ALL

**3528-1.** When speaking to a Flight Service Specialist to obtain a weather briefing, you should state

A—the pilot-in-command's full name and address.
B—a summary of your qualifications.
C—whether the flight is VFR or IFR.

*When requesting a briefing, make known you are a pilot. Give clear and concise facts about your flight:*

1. *Type of flight: VFR or IFR*

2. *Aircraft identification or pilot's name*

3. *Aircraft type*

4. *Departure point*

5. *Route of flight*

6. *Destination*

7. *Altitude*

8. *Estimated time of departure*

9. *Estimated time en route or estimated time of arrival*

*(PLT514, PA.I.C.K1, PH.I.C.K1) – FAA-H-8083-25*

GLI

**3525.** In addition to the standard briefing, what additional information should be asked of the Flight Service Specialist in order to evaluate soaring conditions?

A—The upper soundings to determine the thermal index at all soaring levels.
B—Dry adiabatic rate of cooling to determine the height of cloud bases.
C—Moist adiabatic rate of cooling to determine the height of cloud tops.

*Since thermals depend on sinking cold air forcing warm air upward, strength of thermals depends on the temperature difference between the sinking air and the rising air—the greater the temperature difference, the stronger the thermals. To arrive at an approximation of this difference, a thermal index is computed. A thermal index may be computed for any level using upper soundings. (PLT514) — FAA-H-8083-28*

GLI

**3470.** (Refer to Figure 13.) What effect do the clouds mentioned in the weather briefing have on soaring conditions?

A—All thermals stop at the base of the clouds.
B—Thermals persist to the tops of the clouds at 25,000 feet.
C—The scattered clouds indicate thermals at least to the tops of the lower clouds.

*The telephone weather briefing indicates a few scattered clouds at 5,000 feet AGL, with higher scattered cirrus at 25,000 feet MSL. This briefing shows two different clouds bases and does not give cloud tops. Thermals are a product of instability. The height of thermals depends on the depth of the unstable layer, and their strength depends on the degree of instability. A cloud grows with a rising thermal and scattered cumulus clouds are positive signs of thermals. Whereas an abundant convective cloud cover reduces thermal activity, thermals will exist at least to the tops of the scattered clouds, especially if the outline is firm and sharp, indicating a growing cumulus. (PLT316) — FAA-H-8083-28*

GLI

**3471.** (Refer to Figure 13.) At what time will thermals begin to form?

A—Between 1300Z and 1500Z while the sky is clear.
B—By 1500Z (midmorning) when scattered clouds begin to form.
C—About 2000Z (early afternoon) when the wind begins to increase.

*The telephone weather briefing indicates there should be a few scattered clouds at 5,000 feet AGL by 1500Z. The sky must be clear enough for the sun to warm the earth's surface in order for thermals to develop. (PLT494) — FAA-H-8083-28*

**Answers**

3528-1 [C]        3525   [A]        3470   [C]        3471   [A]

GLI

**3471-1.** (Refer to Figure 13.) When are the thermals at the best?

A—Between 1300Z and 1500Z while the sky is clear.
B—By 1500Z (midmorning) when scattered clouds begin to form.
C—About 2000Z (early afternoon) when the wind begins to form.

*The telephone weather briefing indicates there should be a few scattered clouds at 5,000 feet AGL by 1500Z. Thermals are a product of instability. A cloud grows with a rising thermal and scattered cumulus clouds are positive signs of thermals. Whereas abundant convective cloud cover reduces thermal activity, thermals will exist at least to the tops of the scattered clouds—especially if the outline is firm and sharp, indicating a growing cumulus. (PLT494) — FAA-H-8083-28*

LTA

**3411.** What early morning weather observations indicate the possibility of good weather conditions for balloon flight most of the day?

A—Clear skies and surface winds, 10 knots or less.
B—Low moving, scattered cumulus clouds and surface winds, 5 knots or less.
C—Overcast with stratus clouds and surface winds, 5 knots or less.

*Stratiform clouds indicate no turbulence and 5 knots or less winds are well within safety parameters. (PLT173) — FAA-H-8083-28*

LTA

**3468.** (Refer to Figure 13.) According to the weather briefing, the most ideal time to launch balloons is

A—as soon as possible after 1300Z.
B—at 1500Z when the ground will be partially shaded.
C—at 2000Z when there is enough wind for cross-country.

*The telephone weather briefing given at 1300Z indicates no clouds until 1500Z, and no wind until after 2000Z. The ideal time to launch balloons is as soon after 1300Z as possible before the clouds and wind develop. (PLT316) — FAA-H-8083-28*

LTA

**3469.** (Refer to Figure 13.) According to the weather briefing, good balloon weather will begin to deteriorate

A—soon after 1300Z as the wind starts to increase.
B—about 1500Z when the lower scattered clouds begin to form.
C—at 2000Z due to sharp increase in wind conditions.

*The telephone weather briefing given at 1300Z indicates only a few scattered clouds at 5,000 feet AGL, with higher scattered cirrus at 25,000 feet MSL to form by 1500Z. After 2000Z, however, the wind should pick up to about 15 knots from the south. The marked increase of wind at 2000Z indicates deteriorating ballooning weather. (PLT316) — FAA-H-8083-28*

LTA

**3477.** Which weather reports and forecasts are most important for local area balloon operations?

A—Winds Aloft Forecasts and Radar Summary Charts.
B—Winds Aloft Forecasts and Surface Analysis Charts.
C—Winds Aloft Forecasts and Aviation Routine Weather Reports.

*Local information is provided by the METAR. (PLT515) — FAA-H-8083-28*

Answer (A) is incorrect because it is a local flight. Answer (B) is incorrect because Surface Analysis Charts are a nationwide reference.

# Chapter 10
# Human Factors

# Fitness for Flight

Pilot performance can be seriously degraded by a number of physiological factors. While some of the factors may be beyond the control of the pilot, awareness of cause and effect can help minimize any adverse effects.

**Hypoxia**, a state of oxygen deficiency, impairs functions of the brain and other organs. Headache, drowsiness, dizziness, and euphoria are all symptoms of hypoxia.

For optimum protection, pilots should avoid flying above 10,000 feet MSL for prolonged periods without using supplemental oxygen. Federal Aviation Regulations require that when operating an aircraft at cabin pressure altitudes above 12,500 feet MSL up to and including 14,000 feet MSL, **supplemental oxygen** shall be used by the minimum flight crew during that time in excess of 30 minutes at those altitudes. Every occupant of the aircraft must be provided with supplemental oxygen above 15,000 feet.

Aviatior's breathing oxygen should be used to replenish an aircraft oxygen system for high-altitude flight. Oxygen used for medical purposes or welding normally should not be used because it may contain too much water. The excess water could condense and freeze in oxygen lines when flying at high altitudes and could block oxygen flow. Constant use of oxygen containing too much water may also cause corrosion in the system. Specifications for aviator's breathing oxygen are 99.5% pure oxygen and not more than .005 mg of water per liter of oxygen.

**Hyperventilation**, a deficiency of carbon dioxide within the body, can be the result of rapid or extra deep breathing due to emotional tension, anxiety, or fear. Symptoms will subside after the rate and depth of breathing are brought under control. A pilot should be able to overcome the symptoms or avoid future occurrences of hyperventilation by talking aloud, breathing into a bag, or slowing the breathing rate.

**Carbon monoxide** is a colorless, odorless, and tasteless gas contained in exhaust fumes. Symptoms of carbon monoxide poisoning include headache, drowsiness, or dizziness. Large accumulations of carbon monoxide in the human body result in a loss of muscular power. Susceptibility increases as altitude increases.

A pilot who detects symptoms of carbon monoxide poisoning should immediately shut off the heater and open air vents.

Various complex motions, forces, and visual scenes encountered in flight may result in misleading information being sent to the brain by various sensory organs. **Spatial disorientation** may result if these body signals are used to interpret flight attitude. The best way to overcome spatial disorientation is by relying on the flight instruments rather than taking a chance on the sensory organs. Weight-shift control and powered parachutes can use the compass heading as an instrument indication.

ALL
**3163.** When operating an aircraft at cabin pressure altitudes above 12,500 feet MSL up to and including 14,000 feet MSL, supplemental oxygen shall be used during

A—the entire flight time at those altitudes.
B—that flight time in excess of 10 minutes at those altitudes.
C—that flight time in excess of 30 minutes at those altitudes.

*No person may operate civil aircraft at cabin pressure altitudes above 12,500 feet MSL up to and including 14,000 feet MSL, unless the required minimum flight crew uses supplemental oxygen for that part of the flight at those altitudes that is more than 30 minutes duration. (PLT438, PA.I.H.K1a, PH.I.H.K1a) — 14 CFR §91.211*

**Answers**
3163  [C]

ALL

**3164.** Unless each occupant is provided with supplemental oxygen, no person may operate a civil aircraft of U.S. registry above a maximum cabin pressure altitude of

A—12,500 feet MSL.
B—14,000 feet MSL.
C—15,000 feet MSL.

*No person may operate a civil aircraft at cabin pressure altitudes above 15,000 feet MSL unless each occupant is provided with supplemental oxygen. (PLT438, PA.I.H.K1a, PH.I.H.K1a) — 14 CFR §91.211*

ALL, SPO

**3832.** Large accumulations of carbon monoxide in the human body result in

A—tightness across the forehead.
B—loss of muscular power.
C—an increased sense of well-being.

*A large accumulation of carbon monoxide in the body results in loss of muscular power, vomiting, convulsions, and coma. (PLT097, PA.I.H.K1f, PH.I.H.K1f) — FAA-H-8083-25*

Answers (A) and (C) are incorrect because hypoxia gives you an increased sense of well-being; stress could result in tightness across the forehead.

ALL

**3844.** Which statement best defines hypoxia?

A—A state of oxygen deficiency in the body.
B—An abnormal increase in the volume of air breathed.
C—A condition of gas bubble formation around the joints or muscles.

*Hypoxia is an oxygen deficiency in the body usually caused by flight at higher altitudes. For optimum protection from hypoxia, pilots are encouraged to use supplemental oxygen above 10,000 feet during the day, and above 5,000 feet at night. (PLT330, PA.I.H.K1a, PH.I.H.K1a) — AIM ¶8-1-2*

Answer (B) is incorrect because it describes hyperventilation. Answer (C) is incorrect because it describes the bends.

ALL

**3845.** When a stressful situation is encountered in flight, an abnormal increase in the volume of air breathed in and out can cause a condition known as

A—hyperventilation.
B—aerosinusitis.
C—aerotitis.

*An abnormal increase in the volume of air breathed in and out of the lungs flushes an excessive amount of carbon dioxide from the lungs and blood, causing hyperventilation. (PLT332, PA.I.H.K1b, PH.I.H.K1b) — AIM ¶8-1-3*

ALL, SPO

**3846.** Which would most likely result in hyperventilation?

A—Emotional tension, anxiety, or fear.
B—The excessive consumption of alcohol.
C—An extremely slow rate of breathing and insufficient oxygen.

*Hyperventilation is most likely to occur during periods of stress or anxiety. (PLT332, PA.I.H.K1b, PH.I.H.K1b) — AIM ¶8-1-3*

ALL

**3847.** A pilot experiencing the effects of hyperventilation should be able to restore the proper carbon dioxide level in the body by

A—slowing the breathing rate, breathing into a paper bag, or talking aloud.
B—breathing spontaneously and deeply or gaining mental control of the situation.
C—increasing the breathing rate in order to increase lung ventilation.

*The symptoms of hyperventilation subside within a few minutes after the rate and depth of breathing are consciously brought back under control. The buildup of carbon dioxide in the body can be hastened by controlled breathing in and out of a paper bag held over the nose and mouth. Talking aloud often helps, while normally-paced breathing at all times prevents hyperventilation. (PLT332, PA.I.H.K1b, PH.I.H.K1b) — AIM ¶8-1-3*

ALL

**3848.** Susceptibility to carbon monoxide poisoning increases as

A—altitude increases.
B—altitude decreases.
C—air pressure increases.

---

**Answers**

| | | | | | | | | | | |
|---|---|---|---|---|---|---|---|---|---|---|
| 3164 | [C] | | 3832 | [B] | | 3844 | [A] | 3845 | [A] | |
| 3848 | [A] | | | | | | | | | |

(second answer row: 3846 [A]    3847 [A])

*Susceptibility to carbon monoxide poisoning increases with altitude. As altitude increases, air pressure decreases and the body has difficulty getting oxygen. Add carbon monoxide, which further deprives the body of oxygen, and the situation can become critical. (PLT097, PA.I.H.K1f, PH.I.H.K1f) — FAA-H-8083-25*

ALL

**3850.** The danger of spatial disorientation during flight in poor visual conditions may be reduced by

A—shifting the eyes quickly between the exterior visual field and the instrument panel.
B—having faith in the instruments rather than taking a chance on the sensory organs.
C—leaning the body in the opposite direction of the motion of the aircraft.

*Even if the natural horizon or surface reference is clearly visible, rely on instrument indications to overcome the effects of spatial disorientation. Shifting the eyes quickly from outside to inside, and leaning, will only compound the problem. (PLT334, PA.I.H.K1d, PH.I.H.K1k) — AIM ¶8-1-5*

ALL

**3851.** A lack of orientation with regard to the position, attitude, or movement of the aircraft in space is defined as

A—spatial disorientation.
B—hyperventilation.
C—hypoxia.

*Spatial disorientation is the state of confusion due to misleading information being sent to the brain from various sensory organs, resulting in a lack of awareness of the aircraft position in relation to a specific reference point. (PLT334, PA.I.H.K1d, PH.I.H.K1k) — FAA-H-8083-2*

ALL

**3852.** Pilots are more subject to spatial disorientation if

A—they ignore the sensations of muscles and inner ear.
B—visual cues are taken away, as they are in instrument meteorological conditions (IMC).
C—eyes are moved often in the process of cross-checking the flight instruments.

*Sight, supported by other senses, allows the pilot to maintain orientation. However, during periods of low visibility, the supporting senses sometimes conflict with what is seen. When this happens, a pilot is particularly vulnerable to disorientation and must rely more on flight instruments. (PLT334, PA.I.H.K1d, PH.I.H.K1k) — FAA-H-8083-25*

ALL

**3853.** If a pilot experiences spatial disorientation during flight in a restricted visibility condition, the best way to overcome the effect is to

A—rely upon the aircraft instrument indications.
B—concentrate on yaw, pitch, and roll sensations.
C—consciously slow the breathing rate until symptoms clear and then resume normal breathing rate.

*Even if the natural horizon or surface reference is clearly visible, rely on instrument indications to overcome the effects of spatial disorientation. Shifting the eyes quickly from outside to inside and leaning will only compound the problem. (PLT334, PA.I.H.K1d, PH.I.H.K1k) — AIM ¶8-1-6*

SPO

**2202.** Which will almost always affect your ability to fly?

A—Over-the-counter analgesics and antihistamines.
B—Antibiotics and anesthetic drugs.
C—Prescription analgesics and antihistamines.

*Pilot performance can be seriously degraded by both prescribed and over-the-counter medications, as well as by the medical conditions for which they are taken. Flying is almost always precluded while using prescription analgesics since these drugs may cause side effects such as mental confusion, dizziness, headaches, nausea, and vision problems. Depressants, including antihistamines, lower blood pressure, reduce mental processing, and slow motor and reaction responses. (PLT098) — FAA-H-8083-25*

*Answer (A) is incorrect because over-the-counter analgesics such as aspirin, Tylenol, and Advil, and antihistamines have few side effects when taken in the correct dosage. Answer (B) is incorrect because these drugs do not typically limit flying (but the medical conditions for which they are being taken may indeed limit flying activities).*

SPO

**2089.** As a pilot, flying for long periods in hot summer temperatures increases the susceptibility of dehydration since the

A—dry air at altitude tends to increase the rate of water loss from the body.

B—moist air at altitude helps retain the body's moisture.

C—temperature decreases with altitude.

*As a pilot, flying for long periods in hot summer temperatures or at high altitudes increases the susceptibility of dehydration since the dry air at altitude tends to increase the rate of water loss from the body. If this fluid is not replaced, fatigue progresses to dizziness, weakness, nausea, tingling of hands and feet, abdominal cramps, and extreme thirst. (PLT098) — FAA-H-8083-25*

SPO

**2091.** A pilot should be able to overcome the symptoms or avoid future occurrences of hyperventilation by

A—closely monitoring the flight instruments to control the airplane.

B—slowing the breathing rate or breathing into a bag.

C—increasing the breathing rate in order to increase lung ventilation.

*The symptoms of hyperventilation subside within a few minutes after the rate and depth of breathing are consciously brought back under control. The buildup of carbon dioxide in the body can be hastened by controlled breathing in and out of a paper bag held over the nose and mouth. Talking aloud often helps, while normally-paced breathing at all times prevents hyperventilation. (PLT332) — AIM ¶8-1-3*

SPO

**2090.** If advice is needed concerning possible flight with an illness, a pilot should contact

A—an Aviation Medical Examiner.

B—their family doctor.

C—the nearest hospital.

*The safest rule is not to fly while suffering from any illness. If this rule is considered too stringent for a particular illness, the pilot should contact an Aviation Medical Examiner for advice. (PLT098) — AIM ¶8-1-1*

SPO

**2092.** As hyperventilation progresses a pilot can experience

A—decreased breathing rate and depth.

B—heightened awareness and feeling of well being.

C—symptoms of suffocation and drowsiness.

*As hyperventilation blows off excessive carbon dioxide from the body, a pilot can experience symptoms of light-headedness, suffocation, drowsiness, tingling in the extremities, and coolness and react to them with even greater hyperventilation. Incapacitation can eventually result from uncoordination, disorientation, and painful muscle spasms. Finally, unconsciousness can occur. (PLT332) — AIM ¶8-1-3*

SPO

**2093.** To overcome the symptoms of hyperventilation, a pilot should

A—swallow or yawn.

B—slow the breathing rate.

C—increase the breathing rate.

*The symptoms of hyperventilation subside within a few minutes after the rate and depth of breathing are consciously brought back under control. The buildup of carbon dioxide in the body can be hastened by controlled breathing in and out of a paper bag held over the nose and mouth. (PLT332) — AIM ¶8-1-3*

SPO

**2097.** A state of temporary confusion resulting from misleading information being sent to the brain by various sensory organs is defined as

A—spatial disorientation.

B—hyperventilation.

C—hypoxia.

*Disorientation, or vertigo, is actually a state of temporary spatial confusion resulting from misleading information sent to the brain by various sensory organs. (PLT334) — AIM ¶8-1-5*

**Answers**

| 2089 | [A] | 2091 | [B] | 2090 | [A] | 2092 | [C] | 2093 | [B] | 2097 | [A] |

# Collision Avoidance

Vision is the most important body sense for safe flight. Major factors that determine how effectively vision can be used are the level of illumination and the technique of scanning the sky for other aircraft.

**Atmospheric haze** reduces the ability to see traffic or terrain during flight, making all features appear to be farther away than they actually are.

In preparation for a night flight, the pilot should avoid bright white lights for at least 30 minutes before the flight.

**Scanning** the sky for other aircraft is a key factor in collision avoidance. Pilots must develop an effective scanning technique which maximizes visual capabilities. Because the eyes focus only on a narrow viewing area, effective scanning is accomplished with a series of short, regularly spaced eye movements. Each movement should not exceed 10°, and each area should be observed for at least one second. At night, scan slowly to permit the use of off-center vision.

Prior to starting any maneuver, a pilot should visually scan the entire area for collision avoidance. Any aircraft that appears to have no relative motion and stays in one scan quadrant is likely to be on a collision course. If a target shows neither lateral nor vertical motion, but increases in size, take evasive action.

When climbing or descending VFR on an airway, execute gentle banks, right and left, to provide for visual scanning of the airspace.

ALL, SPO

**3710-1.** Most midair collision accidents occur during

A—hazy days.
B—clear days.
C—cloudy nights.

*The FAA Near Mid-Air Collision Report indicates that 81% of the incidents occurred in clear skies and unrestricted visibility conditions. (PLT194, PA.VI.A.R1, PH.VI.A.R4) — AC 90-48*

ALL, SPO

**3710.** Prior to starting each maneuver, pilots should

A—check altitude, airspeed, and heading indications.
B—visually scan the entire area for collision avoidance.
C—announce their intentions on the nearest CTAF.

*Scanning the sky for other aircraft is a key factor in collision avoidance. (PLT194, PA.VI.A.R1, PH.VI.A.R4) — FAA-H-8083-25*

*Answer (A) is incorrect because checking your instruments is important but secondary to collision avoidance. Answer (C) is incorrect because announcing your intentions on the nearest CTAF does not guarantee that anyone is listening.*

ALL, SPO

**3833.** What effect does haze have on the ability to see traffic or terrain features during flight?

A—Haze causes the eyes to focus at infinity.
B—The eyes tend to overwork in haze and do not detect relative movement easily.
C—All traffic or terrain features appear to be farther away than their actual distance.

*Atmospheric haze can create the illusion of being at a greater distance from objects on the ground and in the air. (PLT333, PA.I.C.K3l, PH.I.C.K3l) — AIM ¶8-1-5*

SPO

**2240.** Haze creates which of the following atmospheric illusions?

A—Being at a greater distance from the runway.
B—Being at a closer distance from the runway.
C—Haze creates no atmospheric illusions.

*Atmospheric haze can create the illusion of being at a greater distance from objects on the ground and in the air. (PLT280) — AIM ¶8-1-5*

**Answers**

3710-1 [B]        3710    [B]        3833    [C]        2240    [A]

SPO
**2066.** Pilots who become apprehensive for their safety for any reason should

A—request assistance immediately.
B—reduce their situational awareness.
C—change their mindset.

*Pilots who become apprehensive for their safety for any reason should request assistance immediately. Ready and willing help is available in the form of radio, radar, direction finding stations and other aircraft. Delay has caused accidents and cost lives. Safety is not a luxury! Take action! (PLT116) — AIM ¶6-1-2*

SPO
**2064.** To scan properly for traffic, a pilot should

A—slowly sweep the field of vision from one side to the other at intervals.
B—concentrate on any peripheral movement detected.
C—use a series of short, regularly spaced eye movements that bring successive areas of the sky into the central visual field.

*Effective scanning is accomplished with a series of short, regularly spaced eye movements that bring successive areas of the sky into the central visual field. Each movement should not exceed 10°, and each area should be observed for at least one second to enable detection. (PLT194) — AIM ¶8-1-6*

SPO
**2062.** Guy wires, which support antenna towers, can extend horizontally; therefore, the towers should be avoided horizontally by at least

A—2,000 feet horizontally.
B—300 feet horizontally.
C—1,000 feet horizontally.

*Most skeletal structures are supported by guy wires which are very difficult to see in good weather and can be invisible at dusk or during periods of reduced visibility. These wires can extend about 1,500 feet horizontally from a structure; therefore, all skeletal structures should be avoided horizontally by at least 2,000 feet. (PLT116) — AIM ¶7-6-4*

ALL, SPO
**3834.** Eye movements during daytime collision avoidance scanning should

A—not exceed 10 degrees and view each sector at least 1 second.
B—be 30 degrees and view each sector at least 3 seconds.
C—use peripheral vision by scanning small sectors and utilizing off-center viewing.

*Effective scanning is accomplished with a series of short, regularly spaced eye movements that bring successive areas of the sky into the central visual field. Each movement should not exceed 10°, and each area should be observed for at least one second to enable detection. (PLT194, PA.VIII.A.R3, PH.I.H.K1d) — AIM ¶8-1-6*

ALL
**3835.** Which technique should a pilot use to scan for traffic to the right and left during straight-and-level flight?

A—Systematically focus on different segments of the sky for short intervals.
B—Concentrate on relative movement detected in the peripheral vision area.
C—Continuous sweeping of the windshield from right to left.

*Effective scanning is accomplished with a series of short, regularly spaced eye movements that bring successive areas of the sky into the central visual field. Each movement should not exceed 10°, and each area should be observed for at least one second to enable detection. (PLT194, PA.VIII.A.R3, PH.I.H.K1d) — AIM ¶8-1-6*

ALL, SPO
**3836.** How can you determine if another aircraft is on a collision course with your aircraft?

A—The other aircraft will always appear to get larger and closer at a rapid rate.
B—The nose of each aircraft is pointed at the same point in space.
C—There will be no apparent relative motion between your aircraft and the other aircraft.

*Any aircraft that appears to have no relative motion and stays in one scan quadrant is likely to be on a collision course. (PLT194, PA.VIII.A.R3, PH.I.H.K1d) — AIM ¶8-1-8*

**Answers**

| 2066 [A] | 2064 [C] | 2062 [A] | 3834 [A] | 3835 [A] | 3836 [C] |
| --- | --- | --- | --- | --- | --- |

**ALL**
**3849.** What preparation should a pilot make to adapt the eyes for night flying?

A—Wear sunglasses after sunset until ready for flight.
B—Avoid red lights at least 30 minutes before the flight.
C—Avoid bright white lights at least 30 minutes before the flight.

*Exposure to total darkness for at least 30 minutes is required for complete dark adaptation. Any degree of dark adaptation is lost within a few seconds of viewing a bright light. Red lights do not affect night vision. (PLT333, PA.XI.A.K1, PH.IX.A.K5) — AIM ¶8-1-6*

**AIR, RTC, LTA, WSC, PPC**
**3712.** What is the most effective way to use the eyes during night flight?

A—Look only at far away, dim lights.
B—Scan slowly to permit offcenter viewing.
C—Concentrate directly on each object for a few seconds.

*During daylight, an object can be seen best by looking directly at it, but at night, a scanning procedure to permit off-center viewing of the object is more effective. In addition, the pilot should consciously practice moving the eyes more slowly than in daylight to optimize night vision. Off-center viewing must be utilized during night flying because of the distribution of rods and cones in the eye. (PLT099, PA.XI.A.K1, PH.IX.A.K5) — FAA-H-8083-25*

**AIR, RTC, LTA, WSC, PPC**
**3713.** The best method to use when looking for other traffic at night is to

A—look to the side of the object and scan slowly.
B—scan the visual field very rapidly.
C—look to the side of the object and scan rapidly.

*During daylight, an object can be seen best by looking directly at it, but at night, a scanning procedure to permit off-center viewing of the object is more effective. In addition, the pilot should consciously practice moving the eyes more slowly than in daylight to optimize night vision. Off-center viewing must be utilized during night flying because of the distribution of rods and cones in the eye. (PLT099, PA.XI.A.K1, PH.IX.A.K5) — FAA-H-8083-25*

**AIR, RTC, LTA, WSC, PPC**
**3714.** The most effective method of scanning for other aircraft for collision avoidance during nighttime hours is to use

A—regularly spaced concentration on the three, nine, and twelve o'clock positions.
B—a series of short, regularly spaced eye movements to search each 30° sector.
C—peripheral vision by scanning small sectors and utilizing offcenter viewing.

*During daylight, an object can be seen best by looking directly at it, but at night, a scanning procedure to permit off-center viewing of the object is more effective. In addition, the pilot should consciously practice moving the eyes more slowly than in daylight to optimize night vision. Off-center viewing must be utilized during night flying because of the distribution of rods and cones in the eye. (PLT099, PA.XI.A.K1, PH.IX.A.K5) — FAA-H-8083-3*

**Answers**

3849 [C]　　3712 [B]　　3713 [A]　　3714 [C]

# Aeronautical Decision Making (ADM)

The pilot is responsible for determining if they are fit to fly for a particular flight. Most preventable accidents have one common factor: human error, rather than a mechanical malfunction. Good aeronautical decision making is necessary to prevent human error. ADM is a systematic approach to the mental process used by aircraft pilots to consistently determine the best course of action in response to a given set of circumstances.

The ADM process addresses all aspects of decision making in the flight deck and identifies the steps involved in good decision making. Steps for good decision making are:

1. Identifying personal attitudes hazardous to safe flight.
2. Learning behavior modification techniques.
3. Learning how to recognize and cope with stress.
4. Developing risk assessment skills.
5. Using all resources in a multicrew situation.
6. Evaluating the effectiveness of one's ADM skills.

There are a number of classic behavioral traps into which pilots have been known to fall. Pilots, particularly those with considerable experience, as a rule always try to complete a flight as planned, please passengers, meet schedules, and generally demonstrate that they have the "right stuff." These tendencies ultimately may lead to practices that are dangerous and often illegal, and may lead to a mishap. All experienced pilots have fallen prey to, or have been tempted by, one or more of these tendencies in their flying careers. These dangerous tendencies or behavior patterns, which must be identified and eliminated, include:

- **Peer pressure.** Poor decision making based upon emotional response to peers rather than evaluating a situation objectively.

- **Mind set.** The inability to recognize and cope with changes in the situation different from those anticipated or planned.

- **Get-there-itis.** This tendency, common among pilots, clouds the vision and impairs judgment by causing a fixation on the original goal or destination combined with a total disregard for any alternative course of action.

- **Duck-under syndrome.** The tendency to sneak a peek by descending below minimums during an approach. Based on a belief that there is always a built-in "fudge" factor that can be used or on an unwillingness to admit defeat and shoot a missed approach.

- **Scud running.** Pushing the capabilities of the pilot and the aircraft to the limits by trying to maintain visual contact with the terrain while trying to avoid physical contact with it. This attitude is characterized by the old pilot's joke: "If it's too bad to go IFR, we'll go VFR."

- **Continuing VFR flight into IMC.** Can lead to spatial disorientation or collision with ground/obstacles. It is even more dangerous if the pilot is not instrument qualified or current.

- **Getting behind the aircraft.** Allowing events or the situation to control your actions rather than the other way around. Characterized by a constant state of surprise at what happens next.

- **Loss of positional or situation awareness.** Another case of getting behind the aircraft which results in not knowing where you are, an inability to recognize deteriorating circumstances, and/or the misjudgment of the rate of deterioration.

- **Operating without adequate fuel reserves.** Ignoring minimum fuel reserve requirements, either VFR or IFR, is generally the result of overconfidence, lack of flight planning, or ignoring the regulations.

- **Descent below the minimum enroute altitude.** Duck-under syndrome manifesting itself during the enroute portion of an IFR flight.

- **Flying outside the envelope.** Unjustified reliance on the (usually mistaken) belief that the aircraft's high performance capability meets the demands imposed by the pilot's (usually overestimated) flying skills.

- **Neglect of flight planning, preflight inspections, checklists, etc.** Unjustified reliance on the pilot's short- and long-term memory, regular flying skills, repetitive and familiar routes, etc.

Each ADM student should take the Self-Assessment Hazardous Attitude Inventory Test in order to gain a realistic perspective on their own attitudes toward flying. The test requires the pilot to provide a response which most accurately reflects the reasoning behind their decision. The pilot must choose one of the five given reasons for making that decision, even though the pilot may not consider any of the five choices acceptable. The test presents extreme cases of incorrect pilot decision making in an effort to introduce the five types of hazardous attitudes.

ADM addresses the following five hazardous attitudes:

1. **Anti-authority (don't tell me!).** This attitude is found in people who do not like anyone telling them what to do. In a sense they are saying "no one can tell me what to do." They may be resentful of having someone tell them what to do or may regard rules, regulations, and procedures as silly or unnecessary. However, it is always your prerogative to question authority if you feel it is in error. The antidote for this attitude is: "Follow the rules. They are usually right."

2. **Impulsivity (do something quickly!).** is the attitude of people who frequently feel the need to do something—anything—immediately. They do not stop to think about what they are about to do, they do not select the best alternative, and they do the first thing that comes to mind. The antidote for this attitude is: "Not so fast. Think first."

3. **Invulnerability (it won't happen to me).** Many people feel that accidents happen to others, but never to them. They know accidents can happen, and they know that anyone can be affected. They never really feel or believe that they will be personally involved. Pilots who think this way are more likely to take chances and increase risk. The antidote for this attitude is: "It could happen to me."

4. **Macho (I can do it).** Pilots who are always trying to prove that they are better than anyone else are thinking "I can do it—I'll show them." Pilots with this type of attitude will try to prove themselves by taking risks in order to impress others. While this pattern is thought to be a male characteristic, women are equally susceptible. The antidote for this attitude is: "Taking chances is foolish."

5. **Resignation (what's the use?).** Pilots who think "what's the use?" do not see themselves as being able to make a great deal of difference in what happens to them. When things go well, the pilot is apt to think that's good luck. When things go badly, the pilot may feel that "someone is out to get me," or attribute it to bad luck. The pilot will leave the action to others, for better or worse. Sometimes, such pilots will even go along with unreasonable requests just to be a "nice guy." The antidote for this attitude is: "I'm not helpless. I can make a difference."

Hazardous attitudes which contribute to poor pilot judgment can be effectively counteracted by redirecting that hazardous attitude so that appropriate action can be taken. Recognition of hazardous thoughts is the first step in neutralizing them in the ADM process. Pilots should become familiar with a means of counteracting hazardous attitudes with an appropriate antidote thought. When a pilot recognizes a thought as hazardous, the pilot should correct that thought by stating the corresponding antidote.

If you hope to succeed at reducing stress associated with crisis management in the air or with your job, it is essential to begin by making a personal assessment of stress in all areas of your life. Good **flight deck stress management** begins with good life stress management. Many of the stress coping techniques practiced for life stress management are not usually practical in flight. Rather, you must condition yourself to relax and think rationally when stress appears. The following checklist outlines some thoughts on flight deck stress management.

1. Avoid situations that distract you from flying the aircraft.

2. Reduce your workload to reduce stress levels. This will create a proper environment in which to make good decisions.

3. If an emergency does occur, be calm. Think for a moment, weigh the alternatives, then act.

4. Maintain proficiency in your aircraft; proficiency builds confidence. Familiarize yourself thoroughly with your aircraft, its systems, and emergency procedures.

5. Know and respect your own personal limits.

6. Do not let little mistakes bother you until they build into a big thing. Wait until after you land, then debrief and analyze past actions.

7. If flying is adding to your stress, either stop flying or seek professional help to manage your stress within acceptable limits.

**The DECIDE model**, comprised of a six-step process, is intended to provide the pilot with a logical way of approaching decision making. The six elements of the DECIDE model represent a continuous loop decision process which can be used to assist a pilot in the decision making process when they are faced with a change in a situation that requires a judgment. This DECIDE model is primarily focused on the intellectual component, but can have an impact on the motivational component of judgment as well. If a pilot practices the DECIDE model in all decision making, its use can become very natural and could result in better decisions being made under all types of situations.

1. **D**etect. The decision maker detects the fact that change has occurred.

2. **E**stimate. The decision maker estimates the need to counter or react to the change.

3. **C**hoose. The decision maker chooses a desirable outcome (in terms of success) for the flight.

4. **I**dentify. The decision maker identifies actions which could successfully control the change.

5. **D**o. The decision maker takes the necessary action.

6. **E**valuate. The decision maker evaluates the effect(s) of their action countering the change.

ALL, SPO

**3931.** What is it often called when a pilot pushes his or her capabilities and the aircraft's limits by trying to maintain visual contact with the terrain in low visibility and ceiling?

A—Scud running.
B—Mind set.
C—Peer pressure.

*Scud running is pushing the capabilities of the pilot and the aircraft to the limits by trying to maintain visual contact with the terrain while trying to avoid physical contact with it. (PLT104, PA.I.H.K4, PH.I.H.K4) — FAA-H-8083-25*

ALL, SPO

**3932.** What antidotal phrase can help reverse the hazardous attitude of anti-authority?

A—Rules do not apply in this situation.
B—I know what I am doing.
C—Follow the rules.

*The anti-authority (don't tell me!) attitude is found in people who do not like anyone telling them what to do. The antidote for this attitude is: follow the rules, they are usually right. (PLT103, PA.I.H.R2, PH.I.H.R2) — FAA-H-8083-25*

**Answers**

3931  [A]  3932  [C]

ALL

**3933.** What antidotal phrase can help reverse the hazardous attitude of impulsivity?

A—It could happen to me.
B—Do it quickly to get it over with.
C—Not so fast, think first.

*Impulsivity (do something quickly!) is the attitude of people who frequently feel the need to do something, anything, immediately. They do not stop to think about what they are about to do, they do not select the best alternative, and they do the first thing that comes to mind. The antidote for this attitude is: Not so fast. Think first. (PLT103, PA.I.H.R2, PH.I.H.R2) — FAA-H-8083-25*

ALL

**3931-1.** Hazardous attitudes occur to every pilot to some degree at some time. What are some of these hazardous attitudes?

A—Poor risk management and lack of stress management.
B—Anti-authority, impulsivity, macho, resignation, and invulnerability.
C—Poor situational awareness, snap judgments, and lack of a decision making process.

*ADM addresses the following five hazardous attitudes: anti-authority (don't tell me!), impulsivity (do something quickly!), invulnerability (it won't happen to me!), macho (I can do it!), resignation (what's the use?). (PLT103, PA.I.H.R2, PH.I.H.R2) — FAA-H-8083-25*

ALL, SPO

**3931-2.** In the aeronautical decision making (ADM) process, what is the first step in neutralizing a hazardous attitude?

A—Making a rational judgement.
B—Recognizing hazardous thoughts.
C—Recognizing the invulnerability of the situation.

*Hazardous attitudes which contribute to poor pilot judgment can be effectively counteracted by redirecting that hazardous attitude so that appropriate action can be taken. Recognition of hazardous thoughts is the first step in neutralizing them in the ADM process. (PLT103, PA.I.H.K4, PH.I.H.K4) — FAA-H-8083-25*

ALL, SPO

**3931-3.** Risk management, as part of the aeronautical decision making (ADM) process, relies on which features to reduce the risks associated with each flight?

A—Application of stress management and risk element procedures.
B—Situational awareness, problem recognition, and good judgment.
C—The mental process of analyzing all information in a particular situation and making a timely decision on what action to take.

*Risk management is the part of ADM which relies on situational awareness, problem recognition, and good judgment to reduce risks associated with each flight. (PLT271, PA.I.H.K4, PH.I.H.K4) — FAA-H-8083-25*

ALL, SPO

**3934.** What antidotal phrase can help reverse the hazardous attitude of invulnerability?

A—It will not happen to me.
B—It can not be that bad.
C—It could happen to me.

*Invulnerability (it won't happen to me) is found in people who think accidents happen to others, but never to them. Pilots who think this way are more likely to take chances and increase risk. The antidote for this attitude is: It could happen to me. (PLT103, PA.I.H.R2, PH.I.H.R2) — FAA-H-8083-25*

ALL

**3935.** What antidotal phrase can help reverse the hazardous attitude of macho?

A—I can do it.
B—Taking chances is foolish.
C—Nothing will happen.

*Macho (I can do it) is the attitude found in pilots who are always trying to prove they are better than anyone else. Pilots with this type of attitude will try to prove themselves by taking risks in order to impress others. The antidote for this attitude is: Taking chances is foolish. (PLT103, PA.I.H.R2, PH.I.H.R2) — FAA-H-8083-25*

**Answers**

3933 [C]    3931-1 [B]    3931-2 [B]    3931-3 [B]    3934 [C]    3935 [B]

ALL

**3936.** What antidotal phrase can help reverse the hazardous attitude of resignation?

A—What is the use.
B—Someone else is responsible.
C—I am not helpless.

*Resignation (what's the use?) is the attitude in pilots who do not see themselves as being able to make a great deal of difference in what happens to them. When things go well, the pilot is apt to think it's due to good luck. When things go badly, the pilot may feel that "someone is out to get me," or attribute it to bad luck. The antidote for this attitude is: I'm not helpless. I can make a difference. (PLT103, PA.I.H.R2, PH.I.H.R2) — FAA-H-8083-25*

ALL

**3937.** Who is responsible for determining whether a pilot is fit to fly for a particular flight, even though he or she holds a current medical certificate?

A—The FAA.
B—The medical examiner.
C—The pilot.

*The pilot is responsible for determining if they are fit to fly for a particular flight. (PLT443, PA.II.A.K1, PH.I.H.K1) — FAA-H-8083-25*

SPO

**2078.** Who is responsible for determining whether a pilot is fit to fly for a particular flight, even though the pilot holds a current and valid U.S. driver's license?

A—The FAA.
B—The pilot.
C—The medical examiner.

*The pilot is responsible for determining if they are fit to fly for a particular flight. (PLT443) — FAA-H-8083-25*

ALL, SPO

**3938.** What is the one common factor which affects most preventable accidents?

A—Structural failure.
B—Mechanical malfunction.
C—Human error.

*Most preventable accidents have one common factor: human error, rather than a mechanical malfunction. (PLT104, PA.II.A.R1, PH.I.H.K1) — FAA-H-8083-25*

ALL

**3939.** What often leads to spatial disorientation or collision with ground/obstacles when flying under visual flight rules (VFR)?

A—Continual flight into instrument conditions.
B—Getting behind the aircraft.
C—Duck-under syndrome.

*Continuing VFR flight into IMC often leads to spatial disorientation or collision with ground/obstacles. It is even more dangerous if the pilot is not instrument qualified or current. (PLT334, PA.I.H.R3, PH.I.H.K1d) — FAA-H-8083-25*

ALL, SPO

**3940.** What is one of the neglected items when a pilot relies on short and long term memory for repetitive tasks?

A—Checklists.
B—Situation awareness.
C—Flying outside the envelope.

*Unjustified reliance on the pilot's short and long term memory, regular flying skills, repetitive and familiar routes usually results in neglect of flight planning, preflight inspections, and checklists. (PLT104, PA.II.B.K2, PH.I.H.K1) — FAA-H-8083-25*

ALL

**3940-1.** A pilot and two passengers landed on a 2,100 foot east-west gravel strip with an elevation of 1,800 feet. The temperature is warmer than expected and after computing the density altitude it is determined the takeoff distance over a 50 foot obstacle is 1,980 feet. The airplane is 75 pounds under gross weight. What would be the best choice?

A—Takeoff off into the headwind will give the extra climb-out time needed.
B—Try a takeoff without the passengers to make sure the climb is adequate.
C—Wait until the temperature decreases, and recalculate the takeoff performance.

*The conditions described provide only 120 feet for a margin of error between required takeoff distance and available runway. This is too risky; the pilot should wait until conditions improve and there is a larger margin of safety between available and needed runway distance. (PLT011, PA.IV.N.K3, PH.I.H.K4) — FAA-H-8083-2*

**Answers**

| | | | | | |
|---|---|---|---|---|---|
| 3936 [C] | 3937 [C] | 2078 [B] | 3938 [C] | 3939 [A] | 3940 [A] |
| 3940-1 [C] | | | | | |

SPO
**2073.** A series of judgmental errors which can lead to a human factors-related accident is sometimes referred to as the

A—error chain.
B—course of action.
C—DECIDE model.

*The poor judgment chain, sometimes referred to as the error chain, is a term used to describe this concept of contributing factors in a human-factors-related accident. Breaking one link in the chain normally is all that is necessary to change the outcome of the sequence of events. (PLT271) — FAA-H-8083-25*

SPO
**2085.** Which of the following is the first step of the Decide Model for effective risk management and Aeronautical Decision Making?

A—Identify.
B—Detect.
C—Evaluate.

*The DECIDE model, comprised of a six-step process, is intended to provide the pilot with a logical way of approaching decision making: detect, estimate, choose, identify, do, and evaluate. (PLT022) — FAA-H-8083-25*

SPO
**2074.** What are some of the hazardous attitudes dealt with in Aeronautical Decision Making (ADM)?

A—Risk management, stress management, and risk elements.
B—Poor decision making, situational awareness, and judgment.
C—Anti-authority (don't tell me), impulsivity (do something quickly without thinking), macho (I can do it).

*ADM addresses the following five hazardous attitudes: Anti-authority (don't tell me!), impulsivity (do something quickly!), invulnerability (it won't happen to me), macho (I can do it), resignation (what's the use?). (PLT103) — FAA-H-8083-25*

SPO
**2195.** What should a pilot do when recognizing a thought as hazardous?

A—Label that thought as hazardous, then correct that thought by stating the corresponding learned antidote.
B—Avoid developing this hazardous thought.
C—Develop this hazardous thought and follow through with modified action.

*When a pilot recognizes a thought as hazardous, the pilot should label that thought as hazardous, then correct that thought by stating the corresponding antidote. (PLT103) — FAA-H-8083-25*

SPO
**2176.** Pilots should be familiar with positive alternatives to

A—Counteract hazardous attitudes.
B—Ensure the right choices have been made.
C—Ensure they are applying the appropriate antidote.

*The pilot must examine decisions carefully to ensure choices have not been influenced by hazardous attitudes and be familiar with positive alternatives to counteract the hazardous attitudes (referred to as antidotes). (PLT103) — FAA-H-8083-25*

SPO
**2079.** Aeronautical decision making (ADM) is a

A—mental process of analyzing all information in a particular situation and making a timely decision on what action to take.
B—systematic approach to the mental process used by pilots to consistently determine the best course of action for a given set of circumstances.
C—decision making process which relies on good judgment to reduce risks associated with each flight.

*ADM is a systematic approach to the mental process used by aircraft pilots to consistently determine the best course of action in response to a given set of circumstances. (PLT022) — FAA-H-8083-25*

**Answers**

| 2073 [A] | 2085 [B] | 2074 [C] | 2195 [A] | 2176 [A] | 2079 [B] |
|---|---|---|---|---|---|

SPO

**2083.** Ignoring minimum fuel reserve requirements is generally the result of overconfidence, disregarding applicable regulations, or

A—lack of flight planning.
B—impulsivity.
C—physical stress.

*Ignoring minimum fuel reserve requirements is generally the result of overconfidence, lack of flight planning, or disregarding applicable regulations. (PLT104) — FAA-H-8083-25*

SPO

**2196.** The basic drive for a pilot to demonstrate the "right stuff" can have an adverse effect on safety, by

A—a total disregard for any alternative course of action.
B—generating tendencies that lead to practices that are dangerous, often illegal, and may lead to a mishap.
C—allowing events, or the situation, to control his or her actions.

*Pilots, particularly those with considerable experience, as a rule always try to complete a flight as planned, please passengers, meet schedules, and generally demonstrate that they have the "right stuff." These tendencies ultimately may lead to practices that are dangerous and often illegal, and may lead to a mishap. (PLT103) — FAA-H-8083-25*

SPO

**2197.** A pilot who relies on short- and long-term memory for repetitive tasks often neglects

A—flying outside the envelope.
B—checklists.
C—situation awareness.

*Unjustified reliance on the pilot's short- and long-term memory, regular flying skills, repetitive and familiar routes usually results in neglect of flight planning, preflight inspections, and checklists. (PLT104) — FAA-H-8083-25*

SPO

**2063.** Consistent adherence to approved checklists is a sign of a

A—disciplined and competent pilot.
B—pilot who lacks the required knowledge.
C—low-time pilot.

*To avoid missing important steps, always use the appropriate checklists whenever they are available. Consistent adherence to approved checklists is a sign of a disciplined and competent pilot. (PLT122) — FAA-H-8083-25*

SPO

**2069.** The positive three-step process in the exchange of flight controls between pilots includes these verbal steps: (1) You have the flight controls, (2) I have the flight controls, and (3)

A—You have the flight controls.
B—I have the aircraft.
C—I have the flight controls.

*There must always be a clear understanding who has control of the aircraft. Prior to flight, a briefing should be conducted that includes the procedure for the exchange of flight controls. A positive three-step process in the exchange of flight controls between pilots is a proven procedure: You have the flight controls, I have the flight controls, You have the flight controls. (PLT340) — FAA-H-8083-9*

SPO

**2068.** To avoid missing important steps, always use the

A—appropriate checklists.
B—placarded airspeeds.
C—airworthiness certificate.

*To avoid missing important steps, always use the appropriate checklists whenever they are available. Consistent adherence to approved checklists is a sign of a disciplined and competent pilot. (PLT122) — FAA-H-8083-25*

SPO

**2082.** An extreme case of a pilot getting behind the aircraft can lead to the operational pitfall of

A—loss of situational awareness.
B—loss of workload.
C—internal stress.

*Getting behind the aircraft can result in not knowing where you are, an inability to recognize deteriorating circumstances, and/or the misjudgment of the rate of deterioration. (PLT104) — FAA-H-8083-25*

---

**Answers**

| 2083 | [A] | 2196 | [B] | 2197 | [B] | 2063 | [A] | 2069 | [A] | 2068 | [A] |
| 2082 | [A] | | | | | | | | | | |

# Cross-Reference A
## Question Number and Page Number

This cross-reference lists all of the questions in this book in sequential order. Use this list in combination with Cross-Reference B to find specific questions to aid your studies. For more information about the questions included in ASA Test Preps, please see pages vii–ix and xxii.

| Question Number | Page Number | Question Number | Page Number | Question Number | Page Number | Question Number | Page Number |
|---|---|---|---|---|---|---|---|
| 2001 | 7–17 | 2064 | 10–8 | 2126 | 5–25 | 2213 | 5–59 |
| 2002 | 6–18 | 2066 | 10–8 | 2127 | 5–25 | 2214 | 5–59 |
| 2003 | 5–29 | 2067 | 4–8 | 2128 | 5–25 | 2215 | 1–9 |
| 2004 | 5–29 | 2068 | 10–16 | 2129 | 5–14 | 2216 | 1–9 |
| 2005 | 5–41 | 2069 | 10–16 | 2130 | 5–6 | 2218 | 6–27 |
| 2006 | 6–43 | 2073 | 10–15 | 2133-1 | 5–44 | 2222 | 7–31 |
| 2007 | 6–43 | 2074 | 10–15 | 2137 | 5–34 | 2223-2 | 4–24 |
| 2007-1 | 6–19 | 2078 | 10–14 | 2138 | 6–14 | 2225 | 1–5 |
| 2007-2 | 6–19 | 2079 | 10–15 | 2138-1 | 6–15 | 2225-1 | 1–5 |
| 2012 | 6–38 | 2082 | 10–16 | 2138-2 | 6–15 | 2226 | 6–46 |
| 2014 | 6–41 | 2083 | 10–16 | 2159 | 8–14 | 2229 | 1–9 |
| 2015 | 6–43 | 2085 | 10–15 | 2163 | 8–19 | 2230 | 4–27 |
| 2016 | 6–43 | 2087 | 5–24 | 2170 | 8–23 | 2232 | 5–23 |
| 2017 | 6–43 | 2089 | 10–6 | 2174 | 4–47 | 2233 | 1–19 |
| 2020 | 2–4 | 2090 | 10–6 | 2175 | 7–39 | 2234 | 4–11 |
| 2024 | 6–21 | 2091 | 10–6 | 2175-1 | 7–39 | 2234-1 | 4–22 |
| 2025 | 6–25 | 2092 | 10–6 | 2176 | 10–15 | 2236 | 4–27 |
| 2026 | 6–24 | 2093 | 10–6 | 2177 | 7–16 | 2238 | 2–7 |
| 2028 | 6–24 | 2097 | 10–6 | 2178 | 7–5 | 2239 | 1–9 |
| 2029 | 6–26 | 2099 | 7–30 | 2179 | 6–14 | 2240 | 10–7 |
| 2030 | 6–25 | 2100 | 7–37 | 2182 | 4–48 | 2242 | 2–7 |
| 2031 | 6–25 | 2101 | 7–30 | 2183 | 4–48 | 2283 | 4–11 |
| 2033 | 5–22 | 2102 | 7–13 | 2186-1 | 5–35 | 2308 | 5–19 |
| 2034-1 | 6–19 | 2103 | 7–16 | 2189 | 5–58 | 2312 | 8–23 |
| 2039 | 4–22 | 2104 | 7–16 | 2192 | 6–12 | 2326 | 2–50 |
| 2040 | 5–34 | 2105 | 7–30 | 2193 | 6–12 | 2327 | 2–50 |
| 2043 | 6–13 | 2106 | 7–5 | 2194 | 6–18 | 2328 | 6–33 |
| 2049 | 6–13 | 2107 | 6–35 | 2195 | 10–15 | 2329 | 2–24 |
| 2050 | 6–13 | 2108 | 7–5 | 2196 | 10–16 | 2331 | 6–33 |
| 2052 | 6–13 | 2109 | 5–55 | 2197 | 10–16 | 2332 | 6–33 |
| 2053 | 5–56 | 2110 | 5–55 | 2198 | 6–14 | 2341 | 2–11 |
| 2054 | 6–45 | 2113-1 | 6–15 | 2199 | 4–11 | 2347 | 2–50 |
| 2055-1 | 6–14 | 2115 | 6–14 | 2201 | 7–13 | 2348 | 2–50 |
| 2056 | 6–13 | 2117 | 5–56 | 2202 | 10–5 | 2350 | 4–48 |
| 2059 | 6–14 | 2118 | 6–36 | 2203 | 5–35 | 2351 | 4–48 |
| 2060 | 6–18 | 2119 | 6–36 | 2204 | 6–14 | 2353 | 2–14 |
| 2061 | 5–8 | 2120 | 5–56 | 2205 | 6–43 | 2354 | 2–15 |
| 2061-1 | 5–8 | 2121 | 5–56 | 2206 | 6–26 | 2356 | 4–7 |
| 2062 | 10–8 | 2122 | 6–8 | 2211 | 5–59 | 2364 | 2–7 |
| 2063 | 10–16 | 2123 | 5–7 | 2212 | 5–59 | 2367 | 6–15 |

# Cross-Reference B
## Airman Knowledge Test Report Codes and Question Numbers

When you take the applicable FAA Knowledge Exam required for an airman certificate or rating, you will receive an Airman Knowledge Test Report (AKTR). This test report will list the Learning Statement Codes (LSC) or Airman Certification Codes (ACS) for questions you have answered incorrectly. Match the codes given on your AKTR to the ones listed in this cross-reference. Use Cross-Reference A in this book to find the page number for the question numbers listed below.

Your AKTR will list the codes accordingly:

- If an ACS exists for the certificate or rating you're seeking, the report will list an ACS code. Reference the ACS specific to the certificate or rating to determine the subject you missed on the test: **faa.gov/training_testing/testing/acs/**

- If an ACS does not yet exist for the certificate or rating you're seeking, the report will list an LSC. Reference the Learning Statement Reference Guide to determine the subject you missed on the test: **faa.gov/training_testing/testing/media/LearningStatementReferenceGuide.pdf**

Your instructor is required to provide instruction on each of the areas of deficiency listed on your AKTR and give you an endorsement for this instruction. The AKTR must be presented to the examiner conducting your practical test. During the oral portion of the practical test, the examiner is required to evaluate the noted areas of deficiency.

If you received a code on your AKTR that is not listed in this cross-reference, email ASA at **cfi@asa2fly.com**. We will provide the definition so you can review that subject area.

## Learning Statement Codes and Question Numbers

| Learning Statement Code | FAA Reference | Subject Description (or **Topic** 〉 **Content** 〉 **Specific** classification) Question Numbers |
|---|---|---|
| PLT003 | FAA-H-8083-25 | Weight and Balance 〉 Center of Gravity 〉 Stability<br>*3287, 3672* |
| PLT005 | FAA-H-8083-25 | Aircraft Performance 〉 Computations 〉 Density Altitude<br>*2356, 3292, 3294* |
| PLT006 | FAA-H-8083-13 | Flight Operations 〉 Soaring Techniques 〉 Performance<br>*3345, 3346, 3347* |
| PLT008 | FAA-H-8083-25 | Aircraft Performance 〉 Computations 〉 Landing Distance<br>*3689, 3690, 3691, 3692, 3693, 3694, 3695, 3696, 3697, 3698* |
| PLT011 | FAA-H-8083-25 | Aircraft Performance 〉 Computations 〉 Takeoff Distance<br>*2113-1, 3705, 3706, 3707, 3708, 3940-1* |
| PLT012 | FAA-H-8083-25<br>SAC | Aircraft Performance 〉 Computations 〉 Cruise<br>Navigation 〉 Pilotage 〉 Aeronautical Charts; Calculations<br>Navigation 〉 Radio 〉 VOR<br>*2001, 2099, 2101, 2105, 2222, 3348, 3349, 3529-1, 3529-3, 3529-4, 3537, 3538, 3539, 3545, 3546, 3547, 3550, 3550-1, 3551, 3556, 3558, 3564, 3564-1, 3564-2, 3565, 3568, 3569, 3571, 3572, 3573, 3574, 3575, 3576, 3634, 3678, 3679, 3680, 3681, 3816, 3817* |

| Learning Statement Code | FAA Reference | Subject Description (or Topic ⟩ Content ⟩ Specific classification) Question Numbers |
|---|---|---|
| PLT013 | FAA-H-8083-25 | Aircraft Performance ⟩ Computations ⟩ Crosswind<br>*3683, 3684, 3685, 3686, 3687, 3688* |
| PLT015 | FAA-H-0883-25 | Calculate flight performance/planning–range<br>*2230* |
| PLT019 | FAA-H-8083-25 | Aircraft Performance ⟩ Computations ⟩ Density Altitude; Pressure Altitude<br>*3293, 3295, 3297, 3298* |
| PLT021 | FAA-H-8083-1<br>FAA-H-8083-21<br>FAA-H-8083-25 | Weight and Balance ⟩ Center of Gravity ⟩ Computations<br>*2350, 2351, 3662, 3663, 3663-1, 3664, 3666, 3667, 3674, 3675, 3676, 3677, 3815, 3861, 3863* |
| PLT022 | AC 60-22 | Define Aeronautical Decision Making (ADM)<br>*2079, 2085* |
| PLT023 | FAA-H-8083-25<br>FAA-H-8083-28 | Aircraft Systems ⟩ Flight Instruments ⟩ Altimeter; Altitude<br>Weather ⟩ Meteorology ⟩ Pressure<br>*3256, 3257, 3258, 3259, 3260, 3388, 3392, 3393* |
| PLT025 | FAA-H-8083-25 | Define Bernoulli's Principle<br>*3201-1* |
| PLT026 | FAA-H-8083-28 | Weather ⟩ Aeronautical Weather Reports ⟩ Aviation Routine Weather Reports (METAR)<br>*3463* |
| PLT039 | AIM | Airport Operations ⟩ Marking/Signs ⟩ Segmented Circle<br>*3805, 3807, 3808, 3809, 3810* |
| PLT040 | AIM<br>SAC | Airspace ⟩ Controlled ⟩ Class B<br>Navigation ⟩ Pilotage ⟩ Airspace<br>*2050, 2138-1, 3599, 3600, 3623* |
| PLT041 | FAA-H-8083-25 | Aircraft Systems ⟩ Flight Instruments ⟩ Altimeter<br>*3250, 3251, 3252, 3253, 3253-1, 3254* |
| PLT044 | AIM | Airport Operations ⟩ Tower Controlled ⟩ Ground Operations<br>*2003, 2012, 3119, 3792-1, 3811* |
| PLT054 | FAA-H-8083-13 | Aerodynamics ⟩ Principles of Flight ⟩ Performance<br>Flight Operations ⟩ X-C ⟩ Performance<br>*3864, 3865, 3866, 3867, 3868* |
| PLT057 | FAA-H-8083-11 | Aircraft Performance ⟩ Computations ⟩ Altitude<br>*3888, 3889, 3890, 3891, 3892, 3893, 3894* |
| PLT059 | FAA-H-8083-28 | Weather ⟩ Aeronautical Weather Reports ⟩ Aviation Routine Weather Reports (METAR)<br>*3462, 3464, 3465, 3466, 3467* |
| PLT061 | AIM<br>FAA-H-8083-28 | Weather ⟩ Aeronautical Weather Reports ⟩ Pilot Weather Reports<br>*3472, 3473, 3474, 3475, 3476* |

| Learning Statement Code | FAA Reference | Subject Description (or Topic ⟩ Content ⟩ Specific classification) Question Numbers |
|---|---|---|
| PLT064 | AIM<br>A/FD<br>FAA-H-8083-25<br>SAC | Airport Operations ⟩ Uncontrolled ⟩ Radio Communications<br>Airspace ⟩ Controlled ⟩ Class E<br>Airspace ⟩ Other ⟩ Military Training Routes<br>Airspace ⟩ Special Use ⟩ MOA<br>Navigation ⟩ Pilotage ⟩ Aeronautical Charts; Airspace; Calculations<br>Navigation ⟩ Radio ⟩ VOR<br>Publications ⟩ Airport Facility Directory ⟩ Parachute Jumping<br><br>*2014, 2055-1, 2059, 2115, 2179, 2198, 2204, 2367, 3068-2, 3520, 3530, 3531, 3535, 3536, 3543, 3553, 3567, 3601, 3601-1, 3603, 3606, 3607, 3608, 3609, 3610, 3611, 3612, 3619, 3620-1, 3620-2, 3621-2, 3621-3, 3627, 3628, 3629, 3631, 3632, 3633, 3635, 3636, 3637, 3638, 3639, 3640, 3644, 3645, 3646, 3647, 3831, 3841-1* |
| PLT072 | FAA-H-8083-28 | Weather ⟩ Aeronautical Weather Forecasts ⟩ Terminal Aerodrome Forecasts (TAF)<br>*3479, 3480, 3481, 3482, 3483, 3484, 3485, 3486* |
| PLT074 | FAA-H-8083-25 | Aerodynamics ⟩ Load Factor ⟩ Steep Turns<br>*2215, 2216, 2371* |
| PLT076 | FAA-H-8083-28 | Weather ⟩ Aeronautical Weather Forecasts ⟩ Winds/Temperatures Aloft Forecast<br>*3500, 3501, 3502, 3503* |
| PLT077 | AIM | Airport Operations ⟩ Marking/Signs ⟩ Airport Markings; Displaced Threshold; Tetrahedron, Traffic Pattern<br>*3773, 3774, 3776, 3806* |
| PLT078 | A/FD | Navigation ⟩ Pilotage ⟩ Aircraft/Facility Directory<br>*2107, 2119, 3513, 3838, 3838-1, 3839, 3840, 3841, 3842* |
| PLT088 | FAA-H-8083-25 | Aircraft Systems ⟩ Flight Instruments ⟩ Airspeed Indicator<br>*3264, 3265, 3266, 3267, 3268, 3269, 3270, 3271, 3272, 3273* |
| PLT090 | FAA-H-8083-25 | Navigation ⟩ Radio ⟩ ADF/NDB; VOR<br>*3533, 3560, 3561, 3570, 3577, 3578, 3579* |
| PLT092 | FAA-H-8083-25 | Weight and Balance ⟩ Center of Gravity ⟩ Computations<br>*3663-2, 3669, 3670, 3671, 3673* |
| PLT097 | FAA-H-8083-25 | Human Factors ⟩ Aeromedical Factors ⟩ Carbon Monoxide Poisoning<br>*3832, 3848* |
| PLT098 | AIM | Human Factors ⟩ Aeromedical Factors ⟩ Fitness for Flight<br>*2089, 2090, 2202* |
| PLT099 | FAA-H-8083-25 | Flight Operations ⟩ Night ⟩ Scan<br>*3712, 3713, 3714* |
| PLT101 | AIM<br>FAA-H-8083-25<br>SAC | Navigation ⟩ Pilotage ⟩ Aeronautical Charts; Airspace; Calculations; Flight Plans<br>Navigation ⟩ Radio ⟩ VOR<br>Publications ⟩ Aeronautical Charts ⟩ Sectionals<br>*3117, 3421, 3530-1, 3559, 3566, 3621-1, 3624, 3625, 3637-1, 3641, 3642, 3643* |
| PLT103 | FAA-H-8083-25 | Human Factors ⟩ ADM ⟩ Hazardous Attitudes<br>*2074, 2176, 2195, 2196, 3931-1, 3931-2, 3932, 3933, 3934, 3935, 3936* |
| PLT104 | FAA-H-8083-25 | Human Factors ⟩ ADM, CRM ⟩ Operational Pitfalls<br>*2082, 2083, 2197, 3931, 3938, 3940* |

| Learning Statement Code | FAA Reference | Subject Description (or Topic 〉 Content 〉 Specific classification) / Question Numbers |
|---|---|---|
| PLT112 | FAA-H-8083-3 | Airport Operations 〉 Taxiing 〉 Flight Controls<br>*2015, 3305, 3306, 3307, 3308* |
| PLT114 | FAA-H-8083-11 | Aircraft Systems 〉 Structures 〉 Balloon<br>*2347, 2348* |
| PLT115 | FAA-H-8083-25 | Aircraft Systems 〉 Powerplant 〉 Fueling; Ignition<br>*3238, 3238-1, 3239* |
| PLT116 | FAA-H-8083-25 | Publications 〉 Advisory Circulars 〉 Acquisition; Subject Numbering<br>*2004, 2052, 2062, 2066, 2106, 2108, 2109, 2110, 2117, 2138-2, 2226, 3709, 3854, 3855, 3856* |
| PLT118 | FAA-H-8083-25 | Aircraft Systems 〉 Flight Instruments 〉 Directional Gyro<br>*3276* |
| PLT119 | FAA-H-8083-3 | Flight Operations 〉 Collision Avoidance 〉 Aircraft Position Lights<br>*2020, 3162, 3715, 3716, 3717, 3916, 3916-1* |
| PLT120 | FAA-H-8083-28 | Weather 〉 Meteorology 〉 Thunderstorms<br>*3449* |
| PLT121 | FAA-H-8083-25 | Weight and Balance 〉 Center of Gravity 〉 Computations<br>*3665, 3668* |
| PLT122 | FAA-H-8083-25 | Recall aircraft operations—checklist usage<br>*2063, 2068* |
| PLT123 | FAA-H-8083-3 | Flight Operations 〉 Climb 〉 Speed<br>*2326, 3011, 3012-1, 3364* |
| PLT124 | FAA-H-8083-25 | Aircraft Performance 〉 Computations 〉 Density Altitude; Landing Distance<br>*3290, 3296, 3299, 3300, 3372* |
| PLT125 | *AIM* | Flight Operations 〉 Normal Procedures 〉 Scan<br>*2229, 3814, 3909* |
| PLT126 | AC 91-13 | Recall airport performance—cold weather operations<br>*2353, 2354* |
| PLT127 | FAA-H-8083-25 | Aircraft Performance 〉 Computations 〉 Density Altitude<br>*2067, 3291* |
| PLT128 | FAA-H-8083-28 | Weather 〉 Meteorology 〉 Icing<br>*3431, 3432, 3956* |
| PLT129 | FAA-H-8083-21 | Flight Operations 〉 Takeoff 〉 Helicopter<br>*2199* |
| PLT130 | FAA-H-8083-25 | Recall aircraft performance—fuel<br>*3907* |
| PLT131 | FAA-H-8083-25 | Aircraft Performance 〉 Atmospheric Effects 〉 Ground Effect<br>*2223-2, 3312, 3313, 3314, 3315, 3324* |
| PLT132 | FAA-H-8083-25 | Aircraft Systems 〉 Flight Instruments 〉 Attitude Indicator<br>*2225-1, 3278, 3341, 3342* |

| Learning Statement Code | FAA Reference | Subject Description (or Topic ⟩ Content ⟩ Specific classification) / Question Numbers |
|---|---|---|
| PLT133 | FAA-H-8083-3 | Flight Operations ⟩ Climb ⟩ Speed<br><br>*3914* |
| PLT134 | FAA-H-8083-25 | Aerodynamics ⟩ Principles of Flight ⟩ Frost<br><br>*2234, 2283, 3206* |
| PLT136 | FAA-H-8083-25 | Aircraft Systems ⟩ Powerplant ⟩ Carburetor<br><br>*3236* |
| PLT140 | AIM | Airport Operations ⟩ LAHSO ⟩ Procedures & Responsibility<br><br>*3951, 3953, 3954* |
| PLT141 | 14 CFR 91<br>AIM<br>FAA-H-8083-3 | Airport Operations ⟩ Lighting ⟩ Rotating Beacon; Taxiway<br>Airport Operations ⟩ Marking/Signs ⟩ Direction Signs; Runway; Taxiway<br>Regulations ⟩ 14 CFR Part 91 ⟩ Light Gun Signals<br><br>*2024, 2025, 2026, 2028, 2029, 2030, 2031, 2206, 2218, 3111, 3112, 3113, 3115, 3116, 3656-1, 3718, 3769, 3770, 3771, 3772, 3777, 3778, 3778-1, 3778-2, 3778-3, 3778-4, 3778-5, 3806-1, 3806-2, 3806-3, 3955, 3955-1, 3955-2, 3955-3, 3955-4, 3955-5, 3955-6, 3957* |
| PLT147 | 14 CFR 91<br>AIM | Airport Operations ⟩ Lighting ⟩ PAPI; VASI<br>Regulations ⟩ 14 CFR Part 91 ⟩ Airport Operations<br><br>*3121, 3760, 3762-1, 3764, 3765, 3766, 3767* |
| PLT149 | FAA-H-8083-21 | Recall airport preflight/taxi operations—procedures<br><br>*2328, 2331* |
| PLT150 | AIM | Airport Operations ⟩ Tower Controlled ⟩ Radio Communications<br><br>*3123-1, 3789, 3804* |
| PLT153 | FAA-H-8083-11 | Aircraft Performance ⟩ Limitations ⟩ Airship<br>Flight Operations ⟩ Landing ⟩ Descents<br>Flight Operations ⟩ Maneuvers ⟩ Advanced; Basic<br>Flight Operations ⟩ Normal Procedures ⟩ Buoyancy<br>Weight and Balance ⟩ Aircraft Loading ⟩ Ballast<br><br>*3368, 3369, 3370, 3371, 3373, 3374, 3375, 3376, 3377, 3378* |
| PLT158 | FAA-H-8083-11 | Recall airship—pressure height/manometers<br><br>*3380* |
| PLT161 | 14 CFR 71<br>14 CFR 91<br>AIM<br>A/FD<br>SAC | Aircraft Systems ⟩ Avionics ⟩ Transponder<br>Airspace ⟩ Controlled ⟩ Class C; Class D<br>Airspace ⟩ Uncontrolled ⟩ Class G<br>Publications ⟩ Airport Facility Directory ⟩ Airport Remarks<br>Regulations ⟩ 14 CFR Part 71 ⟩ Airspace<br>Regulations ⟩ 14 CFR Part 91 ⟩ Aircraft Speed; Airspace; Special VFR;<br>   Transponder Operations<br><br>*2049, 3053, 3054, 3068, 3068-1, 3099, 3100, 3118, 3126, 3127, 3128, 3130, 3153, 3154, 3165, 3166, 3166-1, 3166-2, 3166-3, 3166-4, 3622, 3626, 3779, 3780, 3781, 3782, 3787, 3799, 3802-1, 3803, 3813* |
| PLT162 | AIM | Airspace ⟩ Controlled ⟩ Class D<br><br>*2043, 2056, 2192, 2193, 3787-1, 3788* |
| PLT163 | 14 CFR 91 | Regulations ⟩ 14 CFR Part 91 ⟩ Airspace; Class D Operations<br><br>*2040, 2061-1, 2137, 2138, 2186-1, 2203, 3056, 3057, 3069, 3134, 3135, 3136, 3137, 3142, 3143, 3144, 3145, 3146, 3147, 3148, 3149* |

| Learning Statement Code | FAA Reference | Subject Description (or Topic ⟩ Content ⟩ Specific classification) Question Numbers |
|---|---|---|
| PLT165 | FAA-H-8083-25 FAA-H-8083-28 | Aircraft Systems ⟩ Flight Instruments ⟩ Altimeter<br>Weather ⟩ Meteorology ⟩ Temperature<br><br>*3255, 3382* |
| PLT166 | FAA-H-8083-25 | Aircraft Systems ⟩ Flight Instruments ⟩ Altimeter; Attitude Indicator<br><br>*3261, 3277* |
| PLT167 | FAA-H-8083-25 FAA-H-8083-28 | Aircraft Systems ⟩ Flight Instruments ⟩ Altimeter<br>Weather ⟩ Meteorology ⟩ Pressure<br><br>*3387, 3390, 3391* |
| PLT168 | FAA-H-8083-25 | Aerodynamics ⟩ Principles of Flight ⟩ Angle of Attack<br>Aerodynamics ⟩ Stall/Spins ⟩ Stalls<br><br>*3203, 3204, 3204-1, 3311, 3317* |
| PLT170 | FAA-H-8083-11 | Flight Operations ⟩ Approach ⟩ High-Wind Landing<br><br>*2002, 2017, 2234-1, 3120, 3122, 3308-1, 3339* |
| PLT172 | *AIM* | Recall ATC—system/services<br><br>*2205, 3796* |
| PLT173 | FAA-H-8083-28 | Weather ⟩ Meteorology ⟩ Stability<br><br>*3403, 3404, 3405, 3411, 3758* |
| PLT177 | FAA-8083-1 FAA-H-8083-11 | Flight Operations ⟩ Cruise ⟩ Altitude<br>Flight Operations ⟩ Emergency Procedures ⟩ Balloon<br>Flight Operations ⟩ Landing ⟩ Touchdown<br>Weight and Balance ⟩ Aircraft Loading ⟩ Definitions<br><br>*3351, 3360, 3363, 3887, 3895, 3899* |
| PLT183 | FAA-H-8083-11 | Recall balloon flight operations—ascent/descent<br><br>*3367* |
| PLT184 | FAA-H-8083-11 | Flight Operations ⟩ Normal Procedures ⟩ Preflight<br><br>*3900, 3901* |
| PLT185 | FAA-H-8083-13 | Aerodynamics ⟩ Principles of Flight ⟩ Turns<br><br>*3343, 3344* |
| PLT187 | FAA-H-8083-25 | Aircraft Systems ⟩ Flight Instruments ⟩ Turn Coordinator<br><br>*3275* |
| PLT189 | FAA-H-8083-25 | Aircraft Systems ⟩ Powerplant ⟩ Carburetor Heat<br><br>*3232, 3234* |
| PLT190 | FAA-H-8083-25 | Aircraft Systems ⟩ Powerplant ⟩ Carburetor; Carburetor Heat<br><br>*2341, 3229, 3231, 3235, 3958, 3964, 3975* |
| PLT191 | FAA-H-8083-25 | Aircraft Systems ⟩ Powerplant ⟩ Carburetor<br><br>*3225* |
| PLT192 | FAA-H-8083-28 | Weather ⟩ Meteorology ⟩ Clouds; Stability; Thunderstorms<br><br>*3406, 3407, 3415, 3416, 3417, 3418, 3419, 3420, 3433* |
| PLT194 | *AIM* FAA-H-8083-25 | Air Traffic Control Procedures ⟩ En Route ⟩ Radar<br>Airspace ⟩ Procedures ⟩ Scan<br>Human Factors ⟩ Aero-medical Factors ⟩ Fitness for Flight; Spatial Disorientation<br><br>*2054, 2064, 3710, 3710-1, 3792, 3793, 3794, 3795, 3834, 3835, 3836* |

| Learning Statement Code | FAA Reference | Subject Description (or Topic ⟩ Content ⟩ Specific classification) / Question Numbers |
|---|---|---|
| PLT196 | AIM | Airport Operations ⟩ Tower Controlled ⟩ ATIS<br>3605-2, 3791 |
| PLT198 | FAA-H-8083-3 | Flight Operations ⟩ Cruise ⟩ Ground Track<br>2103, 2104, 2177, 3529-2 |
| PLT200 | FAA-H-8083-25 | Navigation ⟩ Pilotage ⟩ Calculations<br>2100 |
| PLT201 | 14 CFR 91 | Regulations ⟩ 14 CFR Part 91 ⟩ Airport Operations<br>3123 |
| PLT204 | AIM | Instrument Procedures ⟩ Communications ⟩ Reports<br>2007-1, 2007-2, 3613, 3614, 3615, 3790, 3797 |
| PLT205 | AIM | Recall effects of alcohol on the body<br>2087 |
| PLT206 | FAA-H-8083-28 | Weather ⟩ Meteorology ⟩ Pressure<br>3289, 3394 |
| PLT207 | FAA-H-8083-25 | Aircraft Systems ⟩ Electrical ⟩ Charging Systems<br>2238, 2364, 3969 |
| PLT208 | FAA-H-8083-3 | Flight Operations ⟩ Emergency Procedures ⟩ Engine Failure<br>3202-4, 3202-5, 3223-1, 3711, 3902, 3904, 3911, 3915 |
| PLT213 | FAA-H-8083-25 | Aerodynamics ⟩ Stability/Control ⟩ Longitudinal Stability; Stability<br>3210, 3211 |
| PLT214 | FAA-H-8083-5 | Aircraft Systems ⟩ Structures ⟩ Washout<br>3211-1, 3976, 3977, 3979, 3981, 3982 |
| PLT215 | FAA-H-8083-25 | Aircraft Systems ⟩ Flight Instruments ⟩ Compass<br>3279, 3279-2, 3280, 3281, 3282, 3283, 3283-1, 3284, 3285, 3286 |
| PLT219 | FAA-H-8083-3 | Flight Operations ⟩ Maneuvers ⟩ Basic<br>3202-1, 3202-2, 3202-3, 3880, 3897, 3898, 3910 |
| PLT221 | FAA-H-8083-3 | Aerodynamics ⟩ Principles of Flight ⟩ Landings<br>3379, 3719, 3877, 3878, 3879, 3883, 3884, 3912, 3913, 3994, 3995 |
| PLT222 | FAA-H-8083-21 | Flight Operations ⟩ Takeoff ⟩ Helicopter<br>3998 |
| PLT225 | AIM | Navigation ⟩ Pilotage ⟩ Flight Plan<br>2175, 2175-1, 3818 |
| PLT226 | FAA-H-8083-28 | Weather ⟩ Meteorology ⟩ Fog; Icing<br>3443, 3445, 3446, 3447 |
| PLT234 | FAA-H-8083-25 | Recall forces acting on aircraft—3 axis intersect<br>3213 |
| PLT237 | FAA-H-8083-11 | Flight Operations ⟩ Launch Procedures ⟩ False Lift<br>3359, 3365, 3366 |

| Learning Statement Code | FAA Reference | Subject Description (or *Topic* 〉 *Content* 〉 *Specific* classification) Question Numbers |
|---|---|---|
| PLT241 | FAA-H-8083-13 | Aerodynamics 〉 Principles of Flight 〉 Horizontal Lift<br>*3205, 3340* |
| PLT242 | FAA-H-8083-25 | Aerodynamics 〉 Principles of Flight 〉 Forces Acting on Aircraft; Horizontal Lift<br>*3201, 3202, 3301* |
| PLT243 | FAA-H-8083-25 | Aerodynamics 〉Principles of Flight 〉 Torque; Turning Tendency<br>*3207, 3208, 3209* |
| PLT245 | FAA-H-8083-3 | Aerodynamics 〉 Stall/Spins 〉 Spins<br>*3309, 3310, 3382* |
| PLT249 | FAA-H-8083-25 | Aircraft Systems 〉 Powerplant 〉 Carburetor; Carburetor Heat; Mixture Control<br>*3226, 3228* |
| PLT250 | FAA-H-8083-25 | Aircraft Systems 〉 Powerplant 〉 Fuel Grade<br>*3237, 3241, 3242, 3243, 3355, 3886* |
| PLT251 | FAA-H-8083-11 | Flight Operations 〉 Emergency Procedures 〉 Balloon<br>*3356, 3362, 3906* |
| PLT253 | FAA-H-8083-25 | Aircraft Systems 〉 Powerplant 〉 Electric Fuel Pump; Mixture Control<br>*3221-1, 3224, 3227, 3230, 3230-1, 3233, 3243-1, 3352, 3353, 3959, 3960, 3961, 3962, 3963, 3974* |
| PLT254 | FAA-H-8083-11 | Aircraft Systems 〉 Fuel/Oil 〉 Fueling; Tanks<br>*3354, 3357, 3358, 3361, 3885* |
| PLT256 | FAA-H-8083-13 | Recall glider information—effect of loading<br>*3862* |
| PLT257 | FAA-H-8083-3 | Recall glide performance—speed/distance/ballast/lift/drag<br>*2239* |
| PLT260 | FAA-H-8083-21 | Recall gyroplane—aerodynamics/rotor systems<br>*2327, 2332* |
| PLT263 | FAA-H-8083-28 | Weather 〉 Meteorology 〉 Thunderstorms; Turbulence<br>*3425, 3442* |
| PLT271 | FAA-H-8083-25 | Human Factors 〉 ADM 〉 Judgement; Risk Management<br>*2073, 3931-3* |
| PLT274 | FAA-H-8083-28 | Weather 〉 Meteorology 〉 Icing<br>*3429, 3430* |
| PLT278 | FAA-H-8083-25 | Aircraft Systems 〉 Flight Instruments 〉 Airspeed Indicator<br>*3274, 3682* |
| PLT280 | AIM | Recall inflight illusions—causes/sources<br>*2240* |
| PLT281 | FAA-H-8083-25 | Publications 〉 AFD 〉 Revisions<br>*2118, 3619-1* |
| PLT284 | FAA-H-8083-28 | Weather 〉 Aeronautical Weather Forecasts 〉 Winds/Temperatures Aloft Forecast<br>*3505, 3506* |

| Learning Statement Code | FAA Reference | Subject Description (or Topic ⟩ Content ⟩ Specific classification) Question Numbers |
|---|---|---|
| PLT285 | FAA-H-8083-21 | Flight Operations ⟩ Maneuvers ⟩ Basic<br><br>*3735* |
| PLT290 | *AIM*<br>FAA-H-8083-28 | Weather ⟩ Aeronautical Weather Forecasts ⟩ AIRMETS/SIGMETS; SIGMETS<br>Weather ⟩ Hazardous ⟩ Thunderstorms<br><br>*3495, 3496, 3497, 3498, 3499* |
| PLT300 | *AIM* | Recall instrument/navigation system checks/inspections–limits/tuning/<br>identifying/logging<br><br>*3598-1* |
| PLT301 | FAA-H-8083-28 | Weather ⟩ Meteorology ⟩ Moisture; Temperature<br><br>*3383, 3384, 3385, 3402* |
| PLT303 | FAA-H-8083-28 | Recall L/D ratio<br><br>*3350, 3650* |
| PLT304 | FAA-H-8083-13 | Flight Operations ⟩ Launch Procedures ⟩ Aerotow Takeoffs; Climbing Turns<br>*3857, 3858, 3876, 3896* |
| PLT309 | FAA-H-8083-25 | Aerodynamics ⟩ Load Factor ⟩ Flight Maneuvers; Steep Turns<br>*3214, 3215, 3216, 3218* |
| PLT311 | FAA-H-8083-25 | Aerodynamics ⟩ Load Factor ⟩ Airspeed<br><br>*3217* |
| PLT312 | FAA-H-8083-25 | Aerodynamics ⟩ Load Factor ⟩ Stalling Speed<br><br>*3316* |
| PLT313 | FAA-H-8083-1 | Recall loading—limitations/terminology<br><br>*2174, 2182* |
| PLT316 | FAA-H-8083-25 | Weather ⟩ Aeronautical Weather Reports ⟩ Weather Briefings<br><br>*3468, 3469, 3470* |
| PLT320 | FAA-H-8083-25 | Navigation ⟩ Pilotage ⟩ Aeronautical Charts<br><br>*2102, 3279-1* |
| PLT323 | *AIM* | Air Traffic Control Procedures ⟩ Communications ⟩ Flight Service Stations<br>Navigation ⟩ Pilotage ⟩ NOTAMs<br>Publications ⟩ NOTAMs ⟩ FDC NOTAMs<br><br>*2120, 2121* |
| PLT324 | FAA-H-8083-25 | Aircraft Systems ⟩ Powerplant ⟩ Oil System<br><br>*3245* |
| PLT328 | FAA-H-8083-1<br>FAA-H-8083-25 | Weight and Balance ⟩ Aircraft Loading ⟩ Limitations<br>Weight and Balance ⟩ Center of Gravity ⟩ Computations<br><br>*2183, 3288, 3661, 3859, 3860* |
| PLT330 | *AIM* | Human Factors ⟩ Aero-medical Factors ⟩ Fitness for Flight<br><br>*3844* |
| PLT332 | *AIM* | Human Factors ⟩ Aero-medical Factors ⟩ Fitness for Flight<br>*2091, 2092, 2093, 3845, 3846, 3847* |
| PLT333 | *AIM* | Human Factors ⟩ Aero-medical Factors ⟩ Fitness for Flight<br>*3833, 3849* |

| Learning Statement Code | FAA Reference | Subject Description (or *Topic* 〉 *Content* 〉 *Specific* classification) Question Numbers |
|---|---|---|
| PLT334 | FAA-H-8083-25 | Human Factors 〉 Aero-medical Factors 〉 Spatial Disorientation<br>*2097, 3850, 3851, 3852, 3853, 3939* |
| PLT335 | FAA-H-8083-25 | Navigation 〉 Radio 〉 VOR<br>*2178, 2201, 3552* |
| PLT337 | FAA-H-8083-25 | Aircraft Systems 〉 Pitot/Static 〉 Airspeed Indicator; Blockage<br>*3247, 3248, 3249, 3262* |
| PLT340 | FAA-H-8083-3 | Recall positive exchange of flight controls<br>*2069* |
| PLT342 | FAA-H-8083-25 | Aircraft Systems 〉 Powerplant 〉 Mixture Control<br>*3221, 3244, 3651, 3652, 3965, 3966* |
| PLT343 | FAA-H-8083-3<br>FAA-H-8083-25 | Aircraft Systems 〉 Powerplant 〉 Lubrication; Mixture Control<br>*3222, 3653, 3656, 3967, 3968, 3971, 3972, 3973* |
| PLT345 | FAA-H-8083-25<br>FAA-H-8083-28 | Weather 〉 Meteorology 〉 Pressure<br>*3386, 3389* |
| PLT346 | FAA-H-8083-5 | Aircraft Systems 〉 Flight Controls/Primary 〉 Keel Pocket<br>*3978, 3980, 3983, 3984, 3985, 3986, 3987, 3988, 3989, 3990, 3991, 3992, 3993* |
| PLT351 | FAA-H-8083-25 | Aerodynamics 〉 Stability/Control 〉 Downwash<br>Aircraft Systems 〉 Propeller 〉 Adjustable-Pitch; Efficiency<br>*3212, 3246, 3654, 3655* |
| PLT354 | *AIM* | Recall radio—GPS/RNAV/RAIM<br>*3598-2, 3598-3, 3598-4* |
| PLT366 | 49 CFR 830 | Regulations 〉 NTSB Part 830 〉 Immediate Notification to NTSB; Incident Reports; Preservation of Aircraft Wreckage<br>*2189, 2211, 2212, 3194, 3195, 3196, 3197, 3198, 3199, 3200* |
| PLT369 | 14 CFR 91 | Regulations 〉 14 CFR Part 91 〉 Aerobatic Flight<br>*3173* |
| PLT370 | *AIM* | Airspace 〉 Controlled 〉 Clearance; Services Provided<br>*3798, 3837* |
| PLT371 | 14 CFR 1 | Regulations 〉 14 CFR Part 1 〉 Certification of Aircraft; Certification of Airmen<br>*3001, 3002, 3003, 3004* |
| PLT372 | 14 CFR 91 | Regulations 〉 14 CFR Part 91 〉 Annual Inspection; Maintenance Inspections<br>*3182, 3185, 3186, 3189, 3190* |
| PLT373 | 14 CFR 91 | Regulations 〉 14 CFR Part 91 〉 Aircraft Operating Limitations<br>*3075, 3178* |
| PLT374 | 14 CFR 91 | Regulations 〉 14 CFR Part 91 〉 Aircraft Return to Service; Airworthiness; Airworthiness Certificate<br>*3180-1, 3181-1, 3181-2, 3181-3, 3660* |
| PLT375 | 14 CFR 91 | Regulations 〉 14 CFR Part 91 〉 Aircraft Return to Service<br>*3013-2, 3013-3, 3183, 3184* |

| Learning Statement Code | FAA Reference | Subject Description (or *Topic* ⟩ *Content* ⟩ *Specific* classification) / Question Numbers |
|---|---|---|
| PLT376 | 14 CFR 91 *AIM* | Regulations ⟩ 14 CFR Part 91 ⟩ Special VFR / Airspace ⟩ Other ⟩ Wild Life Refuges / *2053, 3150, 3151, 3618* |
| PLT377 | 14 CFR 91 | Regulations ⟩ 14 CFR Part 91 ⟩ Airworthiness Certificate / *3180-2, 3187* |
| PLT378 | 14 CFR 39 | Recall regulations—Airworthiness Directives / *3012-3* |
| PLT381 | 14 CFR 91 | Regulations ⟩ 14 CFR Part 91 ⟩ Altimeter Settings / *3105, 3106, 3107* |
| PLT383 | 14 CFR 91 | Regulations ⟩ 14 CFR Part 91 ⟩ Airworthiness Certificate; Minimum Safe Altitudes / *3097, 3098, 3179* |
| PLT384 | 14 CFR 91 | Regulations ⟩ Briefing of passengers / *3085-1* |
| PLT387 | 14 CFR 61 | Regulations ⟩ 14 CFR Part 61 ⟩ Change of Address / *3035* |
| PLT389 | FAA-H-8083-11 | Flight Operations ⟩ Launch Procedures ⟩ Location and Obstacles / *3908* |
| PLT393 | 14 CFR 91 *AIM* | Airspace ⟩ Special Use ⟩ MOA / Regulations ⟩ 14 CFR Part 91 ⟩ Airspace / *2122, 3125, 3602, 3783, 3783-1, 3784, 3785* |
| PLT395 | 14 CFR 1 | Regulations ⟩ 14 CFR Part 1 ⟩ Night / *2213, 3005, 3025* |
| PLT399 | 14 CFR 61 | Regulations ⟩ 14 CFR Part 61 ⟩ Inspection of Certificate; Medical Certificates; Pilot Certificate / *2129, 3016, 3017, 3018, 3019* |
| PLT400 | 14 CFR 91 | Regulations ⟩ 14 CFR Part 91 ⟩ Aircraft Operating Limitations / *3075-1, 3159* |
| PLT401 | 14 CFR 91 | Regulations ⟩ 14 CFR Part 91 ⟩ PIC Responsibility/Authority / *3059, 3076* |
| PLT402 | 14 CFR 91 *AIM* | Aircraft Systems ⟩ Avionics ⟩ Emergency Locator Transmitter (ELT) / *3160, 3161, 3819, 3820, 3821, 3822* |
| PLT403 | 14 CFR 91 | Regulations ⟩ 14 CFR Part 91 ⟩ ATC Clearances / *3109* |
| PLT405 | 14 CFR 91 | Recall regulations—equipment/instrument/certificate requirements / *3172* |
| PLT407 | 14 CFR 61 | Regulations ⟩ 14 CFR Part 61 ⟩ PIC Recent Flight Experience; Privileges and Limitations / *3036, 3037, 3067-1* |

| Learning Statement Code | FAA Reference | Subject Description (or Topic ⟩ Topic ⟩ Content ⟩ Specific classification) Question Numbers |
|---|---|---|
| PLT411 | 14 CFR 61 | Regulations ⟩ 14 CFR Part 61 ⟩ Certification: Pilots, Flight Instructors, and Ground Instructors<br>3030, 3030-1 |
| PLT413 | 14 CFR 91 | Regulations ⟩ 14 CFR Part 91 ⟩ Fuel Requirements<br>3131, 3132 |
| PLT414 | 14 CFR 91 | Regulations ⟩ 14 CFR Part 91 ⟩ Right-of-Way<br>3089, 3090, 3091, 3092, 3093, 3094, 3095, 3096 |
| PLT416 | 49 CFR 830 | Recall regulations—immediate notification<br>2214 |
| PLT425 | 14 CFR 91 | Recall regulations—maintenance reports/records/entries<br>3193 |
| PLT426 | 14 CFR 91 | Regulations ⟩ 14 CFR Part 91 ⟩ Aircraft Return to Service<br>3012-2, 3188, 3191 |
| PLT427 | 14 CFR 61 | Regulations ⟩ 14 CFR Part 61 ⟩ Medical Certificates<br>3023-1, 3023-2, 3023-3, 3063 |
| PLT430 | 14 CFR 91 | Regulations ⟩ 14 CFR Part 91 ⟩ Minimum Safe Altitudes<br>3101, 3102, 3103, 3104 |
| PLT431 | 14 CFR 91 | Regulations ⟩ 14 CFR Part 91 ⟩ Formation Flight<br>2133-1, 3088 |
| PLT434 | 14 CFR 91 | Recall regulations / operational procedures for a controlled airport<br>3124 |
| PLT435 | AIM | Airport Operations ⟩ Communications ⟩ Inbound<br>2006, 2007, 2034-1, 2060, 2194, 3604, 3605, 3605-1 |
| PLT438 | 14 CFR 91 | Regulations ⟩ 14 CFR Part 91 ⟩ Oxygen Requirements<br>3163, 3164 |
| PLT440 | 14 CFR 91 | Regulations ⟩ 14 CFR Part 91 ⟩ PIC Responsibility/Authority<br>3073, 3083 |
| PLT441 | 14 CFR 91 | Recall regulations—pilot briefing<br>2232 |
| PLT442 | 14 CFR 61 | Regulations ⟩ 14 CFR Part 61 ⟩ PIC Recent Flight Experience<br>3029, 3031, 3032, 3033, 3034, 3040, 3041 |
| PLT443 | FAA-H-8083-25 | Human Factors ⟩ ADM ⟩ Pilot Self-Assessment<br>2078, 3937 |
| PLT444 | 14 CFR 91<br>AIM | Airspace ⟩ Special Use ⟩ Alert Areas<br>Regulations ⟩ 14 CFR Part 91 ⟩ PIC Responsibility/Authority; Preflight Actions<br>2033, 2308, 3070, 3071, 3072, 3074, 3082, 3108, 3108-1, 3110, 3658, 3786, 3952 |
| PLT445 | 14 CFR 91<br>AIM<br>FAA-H-8083-25 | Airport Operations ⟩ Preflight ⟩ Pilot Responsibility<br>Regulations ⟩ 14 CFR Part 91 ⟩ Preflight Actions<br>Weather ⟩ Aeronautical Weather Reports ⟩ Weather Briefings<br>3080, 3081, 3526, 3659 |

| Learning Statement Code | FAA Reference | Subject Description (or Topic ⟩ Content ⟩ Specific classification) Question Numbers |
|---|---|---|
| PLT446 | 14 CFR 43 | Regulations ⟩ 14 CFR Part 43 ⟩ Preventive Maintenance<br>*3013-1, 3014* |
| PLT447 | 14 CFR 61 | Regulations ⟩ 14 CFR Part 61 ⟩ Medical Certificates<br>*3020, 3021, 3022, 3023, 3039, 3062* |
| PLT448 | 14 CFR 61 | Regulations ⟩ 14 CFR Part 61 ⟩ Privileges and Limitations<br>*2123, 2130, 3026, 3027, 3038, 3043, 3044, 3045, 3046, 3047, 3048, 3049, 3050, 3052, 3052-1, 3055, 3058, 3060, 3061, 3064, 3065, 3066, 3067* |
| PLT449 | 14 CFR 61 | Regulations ⟩ 14 CFR Part 61 ⟩ Flight Review<br>*3028* |
| PLT451 | 14 CFR 61 | Regulations ⟩ 14 CFR Part 61 ⟩ Privileges and Limitations; Type Rating<br>*3024* |
| PLT462 | *AIM* | Airport Operations ⟩ Lighting ⟩ Runway Lighting<br>*3768* |
| PLT463 | 14 CFR 61<br>14 CFR 91 | Regulations ⟩ 14 CFR Part 61 ⟩ Drugs/Alcohol<br>Regulations ⟩ 14 CFR Part 91 ⟩ Alcohol or Drugs<br>*2126, 2127, 2128, 3077, 3078, 3079, 3079-1* |
| PLT464 | 14 CFR 91 | Regulations ⟩ 14 CFR Part 91 ⟩ PIC Responsibility/Authority<br>*3084* |
| PLT465 | 14 CFR 91 | Regulations ⟩ 14 CFR Part 91 ⟩ Seat Belts<br>*3085, 3086, 3087* |
| PLT467 | 14 CFR 91 | Regulations ⟩ 14 CFR Part 91 ⟩ Airspace; Flight Rules General; VFR Cruising Altitude/Flight Level<br>*2061, 3051, 3138, 3155, 3156, 3157, 3158* |
| PLT468 | 14 CFR 91 | Regulations ⟩ 14 CFR Part 91 ⟩ Airspace<br>*3139, 3140, 3141* |
| PLT473 | FAA-H-8083-25 | Aircraft Systems ⟩ Flight Controls/Secondary ⟩ Flaps<br>*3219, 3220, 3905* |
| PLT477 | FAA-H-8083-25 | Aerodynamics ⟩ Stall/Spins ⟩ Stalls<br>*2225, 2233, 3263* |
| PLT478 | FAA-H-8083-25 | Aircraft Systems ⟩ Powerplant ⟩ Ignition; Magnetos<br>*2242, 3223, 3223-2, 3240, 3970* |
| PLT479 | FAA-H-8083-3 | Aircraft Systems ⟩ Powerplant ⟩ Engine Starting<br>*3657* |
| PLT486 | FAA-H-8083-3 | Airport Operations ⟩ Taxiing ⟩ Flight Controls<br>*2016, 3302, 3303, 3304, 3903* |
| PLT492 | FAA-H-8083-28 | Weather ⟩ Meteorology ⟩ Stability<br>*3408* |
| PLT493 | FAA-H-8083-28 | Weather ⟩ Meteorology ⟩ Moisture<br>*3401* |

| Learning Statement Code | FAA Reference | Subject Description (or Topic 〉 Content 〉 Specific classification) Question Numbers |
|---|---|---|
| PLT494 | FAA-H-8083-28 | Weather 〉 Meteorology 〉 Thermals<br><br>*3448, 3471, 3471-1, 3751, 3752, 3753, 3754, 3755, 3756, 3757, 3881* |
| PLT495 | FAA-H-8083-28 | Weather 〉 Meteorology 〉 Thunderstorms<br><br>*3434, 3435, 3436, 3437, 3438, 3439, 3440, 3441, 3452, 3521* |
| PLT496 | FAA-H-8083-13 | Recall towrope—strength/safety links/positioning<br><br>*3174, 3175, 3176, 3177* |
| PLT497 | *AIM* | Aircraft Systems 〉 Avionics 〉 Transponder<br><br>*2005, 3129, 3166-5, 3800, 3800-1, 3801, 3802, 3996* |
| PLT501 | FAA-H-8083-28 | Recall turbulence—types/characteristics/reporting/corrective actions<br><br>*2159, 2236* |
| PLT502 | 14 CFR 91 | Regulations 〉 14 CFR Part 91 〉 Light Gun Signals<br><br>*3114, 3812, 3869, 3870, 3871, 3872, 3873, 3874, 3875* |
| PLT506 | 14 CFR 1 | Regulations 〉 14 CFR Part 1 〉 V-speeds<br><br>*3006, 3007, 3008, 3009, 3010* |
| PLT508 | 14 CFR 91 | Recall VOR/altimeter/transponder checks—identification/tuning/identifying/logging<br><br>*3192* |
| PLT509 | *AIM* | Airport Operations 〉 Wake Turbulence 〉 Strength; Vortex Avoidance<br>Flight Operations 〉 Wake Turbulence 〉 Vortex Avoidance; Vortex Behavior<br><br>*2039, 3824, 3825, 3826, 3827, 3828, 3829, 3829-2, 3829-3, 3830* |
| PLT511 | FAA-H-8083-25<br>FAA-H-8083-28 | Weather 〉 Meteorology 〉 Fronts; Stability<br><br>*2312, 3412, 3413, 3414, 3422, 3423, 3424* |
| PLT512 | FAA-H-8083-28 | Weather 〉 Meteorology 〉 Fog; Moisture; Stability; Temperature<br><br>*2369, 3381, 3397, 3398, 3399, 3400, 3409, 3410, 3444* |
| PLT514 | FAA-H-8083-25<br>FAA-H-8083-28 | Weather 〉 Aeronautical Weather Forecasts 〉 Aviation Area Forecasts (FA)<br>Weather 〉 Aeronautical Weather Reports 〉 Aviation Routine Weather Reports (METAR); Weather Briefings<br><br>*3455, 3456, 3457, 3458, 3459, 3460, 3461, 3487, 3525, 3527, 3528, 3528-1* |
| PLT515 | *AIM* | Navigation 〉 Pilotage 〉 Radio Communications<br>Weather 〉 Aeronautical Weather Reports 〉 En Route Flight Advisory Service (EFAS)<br><br>*3477* |
| PLT516 | FAA-H-8083-3<br>FAA-H-8083-28 | Airport Operations 〉 Taxiing 〉 Flight Controls<br>Weather 〉 Meteorology 〉 Wind<br><br>*3395, 3396, 3450, 3451, 3750* |
| PLT517 | FAA-H-8083-28 | Recall winds associated with high/low-pressure systems<br><br>*2170* |
| PLT518 | FAA-H-8083-25<br>FAA-H-8083-28 | Weather 〉 Meteorology 〉 Windshear<br><br>*2163, 3426, 3427, 3428* |

# Airman Certification Codes and Question Numbers

| ACS Code | Question Numbers |
|---|---|
| PA.I.A.K1 | 3024, 3026, 3027, 3028, 3029, 3030, 3030-1, 3031, 3032, 3033, 3034, 3035, 3036, 3037, 3040, 3041, 3172, 3173, 3854 |
| PA.I.A.K2 | 3064, 3065, 3066, 3067, 3070, 3072, 3073, 3076, 3088 |
| PA.I.A.K3 | 3020, 3021, 3022, 3023, 3039 |
| PA.I.A.K4 | 3016, 3017, 3018, 3019 |
| PA.I.A.K5 | 3023-1, 3023-2, 3023-3 |
| PA.I.B.K1 | 3001, 3002, 3003, 3004, 3025, 3074, 3075, 3075-1, 3159, 3178, 3179, 3180-1, 3180-2, 3186 |
| PA.I.B.K1a | 3187 |
| PA.I.B.K1b | 3181-1, 3181-2, 3182, 3183, 3184, 3185, 3188, 3189, 3190, 3191, 3192 |
| PA.I.B.K1c | 3012-2, 3012-3, 3181-3, 3193, 3709 |
| PA.I.B.K2 | 3013-1, 3013-2, 3013-3, 3014 |
| PA.I.C.K1 | 3455, 3456, 3457, 3458, 3459, 3460, 3461, 3526, 3527, 3528, 3528-1 |
| PA.I.C.K2 | 3462, 3463, 3464, 3465, 3466, 3467, 3472, 3473, 3474, 3475, 3476, 3479, 3480, 3481, 3482, 3483, 3484, 3485, 3486, 3487, 3495, 3496, 3497, 3498, 3499, 3500, 3501, 3502, 3503, 3505, 3506 |
| PA.I.C.K3 | 3382 |
| PA.I.C.K3a | 3260, 3381, 3383, 3384, 3385, 3388, 3389, 3391, 3392, 3403, 3404, 3405, 3408, 3412, 3413, 3414 |
| PA.I.C.K3b | 3395, 3426, 3427, 3428, 3450 |
| PA.I.C.K3d | 3397, 3398, 3399, 3400, 3444 |
| PA.I.C.K3e | 3422, 3423 |
| PA.I.C.K3f | 3406, 3407, 3409, 3410, 3415, 3416, 3424, 3433 |
| PA.I.C.K3g | 3417, 3418, 3419, 3420, 3425, 3442 |
| PA.I.C.K3h | 3434, 3435, 3436, 3437, 3438, 3439, 3440, 3441, 3452, 3521 |
| PA.I.C.K3i | 3402, 3429, 3430, 3956 |
| PA.I.C.K3j | 3443, 3445, 3446, 3447 |
| PA.I.C.K3k | 3206, 3401, 3431, 3432 |
| PA.I.C.K3l | 3833 |
| PA.I.D.K2 | 3101, 3102, 3103, 3104, 3155, 3156, 3157, 3158 |
| PA.I.D.K3b | 3571, 3572, 3573, 3574, 3575, 3576 |
| PA.I.D.K4 | 2175, 2175-1 |
| PA.I.D.K5 | 3818 |
| PA.I.E.K1 | 3068, 3068-1, 3069, 3097, 3098, 3099, 3100, 3118, 3119, 3124, 3125, 3126, 3127, 3128, 3130, 3166-5, 3779, 3780, 3781, 3782, 3787, 3787-1, 3788, 3799, 3855 |
| PA.I.E.K2 | 2122, 3068-2, 3117, 3421, 3599, 3600, 3622, 3623, 3624, 3625, 3626, 3627, 3628, 3629, 3631, 3632, 3633, 3634, 3635, 3636, 3637, 3637-1, 3638, 3639, 3640, 3642, 3643 |
| PA.I.E.K3 | 3601, 3601-1, 3602, 3603, 3618, 3783, 3783-1, 3785, 3786, 3831 |
| PA.I.E.S1 | 3136, 3137, 3138, 3139, 3140, 3141, 3142, 3143, 3144, 3145, 3146, 3147, 3148, 3149, 3150, 3151, 3153, 3154, 3520, 3620-1, 3620-2, 3621-1, 3621-2, 3621-3, 3813 |

| ACS Code | Question Numbers |
|---|---|
| PA.I.F.K1 | 3678, 3679, 3680, 3681, 3682, 3683, 3684, 3685, 3686, 3687, 3688, 3689, 3690, 3691, 3692, 3693, 3694, 3695, 3696, 3697, 3698, 3705, 3706, 3707, 3708 |
| PA.I.F.K2 | 3202-1 |
| PA.I.F.K2a | 3246, 3258, 3289, 3290, 3291, 3292, 3293, 3294, 3295, 3296, 3297, 3298, 3299, 3300, 3386, 3394 |
| PA.I.F.K2c | 3265, 3266, 3271, 3272 |
| PA.I.F.K2e | 3287, 3288 |
| PA.I.F.K2f | 3661, 3662, 3663, 3815, 3663-1, 3663-2 |
| PA.I.F.K3 | 3201, 3202, 3203, 3204, 3205, 3207, 3208, 3209, 3210, 3211, 3212, 3214, 3215, 3216, 3217, 3218, 3301, 3316, 3317, 3201-1, 3204-1, 3211-1 |
| PA.I.F.R2 | 3006, 3007, 3008, 3009, 3010, 3264, 3267, 3268, 3270, 3273, 3274 |
| PA.I.F.S1 | 3664, 3665, 3666, 3667, 3668, 3669, 3670, 3671, 3672, 3673, 3674, 3675, 3676, 3677 |
| PA.I.G.K1a | 3213 |
| PA.I.G.K1b | 3219, 3220 |
| PA.I.G.K1c | 3221, 3221-1, 3222, 3238-1, 3240, 3241, 3244, 3653, 3654, 3655, 3656, 3656-1 |
| PA.I.G.K1e | 3224, 3225, 3226, 3228, 3237, 3238, 3242, 3243, 3243-1, 3245 |
| PA.I.G.K1f | 3223, 3223-1, 3223-2 |
| PA.I.G.K1h | 3105, 3106, 3107, 3250, 3251, 3252, 3253, 3253-1, 3254, 3255, 3256, 3257, 3259, 3261, 3262, 3275, 3276, 3277, 3278, 3387, 3390, 3393 |
| PA.I.G.K2 | 3239, 3651, 3652 |
| PA.I.H.K1a | 3163, 3164, 3844 |
| PA.I.H.K1b | 3845, 3846, 3847 |
| PA.I.H.K1d | 3850, 3851, 3852, 3853 |
| PA.I.H.K1f | 3832, 3848 |
| PA.I.H.K2 | 3077, 3078, 3079, 3079-1 |
| PA.I.H.K4 | 3931, 3931-2, 3931-3 |
| PA.I.H.R2 | 3931-1, 3932, 3933, 3934, 3935, 3936 |
| PA.I.H.R3 | 3939 |
| PA.II.A.K1 | 3937 |
| PA.II.A.K2 | 3658, 3659 |
| PA.II.A.K3d | 3080, 3081, 3082, 3131, 3132, 3660 |
| PA.II.A.K4 | 3940-1 |
| PA.II.A.R1 | 3938 |
| PA.II.B.K1 | 3083, 3084, 3085, 3085-1, 3086, 3087 |
| PA.II.B.K2 | 3490 |
| PA.II.C.R1 | 3657 |
| PA.II.D.K1 | 3513, 3619, 3619-1, 3838, 3838-1, 3839, 3840, 3841, 3841-1, 3842 |
| PA.II.D.K3 | 3718, 3768, 3769, 3770, 3771, 3772, 3773, 3774, 3776, 3777, 3778, 3778-1, 3778-2, 3778-3, 3778-4, 3778-5, 3806-1, 3806-2, 3806-3, 3955-1, 3955-2, 3955-3, 3955-4, 3955-5, 3955-6, 3957 |
| PA.II.D.K4 | 3805, 3806 |

| ACS Code | Question Numbers |
|---|---|
| PA.II.D.S3 | 3302, 3303, 3304, 3305, 3306, 3307, 3308, 3308-1 |
| PA.II.F.R3 | 3824, 3825, 3826, 3829-3 |
| PA.III.A.K1 | 2004, 3606, 3607, 3608, 3609, 3611, 3612, 3641, 3790, 3791, 3856 |
| PA.III.A.K2 | 3604, 3605, 3605-1, 3605-2, 3610, 3613, 3614, 3615, 3811, 3812, 3998 |
| PA.III.A.K3 | 3111, 3112, 3113, 3114, 3115, 3116, 3804 |
| PA.III.A.K4 | 3129, 3165, 3800, 3800-1, 3801, 3802, 3803, 3996 |
| PA.III.A.K7 | 3792, 3792-1, 3793, 3794, 3795, 3796, 3797, 3798 |
| PA.III.A.K8 | 3194, 3195, 3196, 3197, 3198, 3199, 3200 |
| PA.III.B.K1 | 3123, 3123-1 |
| PA.III.B.K2 | 3120, 3121 |
| PA.III.B.K3 | 3089, 3090, 3091, 3092, 3093, 3094, 3095, 3096 |
| PA.III.B.K4 | 3807, 3808, 3809, 3810 |
| PA.III.B.R3 | 3827 |
| PA.III.B.S1 | 3760, 3762-1, 3764, 3765, 3766, 3767 |
| PA.IV.A.K2 | 3011, 3012-1 |
| PA.IV.A.R2d | 3830 |
| PA.IV.B.K1 | 3719 |
| PA.IV.B.R2d | 3828, 3829, 3829-2 |
| PA.IV.B.R3b | 3951, 3952, 3953, 3954, 3955 |
| PA.IV.C.K4 | 3312, 3313, 3314, 3315 |
| PA.V.B.K2 | 3202-2, 3203-3 |
| PA.VI.A.K1 | 3530, 3530-1, 3535, 3536, 3543, 3567 |
| PA.VI.A.K2 | 3279, 3279-1, 3279-2, 3280, 3281, 3282, 3283, 3283-1, 3284, 3286 |
| PA.VI.A.K5a | 3531, 3538, 3545, 3546, 3547, 3550, 3551, 3556, 3564, 3565, 3568 |
| PA.VI.A.K5b | 2001, 3816, 3817, 3529-1, 3529-2 |
| PA.VI.A.K5c | 3529-3, 3529-4, 3550-1, 3564-1, 3564-2 |
| PA.VI.A.R1 | 3710, 3710-1 |
| PA.VI.B.K1 | 3533, 3539, 3552, 3553, 3559, 3560, 3561, 3566, 3570, 3577, 3578, 3579, 3598-1, 3814 |
| PA.VI.B.K2 | 3598-3, 3598-4 |
| PA.VI.B.K4 | 3166, 3166-1, 3166-2, 3166-3, 3166-4 |
| PA.VII.B.K2 | 3269 |
| PA.VII.C.K1 | 3263 |
| PA.VII.D.K1 | 3310, 3311 |
| PA.VII.D.K2 | 3309 |
| PA.VIII.A.R3 | 3834, 3835, 3836 |
| PA.VIII.F.K1 | 3108, 3108-1, 3109, 3110, 3837 |
| PA.IX.B.K2a | 3202-5, 3711 |

| ACS Code | Question Numbers |
|---|---|
| PA.IX.B.K2c | 3202-4 |
| PA.IX.C.K1 | 3227, 3229, 3230, 3230-1, 3231, 3232, 3233, 3234, 3235, 3236 |
| PA.IX.C.K2c | 3247, 3248, 3249 |
| PA.IX.D.K1 | 3160, 3161, 3819, 3820, 3821, 3822 |
| PA.XI.A.K1 | 3712, 3713, 3714, 3849 |
| PA.XI.A.K3 | 3005, 3162, 3715, 3716, 3717, 3916, 3916-1 |
| PH.I.A.K1 | 3001, 3002, 3024, 3028, 3029, 3030, 3030-1, 3031, 3033, 3034, 3035, 3040, 3041, 3070, 3072, 3073, 3074, 3172, 3713 |
| PH.I.A.K2 | 3064, 3065, 3066, 3067, 3076, 3088 |
| PH.I.A.K3 | 3020, 3021, 3022, 3023, 3039 |
| PH.I.A.K4 | 3016, 3017, 3018, 3019 |
| PH.I.A.K5 | 3023-1, 3023-2, 3023-3 |
| PH.I.B.K1 | 3003, 3004, 3013-1, 3075, 3075-1, 3159, 3178, 3179, 3180-1, 3180-2, 3181-1, 3181-2, 3182, 3183, 3184, 3185, 3186, 3187, 3188, 3189, 3190, 3191, 3192 |
| PH.I.B.K1c | 3012-2, 3012-3, 3181-3, 3193, 3709, 3854, 3855, 3856 |
| PH.I.B.K2 | 3013-2, 3013-3, 3014 |
| PH.I.B.K3 | 3162, 3916, 3916-1 |
| PH.I.C.K1 | 3455, 3456, 3457, 3458, 3459, 3460, 3461, 3526, 3527, 3528, 3528-1 |
| PH.I.C.K2a | 3462, 3463, 3464, 3465, 3466, 3467, 3472, 3473, 3474, 3475, 3476 |
| PH.I.C.K2c | 3479, 3480, 3481, 3482, 3483, 3484, 3485, 3486 |
| PH.I.C.K2d | 3487 |
| PH.I.C.K2e | 3500, 3501, 3502, 3503, 3505, 3506 |
| PH.I.C.K2g | 3495, 3496, 3497, 3498, 3499 |
| PH.I.C.K3 | 3382 |
| PH.I.C.K3a | 3385, 3403, 3404, 3405, 3408, 3412, 3413, 3414 |
| PH.I.C.K3b | 3395, 3426, 3427, 3428, 3450 |
| PH.I.C.K3c | 3381, 3383, 3384 |
| PH.I.C.K3d | 3397, 3398, 3399, 3400, 3444 |
| PH.I.C.K3e | 3422, 3423 |
| PH.I.C.K3f | 3406, 3407, 3409, 3410, 3415, 3416, 3424, 3433 |
| PH.I.C.K3g | 3417, 3418, 3419, 3420, 3425, 3442 |
| PH.I.C.K3h | 3434, 3435, 3436, 3437, 3438, 3439, 3440, 3441, 3452, 3521 |
| PH.I.C.K3i | 3402, 3429, 3430, 3956 |
| PH.I.C.K3j | 3443, 3445, 3446, 3447 |
| PH.I.C.K3k | 3206, 3401, 3431, 3432 |
| PH.I.C.K3l | 3833 |
| PH.I.D.K2 | 3101, 3155, 3156, 3157, 3158 |
| PH.I.D.K5 | 2175, 2175-1, 3818 |

| ACS Code | Question Numbers |
|---|---|
| PH.I.E.K1 | 2122, 3068, 3068-1, 3069, 3097, 3098, 3099, 3100, 3118, 3119, 3124, 3125, 3126, 3127, 3128, 3626, 3779, 3780, 3781, 3782, 3787, 3788, 3799 |
| PH.I.E.K2 | 3068-2, 3117, 3421, 3599, 3600, 3601, 3601-1, 3622, 3623, 3624, 3625, 3627, 3628, 3629, 3787-1 |
| PH.I.E.K3 | 3602, 3603, 3618, 3783, 3783-1, 3785, 3786, 3831 |
| PH.I.E.K4 | 3150, 3151, 3152, 3813 |
| PH.I.E.S1 | 3136, 3137, 3138, 3139, 3140, 3141, 3142, 3143, 3144, 3145, 3146, 3147, 3148, 3149, 3520, 3620-1, 3620-2, 3621-1, 3621-2, 3621-3 |
| PH.I.F.K1 | 3683, 3684, 3685, 3686, 3687, 3688, 3699, 3700, 3701, 3703, 3704, 3732 |
| PH.I.F.K2a | 3289, 3290, 3291, 3292, 3293, 3294, 3295, 3296, 3297, 3298, 3299, 3300, 3386, 3394, 3702, 3733 |
| PH.I.F.K3 | 3661, 3662, 3663, 3663-1, 3663-2, 3720, 3721, 3722, 3723, 3724, 3725, 3726, 3727, 3728, 3729, 3730, 3731, 3815 |
| PH.I.F.K4 | 3201, 3201-1, 3202-1, 3203, 3204, 3204-1, 3317, 3318, 3319, 3320, 3321, 3322 |
| PH.I.F.R7 | 3330, 3331 |
| PH.I.G.K1a | 3326, 3327, 3337, 3742 |
| PH.I.G.K1b | 3221, 3221-1, 3222, 3223-2, 3238, 3238-1, 3240, 3241, 3244, 3245, 3651, 3652, 3656, 3656-1 |
| PH.I.G.K1c | 3328, 3333, 3334 |
| PH.I.G.K1e | 3225, 3226, 3228, 3237, 3242, 3243, 3243-1 |
| PH.I.G.K1h | 3223-1 |
| PH.I.G.K1i | 3006, 3105, 3106, 3107, 3250, 3251, 3252, 3253, 3253-1, 3254, 3255, 3256, 3257, 3258, 3259, 3260, 3261, 3264, 3268, 3276, 3277, 3278, 3387, 3388, 3389, 3390, 3391, 3392, 3393 |
| PH.I.G.K1j | 3329 |
| PH.I.G.K1k | 3229, 3230, 3230-1, 3232, 3233, 3234, 3236 |
| PH.I.H.K1 | 3937, 3938, 3940 |
| PH.I.H.K1a | 3163, 3164, 3844 |
| PH.I.H.K1b | 3845, 3846, 3847 |
| PH.I.H.K1d | 3834, 3835, 3836, 3939 |
| PH.I.H.K1f | 3832, 3848 |
| PH.I.H.K1k | 3850, 3851, 3852, 3853 |
| PH.I.H.K2 | 3077, 3078, 3079, 3079-1 |
| PH.I.H.K4 | 3931, 3931-2, 3931-3, 3940-1 |
| PH.I.H.R2 | 3931-1, 3932, 3933, 3934, 3935, 3936 |
| PH.II.A.K2 | 3660 |
| PH.II.A.K3 | 3080, 3081, 3082, 3131, 3132, 3133 |
| PH.II.A.K3a | 3659 |
| PH.II.A.K3d | 3658 |
| PH.II.A.K4 | 3739 |
| PH.II.B.K1 | 3083, 3084, 3085, 3085-1, 3086, 3087 |

| ACS Code | Question Numbers |
|---|---|
| PH.III.A.K1 | 3120, 3121, 3718, 3760, 3762-1, 3764, 3765, 3766, 3767, 3768, 3769, 3770, 3771, 3772, 3773, 3774, 3776, 3777, 3778, 3778-1, 3778-2, 3778-3, 3778-4, 3778-5, 3805, 3806, 3806-1, 3806-2, 3806-3, 3955-1, 3955-2, 3955-3, 3955-4, 3955-5, 3955-6, 3957 |
| PH.III.A.K2 | 3951, 3952, 3953, 3954, 3955 |
| PH.III.B.K2 | 2004, 3108, 3108-1, 3109, 3110, 3604, 3605, 3605-1, 3605-2, 3606, 3607, 3608, 3609, 3610, 3611, 3612, 3613, 3614, 3615, 3641, 3790, 3791, 3811, 3812, 3837, 3998 |
| PH.III.B.K3 | 3111, 3112, 3113, 3114, 3115, 3116, 3804 |
| PH.III.B.K4 | 3129, 3165, 3166, 3166-1, 3166-2, 3166-3, 3166-4, 3166-5, 3800, 3800-1, 3801, 3802, 3803, 3996 |
| PH.III.B.K7 | 3792, 3792-1, 3793, 3794, 3795, 3796, 3797, 3798 |
| PH.III.B.K8 | 3194, 3195, 3196, 3197, 3198, 3199, 3200 |
| PH.III.C.K2 | 3122, 3123, 3123-1, 3719, 3807, 3808, 3809, 3810 |
| PH.III.C.K3 | 3089, 3090, 3091, 3092, 3093, 3095 |
| PH.IV.A.K3 | 3323 |
| PH.IV.B.K1 | 3513, 3619, 3619-1, 3838, 3838-1, 3839, 3840, 3841, 3841-1, 3842 |
| PH.IV.B.R7 | 3335 |
| PH.IV.D.R4 | 3336 |
| PH.IV.E.K1 | 3744, 3745 |
| PH.V.A.R3b | 3711 |
| PH.V.B.K1 | 3740 |
| PH.V.B.R6 | 3734-2, 3734-3 |
| PH.V.F.K2 | 3746 |
| PH.V.F.K3 | 3747 |
| PH.V.G.K1 | 3748, 3749 |
| PH.V.I.K4 | 3325 |
| PH.VI.A.K1 | 3743 |
| PH.VI.A.R4 | 3710, 3710-1 |
| PH.VI.B.K5 | 3736, 3737 |
| PH.VII.A.K1 | 3530, 3530-1, 3535, 3536, 3543, 3567 |
| PH.VII.A.K2 | 3279, 3279-1, 3279-2, 3280, 3281, 3282, 3283, 3283-1, 3284, 3286 |
| PH.VII.A.K3 | 3631, 3632, 3633, 3634, 3635, 3636, 3637, 3637-1, 3638, 3639, 3640, 3642 |
| PH.VII.A.K5a | 3531, 3538, 3545, 3546, 3547, 3550, 3551, 3556, 3564, 3565, 3568 |
| PH.VII.A.K5b | 2001, 3529-1, 3529-2, 3816, 3817 |
| PH.VII.A.K5c | 3529-3, 3529-4, 3550-1, 3564-1, 3564-2, 3571, 3572, 3573, 3574, 3575, 3576 |
| PH.VII.B.K1 | 3533, 3539, 3552, 3553, 3559, 3560, 3561, 3566, 3570, 3577, 3578, 3579, 3598-1, 3643, 3814 |
| PH.VII.B.K2 | 3598-3, 3598-4 |
| PH.VIII.B.K1 | 3741 |
| PH.VIII.D.K2c | 3247, 3248, 3249, 3262 |
| PH.VIII.E.K4 | 3734-1 |

| ACS Code | Question Numbers |
|---|---|
| PH.VIII.E.K5 | 3734 |
| PH.VIII.G.R3 | 3738 |
| PH.VIII.I.K1 | 3332 |
| PH.VIII.I.K1b | 2329, 3338 |
| PH.VIII.K.K1 | 3160, 3161, 3819, 3820, 3821, 3822 |
| PH.IX.A.K3 | 3005 |
| PH.IX.A.K4 | 3162, 3916, 3916-1, 3715, 3716, 3717 |
| PH.IX.A.K5 | 3712, 3713, 3714, 3715, 3716, 3717, 3849 |

# Are you checkride ready?

Yes—with ASA materials, you are ready. The *Private Pilot Oral Exam Guide*, Checkride App, and *Private Pilot Airplane Airman Certification Standards* will prepare you for the final exam by providing a review of what you must know, consider, and do to earn your Private Pilot Certificate.

**asa2fly.com/Checkride**

— Since 1940 —

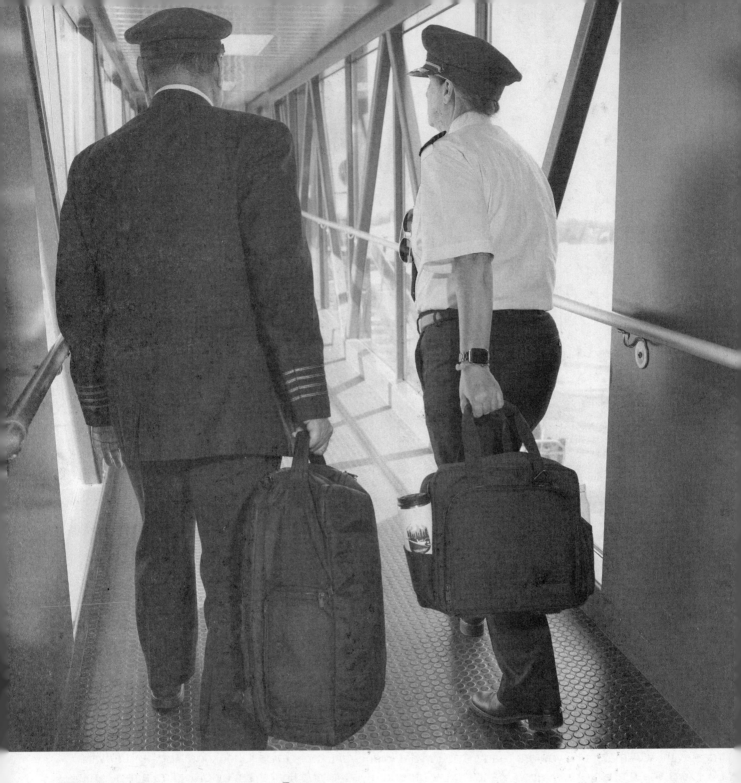

# Pack your bag.

Flight deck needs evolve with the mission. The tools you carry now may be different than the ones in your old flight bag. Maybe it's time for a new one. ASA flight bags—for student pilots to crewmembers.

**asa2fly.com/FlightBags**

— Since 1940 —

FAA-CT-8080-2H

# Airman Knowledge Testing Supplement for Sport Pilot, Recreational Pilot, Remote Pilot, and Private Pilot

# 2018

U.S. Department of Transportation
**FEDERAL AVIATION ADMINISTRATION**
Flight Standards Service

# Preface

This testing supplement supersedes FAA-CT-8080-2G, Airman Knowledge Testing Supplement for Sport Pilot, Recreational Pilot, and Private Pilot, dated 2016.

This Airman Knowledge Testing Supplement is designed by the Federal Aviation Administration (FAA) Flight Standards Service. It is intended for use by Airman Knowledge Testing (AKT) Organization Designation Authorization (ODA) Holders and other entities approved and/or authorized to administer airman knowledge tests on behalf of the FAA in the following knowledge areas:

Sport Pilot–Airplane (ASEL and ASES)
Sport Pilot–Gyroplane
Sport Pilot–Glider
Sport Pilot–Airship (LTA)
Sport Pilot–Balloon (LTA)
Sport Pilot–Weight-Shift Control (WSCS and WSCL)
Sport Pilot–Powered Parachute (PPL and PPS)

Recreational Pilot–Airplane (RPA)
Recreational Pilot–Rotorcraft/Helicopter (RPH)

Recreational Pilot–Rotorcraft/Gyroplane (RPG)
Private Pilot–Airplane/Recreational Pilot–Transition (PAT)
Private Pilot–Helicopter/Recreational Pilot–Transition (PHT)
Private Pilot–Gyroplane/Recreational Pilot–Transition (POT)
Private Pilot–Airplane (PAR)
Private Pilot–Rotorcraft/Helicopter (PRH)
Private Pilot–Rotorcraft/Gyroplane (PRO)
Private Pilot–Glider (POL)
Private Pilot–Free Balloon–Hot Air (PBH)
Private Pilot–Free Balloon–Gas (PBG)
Private Pilot–Lighter-Than-Air–Airship (PLA)
Private Pilot–Powered-Parachute (PPP)
Private Pilot–Weight-shift Control (PWS)

Unmanned Aircraft General–Small (UAG)

Comments regarding this supplement, or any Airman Testing publication, should be emailed to AFS630comments@faa.gov.

# Contents

# Appendix 1

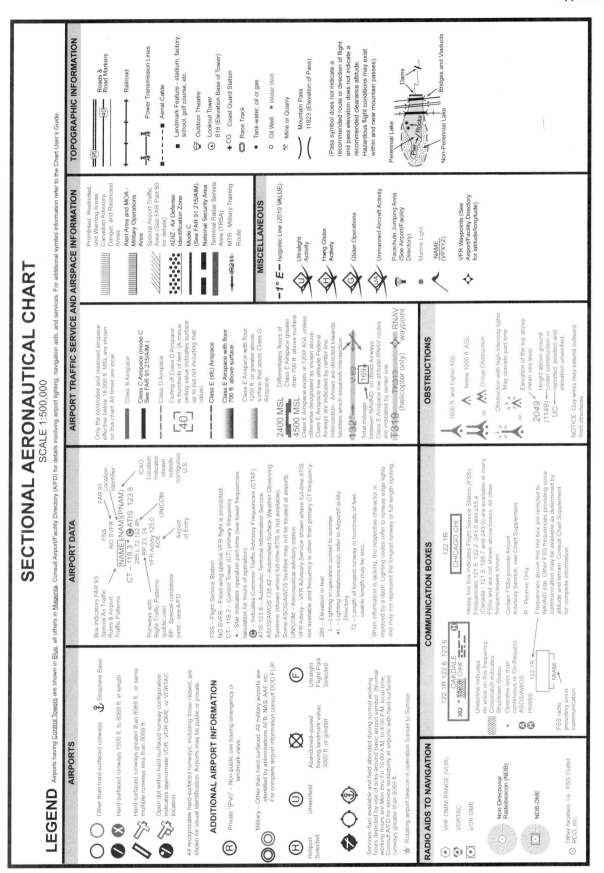

**Legend 1.** Sectional Aeronautical Chart.

4

# DIRECTORY LEGEND
## SAMPLE

CITY NAME
AIRPORT NAME (ALTERNATE NAME) (LTS) (KLTS) CIV/MIL 3 N UTC–6(–5DT) N34°41.93' W99°20.20' JACKSONVILLE

200 B S4 FUEL 100 OX 1 TPA—1000(800) AOE Class IV, ARFF Index A NOTAM FILE ORL Not insp. COPTER
H–4G, L–19C
IAP, DIAP, AD

RWY 18–36: H12004X200 (ASPH–CONC–GRVD)
    S–90, D–160, 2D–300 PCN 80 R/B/W/T    HIRL    CL
    RWY 18: LDIN. MALSF. TDZL. REIL. PAPI(P2R)—GA 3.0° TCH 36'.
        Thld dsplcd 300'. Trees. Rgt tfc.    0.3% up.
    RWY 36: ALSF1.    0.4% down.
    RWY 09–27: H6000X150 (ASPH) MIRL
    RWY 173–353: H3515X150 (ASPH–PFC)    AUW PCN 59 F/A/W/T
    LAND AND HOLD SHORT OPERATIONS
    LANDING    HOLD SHORT POINT    DIST AVBL
    RWY 18        09–27                6500
    RWY 36        09–27                5400
    RUNWAY DECLARED DISTANCE INFORMATION
    RWY 18: TORA–12004    TODA–12704    ASDA–11704    LDA–11504
    RWY 36: TORA–12004    TODA–12004    ASDA–12004    LDA–11704
ARRESTING GEAR/SYSTEM
    RWY 18 → HOOK E5 (65' OVRN) BAK–14 BAK–12B (1650')
        BAK–14 BAK–12 (B) (1087') HOOK E5 (74' OVRN) ← RWY 36
MILITARY SERVICE: A–GEAR E–5 connected on dep end, disconnected on
    apch end.    JASU 3(AM32A–60) 2(A/M32A–86)

FUEL J8(Mil) (NC–100, A)    FLUID W SP PRESAIR LOX
OIL O–128    TRAN ALERT Avbl 1300–0200Z‡, svc limited weekends.

AIRPORT REMARKS: Special Air Traffic Rules—Part 93, see Regulatory Notices. Attended 1200–0300Z‡. Parachute
    Jumping. Deer invof arpt. Heavy jumbo jet training surface to 9000'. Twy A clsd indef. Flight Notification Service
    (ADCUS) avbl.
MILITARY REMARKS: ANG PPR/Official Business Only. Base OPS DSN 638–4390, C503–335–4222. Ctc Base OPS 15
    minutes prior to ldg and after dep. Limited tran parking.
WEATHER DATA SOURCES: AWOS–1 120.3 (202) 426–8000. LLWAS.
COMMUNICATIONS: SFA    ATIS 127.25 273.5 (202) 426–8003    UNICOM 122.95    PTD 372.2
    NAME FSS (ORL) on arpt. 123.65 122.65 122.2
    NAME RCO 112.2T 112.1R (NAME RADIO)
Ⓡ NAME APP/DEP CON 128.35 257.725 (1200–0400Z‡)
    TOWER 119.65 255.6 (1200–0400Z‡)    GND CON 121.7    GCO 135.075 (ORLANDO CLNC)    CLNC DEL 125.55
    NAME COMD POST (GERONIMO) 311.0 321.4 6761    PMSV METRO 239.8    NAME OPS 257.5
AIRSPACE: CLASS B See VFR Terminal Area Chart.
RADIO AIDS TO NAVIGATION: NOTAM FILE ORL. VHF/DF ctc FSS.
    (H) VORTAC 112.2    MCO    Chan 59    N28°32.55' W81°20.12'    at fld.    1110/8E.
    (H) TACAN Chan 29    CBU (109.2)    N28°32.65' W81°21.12'    at fld.    1115/8E.
    HERNY NDB (LOM) 221    OR    N28°37.40' W81°21.05'    177° 5.4 NM to fld.
    ILS/DME 108.5    I–ORL    Chan 22    Rwy 18.    Class IIE.    LOM HERNY NDB.
    ASR/PAR (1200–0400Z‡)
COMM/NAV/WEATHER REMARKS: Emerg frequency 121.5 not avbl at twr.

HELIPAD H1: H100X75 (ASPH)
HELIPAD H2: H60X60 (ASPH)
HELIPORT REMARKS: Helipad H1 lctd on general aviation side and H2 lctd on air carrier side of arpt.

187    TPA 1000(813)
WATERWAY 15–33: 5000X425 (WATER)
SEAPLANE REMARKS: Birds roosting and feeding areas along river banks. Seaplanes operating adjacent to SW side of
    arpt not visible from twr and are required to ctc twr.

All bearings and radials are magnetic unless otherwise specified.
All mileages are nautical unless otherwise noted.
All times are Coordinated Universal Time (UTC) except as noted.
All elevations are in feet above/below Mean Sea Level (MSL) unless otherwise noted.
The horizontal reference datum of this publication is North American Datum of 1983 (NAD83), which for charting purposes
is considered equivalent to World Geodetic System 1984 (WGS 84).

**NE, 09 FEB 20XX to 05 APR 20XX**

**Legend 2.** Chart Supplement.

## SKETCH LEGEND

### RUNWAYS/LANDING AREAS

Hard Surfaced . . . . . . . .

Metal Surface . . . . . . . .

Sod, Gravel, etc. . . . . . . .

Light Plane, . . . . . . . . . .
Ski Landing Area or Water
Under Construction . . . . .

Closed . . . . . . . . . . . .

Helicopter Landings Area . . . . . . . . . . . ⒣

Displaced Threshold . . . . . . . .

Taxiway, Apron and Stopways . .

### RADIO AIDS TO NAVIGATION

VORTAC . . . ⬡        VOR . . . . . . . . ⬡

VOR/DME . . ▢        NDB . . . . . . . . ⊙

TACAN . . . . ⬠        NDB/DME . . . . ▣

### MISCELLANEOUS AERONAUTICAL FEATURES

Airport Beacon . . . . . . . . . . . .        ☆  ✪
Wind Cone . . . . . . . . . . . . . .        ⊷  ⊸
Landing Tee . . . . . . . . . . . . .        ⊢  ⊣
Tetrahedron . . . . . . . . . . . . .        ▶  ▷
Control Tower . . . . . . . . . .        ♙  or  TWR

When control tower and rotating beacon
are co-located beacon symbol will be
used and further identified as TWR.

### MISCELLANEOUS BASE AND CULTURAL FEATURES

Buildings . . . . . . . . . .

Power Lines . . . . . . . . . . .

Fence . . . . . . . . . . .

Towers . . . . . . . . . . . . . .

Tanks . . . . . . . . . . . . .

Oil Well . . . . . . . . . . . . .

Smoke Stack . . . . . . . . . . . . . . . .

Obstruction . . . . . . . . . . . . . .        5812  ⋀

Controlling Obstruction . . . . . . . . . .        +5812

Trees . . . . . . . . . . . . . . . . . . .

Populated Places . . . . . . . . . . . . .

Cuts and Fills . . . . . .    Cut        Fill

Cliffs and Depressions . .

Ditch . . . . . . . . . . . . . .

Hill . . . . . . . . . . . . . . . . . . .

### APPROACH LIGHTING SYSTEMS

A dot '•' portrayed with approach lighting
letter identifier indicates sequenced flashing
lights (F) installed with the approach lighting
system e.g. Ⓐ₁ Negative symbology, e.g., Ⓐ₁
Ⓥ indicates Pilot Controlled Lighting (PCL).

Runway Centerline Lighting . . . . .

Ⓐ  Approach Lighting System ALSF-2 . .

Ⓐ₁  Approach Lighting System ALSF-1 . .

Ⓐ₂  Short Approach Lighting System
    SALS/SALSF

Ⓐ₃  Simplified Short Approach Lighting
    System (SSALR) with RAIL . . . . .

Ⓐ₄  Medium Intensity Approach Lighting System
    (MALS and MALSF)/(SSALS
    and SSALF) . . . . . . . . . . .

Ⓐ₅  Medium Intensity Approach Lighting
    System (MALSR) and RAIL . . . .

    Omnidirectional Approach
    Lighting System (ODALS) . . . . . . .

Ⓓ  Navy Parallel Row and Cross Bar . . .

✝  Air Force Overrun . . . . . . . . . .

Ⓥ  Visual Approach Slope Indicator with
    Standard Threshold Clearance provided

Ⓥ₂  Pulsating Visual Approach Slope Indicator
    (PVASI)

Ⓥ₃  Visual Approach Slope Indicator with a
    threshold crossing height to accomodate
    long bodied or jumbo aircraft

Ⓥ₄  Tri-color Visual Approach Slope Indicator
    (TRCV)

Ⓥ₅  Approach Path Alignment Panel (APAP)

Ⓟ  Precision Approach Path Indicator (PAPI)

**Legend 3.**  Chart Supplement.

## 6        DIRECTORY LEGEND

### LEGEND

This directory is a listing of data on record with the FAA on all open to the public airports, military facilities and selected private use facilities specifically requested by the Department of Defense (DoD) for which a DoD Instrument Approach Procedure has been published in the U.S. Terminal Procedures Publication. Additionally this listing contains data for associated terminal control facilities, air route traffic control centers, and radio aids to navigation within the conterminous United States, Puerto Rico and the Virgin Islands. Joint civil/military and civil airports are listed alphabetically by state, associated city and airport name and cross-referenced by airport name. Military facilities are listed alphabetically by state and official airport name and cross-referenced by associated city name. Navaids, flight service stations and remote communication outlets that are associated with an airport, but with a different name, are listed alphabetically under their own name, as well as under the airport with which they are associated.

The listing of an open to the public airport in this directory merely indicates the airport operator's willingness to accommodate transient aircraft, and does not represent that the facility conforms with any Federal or local standards, or that it has been approved for use on the part of the general public. Military and private use facilities published in this directory are open to civil pilots only in an emergency or with prior permission. See Special Notice Section, Civil Use of Military Fields.

The information on obstructions is taken from reports submitted to the FAA. Obstruction data has not been verified in all cases. Pilots are cautioned that objects not indicated in this tabulation (or on the airports sketches and/or charts) may exist which can create a hazard to flight operation. Detailed specifics concerning services and facilities tabulated within this directory are contained in the Aeronautical Information Manual, Basic Flight Information and ATC Procedures.

The legend items that follow explain in detail the contents of this Directory and are keyed to the circled numbers on the sample on the preceding pages.

 **CITY/AIRPORT NAME**

Civil and joint civil/military airports and facilities in this directory are listed alphabetically by state and associated city. Where the city name is different from the airport name the city name will appear on the line above the airport name. Airports with the same associated city name will be listed alphabetically by airport name and will be separated by a dashed rule line. A solid rule line will separate all others. FAA approved helipads and seaplane landing areas associated with a land airport will be separated by a dotted line. Military airports are listed alphabetically by state and official airport name.

 **ALTERNATE NAME**

Alternate names, if any, will be shown in parentheses.

 **LOCATION IDENTIFIER**

The location identifier is a three or four character FAA code followed by a four-character ICAO code assigned to airports. ICAO codes will only be published at joint civil/military, and military facilities. If two different military codes are assigned, both codes will be shown with the primary operating agency's code listed first. These identifiers are used by ATC in lieu of the airport name in flight plans, flight strips and other written records and computer operations. Zeros will appear with a slash to differentiate them from the letter "O".

 **OPERATING AGENCY**

Airports within this directory are classified into two categories, Military/Federal Government and Civil airports open to the general public, plus selected private use airports. The operating agency is shown for military, private use and joint civil/military airports. The operating agency is shown by an abbreviation as listed below. When an organization is a tenant, the abbreviation is enclosed in parenthesis. No classification indicates the airport is open to the general public with no military tenant.

| | | | |
|---|---|---|---|
| A | US Army | MC | Marine Corps |
| AFRC | Air Force Reserve Command | N | Navy |
| AF | US Air Force | NAF | Naval Air Facility |
| ANG | Air National Guard | NAS | Naval Air Station |
| AR | US Army Reserve | NASA | National Air and Space Administration |
| ARNG | US Army National Guard | P | US Civil Airport Wherein Permit Covers |
| CG | US Coast Guard | | Use by Transient Military Aircraft |
| CIV/MIL | Joint Use Civil/Military | PVT | Private Use Only (Closed to the Public) |
| DND | Department of National Defense Canada | | |

 **AIRPORT LOCATION**

Airport location is expressed as distance and direction from the center of the associated city in nautical miles and cardinal points, e.g., 4 NE.

 **TIME CONVERSION**

Hours of operation of all facilities are expressed in Coordinated Universal Time (UTC) and shown as "Z" time. The directory indicates the number of hours to be subtracted from UTC to obtain local standard time and local daylight saving time UTC–5(–4DT). The symbol ‡ indicates that during periods of Daylight Saving Time effective hours will be one hour earlier than shown. In those areas where daylight saving time is not observed the (–4DT) and ‡ will not be shown. Daylight saving time is in effect from 0200 local time the second Sunday in March to 0200 local time the first Sunday in November. Canada and all U.S. Conterminous States observe daylight saving time except Arizona and Puerto Rico, and the Virgin Islands. If the state observes daylight saving time and the operating times are other than daylight saving times, the operating hours will include the dates, times and no ‡ symbol will be shown, i.e., April 15–Aug 31 0630–1700Z, Sep 1–Apr 14 0600–1700Z.

**NE, 09 FEB 20XX to 05 APR 20XX**

**Legend 4.** Chart Supplement.

## DIRECTORY LEGEND 7

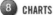 **GEOGRAPHIC POSITION OF AIRPORT—AIRPORT REFERENCE POINT (ARP)**

Positions are shown as hemisphere, degrees, minutes and hundredths of a minute and represent the approximate geometric center of all usable runway surfaces.

**8 CHARTS**

Charts refer to the Sectional Chart and Low and High Altitude Enroute Chart and panel on which the airport or facility is located. Helicopter Chart locations will be indicated as COPTER. IFR Gulf of Mexico West and IFR Gulf of Mexico Central will be depicted as GOMW and GOMC.

**9 INSTRUMENT APPROACH PROCEDURES, AIRPORT DIAGRAMS**

IAP indicates an airport for which a prescribed (Public Use) FAA Instrument Approach Procedure has been published. DIAP indicates an airport for which a prescribed DoD Instrument Approach Procedure has been published in the U.S. Terminal Procedures. See the Special Notice Section of this directory, Civil Use of Military Fields and the Aeronautical Information Manual 5–4–5 Instrument Approach Procedure Charts for additional information. AD indicates an airport for which an airport diagram has been published. Airport diagrams are located in the back of each A/FD volume alphabetically by associated city and airport name.

**10 AIRPORT SKETCH**

The airport sketch, when provided, depicts the airport and related topographical information as seen from the air and should be used in conjunction with the text. It is intended as a guide for pilots in VFR conditions. Symbology that is not self-explanatory will be reflected in the sketch legend. The airport sketch will be oriented with True North at the top. Airport sketches will be added incrementally.

**11 ELEVATION**

The highest point of an airport's usable runways measured in feet from mean sea level. When elevation is sea level it will be indicated as "00". When elevation is below sea level a minus "−" sign will precede the figure.

**12 ROTATING LIGHT BEACON**

B indicates rotating beacon is available. Rotating beacons operate sunset to sunrise unless otherwise indicated in the AIRPORT REMARKS or MILITARY REMARKS segment of the airport entry.

 **SERVICING—CIVIL**

| | |
|---|---|
| S1: Minor airframe repairs. | S5: Major airframe repairs. |
| S2: Minor airframe and minor powerplant repairs. | S6: Minor airframe and major powerplant repairs. |
| S3: Major airframe and minor powerplant repairs. | S7: Major powerplant repairs. |
| S4: Major airframe and major powerplant repairs. | S8: Minor powerplant repairs. |

 **FUEL**

| CODE | FUEL | CODE | FUEL |
|---|---|---|---|
| 80 | Grade 80 gasoline (Red) | B+ | Jet B, Wide-cut, turbine fuel with FS–II*, FP** minus 50° C. |
| 100 | Grade 100 gasoline (Green) | | |
| 100LL | 100LL gasoline (low lead) (Blue) | J4 (JP4) | (JP–4 military specification) FP** minus 58° C. |
| 115 | Grade 115 gasoline (115/145 military specification) (Purple) | | |
| A | Jet A, Kerosene, without FS–II*, FP** minus 40° C. | J5 (JP5) | (JP–5 military specification) Kerosene with FS–11, FP** minus 46°C. |
| A+ | Jet A, Kerosene, with FS–II*, FP** minus 40°C. | J8 (JP8) | (JP–8 military specification) Jet A–1, Kerosene with FS–II*, FP** minus 47°C. |
| A1 | Jet A–1, Kerosene, without FS–II*, FP** minus 47°C. | J8+100 | (JP–8 military specification) Jet A–1, Kerosene with FS–II*, FP** minus 47°C, with-fuel additive package that improves thermo stability characteristics of JP–8. |
| A1+ | Jet A–1, Kerosene with FS–II*, FP** minus 47° C. | | |
| B | Jet B, Wide-cut, turbine fuel without FS–II*, FP** minus 50° C. | J | (Jet Fuel Type Unknown) |
| | | MOGAS | Automobile gasoline which is to be used as aircraft fuel. |

*(Fuel System Icing Inhibitor)

**(Freeze Point)

NOTE: Certain automobile gasoline may be used in specific aircraft engines if a FAA supplemental type certificate has been obtained. Automobile gasoline, which is to be used in aircraft engines, will be identified as "MOGAS", however, the grade/type and other octane rating will not be published.

Data shown on fuel availability represents the most recent information the publisher has been able to acquire. Because of a variety of factors, the fuel listed may not always be obtainable by transient civil pilots. Confirmation of availability of fuel should be made directly with fuel suppliers at locations where refueling is planned.

 **OXYGEN—CIVIL**

| | |
|---|---|
| OX 1 High Pressure | OX 3 High Pressure—Replacement Bottles |
| OX 2 Low Pressure | OX 4 Low Pressure—Replacement Bottles |

 **TRAFFIC PATTERN ALTITUDE**

Traffic Pattern Altitude (TPA)—The first figure shown is TPA above mean sea level. The second figure in parentheses is TPA above airport elevation. Multiple TPA shall be shown as "TPA—See Remarks" and detailed information shall be shown in the Airport or Military Remarks Section. Traffic pattern data for USAF bases, USN facilities, and U.S. Army airports (including those on which ACC or U.S. Army is a tenant) that deviate from standard pattern altitudes shall be shown in Military Remarks.

**NE, 09 FEB 20XX to 05 APR 20XX**

**Legend 5.** Chart Supplement.

# 8     DIRECTORY LEGEND

**17 AIRPORT OF ENTRY, LANDING RIGHTS, AND CUSTOMS USER FEE AIRPORTS**

U.S. CUSTOMS USER FEE AIRPORT—Private Aircraft operators are frequently required to pay the costs associated with customs processing.

AOE—Airport of Entry. A customs Airport of Entry where permission from U.S. Customs is not required to land. However, at least one hour advance notice of arrival is required.

LRA—Landing Rights Airport. Application for permission to land must be submitted in advance to U.S. Customs. At least one hour advance notice of arrival is required.

NOTE: Advance notice of arrival at both an AOE and LRA airport may be included in the flight plan when filed in Canada or Mexico. Where Flight Notification Service (ADCUS) is available the airport remark will indicate this service. This notice will also be treated as an application for permission to land in the case of an LRA. Although advance notice of arrival may be relayed to Customs through Mexico, Canada, and U.S. Communications facilities by flight plan, the aircraft operator is solely responsible for ensuring that Customs receives the notification. (See Customs, Immigration and Naturalization, Public Health and Agriculture Department requirements in the International Flight Information Manual for further details.)

US Customs Air and Sea Ports, Inspectors and Agents

| | |
|---|---|
| Northeast Sector (New England and Atlantic States—ME to MD) | 407–975–1740 |
| Southeast Sector (Atlantic States—DC, WV, VA to FL) | 407–975–1780 |
| Central Sector (Interior of the US, including Gulf states—MS, AL, LA) | 407–975–1760 |
| Southwest East Sector (OK and eastern TX) | 407–975–1840 |
| Southwest West Sector (Western TX, NM and AZ) | 407–975–1820 |
| Pacific Sector (WA, OR, CA, HI and AK) | 407–975–1800 |

**18 CERTIFICATED AIRPORT (14 CFR PART 139)**

Airports serving Department of Transportation certified carriers and certified under 14 CFR part 139 are indicated by the Class and the ARFF Index; e.g. Class I, ARFF Index A, which relates to the availability of crash, fire, rescue equipment. Class I airports can have an ARFF Index A through E, depending on the aircraft length and scheduled departures. Class II, III, and IV will always carry an Index A.

14 CFR PART 139 CERTIFICATED AIRPORTS
AIRPORT CLASSIFICATIONS

| Type of Air Carrier Operation | Class I | Class II | Class III | Class IV |
|---|---|---|---|---|
| Scheduled Air Carrier Aircraft with 31 or more passenger seats | X | | | |
| Unscheduled Air Carrier Aircraft with 31 or more passengers seats | X | X | | X |
| Scheduled Air Carrier Aircraft with 10 to 30 passenger seats | X | X | X | |

## 14 CFR–PART 139 CERTIFICATED AIRPORTS
INDICES AND AIRCRAFT RESCUE AND FIRE FIGHTING EQUIPMENT REQUIREMENTS

| Airport Index | Required No. Vehicles | Aircraft Length | Scheduled Departures | Agent + Water for Foam |
|---|---|---|---|---|
| A | 1 | <90' | ≥1 | 500#DC or HALON 1211 or 450#DC + 100 gal $H_2O$ |
| B | 1 or 2 | ≥90', <126' | ≥5 | Index A + 1500 gal $H_2O$ |
| | | ≥126', <159' | <5 | |
| C | 2 or 3 | ≥126', <159' | ≥5 | Index A + 3000 gal $H_2O$ |
| | | ≥159', <200' | <5 | |
| D | 3 | ≥159', <200' | | Index A + 4000 gal $H_2O$ |
| | | >200' | <5 | |
| E | 3 | ≥200' | ≥5 | Index A + 6000 gal $H_2O$ |

> Greater Than; < Less Than; ≥ Equal or Greater Than; ≤ Equal or Less Than; $H_2O$–Water; DC–Dry Chemical.

NOTE: The listing of ARFF index does not necessarily assure coverage for non-air carrier operations or at other than prescribed times for air carrier. ARFF Index Ltd.—indicates ARFF coverage may or may not be available, for information contact airport manager prior to flight.

**19 NOTAM SERVICE**

All public use landing areas are provided NOTAM service. A NOTAM FILE identifier is shown for individual langing areas, e.g., "NOTAM FILE BNA". See the AIM, Basic Flight Information and ATC Procedures for a detailed description of NOTAMs.

NE, 09 FEB 20XX to 05 APR 20XX

**Legend 6.** Chart Supplement.

# DIRECTORY LEGEND 9

Current NOTAMs are available from flight service stations at 1–800–WX–BRIEF (992–7433) or online through the FAA PilotWeb at https://pilotweb.nas.faa.gov. Military NOTAMs are available using the Defense Internet NOTAM Service (DINS) at https://www.notams.jcs.mil.

Pilots flying to or from airports not available through the FAA PilotWeb or DINS can obtain assistance from Flight Service.

 **FAA INSPECTION**

All airports not inspected by FAA will be identified by the note: Not insp. This indicates that the airport information has been provided by the owner or operator of the field.

**21 RUNWAY DATA**

Runway information is shown on two lines. That information common to the entire runway is shown on the first line while information concerning the runway ends is shown on the second or following line. Runway direction, surface, length, width, weight bearing capacity, lighting, and slope, when available are shown for each runway. Multiple runways are shown with the longest runway first. Direction, length, width, and lighting are shown for sea-lanes. The full dimensions of helipads are shown, e.g., 50X150. Runway data that requires clarification will be placed in the remarks section.

### RUNWAY DESIGNATION

Runways are normally numbered in relation to their magnetic orientation rounded off to the nearest 10 degrees. Parallel runways can be designated L (left)/R (right)/C (center). Runways may be designated as Ultralight or assault strips. Assault strips are shown by magnetic bearing.

### RUNWAY DIMENSIONS

Runway length and width are shown in feet. Length shown is runway end to end including displaced thresholds, but excluding those areas designed as overruns.

### RUNWAY SURFACE AND LENGTH

Runway lengths prefixed by the letter ''H'' indicate that the runways are hard surfaced (concrete, asphalt, or part asphalt–concrete). If the runway length is not prefixed, the surface is sod, clay, etc. The runway surface composition is indicated in parentheses after runway length as follows:

| | | |
|---|---|---|
| (AFSC)—Aggregate friction seal coat | (GRVD)—Grooved | (PSP)—Pierced steel plank |
| (AMS)—Temporary metal planks coated with nonskid material | (GRVL)—Gravel, or cinders | (RFSC)—Rubberized friction seal coat |
| | (MATS)—Pierced steel planking, landing mats, membranes | (TURF)—Turf |
| (ASPH)—Asphalt | | (TRTD)—Treated |
| (CONC)—Concrete | (PEM)—Part concrete, part asphalt | (WC)—Wire combed |
| (DIRT)—Dirt | (PFC)—Porous friction courses | |

### RUNWAY WEIGHT BEARING CAPACITY

Runway strength data shown in this publication is derived from available information and is a realistic estimate of capability at an average level of activity. It is not intended as a maximum allowable weight or as an operating limitation. Many airport pavements are capable of supporting limited operations with gross weights in excess of the published figures. Permissible operating weights, insofar as runway strengths are concerned, are a matter of agreement between the owner and user. When desiring to operate into any airport at weights in excess of those published in the publication, users should contact the airport management for permission. Runway strength figures are shown in thousand of pounds, with the last three figures being omitted. Add 000 to figure following S, D, 2S, 2T, AUW, SWL, etc., for gross weight capacity. A blank space following the letter designator is used to indicate the runway can sustain aircraft with this type landing gear, although definite runway weight bearing capacity figures are not available, e.g., S, D. Applicable codes for typical gear configurations with S=Single, D=Dual, T=Triple and Q=Quadruple:

| CURRENT | NEW | NEW DESCRIPTION |
|---|---|---|
| S | S | Single wheel type landing gear (DC3), (C47), (F15), etc. |
| D | D | Dual wheel type landing gear (BE1900), (B737), (A319), etc. |
| T | D | Dual wheel type landing gear (P3, C9). |
| ST | 2S | Two single wheels in tandem type landing gear (C130). |
| TRT | 2T | Two triple wheels in tandem type landing gear (C17), etc. |
| DT | 2D | Two dual wheels in tandem type landing gear (B707), etc. |
| TT | 2D | Two dual wheels in tandem type landing gear (B757, KC135). |
| SBTT | 2D/D1 | Two dual wheels in tandem/dual wheel body gear type landing gear (KC10). |
| None | 2D/2D1 | Two dual wheels in tandem/two dual wheels in tandem body gear type landing gear (A340–600). |
| DDT | 2D/2D2 | Two dual wheels in tandem/two dual wheels in double tandem body gear type landing gear (B747, E4). |
| TTT | 3D | Three dual wheels in tandem type landing gear (B777), etc. |
| TT | D2 | Dual wheel gear two struts per side main gear type landing gear (B52). |
| TDT | C5 | Complex dual wheel and quadruple wheel combination landing gear (C5). |

**NE, 09 FEB 20XX to 05 APR 20XX**

**Legend 7.** Chart Supplement.

## 10                 DIRECTORY LEGEND

AUW—All up weight. Maximum weight bearing capacity for any aircraft irrespective of landing gear configuration.

SWL—Single Wheel Loading. (This includes information submitted in terms of Equivalent Single Wheel Loading (ESWL) and Single Isolated Wheel Loading).

PSI—Pounds per square inch. PSI is the actual figure expressing maximum pounds per square inch runway will support, e.g., (SWL 000/PSI 535).

Omission of weight bearing capacity indicates information unknown.

The ACN/PCN System is the ICAO standard method of reporting pavement strength for pavements with bearing strengths greater than 12,500 pounds. The Pavement Classification Number (PCN) is established by an engineering assessment of the runway. The PCN is for use in conjunction with an Aircraft Classification Number (ACN). Consult the Aircraft Flight Manual, Flight Information Handbook, or other appropriate source for ACN tables or charts. Currently, ACN data may not be available for all aircraft. If an ACN table or chart is available, the ACN can be calculated by taking into account the aircraft weight, the pavement type, and the subgrade category. For runways that have been evaluated under the ACN/PCN system, the PCN will be shown as a five-part code (e.g. PCN 80 R/B/W/T). Details of the coded format are as follows:

(1) The PCN NUMBER—The reported PCN indicates that an aircraft with an ACN equal or less than the reported PCN can operate on the pavement subject to any limitation on the tire pressure.

(2) The type of pavement:
    R — Rigid
    F — Flexible

(3) The pavement subgrade category:
    A — High
    B — Medium
    C — Low
    D — Ultra-low

(4) The maximum tire pressure authorized for the pavement:
    W — High, no limit
    X — Medium, limited to 217 psi
    Y — Low, limited to 145 psi
    Z — Very low, limited to 73 psi

(5) Pavement evaluation method:
    T — Technical evaluation
    U — By experience of aircraft using the pavement

NOTE: Prior permission from the airport controlling authority is required when the ACN of the aircraft exceeds the published PCN or aircraft tire pressure exceeds the published limits.

### RUNWAY LIGHTING

Lights are in operation sunset to sunrise. Lighting available by prior arrangement only or operating part of the night and/or pilot controlled lighting with specific operating hours are indicated under airport or military remarks. At USN/USMC facilities lights are available only during airport hours of operation. Since obstructions are usually lighted, obstruction lighting is not included in this code. Unlighted obstructions on or surrounding an airport will be noted in airport or military remarks. Runway lights nonstandard (NSTD) are systems for which the light fixtures are not FAA approved L-800 series: color, intensity, or spacing does not meet FAA standards. Nonstandard runway lights, VASI, or any other system not listed below will be shown in airport remarks or military service. Temporary, emergency or limited runway edge lighting such as flares, smudge pots, lanterns or portable runway lights will also be shown in airport remarks or military service. Types of lighting are shown with the runway or runway end they serve.

NSTD—Light system fails to meet FAA standards.
LIRL—Low Intensity Runway Lights.
MIRL—Medium Intensity Runway Lights.
HIRL—High Intensity Runway Lights.
RAIL—Runway Alignment Indicator Lights.
REIL—Runway End Identifier Lights.
CL—Centerline Lights.
TDZL—Touchdown Zone Lights.
ODALS—Omni Directional Approach Lighting System.
AF OVRN—Air Force Overrun 1000' Standard Approach Lighting System.
LDIN—Lead-In Lighting System.
MALS—Medium Intensity Approach Lighting System.
MALSF—Medium Intensity Approach Lighting System with Sequenced Flashing Lights.
MALSR—Medium Intensity Approach Lighting System with Runway Alignment Indicator Lights.

SALS—Short Approach Lighting System.
SALSF—Short Approach Lighting System with Sequenced Flashing Lights.
SSALS—Simplified Short Approach Lighting System.
SSALF—Simplified Short Approach Lighting System with Sequenced Flashing Lights.
SSALR—Simplified Short Approach Lighting System with Runway Alignment Indicator Lights.
ALSAF—High Intensity Approach Lighting System with Sequenced Flashing Lights.
ALSF1—High Intensity Approach Lighting System with Sequenced Flashing Lights, Category I, Configuration.
ALSF2—High Intensity Approach Lighting System with Sequenced Flashing Lights, Category II, Configuration.
SF—Sequenced Flashing Lights.
OLS—Optical Landing System.
WAVE-OFF.

NOTE: Civil ALSF2 may be operated as SSALR during favorable weather conditions. When runway edge lights are positioned more than 10 feet from the edge of the usable runway surface a remark will be added in the ''Remarks'' portion of the airport entry. This is applicable to Air Force, Air National Guard and Air Force Reserve Bases, and those joint civil/military airfields on which they are tenants.

**NE, 09 FEB 20XX to 05 APR 20XX**

**Legend 8.** Chart Supplement.

# DIRECTORY LEGEND 11

## VISUAL GLIDESLOPE INDICATORS

APAP—A system of panels, which may or may not be lighted, used for alignment of approach path.

| | | | |
|---|---|---|---|
| PNIL | APAP on left side of runway | PNIR | APAP on right side of runway |

PAPI—Precision Approach Path Indicator

| | | | |
|---|---|---|---|
| P2L | 2-identical light units placed on left side of runway | P4L | 4-identical light units placed on left side of runway |
| P2R | 2-identical light units placed on right side of runway | P4R | 4-identical light units placed on right side of runway |

PVASI—Pulsating/steady burning visual approach slope indicator, normally a single light unit projecting two colors.

| | | | |
|---|---|---|---|
| PSIL | PVASI on left side of runway | PSIR | PVASI on right side of runway |

SAVASI—Simplified Abbreviated Visual Approach Slope Indicator

| | | | |
|---|---|---|---|
| S2L | 2-box SAVASI on left side of runway | S2R | 2-box SAVASI on right side of runway |

TRCV—Tri-color visual approach slope indicator, normally a single light unit projecting three colors.

| | | | |
|---|---|---|---|
| TRIL | TRCV on left side of runway | TRIR | TRCV on right side of runway |

VASI—Visual Approach Slope Indicator

| | | | |
|---|---|---|---|
| V2L | 2-box VASI on left side of runway | V6L | 6-box VASI on left side of runway |
| V2R | 2-box VASI on right side of runway | V6R | 6-box VASI on right side of runway |
| V4L | 4-box VASI on left side of runway | V12 | 12-box VASI on both sides of runway |
| V4R | 4-box VASI on right side of runway | V16 | 16-box VASI on both sides of runway |

NOTE: Approach slope angle and threshold crossing height will be shown when available; i.e., –GA 3.5° TCH 37'.

## PILOT CONTROL OF AIRPORT LIGHTING

| Key Mike | Function |
|---|---|
| 7 times within 5 seconds | Highest intensity available |
| 5 times within 5 seconds | Medium or lower intensity (Lower REIL or REIL-Off) |
| 3 times within 5 seconds | Lowest intensity available (Lower REIL or REIL-Off) |

Available systems will be indicated in the airport or military remarks, e.g., ACTIVATE HIRL Rwy 07–25, MALSR Rwy 07, and VASI Rwy 07—122.8.

Where the airport is not served by an instrument approach procedure and/or has an independent type system of different specification installed by the airport sponsor, descriptions of the type lights, method of control, and operating frequency will be explained in clear text. See AIM, ''Basic Flight Information and ATC Procedures,'' for detailed description of pilot control of airport lighting.

## RUNWAY SLOPE

When available, runway slope data will only be provided for those airports with an approved FAA instrument approach procedure. Runway slope will be shown only when it is 0.3 percent or greater. On runways less than 8000 feet, the direction of the slope up will be indicated, e.g., 0.3% up NW. On runways 8000 feet or greater, the slope will be shown (up or down) on the runway end line, e.g., RWY 13: 0.3% up., RWY 21: Pole. Rgt tfc. 0.4% down.

## RUNWAY END DATA

Information pertaining to the runway approach end such as approach lights, touchdown zone lights, runway end identification lights, visual glideslope indicators, displaced thresholds, controlling obstruction, and right hand traffic pattern, will be shown on the specific runway end. ''Rgt tfc''—Right traffic indicates right turns should be made on landing and takeoff for specified runway end.

## LAND AND HOLD SHORT OPERATIONS (LAHSO)

LAHSO is an acronym for ''Land and Hold Short Operations.'' These operations include landing and holding short of an intersection runway, an intersecting taxiway, or other predetermined points on the runway other than a runway or taxiway. Measured distance represents the available landing distance on the landing runway, in feet.

Specific questions regarding these distances should be referred to the air traffic manager of the facility concerned. The Aeronautical Information Manual contains specific details on hold–short operations and markings.

## RUNWAY DECLARED DISTANCE INFORMATION

TORA—Take-off Run Available. The length of runway declared available and suitable for the ground run of an aeroplane take–off.

TODA—Take-off Distance Available. The length of the take–off run available plus the length of the clearway, if provided.

ASDA—Accelerate-Stop Distance Available. The length of the take–off run available plus the length of the stopway, if provided.

LDA—Landing Distance Available. The length of runway which is declared available and suitable for the ground run of an aeroplane landing.

## 22 ARRESTING GEAR/SYSTEMS

Arresting gear is shown as it is located on the runway. The a–gear distance from the end of the appropriate runway (or into the overrun) is indicated in parentheses. A–Gear which has a bi–direction capability and can be utilized for emergency approach end engagement is indicated by a (B). The direction of engaging device is indicated by an arrow. Up to 15 minutes advance notice may be required for rigging A–Gear for approach and engagement. Airport listing may show availability of other than US Systems. This information is provided for emergency requirements only. Refer to current aircraft operating manuals for specific engagement weight and speed criteria based on aircraft structural restrictions and arresting system limitations.

Following is a list of current systems referenced in this publication identified by both Air Force and Navy terminology:

**NE, 09 FEB 20XX to 05 APR 20XX**

**Legend 9.** Chart Supplement.

## 12          DIRECTORY LEGEND

BI–DIRECTIONAL CABLE (B)

| TYPE | DESCRIPTION |
|------|-------------|
| BAK–9 | Rotary friction brake. |
| BAK–12A | Standard BAK–12 with 950 foot run out, 1–inch cable and 40,000 pound weight setting. Rotary friction brake. |
| BAK–12B | Extended BAK–12 with 1200 foot run, 1¼ inch Cable and 50,000 pounds weight setting. Rotary friction brake. |
| E28 | Rotary Hydraulic (Water Brake). |
| M21 | Rotary Hydraulic (Water Brake) Mobile. |

The following device is used in conjunction with some aircraft arresting systems:

| | |
|------|-------------|
| BAK–14 | A device that raises a hook cable out of a slot in the runway surface and is remotely positioned for engagement by the tower on request. (In addition to personnel reaction time, the system requires up to five seconds to fully raise the cable.) |
| H | A device that raises a hook cable out of a slot in the runway surface and is remotely positioned for engagement by the tower on request. (In addition to personnel reaction time, the system requires up to one and one–half seconds to fully raise the cable.) |

UNI–DIRECTIONAL CABLE

| TYPE | DESCRIPTION |
|------|-------------|
| MB60 | Textile brake—an emergency one–time use, modular braking system employing the tearing of specially woven textile straps to absorb the kinetic energy. |
| E5/E5–1/E5–3 | Chain Type. At USN/USMC stations E–5 A–GEAR systems are rated, e.g., E–5 RATING–13R–1100 HW (DRY), 31L/R–1200 STD (WET). This rating is a function of the A–GEAR chain weight and length and is used to determine the maximum aircraft engaging speed. A dry rating applies to a stabilized surface (dry or wet) while a wet rating takes into account the amount (if any) of wet overrun that is not capable of withstanding the aircraft weight. These ratings are published under Military Service. |

FOREIGN CABLE

| TYPE | DESCRIPTION | US EQUIVALENT |
|------|-------------|---------------|
| 44B–3H | Rotary Hydraulic) (Water Brake) | |
| CHAG | Chain | E–5 |

UNI–DIRECTIONAL BARRIER

| TYPE | DESCRIPTION |
|------|-------------|
| MA–1A | Web barrier between stanchions attached to a chain energy absorber. |
| BAK–15 | Web barrier between stanchions attached to an energy absorber (water squeezer, rotary friction, chain). Designed for wing engagement. |

NOTE: Landing short of the runway threshold on a runway with a BAK–15 in the underrun is a significant hazard. The barrier in the down position still protrudes several inches above the underrun. Aircraft contact with the barrier short of the runway threshold can cause damage to the barrier and substantial damage to the aircraft.

OTHER

| TYPE | DESCRIPTION |
|------|-------------|
| EMAS | Engineered Material Arresting System, located beyond the departure end of the runway, consisting of high energy absorbing materials which will crush under the weight of an aircraft. |

### 23 MILITARY SERVICE

Specific military services available at the airport are listed under this general heading. Remarks applicable to any military service are shown in the individual service listing.

### 24 JET AIRCRAFT STARTING UNITS (JASU)

The numeral preceding the type of unit indicates the number of units available. The absence of the numeral indicates ten or more units available. If the number of units is unknown, the number one will be shown. Absence of JASU designation indicates non–availability.

The following is a list of current JASU systems referenced in this publication:

USAF JASU (For variations in technical data, refer to T.O. 35–1–7.)

ELECTRICAL STARTING UNITS:

| | |
|------|-------------|
| A/M32A–86 | AC: 115/200v, 3 phase, 90 kva, 0.8 pf, 4 wire |
| | DC: 28v, 1500 amp, 72 kw (with TR pack) |
| MC–1A | AC: 115/208v, 400 cycle, 3 phase, 37.5 kva, 0.8 pf, 108 amp, 4 wire |
| | DC: 28v, 500 amp, 14 kw |
| MD–3 | AC: 115/208v, 400 cycle, 3 phase, 60 kva, 0.75 pf, 4 wire |
| | DC: 28v, 1500 amp, 45 kw, split bus |
| MD–3A | AC: 115/208v, 400 cycle, 3 phase, 60 kva, 0.75 pf, 4 wire |
| | DC: 28v, 1500 amp, 45 kw, split bus |
| MD–3M | AC: 115/208v, 400 cycle, 3 phase, 60 kva, 0.75 pf, 4 wire |
| | DC: 28v, 500 amp, 15 kw |

**NE, 09 FEB 20XX to 05 APR 20XX**

**Legend 10.** Chart Supplement.

## DIRECTORY LEGEND 13

| | |
|---|---|
| MD–4 | AC: 120/208v, 400 cycle, 3 phase, 62.5 kva, 0.8 pf, 175 amp, "WYE" neutral ground, 4 wire, 120v, 400 cycle, 3 phase, 62.5 kva, 0.8 pf, 303 amp, "DELTA" 3 wire, 120v, 400 cycle, 1 phase, 62.5 kva, 0.8 pf, 520 amp, 2 wire |

AIR STARTING UNITS

| | |
|---|---|
| AM32–95 | 150 +/– 5 lb/min (2055 +/– 68 cfm) at 51 +/– 2 psia |
| AM32A–95 | 150 +/– 5 lb/min @ 49 +/– 2 psia (35 +/– 2 psig) |
| LASS | 150 +/– 5 lb/min @ 49 +/– 2 psia |
| MA–1A | 82 lb/min (1123 cfm) at 130° air inlet temp, 45 psia (min) air outlet press |
| MC–1 | 15 cfm, 3500 psia |
| MC–1A | 15 cfm, 3500 psia |
| MC–2A | 15 cfm, 200 psia |
| MC–11 | 8,000 cu in cap, 4000 psig, 15 cfm |

COMBINED AIR AND ELECTRICAL STARTING UNITS:

| | |
|---|---|
| AGPU | AC: 115/200v, 400 cycle, 3 phase, 30 kw gen |
| | DC: 28v, 700 amp |
| | AIR: 60 lb/min @ 40 psig @ sea level |
| AM32A–60* | AIR: 120 +/– 4 lb/min (1644 +/– 55 cfm) at 49 +/– 2 psia |
| | AC: 120/208v, 400 cycle, 3 phase, 75 kva, 0.75 pf, 4 wire, 120v, 1 phase, 25 kva |
| | DC: 28v, 500 amp, 15 kw |
| AM32A–60A | AIR: 150 +/– 5 lb/min (2055 +/– 68 cfm at 51 +/– psia |
| | AC: 120/208v, 400 cycle, 3 phase, 75 kva, 0.75 pf, 4 wire |
| | DC: 28v, 200 amp, 5.6 kw |
| AM32A–60B* | AIR: 130 lb/min, 50 psia |
| | AC: 120/208v, 400 cycle, 3 phase, 75 kva, 0.75 pf, 4 wire |
| | DC: 28v, 200 amp, 5.6 kw |

*NOTE: During combined air and electrical loads, the pneumatic circuitry takes preference and will limit the amount of electrical power available.

USN JASU

ELECTRICAL STARTING UNITS:

| | |
|---|---|
| NC–8A/A1 | DC: 500 amp constant, 750 amp intermittent, 28v; |
| | AC: 60 kva @ .8 pf, 115/200v, 3 phase, 400 Hz. |
| NC–10A/A1/B/C | DC: 750 amp constant, 1000 amp intermittent, 28v; |
| | AC: 90 kva, 115/200v, 3 phase, 400 Hz. |

AIR STARTING UNITS:

| | |
|---|---|
| GTC–85/GTE–85 | 120 lbs/min @ 45 psi. |
| MSU–200NAV/A/U47A–5 | 204 lbs/min @ 56 psia. |
| WELLS AIR START SYSTEM | 180 lbs/min @ 75 psi or 120 lbs/min @ 45 psi. Simultaneous multiple start capability. |

COMBINED AIR AND ELECTRICAL STARTING UNITS:

| | |
|---|---|
| NCPP–105/RCPT | 180 lbs/min @ 75 psi or 120 lbs/min @ 45 psi. 700 amp, 28v DC. 120/208v, 400 Hz AC, 30 kva. |

JASU (ARMY)

| | |
|---|---|
| 59B2–1B | 28v, 7.5 kw, 280 amp. |

OTHER JASU

ELECTRICAL STARTING UNITS (DND):

| | |
|---|---|
| CE12 | AC 115/200v, 140 kva, 400 Hz, 3 phase |
| CE13 | AC 115/200v, 60 kva, 400 Hz, 3 phase |
| CE14 | AC/DC 115/200v, 140 kva, 400 Hz, 3 phase, 28vDC, 1500 amp |
| CE15 | DC 22–35v, 500 amp continuous 1100 amp intermittent |
| CE16 | DC 22–35v, 500 amp continuous 1100 amp intermittent soft start |

AIR STARTING UNITS (DND):

| | |
|---|---|
| CA2 | ASA 45.5 psig, 116.4 lb/min |

COMBINED AIR AND ELECTRICAL STARTING UNITS (DND)

| | |
|---|---|
| CEA1 | AC 120/208v, 60 kva, 400 Hz, 3 phase DC 28v, 75 amp |
| | AIR 112.5 lb/min, 47 psig |

ELECTRICAL STARTING UNITS (OTHER):

| | |
|---|---|
| C–26 | 28v 45kw 115–200v 15kw 380–800 Hz 1 phase 2 wire |
| C–26–B, C–26–C | 28v 45kw: Split Bus: 115–200v 15kw 380–800 Hz 1 phase 2 wire |
| E3 | DC 28v/10kw |

AIR STARTING UNITS (OTHER):

| | |
|---|---|
| A4 | 40 psi/2 lb/sec (LPAS Mk12, Mk12L, Mk12A, Mk1, Mk2B) |
| MA–1 | 150 Air HP, 115 lb/min 50 psia |
| MA–2 | 250 Air HP, 150 lb/min 75 psia |

CARTRIDGE:

| | |
|---|---|
| MXU–4A | USAF |

**NE, 09 FEB 20XX to 05 APR 20XX**

**Legend 11.** Chart Supplement.

**14**  **DIRECTORY LEGEND**

 **FUEL—MILITARY**

Fuel available through US Military Base supply, DESC Into–Plane Contracts and/or reciprocal agreement is listed first and is followed by (Mil). At commercial airports where Into–Plane contracts are in place, the name of the refueling agent is shown. Military fuel should be used first if it is available. When military fuel cannot be obtained but Into–Plane contract fuel is available, Government aircraft must refuel with the contract fuel and applicable refueling agent to avoid any breach in contract terms and conditions. Fuel not available through the above is shown preceded by NC (no contract). When fuel is obtained from NC sources, local purchase procedures must be followed. The US Military Aircraft Identaplates DD Form 1896 (Jet Fuel), DD Form 1897 (Avgas) and AF Form 1245 (Avgas) are used at military installations only. The US Government Aviation Into–Plane Reimbursement (AIR) Card (currently issued by AVCARD) is the instrument to be used to obtain fuel under a DESC Into–Plane Contract and for NC purchases if the refueling agent at the commercial airport accepts the AVCARD. A current list of contract fuel locations is available online at www.desc.dla.mil/Static/ProductsAndServices.asp; click on the Commercial Airports button.

See legend item 14 for fuel code and description.

**26** **SUPPORTING FLUIDS AND SYSTEMS—MILITARY**

CODE

| | |
|---|---|
| ADI | Anti–Detonation Injection Fluid—Reciprocating Engine Aircraft. |
| W | Water Thrust Augmentation—Jet Aircraft. |
| WAI | Water–Alcohol Injection Type, Thrust Augmentation—Jet Aircraft. |
| SP | Single Point Refueling. |
| PRESAIR | Air Compressors rated 3,000 PSI or more. |
| De–Ice | Anti–icing/De–icing/Defrosting Fluid (MIL–A–8243). |

**OXYGEN:**

| | |
|---|---|
| LPOX | Low pressure oxygen servicing. |
| HPOX | High pressure oxygen servicing. |
| LHOX | Low and high pressure oxygen servicing. |
| LOX | Liquid oxygen servicing. |
| OXRB | Oxygen replacement bottles. (Maintained primarily at Naval stations for use in acft where oxygen can be replenished only by replacement of cylinders.) |
| OX | Indicates oxygen servicing when type of servicing is unknown. |

NOTE: Combinations of above items is used to indicate complete oxygen servicing available;

| | |
|---|---|
| LHOXRB | Low and high pressure oxygen servicing and replacement bottles; |
| LPOXRB | Low pressure oxygen replacement bottles only, etc. |

NOTE: Aircraft will be serviced with oxygen procured under military specifications only. Aircraft will not be serviced with medical oxygen.

**NITROGEN:**

LPNIT — Low pressure nitrogen servicing.
HPNIT — High pressure nitrogen servicing.
LHNIT — Low and high pressure nitrogen servicing.

**27** **OIL—MILITARY**

US AVIATION OILS (MIL SPECS):

| CODE | GRADE, TYPE |
|---|---|
| O–113 | 1065, Reciprocating Engine Oil (MIL–L–6082) |
| O–117 | 1100, Reciprocating Engine Oil (MIL–L–6082) |
| O–117+ | 1100, O–117 plus cyclohexanone (MIL–L–6082) |
| O–123 | 1065, (Dispersant), Reciprocating Engine Oil (MIL–L–22851 Type III) |
| O–128 | 1100, (Dispersant), Reciprocating Engine Oil (MIL–L–22851 Type II) |
| O–132 | 1005, Jet Engine Oil (MIL–L–6081) |
| O–133 | 1010, Jet Engine Oil (MIL–L–6081) |
| O–147 | None, MIL–L–6085A Lubricating Oil, Instrument, Synthetic |
| O–148 | None, MIL–L–7808 (Synthetic Base) Turbine Engine Oil |
| O–149 | None, Aircraft Turbine Engine Synthetic, 7.5c St |
| O–155 | None, MIL–L–6086C, Aircraft, Medium Grade |
| O–156 | None, MIL–L–23699 (Synthetic Base), Turboprop and Turboshaft Engines |
| JOAP/SOAP | Joint Oil Analysis Program. JOAP support is furnished during normal duty hours, other times on request. (JOAP and SOAP programs provide essentially the same service, JOAP is now the standard joint service supported program.) |

**28** **TRANSIENT ALERT (TRAN ALERT)—MILITARY**

Tran Alert service is considered to include all services required for normal aircraft turn–around, e.g., servicing (fuel, oil, oxygen, etc.), debriefing to determine requirements for maintenance, minor maintenance, inspection and parking assistance of transient aircraft. Drag chute repack, specialized maintenance, or extensive repairs will be provided within the capabilities and priorities of the base. Delays can be anticipated after normal duty hours/holidays/weekends regardless of the hours of transient maintenance operation. Pilots should not expect aircraft to be serviced for TURN–AROUNDS during time periods when servicing or maintenance manpower is not available. In the case of airports not operated exclusively by US military, the servicing indicated by the remarks will not always be available for US military

**NE, 09 FEB 20XX to 05 APR 20XX**

**Legend 12.** Chart Supplement.

aircraft. When transient alert services are not shown, facilities are unknown. NO PRIORITY BASIS—means that transient alert services will be provided only after all the requirements for mission/tactical assigned aircraft have been accomplished.

 **AIRPORT REMARKS**

The Attendance Schedule is the months, days and hours the airport is actually attended. Airport attendance does not mean watchman duties or telephone accessibility, but rather an attendant or operator on duty to provide at least minimum services (e.g., repairs, fuel, transportation).

Airport Remarks have been grouped in order of applicability. Airport remarks are limited to those items of information that are determined essential for operational use, i.e., conditions of a permanent or indefinite nature and conditions that will remain in effect for more than 30 days concerning aeronautical facilities, services, maintenance available, procedures or hazards, knowledge of which is essential for safe and efficient operation of aircraft. Information concerning permanent closing of a runway or taxiway will not be shown. A note "See Special Notices" shall be applied within this remarks section when a special notice applicable to the entry is contained in the Special Notices section of this publication.

Parachute Jumping indicates parachute jumping areas associated with the airport. See Parachute Jumping Area section of this publication for additional Information.

Landing Fee indicates landing charges for private or non-revenue producing aircraft. In addition, fees may be charged for planes that remain over a couple of hours and buy no services, or at major airline terminals for all aircraft.

Note: Unless otherwise stated, remarks including runway ends refer to the runway's approach end.

 **MILITARY REMARKS**

Military Remarks published at a joint Civil/Military facility are remarks that are applicable to the Military. At Military Facilities all remarks will be published under the heading Military Remarks. Remarks contained in this section may not be applicable to civil users. The first group of remarks is applicable to the primary operator of the airport. Remarks applicable to a tenant on the airport are shown preceded by the tenant organization, i.e., (A) (AF) (N) (ANG), etc. Military airports operate 24 hours unless otherwise specified. Airport operating hours are listed first (airport operating hours will only be listed if they are different than the airport attended hours or if the attended hours are unavailable) followed by pertinent remarks in order of applicability. Remarks will include information on restrictions, hazards, traffic pattern, noise abatement, customs/agriculture/immigration, and miscellaneous information applicable to the Military.

Type of restrictions:

CLOSED: When designated closed, the airport is restricted from use by all aircraft unless stated otherwise. Any closure applying to specific type of aircraft or operation will be so stated. USN/USMC/USAF airports are considered closed during non-operating hours. Closed airports may be utilized during an emergency provided there is a safe landing area.

OFFICIAL BUSINESS ONLY: The airfield is closed to all transient military aircraft for obtaining routine services such as fueling, passenger drop off or pickup, practice approaches, parking, etc. The airfield may be used by aircrews and aircraft if official government business (including civilian) must be conducted on or near the airfield and prior permission is received from the airfield manager.

AF OFFICIAL BUSINESS ONLY OR NAVY OFFICIAL BUSINESS ONLY: Indicates that the restriction applies only to service indicated.

PRIOR PERMISSION REQUIRED (PPR): Airport is closed to transient aircraft unless approval for operation is obtained from the appropriate commander through Chief, Airfield Management or Airfield Operations Officer. Official Business or PPR does not preclude the use of US Military airports as an alternate for IFR flights. If a non–US military airport is used as a weather alternate and requires a PPR, the PPR must be requested and confirmed before the flight departs. The purpose of PPR is to control volume and flow of traffic rather than to prohibit it. Prior permission is required for all aircraft requiring transient alert service outside the published transient alert duty hours. All aircraft carrying hazardous materials must obtain prior permission as outlined in AFJI 11–204, AR 95–27, OPNAVINST 3710.7.

Note: OFFICIAL BUSINESS ONLY AND PPR restrictions are not applicable to Special Air Mission (SAM) or Special Air Resource (SPAR) aircraft providing person or persons on aboard are designated Code 6 or higher as explained in AFJMAN 11–213, AR 95–11, OPNAVINST 3722–8J. Official Business Only or PPR do not preclude the use of the airport as an alternate for IFR flights.

 **WEATHER DATA SOURCES**

Weather data sources will be listed alphabetically followed by their assigned frequencies and/or telephone number and hours of operation.

ASOS—Automated Surface Observing System. Reports the same as an AWOS–3 plus precipitation identification and intensity, and freezing rain occurrence;

AWOS—Automated Weather Observing System

    AWOS–A—reports altimeter setting (all other information is advisory only).

    AWOS–AV—reports altimeter and visibility.

    AWOS–1—reports altimeter setting, wind data and usually temperature, dew point and density altitude.

    AWOS–2—reports the same as AWOS–1 plus visibility.

    AWOS–3—reports the same as AWOS–1 plus visibility and cloud/ceiling data.

    AWOS–3P reports the same as the AWOS–3 system, plus a precipitation identification sensor.

    AWOS–3PT reports the same as the AWOS–3 system, plus precipitation identification sensor and a thunderstorm/lightning reporting capability.

    AWOS–3T reports the same as AWOS–3 system and includes a thunderstorm/lightning reporting capability.

**NE, 09 FEB 20XX to 05 APR 20XX**

**Legend 13.** Chart Supplement.

## 16                    DIRECTORY LEGEND

See AIM, Basic Flight Information and ATC Procedures for detailed description of Weather Data Sources.

AWOS-4—reports same as AWOS-3 system, plus precipitation occurence, type and accumulation, freezing rain, thunderstorm, and runway surface sensors.

HIWAS—See RADIO AIDS TO NAVIGATION

LAWRS—Limited Aviation Weather Reporting Station where observers report cloud height, weather, obstructions to vision, temperature and dewpoint (in most cases), surface wind, altimeter and pertinent remarks.

LLWAS—indicates a Low Level Wind Shear Alert System consisting of a center field and several field perimeter anemometers.

SAWRS—identifies airports that have a Supplemental Aviation Weather Reporting Station available to pilots for current weather information.

SWSL—Supplemental Weather Service Location providing current local weather information via radio and telephone.

TDWR—indicates airports that have Terminal Doppler Weather Radar.

WSP—indicates airports that have Weather System Processor.

When the automated weather source is broadcast over an associated airport NAVAID frequency (see NAVAID line), it shall be indicated by a bold ASOS, AWOS, or HIWAS followed by the frequency, identifier and phone number, if available.

 **COMMUNICATIONS**

Airport terminal control facilities and radio communications associated with the airport shall be shown. When the call sign is not the same as the airport name the call sign will be shown. Frequencies shall normally be shown in descending order with the primary frequency listed first. Frequencies will be listed, together with sectorization indicated by outbound radials, and hours of operation. Communications will be listed in sequence as follows:

Single Frequency Approach (SFA), Common Traffic Advisory Frequency (CTAF), Automatic Terminal Information Service (ATIS) and Aeronautical Advisory Stations (UNICOM) or (AUNICOM) along with their frequency is shown, where available, on the line following the heading ''COMMUNICATIONS.'' When the CTAF and UNICOM frequencies are the same, the frequency will be shown as CTAF/UNICOM 122.8.

The FSS telephone nationwide is toll free 1–800–WX–BRIEF (1–800–992–7433). When the FSS is located on the field it will be indicated as ''on arpt''. Frequencies available at the FSS will follow in descending order. Remote Communications Outlet (RCO) providing service to the airport followed by the frequency and FSS RADIO name will be shown when available.

FSS's provide information on airport conditions, radio aids and other facilities, and process flight plans. Airport Advisory Service (AAS) is provided on the CTAF by FSS's for select non-tower airports or airports where the tower is not in operation.

(See AIM, Para 4–1–9 Traffic Advisory Practices at Airports Without Operating Control Towers or AC 90–42C.)

Aviation weather briefing service is provided by FSS specialists. Flight and weather briefing services are also available by calling the telephone numbers listed.

Remote Communications Outlet (RCO)—An unmanned air/ground communications facility that is remotely controlled and provides UHF or VHF communications capability to extend the service range of an FSS.

Civil Communications Frequencies-Civil communications frequencies used in the FSS air/ground system are operated on 122.0, 122.2, 123.6; emergency 121.5; plus receive-only on 122.1.

    a.  122.0 is assigned as the Enroute Flight Advisory Service frequency at selected FSS RADIO outlets.

    b.  122.2 is assigned as a common enroute frequency.

    c.  123.6 is assigned as the airport advisory frequency at select non-tower locations. At airports with a tower, FSS may provide airport advisories on the tower frequency when tower is closed.

    d.  122.1 is the primary receive-only frequency at VOR's.

    e.  Some FSS's are assigned 50 kHz frequencies in the 122–126 MHz band (eg. 122.45). Pilots using the FSS A/G system should refer to this directory or appropriate charts to determine frequencies available at the FSS or remoted facility through which they wish to communicate.

Emergency frequency 121.5 and 243.0 are available at all Flight Service Stations, most Towers, Approach Control and RADAR facilities.

Frequencies published followed by the letter ''T'' or ''R'', indicate that the facility will only transmit or receive respectively on that frequency. All radio aids to navigation (NAVAID) frequencies are transmit only.

### TERMINAL SERVICES

SFA—Single Frequency Approach.

CTAF—A program designed to get all vehicles and aircraft at airports without an operating control tower on a common frequency.

ATIS—A continuous broadcast of recorded non-control information in selected terminal areas.

D–ATIS—Digital ATIS provides ATIS information in text form outside the standard reception range of conventional ATIS via landline & data link communications and voice message within range of existing transmitters.

AUNICOM—Automated UNICOM is a computerized, command response system that provides automated weather, radio check capability and airport advisory information selected from an automated menu by microphone clicks.

UNICOM—A non-government air/ground radio communications facility which may provide airport information.

PTD—Pilot to Dispatcher.

APP CON—Approach Control. The symbol ® indicates radar approach control.

TOWER—Control tower.

GCA—Ground Control Approach System.

GND CON—Ground Control.

GCO—Ground Communication Outlet—An unstaffed, remotely controlled, ground/ground communications facility. Pilots at

**NE, 09 FEB 20XX to 05 APR 20XX**

## Legend 14. Chart Supplement.

## DIRECTORY LEGEND 17

uncontrolled airports may contact ATC and FSS via VHF to a telephone connection to obtain an instrument clearance or close a VFR or IFR flight plan. They may also get an updated weather briefing prior to takeoff. Pilots will use four ''key clicks'' on the VHF radio to contact the appropriate ATC facility or six ''key clicks'' to contact the FSS. The GCO system is intended to be used only on the ground.

DEP CON—Departure Control. The symbol Ⓡ indicates radar departure control.

CLNC DEL—Clearance Delivery.

PRE TAXI CLNC—Pre taxi clearance.

VFR ADVSY SVC—VFR Advisory Service. Service provided by Non-Radar Approach Control.

  Advisory Service for VFR aircraft (upon a workload basis) ctc APP CON.

COMD POST—Command Post followed by the operator call sign in parenthesis.

PMSV—Pilot-to-Metro Service call sign, frequency and hours of operation, when full service is other than continuous. PMSV installations at which weather observation service is available shall be indicated, following the frequency and/or hours of operation as ''Wx obsn svc 1900–0000Z‡'' or ''other times'' may be used when no specific time is given. PMSV facilities manned by forecasters are considered ''Full Service''. PMSV facilities manned by weather observers are listed as ''Limited Service''.

OPS—Operations followed by the operator call sign in parenthesis.

CON

RANGE

FLT FLW—Flight Following

MEDIVAC

NOTE: Communication frequencies followed by the letter ''X'' indicate frequency available on request.

### 🜲 AIRSPACE

Information concerning Class B, C, and part–time D and E surface area airspace shall be published with effective times. Class D and E surface area airspace that is continuous as established by Rulemaking Docket will not be shown.

CLASS B—Radar Sequencing and Separation Service for all aircraft in CLASS B airspace.

CLASS C—Separation between IFR and VFR aircraft and sequencing of VFR arrivals to the primary airport.

TRSA—Radar Sequencing and Separation Service for participating VFR Aircraft within a Terminal Radar Service Area.

Class C, D, and E airspace described in this publication is that airspace usually consisting of a 5 NM radius core surface area that begins at the surface and extends upward to an altitude above the airport elevation (charted in MSL for Class C and Class D). Class E surface airspace normally extends from the surface up to but not including the overlying controlled airspace.

When part–time Class C or Class D airspace defaults to Class E, the core surface area becomes Class E. This will be formatted as:

AIRSPACE: CLASS C svc ''times'' ctc APP CON other times CLASS E:

or

AIRSPACE: CLASS D svc ''times'' other times CLASS E.

When a part–time Class C, Class D or Class E surface area defaults to Class G, the core surface area becomes Class G up to, but not including, the overlying controlled airspace. Normally, the overlying controlled airspace is Class E airspace beginning at either 700' or 1200' AGL and may be determined by consulting the relevant VFR Sectional or Terminal Area Charts. This will be formatted as:

AIRSPACE: CLASS C svc ''times'' ctc APP CON other times CLASS G, with CLASS E 700' (or 1200') AGL & abv:

or

AIRSPACE: CLASS D svc ''times'' other times CLASS G with CLASS E 700' (or 1200') AGL & abv:

or

AIRSPACE: CLASS E svc ''times'' other times CLASS G with CLASS E 700' (or 1200') AGL & abv.

NOTE: AIRSPACE SVC ''TIMES'' INCLUDE ALL ASSOCIATED ARRIVAL EXTENSIONS. Surface area arrival extensions for instrument approach procedures become part of the primary core surface area. These extensions may be either Class D or Class E airspace and are effective concurrent with the times of the primary core surface area. For example, when a part–time Class C, Class D or Class E surface area defaults to Class G, the associated arrival extensions will default to Class G at the same time. When a part–time Class C or Class D surface area defaults to Class E, the arrival extensions will remain in effect as Class E airspace.

NOTE: CLASS E AIRSPACE EXTENDING UPWARD FROM 700 FEET OR MORE ABOVE THE SURFACE, DESIGNATED IN CONJUNCTION WITH AN AIRPORT WITH AN APPROVED INSTRUMENT PROCEDURE.

Class E 700' AGL (shown as magenta vignette on sectional charts) and 1200' AGL (blue vignette) areas are designated when necessary to provide controlled airspace for transitioning to/from the terminal and enroute environments. Unless otherwise specified, these 700'/1200' AGL Class E airspace areas remain in effect continuously, regardless of airport operating hours or surface area status. These transition areas should not be confused with surface areas or arrival extensions.

(See Chapter 3, AIRSPACE, in the Aeronautical Information Manual for further details)

**NE, 09 FEB 20XX to 05 APR 20XX**

**Legend 15.** Chart Supplement.

**18**            **DIRECTORY LEGEND**

 **RADIO AIDS TO NAVIGATION**

The Airport/Facility Directory lists, by facility name, all Radio Aids to Navigation that appear on FAA, AeroNav Products Visual or IFR Aeronautical Charts and those upon which the FAA has approved an Instrument Approach Procedure, with exception of selected TACANs. Military TACAN information will be published for Military facilities contained in this publication. All VOR, VORTAC, TACAN, ILS and MLS equipment in the National Airspace System has an automatic monitoring and shutdown feature in the event of malfunction. Unmonitored, as used in this publication, for any navigational aid, means that monitoring personnel cannot observe the malfunction or shutdown signal. The NAVAID NOTAM file identifier will be shown as "NOTAM FILE IAD" and will be listed on the Radio Aids to Navigation line. When two or more NAVAIDS are listed and the NOTAM file identifier is different from that shown on the Radio Aids to Navigation line, it will be shown with the NAVAID listing. NOTAM file identifiers for ILSs and its components (e.g., NDB (LOM) are the same as the associated airports and are not repeated. Automated Surface Observing System (ASOS), Automated Weather Observing System (AWOS), and Hazardous Inflight Weather Advisory Service (HIWAS) will be shown when this service is broadcast over selected NAVAIDs.

NAVAID information is tabulated as indicated in the following sample:

VOR unusable 020°–060° byd 26 NM blo 3,500'

Restriction within the normal altitude/range of the navigational aid (See primary alphabetical listing for restrictions on VORTAC and VOR/DME).

Note: Those DME channel numbers with a (Y) suffix require TACAN to be placed in the "Y" mode to receive distance information.

**HIWAS**—Hazardous Inflight Weather Advisory Service is a continuous broadcast of inflight weather advisories including summarized SIGMETs, convective SIGMETs, AIRMETs and urgent PIREPs. HIWAS is presently broadcast over selected VOR's throughout the U.S.

**ASR/PAR**—Indicates that Surveillance (ASR) or Precision (PAR) radar instrument approach minimums are published in the U.S. Terminal Procedures. Only part-time hours of operation will be shown.

### RADIO CLASS DESIGNATIONS

VOR/DME/TACAN Standard Service Volume (SSV) Classifications

| SSV Class | Altitudes | Distance (NM) |
|-----------|-----------|---------------|
| (T) Terminal | 1000' to 12,000' | 25 |
| (L) Low Altitude | 1000' to 18,000' | 40 |
| (H) High Altitude | 1000' to 14,500' | 40 |
| | 14,500' to 18,000' | 100 |
| | 18,000' to 45,000' | 130 |
| | 45,000' to 60,000' | 100 |

NOTE: Additionally, (H) facilities provide (L) and (T) service volume and (L) facilities provide (T) service. Altitudes are with respect to the station's site elevation. Coverage is not available in a cone of airspace directly above the facility.

**CONTINUED ON NEXT PAGE**

**NE, 09 FEB 20XX to 05 APR 20XX**

**Legend 16.** Chart Supplement.

## DIRECTORY LEGEND

19

### CONTINUED FROM PRECEDING PAGE

The term VOR is, operationally, a general term covering the VHF omnidirectional bearing type of facility without regard to the fact that the power, the frequency protected service volume, the equipment configuration, and operational requirements may vary between facilities at different locations.

| | |
|---|---|
| AB | Automatic Weather Broadcast. |
| DF | Direction Finding Service. |
| DME | UHF standard (TACAN compatible) distance measuring equipment. |
| DME(Y) | UHF standard (TACAN compatible) distance measuring equipment that require TACAN to be placed in the ''Y'' mode to receive DME. |
| GS | Glide slope. |
| H | Non-directional radio beacon (homing), power 50 watts to less than 2,000 watts (50 NM at all altitudes). |
| HH | Non-directional radio beacon (homing), power 2,000 watts or more (75 NM at all altitudes). |
| H-SAB | Non-directional radio beacons providing automatic transcribed weather service. |
| ILS | Instrument Landing System (voice, where available, on localizer channel). |
| IM | Inner marker. |
| ISMLS | Interim Standard Microwave Landing System. |
| LDA | Localizer Directional Aid. |
| LMM | Compass locator station when installed at middle marker site (15 NM at all altitudes). |
| LOM | Compass locator station when installed at outer marker site (15 NM at all altitudes). |
| MH | Non-directional radio beacon (homing) power less than 50 watts (25 NM at all altitudes). |
| MLS | Microwave Landing System. |
| MM | Middle marker. |
| OM | Outer marker. |
| S | Simultaneous range homing signal and/or voice. |
| SABH | Non-directional radio beacon not authorized for IFR or ATC. Provides automatic weather broadcasts. |
| SDF | Simplified Direction Facility. |
| TACAN | UHF navigational facility-omnidirectional course and distance information. |
| VOR | VHF navigational facility-omnidirectional course only. |
| VOR/DME | Collocated VOR navigational facility and UHF standard distance measuring equipment. |
| VORTAC | Collocated VOR and TACAN navigational facilities. |
| W | Without voice on radio facility frequency. |
| Z | VHF station location marker at a LF radio facility. |

**NE, 09 FEB 20XX to 05 APR 20XX**

**Legend 17.** Chart Supplement.

## 20    DIRECTORY LEGEND

### ILS FACILITY PEFORMANCE CLASSIFICATION CODES

Codes define the ability of an ILS to support autoland operations. The two portions of the code represent Official Category and farthest point along a Category I, II, or III approach that the Localizer meets Category III structure tolerances.

Official Category: I, II, or III; the lowest minima on published or unpublished procedures supported by the ILS.

Farthest point of satisfactory Category III Localizer performance for Category I, II, or III approaches: A – 4 NM prior to runway threshold, B – 3500 ft prior to runway threshold, C – glide angle dependent but generally 750–1000 ft prior to threshold, T – runway threshold, D – 3000 ft after runway threshold, and E – 2000 ft prior to stop end of runway.

ILS information is tabulated as indicated in the following sample:

ILS/DME    108.5    I–ORL    Chan 22    Rwy 18.    Class IIE.    LOM HERNY NDB.

ILS Facility Performance
Classification Code

### FREQUENCY PAIRING PLAN AND MLS CHANNELING

| MLS CHANNEL | VHF FREQUENCY | TACAN CHANNEL | MLS CHANNEL | VHF FREQUENCY | TACAN CHANNEL | MLS CHANNEL | VHF FREQUENCY | TACAN CHANNEL |
|---|---|---|---|---|---|---|---|---|
| 500 | 108.10 | 18X | 568 | 109.45 | 31Y | 636 | 114.15 | 88Y |
| 502 | 108.30 | 20X | 570 | 109.55 | 32Y | 638 | 114.25 | 89Y |
| 504 | 108.50 | 22X | 572 | 109.65 | 33Y | 640 | 114.35 | 90Y |
| 506 | 108.70 | 24X | 574 | 109.75 | 34Y | 642 | 114.45 | 91Y |
| 508 | 108.90 | 26X | 576 | 109.85 | 35Y | 644 | 114.55 | 92Y |
| 510 | 109.10 | 28X | 578 | 109.95 | 36Y | 646 | 114.65 | 93Y |
| 512 | 109.30 | 30X | 580 | 110.05 | 37Y | 648 | 114.75 | 94Y |
| 514 | 109.50 | 32X | 582 | 110.15 | 38Y | 650 | 114.85 | 95Y |
| 516 | 109.70 | 34X | 584 | 110.25 | 39Y | 652 | 114.95 | 96Y |
| 518 | 109.90 | 36X | 586 | 110.35 | 40Y | 654 | 115.05 | 97Y |
| 520 | 110.10 | 38X | 588 | 110.45 | 41Y | 656 | 115.15 | 98Y |
| 522 | 110.30 | 40X | 590 | 110.55 | 42Y | 658 | 115.25 | 99Y |
| 524 | 110.50 | 42X | 592 | 110.65 | 43Y | 660 | 115.35 | 100Y |
| 526 | 110.70 | 44X | 594 | 110.75 | 44Y | 662 | 115.45 | 101Y |
| 528 | 110.90 | 46X | 596 | 110.85 | 45Y | 664 | 115.55 | 102Y |
| 530 | 111.10 | 48X | 598 | 110.95 | 46Y | 666 | 115.65 | 103Y |
| 532 | 111.30 | 50X | 600 | 111.05 | 47Y | 668 | 115.75 | 104Y |
| 534 | 111.50 | 52X | 602 | 111.15 | 48Y | 670 | 115.85 | 105Y |
| 536 | 111.70 | 54X | 604 | 111.25 | 49Y | 672 | 115.95 | 106Y |
| 538 | 111.90 | 56X | 606 | 111.35 | 50Y | 674 | 116.05 | 107Y |
| 540 | 108.05 | 17Y | 608 | 111.45 | 51Y | 676 | 116.15 | 108Y |
| 542 | 108.15 | 18Y | 610 | 111.55 | 52Y | 678 | 116.25 | 109Y |
| 544 | 108.25 | 19Y | 612 | 111.65 | 53Y | 680 | 116.35 | 110Y |
| 546 | 108.35 | 20Y | 614 | 111.75 | 54Y | 682 | 116.45 | 111Y |
| 548 | 108.45 | 21Y | 616 | 111.85 | 55Y | 684 | 116.55 | 112Y |
| 550 | 108.55 | 22Y | 618 | 111.95 | 56Y | 686 | 116.65 | 113Y |
| 552 | 108.65 | 23Y | 620 | 113.35 | 80Y | 688 | 116.75 | 114Y |
| 554 | 108.75 | 24Y | 622 | 113.45 | 81Y | 690 | 116.85 | 115Y |
| 556 | 108.85 | 25Y | 624 | 113.55 | 82Y | 692 | 116.95 | 116Y |
| 558 | 108.95 | 26Y | 626 | 113.65 | 83Y | 694 | 117.05 | 117Y |
| 560 | 109.05 | 27Y | 628 | 113.75 | 84Y | 696 | 117.15 | 118Y |
| 562 | 109.15 | 28Y | 630 | 113.85 | 85Y | 698 | 117.25 | 119Y |
| 564 | 109.25 | 29Y | 632 | 113.95 | 86Y | | | |
| 566 | 109.35 | 30Y | 634 | 114.05 | 87Y | | | |

### FREQUENCY PAIRING PLAN AND MLS CHANNELING

The following is a list of paired VOR/ILS VHF frequencies with TACAN channels and MLS channels.

| TACAN CHANNEL | VHF FREQUENCY | MLS CHANNEL | TACAN CHANNEL | VHF FREQUENCY | MLS CHANNEL | TACAN CHANNEL | VHF FREQUENCY | MLS CHANNEL |
|---|---|---|---|---|---|---|---|---|
| 2X | 134.5 | - | 19Y | 108.25 | 544 | 25X | 108.80 | - |
| 2Y | 134.55 | - | 20X | 108.30 | 502 | 25Y | 108.85 | 556 |
| 11X | 135.4 | - | 20Y | 108.35 | 546 | 26X | 108.90 | 508 |
| 11Y | 135.45 | - | 21X | 108.40 | - | 26Y | 108.95 | 558 |
| 12X | 135.5 | - | 21Y | 108.45 | 548 | 27X | 109.00 | - |
| 12Y | 135.55 | - | 22X | 108.50 | 504 | 27Y | 109.05 | 560 |
| 17X | 108.00 | - | 22Y | 108.55 | 550 | 28X | 109.10 | 510 |
| 17Y | 108.05 | 540 | 23X | 108.60 | - | 28Y | 109.15 | 562 |
| 18X | 108.10 | 500 | 23Y | 108.65 | 552 | 29X | 109.20 | - |
| 18Y | 108.15 | 542 | 24X | 108.70 | 506 | 29Y | 109.25 | 564 |
| 19X | 108.20 | - | 24Y | 108.75 | 554 | 30X | 109.30 | 512 |

**NE, 09 FEB 20XX to 05 APR 20XX**

**Legend 18.** Chart Supplement.

## DIRECTORY LEGEND 21

| TACAN CHANNEL | VHF FREQUENCY | MLS CHANNEL | TACAN CHANNEL | VHF FREQUENCY | MLS CHANNEL | TACAN CHANNEL | VHF FREQUENCY | MLS CHANNEL |
|---|---|---|---|---|---|---|---|---|
| 30Y | 109.35 | 566 | 63X | 133.60 | - | 95Y | 114.85 | 650 |
| 31X | 109.40 | - | 63Y | 133.65 | - | 96X | 114.90 | - |
| 31Y | 109.45 | 568 | 64X | 133.70 | - | 96Y | 114.95 | 652 |
| 32X | 109.50 | 514 | 64Y | 133.75 | - | 97X | 115.00 | - |
| 32Y | 109.55 | 570 | 65X | 133.80 | - | 97Y | 115.05 | 654 |
| 33X | 109.60 | - | 65Y | 133.85 | - | 98X | 115.10 | - |
| 33Y | 109.65 | 572 | 66X | 133.90 | - | 98Y | 115.15 | 656 |
| 34X | 109.70 | 516 | 66Y | 133.95 | - | 99X | 115.20 | - |
| 34Y | 109.75 | 574 | 67X | 134.00 | - | 99Y | 115.25 | 658 |
| 35X | 109.80 | - | 67Y | 134.05 | - | 100X | 115.30 | - |
| 35Y | 109.85 | 576 | 68X | 134.10 | - | 100Y | 115.35 | 660 |
| 36X | 109.90 | 518 | 68Y | 134.15 | - | 101X | 115.40 | - |
| 36Y | 109.95 | 578 | 69X | 134.20 | - | 101Y | 115.45 | 662 |
| 37X | 110.00 | - | 69Y | 134.25 | - | 102X | 115.50 | - |
| 37Y | 110.05 | 580 | 70X | 112.30 | - | 102Y | 115.55 | 664 |
| 38X | 110.10 | 520 | 70Y | 112.35 | - | 103X | 115.60 | - |
| 38Y | 110.15 | 582 | 71X | 112.40 | - | 103Y | 115.65 | 666 |
| 39X | 110.20 | - | 71Y | 112.45 | - | 104X | 115.70 | - |
| 39Y | 110.25 | 584 | 72X | 112.50 | - | 104Y | 115.75 | 668 |
| 40X | 110.30 | 522 | 72Y | 112.55 | - | 105X | 115.80 | - |
| 40Y | 110.35 | 586 | 73X | 112.60 | - | 105Y | 115.85 | 670 |
| 41X | 110.40 | - | 73Y | 112.65 | - | 106X | 115.90 | - |
| 41Y | 110.45 | 588 | 74X | 112.70 | - | 106Y | 115.95 | 672 |
| 42X | 110.50 | 524 | 74Y | 112.75 | - | 107X | 116.00 | - |
| 42Y | 110.55 | 590 | 75X | 112.80 | - | 107Y | 116.05 | 674 |
| 43X | 110.60 | - | 75Y | 112.85 | - | 108X | 116.10 | - |
| 43Y | 110.65 | 592 | 76X | 112.90 | - | 108Y | 116.15 | 676 |
| 44X | 110.70 | 526 | 76Y | 112.95 | - | 109X | 116.20 | - |
| 44Y | 110.75 | 594 | 77X | 113.00 | - | 109Y | 116.25 | 678 |
| 45X | 110.80 | - | 77Y | 113.05 | - | 110X | 116.30 | - |
| 45Y | 110.85 | 596 | 78X | 113.10 | - | 110Y | 116.35 | 680 |
| 46X | 110.90 | 528 | 78Y | 113.15 | - | 111X | 116.40 | - |
| 46Y | 110.95 | 598 | 79X | 113.20 | - | 111Y | 116.45 | 682 |
| 47X | 111.00 | - | 79Y | 113.25 | - | 112X | 116.50 | - |
| 47Y | 111.05 | 600 | 80X | 113.30 | - | 112Y | 116.55 | 684 |
| 48X | 111.10 | 530 | 80Y | 113.35 | 620 | 113X | 116.60 | - |
| 48Y | 111.15 | 602 | 81X | 113.40 | - | 113Y | 116.65 | 686 |
| 49X | 111.20 | - | 81Y | 113.45 | 622 | 114X | 116.70 | - |
| 49Y | 111.25 | 604 | 82X | 113.50 | - | 114Y | 116.75 | 688 |
| 50X | 111.30 | 532 | 82Y | 113.55 | 624 | 115X | 116.80 | - |
| 50Y | 111.35 | 606 | 83X | 113.60 | - | 115Y | 116.85 | 690 |
| 51X | 111.40 | - | 83Y | 113.65 | 626 | 116X | 116.90 | - |
| 51Y | 111.45 | 608 | 84X | 113.70 | - | 116Y | 116.95 | 692 |
| 52X | 111.50 | 534 | 84Y | 113.75 | 628 | 117X | 117.00 | - |
| 52Y | 111.55 | 610 | 85X | 113.80 | - | 117Y | 117.05 | 694 |
| 53X | 111.60 | - | 85Y | 113.85 | 630 | 118X | 117.10 | - |
| 53Y | 111.65 | 612 | 86X | 113.90 | - | 118Y | 117.15 | 696 |
| 54X | 111.70 | 536 | 86Y | 113.95 | 632 | 119X | 117.20 | - |
| 54Y | 111.75 | 614 | 87X | 114.00 | - | 119Y | 117.25 | 698 |
| 55X | 111.80 | - | 87Y | 114.05 | 634 | 120X | 117.30 | - |
| 55Y | 111.85 | 616 | 88X | 114.10 | - | 120Y | 117.35 | - |
| 56X | 111.90 | 538 | 88Y | 114.15 | 636 | 121X | 117.40 | - |
| 56Y | 111.95 | 618 | 89X | 114.20 | - | 121Y | 117.45 | - |
| 57X | 112.00 | - | 89Y | 114.25 | 638 | 122X | 117.50 | - |
| 57Y | 112.05 | - | 90X | 114.30 | - | 122Y | 117.55 | - |
| 58X | 112.10 | - | 90Y | 114.35 | 640 | 123X | 117.60 | - |
| 58Y | 112.15 | - | 91X | 114.40 | - | 123Y | 117.65 | - |
| 59X | 112.20 | - | 91Y | 114.45 | 642 | 124X | 117.70 | - |
| 59Y | 112.25 | - | 92X | 114.50 | - | 124Y | 117.75 | - |
| 60X | 133.30 | - | 92Y | 114.55 | 644 | 125X | 117.80 | - |
| 60Y | 133.35 | - | 93X | 114.60 | - | 125Y | 117.85 | - |
| 61X | 133.40 | - | 93Y | 114.65 | 646 | 126X | 117.90 | - |
| 61Y | 133.45 | - | 94X | 114.70 | - | 126Y | 117.95 | - |
| 62X | 133.50 | - | 94Y | 114.75 | 648 | | | |
| 62Y | 133.55 | - | 95X | 114.80 | - | | | |

**(35) COMM/NAV/WEATHER REMARKS:**
These remarks consist of pertinent information affecting the current status of communications, NAVAIDs and weather.

**NE, 09 FEB 20XX to 05 APR 20XX**

**Legend 19.** Chart Supplement.

# Appendix 2

**Figure 1.** Lift Vector.

| Angle of bank ϕ | Load factor n |
|---|---|
| 0° | 1.0 |
| 10° | 1.015 |
| 30° | 1.154 |
| 45° | 1.414 |
| 60° | 2.000 |
| 70° | 2.923 |
| 80° | 5.747 |
| 85° | 11.473 |
| 90° | ∞ |

**Figure 2.** Load Factor Chart.

**Figure 3.** Altimeter.

**Figure 4.** Airspeed Indicator.

**Figure 5.** Turn Coordinator.

**Figure 6.** Heading Indicator.

**Figure 7.** Attitude Indicator.

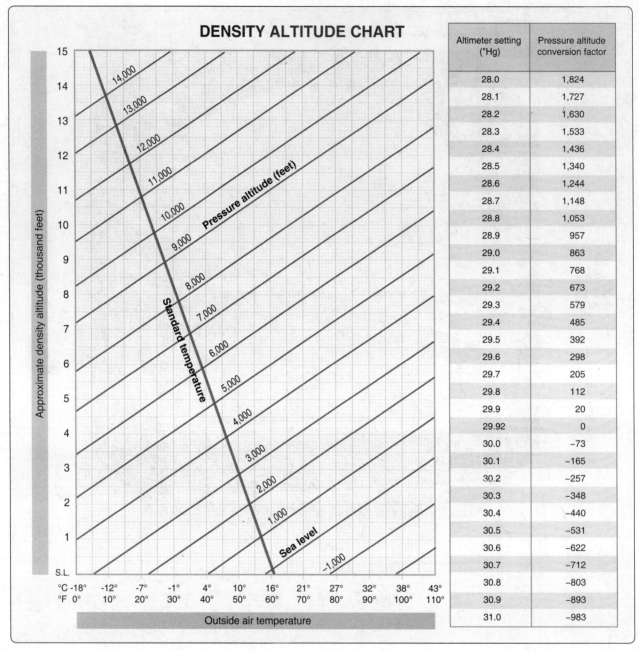

**Figure 8.** Density Altitude Chart.

**Figure 9.** Control Position for Taxi.

**Figure 10.** Gyroplane Rotor Blade Position.

**Figure 11.** Glider Yaw String.

METAR KINK 121845Z 11012G18KT 15SM SKC 25/17 A3000

METAR KBOI 121854Z 13004KT 30SM SCT150 17/6 A3015

METAR KLAX 121852Z 25004KT 6SM BR SCT007 SCT250 16/15 A2991

SPECI KMDW 121856Z 32005KT 1 1/2SM RA OVC007 17/16 A2980 RMK RAB35

SPECI KJFK 121853Z 18004KT 1/2SM FG R04/2200 OVC005 20/18 A3006

**Figure 12.** Aviation Routine Weather Reports (METAR).

This is a telephone weather briefing from the Dallas FSS for local operation of gliders and lighter-than-air at Caddo Mills, Texas (about 30 miles east of Dallas). The briefing is at 13Z.

"There are no adverse conditions reported or forecast for today."

"A weak low pressure over the Texas Panhandle and eastern New Mexico is causing a weak southerly flow over the area."

"Current weather here at Dallas is wind south 5 knots, visibility 12 miles, clear, temperature 21, dewpoint 9, altimeter 29 point 78."

"By 15Z, we should have a few scattered cumuliform clouds at 5 thousand AGL, with higher scattered cirrus at 25 thousand MSL. After 20Z, the wind should pick up to about 15 knots from the south."

"The winds aloft are: 3 thousand 170 at 7, temperature 20; 6 thousand 200 at 18, temperature 14; 9 thousand 210 at 22, temperature 8; 12 thousand 225 at 27, temperature 0; 18 thousand 240 at 30, temperature −7."

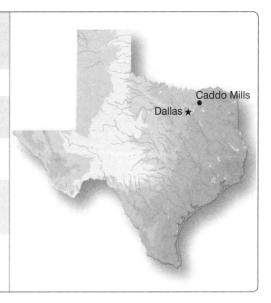

**Figure 13.** Telephone Weather Briefing.

UA/OV KOKC-KTUL/TM 1800/FL120/TP BE90/SK BKN018-TOP055/OVC072-TOP089/CLR ABV/TA M7/WV 08021/TB LGT 055-072/IC LGT-MOD RIME 072-089

**Figure 14.** Pilot Weather Report.

2-15

TAF

KMEM 121720Z 1218/1324 20012KT 5SM HZ BKN030 PROB40 1220/1222 1SM TSRA OVC008CB
    FM122200 33015G20KT P6SM BKN015 OVC025 PROB40 1220/1222 3SM SHRA
    FM120200 35012KT OVC008 PROB40 1202/1205 2SM-RASN BECMG 1306/1308 02008KT BKN012
    BECMG 1310/1312 00000KT 3SM BR SKC TEMPO 1212/1214 1/2SM FG
    FM131600 VRB06KT P6SM SKC=

KOKC 051130Z 0512/0618 14008KT 5SM BR BKN030 TEMPO 0513/0516 1 1/2SM BR
    FM051600 18010KT P6SM SKC BECMG 0522/0524 20013G20KT 4SM SHRA OVC020
    PROB40 0600/0606 2SM TSRA OVC008CB BECMG 0606/0608 21015KT P6SM SCT040=

**Figure 15.** Terminal Aerodrome Forecasts (TAF).

FB WBC 151745
DATA BASED ON 151200Z
VALID 1600Z FOR USE 1800-0300Z. TEMPS NEG ABV 24000

| FT | 3000 | 6000 | 9000 | 12000 | 18000 | 24000 | 30000 | 34000 | 39000 |
|----|------|------|------|-------|-------|-------|-------|-------|-------|
| ALS | | | 2420 | 2635-08 | 2535-18 | 2444-30 | 245945 | 246755 | 246862 |
| AMA | | 2714 | 2725+00 | 2625-04 | 2531-15 | 2542-27 | 265842 | 256352 | 256762 |
| DEN | | | 2321-04 | 2532-08 | 2434-19 | 2441-31 | 235347 | 236056 | 236262 |
| HLC | | 1707-01 | 2113-03 | 2219-07 | 2330-17 | 2435-30 | 244145 | 244854 | 245561 |
| MKC | 0507 | 2006+03 | 2215-01 | 2322-06 | 2338-17 | 2348-29 | 236143 | 237252 | 238160 |
| STL | 2113 | 2325+07 | 2332+02 | 2339-04 | 2356-16 | 2373-27 | 239440 | 730649 | 731960 |

**Figure 17.** Winds and Temperatures Aloft Forecast.

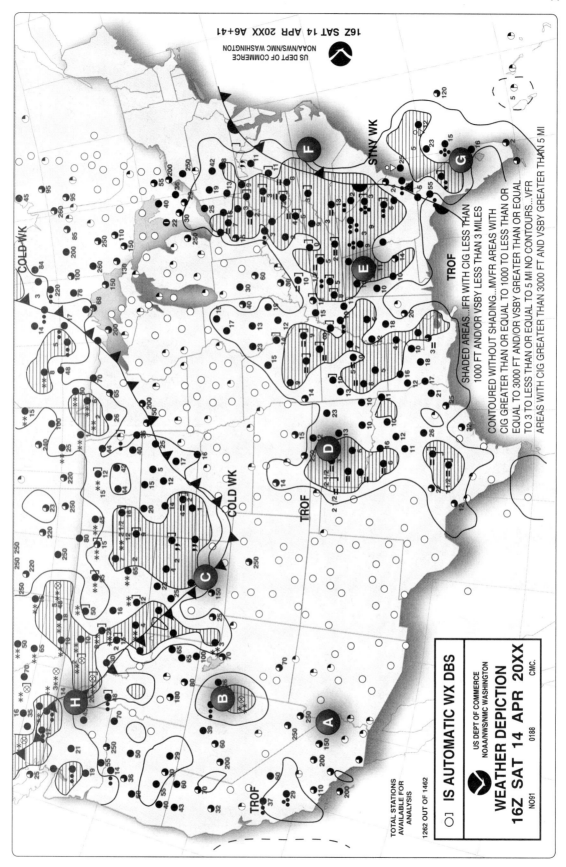

**Figure 18.** Weather Depiction Chart.

**Figure 19.** Low-Level Significant Weather (SIGWX) Prognostic Charts.

**Figure 20.** Sectional Chart Excerpt.

*NOTE: Chart is not to scale and should not be used for navigation. Use associated scale.*

**Figure 21.** Sectional Chart Excerpt.

*NOTE: Chart is not to scale and should not be used for navigation. Use associated scale.*

**Figure 22.** Sectional Chart Excerpt.

*NOTE: Chart is not to scale and should not be used for navigation. Use associated scale.*

**Figure 23.** Sectional Chart Excerpt.
*NOTE: Chart is not to scale and should not be used for navigation. Use associated scale.*

**Figure 24.** Sectional Chart Excerpt.

*NOTE: Chart is not to scale and should not be used for navigation. Use associated scale.*

**Figure 25.** Sectional Chart Excerpt.

*NOTE: Chart is not to scale and should not be used for navigation. Use associated scale.*

**Figure 26.** Sectional Chart Excerpt.

*NOTE: Chart is not to scale and should not be used for navigation. Use associated scale.*

**Figure 27.** Time Conversion Table.

**Figure 28.** VOR.

**COEUR D'ALENE—PAPPY BOYINGTON FLD** (COE)   9 NW   UTC−8(−7DT)                    GREAT FALLS
　　　N47°46.46' W116°49.18'                                                           H−1C, L−13B
2320   B   S4   **FUEL** 100, JET A   OX 1, 2, 3, 4   Class IV, ARFF Index A   NOTAM FILE COE
RWY 05−23: H7400X100 (ASPH−GRVD)   S−57, D−95, 2S−121, 2D−165   HIRL   0.6% up NE      IAP
　RWY 05: MALSR (NSTD). PAPI(P4R)—GA 3.0° TCH 56'.
　RWY 23: REIL. PAPI(P4R)—GA 3.0° TCH 50'.
RWY 01−19: H5400X75 (ASPH)   S−50, D−83, 2S−105, 2D−150
　MIRL   0.3% up N
　RWY 01: REIL. PAPI(P2L)—GA 3.0° TCH 39'. Rgt tfc.
　RWY 19: PAPI(P2L)—GA 3.0° TCH 41'.
**RUNWAY DECLARED DISTANCE INFORMATION**
　RWY 01:   TORA−5400   TODA−5400   ASDA−5400   LDA−5400
　RWY 05:   TORA−7400   TODA−7400   ASDA−7400   LDA−7400
　RWY 19:   TORA−5400   TODA−5400   ASDA−5400   LDA−5400
　RWY 23:   TORA−7400   TODA−7400   ASDA−7400   LDA−7400
**AIRPORT REMARKS:** Attended Mon−Fri 1500−0100Z‡. For after hrs
fuel-self svc avbl or call 208−772−6404, 208−661−4174,
208−661−7449, 208−699−5433. Self svc fuel avbl with credit
card. 48 hr PPR for unscheduled ops with more than 30
passenger seats call arpt manager 208−446−1860. Migratory
birds on and invof arpt Oct−Nov. Remote cntl airstrip is 2.3 miles
west AER 05. Arpt conditions avbl on AWOS. Rwy 05 NSTD
MALSR, thld bar extends 5' byd rwy edge lgts each side. ACTIVATE
MIRL Rwy 01−19, HIRL Rwy 05−23, REIL Rwy 01 and Rwy 23, MALSR Rwy 05—CTAF. PAPI Rwy 01, Rwy 19, Rwy
05, and Rwy 23 opr continuously.
**WEATHER DATA SOURCES:** AWOS−3 135.075 (208) 772−8215.
　HIWAS 108.8 COE.
**COMMUNICATIONS:** CTAF/UNICOM 122.8
　RCO 122.05 (BOISE RADIO)
Ⓡ SPOKANE APP/DEP CON 132.1
**AIRSPACE: CLASS E** svc continuous.
**RADIO AIDS TO NAVIGATION:** NOTAM FILE COE.
　(T) VORW/DME 108.8   COE   Chan 25   N47°46.42' W116°49.24'   at fld. 2320/19E.   HIWAS.
　　DME portion unusable:
　　　220°−240° byd 15 NM                               280°−315° byd 15 NM blo 11,000'.
　POST FALLS NDB (MHW) 347   LEN   N47°44.57' W116°57.66'   053° 6.0 NM to fld.
　ILS 110.7   I−COE   Rwy 05   Class ID.   Localizer unusable 25° left and right of course.

**Figure 31.** Chart Supplement.

## Useful load weights and moments

### Baggage or 5th seat occupant

| ARM 140 | |
| --- | --- |
| Weight | Moment/100 |
| 10 | 14 |
| 20 | 28 |
| 30 | 42 |
| 40 | 56 |
| 50 | 70 |
| 60 | 84 |
| 70 | 98 |
| 80 | 112 |
| 90 | 126 |
| 100 | 140 |
| 110 | 154 |
| 120 | 168 |
| 130 | 182 |
| 140 | 196 |
| 150 | 210 |
| 160 | 224 |
| 170 | 238 |
| 180 | 252 |
| 190 | 266 |
| 200 | 280 |
| 210 | 294 |
| 220 | 308 |
| 230 | 322 |
| 240 | 336 |
| 250 | 350 |
| 260 | 364 |
| 270 | 378 |

### Occupants

| Front seats ARM 85 | | Rear seats ARM 121 | |
| --- | --- | --- | --- |
| Weight | Moment/100 | Weight | Moment/100 |
| 120 | 102 | 120 | 145 |
| 130 | 110 | 130 | 157 |
| 140 | 119 | 140 | 169 |
| 150 | 128 | 150 | 182 |
| 160 | 136 | 160 | 194 |
| 170 | 144 | 170 | 206 |
| 180 | 153 | 180 | 218 |
| 190 | 162 | 190 | 230 |
| 200 | 170 | 200 | 242 |

### Usable fuel

| Main wing tanks ARM 75 | | |
| --- | --- | --- |
| Gallons | Weight | Moment/100 |
| 5 | 30 | 22 |
| 10 | 60 | 45 |
| 15 | 90 | 68 |
| 20 | 120 | 90 |
| 25 | 150 | 112 |
| 30 | 180 | 135 |
| 35 | 210 | 158 |
| 40 | 240 | 180 |
| 44 | 264 | 198 |

| Auxiliary wing tanks ARM 94 | | |
| --- | --- | --- |
| Gallons | Weight | Moment/100 |
| 5 | 30 | 28 |
| 10 | 60 | 56 |
| 15 | 90 | 85 |
| 19 | 114 | 107 |

**Empty weight~2,015**

**MOM/100~1,554**

**Moment limits vs weight**

Moment limits are based on the following weight and center of gravity limit data (landing gear down).

| *Oil | | |
| --- | --- | --- |
| Quarts | Weight | Moment/100 |
| 10 | 19 | 5 |

*Included in basic empty weight.

| Weight condition | Forward CG limit | AFT CG limit |
| --- | --- | --- |
| 2,950 lb (takeoff or landing) | 82.1 | 84.7 |
| 2,525 lb | 77.5 | 85.7 |
| 2,475 lb or less | 77.0 | 85.7 |

**Figure 32.** Airplane Weight and Balance Tables.

| Moment limits vs weight (continued) | | | | | | | |
|---|---|---|---|---|---|---|---|

| Weight | Minimum Moment 100 | Maximum Moment 100 | Weight | Minimum Moment 100 | Maximum Moment 100 |
|---|---|---|---|---|---|
| 2,100 | 1,617 | 1,800 | 2,500 | 1,932 | 2,143 |
| 2,110 | 1,625 | 1,808 | 2,510 | 1,942 | 2,151 |
| 2,120 | 1,632 | 1,817 | 2,520 | 1,953 | 2,160 |
| 2,130 | 1,640 | 1,825 | 2,530 | 1,963 | 2,168 |
| 2,140 | 1,648 | 1,834 | 2,540 | 1,974 | 2,176 |
| 2,150 | 1,656 | 1,843 | 2,550 | 1,984 | 2,184 |
| 2,160 | 1,663 | 1,851 | 2,560 | 1,995 | 2,192 |
| 2,170 | 1,671 | 1,860 | 2,570 | 2,005 | 2,200 |
| 2,180 | 1,679 | 1,868 | 2,580 | 2,016 | 2,208 |
| 2,190 | 1,686 | 1,877 | 2,590 | 2,026 | 2,216 |
| 2,200 | 1,694 | 1,885 | 2,600 | 2,037 | 2,224 |
| 2,210 | 1,702 | 1,894 | 2,610 | 2,048 | 2,232 |
| 2,220 | 1,709 | 1,903 | 2,620 | 2,058 | 2,239 |
| 2,230 | 1,717 | 1,911 | 2,630 | 2,069 | 2,247 |
| 2,240 | 1,725 | 1,920 | 2,640 | 2,080 | 2,255 |
| 2,250 | 1,733 | 1,928 | 2,650 | 2,090 | 2,263 |
| 2,260 | 1,740 | 1,937 | 2,660 | 2,101 | 2,271 |
| 2,270 | 1,748 | 1,945 | 2,670 | 2,112 | 2,279 |
| 2,280 | 1,756 | 1,954 | 2,680 | 2,123 | 2,287 |
| 2,290 | 1,763 | 1,963 | 2,690 | 2,133 | 2,295 |
| 2,300 | 1,771 | 1,971 | 2,700 | 2,144 | 2,303 |
| 2,310 | 1,779 | 1,980 | 2,710 | 2,155 | 2,311 |
| 2,320 | 1,786 | 1,988 | 2,720 | 2,166 | 2,319 |
| 2,330 | 1,794 | 1,997 | 2,730 | 2,177 | 2,326 |
| 2,340 | 1,802 | 2,005 | 2,740 | 2,188 | 2,334 |
| 2,350 | 1,810 | 2,014 | 2,750 | 2,199 | 2,342 |
| 2,360 | 1,817 | 2,023 | 2,760 | 2,210 | 2,350 |
| 2,370 | 1,825 | 2,031 | 2,770 | 2,221 | 2,358 |
| 2,380 | 1,833 | 2,040 | 2,780 | 2,232 | 2,366 |
| 2,390 | 1,840 | 2,048 | 2,790 | 2,243 | 2,374 |
| 2,400 | 1,848 | 2,057 | 2,800 | 2,254 | 2,381 |
| 2,410 | 1,856 | 2,065 | 2,810 | 2,265 | 2,389 |
| 2,420 | 1,863 | 2,074 | 2,820 | 2,276 | 2,397 |
| 2,430 | 1,871 | 2,083 | 2,830 | 2,287 | 2,405 |
| 2,440 | 1,879 | 2,091 | 2,840 | 2,298 | 2,413 |
| 2,450 | 1,887 | 2,100 | 2,850 | 2,309 | 2,421 |
| 2,460 | 1,894 | 2,108 | 2,860 | 2,320 | 2,428 |
| 2,470 | 1,902 | 2,117 | 2,870 | 2,332 | 2,436 |
| 2,480 | 1,911 | 2,125 | 2,880 | 2,343 | 2,444 |
| 2,490 | 1,921 | 2,134 | 2,890 | 2,354 | 2,452 |
| | | | 2,900 | 2,365 | 2,460 |
| | | | 2,910 | 2,377 | 2,468 |
| | | | 2,920 | 2,388 | 2,475 |
| | | | 2,930 | 2,399 | 2,483 |
| | | | 2,940 | 2,411 | 2,491 |
| | | | 2,950 | 2,422 | 2,499 |

**Figure 33.** Airplane Weight and Balance Tables.

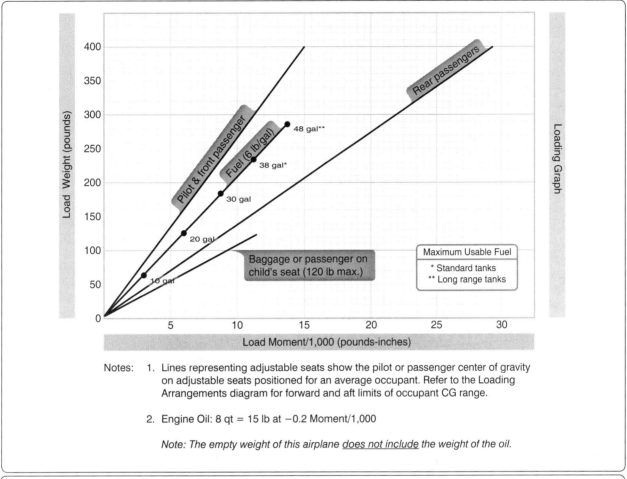

Notes: 1. Lines representing adjustable seats show the pilot or passenger center of gravity on adjustable seats positioned for an average occupant. Refer to the Loading Arrangements diagram for forward and aft limits of occupant CG range.

2. Engine Oil: 8 qt = 15 lb at −0.2 Moment/1,000

*Note: The empty weight of this airplane does not include the weight of the oil.*

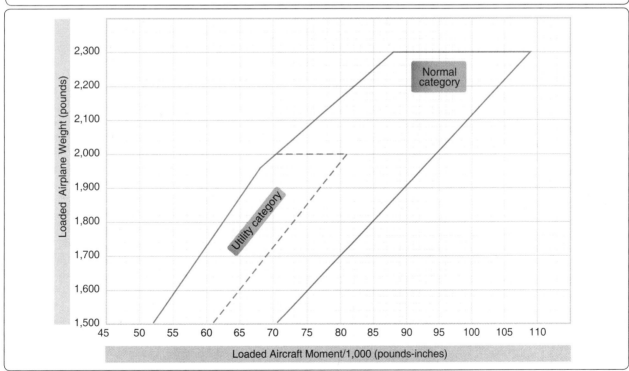

**Figure 34.** Airplane Weight and Balance Graphs.

## Cruise power settings
### 65% Maximum continuous power (or full throttle 2,800 pounds)

| Press ALT. | ISA −20 °C (−36 °F) IOAT °F | °C | Engine speed RPM | MAN. press IN HG | Fuel flow per engine PSI | GPH | TAS KTS | MPH | Standard day (ISA) IOAT °F | °C | RPM | IN HG | PSI | GPH | KTS | MPH | ISA +20 °C (+36 °F) IOAT °F | °C | RPM | IN HG | PSI | GPH | KTS | MPH |
|---|---|---|---|---|---|---|---|---|---|---|---|---|---|---|---|---|---|---|---|---|---|---|---|---|
| SL | 27 | −3 | 2,450 | 20.7 | 6.6 | 11.5 | 147 | 169 | 63 | 17 | 2,450 | 21.2 | 6.6 | 11.5 | 150 | 173 | 99 | 37 | 2,450 | 21.8 | 6.6 | 11.5 | 153 | 176 |
| 2,000 | 19 | −7 | 2,450 | 20.4 | 6.6 | 11.5 | 149 | 171 | 55 | 13 | 2,450 | 21.0 | 6.6 | 11.5 | 153 | 176 | 91 | 33 | 2,450 | 21.5 | 6.6 | 11.5 | 156 | 180 |
| 4,000 | 12 | −11 | 2,450 | 20.1 | 6.6 | 11.5 | 152 | 175 | 48 | 9 | 2,450 | 20.7 | 6.6 | 11.5 | 156 | 180 | 84 | 29 | 2,450 | 21.3 | 6.6 | 11.5 | 159 | 183 |
| 6,000 | 5 | −15 | 2,450 | 19.8 | 6.6 | 11.5 | 155 | 178 | 41 | 5 | 2,450 | 20.4 | 6.6 | 11.5 | 158 | 182 | 79 | 26 | 2,450 | 21.0 | 6.6 | 11.5 | 161 | 185 |
| 8,000 | −2 | −19 | 2,450 | 19.5 | 6.6 | 11.5 | 157 | 181 | 36 | 2 | 2,450 | 20.2 | 6.6 | 11.5 | 161 | 185 | 72 | 22 | 2,450 | 20.8 | 6.6 | 11.5 | 164 | 189 |
| 10,000 | −8 | −22 | 2,450 | 19.2 | 6.6 | 11.5 | 160 | 184 | 28 | −2 | 2,450 | 19.9 | 6.6 | 11.5 | 163 | 188 | 64 | 18 | 2,450 | 20.3 | 6.5 | 11.4 | 166 | 191 |
| 12,000 | −15 | −26 | 2,450 | 18.8 | 6.4 | 11.5 | 162 | 186 | 21 | −6 | 2,450 | 18.8 | 6.1 | 10.9 | 163 | 188 | 57 | 14 | 2,450 | 18.8 | 5.9 | 10.6 | 163 | 188 |
| 14,000 | −22 | −30 | 2,450 | 17.4 | 5.8 | 10.5 | 159 | 183 | 14 | −10 | 2,450 | 17.4 | 5.6 | 10.1 | 160 | 184 | 50 | 10 | 2,450 | 17.4 | 5.4 | 9.8 | 160 | 184 |
| 16,000 | −29 | −34 | 2,450 | 16.1 | 5.3 | 9.7 | 156 | 180 | 7 | −14 | 2,450 | 16.1 | 5.1 | 9.4 | 156 | 180 | 43 | 6 | 2,450 | 16.1 | 4.9 | 9.1 | 155 | 178 |

Note: 1. Full throttle manifold pressure settings are approximate.
2. Shaded area represents operation with full throttle.

**Figure 35.** Airplane Power Setting Table.

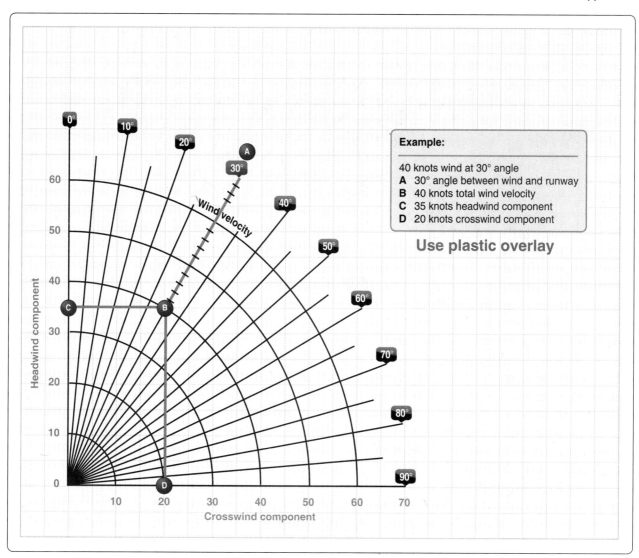

**Figure 36.** Crosswind Component Graph.

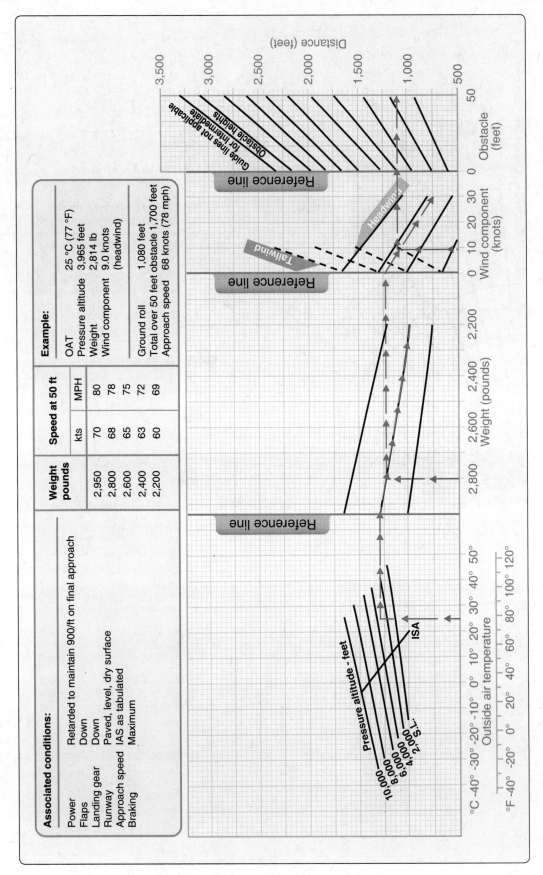

**Figure 37.** Airplane Landing Distance Graph.

## Landing distance

Flaps lowered to 40° – Power off
Hard surface runway – Zero wind

| Gross weight lb | Approach speed, IAS, MPH | At sea level & 59 °F | | At 2,500 feet & 50 °F | | At 5,000 feet & 41 °F | | At 7,500 feet & 32 °F | |
| --- | --- | --- | --- | --- | --- | --- | --- | --- | --- |
| | | Ground roll | Total to clear 50 feet OBS | Ground roll | Total to clear 50 feet OBS | Ground roll | Total to clear 50 feet OBS | Ground roll | Total to clear 50 feet OBS |
| 1,600 | 60 | 445 | 1,075 | 470 | 1,135 | 495 | 1,195 | 520 | 1,255 |

NOTE:
1. Decrease the distances shown by 10% for each 4 knots of headwind.
2. Increase the distance by 10% for each 60 °F temperature increase above standard.
3. For operation on a dry, grass runway, increase distance (both "ground roll" and "total to clear 50 feet obstacle") by 20% of the "total to clear 50 feet obstacle" figure.

**Figure 38.** Airplane Landing Distance Table.

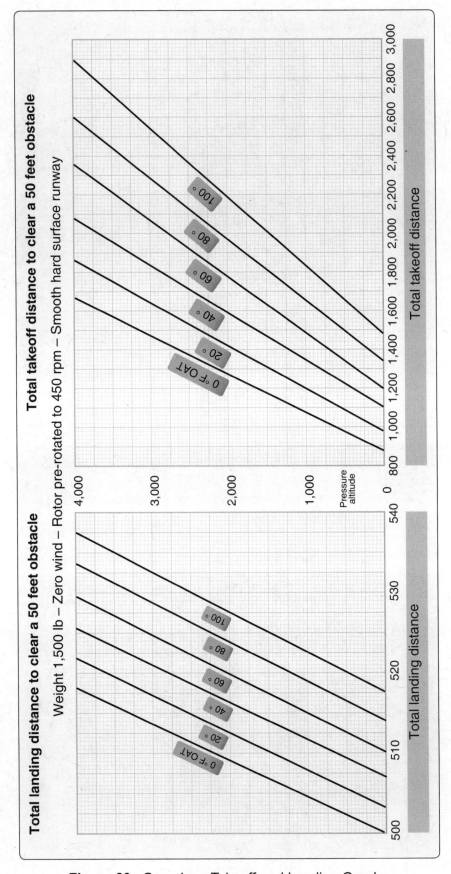

**Figure 39.** Gyroplane Takeoff and Landing Graphs.

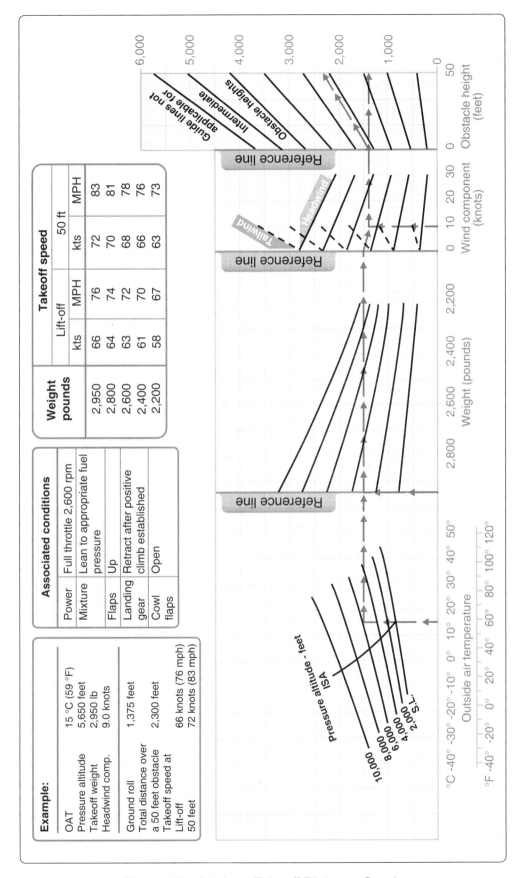

**Figure 40.** Airplane Takeoff Distance Graph.

**Figure 41.** Helicopter Weight and Balance Graph.

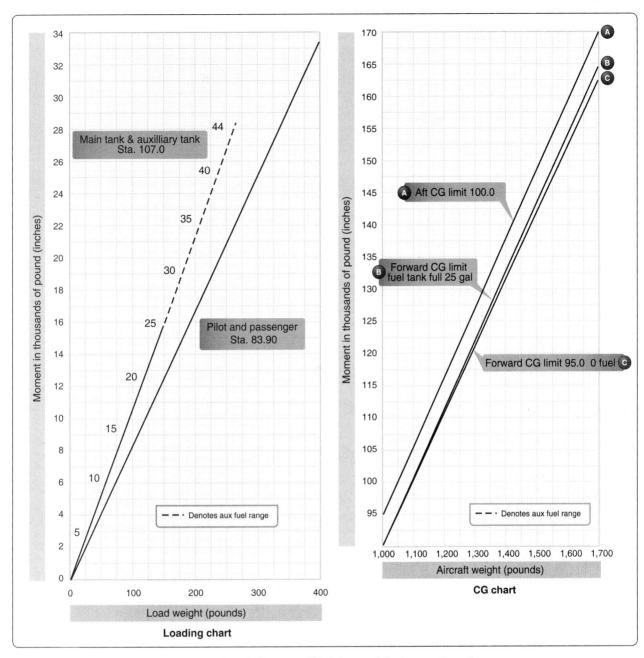

**Figure 42.** Helicopter Weight and Balance Graphs.

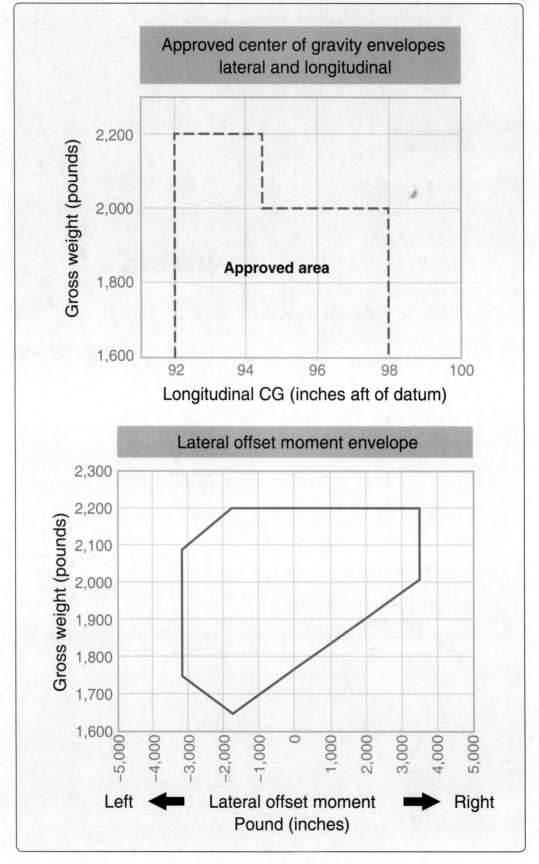

**Figure 43.** Helicopter CG Envelopes.

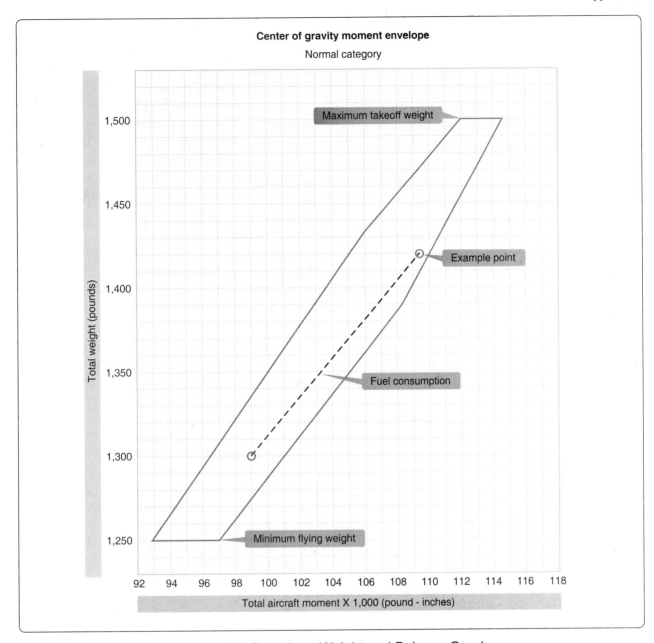

**Figure 44.** Gyroplane Weight and Balance Graph.

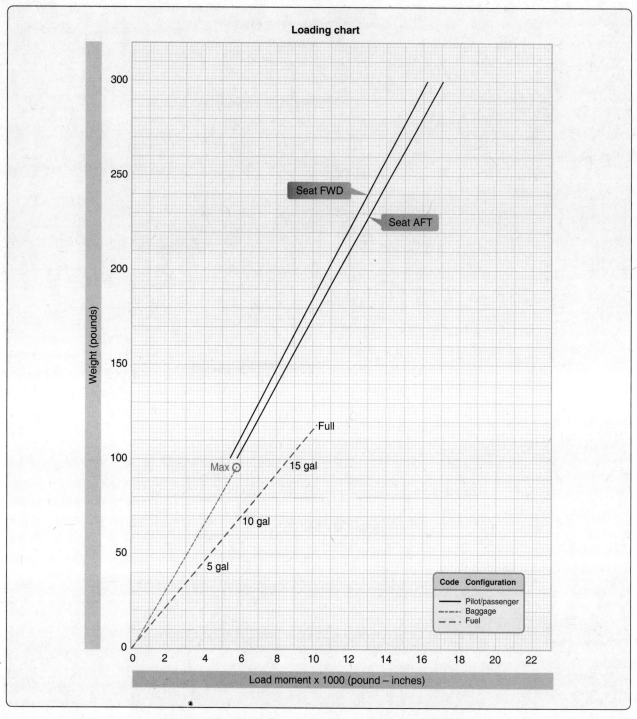

**Figure 45.** Gyroplane Weight and Balance Graph.

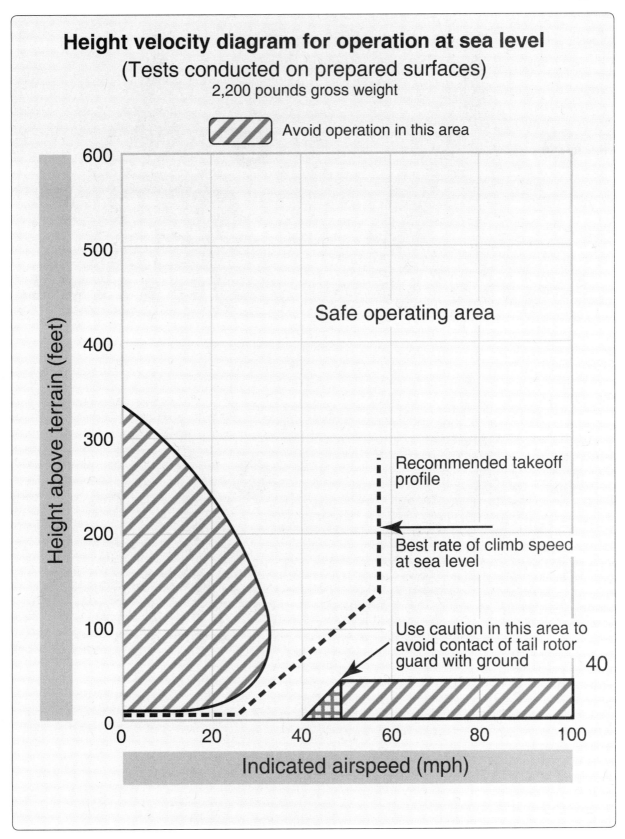

**Figure 46.** Helicopter Height Velocity Diagram.

**Figure 47.** VASI Illustrations.

**Figure 48.** Airport Diagram.

**Figure 49.** Airport Diagram.

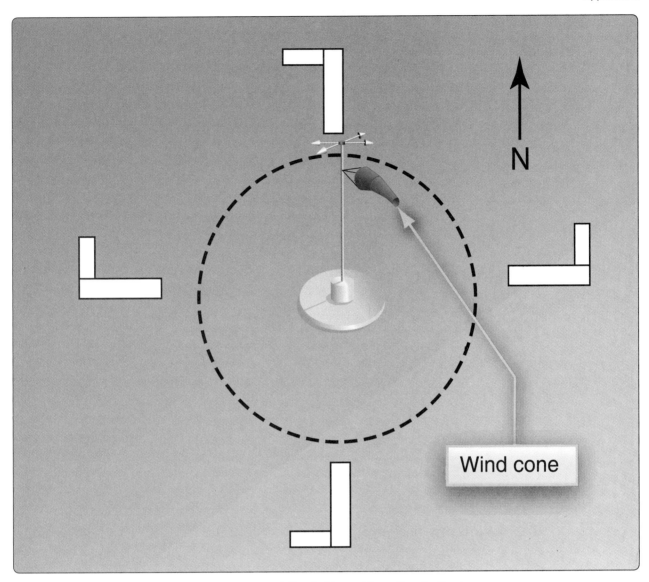

**Figure 50.** Wind Sock Airport Landing Indicator.

Approved OMB No. 2120-0026
Exp. 5/31/2017

# International Flight Plan

U S Department of Transportation
Federal Aviation Administration

PRIORITY     ADDRESSEE(S)

**<=FF**

FILING TIME     ORIGINATOR     **<=**

SPECIFIC IDENTIFICATION OF ADDRESSEE(S) AND / OR ORIGINATOR

---

3 MESSAGE TYPE     7 AIRCRAFT IDENTIFICATION     8 FLIGHT RULES     TYPE OF FLIGHT

**<=(FPL**     —     —     —     **<=**

9 NUMBER     TYPE OF AIRCRAFT     WAKE TURBULENCE CAT.     10 EQUIPMENT

—     /     —     /     **<=**

13 DEPARTURE AERODROME     TIME

—     **<=**

15 CRUISING SPEED     LEVEL     ROUTE

—

     **<=**

---

TOTAL EET

16 DESTINATION AERODROME     HR   MIN     ALTN AERODROME     2ND ALTN AERODROME     **<=**

18 OTHER INFORMATION

—

     **<=**

---

SUPPLEMENTARY INFORMATION (NOT TO BE TRANSMITTED IN FPL MESSAGES)

19     ENDURANCE     EMERGENCY RADIO
     HR   MIN                                              UHF     VHF     ELT

—**E/**          **P/** PERSONS ON BOARD          **R/**  U     V     E

SURVIVAL EQUIPMENT          JACKETS
     POLAR DESERT MARITIME JUNGLE          LIGHT FLUORES UHF  VHF
     / P     D     M     J          / L     F     U     V

DINGHIES
NUMBER CAPACITY COVER          COLOR
**D** /          C          **<=**

AIRCRAFT COLOR AND MARKINGS
**A/**

REMARKS
**N** /          **<=**

PILOT-IN-COMMAND
**C/**          **)<=**

FILED BY          ACCEPTED BY          ADDITIONAL INFORMATION

FAA Form 7233-4 (7/15)

**Figure 51.** Flight Plan Form.

## NEBRASKA

**LINCOLN**  (LNK)   4 NW   UTC−6(−5DT)   N40°51.05′ W96°45.55′    OMAHA
  1219   B   S4   **FUEL** 100LL, JET A   TPA—See Remarks   ARFF Index—See Remarks    H−5C, L−10I
    NOTAM FILE LNK    IAP, AD
  **RWY 18−36:** H12901X200 (ASPH−CONC−GRVD)   S−100, D−200,
    2S−175, 2D−400   HIRL
    **RWY 18:** MALSR. PAPI(P4L)—GA 3.0° TCH 55′. Rgt tfc.   0.4%
      down.
    **RWY 36:** MALSR. PAPI(P4L)—GA 3.0° TCH 57′.
  **RWY 14−32:** H8649X150 (ASPH−CONC−GRVD)   S−80, D−170,
    2S−175, 2D−280   MIRL
    **RWY 14:** REIL. VASI(V4L)—GA 3.0° TCH 48′. Thld dsplcd 363′.
    **RWY 32:** VASI(V4L)—GA 3.0° TCH 50′. Thld dsplcd 470′.
      Pole.   0.3% up.
  **RWY 17−35:** H5800X100 (ASPH−CONC−AFSC)   S−49, D−60
      HIRL   0.8% up S
    **RWY 17:** REIL. PAPI(P4L)—GA 3.0° TCH 44′.
    **RWY 35:** ODALS. PAPI(P4L)—GA 3.0° TCH 30′. Rgt tfc.
  **RUNWAY DECLARED DISTANCE INFORMATION**
    **RWY 14:** TORA−8649   TODA−8649   ASDA−8649   LDA−8286
    **RWY 17:** TORA−5800   TODA−5800   ASDA−5400   LDA−5400
    **RWY 18:** TORA−12901  TODA−12901  ASDA−12901  LDA−12901
    **RWY 32:** TORA−8649   TODA−8649   ASDA−8286   LDA−7816
    **RWY 35:** TORA−5800   TODA−5800   ASDA−5800   LDA−5800
    **RWY 36:** TORA−12901  TODA−12901  ASDA−12901  LDA−12901
  **AIRPORT REMARKS:** Attended continuously. Birds invof arpt. Rwy 18 designated calm wind rwy. Rwy 32 apch holdline
    on South A twy. TPA−2219 (1000), heavy military jet 3000 (1781). Class I, ARFF Index B. ARFF Index C level
    equipment provided. Rwy 18−36 touchdown and rollout rwy visual range avbl. When twr clsd MIRL Rwy 14−32
    preset on low ints, HIRL Rwy 18−36 and Rwy 17−35 preset on med ints, ODALS Rwy 35 operate continuously on
    med ints, MALSR Rwy 18 and Rwy 36 operate continuously and REIL Rwy 14 and Rwy 17 operate continuously
    on low ints. VASI Rwy 14 and Rwy 32, PAPI Rwy 17, Rwy 35, Rwy 18 and Rwy 36 on continuously.
  **WEATHER DATA SOURCES:** ASOS (402) 474−9214. LLWAS
  **COMMUNICATIONS: CTAF** 118.5   **ATIS** 118.05   **UNICOM** 122.95
    **RCO** 122.65 (COLUMBUS RADIO)
  Ⓡ **APP/DEP CON** 124.0 (180°−359°) 124.8 (360°−179°)
    **TOWER** 118.5 125.7 (1130−0600Z‡)   **GND CON** 121.9   **CLNC DEL** 120.7
  **AIRSPACE: CLASS C** svc 1130−0600Z‡ ctc **APP CON** other times **CLASS E.**
  **RADIO AIDS TO NAVIGATION:** NOTAM FILE LNK.
    **(H) VORTACW** 116.1   LNK   Chan 108   N40°55.43′ W96°44.52′   181° 4.4 NM to fld. 1370/9E
    **POTTS NDB (MHW/LOM)** 385   LN   N40°44.83′ W96°45.75′   355° 6.2 NM to fld. Unmonitored when twr clsd.
    **ILS** 111.1   I−OCZ   Rwy 18.   Class IB   OM unmonitored.
    **ILS** 109.9   I−LNK   Rwy 36   Class IA   LOM POTTS NDB. MM unmonitored. LOM unmonitored when twr
      clsd.
  **COMM/NAV/WEATHER REMARKS:** Emerg frequency 121.5 not available at twr.

**LOUP CITY MUNI**  (ØF4)   1 NW   UTC−6(−5DT)   N41°17.20′ W98°59.41′    OMAHA
  2071   B   **FUEL** 100LL   NOTAM FILE OLU    L−10H, 12H
  **RWY 16−34:** H3200X60 (CONC)   S−12.5   MIRL
    **RWY 34:** Trees.
  **RWY 04−22:** 2040X100 (TURF)
    **RWY 04:** Tree.   **RWY 22:** Road.
  **AIRPORT REMARKS:** Unattended. For svc call 308−745−1344/1244/0664.
  **COMMUNICATIONS: CTAF** 122.9
  **RADIO AIDS TO NAVIGATION:** NOTAM FILE OLU.
    **WOLBACH (H) VORTAC** 114.8   OBH   Chan 95   N41°22.54′ W98°21.22′   253° 29.3 NM to fld. 2010/7E.

**MARTIN FLD**   (See SO SIOUX CITY)

**Figure 52.**  Chart Supplement.

## Stations diagram

Rear seat STA. 74.70

Front seat
STA. 43.80

STA. 0

Empty weight...............................................610 pounds
Empty weight station ............................... 96.47 inches
Maximum gross weight............................1,040 pounds
Center of gravity limits...............Stations 78.20 to 86.10

**Figure 53.** Glider Weight and Balance Diagram.

**Figure 54.** Glider Performance Graph.

**Figure 55.** Standard Soaring Signals.

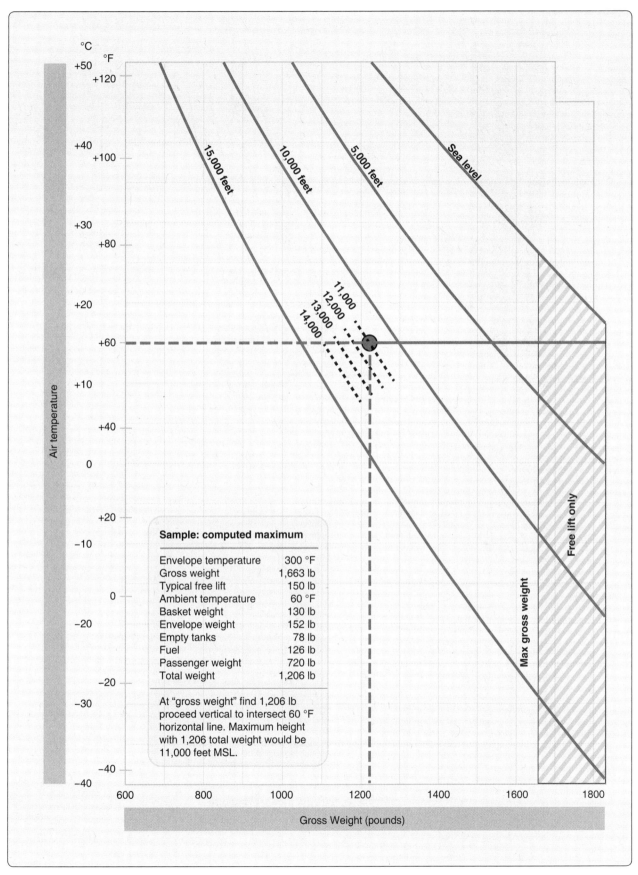

**Figure 56.** Hot Air Balloon Performance Graph.

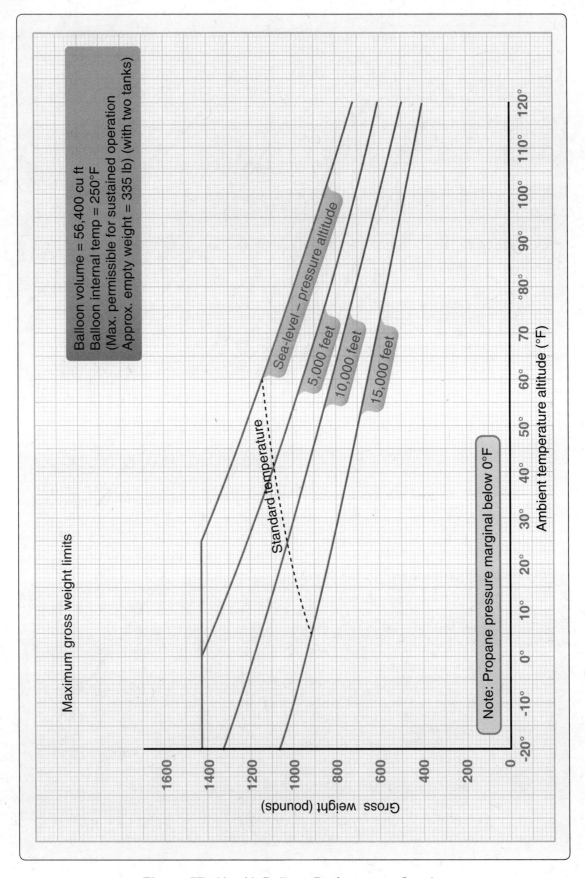

**Figure 57.** Hot Air Balloon Performance Graph.

| For | N | 30 | 60 | E | 120 | 150 |
|---|---|---|---|---|---|---|
| Steer | 0 | 27 | 56 | 85 | 116 | 148 |
| For | S | 210 | 240 | W | 300 | 330 |
| Steer | 181 | 214 | 244 | 274 | 303 | 332 |

**Figure 58.** Compass Card.

**Figure 59.** Sectional Chart Excerpt.

*Note: Chart is not to scale and should not be used for navigation. Use associated scale.*

**Figure 60.** Weight and Balance Diagram.

**Figure 61.** Weight and Balance Diagram.

**Figure 62.** Rectangular Course.

## OHIO

# TOLEDO

**TOLEDO EXECUTIVE** (TDZ) 6 SE UTC−5(−4DT) N41°33.90′ W83°28.93′     DETROIT
623 B S4 **FUEL** 100LL, JET A OX 1, 3 NOTAM FILE TDZ     H−10G, L−28J
**RWY 14−32:** H5829X100 (ASPH−GRVD) S−63, D−85, 2S−107 MIRL     IAP
  **RWY 14:** REIL. PAPI(P4L)—GA 3.0° TCH 34′. Thld dsplcd 225′.
  Tower.
  **RWY 32:** VASI(V4L)—GA 3.0° TCH 43′. Thld dsplcd 351′. Road.
**RWY 04−22:** H3799X75 (ASPH) S−63, D−85, 2S−107 MIRL
  **RWY 04:** REIL. PAPI(P4L)—GA 3.5° TCH 35′. Thld dsplcd 100′.
  Road.
  **RWY 22:** REIL. PAPI(P4L)—GA 3.0° TCH 25′. Thld dsplcd 380′.
  Railroad.
**AIRPORT REMARKS:** Attended Mon–Fri continuously, Sat–Sun
  1300–0100Z‡. Parallel twy Rwy 04–22 and Rwy 14–32 35′ wide.
  Seagulls on and invof arpt. Ldg fee. ACTIVATE MIRL Rwy 04–22
  and Rwy 14–32, REIL and PAPI Rwy 04, Rwy 22, Rwy 14 and VASI
  Rwy 32—CTAF.
**WEATHER DATA SOURCES:** ASOS 121.575 (419) 838−5034.
**COMMUNICATIONS: CTAF/UNICOM** 123.05
Ⓡ **APP/DEP CON** 126.1 **CLNC DEL** 125.6
**RADIO AIDS TO NAVIGATION:** NOTAM FILE CLE.
  WATERVILLE (L) VOR/DME 113.1 VWV Chan 78 N41°27.09′
  W83°38.32′ 048° 9.8 NM to fld. 664/2W.

---

**TOLEDO EXPRESS** (TOL) 10 W UTC−5(−4DT) N41°35.21′ W83°48.47′     DETROIT
683 B S4 **FUEL** 100LL, JET A OX 3 LRA Class I, ARFF Index B NOTAM FILE TOL     H−10G, L−28J
**RWY 07−25:** H10599X150 (ASPH−GRVD) S−100, D−174, 2S−175, 2D−300, 2D/2D2−550     IAP, AD
  HIRL CL
  **RWY 07:** ALSF2. TDZL. Trees.
  **RWY 25:** MALSR. VASI(V4L)—GA 3.0° TCH 51′. Trees. 0.3% up.
**RWY 16−34:** H5599X150 (ASPH−GRVD) S−100, D−174, 2S−175,
  2D−300 MIRL
  **RWY 16:** REIL. PAPI(P4L)—GA 3.0° TCH 48′. Trees.
  **RWY 34:** REIL.
**RUNWAY DECLARED DISTANCE INFORMATION**

| | | | |
|---|---|---|---|
| **RWY 07:** TORA 10599 | TODA 10599 | ASDA 10599 | LDA 10599 |
| **RWY 16:** TORA 5599 | TODA 5599 | ASDA 5599 | LDA 5599 |
| **RWY 25:** TORA 10599 | TODA 10599 | ASDA 10599 | LDA 10599 |
| **RWY 34:** TORA 5599 | TODA 5599 | ASDA 5599 | LDA 5599 |

**ARRESTING GEAR/SYSTEM**
  RWY 07 ←BAK−12          BAK−12 →RWY 25
**AIRPORT REMARKS:** Attended continuously. Fuel and svc avbl
  1300–0500Z‡. Birds on and invof arpt. Twy A west of Rwy 16 and
  the ramp between Twy B9 and B13 not visible from twr. Twy D
  intersection of Twy D1, heavy acft use minimal power to reduce
  foreign object damage on Air National Guard ramp. Customs:
  Sat–Sun req must be made prior to 2200Z‡ on Fri, phone 419−259−6424.
**WEATHER DATA SOURCES:** ASOS (419) 865−8351.
**COMMUNICATIONS: ATIS** 118.75 **UNICOM** 122.95
Ⓡ **APP/DEP CON** 126.1 (360°−179°) 134.35 (180°−359°) 123.975
  **TOWER** 118.1 **GND CON** 121.9 **CLNC DEL** 121.75
**AIRSPACE: CLASS C** svc continuous ctc **APP CON**
**RADIO AIDS TO NAVIGATION:** NOTAM FILE CLE.
  WATERVILLE (L) VOR/DME 113.1 VWV Chan 78 N41°27.09′ W83°38.32′ 319° 11.1 NM to fld. 664/2W.
  TOPHR NDB (LOM) 219 TO N41°33.21′ W83°55.27′ 074° 5.5 NM to fld. Unmonitored. NOTAM FILE TOL.
  ILS 109.7. I−TOL Rwy 07. Class IE. LOM TOPHR NDB.
  ILS 108.7 I−BQE Rwy 25. Class IA. LOC unusable 0.4 NM inbound. ILS unmonitored when twr clsd.
  ASR

---

**SEAGATE HELISTOP** (6T2) 00 N UTC−5(−4DT) N41°39.25′ W83°31.88′     DETROIT
650 NOTAM FILE CLE
**HELIPAD H1:** H50X50 (CONC)
**HELIPORT REMARKS:** Unattended. ACTIVATE orange perimeter lgts—CTAF. Helipad H1 NSTD 1−box (2 VASIS). Helipad
  H1 not marked with ''H.'' Helipad H1 perimeter lgts.
**COMMUNICATIONS: CTAF/UNICOM** 123.05

**Figure 63.** Chart Supplement.

**Figure 64.** Airport Markings.

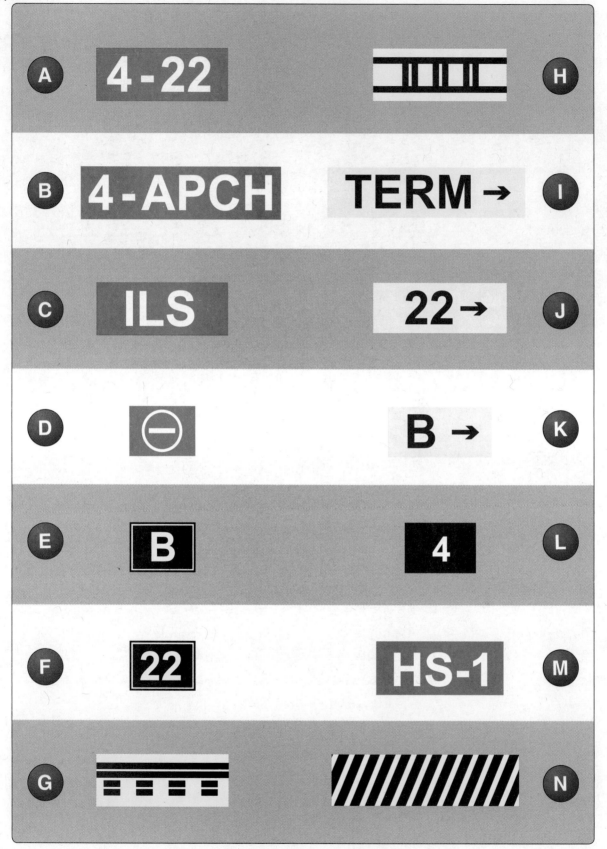

**Figure 65.** U.S. Airport Signs.

**Figure 66.** S-Turn Diagram.

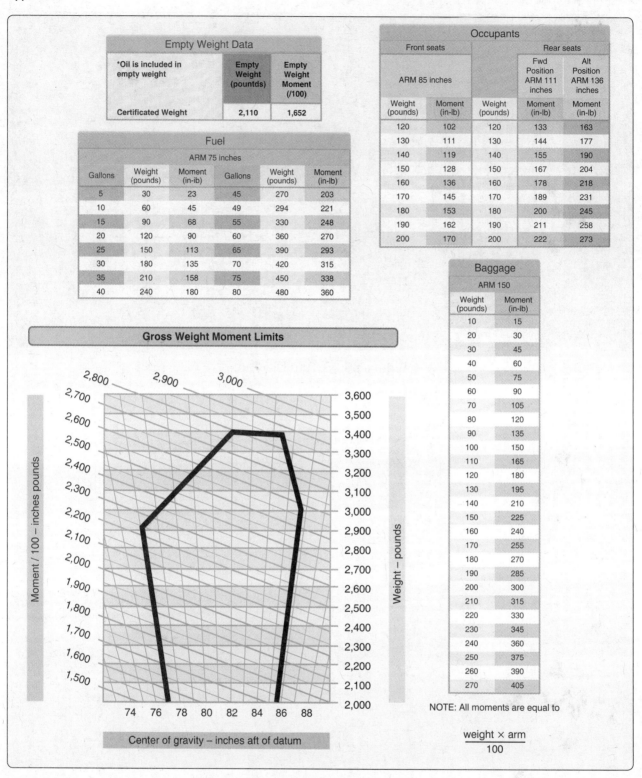

**Figure 67.** Weight and Balance Chart.

Empty Weight Data

| *Oil is included in empty weight | Empty Weight (pountds) | Empty Weight Moment (/100) |
|---|---|---|
| Certificated Weight | 2,110 | 1,652 |

Fuel

ARM 75 inches

| Gallons | Weight (pounds) | Moment (in-ib) | Gallons | Weight (pounds) | Moment (in-lb) |
|---|---|---|---|---|---|
| 5 | 30 | 23 | 45 | 270 | 203 |
| 10 | 60 | 45 | 49 | 294 | 221 |
| 15 | 90 | 68 | 55 | 330 | 248 |
| 20 | 120 | 90 | 60 | 360 | 270 |
| 25 | 150 | 113 | 65 | 390 | 293 |
| 30 | 180 | 135 | 70 | 420 | 315 |
| 35 | 210 | 158 | 75 | 450 | 338 |
| 40 | 240 | 180 | 80 | 480 | 360 |

Occupants

| Front seats | | | Rear seats | |
|---|---|---|---|---|
| ARM 85 inches | | | Fwd Position ARM 111 inches | Alt Position ARM 136 inches |
| Weight (pounds) | Moment (in-lb) | Weight (pounds) | Moment (in-lb) | Moment (in-lb) |
| 120 | 102 | 120 | 133 | 163 |
| 130 | 111 | 130 | 144 | 177 |
| 140 | 119 | 140 | 155 | 190 |
| 150 | 128 | 150 | 167 | 204 |
| 160 | 136 | 160 | 178 | 218 |
| 170 | 145 | 170 | 189 | 231 |
| 180 | 153 | 180 | 200 | 245 |
| 190 | 162 | 190 | 211 | 258 |
| 200 | 170 | 200 | 222 | 273 |

Baggage

ARM 150

| Weight (pounds) | Moment (in-lb) |
|---|---|
| 10 | 15 |
| 20 | 30 |
| 30 | 45 |
| 40 | 60 |
| 50 | 75 |
| 60 | 90 |
| 70 | 105 |
| 80 | 120 |
| 90 | 135 |
| 100 | 150 |
| 110 | 165 |
| 120 | 180 |
| 130 | 195 |
| 140 | 210 |
| 150 | 225 |
| 160 | 240 |
| 170 | 255 |
| 180 | 270 |
| 190 | 285 |
| 200 | 300 |
| 210 | 315 |
| 220 | 330 |
| 230 | 345 |
| 240 | 360 |
| 250 | 375 |
| 260 | 390 |
| 270 | 405 |

NOTE: All moments are equal to

$$\frac{weight \times arm}{100}$$

**Figure 68.** Wind Triangle.

**Figure 69.** Sectional Chart Excerpt.

*NOTE: Chart is not to scale and should not be used for navigation. Use associated scale.*

**Figure 70.** Sectional Chart Excerpt.
*NOTE: Chart is not to scale and should not be used for navigation. Use associated scale.*

**Figure 71.** Sectional Chart Excerpt.
*NOTE: Chart is not to scale and should not be used for navigation. Use associated scale.*

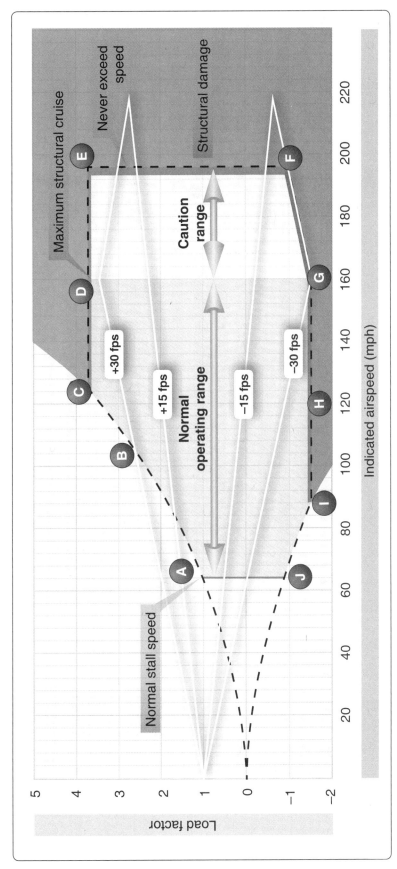

**Figure 72.** Velocity vs. G-Loads.

**Figure 73.** Glider Hand Signals.

**Figure 74.** Sectional Chart Excerpt.

*NOTE: Chart is not to scale and should not be used for navigation. Use associated scale.*

**Figure 75.** Sectional Chart Excerpt.
*NOTE: Chart is not to scale and should not be used for navigation. Use associated scale.*

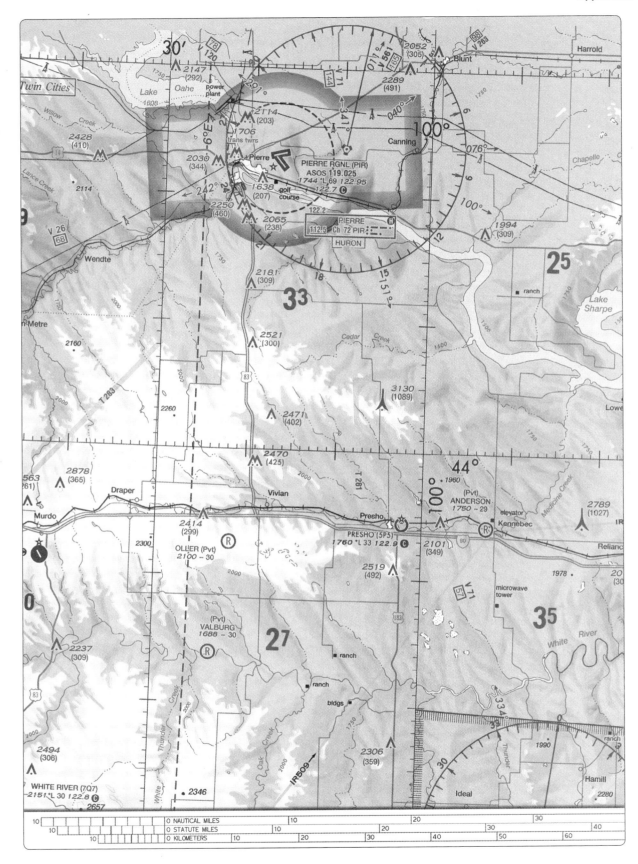

**Figure 76.** Sectional Chart Excerpt.
*NOTE: Chart is not to scale and should not be used for navigation. Use associated scale.*

**SOUTH DAKOTA**

**PIERRE RGNL** (PIR)   3 E   UTC −6(−5DT)   N44°22.96′ W100°17.16′   **OMAHA**
1744   B   S4   **FUEL** 100LL, JET A   OX 1, 2, 3, 4   Class I, ARFF Index A   NOTAM FILE PIR   H−2I, L−12H
**RWY 13−31:** H6900X100 (ASPH−GRVD)   S−91, D−108, 2S−137, 2D−168   HIRL   IAP
   **RWY 13:** REIL. PAPI(P4L)—GA 3.0 ° TCH 52′.
   **RWY 31:** MALSR. PAPI(P4L)—GA 3.0 ° TCH 52′.
**RWY 07−25:** H6881X150 (ASPH−GRVD)   S−91, D−114, 2S−145,
   2D−180   HIRL   0.6% up W
   **RWY 07:** REIL. PAPI(P4L)—GA 3.0 ° TCH 47′. Tank.
   **RWY 25:** REIL. PAPI(P4L)—GA 3.0 ° TCH 54′.
**RUNWAY DECLARED DISTANCE INFORMATION**
   **RWY 07:**   TORA−6881   TODA−6881   ASDA−6830   LDA−6830
   **RWY 13:**   TORA−6900   TODA−6900   ASDA−6900   LDA−6900
   **RWY 25:**   TORA−6881   TODA−6881   ASDA−6881   LDA−6881
   **RWY 31:**   TORA−6900   TODA−6900   ASDA−6900   LDA−6900
**AIRPORT REMARKS:** Attended Mon−Fri 1100−0600Z‡, Sat−Sun
1100−0400Z‡. For attendant other times call
605−224−9000/8621. Arpt conditions unmonitored during
0530−1000Z‡. Numerous non−radio acft operating in area. Birds
on and invof arpt and within a 25 NM radius. No line of sight
between rwy ends of Rwy 07−25. ARFF provided for part 121 air
carrier ops only. 48 hr PPR for unscheduled acr ops involving acft
designed for 31 or more passenger seats call 605−773−7447 or
605−773−7405. Taxiway C is 50′ wide and restricted to acft 75,000 pounds or less. ACTIVATE HIRL Rwy 13−31
and Rwy 07−25, MALSR Rwy 31, REIL Rwy 07, Rwy 13 and Rwy 25, PAPI Rwy 07, Rwy 25, Rwy 13 and Rwy
31—CTAF 122.7. NOTE: See Special Notices Section—
Aerobatic Practice Areas.
**WEATHER DATA SOURCES:** ASOS 119.025 (605) 224−6087.   **HIWAS** 112.5 PIR.
**COMMUNICATIONS: CTAF** 122.7   **UNICOM** 122.95
   **RCO** 122.2 (HURON RADIO)
Ⓡ **MINNEAPOLIS CENTER APP/DEP CON** 125.1
**RADIO AIDS TO NAVIGATION:** NOTAM FILE PIR.
   **(L) VORTACW** 112.5   PIR   Chan 72   N44°23.67′ W100°09.77′   251° 5.3 NM to fld. 1789/11E.   **HIWAS.**
   **ILS/DME** 111.9   I−PIR   Chan 56   Rwy 31.   Class IA   ILS GS unusable for coupled apch blo 2,255′. GS
      unusable blo 2135′.

**PINE RIDGE** (IEN)   2 E   UTC −7(−6DT)   N43°01.35′ W102°30.66′   **CHEYENNE**
3333   B   NOTAM FILE IEN   H−5B, L−12G
**RWY 12−30:** H5000X60 (ASPH)   S−12   MIRL   0.7% up SE   IAP
   **RWY 12:** P−line.
   **RWY 30:** PAPI(P2L)—GA 3.0 ° TCH 26′. Fence.
**RWY 06−24:** H3003X50 (ASPH)   S−12   0.7% up NE
   **RWY 24:** Fence.
**AIRPORT REMARKS:** Unattended. Rwy 06−24 CLOSED indef. MIRL Rwy
12−30 and PAPI Rwy 30 opr dusk−0530Z‡, after 0530Z‡
ACTIVATE—CTAF.
**WEATHER DATA SOURCES:** ASOS 126.775 (605) 867−1584.
**COMMUNICATIONS: CTAF** 122.9
**DENVER CENTER APP/DEP CON** 127.95
**RADIO AIDS TO NAVIGATION:** NOTAM FILE RAP.
   **RAPID CITY (H) VORTAC** 112.3   RAP   Chan 70   N43°58.56′
      W103°00.74′   146° 61.3 NM to fld. 3160/13E.

**Figure 77.** Chart Supplement.

**Figure 78.** Sectional Chart Excerpt.

*NOTE: Chart is not to scale and should not be used for navigation. Use associated scale.*

**64**　　　　　　　　　　　　　　　**IOWA**

**SIOUX CITY**　N42°20.67′ W96°19.42′　　NOTAM FILE SUX　　　　　　　　　　　OMAHA
　(L) **VORTAC** 116.5　SUX　Chan 112　　313 ° 4.4 NM to Sioux Gateway/Col Bud Day Fld. 1087/9E.　**HIWAS.**　**L–12I**
　　VOR unusable:
　　280°–292° byd 25 NM　　　　　　　　　　　　　306°–350° byd 20 NM blo 3,000′
　　293°–305° byd 20 NM blo 4,500′　　　　　　　 350°–280° byd 30 NM blo 3,000′
　　293°–305° byd 35 NM
　**RCO** 122.45 122.1R 116.5T (FORT DODGE RADIO)

## SIOUX CITY
**SIOUX GATEWAY/COL BUD DAY FLD**　(SUX)　6 S　UTC –6(–5DT)　N42°24.16′ W96°23.06′　　OMAHA
　1098　B　S4　**FUEL** 100LL, 115, JET A　OX 1, 2, 3, 4　Class I, ARFF Index—See Remarks　**H–5C, L–12I**
　NOTAM FILE SUX　　　　　　　　　　　　　　　　　　　　　　　　　　　　**IAP, AD**
　**RWY 13–31:** H9002X150 (CONC–GRVD)　S–100, D–120, 2S–152,
　　2D–220　HIRL
　**RWY 13:** MALS. VASI(V4L)—GA 3.0 ° TCH 49′. Tree.
　**RWY 31:** MALSR. VASI(V4L)—GA 3.0 ° TCH 50′.
　**RWY 17–35:** H6600X150 (ASPH–PFC)　S–65, D–80, 2S–102,
　　2D–130　MIRL
　**RWY 17:** REIL. VASI(V4R)—GA 3.0 ° TCH 50′. Trees.
　**RWY 35:** PAPI(P4L)—GA 3.0 ° TCH 54′. Pole.
　**LAND AND HOLD SHORT OPERATIONS**

| LANDING | HOLD SHORT POINT | DIST AVBL |
|---|---|---|
| RWY 13 | 17–35 | 5400 |
| RWY 17 | 13–31 | 5650 |

　**ARRESTING GEAR/SYSTEM**
　　RWY 13 ←BAK–14 BAK–12B(B) (1392′)
　　　　　　　　　　　　BAK–14 BAK–12B(B) (1492′) →RWY 31
　**AIRPORT REMARKS:** Attended continuously. PAEW 0330–1200Z ‡ during
　　inclement weather Nov–Apr. AER 31–BAK–12/14 located (1492′)
　　from thld. Airfield surface conditions not monitored by arpt
　　management between 0600–1000Z ‡ daily. Rwy 13–BAK–12/14
　　located (1392′) from thld. All A–gear avbl only during ANG flying ops. Twr has limited visibility southeast of
　　ramp near ARFF bldg and northeast of Rwy 31 touchdown zone. Rwy 31 is calm wind rwy. Class I, ARFF Index
　　B. ARFF Index E fire fighting equipment avbl on request. Twy F unlit, retro–reflective markers in place. Portions
　　of Twy A SE of Twy B not visible by twr and is designated a non–movement area. Rwy 13–31 touchdown and
　　rollout rwy visual range avbl. When twr clsd, ACTIVATE HIRL Rwy 13–31; MIRL Rwy 17–35; MALS Rwy 13;
　　MALSR Rwy 31; and REIL Rwy 17—CTAF.
　**WEATHER DATA SOURCES:** ASOS (712) 255–6474.　**HIWAS** 116.5 SUX. LAWRS.
　**COMMUNICATIONS: CTAF** 118.7　**ATIS** 119.45　**UNICOM** 122.95
　　SIOUX CITY RCO 122.45 122.1R 116.5T (FORT DODGE RADIO)
　Ⓡ **SIOUX CITY APP/DEP CON** 124.6 (1200–0330Z‡)
　Ⓡ **MINNEAPOLIS CENTER APP/DEP CON** 124.1 (0330–1200Z‡)
　　**SIOUX CITY TOWER** 118.7 (1200–0330Z‡)　**GND CON** 121.9
　**AIRSPACE: CLASS D** svc 1200–0330Z‡ other times CLASS E.
　**RADIO AIDS TO NAVIGATION:** NOTAM FILE SUX.
　　**SIOUX CITY (L) VORTAC** 116.5　SUX　Chan 112　N42 °20.67′ W96°19.42′　313° 4.4 NM to fld. 1087/9E.
　　　HIWAS.
　　**NDB (MHW)** 233　GAK　N42°24.49′ W96°23.16′　at fld.
　　**SALIX NDB (MHW/LOM)** 414　SU　N42°19.65′ W96°17.43′　311° 6.1 NM to fld. Unmonitored.
　　**TOMMI NDB (MHW/LOM)** 305　OI　N42°27.61′ W96°27.73′　128° 4.9 NM to fld. Unmonitored.
　　**ILS** 109.3　I–SUX　Rwy 31　Class IT.　LOM SALIX NDB. ILS Unmonitored when twr clsd. Glide path
　　　unusable coupled approach (CPD) blo 1805′.
　　**ILS** 111.3　I–OIQ　Rwy 13　LOM TOMMI NDB. Localizer shutdown when twr clsd.
　　**ASR** (1200–0330Z‡)

**SNORE**　N43°13.96′ W95°19.66′　　NOTAM FILE SPW.　　　　　　　　　　　OMAHA
　**NDB (LOM)** 394　SP　121° 6.8 NM to Spencer Muni.

**SOUTHEAST IOWA RGNL**　(See BURLINGTON)

**Figure 79.** Chart Supplement.

**Figure 80.** Sectional Chart Excerpt.

*NOTE: Chart is not to scale and should not be used for navigation. Use associated scale.*

**COLORADO**

**CRAWFORD**   (99V)   2 W   UTC −7(−6DT)   N38°42.25′ W107°38.62′                                    DENVER
6470   S2   OX 4   TPA—7470(1000)   NOTAM FILE DEN                                                    L–9E
RWY 07–25: H4900X20 (ASPH)      LIRL (NSTD)
  RWY 07: VASI (NSTD). Trees.         RWY 25: VASI (NSTD) Tank. Rgt tfc.
RWY E–W: 2500X125 (TURF)
  RWY E: Rgt tfc.           RWY W: Trees.
AIRPORT REMARKS: Attended continuously. Rwy 07–25 west 1300 ′ only 25′ wide. Heavy glider ops at arpt. Land to the
  east tkf to the west winds permitting. 100LL fuel avbl for emergency use only. Pedestrians, motor vehicles, deer
  and wildlife on and invof arpt. Unlimited vehicle use on arpt. Rwy West has +15 ′ building 170′ from thld 30′ left,
  +10′ road 100′ from thld centerline. +45′ tree 100′ L of Rwy 07 extended centerline 414 ′ from rwy end. −8′ to
  −20′ terrain off both sides of first 674 ′ of Rwy 25 end. E–W rwy occasionally has 6 inch diameter irrigation
  pipes crossing rwy width in various places. Rwy 07 has 20 ′ trees and −10′ to 20′ terrain 20′ right of rwy first
  150′. E–W rwy consists of +12 inch alfalfa vegetation during various times of the year. Arpt lgts opr
  dusk–0800Z‡. Rwy 07 1 box VASI left side for local operators only or PPR call 970–921–7700 or
  970–921–3018. Rwy 07–25 LIRL on N side from Rwy 25 end W 3800 ′. Rwy 07 1300′ from end E 300′. No thld
  lgts Rwy 07–25 3800′ usable for ngt ops.
COMMUNICATIONS: CTAF/UNICOM 122.8
RADIO AIDS TO NAVIGATION: NOTAM FILE MTJ.
  MONTROSE (H) VORW/DME 117.1   MTJ   Chan 118   N38 °30.39′ W107°53.96′   033° 16.9 NM to fld. 5713/12E.

**CREEDE**
  **MINERAL CO MEM**   (C24)   2 E   UTC −7(−6DT)   N37°49.33′ W106°55.79′                              DENVER
  8680   NOTAM FILE DEN                                                                                H–3E, L–9E
  RWY 07–25: H6880X60 (ASPH)      S-12.5, D-70, 2D-110
    RWY 07: Thld dsplcd 188 ′.        RWY 25: Road.
  AIRPORT REMARKS: Unattended. Elk and deer on and invof arpt. Glider and hang glider activity on and in vicinity of
    arpt. Mountains in all directions. Departure to NE avoid over flight of trailers and resident homes, climb to 200  ′
    above ground level on centerline extended prior to turn. Acft stay to right of valley on apch and/or departure
    route. 2′ cable fence around apron.
  COMMUNICATIONS: CTAF 122.9
  RADIO AIDS TO NAVIGATION: NOTAM FILE DEN.
    BLUE MESA (H) VORW/DME 114.9   HBU   Chan 96   N38 °27.13′ W107°02.39′   158° 38.1 NM to fld. 8730/14E.

  **CUCHARA VALLEY AT LA VETA**   (See LA VETA)

**DEL NORTE**
  **ASTRONAUT KENT ROMINGER**   (8V1)   3 N   UTC −7(−6DT)   N37°42.83′ W106°21.11′                     DENVER
  7949   NOTAM FILE DEN                                                                                H–3E, L–9E
  RWY 06–24: 6050X75 (ASPH)      1.1% up SW
  RWY 03–21: 4670X60 (TURF–DIRT)
    RWY 21: Mountain.
  AIRPORT REMARKS: Unattended. Wildlife on and invof arpt. Unlimited vehicle access on arpt. Mountainous terrain
    surrounds arpt in all directions.
  COMMUNICATIONS: CTAF 122.9
  RADIO AIDS TO NAVIGATION: NOTAM FILE ALS.
    ALAMOSA (H) VORTACW 113.9   ALS   Chan 86   N37 °20.95′ W105°48.93′   298° 33.7 NM to fld. 7535/13E.

**Figure 81.** Chart Supplement.

**Figure 82.** Altimeter.